THE PALGRAVE GUIDE TO ENGLISH LITERATURE AND ITS CONTEXTS, 1500–2000

RELATED TITLES FROM PALGRAVE MACMILLAN

Michael Alexander, *A History of English Literature* (2000)

John Peck and Martin Coyle, *A Brief History of English Literature* (2002)

Rick Rylance and Judy Simons (eds), *Literature in Context* (2001)

The Palgrave Guide to English Literature and its Contexts, 1500–2000

PETER WIDDOWSON

First published 2004 by
PALGRAVE MACMILLAN
Houndmills, Basingstoke, Hampshire RG21 6XS and
175 Fifth Avenue, New York, N.Y. 10010
Companies and representatives throughout the world

PALGRAVE MACMILLAN is the global academic imprint of the Palgrave Macmillan division of St. Martin's Press, LLC and of Palgrave Macmillan Ltd. Macmillan® is a registered trademark in the United States, United Kingdom and other countries. Palgrave is a registered trademark in the European Union and other countries.

ISBN 0–333–79217–3 hardback
ISBN 0–333–79218–1 paperback

This book is printed on paper suitable for recycling and made from fully managed and sustained forest sources.

A catalogue record for this book is available from the British Library.

Library of Congress Cataloging-in-Publication Data
Widdowson, Peter.
  The Palgrave guide to English literature and its contexts, 1500–2000 / Peter Widdowson.
    p. cm.
  Includes bibliographical references and index.
  ISBN 0–333–79217–3 — ISBN 0–333–79218–1 (pbk.)
    1. English literature—History and criticism—Handbooks, manuals, etc.
2. Literature and society—Great Britain—Handbooks, manuals, etc. 3. Great Britain—Civilization—Handbooks, manuals, etc. I. Title.

PR401.W54 2004
820.9—dc22   2003069646

10 9 8 7 6 5 4 3 2 1
13 12 11 10 09 08 07 06 05 04

Printed in China

This book is dedicated to Simon Dentith,
great friend, colleague and adviser-in-chief

Contents

Acknowledgements

My principal acknowledgement is to the University of Gloucestershire, and more specifically the School of Humanities, for giving me the time and space in which to compile this book (including two periods of research leave without which such a monstrous undertaking could never have been completed). My heartfelt thanks go to my colleagues in English and elsewhere in the University who have both endured interminable 'tales from the timelines' without visibly falling asleep and have supplied me with essential pieces of information in the long-running game of 'Serious Pursuits' I have foisted on them over the past few years. I am particularly grateful to Professor Simon Dentith, to whom this book is dedicated, for his continuous support, humorous exasperation and witheringly apt advice on when to stop. My thanks also, as always, to long-suffering Jane and Tom who must have thought it would never stop, but silently prayed that it might.

Introduction

Premises and Procedures

1 PREMISES

The fundamental premise on which this book rests is that literature – and indeed every other form of cultural production – exists within history and should be studied with its contexts and chronologies clearly in view. This is not to say that matters of form and interpretation are secondary, nor to preclude the practice of any of the multiple critical approaches currently available to us; it is merely to assume that historical knowledge is an essential tool in understanding the significance of any individual artefact, whether at the moment of its production or in the diverse process of its consumption thereafter.

The second premise – and one that accounts for the particular format of this book – is that historical knowledge of a kind useful to students of literature, if no other, is difficult to access in direct relation to specific movements, authors and texts and over long periods of time. Narrative histories, including literary histories, are normally extended prose accounts which often disturb historical chronology and disperse both contextual and literary data according to the sectionalisation which structures their narrative. Without a considerable degree of prior knowledge, a linear reading of a literary history for specific information about either text or context can be a time-consuming and frustrating business. The presentation here of literary writing in relation to its historical and cultural contexts by way of timeline tables proceeding chronologically from 1500 to the end of 1999 aims to provide sequences and correlations which are immediately perceptible and comprehensible. Every year of the 500 years between those two dates receives an individual entry across four major columns containing historical, cultural and literary information.

Eng. Lit.

A further premise underlying the volume might be flagged by substituting the familiar diminutive 'Eng. Lit.' in the book's title, thereby acknowledging that the authors and texts indicated in the two columns on the right of the timeline tables are by and large those which comprise the received canon of 'English Literature'. This delimited focus is based on two very basic practical considerations: one on the well-known dictum that 'literature is what gets taught', thus overtly directing the book's emphasis to the still normative curriculum in secondary and higher education in the UK and elsewhere in the world; the other on the recognition that if the tables were to include both the canon and all its diverse potential alternatives, the book would become impossibly unwieldy (and never finished). However, attempts have been made to mitigate the predominance of the 'English Canon' by offering examples of literary works from other countries in the 'International Literature' sections of the 'Social and Cultural Contexts' columns, and where appropriate, by including British and Irish authors and works other than those found in conventional literary history in the 'Authors'/'Indicative Texts' columns (this is especially the case for the later decades of the 20th Century).

Historical Range

The period covered by the present volume, 1500–2000, takes as its starting-point the beginnings of the English Reformation and Renaissance and the gradual appearance of a recognisably modern English Literature (while regretting the sacrifice of earlier writing – especially the poetry of the Gawain Poet, Langland and Chaucer), and ends with the close of the 20th Century and the second millennium. Hence, and in relation to the notion above that 'literature is what gets taught', the five centuries represented here contain the vast proportion of literature currently studied in secondary and tertiary education.

Timelines

The Palgrave Guide to English Literature and its Contexts is designed, therefore, to be used as a comprehensive reference work for students and teachers of English Literature at all levels (although a less specialist use for it might be to prepare for Quiz Nights). Accuracy of dating has been striven for throughout, and as much contextual material included as seemed relevant and/or interesting without destroying the book's portability. It is divided into nine 'Period' chapters consisting of timeline tables in six columns (for more detail on the main columns' composition, see **Procedures** below). The first vertical column gives the commonly used term(s) for the period (e.g. 'Tudor', 'Jacobean', 'Restoration', 'Fin-de-Siècle', 'Modernist'); the second gives the individual year date (e.g. '1642'); and the four substantive ones are divided into 'International and Political Contexts', 'Social and Cultural Contexts', 'Authors' and 'Indicative Titles'.

The tables can be read diachronically (vertically) or synchronically (horizontally), so that while the former enables a sequential chronological history to be pursued, the latter allows a specific year to be singled out to overview the historical, cultural and literary events that occurred in it. In addition, each chapter has a short introductory paragraph outlining the concepts relevant to that period as well as headnote glosses on key terms and concepts preceding the tables themselves (glossed terms and concepts appear in bold the first time they are mentioned in a chapter). The use of an asterisk after key terms and concepts within the the text indicates cross-reference to another gloss in that chapter or others. The glosses have two principal purposes: first, to offer succinct working definitions of terms commonly used in literary history which students may recognise but not be fully conversant with (e.g. 'Jacobean', 'Caroline', 'Interregnum', 'Restoration', 'Augustan', 'Regency', 'Georgian', 'Inter-War'); and second, to pull into view historical, cultural and literary 'narratives' from the detailed material in the timeline tables which may be initially obscured by the detail but which can then be tracked back through the timelines. Examples might include 'Succession' crises for the British monarchy at various historical moments; the growth of Britain as a trading nation and the acquisition of Empire; the reasons for the independence struggle of the American colonies in becoming the USA; the shift from Neo-Classical values in the arts to those espoused by the Romantics; the progress of nationalist movements in 19th-Century Europe; the 'Irish Question' throughout 500 years of British history; the predominance of one genre over others in different literary periods; the rise to power of totalitarian regimes in inter-war Europe; the technological innovations of the later 20th Century, and the accelerating global concern about the environment and health. In effect, the headnote glosses and their extrapolated 'narratives' offer a condensed history of the period between 1500 and 2000, supported by the year-on-year detail in the timeline tables.

2 PROCEDURES

Periodicity

Periodicity is a key problem for any kind of history: ruling dynasties or monarchs' reigns do not fit neatly into decades or centuries (the Tudors give way to the Stuarts in 1603 – are the 1600s then 'Elizabethan' or 'Jacobean'?); political or artistic movements do not start and end in precise time-frames and will have different chronologies in different national locations (when does the Renaissance begin and end in Italy and in England?); descriptive labels distort by generalisation (why is the so-called 'last Augustan', Jane Austen, writing throughout the height of the 'Romantic' period?); even centuries seem not to have definite limits (why do some modern historians conceive of 'the long 18th Century', or see the end of the 19th Century as occurring in 1914?). The basic principle of the present book has been to organise periods in the timeline tables into groupings which seem to make sense in generally accepted historical periodisations (e.g. 1830–99: the 'Victorian Period'), while drawing attention in the chapter headnotes to the difficulties and anomalies incident upon this (e.g. that the 'Victorian Period' includes the reign of William IV and that Queen Victoria did not die until 1901). In addition, a descriptive label to the chapter grouping is added where the movement it alludes to retains common currency in literary history and the curriculum (e.g. the 'Augustan Period', the 'Modernist Period'), but a cautionary gloss on it is also included in the headnotes.

Dates

Great care has been taken to establish the correct date for events and texts, but this is by no means a straightforward process. One of the most disturbing features of compiling a book like the present one has been to discover how often, and how significantly, apparently authoritative reference books give different dates for the same event, author or text. This can be the result of a simple typo or error of transcription (e.g. 1803 for 1808, 1668 for 1686), but it is often more complex. For example, events will run across calendar years (December to January), and some commentators will cite the start date and others the end date; some authorities will give the date of a piece of parliamentary legislation as that of the Bill introducing it, while others that of the Act as passed – which can also, of course, be in different years; publishers bringing out a book late one year will often give the following year as the date of publication, and literary historians will cite either depending on their source or inclination; the date given for plays from the Elizabethan and Jacobean periods will vary from the (speculated) date of composition to the date of first performance to the date of printed publication – which can be many years apart; with literary works in other languages, the date of translation into English may be the one given rather than the date of original publication, especially if accompanying the English title. (Similar problems occur with the other arts: date of composition of a piece of music may be very different from the date of first performance; date of painting very different from date of exhibition; cited dates for films will vary on place of first release – e.g. whether in the USA or the UK.) While accepting that *The Palgrave Guide* will be as susceptible to error as any other reference book, its rule of thumb when faced with these difficulties has been to go for consistency (e.g. Acts of Parliament not Bills; date of first performance for plays unless otherwise indicated); to give dual dates (e.g. 1912–13) or to accept a majority verdict when it is genuinely uncertain which is the accepted date for an event or a text's publication; to take the publication date given in one of the British copyright libraries' catalogues as the final adjudicator in cases of unresolved dispute; and to use the device [*c.*] (*circa* = 'about', 'around this time') for all art-works of uncertain date, especially in earlier periods (e.g. '*c.*1515' for a painting by Titian).

Selection

It will be immediately obvious on flicking through the book that the balance in terms of size of entry for individual years is markedly different from the earlier centuries to the later ones – and especially the second half of the 20th Century. This is inevitable, to state the obvious: literacy in the distant past was extremely limited; relatively few books and no newspapers or magazines were published until well into the 17th Century; there were no mass-communications media; historical records are patchy or non-existent; there is simply less that we know about to include. The problem is very different the nearer we come to the present day: there is so much potential material available that the question is: what goes in and what is left out, and on what principles for either? Leaving aside the simple fact that everyone will have a different view of what should or should not be included, the process of selection is probably the most fraught ideologically of all the problems that beset a project of the present kind – which will almost inevitably be seen as Anglo/Eurocentric, sexist, racist, elitist.

The book has tried hard to keep these anticipated charges at bay, but given the nature of the project – a historical guide to English Literature – there comes a point of resigned but realistic acceptance that inequities and imbalances will occur: that principles of selection will be subjective (what do I know enough about and think relevant?) and will vary depending on the period and the literary/cultural production thereof (e.g. an increased proliferation of women writers from the 18th Century onwards means that the gender balance of the timeline tables changes; achievements in the visual arts from about 1870 to 1930 explains the prominence given to them in that period; film becomes a dominant art form in the mid-20th Century and thereby explains its enlarged presence; region and ethnicity become increasingly important factors in British literary writing in the later 20th Century and are therefore given more emphasis). However, the fundamental defence of selectivity and partiality must be: first, the book's length (theoretically, it could be literally encyclopaedic); and second, that the material it contains is cited as representative or 'indicative' rather than exhaustive. But even this becomes increasingly problematical with contemporary mass cultural forms like TV and pop music: just ask yourself how you would select 'indicative' examples of either for each of the past 50 years while keeping the book to a publishable length.

How to Use this Book

1 STRUCTURE

The fundamental premise of this book is that literature exists within history and should be studied with its chronologies and contexts clearly in view. It assumes that historical knowledge is an essential tool in understanding the significance of any literary text, whether at the moment of its production or during its consumption thereafter.

The Palgrave Guide to English Literature and its Contexts is designed to be used as a comprehensive reference work for students and teachers of English Literature at all levels (although a less specialist use for it might be to prepare for Quiz Nights). The period covered, 1500–1999, takes as its starting-point the English Reformation and Renaissance and the appearance of a recognisably modern English Literature, and ends with the close of the 20th Century and the second millennium. The authors and works presented in the timeline tables are mainly those of the received canon of English Literature. However, it also offers contextualising examples of literary works from other countries, and includes a wider range of British and Irish authors and works than those found in conventional literary history.

Each chapter focuses on a key period in English Literature and History and introduces and outlines key terms, concepts and developments during that period. Each chapter also includes a series of timelines showing political, social and cultural events for each year, alongside the key literary authors and works. The timelines can be read either vertically or horizontally, allowing you to follow a chronological history or to single out a specific year to overview the historical, cultural and literary events that occurred in it.

The chapters begin with a short **Introduction** providing an overview of the period. The second section – **Key Terms and Concepts** – provides a working definition of key terms commonly used in literary history which you may recognise but not fully understand; and second, to pull into view from the detailed material in the timeline tables historical and cultural **'narratives'** which may be obscured by the detail but which can then be tracked back through the timelines (for example: 'Succession' crises for the British monarchy at various historical moments; the growth of Britain as a trading nation and the acquisition of Empire; the 'Irish Question' throughout 500 years of British history; the accelerating global concern about the environment in the later 20th Century). The **timelines** that follow provide an entry for each year from 1500–1999, with information on **International and Political Contexts**, **Social and Cultural Contexts**, **Authors** and **Literary Works**.

2 SUBSTANTIVE TIMELINE COLUMNS

The general structure of the book's chapters, headnote glosses and timeline tables has been outlined above. What follows here is a fuller indication of the nature of the four substantive columns and their contents.

NB: the first reference to any monarch, politician, author, artist, and so on indicates their nationality and gives their name in full as it is commonly used; thereafter, only a shortened version is used (e.g. George III, Cavour, de Staël, Picasso); a consistent use of abbreviations is also deployed throughout, and these can be found in a separate list which follows this introduction.

International and Political Contexts   The sequencing of this column is normally as follows: first, British and Irish political events (including major social developments related to affairs of state); second, European events and movements which have some bearing on Britain; third, events and movements in the rest of the world which have international resonances or repercussions (the order of these varies, but once the USA comes into existence, events involving it tend to follow those in Europe, with the 'old' British Empire colonies coming next).

Social and Cultural Contexts   Here 'Social' and 'Cultural' are interpreted in the broadest terms to include material from across the spectrum of social and cultural life. First come developments in British society and general culture, followed by those in other countries; second, works of theological, political, philosophical and historical significance in any language; third, an **Int. Lit.** (International Literature) section which includes examples of literary writing from other countries (note that works in other languages appear in their year of original publication, with the [usually later] date of English translation appended whenever possible); fourth, a **Music** section which includes developments in music and examples of compositions; fifth, an **Art** section which does the same for painting, sculpture, architecture, and so on (NB: the first reference to an artist's work indicates which genre s/he normally works in – e.g. following their name, '[pnt]', '[sculpt.]', etc.; where a work is accessible to view in the UK, the relevant collection is indicated after the title – e.g. '[NG]', '[Tate]', etc. [see list of abbreviations below]). In the 20th Century, a sixth section is appended on **Film**, which gives the name of the director, country of origin (where it is other than the USA), title and principal actors. In addition, and where appropriate, there may be a **Lit.** [Literary] **Events** section indicating events in the general culture which are of literary interest, and a section entitled **Theory/Crit** (Theory and Criticism) which highlights significant contributions to the definition, analysis and study of literature (note that in the later part of the 20th Century – and especially from the 1960s onwards – this becomes a concise history of movements in contemporary cultural and critical theory and practice).

Authors   This is linked across to the **Indicative Titles** column; see below. The first reference to British authors gives the full name by which they are best known, and their dates of birth and death (e.g. '1867–1908'; and birth date only for living authors – e.g. 'b.1956'). Titles are included where they are a familiar part of the name or are often substituted for a forename (e.g. 'Sir Walter Scott', '[Mrs] Elizabeth Gaskell', 'Lord Byron'). Where an author is commonly known only by their surname and forename initials, that is all that is given (e.g. 'G. K. Chesterton'; 'L. P. Hartley'), but where they are known variously by initials or forenames both are given as follows: 'G.[eorge] B.[ernard] Shaw'; 'T.[homas] S.[tearns] Eliot'. After the first reference, only the surname is given, but where confusion may occur, an initial is also included (e.g. 'H. Fielding', 'S. Fielding'; 'P. B.

Shelley', 'M. Shelley'). In the later part of the 20th Century, the place of birth or origin is also cited where possible, either to indicate 'anomalies' (e.g. Sylvia Plath and Timberlake Wertenbaker, who are not strictly British but may reasonably be thought of as contributing centrally to British literary culture), or to establish the significance of region or ethnicity (e.g. originating in the Caribbean, Ulster, Eire, Scotland).

Indicative Titles   This column is divided into three sections, always in the same order (except where one genre does not feature in a particular year): 'Poetry' (represented by **P:**), 'Prose and Fiction' (**Pr/F:**) and 'Drama' (**Dr:**), and gives the titles of works by authors in the preceding column. For poetry, prose and fiction, the year in which they were first published is the one cited (unless otherwise explained), but for plays, it is the year of first performance (unless otherwise indicated). Where it is not immediately apparent what the nature of the work cited may be, a brief explanatory comment is appended in square brackets thus: '[long narrative poem]'; '[historical romance]'; '[melodrama]; '[misc. (for 'miscellaneous') essays]'; a work published after the author's death will have '[posthm. (for 'posthumous')]' after it; works which comprise, for example, a trilogy will have '[trilogy*]' after the first volume and the asterisk repeated after the succeeding volumes. A work whose date is uncertain will have '[*c.*]' preceding its title [see 'Dates' in **Procedures** above], and one which is published over a number of years will be located in the year of its first appearance (e.g. 1771), but its title will be preceded by '[–1776]'.

3 INDEX

The Palgrave Guide to English Literature and its Contexts, 1500–2000 contains two indexes in order to facilitate movement around the mass of information it contains. The first is an alphabetical list of all the British authors who appear in the **Authors** column, together with their dates and the year their work is first cited in the **Indicative Titles** column. This will enable the reader to find the first citation easily and then have a parameter within which to search for later works by the same author. The second index is an alphabetical list of the major period names, movements and concepts which appear in the headnote glosses to the chapters. Detailed contents lists, which may be used in conjunction with the second index, enable easy navigation to the locations of definitions to key terms and concepts.

Abbreviations Used Throughout

GENERAL

[>]	henceforward, continuing thereafter
adaptn	adaptation
aka	also known as
anthol.	anthology
archit.	architecture/al
attrib.	attributed (to)
autobiog.	autobiography/ical
b.	born; or (after number) billion
biog.	biography/ical
bk/s	book/books
b-s.	best-selling/er
c.	*circa* ('about', 'around this time')
C	century (as in 18thC)
CC	County Council
C. in C.	Commander in Chief
C of E	Church of England
Co.	company (as in East India Co.)
Coll.	Collection (especially of art collections)
coll.	collection (of poems, stories, etc.)
comp.	composes (usually in music)
Cons.	Conservative (political party)
contemp.	contemporary
conts/cont.d	continues/continued
d.	dies/died
discvs/.d	discovers/ed
E.	East
edtn	edition
EEC/EU	European Economic Community/European Union
engrv.	engrave (in art)
esp.ly	especially
estabs/.d	establishes/ed
et al	and others (as in Smith et al [eds] . . .)
exhib.d	exhibited
fnds/fnd.d	founds/founded
Gen.	General (as title: Gen. Eisenhower)
gvnmt	government
HE	higher education
illstrs/illstr.d	illustrates/illustrated by
incls/incl.d	includes/included
intros/intro.d	introduces/introduced
Lab.	Labour (political party)
Lat.	Latin
LCC	London County Council
Lib.	Liberal (political party)
litho.	lithograph
L of Ns	League of Nations
l.s.d.	pounds, shillings and pence (old UK currency)
m.	marries/marriage; or (after number) million
misc.	miscellaneous
ms(s)	manuscript/manuscripts
mth/s	month/months
N.	North
nda	no date available
NJ	New Jersey
NY	New York

p.a.	per annum	W.	West
pf.d	performed (usually first performance of play, symphony, etc.)	w/c.	watercolour
		wk/s	week/s
		wrtn	written
phil.	philosophy/ical	Xian	Christian
PM	Prime Minister	yr/s	year/years
pnt	paint (in art)		
posthm.	posthumous (usually of publication)		

NATIONAL DESCRIPTORS (AS ADJECTIVES)

Pres.	President (as title: Pres. Kennedy)	Amer.	American
prnt.d	printed	Aust.	Austrian
prog./s	programme/programmes	Austrl.	Australian
Pt	Part (as in 'Parts I + II')	Belg.	Belgian
pubs/pub.d	publishes/published	Chin.	Chinese
p.w.	per week	Dan.	Danish
R.	River (as prefix to name: River Thames)	Eng.	English
		Fr.	French
RC/ism	Roman Catholic/ism	Ger.	German
re.	concerning, about	Grk	Greek
ref.	reference	Ind.	Indian
rev.d	revised (as in 'rev.d edtn')	Ir.	Irish
RN	Royal Navy	It.	Italian
S.	South	Jap.	Japanese
sci. fi.	science fiction	Norw.	Norwegian
sculpt.	to make a sculpture/a sculptor	Pol.	Polish
		Portug.	Portuguese
Sec.	Secretary (as in 'Sec. of State')	Pruss.	Prussian
		Russ.	Russian
ser.	series	SA	South African (also for the state)
SNP	Scottish Nationalist Party		
sociol.	sociology/sociological	Scots	Scottish
St	street	Sp.	Spanish
trans	translation	Swed.	Swedish
UC	University College	Turk.	Turkish
UN	United Nations	US	United States
USSR	Union of Soviet Socialist Republics		
v.	vide ('see' – as in 'cross-refer'); or versus		
vol./vols	volume/volumes		

UK ART COLLECTIONS

Aberconway Coll.	Aberconway Collection, London
Aberdeen AG	Aberdeen City Art Gallery
Alfreton Hall	. . . Derbyshire
Apsley House	Wellington Collection, Apsley House, London
Astor Coll.	Astor Collection, London
Arts Council	. . . London
Ashmolean	Ashmolean Museum, Oxford
BAG	Birmingham City Art Gallery
Barber Inst.	Barber Institute, University of Birmingham
Beit Coll.	Beit Collection, Russborough
Blenheim	Blenheim Palace
BM	British Museum, London
Bradford AG	Bradford City Art Gallery
British Council	. . . London
Burrell Coll.	Burrell Collection, Glasgow
Cadbury Coll.	Cadbury Collection, Birmingham
Christ's Hosp.	Christ's Hospital, London
Clark Coll.	Clark Collection, London
Colston Coll.	. . . East Lothian
Courtauld	Courtauld Institute, University of London
Derby AG	Derby City Art Gallery
Dewar Coll.	Dewar Collection, London
Dulwich	Dulwich College, London
Dunvegan Castle	. . . Isle of Skye
Foundling Hosp.	Foundling Hospital, London
Glasgow AG	Glasgow City Art Gallery
Guildhall	Guildhall Art Gallery, London
Hampton Court	Hampton Court Palace, Surrey
Harewood House	. . . Yorkshire
Helly Nahmad Gall.	Helly Nahmad Gallery, London
Hull AG	Hull City Art Gallery
Hunterian	Hunterian Collection, University of Glasgow
IWM	Imperial War Museum, London
Keble	Keble College, Oxford
Kensington Palace	. . . London
Kenwood	Kenwood House, London
Knole, Kent	Knole House, Kent (National Trust)
Lady Lever AG	Lady Lever Art Gallery, Port Sunlight
Laing AG	Laing Art Gallery, Newcastle-upon-Tyne
Leeds AG	Leeds City Art Gallery
Lefevre Coll.	Lefevre Collection, London
Londesborough Estates	. . . E. Riding of Yorkshire
London Mus.	London Museum
MAG	Manchester City Art Gallery
Marlborough AG	Marlborough Art Gallery, London
Meir Coll.	Meir Collection, London
NAG	Nottingham City Art Gallery
NG	National Gallery, London
NMM	National Maritime Museum, Greenwich, London
NMW	National Museum of Wales, Cardiff
Norwich	Castle Museum, Norwich
NPG	National Portrait Gllery, London

Penrose Coll.	Penrose Collection, London	Southampton AG	Southampton City Art Gallery
Petworth	Petworth House, Sussex	Spencer Coll.	Spencer Collection, Althorpe
RCA	Royal College of Art, London	St Barts	St Bartholomew's Hospital, London
R. Coll. Surgeons	Royal College of Surgeons Collection, London	St Paul's	St Paul's Cathedral, London
Rosebery Coll.	Rosebery Collection, Dalmeny	Sudeley	Sudeley Castle, Gloucestershire
Rothschild Coll.	Rothschild Collection, Cambridge	Syon House	. . . Brentford, London
Royal Co. of Archers	Royal Company of Archers, Edinburgh	V&A	Victoria and Albert Museum, London
Royal Coll.	Royal Collection (at Buckingham Palace or Windsor Castle)	Wallace Coll.	Wallace Collection, Hertford House, London
Royal Holloway	Royal Holloway College, Egham	Walker AG	Walker Art Gallery, Liverpool
Saatchi Coll.	Saatchi Collection, London	Wrotham Park	. . . Kent
		Zoological Soc.	Zoological Society, London
Sloane	Sloane Museum, London		
SNG	National Gallery of Scotland, Edinburgh		

1

1500–1649

The English Reformation and Renaissance

INTRODUCTION

The long period covered in this chapter takes us from the reign of the **Tudor*** monarch, King Henry VII (died 1509 – succeeded by Henry VIII), to the execution by Parliament of the **Stuart*** King Charles I in 1649. It is a period which establishes the foundations of the modern United Kingdom, and includes **The (English) Reformation***, **The (English) Renaissance***, the **Elizabethan*** period (with its great flowering of a national literature), the first part of the Stuart* reign [see Chapter 2 for its continuation after 1660], the **Jacobean*** and **Caroline*** periods, and **The English Civil War***.

Chapter contents

1.1 TUDOR

The family name of the line of monarchs – 'The Tudors' – who held the English throne from 1485 to 1603, and hence the name of the period from the accession of Henry VII to the death of Elizabeth I.

With the murder of Edward V and his brother Richard ('the Princes in the Tower') in 1483, the death of the Yorkist Richard III at the Battle of Bosworth Field, and the end of the Wars of the Roses (1455–85, an intermittent civil war was waged between the houses of York [white] and Lancaster [red] which had deeply divided the kingdom), the Plantagenet line ended, and the Lancastrian Henry Tudor acceded to the throne. He was descended from John of Gaunt, Duke of Lancaster, on his mother's side, and from the kings of France and native Welsh princes on his father's, his family name deriving from Owen Tudor whom his maternal grandmother, Catherine, daughter of Charles VI of France, had married after the death of her husband, Henry V of England. The self-pronounced Welsh origins of the usurping Tudors were central to the *Tudor Myth*, which claimed the dynasty's descent from ancient British rulers, including King Arthur, and promised to restore the power and glory of Camelot. The stylised figure of the *Tudor Rose* – red and white to symbolise the houses of Lancaster and York, and thus the end of hostilities between them – was adopted as a badge by Henry VII. It features prominently in *Tudor Architecture*, which is characterised by half-timbering and patterned brickwork.

Key Timeline Narratives 1500–1603

➲ **The Succession**   The problem of protecting a line of succession for the Tudor dynasty, especially the failure of Henry VIII and his queen, Catherine of Aragon, to produce a son and heir, which helped to instigate the English **Reformation***, and the youthfulness and then the early death of Henry's only son (by Jane Seymour), King Edward VI.

➲ **Religion**   The inception of religious strife in what was later to become 'Great Britain', and which dominated its history for at least the next three centuries. A crucial instance of this was the furore, after the death of Edward VI (1553), around the accession of Henry VIII's legitimate daughter by Catherine of Aragon, Mary I (Mary Tudor), a Roman Catholic who married Philip II, King of Spain, and whose persecution of English Protestants in an attempt to restore England to the Roman Catholic fold resulted in the sobriquet 'Bloody Mary'. When she died childless in 1558, her half-sister, Queen Elizabeth I (daughter of Ann Boleyn, Henry VIII's second wife), acceded to the throne, but Elizabeth's failure to marry and produce an heir in her turn led, on her death in 1603, to the end the Tudor line and the start of the **Stuart*** succession.

➲ **Politics**   The gradual development of an English national state and identity, distinct from the still largely Catholic mainland Europe.

1.2 THE (ENGLISH) REFORMATION

Literally, 'reformation' means an act of reforming, amending and improving. Capitalised and preceded by the definite article, 'The Reformation' identifies that period and process in the 16th

Century in Europe which saw the doctrine and power of the Roman Catholic Church challenged and in many cases replaced by the various forms of Protestant religion.

However, political and economic factors also determined its course and nature: the hostility of rulers and jurists to the temporal encroachments of the Vatican; the growing wealth of the clergy, and the religious and moral laxity of many; the development of printing, which assisted the spread of ideas; and related to this, the humanism of the **Renaissance***, which encouraged a new critical and enquiring attitude of mind. The individualism at the heart of Reformation religions, combined with their embattled location in diverse Northern European states, also helped to foster the growth of nationalism and the economic prosperity of the mercantile classes.

The Dutch humanist scholar, Erasmus, who introduced a Greek edition of the Scriptures in 1516 to replace the Vatican's Latin one, is usually regarded as the principal intellectual force behind the Reformation (as, indeed, behind the later Renaissance*, too). Whilst not attacking the authority of the Pope himself, Erasmus nevertheless castigated the Church for its abuses (selling pardons and religious relics) and for its pedantry (e.g. in *In Praise of Folly*, 1509). The start of the Reformation proper is normally dated to 1517, when the German theologian, Martin Luther, nailed his *95 Theses Against the Sale of Papal Indulgencies* to a church door in Wittenberg. Unlike Erasmus (who was to attack the reformers' zeal in 1523), Luther refused to submit to the Pope's authority, which led to his excommunication in 1521, and the consequent spread of Protestantism across much of Northern Europe. The Lutheran reformers sought to restore Christianity to its early purity, their main tenets being justification by faith and the absolute authority of the Scriptures in all matters of faith, in contradistinction to ecclesiastical tradition (i.e. that of the authority of the Roman Catholic Church). The new religion was then driven by the far stricter religious and moral teachings of, for example, the French reformer, Jean Calvin, based in the middle years of the 16th Century in Geneva, from where was exported a widely influential, severe and doctrinaire brand of Protestant individualism (including the doctrine of predestination). Calvinism flourished in Switzerland, the Low Countries, and in Scotland under John Knox. The reaction against such developments in Roman Catholic Europe is known as the 'Counter-Reformation'.

The English Reformation should be seen in the context of the European movement, but it was rather differently motivated and inflected. In 1519, Henry VIII had written a book against Luther entitled *Defence of the Seven Sacraments*. For this, the Pope bestowed on him the title, 'Fidei Defensor' ('Defender of the Faith'), but the failure of Henry's marriage to Catherine of Aragon to produce a male heir led him to seek permission from Rome to divorce her, so that he could marry the already pregnant Ann Boleyn. The Vatican demurred, Henry married Ann regardless and was excommunicated. He made Thomas Cranmer Archbishop of Canterbury, and by the Act of Supremacy in 1534, declared himself 'the only supreme head on earth of the Church of England'. Although Henry continued to claim to be a Catholic, from 1536 to 1539, he carried out the Dissolution of the Monastries, whereby the hundreds of religious houses in England were ransacked for their wealth, their abbeys often destroyed, and their lands confiscated and sold.

During the minority reign of his son, Edward VI, who succeeded Henry at the age of nine, the powerful men in his Protectorate introduced stringent Protestant reforms which inclined the country towards Calvinism. On Edward's death, Mary I [see **Tudor*** above] attempted to reintroduce Catholicism as the national religion with considerable support, but her unpopular marriage to the king of Catholic Spain, together with the increasing ferocity of the persecution of Protestants (Bishops Ridley, Latimer and Cranmer, amongst many others, were burnt at the stake), turned the tide against her. Her half-sister, Elizabeth I, succeeded her in 1558, and managed, in the course of her long and eventful reign [see **Elizabethan*** below], to effect a compromise between Catholic liturgy (which she enjoyed) and Protestant faith (which she believed in). A major Catholic uprising occurred in the north of England in 1569 (it was suppressed), but after 1570, in reaction to Rome's deeply resented declaration that Elizabeth was illegitimate, the so-called Elizabethan Church Settlement increasingly gained popular support.

1.3 THE (ENGLISH) RENAISSANCE

The noun 'renaissance', from the French 'renascence', literally means 'rebirth'. Capitalised, and with the direct article, 'The Renaissance' defines the artistic, literary and scientific revival which took place in Europe from the 14th Century to the mid-17th Century (the end-date is disputed).

This period has been seen as an intermediate period between the Middle Ages and the full development of the modern world (even so, its later phases are now more usually described by historians as belonging to 'the Early Modern Period', a less loaded term than 'The Renaissance'). The movement originated in Italy, where the word 'rinascità' was in use by the mid-16th Century to describe the great flowering of the Italian arts in the 14th Century ('Quattrocento'), and later spread throughout Europe. However, the term was first used in English only in 1840, and its general currency was established in the mid-19th Century by the Swiss historian, Jacob Burckhardt, in his work, *The Civilization of the Renaissance in Italy* (1860). 'Renaissance' can also be used as an adjective, as in 'Renaissance painting' or 'Renaissance Man' [see below].

In general terms, the Renaissance was characterised by the renewed influence of classical culture and values; a new humanism in part derived from these; and the beginning of objective scientific enquiry. It represents a contrast to the Church-centred culture of the medieval period in its celebration of humanity and individuality; but although the the notion of 'rebirth' suggests a sudden rupture with the past, the Renaissance is probably better thought of as a process of gradual change. In 14th-century Italy, a humanist and classical literary revival began with the writings of Petrarch and Boccaccio, while Giotto established the foundations of Renaissance painting. In the 15th Century, Byzantine scholars founded a Platonic Academy in Florence, and with the the fall of Constantinople to the Turks in 1453, Greek scholars brought classical manuscripts to Italy, the invention of printing thereafter allowing the 'new learning' to spread throughout Europe. Fifteenth-century Italian art includes the work of Fra Angelico, Mantegna and Botticelli in painting, Donatello and Ghiberti in sculpture, and Brunelleschi in architecture, while at its height in the 16th Century, the great names of the Italian Renaissance are: in painting and sculpture, Michelangelo, Leonardo da Vinci, Raphael, Titian, Giovanni Bellini; in literature, Tasso and Ariosto; in political thought, Machiavelli; and in music, Palestrina. It is the multiple talents of, for example, Michaelangelo (painter, poet, architect, sculptor) and da Vinci (painter, anatomist, scientific inventor) which give us the notion of *Renaissance Man*: someone equally capable of high success in several different fields of expertise, and himself both an examplar and celebrant of that proud humanity, physical and mental, which characterises the Renaissance world-view and which is otherwise expressed in its valorisation of the fully rounded 'gentleman' or 'courtier' (Castiglione's *Il Cortegiano*; translated into English by Sir Thomas Hoby in 1552–3). Elsewhere in Europe, this is also the period of such writers as Ronsard, Rabelais, Lope de Vega, Cervantes and Montaigne, and visual artists, Dürer, El Greco, Holbein and the Bruegel family.

In experimental science, mathematics, geography and astronomy, too, a new inquiring spirit was developing which freed human beings to explore, understand and enjoy the physical world in ways impossible under the medieval Church's dispensation. Copernicus placed the sun, not the earth, at the centre of the universe, which Galileo was later to verify using a telescope, and all sorts of other instruments for investigating and measuring the universe were invented; the Spanish and Portuguese 'discovered' the New World of the Americas and first circumnavigated the globe; anatomy developed rapidly; Erasmus and other scholars promoted a neo-classical humanism in philosophical thinking based on notions of a harmonious universe with Man at the centre of it, of a more heroic humanity capable of perfectibility, reason not religion as the principle governing human behaviour, and above all, an elation mixed with anxiety about the apparently boundless freedom to think everything anew: as John Donne famously put it: 'The new philosophy calls all in doubt.'

The English Renaissance is normally dated from either *c.*1476, with the introduction of printing into England by William Caxton, or 1485 with the arrival of the Tudor* dynasty, and reaching its apogee in the Elizabethan* and **Jacobean*** periods. There were signs of the times in Henry VIII's reign: Sir Thomas More, a friend of Erasmus, published his *Utopia*; another humanist, Sir Thomas Elyot, published *The Boke named the Govenour*; King Henry himself had the education, abilities and tastes of a Renaissance 'courtier' [see above]; the poetry of John Skelton, Sir Thomas Wyatt and Henry Howard, Earl of Surrey, belongs to this period; and a number of colleges at Oxford and Cambridge Universities were founded. But cultural historians believe that the effects of the Reformation slowed the Renaissance process down in England, and there is certainly no achievement in the visual arts to match that of 15th-and 16th-century Italy. The height of the English Renaissance, then, and especially so in literature (although also in music, architecture and art), belongs to the later Elizabethan period, indicative events in the late 1570s and early 1580s being the building and opening of the first public theatres in London and the composition by Sir Philip Sidney, a quintessential type of the Renaissance 'gentleman', of his *Arcadia* (the 'Old' version) and *Defence of Poetry*. However, general characteristics of cultural developments throughout the period would include: as a reflex of the Reformation, a great increase in printed works in the English language, resulting in a rapid rise in literacy; the enforced spread of English in Wales and Ireland, and then its exportation to the New World; a new sense of national identity and pride which fostered confidence in using English for serious writing (rather than Latin) and for the creation of a national literature which would compete with those in classical and other European languages; a huge expansion in vocabulary (it is estimated that during the century and a half from c.1500, exploration, trade, translation and scholarship caused well over 10,000 new words to enter English from Latin, Greek, European and other languages, as well as neologisms created by native authors); a consequent linguistic exuberance and innovativeness in literary style, form and genre; and the development of a literature which enthusiastically explored the social, political, religious, cultural and emotional implications of newly liberated, human-centred experience.

1.4 ELIZABETHAN

As an adjective, 'Elizabethan' designates the reign of Queen Elizabeth I of England and Ireland, 1558–1603, and the literature, art, music and architecture produced in those years; as a noun, it identifies someone living during the period – although it tends to be used more specifically for the literary writers of the second half of the era ('Sidney and Spenser were distinguished Elizabethans').

On the death of Mary I [see Tudor*], Elizabeth acceded to the throne, and immediately faced religious strife, economic instability and war with France. But while the history of her reign shows the resolution of many such problems, it is also marked throughout by domestic unrest and rebellion in Ireland, hostile relations with much of continental Europe, and religious opposition by, and suppression of, both Catholics and Puritans. Nevertheless, it is also witness to a great enhancement of national identity and pride, the major achievements of the English Renaissance*, an increase in English international power, and the inception of a capitalist economy.

Key Timeline Narratives

⮑ **Religion**   The re-establishment of the Church of England on a moderate basis; a string of Catholic plots against Elizabeth, focused after 1568 around the exiled and imprisoned Mary, Queen of Scots (finally executed in 1587), the severe repression of English Catholics, and the related chronic crisis about the succession throughout the unmarried and childless Elizabeth's reign; relations with Protestant Scotland; the increasing opposition of the Puritans to Anglicanism, their growing power in Parliament and resistance to the Crown, and the resulting attempts to suppress them.

⮑ **Ireland and Europe**   The 'planting' (colonising) of Ireland by English and Scottish Protestants, and the series of Irish revolts from 1569 until the reconquest and 'pacification' of 1600–3; strained relations with Catholic Europe over religion and the execution of Mary, Queen of Scots, but also exacerbated by England's rapid development as a major maritime power – both in terms of international trade and of the licensed piracy of, for example, Sir John Hawkins and Sir Francis Drake who plundered Spanish ships in the Americas – culminating in the defeat of the Spanish Armada in 1588.

⮱ **North America**   The start of the settling and colonising of North America with Sir Walter Raleigh's ventures in Virginia.

⮱ **Social and Economic Developments**   The beginnings of social legislation in Parliament in respect of Poor Relief Acts and associated initiatives; the physical and symbolic expansion of London as capital city; the development of banking and other financial institutions to facilitate and expand a fledgling capitalist economy, but also economic depression and social unrest caused by a combination of Elizabeth's fiscal policies, heavy taxation and a series of bad harvests in the 1590s.

⮱ **Literary and Cultural Events**   The continued founding of new schools, Oxbridge colleges and libraries; the widespread translation of religious, classical and other literary works into English; the extensive building of theatres in London, and the rapid upsurge in dramatic writing; the appearance in the later part of the period not only of a significant literature in English, but also accompanying it, a literary critical discourse in which to discuss and promote it; developments in English painting (especially portraiture), music (especially songs and madrigals), and architecture (especially the erection of great houses and other public buildings across the country).

1.5 STUART (ALSO STEWART)

*The family name of the line of monarchs – 'the Stuarts' – who occupied the British throne from the accession of King James I in 1603 to the deposition and execution of King Charles I in 1649; and from the **Restoration*** of King Charles II in 1660 to the death of Queen Anne in 1714.*

The 'missing' period between 1649 and 1660 is the **Interregnum***, during which Great Britain was governed first as a **Commonwealth*** under Parliament and then as a **Protectorate*** under Oliver Cromwell. [Commentary and suggested timeline narratives in respect of the restored Stuart line after 1660 will be found in the glosses to Chapter 2.]

The Stuarts, in fact, were monarchs of Scotland from 1371 to 1714, and on the death of Elizabeth I without an heir, her cousin, the then James VI of Scotland, acceded to the English throne as James I of England [see also Jacobean*]. James, the son of Mary, Queen of Scots, who had become King of Scotland on his mother's forced abdication in 1567, and who made only token protest at her execution in 1587 [see under Elizabethan*], was a staunch Protestant whose claim to the throne, accepted by both Elizabeth and Parliament, derived from the marriage of James IV of Scotland to Margaret Tudor, daughter of Henry VII of England. James's joint monarchy effectively brought about the union of England and Scotland, and in 1604, he was declared king of 'Great Britain, France and Ireland' – the reference to France by this point being anachronistic wishful thinking. [It is from this point, then, that the present volume will normally use 'Great Britain'/'British' and not 'English' when referring to historical and cultural events – except where the latter term is specifically correct. After 1800, when the Act of Union united the Parliaments of Great Britain and Ireland to form 'The United Kingdom of Great Britain and Ireland', 'UK' will tend to be substituted for 'British/Britain'.]

1.6   JACOBEAN

*Derived from the Latin for James, 'Jacobus', the adjective 'Jacobean' is used solely to identify the period of the reign of King James I of England, Scotland and Ireland, 1603–25 [see **Stuart*** above], and the literature, architecture, furniture and style of decoration produced during it.*

James was a devout but not extreme Protestant, and did much to establish his religion as the national one (he played a central role in organising a new standardised translation of the Bible: the 'Authorised Version' or 'King James Bible' of 1611). However, his religious beliefs brought him into serious conflict with both Catholics and Puritans, while his dogmatic insistence on the Divine Right of Kings caused him to clash bitterly with Parliament, and especially a House of Commons which was developing a growing sense of independence. James himself was a scholar who wrote learned treatises on several subjects, and was a strong supporter of the arts, especially the theatre (Shakespeare's company was called the 'King's Men', and it is possible that James saw an early production of Shakespeare's topical tragedy, *Macbeth*, in 1606). The combination of intellectual talent and stubborn personality led to him being dubbed 'the wisest fool in Christendom'.

Key Timeline Narratives 1603–1625

- **Religion**   The continuing religious strife between Catholics and Protestants, and the rapidly growing power of the Puritans, especially in Parliament (the Gunpowder Plot in 1605 is the most famous event in this narrative, which led to severe persecution of Catholics).

- **Government**   The increasingly divisive tensions between King and Parliament, initially instigated by dislike in some quarters for James's scheme for the 'perfect union' of England and Scotland, and by his hostility to Puritanism at the Hampton Court Conference (1604) – this being compounded by his dubious financial devices (sale of monopolies and titles, royal duties levied at ports); his ambivalent relationship with Spain; and resentment at his reliance on favourites (especially the Duke of Buckingham).

- **Naval Expansion and Colonisation**   The continuing development of British maritime power, its underpinning of national mercantile interests abroad (e.g. those of the East India Company), and the resulting conflicts with the Dutch in particular; the colonisation of the east coast of North America, and the sailing of the Pilgrim Fathers to 'New England' in 1620; the authorised 'plantation' of confiscated Irish land, especially in Ulster, by English and Scottish settlers.

- **Social and Economic Events**   The incidence of plague in London, which had the effect of frequently closing the proliferating theatres there; the continuing foundation of schools and university colleges, and the rise of 'Jacobean' architectural design for houses and public buildings (Inigo Jones, as Surveyor of the King's Works, built the Queen's House, Greenwich, and the new Palace of Whitehall).

- **Theatre**   It is not fortuitous that the commonest present-day use of the word 'Jacobean' is in the phrase 'Jacobean Drama', for it was during James's reign that many of the most famous tragedies and comedies in English were written and first performed (e.g. by Shakespeare, Jonson, Webster, Beaumont and Fletcher, Middleton, Massinger and Ford).

1.7   CAROLINE

The adjective 'Caroline' (less frequently 'Carolean') is derived from the Latin for Charles, 'Carolus', and is used to describe the period of the reign of King Charles I of England, Scotland and Ireland, 1625–49.

'Caroline' is occasionally also applied to the reign of King Charles II, 1660–85, but **The Restoration*** [see Chapter 2] is now the conventionally accepted term for this period. Unlike 'Jacobean', 'Caroline' is far less commonly used either as a period descriptor or for the literature and other arts of the time, perhaps because there is not a substantive body of work with enough characteristics in common to have given the word equal currency. The verse of the so-called 'Cavalier Poets' (Herrick, Cowley, Suckling, Lovelace, Waller, Denham), however, is the most coherent corpus of work to be properly called 'Caroline', but it is worth remembering that Donne died six years into Charles's reign and that his poems were first published only in 1633; that the devotional 'Metaphysical Poets' (Crashaw, Vaughan, Herbert, Traherne) were writing in this period; and that the writing careers of Milton and Marvell straddled the Interregnum* [see Chapter 2].

James I bequeathed to his son Charles a situation marked by hostility between Crown and Parliament, one Charles immediately compounded by marrying the Catholic French princess, Henrietta Maria, only a matter of weeks after his accession to the throne. Her influence on the king was abhorred by Parliament, and by 1642, just before the Civil War started, she was herself in danger of impeachment. Like his father, Charles was talented, autocratic and a firm believer in the Divine Right of Kings; he also indulged the same favourite, Buckingham, until the latter's assassination in 1628. In addition, Charles promoted the High Church Anglicanism of Archbishop Laud, which was anathema to an extreme Protestant Parliament; but it was the king's penurious financial situation and the strategies he then deployed to raise money without accountability which produced the most persistent, and ultimately terminal, conflict with the Commons.

It is clear from the timelines that the dominant narrative of this period is the one flagged in the previous paragraph: Charles's dissolution of three Parliaments between 1625 and 1629, and his collection of revenues without consent; his acceptance under duress of the Petition of Right in 1628; his 11 years of 'personal rule' without Parliament (1629–40), using the Earl of Strafford (Thomas Wentworth) and the Courts of the Star Chamber and High Commission to enforce his government in the kingdom; his imposition of the hated 'Ship Money' tax on maritime and then inland counties, which resulted in the John Hampden trial; the necessity of recalling Paliament in 1640 under threat of a Scottish invasion [see below], first as the 'Short Parliament' and then as the 'Long Parliament' (which outlasted Charles himself); the execution by the 'Long Parliament' of

Strafford and Laud, and the drawing up of the 'Grand Remonstrance' (1641) by John Pym and other leaders of the resistance to the king; Charles's failed attempt in early 1642 to arrest the 'Five Members' responsible for the document; his raising of his standard at Nottingham, the commencement of the **English Civil War***, and Charles's ultimate defeat, imprisonment, trial and execution.

1.8 THE ENGLISH CIVIL WAR

*Although England had been ravaged by civil war in the past – most especially by the Wars of the Roses (1455–85; see **Tudor*** above) – the term 'The English Civil War' (aka 'The Great Rebellion') refers exclusively to the struggle between Parliament and King Charles I (then his son, Charles Stuart – later King Charles II) from 1642 to 1651.*

The English Civil War was caused principally by Puritan and emerging middle-class opposition to the king's claims to rule by divine right and the Long Parliament's consequent attempts to curb royal policy by withholding resources from him. The country was divided between the 'Royalist' or 'Cavalier' interest and the 'Parliamentarians' or 'Roundheads' (Puritans tended to have their hair cut short, unlike the Cavaliers' flowing locks). The king raised his standard at Nottingham in 1642, and the Civil War began.

The detailed course of the war can be followed in the timeline tables (including those at the beginning of Chapter 2), but key moments are: Parliament's covenant with the Scots (1643); the calling of the Royalist Parliament at Oxford (1644); Charles's flight from Oxford and surrender to the Scots (1646; end of '1st Civil War'); the king's signing of an 'Engagement' with the Scots (1647); their subsequent invasion of England on the king's behalf and defeat at Preston (1648; end of '2nd Civil War'); the trial and beheading of Charles I (1649), and the declaration of England as a 'Free Commonwealth*' [see Chapter 2]; the proclamation of Charles Stuart as king in Edinburgh (1649); a further Scottish Royalist invasion of England, and its defeat at the Battle of Worcester (1651). Charles Stuart fled to France, and the period of the Interregnum* (see Chapter 2) begins.

Key Timeline Narratives

➲ *Religion*   Attempts by Charles and Laud to anglicise the Presbyterian Scottish Kirk, leading to serious rebellions, the 'Bishops' Wars' of 1639–40, and the threat of a Scottish invasion which forced the king to recall Parliament in 1640 [see above]; further Irish Catholic rebellions in the 1640s, and in 1649, the invasion of Ireland by Oliver Cromwell.

➲ *Colonisation*   The expansion of British colonisation of North America, including parts of what was to become Canada; expansion of British trading activity in India and then China, and continuing conflict with the Dutch and French over areas of influence for trade and for colonisation.

➲ *Science*   The start of the draining of the Fens in the eastern counties of England by Dutch engineers;

the continuation of scientific development (Sir William Harvey proved the circulation of the blood in 1628), with the seeds of the establishment of the Royal Society (1662) sown during this period.

⮑ *Law*   Censorship by Crown and Parliament featured throughout the period, but so too did the begininngs of copyright.

⮑ *Theatre*   The drama continued to flourish – although many of the major Jacobean names had disappeared by the 1630s – until the theatres were closed by the Puritans in 1642 (reopened at The Restoration* in 1660; see Chapter 2).

Timelines: 1500–1649

PERIOD	YEAR	INTERNATIONAL AND POLITICAL CONTEXTS	SOCIAL AND CULTURAL CONTEXTS	AUTHORS	INDICATIVE TITLES
TUDOR	1500	Henry VII king [since 1485]; Great Jubilee Year. [During this century, Renaissance spreads from Italy thro'out W. Europe.]	**Music:** 1st virginals & violins. **Art:** [c.] Giorgione [pnt] 'Judith'; [c.] Giovanni Bellini [pnt] 'Madonna and Child in a Landscape'; Albrecht Dürer [pnt] 'Young Man Wearing a Cap'; [c.] Lucas Cranach the Elder [pnt] 'Crucifixion'	Lit. **'Events':**	1st printing press estab.d in Fleet Street
	1501	Prince Arthur, Henry's heir, m. Catherine of Aragon – Arthur dies 6 mths later; 1st voyage of Anglo-Portugese Syndicate to N. America carrying slaves	**Art:** Holyrood House, Edinburgh, 1st built; [–1504] Michelangelo [sculpt] 'David'	P: Gavin Douglas (c.1447–1522) Lit. **'Events':**	The Palace of Honour [Scots poem; prnt.d 1553] Aldine Press edtn of Virgil pub.d
	1502	[>] Expanding discovery of 'The New World'	**Art:** Bellini, 'Baptism of Christ'; [–1503] Raphael [pnt], 'Coronation of the Virgin' & [–1503] 'Madonna Conestabile; Dürer, 'Hare'	Lit. **'Events':**	Further Aldine Press edtns of classical authors pub.d
	1503	Catherine of Aragon betrothed to 11-yr-old Prince Henry, next in line to throne [becomes Henry VIII]; 1st gold sovereigns struck	Desiderius Erasmus, Handbook of a Christian Soldier. **Art:** Raphael, 'Crucifixion' [NG] & [–1504] 'The Knight's Dream (Vision of a Knight)' [NG]; Michelangelo [pnt] 'Doni Tondo (The Holy Family)'; [–1507] Leonardo da Vinci [pnt] 'Mona Lisa'; Matthias Grünewald [pnt] 'Lindenhardt Altarpiece'	P: William Dunbar (c.1460–c.1520)	The Thistle and the Rose [allegorical poem]
	1504	Henry VII institutes state supervision of guilds & companies; 1st silver shilling minted	Int. Lit. Jacopo Sannazaro, Arcadia [It. pastoral romance]. **Art:** Giorgione, 'Madonna with Sts Francis and Liberale'; Raphael, 'Marriage of the Virgin'; Dürer, 'Adoration of the Magi'; Cranach, 'The Flight into Egypt'		
	1505	Henry issues new Charter to Merchant Adventurers; [>] Portuguese trading empire expands in Indian Ocean & Far East	Christ's College, Cambridge, fnd.d. **Art:** Hieronymus Bosch [pnt] 'The Garden of Earthly Delights' [triptych; begun c.1485] & [c.] 'The Hay Wagon' [triptych]	P: John Skelton (c.1460–1529) Lit. **'Events':**	[c.] Ware the Hawk & Philip Sparrow [wrtn] By now, Skelton is recognised as the 'Laureate' poet
	1506	Commercial treaty between England & Netherlands	Columbus dies. **Art:** 1st-century BC Laocoön sculpture group discovered in Rome; [–1626] Donato Bramante builds the new Basilica of St Peter's, Rome; Giorgione, 'Tempesta'; Lorenzo Lotto [pnt] 'St Jerome in the Wilderness'		
	1507		Martin Waldseemüller, Ger. cartographer, 1st names 'America' on his new world map & globe. **Art:** Leonardo, 'Virgin of the Rocks' [NG has copy] & [c.] 'Madonna and Child with St Anne' [cartoon; NG]; Giorgione, 'Sleeping Venus'	P: Dunbar	[c.] Dance of the Seven Deadly Sins
	1508		Martin Luther becomes Professor of Divinity at Wittenberg. **Art:** [–1511] Baldassarre Peruzzi builds Villa Farnesina, Florence; [c.] Michelangelo [pnt]	Lit. **'Events':**	7 of Dunbar's poems prnt.d [1st e.g. of Scots typography]

Year	History	Arts & Society	Author	Work
1509	Henry VII dies, Henry VIII becomes king of England – m. to Catherine of Aragon [v.1503]	'Entombment of Christ' [NG] & [–1512] pnts Sistine Chapel ceiling, Vatican, Rome; Lucas van Leyden [engrv.] 'David Playing Before Saul'	**P:** Alexander Barclay (1475?–1552)	*The Ship of Fools* [Eng. trans/imitation of earlier Ger. poem]
1510	Parliament grants Henry VIII life-long duties on tonnage, poundage & wool	Peter Henlein invents 'Nuremberg Egg' – 1st watch; Brasenose College, Oxford & St Paul's School, London, fnd.d; Erasmus, *In Praise of Folly* [pub.d Paris, 1511]. **Art:** [–1511] Raphael decorates Stanza della Segnatura, Vatican [incls 'School of Athens']; Cranach, 'Adam and Eve'		
1511		[c.–1514] Erasmus, Professor of Greek at Cambridge. **Art:** [–1517] van Leyden [engrv.] 'Return of the Prodigal Son', 'Ecce Homo' & 'Ascent to Calvary'		
1512		[c.] St. John's College, Cambridge, fnd.d. **Art:** [–1512] Raphael, 'Galatea' [fresco; Villa Farnesina, Florence]		
1513	Scots, allied with French, beaten at Battle of Flodden; Balboa crosses Isthmus of Panama & discovers the Pacific; Florida discovered	**Art:** Dürer [engrv.] 'St Jerome' [BM]; [c.–1515] Grünewald, 'Isenheim Altarpiece'; [–1518] Pietro Torrigiano [sculpt] tomb of Henry VII & Elizabeth of York [Westminster Abbey]	**P:** Douglas	Virgil's *Aeneid* [Eng. trans wrtn; prnt.d 1553]
1514	Peace and treaty between England & France – Spain now recognised as England's main rival	[–1514] Niccolo Machiavelli, *The Prince* [wrtn; pub.d 1532; Eng. trans, 1540]. **Art:** [–1514] Raphael, 'Sistine (Dresden) Madonna'; Dürer [engrv.] 'Knight, Death and the Devil' [BM]	**P:** Barclay **Pr/F:** Sir Thomas More (1477/8?–1535)	*Eclogues* [completed; Eng. trans of Lat. history by Sallust] [–1518] *History of King Richard III* [prnt.d 1557]
1515	Commercial treaty between England & Spain; Thomas Wolsey created Cardinal & becomes Lord Chancellor	**Art:** [–1515] Raphael, 'Madonna della Sedia'; Dürer [engrv.] 'Melancholia' & 'St Jerome in his Study'; [–1515] Antonio Correggio [pnt] 'Madonna with St Francis' [altarpiece]	**Dr:** Skelton	[c.] *Magnificence* [morality play wrtn; pub. posthm. 1533]
1516	Princess Mary born [later Queen Mary I, 'Mary Tudor']	**Art:** [–1530] Thomas Wolsey builds Hampton Court Palace – presented to Henry VIII, 1526; [–1516] Raphael, 'Baldassare Castiglione'; [–1516] Michelangelo [sculpt] 'Moses' & [c.] 'Bound Slaves'; [c.] Titian [pnt] 'Sacred and Profane Love'	**Pr/F:** More	Erasmus edits Greek New Testament. **Int. Lit:** Ludovico Ariosto, *Orlando Furioso* [completed in 3rd edtn, 1532]. **Art:** St George's Chapel, Windsor, completed; [c.–1518] Titian, 'Assumption of the Virgin' [altarpiece] — *Utopia* [pub.d in Latin at Louvain by Erasmus; Eng. trans 1551]

PERIOD	YEAR	INTERNATIONAL AND POLITICAL CONTEXTS	SOCIAL AND CULTURAL CONTEXTS	AUTHORS	INDICATIVE TITLES
TUDOR	1517	'Evil May Day' riots in London against foreign merchants & craftsmen	Luther nails his 95 'Theses' [against sale of indulgences] to Wittenberg church door: start of Reformation; Corpus Christi College, Oxford, fnd.d; coffee 1st imported to Europe. **Art:** [–1519] Raphael et al, 'Loggia di Psiche' [frescoes; Rome]; Andrea del Sarto [pnt] 'Madonna of the Harpies'	P: Skelton	[c.] *The Tunning of Elynour Rummyng* [wrtn; prnt.d, c.1521]
	1518	Wolsey's diplomacy brings Peace of London between England & continental powers; agreement between English merchants & Antwerp	Royal College of Physicians fnd.d; interrogation of Luther – refuses to recant. **Art:** Dürer [etch] 'Landscape with a Cannon' [BM]; [–c.1520] Titian, 'Bacchanal'	Lit. 'Events':	1st copyright awarded to the King's Printer
	1519	[–1521] Cortez conquers Mexico; [–1522] Magellan's voyage round the world begins	Da Vinci dies; Zwingli begins Protestant preaching in Zurich. **Art:** [–1526] Titian 'Madonna of the Pesaro Family' [altarpiece]		
	1520	Henry VIII meets Charles V, Holy Roman Emperor & King of Spain, signs secret treaty [hostile to France] at Calais; commercial treaty also made between England & Emperor; Henry meets Francis I of France on the Field of Cloth of Gold, but no treaty against Holy Roman Empire; Suleiman the Magnificent, Sultan of Turkey – empire stretches from Baghdad to Hungary; Magellan discovers Chile & 'Magellan Strait', enters & names 'Pacific'	Raphael dies; Luther declared a heretic by Pope, burns excommunication bull, pub.s reform pamphlets – Reformation movement in Netherlands; chocolate 1st imported to Europe. **Art:** [–c.1534] Michelangelo designs tombs & chapel for Medicis, Florence; Dürer [draws] 'Erasmus'; Cranach [engrv.] 'Luther'		
	1521	Secret treaty against France made in Bruges between Wolsey & Charles V; Henry VIII declared 'Defender of the Faith' by Pope Leo X for his *Golden Book* [riposte to Luther]; Magellan dies [v.1522]	Luther condemned as heretic before the Diet of Worms – Edict outlaws him & his followers; silk 1st manufactured in France. **Art:** [–1522] Hans Holbein the Younger [pnt] 'The Dead Christ in the Tomb'	P: Skelton	[–1522] *Speke Parott, Collyn Clout, Why Come Ye Nat to Courte?* [wrtn; satirical attacks on Cardinal Wolsey]
	1522	England declares war on France – Scot.-Fr. alliance; Magellan's ship returns to Spain – 1st circumnavigation of world	Luther's trans of New Testament 1st pub.d. **Art:** [–1523] Titian, 'Bacchus and Ariadne'; Correggio, 'Adoration of the Shepherds (Night)' [NG]	Lit. 'Events':	Books 1st printed in Cambridge
	1523	Statutes regulating trade intro.d – esp.ly against foreign merchants; invasion of France by Allies; Diet of Nuremberg – Pope promises to abolish abuses	Zwingli brings reformation to Zurich; John Fitzherbert, *Husbandry* [1st Eng. agricultural handbook]. **Art:** Holbein, 'Erasmus' [NG];	P: Skelton Lit. 'Events':	*Garlande of Laurell* Tudor Aled, major poet at Caerwys Eisteddfod
	1524	Allies besiege Marseilles; Francisco Pizarro explores S. American coast, lands in Ecuador	1st Lutheran hymn book; Erasmus, *De Libero Arbitrio* [refutes Luther]. **Art:** Michelangelo begins building Biblioteca Laurenziana, Florence; [–1525] Holbein [woodcuts] 'The Dance of Death'; [–1530] Correggio, 'Assumption of the Virgin'		

1525	French defeated by Germans & Spanish at Pavia; peace between England & France; peasants' revolt in Germany violently suppressed – end of free peasantry	William Tyndale forced out of England – [-1526] his Eng. trans of New Testament pub.d at Worms; Wolsey founds Cardinal College, Oxford, [re-endowed as Christchurch, 1546]; Galen's medical works 1st pubd in original Grk. **Art:** Holbein, 'The Passion of Christ' [4 panels of altarpiece]; del Sarto, 'Madonna del Sacco'	
1526	Peace of Madrid between Charles V & Francis I; [-1761] Mogul dynasty established at Delhi by Babar – takes Koh-i-Noor diamond from Agra; Cabot sails to River Plate estuary; Pizarro reaches Peru	Tyndale's New Testament burned; Luther pubs Order of Service in German & De Servo Arbitrio [against Erasmus]; Paracelsus extends use of medicine; Hippocrates's medical work 1st pub.d in original Grk. **Art:** Dürer, 'Four Apostles'; [c.] Cranach, 'Judith'; Lotto, 'Young Man in a Striped Coat'; van Leyden [pnt] 'The Last Judgment' [triptych]; Albrecht Altdorfer [pnt] 'Susannah at the Bath'	**Pr/F:** Hector Boece (c.1465–1536) *History of Scotland* [in Latin]
1527	Henry VIII seeks annulment of marriage to Catherine of Aragon; Anglo-Fr. alliance of Amiens; Rome sacked by Charles V, Holy Roman Emperor; Babar defeats Hindus at Kanwaha; John Rut's voyage in search of NW Passage	Reformation spreading through Germany & Scandinavia. **Art:** Lotto, 'Portrait of Andrea Odoni' [Hampton Court]; Holbein, 'Sir Henry Guildford' [Royal Coll.], 'Sir Thomas More' & 'Lady with a Squirrel and Starling' [NG]	
1528	England declares war on Charles V & Holy Roman Empire; Eng. merchants arrested in Spain & Flanders as reprisal for Wolsey's wool trade policy	Cocoa beans 1st imported to Europe; Baldassare Castiglione, *Il Cortegiano* [Eng. trans as *The Courtier*, 1561]. **Art:** Le Breton designs Palace of Fontainbleau for Francis I; [-1530] Holbein, 'St Mary with Burgomaster Jakob Meyer (The Darmstadt Madonna)'; [-1530] Parmigianino [pnt] 'Madonna of the Rose'	
1529	Henry VIII accedes to Peace of Cambrai between Charles V & Francis I; fall of Wolsey [failure to secure Pope's acceptance of king's wish to divorce]; [-1532] Sir Thomas More, Lord Chancellor; rise of Thomas Cromwell; [-1536] Henry summons 'Reformation Parliament'; Treaty of Saragossa defines frontier between Sp. & Portug. territories in Pacific; 1st siege of Vienna by Turks	Simon Fish, *A Supplication for the Beggars*; Diego Ribero produces accurate map of Pacific. **Art:** Michelangelo becomes overseer of fortifications, Florence; Titian, 'Pesaro Madonna'; Altdorfer, 'Battle of Arbela'	**P:** Sir David Lindsay (1486–1555) **Lit. 'Events':** *Complaynt to the King* [Scots poem] Skelton dies
1530	Charles V crowned Holy Roman Emperor by Pope; Portuguese begin to colonise Brazil; [-1532] William Hawkins makes 3 expeditions to Brazil	Henry VIII takes over & rebuilds Whitehall Palace; 'lepra'/'the pox' now indentified as 'syphilis'. **Art:** [-1580] Limoges enamels on copper produced; Michelangelo [sculpt in marble] 'The Virgin and the Child Jesus', Medici Chapel; Titian, 'Virgin and Child with St Catherine (Virgin with the Rabbit)'; [c.] Correggio, 'Madonna della Scodella', 'Leda and the Swan' & [-1532] 'Danaë'	

PERIOD	YEAR	INTERNATIONAL AND POLITICAL CONTEXTS	SOCIAL AND CULTURAL CONTEXTS	AUTHORS	INDICATIVE TITLES
TUDOR	1531	Henry VIII declared 'Head of the Church in England'; Beggars Act distinguishes between able-bodied & impotent poor – unlicensed beggars to be whipped; Act regulates construction of London sewers; Charles V bans Reformation doctrines in Netherlands; Inquisition established in Portugal	Erasmus, 1st complete edtn of Aristotle. **Art:** Cranach, 'Venus and Amor'	**Pr/F:** Sir Thomas Elyot (c.1490–1546)	*The Boke named the Governour* [humanist treatise on moral education]
	1532	Submission of the clergy to Henry VIII – start of Reformation in England; Sir Thomas More resigns; Gvnmt regulates various trades [e.g. wholesale price of wine]; Turks invade Hungary; [–1534] Pizarro conquers Peru	Jean Calvin begins Reformation work in Paris. **Int. Lit.:** François Rabelais, *Pantagruel* [Fr. satirical fiction; v.1534]. **Art:** St James's Palace Chapel built; Holbein settles in London; [c.] Correggio, 'Jupiter and Io'; Cranach, 'Venus'; [–1536] Baldassare Peruzzi builds Palazzo Massimi alle Colonne, Rome	**Lit. 'Events':**	1st complete edtn of Chaucer's works pub.d
	1533	Henry declares his marriage to Catherine of Aragon void – secret m. to Anne Boleyn – Princess Elizabeth born [later Queen Elizabeth I] – Henry excommunicated by Pope Clement VII; Thomas Cranmer, Archbishop of Canterbury; Thomas Cromwell, Privy Councillor & Secretary of State; all farmers must grow flax – to check unemployment caused by linen imports; [–1584] Ivan the Terrible begins to rule Russia	Meat to be sold by weight – gvnmt statute fixes maximum price for it; 1st cultivation of sugar-cane in Brazil. **Art:** Holbein, 'The Ambassadors: Jean de Dinteville and Georges de Selve' [NG], 'Robert Cheeseman of Dormanswell' & [c.] 'Thomas Cromwell' [miniature; NPG]; Titian, 'Charles V'	**Pr/F:** More **Dr:** John Heywood (c.1497–c.1580) **Lit. 'Events':**	*An Apologie of Syr Thomas More* [c.] *Play of the Weather* 'Morality Plays' were being performed in the early to mid-16th Century
	1534	Papal decree declares Henry VIII's marriage to Catherine of Aragon valid – Parliament passes Act of Supremacy [Henry takes over Pope's powers & becomes Supreme Head of Church in England (1535)] & Act of Succession [Anne Boleyn's children by king to succeed him] – Sir Thomas More & Bishop Fisher refuse to swear to Acts – clergy forced to submit to king – no further money ['Peter's Pence'] to be paid to Rome; Jacques Cartier claims Labrador, N. America, for France	Act permits farmers only 2000 sheep to limit enclosure for pasture; wool cloth manufacture in Worcestershire limited to county's 5 towns; Ignatius Loyola fnds Society of Jesus [Jesuit Order] in Paris; Luther's trans of whole Bible completed. **Int. Lit.:** Rabelais, *Gargantua* [final full version of *Pantagruel and Gargantua*, 1564]. **Art:** [–1545] Michelangelo builds Palazzo Farnese, Rome; [–1540] Parmigianino, 'Madonna with the Long Neck'	**Dr:** J. Heywood	[c.] *A Play of Love*
	1535	English bishops abjure Pope's authority in England; Cromwell, Vicar General – orders visitation of churches & monasteries; trial and execution of More & Fisher; Statute of Uses restricts testamentary rights of landowners; [>] S. America being opened up – esp.ly by Spain – thro'out this period; Cartier discovers St Lawrence river	Miles Coverdale, 1st complete Eng. trans of Bible. **Art:** [c.] Holbein, 'Allegory of the Old and New Testaments' [SNG]		
	1536	Authority of Bishop of Rome declared void for England; [–1539] Act of Suppression begins dissolution of monasteries; reform of universities; Catherine of Aragon dies; Anne Boleyn executed – Henry m. Jane Seymour; Act of Union unites England & Wales [Welsh language excluded from official use]; [–1537] 'Pilgrimage of Grace' – insurrection in northern counties – crushed; law	Calvin goes to Geneva – 1st *Institutes* [in Latin]; at instigation of Henry VIII, Tyndale burned at stake in Netherlands. **Art:** Holbein becomes court painter to Henry VIII – [–1537] pnts 'Portrait of Jane Seymour'; [c.–1541] Michelangelo, 'Last Judgement' [Sistine Chapel]; [–1538] Titian, 'Duke of Urbino' & 'Eleonora Gonzaga' [Duke's wife]; Jacopo Sansovino begins the Old Library, Piazzetta San Marco, Venice		

...introduced for relief of poor; Cartier claims Canada for France

Year			Dr / Lit	
1537	Henry VIII orders *Bishops' Book* to be pub.d – strictly orthodox to RC doctrine, except for authority of Pope; Jane Seymour dies, leaving son, Prince Edward [later King Edward VI]; Act of Parliament orders all Irish to speak English & wear English-style dress	Sansovino begins Palazzo Corner (Ca' Grande), Venice [designed, 1532]	**Dr:** John Bale (1495–1563) **Lit. 'Events':**	[c.] *King John* [1st Eng. history play] Licensing of books commences as monastry libraries continue to be destroyed
1538	Pope Paul III issues Bull of excommunication & deposition against Henry VIII; Thomas à Becket's shrine at Canterbury & other holy places destroyed; Turks capture Aden	Sir Thomas Elyot pubs a Latin-English dictionary; **Art:** Holbein issues woodcut series, 'The Dance of Death' [begun 1523] & [c.] pnts 'Edward, Prince of Wales'; Titian, 'The Venus of Urbino'	**Lit. 'Events':**	[c.] Sir Thomas Wyatt (1503–1542) & Henry Howard, Earl of Surrey (1518–1547), write their poetry – 1st pub.d in *Tottel's Miscellany* (1557)
1539	Act of the Six Articles (the 'Bloody Statute') abolishes 'diversity of opinions' & insists on fundamental RC doctrines for worship in England – burning at stake punishment for breach of Act; marriage contract between Henry VIII & Anne of Cleves [to cement ties with Protestant Germany]; merchants granted free trade for 7 years; Spain annexes Cuba	Henry VIII licenses the 'Great Bible' [based on combination of Tyndale's & Coverdale's Eng. trans – preface by Cranmer – copies to be placed in every parish church]. **Art:** [–1540] Holbein, 'Anne of Cleves' [watercolour; V&A]		
1540	Henry m. Anne of Cleves – marriage annulled in 6 mths – Henry m. Catherine Howard; Cromwell executed; barbers & surgeons joined in one Guild; Spain discovers California	Henry VIII fnds 1st Cambridge Regius Professorship; Pope approves Jesuit Order. **Int. Lit.:** Aretino, *Orazia*. **Art:** Stirling Palace begun by James V of Scotland; [c.] Holbein, 'Catherine Howard'	**Dr:** Sir David Lyndsay [or Lindsay] (c.1486–1555)	*Satyre of the Thrie Estaits* [morality play]
1541	Henry declares himself King of Ireland & Head of Irish Church; Wales given representation in Parliament; Catholic conspiracy to raise N. of England – Henry makes a 'progress' there; Hungary conquered & [–1688] becomes a province of Turkey; [>] N. America being opened up thro'out this period	Henry VIII fnds King's Schools at Chester & Worcester; Southwell Minster fnd.d; John Knox begins Reformation in Scotland; Calvin estabs Protestant church at Geneva; Loyola, 1st General of Jesuit missionaries	**Dr:** J. Heywood	[c.] *The Playe called the Four P's* [prnt.d, 1569]
1542	War between England & Scotland; Catherine Howard beheaded; Mary, Queen of Scots, born – James V dies – his widow, Mary of Guise, regent of Scotland; Inquisition estab.d in Cologne & Rome	Magdalene College, Cambridge, fnd.d; Robert Recorde, *Ground of Artes* – 1st maths book in English. **Art:** [–1545] Michelangelo, 'Crucifixion of St Peter' & 'Conversion of St Paul' [frescoes, Pauline Chapel, Vatican]; [c.–1546] Bronzino [pnt] 'Allegory of Venus, Cupid, Folly, and Time' [NG]		
1543	Henry VIII m. Catherine Parr; Anglo-Scots war ends with proposal that Mary Q of S should m. Prince Edward – Scots repudiate this [v.1544]; Wales integrated further into England by creation of 12 counties, introduction of English common law & allocation of seats at Westminster; Henry VIII in alliance with Charles V against France	Copernicus, *De revolutionibus* [treatise on sun-centred universe – supersedes Ptolemaic system – banned by RC Church until 1758]; Andreas Vesalius, *De Humani Corporis Fabrica* [repudiates Galen & advances biological science]. **Art:** Benvenuto Cellini completes gold salt-cellar for Francis I of France		

PERIOD	YEAR	INTERNATIONAL AND POLITICAL CONTEXTS	SOCIAL AND CULTURAL CONTEXTS	AUTHORS	INDICATIVE TITLES
TUDOR	1544	'Rough Wooing' [v.1543]: Eng. army invades Scotland & devastates South & Edinburgh; 3rd Succession Act places Princesses Mary & Elizabeth in line to throne; Henry VIII & Charles V invade France – Henry captures Boulogne	Litany issued in English; 'lion passant' 1st regularly stamped on Eng. silver; Holyrood House, Scotland, destroyed by English – immediately rebuilt		
	1545	Scots defeat English at Ancram Moor – English immediately re-invade; Fr. invasion scare – loss of royal ship, 'Mary Rose' – England in command of Channel; [–1547] Council of Trent reformulates RC doctrine & administration – begins Counter-Reformation against Protestantism [also meets 1551–2, 1562–3]	Services for morning & evening prayer issued in English; 1st complete edtn of Luther's works. **Art:** [c.] Titian, 'Portrait of a Man (Young Englishman)', 'Pietro Aretino' & [c.] 'Danaë'; [–1554] Cellini [sculpt] 'Perseus with the Head of Medusa'	**Pr/F:** Elyot Roger Ascham (1515–68)	*Defence of Good Women* *Toxophilus* [treatise on archery]
	1546	Anglo-French war ends – Boulogne remains English for 8 yrs; Henry fnds Eng. Navy Board; large weaving factory estab.d by William Stumpe – employs 500 workers; Scottish revolt against Rome begins; Empire & Papacy allied against Protestants	Henry VIII fnds Trinity College, Cambridge & Oxford Regius Professorships; 1st accurate map of Britain produced in Rome. **Art:** Louvre, Paris, rebuilt; [–1564] Michelangelo, chief architect, St Peter's, Rome; [–1580] Andrea Palladio estabs Palladian architecture in Italy [incls Villa Capra (Villa Rotunda), Vicenza, 1550–1 & Teatro Olimpico, Vicenza, begun 1580]; [–1547] Cellini [sculpt] 'Cosimo I de' Medici'; Gerlach Flicke [pnt] 'Thomas Cranmer' [NPG]; [c. & attrib.] William Scrots [pnt] 'Henry Howard, Earl of Surrey' [NPG]	**Lit. 'Events':**	*Yn y Llyyr hwnn* [1st book prnt.d in Welsh]
	1547	Death of Henry VIII, King Edward VI [aged 4] accedes – Duke of Somerset, Protector [–1552] – [> period of radical Protestantism in Eng. Church ensues – Six Articles repealed [v.1539]; Three Acts to combat enclosure; fierce vagrancy laws introduced; 1st Poor Law raised in London; Treasons Act removes much repressive legislation; English invade & defeat Scotland	*Book of Homilies* [for use by clergy]] 1st issued; [c.] Knox exiled to France; [c.] Nostradamus begins to make predictions. **Art:** Tintoretto [pnt] 'The Last Supper'	**Lit. 'Events':**	Henry Howard, Earl of Surrey [poet] executed
	1548	Mary Q of S sent to France to be betrothed to the Dauphin [v.1558]; Craft Guilds [except London's] & Chantry chapels abolished; religious unrest in 'liberal' atmosphere created by Treasons Act of 1547	Roger Ascham becomes tutor to Princess Elizabeth; 7 professorships fnd.d at London, but no university estab.d until 1828; Knox, *Epistle on Justification by Faith*. **Art:** Palazzo Pitti, Florence begun; Titian, 'Emperor Charles V'; Tintoretto, 'Miracle of the Slave (St Mark Rescuing a Slave)'	**Pr/F:** Edward Hall [or Halle] (c. 1499–1547)	*The Union of the Two Noble and Illustrate Families of York and Lancaster* [posthm.; aka *Hall's Chronicle*]
	1549	Act of Uniformity: mass & use of Latin abolished in Eng. church services; fierce Treason Act reverses 'liberal' legislation of 1547–8 – rebellions suppressed in Eng. counties [against enclosures & new religious policies]; price-rings by provision dealers made illegal; tax on sheep & cloth; 1st bad harvest of Edward VI's reign; England & France at war; Jesuit missionaries reach Japan	1st *English Book of Common Prayer* pub.d [mainly edited by Cranmer] – use enforced from now on; [c.] Lindisfarne Castle, Holy Island, begun; Somerset House fnd.d. **Art:** [c.] Tintoretto, 'St Augustine Healing the Plague-Stricken'	**Theory/Crit:**	Joachim du Bellay pubs manifesto of the Pléiade [group of modernising Fr. poets, incls Pierre de Ronsard, v.1550], *Defence and Illustration of the French Language* [advocates use of French not Latin for literature & classical & Italian models not medieval traditions

1550	Peace of Boulogne between England & France & England & Scotland relinquished to France; 2nd bad harvest of Edward VI's reign – local uprisings continue; boom in Eng. cloth exports	**Int. Lit:** Pierre de Ronsard, *Odes* [Fr. Pléiade movement, v.1549]. **Art:** Giorgio Vasari, *Lives of the Most Eminent Painters, Sculptors, and Architects* [enlarged edtn, 1568]; [–1551] Titian, 'King Philip II of Spain' & 'Johann Friedrich, Elector of Saxony'; [c.] Tintoretto, 'Christ Washing the Disciples' Feet'	**Int. Lit:** **Pr/F:** More — *Utopia* [posthm. Eng. trans.]
1551	42 Articles intro.d to give Eng. Protestant religion a definitive creed; 'Great debasement' & revaluation of Eng. coinage; 3rd bad harvest – unrest continues; fall in cloth exports – 16C boom over; [–1552] 2nd session of Council of Trent [v.1545]	[c.] coaches 1st intro.d in England. **Music:** [>] Giovanni da Palestrina comp. many masses as master of the Julian choir, St Peter's, Rome. **Art:** Tintoretto, 'Susanna and the Elders'	
1552	2nd Act of Uniformity [v. also 1549, 1559, 1562] confirms 42 Articles of 1551 & prescribes use of new & more clearly Protestant Book of Common Prayer [withdrawn on Mary's accession, 1553]; Act passed for collection of funds in churches to assist 'deserving' poor; 1st 'Bridewell' [gaol] estab.d in London	Christ's Hospital, London & Shrewsbury Schools fnd.d. **Int. Lit:** de Ronsard, *Les Amours de Cassandre* [Petrarchan sonnets]. **Music:** Thomas Tallis ['father of Eng. cathedral music'] comp. 'Service in the Dorian Mode' [1st pub.d 1641]	**Dr:** Anon [attrib. to William Stevenson (d. 1575)] — [c.] *Gammer Gurton's Needle* [early Eng. comedy; pf.d Christ's College, Cambridge, c.1566; prnt.d, 1575]
1553	Edward VI dies – leading Protestants proclaim Lady Jane Grey queen to ensure Protestant succession – reigns for 10 days – replaced by Mary I (Mary Tudor) – RC monarchy restored – England reconciled with Rome – RC bishops reinstated – Protestant bishops arrested; Richard Chancellor's voyage to Moscow – treaty gives trading freedom to Eng. ships	The 'Great Harry' [largest Eng. ship] burned; Tonbridge School fnd.d; [–1594] Richard Hooker, *The Laws of Ecclesiastical Polity* [defence of C of E; last 3 vols pub.d posthm. in 17C]. **Art:** [c.] Titian, 'Danaë'; Paolo Veronese [pnt] 'Temptation of St Anthony' & 'Juno Bestowing Her Gifts on Venice'	**Dr:** Nicholas Udall (1505–56) — [c.] *Ralph Roister Doister* [early Eng. comedy]; **Theory/Crit:** Thomas Wilson, *Arte of Rhetorique*
1554	Lady Jane Grey executed; Sir Thomas Wyatt [son of poet] leads failed rebellion of Kentish men against Mary – executed; Mary m. Philip (later II) of Spain, son & heir to Charles V; Act of Supremacy revoked [v.1534] – RCism re-estab.d in England – Cardinal Pole arrives as Papal Legate; [–1555] Muscovy Trading Co. estab.d to develop Anglo-Russian trade [1st joint-stock Co.]	**Int. Lit:** Matteo Bendello, *Novelle* [214 It. stories]. **Music:** [c.] Palestrina [comp] church music & part-songs. **Art:** Cellini, 'Perseus holding the head of Medusa' [bronze statue]; [c.] Titian, 'Venus and Adonis'	**P:** Elizabeth Tudor (later Queen Elizabeth I; 1533–1603) — 'Woodstock' poems [wrtn while imprisoned there]
1555	Act restores papal supremacy; [–1558] Queen ('Bloody Mary') begins persecution of Eng. Protestants – Bishops Hooper, Ridley and Latimer burned – Cranmer deprived of Archbishopric of Canterbury; Knox returns from exile in France – unites Scottish Protestants; Peace of Augsburg accepts Protestantism as dominant in Germany	St John's & Trinity Colleges, Oxford & Gresham's School fnd.d; Gray's Inn Hall, London, begun. **Int. Lit:** Ronsard, *Hymnes*. **Art:** [–1572] Vasari redesigns Palazzo Vecchio, Florence, for Cosimo de' Medici & decorates interior with frescoes; Michelangelo [sculpt] 'Rondanini Pietà'; Tintoretto, 'Venus, Vulcan and Mars' [completed]	
1556	Cranmer burned at stake – Pole, Archbishop of Canterbury; Charles V abdicates – Philip II, king of Spain – Mary supports Spain in war with France; worst harvest of century – series of epidemics begins; [–1605] Akbar the Great, Mogul emperor – defeats Hindus at Panipat	1st trucks run on rails in Germany. **Int. Lit:** Ronsard, *Les Amours de Marie*. **Music:** 'Old Hundredth' psalm tune in Knox's Psalter].	**Lit. 'Events':** Stationers' Co. acquires monopoly of Eng. printing [Royal Charter, 1557] – industry required to censor the works it was publishing

Period	Year	International and Political Contexts	Social and Cultural Contexts	Authors	Indicative Titles
TUDOR/ELIZABETHAN	1557	Anglo-Fr. war – France defeated by English & Spanish; Disputation at Worms – last attempt by Holy Roman Empire to reconcile RC & Lutheran views	1st Covenant signed in Scotland; Gonville & Caius College, Cambridge, fnd.d; Repton College fnd.d. **Int. Lit.:** Jörg Wickram, *Der Goldfaden* [early Ger. novel]. **Art:** Mosque of Suleiman I, Constantinople, built	**P:** Henry Howard, Earl of Surrey (1518–47) **Lit. 'Events':**	Virgil's *Aeneid*, Bks II, IV [posthm.; Eng. trans] Richard Tottel (ed.), *Songes and Sonnetts* ['Tottel's Miscellany'; incls poetry of Surrey & Wyatt]; play entitled *A Sack Full of News* pf.d & suppressed at Boar's Head Inn Theatre, Aldgate
	1558	English lose Calais to France [last Eng. possession in Europe]; Mary I dies – Queen Elizabeth I accedes; William Cecil, Secretary of State; Mary Q of S m. Francis, Dauphin of France; 1st Russian trade delegation to London	[c.] 1st firearms manufactured; Knox, *First Blast of the Trumpet Against the Monstrous Regiment of Women* [attack on the rule of Mary I in England & Mary of Guise in Scotland, regent & mother of Mary, Q of S]. **Int. Lit.:** Marguérite d'Angoulême, *The Heptaméron*. **Art:** Sir Thomas Lucy builds Charlecote Park, Warwickshire; [c.] Pieter Brueghel the Elder [pnt] 'The Alchemist at Work'	**Lit. 'Events':**	Thomas Phaer's trans of Virgil pub.d
	1559	Acts of Supremacy & Uniformity restore & fully establish C of E [Queen, 'Supreme Governor'] – England severed from Rome – Court of High Commission estab.d to enforce Acts & religious conformity; Philip II of Spain [Mary I's widower] offers to m. Elizabeth – refused; Francis II accedes to Fr. throne – Mary Q of S now also Queen of France; Hugenots estab. reformed churches in France	Revised [less extreme] Prayer Book of Elizabeth I issued – a Bible to be placed in every church – priests can marry; [>] beginnings of Puritanism; Amyot's Fr. trans of Plutarch's *Lives*. **Art:** Titian, 'Diana and Actaeon' [on loan to SNG]	**Pr/F:** Anon	*Mirror for Magistrates* [didactic chronicles; 5 edtns by 1610]
	1560	Treaty of Berwick: Eng. military help given to Scottish rebels; Treaty of Edinburgh: Fr. toops to withdraw – Francis II & Mary reject it; Scots Parliament estab.s Reformed Church – papal authority abolished – only Protestant faith recognised; [–1561] Sir Thomas Gresham reforms currency ['Gresham's Law': coins of lower intrinsic value will drive coins of higher intrinsic value but equal legal exchange value out of circulation]; Parliament in Ireland imposes Royal Supremacy & Book of Common Prayer; Francis II of France dies	[>] Eng. & Scot. settlers begin to estab. Eng. language in Ireland & Scots in Ulster; 'Geneva Bible' pub.d by reformers; Knox's writings form framework for Scottish Presbyterianism; Elizabeth I fnd.s Westminster School; Peter Whithorne, Eng. trans of Machiavelli, *The Art of War*. **Art:** [–1580] Vasari builds Uffizi Palace, Florence; formal gardens at Penshurst Place, Kent, laid out; [c.–1570] Tintoretto, 'Susannah and the Elders'; Titian, 'Death of Actaeon' [NG]	**Dr:** Jasper Heywood (1535–98)	*Thyestes* [trans of Seneca; prnt.d]
	1561	Mary Q of S [as widowed Q of France] returns to Scotland – Elizabeth I refuses her passage over English soil	Knox estab.s Scottish Church constitution; [–20C] sterling standard silver coinage estab.d; Merchant Taylor's School, London, fnd.d; Fallopius undertakes research on female anatomy **Theory/Crit:** Julius Caesar Scaliger, *Poetics* [posthm.; Fr. neo-classical literary theory]	**Dr:** Thomas Norton (1532–84) & Thomas Sackville (1536–1608) **Lit. 'Events':**	*Gorbaduc* [1st Eng. blank verse tragedy – pf.d for Elizabeth I; prnt.d 1565; rev.d edtn 1570, with title *The Tragidie of Ferrex and Porrex*] Sir Thomas Hoby, Eng. trans of Castiglione's *The Courtier* (1528)
	1562	4th Act of Uniformity prescribes use of Book of Common Prayer [v. also 1549, 1552, 1559]; Elizabeth I nearly dies of smallpox – succession	[–1572] Middle Temple Hall, London, built; Torquato Tasso, *Rinaldo* [Ital. poem]. **Art:** Tintoretto, 'Christ at the Sea of Galilee', & [–1566] 'Miracles of St Mark'		

Year	International/Political Events	Science / Art / Music	Author	Literature
(1562, cont.)	dilemma; Treaty of Hampton Court between Elizabeth & Fr. Protestant Huguenots – Fr. religious wars begin; Eng. occupy Le Havre; [-1563] Council of Trent re-opens [v.1545]; 1st voyage of Sir John Hawkins to W. Indies carrying W. African slaves	[3 canvases]; [-1565] Brueghel, 'Fall of Icarus'; Veronese, 'The Marriage at Cana'		
1563	Convocation of Anglican Church approves 'Thirty-Nine Articles' [rev.d 1562] setting out its doctrine; [-1814] Statute of Apprentices seeks to solve unemployment & poverty by giving every man a trade [regulates conditions of employment for mass of population]; Act against enclosure; serious outbreak of plague in London & elsewhere – 1000s die; French regain Le Havre	2nd Book of Homilies; John Foxe, *Acts and Monuments* ['Foxe's Book of Martyrs' – defence of Protestant reformers – Eng. trans from Latin]. **Music:** William Byrd appointed organist at Lincoln Cathedral. **Art:** John Shute, *First and Chief Grounds of Architecture*; Brueghel, 'Tower of Babel'	**P:** Barnabe Googe (1540–94)	*Eclogues, Epitaphs and Sonnets* [1st Eng. pastorals]
1564	Elizabeth I suggests Robert Dudley, Earl of Leicester, might m. Mary Q of S; 1st Puritan opposition to Anglicanism; Court of High Commission estab.d in Ireland to enforce conformity – riots against Eng. 'plantation' [colonisation] of Ireland; Anglo-Fr. peace; Anglo-Sp. trade war; Eng. merchants make trading agreements with Ger. & Dutch counterparts; [-1565] Hawkins 2nd voyage to W. Indies	1st horse-drawn coach intro.d in England from Holland; 1st complete *Index* of prohibited books issued by Pope. **Art:** Michelangelo dies; Philibert Delorme begins building Tuileries, Paris; [-1587] Tintoretto, 'The Life of Christ' [cycle of paintings; incls 'The Flight into Egypt']		
1565	Mary Q of S m. her cousin, Lord Darnley	[>] sweet potatoes, etc. intro.d into Britain from America; pencils 1st made in England; John Stow, *Summary of English Chronicles*. **Art:** Brueghel, 'The Seasons'; [c.] Titian, 'Annunciation'; [c.] Tintoretto, 'Crucifixion'; Giambologna [sculpt] 'Samson Slaying a Philistine' [V&A]	**Lit. 'Events':** / **Theory/Crit:** Pierre de Ronsard	[-1567] Arthur Golding, Eng. trans of Ovid, *Metamorphoses*, Bks I–IV / *Abrégé de l'art poétique français*
1566	Succession issue between Elizabeth I & Parliament – she forbids discussion of possible marriage; [>] many Puritan Bills brought before Commons; [-1568] Gresham builds & fnd.s Royal Exchange, London; Mary Q of S's secretary, David Rizzio, murdered in Holyrood Palace	**Art:** [-1580] Longleat House, Wiltshire, built; [c.] Veronese, 'Family of Darius before Alexander' [NG]	**Pr/F:** George Gascoigne (c.1539–78) / **Dr:** Gascoigne / **Lit. 'Events':**	*The Supposes* [trans & adaptn of Ariosto – prose comedy] / *Jocasta* [adaptn of Euripedes] / William Adlington, Eng. trans of Apuleius, *The Golden Ass*
1567	Darnley murdered by Earl of Bothwell [perhaps at Mary Q of S's instigation] – Mary m. Bothwell – defeated by Scots lords – forced to abdicate – is imprisoned – her 1-yr-old son becomes King James VI [later also James I of England] – regency in Scotland; [-1568] 1st revolt of Netherlands suppressed by Sp. troops under Duke of Alba; [-1568] Hawkins 3rd voyage to W. Indies [with Francis Drake]	Welsh trans of New Testament & Prayer Book; Rugby School fnd.d. **Music:** Palestrina [comp] 'Missa Papae Marcelli'; [c.] Thomas Tallis, Eng. composer of church music, etc., active. **Art:** Titian, 'Ecce Home'; [c.] Giambologna, 'Venus'	**P:** George Turberville (c.1540–1610) / **Lit. 'Events':**	*Epitaphes, Epigrams, Songs, and Sonets* / play entitled *Samson* pf.d at Red Lion Inn Theatre, Stepney

Period	Year	International and Political Contexts	Social and Cultural Contexts	Authors	Indicative Titles
	1568	Mary Q of S escapes captivity – again defeated – flees to England – Elizabeth I imprisons her for life; Elizabeth orders seizure of Sp. ships carrying bullion to pay Alba's troops – Alba's 'Bloody Council' condemns all Protestants in Netherlands to death as heretics – 1000s of Hugenot artisans flee to England; Hawkins's ships attacked by Spanish off Mexico; wars between Huguenots & Catholics in France continue	Matthew Parker, Archbishop of Canterbury, supervises preparation of the 'Bishops' Bible'; Eisteddfod held at Flint, Wales; school for Eng. Jesuits fnd.d at Douai. Art: Brueghel, 'Peasant Dance' & 'Peasant Wedding'		
	1569	Pro-Catholic 'rising of Northern Earls' to replace Elizabeth I with Mary Q of S – quelled	Gerardus Mercator's Chart & 'Cosmographia' [map of the world] fnds modern cartography. Art: [c.] El Greco [pnt] 'Coronation of a Saint or King' ['Modena polyptych']		
	1570	Elizabeth I declared usurper by Pope & excommunicated – RC subjects absolved from allegiance to crown; Ridolfo plot against Elizabeth foiled [RC conspiracy supported by Spain to overthrow Queen & substitute Mary Q of S]; 1st voyage of Francis Drake to W. Indies	Art: Palladio, Treatise on Architecture; [–1580] Veronese, 'The Finding of Moses'; [–1580] Giambologna [sculpt] 'Flying Mercury' [bronze]; El Greco, 'Christ Expelling the Merchants from the Temple'	Pr/F: Ascham	The Scholemaster [posthm.; wrtn c. 1558–63; treatise on education]
	1571	Further tension between Parliament & Elizabeth over Succession issue [re Mary Q of S]; Parliament prohibits papal bulls in England; Treasons Act – high treason to deny Royal Supremacy or call Queen a heretic; Elizabeth opens Royal Exchange [London Stock Exchange; v.1566] – [>] England's capitalist economy grows – extensive overseas trade; sea battle of Lepanto destroys invading Turks' naval power	Statutory confirmation of [revised] Thirty-Nine Articles – now printed in Prayer Book; Jesus College, Oxford & Harrow School fnd.d. Art: [c.] Veronese, 'Feast in the House of the Pharisee'		
	1572	Duke of Norfolk executed for part in Ridolfi plot [v.1570]; Succession issue continues; Duke of Alençon, suitor to Elizabeth; Poor Relief Act levies 1st compulsory rate on each parish & defines vagrancy; St Bartholomew's Day massacre of 1000s of Protestants in Paris; Drake's expedition to attack Sp. harbours in the Americas & seize treasure – 1st Englishman to see the Pacific	Society of Antiquaries fnd.d; Bombelli, Algebra; Etienne, Thesaurus Linguae Graecae. Art: Nicholas Hilliard [pnt] 'Elizabeth I' [miniature; NPG] & 'Portrait of a Man of Twenty-Four' [miniature; V&A]	Lit. 'Events':	Actors not under aristocratic patronage declared vagabonds
	1573	Sir Francis Walsingham, Sec. of State – creates 'trained bands' of militia; Edinburgh Castle falls to Anglo-Scottish force; 1st Earl of Essex granted 'plantation' rights in Ireland – [>] ruthless colonisation underway; Hawkins, Treasurer of Navy Board – promotes greater efficiency	Int. Lit.: Tasso, Aminta [It. pastoral play]. Art: [c.] Titian, 'Pietà' [unfinished]; Veronese, 'Adoration of the Magi' [NG]; Giambologna, 'Astronomy' [gilt bronze]	P: Isabella Whitney (late-1540s–date unknown)	A Sweet Nosegay
	1574	1st RC priests' mission from continent to reconvert England; Anglo-Sp. settlement of claims & counter-claims since 1568	Art Taddeo Zuccaro [pnt] 'Elizabeth I' & 'Mary, Queen of Scots'		

TUDOR/ELIZABETHAN

1575	Elizabeth I declines sovereignty of Netherlands; Parliament wins right of freedom from arrest for members & their servants; Essex's army massacres inhabitants of Rathlin Island off the NE coast of Ireland	**Music:** Tallis & Byrd [compl] *Cantiones Sacrae*. **Art:** [c.] Veronese, 'Mystic Marriage of St Catherine'	**Pr/F:** Turberville **Lit. 'Events':** **Theory/Crit:** George Gascoigne	*The Book of Falconrie* Paul's Theatre [private] opens *Certain Notes of Instruction on Making of Verse* [early Eng. essay on subject]
1576	Poor Relief Act makes materials available for able-bodied poor to work & requires all corporate towns to estab. workhouses & Bridewells for vagabonds; Jesuit priests arrive in England from Douai; unpaid Sp. troops sack Antwerp – Sp. control of Netherlands collapses; [–1579] Martin Frobisher's 3 voyages to find NW Passage – annexes Frobisher Bay	Sir Humphrey Gilbert, *Discourse of a discovery for a new passage to Cataia* [in favour of Eng. colonisation]. Leonard Digges, Eng. trans of Copernicus. **Art:** [–1584] Veronese, 'Mars and Venus'	**Pr/F:** Turberville **Lit. 'Events':**	*The Noble Art of Venerie* James Burbage's 'The Theatre', Shoreditch, opens [outside city limits], replacing one at Red Lion Inn [v. 1567]; 1st [private] Blackfriars Theatre opens [with child actors], [>] theatrical activity at Newington Butts [Elephant & Castle]
1577	1st Jesuit missionary executed at Tyburn; complaints about enclosure of commons for breeding; [–1580] Drake begins voyage round the world	William Harrison, *Description of England & Description of Britain* [wrtn for] Raphael Holinshed [compiler], *Chronicles of England, Scotland and Ireland* ['Holinshed's Chronicles'; reissued posthm. in 3 vols, 1586–7]. **Art:** El Greco, 'The Assumption of the Virgin'; Hilliard, 'Self-Portrait' [miniature; V&A]	**Pr/F:** Sir Philip Sidney (1554–86) **Lit. 'Events':**	[–1580] 'Old' *Arcadia* [wrtn; prose romance; v. also 1580, 1590 & 1593] Curtain Theatre, Finsbury Fields, opens
1578	Levant Trading Co. [for Turkey] fnd.d; Drake sails through Magellan Strait into Pacific; King James VI assumes personal rule [gvnmt] of Scotland	Jesuit Eng. College, Douai, moves to Rheims. **Int.** **Lit.:** Ronsard, *Les Amours d'Hélèn*	**Pr/F:** John Lyly (c.1554–1606) **Dr:** Sidney	*Euphues, The Anatomie of Wit* [Pt I] [c.] *The Lady of May* [masque pf.d before Q. Elizabeth]
1579	Duke of Alençon visits England to woo Elizabeth I; [–1583] Earl of Desmond's rebellion in Ireland; a further Jesuit mission to England underway; Eastland Trading Co. [for Baltic] granted Charter; Sp. reconquest of Netherlands begins; Drake claims 'New Albion' [California] for England	Jesuit Eng. College moves to Rome; Christopher Saxton pubs atlas of England & Wales [commissioned by Elizabeth I; 1st national atlas of any country]. **Art:** El Greco, 'Espolio (Disrobing of Christ)'; [–1583] Giambologna [sculpt] 'Rape of the Sabines' [Florence]	**P:** Edmund Spenser (1552–99) **Pr/F:** Sir Thomas North (1535–1600) **Theory/Crit:** Stephen Gosson	*The Shepheard's Calendar* *Plutarch's Lives of the Noble Grecians and Romans* [Eng. trans from French] *School of Abuse* [satirical attack on the theatre]
1580	New mission of RC priests to England [incls Edmund Campion]; earthquake in London; Lord Grey, Lord Deputy of Ireland, & Sir Walter Raleigh ruthlessly suppress rebellion – many massacred; treaty with Turkey opens up trade; Drake returns laden with treasure – 1st Englishman to circumnavigate the globe	[c.] coffee 1st imported to Italy; John Stow, *Annals, or a General Chronicle of England*; Michel de Montaigne, *Essais* [& 1588; v.1603]. **Music:** [c.] early ref. made to song 'Greensleeves'. **Art:** Palladio builds Teatro Olimpico, Vicenza; Woolaton Hall, Nottinghamshire, begun; El Greco, 'Adoration of the Name of Jesus (Dream of Philip II)' &'The Martyrdom of St Maurice'. **Lit. 'Events':** Spenser & Raleigh go to Ireland; performance of plays on Sunday banned; last Miracle Plays pf.d at Coventry	**P:** Sidney **Pr/F:** Lyly **Theory/crit:** Sidney	*Astrophil and Stella* [sonnet sequence wrtn; pub.d posthm., 1591] *Euphues and his England* [Pt II] [c. –1583] *An Apologie for Poetrie* [wrtn; pub.d posthm., 1595; also pub.d as *The Defence of Poesie*, 1595]

PERIOD	YEAR	INTERNATIONAL AND POLITICAL CONTEXTS	SOCIAL AND CULTURAL CONTEXTS	AUTHORS	INDICATIVE TITLES
TUDOR/ELIZABETHAN	1581	Campion executed; [>] Gvnmt repression of Eng. RCs increases – heavy fines for recusancy [refusal to attend C of E when legally compulsory]; Elizabeth I's proposed m. to Duke Francis of Anjou under negotiation; Levant [trading] Co. fnd.d	Sedan chairs intro.d in England; Galileo discovers regular periodicity of the pendulum. **Int. Lit.::** Tasso, *Jerusalem Delivered* [epic of 1st Crusade]; **Music:** [c.] 1st dramatic ballet pf.d at Versailles. **Art:** [–1584] Tintoretto, 'Triumph of Venice as Queen of the Seas' [ceiling decoration]	**Lit. 'Events':**	Jasper Heywood [& others], Eng. trans, *Seneca his Ten Tragedies*; Joseph Hall, Eng. trans *Ten Books of Homer's Iliads*
	1582	All Jesuits & seminary priests declared traitors; Duke Francis leaves – m. negotiations end; Elizabeth I revises weights standards [unchanged until 1824]; 1st London waterworks constructed; 'Raid of Ruthven' – King James VI kidnapped by Scots Protestants to protect him from RCs	Pope Gregory XIII intros the Gregorian Calendar [11 days ahead of the old one] – England resists it until 1752; Edinburgh University fnd.d; Richard Hakluyt, *Divers Voyages touching the Discovery of America* [advocates colonisation of N. America]; George Buchanan, *Rerum Scoticarum Historia* [20 vols]	**P:** Thomas Watson (c.1557–92) **Pr/F:** Sidney **Lit. 'Events':**	*Hecatompathia or the Passionate Century of Love* [100 18-line 'sonnets'] [–1584] 'New' *Arcadia* [wrtn; unfinished revision; v.1577, 1590 & 1593] Richard Stanyhurst, Eng. trans *The First Four Books of Virgil his Æneis*
	1583	Somerville plot to assassinate Elizabeth I discv.d – also Throckmorton plot for Sp. invasion on behalf of Mary, Q of S; John Whitgift becomes Archbishop of Canterbury – to check Puritanism & ensure conformity; Earl of Desmond killed – Ir. rebellion ends [v.1579]; Sir Humphrey Gilbert annexes Newfoundland for Eng. crown & estabs 1st colony of British Empire	A life assurance policy 1st issued; Edinburgh University fnd.d; Thomas Smith, *De Republica Anglorum* [describes Elizabethan constitution]; Philip Stubbes, *Anatomie of Abuses* [Puritan pamphlet denouncing luxury of the times]; Joseph Julius Scaliger estab.s scientific basis for ancient chronology	**Lit. 'Events':**	'Queen Elizabeth's Men' [theatre Co.] formed; 1st Cambridge University Press printer employed
	1584	Pope launches 'Enterprise of England' to restore RCism to England; Sp. ambassador expelled; alliance between Elizabeth I & James VI of Scotland to defend religion; Elizabeth frustrates Puritan campaign in Parliament to further reform Church; [–1589] Sir Walter Raleigh sends expedition to N. America to annexe lands in the Queen's name	Emmanuel College, Cambridge & Uppingham School fnd.d; Knox, *History of the Reformation in Scotland* [posthm.]; Hakluyt, *A Discourse Concerning the Western Planting* [supports Raleigh's plan to colonise Virginia]. **Music:** Palestrina [compl] setting for the 'Song of Soloman'. **Art:** Tintoretto, 'Life of the Virgin' [series; incls 'Mary Magdalene in the Wilderness']	**P:** Anne Cecil de Vere (1556–89) **Pr/F:** Robert Greene (1558–92) **Dr:** Lyly George Peele (c.1558–c.1598) **Lit. 'Events':**	*Sonnets* *Myrror of Modestie* *Campaspe* [romantic comedy] *The Arraignment of Paris* [prnt.d; pf.d at Court, 1581?] 1st Blackfriars theatre closes
	1585	Elizabeth I sends Earl of Leicester to aid Dutch & wage undeclared war on Spain – also sends Drake to plunder Sp. possessions in W. Indies; Parliament passes Act against Jesuits & priests; Roanoke Island, Virginia – Raleigh's 1st settlement in N. America fnd.d [abandoned 1586]; Barbary Co. fnd.d [N. Africa trade]; [–1587] John Davis, seeking NW Passage, discovers Davis Strait	Court of Star Chamber suppresses all printing offices outside London; earliest spring-driven Eng. clocks made; [–1587] William Camden, *Britannia* [in Latin; Eng. trans, Philemon Holland, 1610 – topographical survey & history of British Isles]. **Int. Lit:** Miguel de Cervantes, *La Galatea* [pastoral romance; prnt.d]. **Art:** [c.] Delft pottery begins to be made	**P:** Watson **Lit. 'Events':**	*Amyntas* ['sonnets'] [c.] Shakespeare leaves Stratford for London

Year	History/Politics	Society/Culture/Arts	Authors	Literature
1586	Babington Plot to kill Eliz. – Mary Q of S tried for complicity – sentenced to death; Treaty of Berwick between Scots & English; 3rd circumnavigation of the world by Cavendish; Drake returns with large booty	[c.] potatoes & tobacco 1st intro.d into England from N. America. **Art:** El Greco, 'Burial of Count Orgaz' **Theory/Crit:** William Webbe, *Discourse of English Poetrie*	**P:** William Warner (c.1558–1609) **Pr/F:** Sidney **Dr:** Anon **Lit. 'Events':**	[–1606] *Albion's England* [long historical poem] 'New' *Arcadia* [wrtn] [c.] *The Famous Victories of Henry V* Sidney killed fighting Spanish in Netherlands
1587	Mary Q of S executed – James VI of Scotland now heir apparent to English throne; an MP challenges Elizabeth's absolutism in Church affairs & defends free speech; Leicester's Dutch expedition fails; Pope proclaims crusade against England; Drake destroys Sp. fleet at Cadiz – delays Armada for a year; new attempt to colonise Virginia [fails 1591]	**Music:** Claudio Monteverdi [comp] 1st book of madrigals. **Art:** [–1591] Rialto Bridge, over Grand Canal, Venice, built; [c.] Hilliard, 'Young Man Leaning Against a Rose Tree' [miniature; V&A]. **Lit. 'Events':** Philip Henslowe's Rose Theatre, Bankside, opens; Holinshed, *Chronicles* [3-vol. 2nd edtn]	**Dr:** Thomas Kyd (1558–94) Christopher Marlowe (1564–93)	[c.] The *Spanish Tragedy* [prnt.d c.1592; reprnt.d with additions 1602] [c.–1588] *Tamburlaine the Great* Pts I & II [prnt.d, 1590] & [c.] *Dr Faustus* [earliest extant prnt.d edtn, 1604]
1588	Defeat of Spanish Armada – Elizabeth I addresses troops at Tilbury; Elizabeth builds 1st Chatham Dockyard; Billingsgate, London, opens as landing-stage	William Morgan's trans of Bible into Welsh [has enabled survival of Welsh language into modern times]; [–1589] 'Martin Marprelate' tracts attack episcopacy; Thomas Harriot, *A Brief and True Report of the New Found Land of Virginia*. **Art:** [–1591] cupola of St Peter's, Rome, built; Tintoretto, 'Paradise' [claimed to be the largest painting in the world]	**Pr/F:** Greene **Dr:** Lyly **Lit. 'Events':**	*Pandosto, or The Triumph of Time* [romance] [c.] *Endimion, the Man in the Moon* [prnt.d 1591] Eng. trans of 1st Ger. book on Dr Faustus pub.d; Vatican Library opens
1589	1st Standing Committee on Privileges set up by Commons; [–1592] Archbishop Whitgift's onslaught on Presbyterianism; London merchants seek to send trading mission to India; Eng. attacks on Portugese coast; Henry of Navarre as Henry IV of France starts Bourbon dynasty – Elizabeth I forms alliance – Eng. troops help in reconquest of France	1st Eng. knitting machine made; Hakluyt, *Principal Navigations, Voyages, Traffics and Discoveries of the English Nation* [1st edtn; expanded, 3 vols, 1598–1600]. **Lit. 'Events':** Spenser returns with Raleigh from Ireland to Court	**Dr:** Greene Marlowe **Theory/Crit:** Thomas Nashe George Puttenham	[c.] *Friar Bacon and Friar Bungay* [prnt.d, 1594] [c.] *The Jew of Malta* [earliest extant prnt.d text, 1633] *The Anatomie of Absurditie* [attack on contemp. writing] *The Arte of English Poesie*
1590	Archbishop Whitgift & Bishop Bancroft of London launch offensive against Puritan ministers; relief expedition to Roanoke colony (Virginia) finds settlers have inexplicably vanished	1st Eng. paper mill estab.d at Dartford. **Music:** Monteverdi, 2nd madrigal book; Thomas Watson, *First Sett of Italian Madrigals Englished*. **Art:** [–1597] Hardwick Hall, Derbys, built; El Greco, 'St Jerome'; [c.] Hilliard, 'George Clifford, 3rd Earl of Cumberland' [NMM, Greenwich]. **Lit. 'Events':** Paul's Playhouse closes	**P:** Spenser **Pr/F:** Sidney **Dr:** Peele William Shakespeare (1564–1616)	*The Faerie Queene* [Bks I–III] 'New' *Arcadia* [pub.d posthm. unfinished] [c.] *The Old Wives' Tale* [prnt.d 1595] [c.–1594] early comedies & history plays, *Richard III* & *Titus Andronicus*
1591	The 'Revenge' in battle with Sp. fleet – Sir Richard Grenville killed; [–1594] 1st Eng. voyage to reach E. Indies	Elizabeth I fnds Trinity College, Dublin; Raleigh, *A Report about ... the Isles of Azores*. **Lit. 'Events':** [c.] posthm. pub. of Sidney's *Astrophil and Stella* popularises sonnet form; Sir John Harington, Eng. trans of Ariosto's *Orlando Furioso*	**P:** Spenser Michael Drayton (1563–1631) **Dr:** Anon Greene	*Complaints* [misc. short poems] *The Harmonie of the Church* [metrical rendition of passages from scripture] [c.] *Arden of Faversham* [prnt.d 1592] [c.] *James IV* [prnt.d 1598]
1592	Raleigh disgraced after secret affair with, and later m. to, Elizabeth I's maid of honour; Presbyterian Church estab.d in Scotland; Davis discovers Falkland Islands	Ruins of Pompeii 1st discv.d; Galileo, *Della Scienza Meccanicca*. **Music:** Monteverdi, 3rd madrigal book. **Art:** [c.] Marcus Gheeraerts the Younger [pnt] 'Elizabeth I' ('The Ditchley Portrait') [NPG] **Lit. 'Events':** [–1594] plague in London closes theatres	**P:** Shakespeare Samuel Daniel (1562–1619) **Pr/F:** Nashe **Dr:** Lyly Marlowe	[–1593] *Venus and Adonis* *Delia* [sonnets] & *The Complaint of Rosalind* *Pierce Penniless his Supplication to the Divell* *Gallathea and Midas* *Edward II* [prnt.d 1594]

PERIOD	YEAR	INTERNATIONAL AND POLITICAL CONTEXTS	SOCIAL AND CULTURAL CONTEXTS	AUTHORS	INDICATIVE TITLES
	1593	Elizabeth I defines freedom of speech in Parliament as the privilege to say 'Aye' or 'No' – Parliament dissolved; all absentees from church over 16 to be imprisoned; Act passed against the seditious & disloyal – opponents of royal supremacy to be executed; [–1603] widespread rebellion in N. Ireland – supported by Spain	Music: Thomas Morley [comp] 5 books of madrigals. Art: [c.] El Greco, 'The Crucifixion' & 'The Resurrection'; [–1594] Caravaggio, 'Boy with a Basket of Fruit' Lit. 'Events': Marlowe killed	P: Drayton Marlowe Watson John Donne (c.1572–1631) Mary Sidney, Duchess of Pembroke (1561–1621) Pr/F: Nashe P. Sidney Dr: Marlowe	The Shepherd's Garland & Piers Gaveston [verse history] Hero and Leander [cont.d by Chapman & pub.d, 1598] The Teares of Fancie [sonnets] [c.1593–1601] Songs and Sonets, Elegies, Satyres & Verse Letters [wrtn] [–1600] Psalms [revises & conts her brother Philip's trans; 1st pub.d 1623] Christ's Tears over Jerusalem 'New' Arcadia [repub.d with parts of 'Old' incorporated] The Massacre at Paris
	1594	[–1597] 1st of bad harvests leads to high prices, famine, plague & riots; Lord Mayor's conference on problem of rogues in London; English sack Portug. colony of Pernambuco & open up trade in E. Indies	Lit. 'Events': theatres reopen	P: Drayton Shakespeare Pr/F: Nashe Dr: Lyly Shakespeare Thomas Heywood (c.1574–1641)	[–1619] Idea [sonnet sequence] The Rape of Lucrece & [>] Sonnets [pub.d, 1609] The Unfortunate Traveller [c.] Mother Bombie [comedy] [c.1594–1600] incls: Romeo and Juliet, MND, Henry IV, Richard II, Henry V, Merchant of Venice, Much Ado, Julius Caesar, As You Like It, [c.] The Four Prentices of London
	1595	Apprentices & masterless men riot in Southwark; Hugh O'Neill, earl of Tyrone, openly joins Ir. rebellion; Raleigh voyages to Guiana, S. America seeking 'El Dorado' [legendary place rich in gold] – explores Orinoco river; Dutch begin to colonise E. Indies	[c.] 1st heels on shoes; bows & arrows finally abolished as weapons of war. Art: [c.] Caravaggio, 'Lute Player' Lit. 'Events': Swan theatre, Bankside, built; Robert Southwell, Jesuit poet, hanged – St Peter's Complaint [poems] prnt.d	P: Daniel Spenser Dr: M. Sidney George Chapman (c.1557–1634) Anthony Munday (1553–1633) et al	[–1609] A History of the Civil Wars between York and Lancaster [poem in 8 Bks] Amoretti [sonnets] & [–1596] Epithalamion & Colin Clout Comes Home Againe The Tragedy of Antonie [trans] The Blind Beggar of Alexandria Sir Thomas More [Shakespeare may have collaborated]
	1596	Peasants' uprising in S. Oxfordshire over grain prices & enclosures; Earl of Essex's force sacks Cadiz; Eng, Fr. & Dutch allied against Spain – storms prevent 2nd Sp. Armada; Barents Sea discv.d	Drake dies; tomatoes intro.d into England; Sidney Sussex College, Cambridge & Whitgift School, Croydon, fnd.d; Raleigh, The Discovery of Guiana Lit. 'Events': 2nd Blackfriars theatre built [residents' petition prohibits opening]	P: Spenser Sir John Davies (1569–1626)	The Faerie Queene [Bks IV–VI], Prothalamiom & Four Hymns Orchestra, or a Poeme of Dauncing
	1597	1576 Act for poor relief reinstated [in effect till 1834] – workhouses built; vagrancy law provides for punishment of beggars & 'masterless men'; complaint [from Durham] about huge reduction of tillage by enclosure; [–1602] Ir. rebellion under	Gresham's College, London, fnd.d; King James VI [of Scotland], Demonologie [on witchcraft]. Music: Morley, A Plaine and Easie Introduction to Practicall Musicke; John Dowland [comp] 1st book of Eng. airs, with lute accompaniment; [c.] Ottavio Rinuccini	P: Joseph Hall (1574–1656) Pr/F: Sir Francis Bacon (1561–1626)	Virgidemiarum [satires] Essays [v.1612 & 1622]

TUDOR/ELIZABETHAN

Year	History / Politics	Science / Art / Music / Lit. 'Events'	Authors	Works
	Hugh O'Neill, 2nd Earl of Tyrone ('the O'Neill'): Eng. routed near Armagh – whole province in revolt; storms destroy 3rd Sp. Armada; Eng. raiders sack Portug. Azores	[compl] 'La Dafne' [early It. opera]. **Art:** [–1599] El Greco, 3 altarpieces, S. José Chapel, Toledo [incls 'St Joseph Leading the Child Jesus']; [–1600] Annibale Carraci pnts frescoes in Gallery of Farnese Palace, Rome	Thomas Deloney (c.1560–1600) **Dr:** Chapman	[–1600] *Thomas of Reading, Jack of Newbury & The Gentle Craft* [short novels] *A Humorous Day's Mirth*
1598	Edict of Nantes: Henri IV (Henri of Navarre) grants freedom of worship to Fr. Protestants [v.1685]	1st ref. to game of cricket; [–1602] Sir Thomas Bodley rebuilds university library, Oxford; [–1600] Hakluyt, *Principal Navigations* [2nd edtn, 3 vols]; Stow, *A Survey of London and Westminster*. **Art:** [c.–1600] El Greco, 'Portrait of Cardinal Niño de Guevara'; [c.] Caravaggio, 'Sick Little Bacchus'. **Lit. 'Events':** Spenser flees to London from rebellion in Ireland – writes *View of the Present State of Ireland* [banned – pub.d 1633]; George Chapman, Eng. trans of Homer's *Iliad*, I–II, VII–XI [& 1610, 1611]; Burbage's 'The Theatre' [v.1576] dismantled – timbers used to construct Globe Theatre [v.1599]	**P:** Chapman **Dr:** Munday & Henry Chettle (c.1560–c.1607) Ben Jonson (1572–1637)	*Hero and Leander* [conts & pubs Marlowe's poem] *Robin Hood* [2 plays; prnt.d 1601?] *Everyman in His Humour* [1st version; prnt.d 1601]
1599	Essex concludes unfavourable treaty with Tyrone in Ireland – banished by Elizabeth I; King James VI of Scotland pubs *Basilikon Doron, the True Law of Free Monarchies* condemning Prebyterianism & asserting Divine Right of Kings	**Lit. 'Events':** Spenser dies; Samuel Daniel, Poet Laureate – pubs *Poetical Essays* & *Musophilus, or A General Defence of Learning*; bishops attack satire & erotic poetry; Burbage's Globe Theatre, Bankside, opens [in use until closing of the theatres in 1642; pulled down, 1644]; 2nd Blackfriars Theatre opens; Paul's Playhouse reopens	**P:** Davies **Pr/F:** John Marston (c.1576–1634) **Dr:** Anon Thomas Dekker (c.1570–c.1632) Jonson Marston Henry Porter (dates unknown)	*Nosce Teipsum* *The Scourge of Villainie* [satires] *A Warning for Fair Women* [prnt.d] *The Shoemaker's Holiday & Old Fortunatus* [both prnt.d 1600] *Everyman Out of His Humour* *Histriomastix & Antonio and Mellida* [prnt.d 1602] *The Two Angry Women of Abingdon*
1600	[–1603] Lord Mountjoy achieves victory over Tyrone at Battle of Kinsale – systematically ravages Ir. districts & starves them into surrender; Elizabeth I grants charter to London merchants to estab. East India Company [active until 1858]; 1st Englishman, William Adams, lands in Japan	William Gilbert, *De Magnete* [on magnetism & electricity]. **Music:** recorders become popular in England; Dowland, 2nd book of songs; Jacopo Peri [compl] 'Euridice' [early It. opera]. **Art:** [–1601] Caravaggio, 'Crucifixion of St Peter' & 'Conversion of St Paul' [Rome]. **Lit. 'Events':** Fortune Theatre, Cripplegate, opens; *England's Helicon* pub.d [anthology of Eng. lyrics – incls Marlowe's 'Come live with me and be my love' & Raleigh's 'reply']; Edward Fairfax, Eng. trans of Tasso's *Gerusalemme Liberata* [v.1581]	**Dr:** T. Heywood Jonson Marston Shakespeare	*The Fair Maid of the West; or, A Girl Worth Gold* [Pt I; v.1630] [–1601] *Cynthia's Revels* *Antonio's Revenge* [prnt.d 1602] [c.1600–4] incls: *Hamlet, Twelfth Night, All's Well, Measure for Measure, Troilus and Cressida, Othello*
1601	Essex's rebellion against Elizabeth I fails – Essex executed; Poor Law Act codifies all Tudor poor laws; Parliament abolishes Monopolies; Sp. troops land in Ireland to aid Tyrone – Mountjoy routs them; 1st E. India Co. trading voyage; Jesuit missionaries reach China	Trinity College Library, Cambridge, fnd.d. **Music:** Morley compiles collection in honour of Elizabeth I, 'The Triumphs of Oriana'; [–1617] Thomas Campion pubs 5 'Books of Airs' [lyrics set to music – see 1610 & 1612]. **Art:** Montacute House, Somerset completed. **Lit. 'Events':** Elizabeth I's 'Golden speech'; Boar's Head Theatre, Whitechapel, opens	**Dr:** Anon Jonson Marston & Dekker	*Two Lamentable Tragedies* [prnt.d] *The Poetaster* [attacks Dekker & Marston] *Satiromastix* [riposte to Jonson]

PERIOD	YEAR	INTERNATIONAL AND POLITICAL CONTEXTS	SOCIAL AND CULTURAL CONTEXTS	AUTHORS	INDICATIVE TITLES
	1602	Sp. surrender – reconquest of Ireland begins; Dutch East India Co. estab.d	Bodleian Library, Oxford, so named & opens. **Art:** Long Gallery, Haddon Hall, Derbyshire, built	**Dr:** Chettle Dekker **Theory/Crit:** Thomas Campion Samuel Daniel	[c.] *The Tragedy of Hoffman* *The Merry Devil of Edmonton* *Observations on The Art of English Poesie* [advocates classical metre] *Defence of Rhyme* [reply: champions native Eng. use of rhyme]
	1603	Elizabeth I dies – James VI of Scotland becomes King James I – creates Union of England & Scotland – Succession plots against him – Raleigh implicated & imprisoned in Tower; under James I, witchcraft becomes a punishable offence in Eng. law; plague kills 33,500 in London	**Music:** Dowland, 3rd book of songs. **Art:** Audley End House, Essex, built **Lit. 'Events':** James I becomes patron of 2 boys theatre companies; [–1604] plague closes theatres; John Florio, Eng. trans of Montaigne, *Essays*	**Pr/F:** Dekker **Dr:** T. Heywood Jonson	*The Wonderful Year* [pamphlet describing the plague] *A Woman Killed with Kindness* [prnt.d 1607] *Sejanus*
	1604	James I declared king of 'Great Britain, France & Ireland'; James's 1st Parliament; Act confirms anti-RC recusancy statutes – James orders RC priests to be banished; [–1605] campaign against Nonconformist ministers – some ejected from livings; Eng. priests given statutory authority to marry; 1597 vagrancy law expanded; peace treaty with Spain	Hampton Court Conference: C of E bishops denounce both RCism & Puritanism – also consider Church reform & standard text of the Bible – James I orders new trans [by Lancelot Andrewes & others; completed 1611]; Blundell's School, Tiverton, fnd.d; Robert Cawdrey, *The Table Alphabetical/* [1st Eng. dictionary]. **Music:** Company of Musicians, London, fnd.d. **Art:** Caravaggio, 'Deposition of Christ' **Lit. 'Events':** Red Bull theatre, Clerkenwell, replaces Boars Head	**Dr:** Chapman Dekker & John Webster (c.1578–c.1632) Dekker & Thomas Middleton (c.1580–1627) Marston Shakespeare	*Bussy d'Ambois* [prnt.d 1607] *Westward Ho!* *The Honest Whore* [Pt I; Pt II (by Dekker), 1630] *The Dutch Courtezan & The Malcontent* [& prnt.d] [c.1604–9] incls: *King Lear, Macbeth, Antony and Cleopatra, Coriolanus, Pericles*
	1605	Gunpowder Plot: RC conspirators led by Guy Fawkes unsuccessfully attempt to blow up king & Parliament because of C of E intolerance; Ir. settlement attempted on Eng. legal lines; [>] thro'out this period, many London trades companies incorporated	**Int. Lit.:** Miguel de Cervantes, *Don Quixote*, Pt. I [Eng. trans, 1612]. **Art:** [c.] El Greco, 'St Bartholomew'	**Pr/F:** Bacon **Dr:** Chapman, Jonson & Marston Jonson Middleton	*The Advancement of Learning* *Eastward Ho!* [& prnt.d] *The Masque of Blackness* [designed by Inigo Jones] *Michaelmas Term & A Trick to Catch the Old One* [prnt.d 1607–8]
	1606	Gunpowder Plotters executed; persecution of RCs by Parliament; Courts & merchants in conflict over royal duties levied at ports; Royal Charter granted to Virginia Co. – expedition to recolonise it; Sp. discover Torres Strait – Dutch explore N. coast of 'New Holland' (Australia)	**Art:** [c.] El Greco, 'The Feast in the House of Simon'; Peter Paul Rubens [pnt] 'The Circumcision' [Genoa altarpiece] & 'Virgin in a Glory of Angels'. **Lit. 'Events':** Whitefriars [private] theatre built; Rose theatre demolished; Paul's Playhouse closes	**P:** Drayton **Dr:** Jonson Middleton Middleton & Dekker John Day (1574–1640)	[c.] *Poems, Lyric and Pastoral* [incls 'Ballad of Agincourt': 'Faire stood the wind for France'] *Volpone* [prnt.d 1607] & *Hymenaei* [masque] [attrib.] *The Revenger's Tragedy* & [c.] *A Mad World, My Masters* [prnt.d 1608] *The Roaring Girl* [prnt.d 1611] *The Isle of Gulls*
	1607	Confiscated Ir. lands given to Eng. & Scots settlers – 'Plantation' [colonisation] of Ulster recommences; Eng. Parliament rejects Union of England &	[c.] forks 1st in use in Italy. **Int. Lit.:** [c.–1623] Honoré d'Urfé, *L'Astrée* [much imitated Fr. pastoral romance; many different edtns]. **Music:** [c.] Anon,	**P:** Donne **Dr:** Francis Beaumont	*La Corona* [divine poems; wrtn] *The Woman Hater* [pf.d?] &

STUART/JACOBEAN

	Events / Context	Authors	Literary & Other Works
	Scotland; Jamestown colony, Virginia, estab.d – 1st permanent Eng. settlement – Chesapeake Bay explored	(c.1584–1616)	[-1608] *The Knight of the Burning Pestle* [prnt.d 1613; possibly co-authored by John Fletcher]
	'There is a Lady Sweet and Kind' [madrigal]; Monteverdi, 'Orpheus' [It. opera]. **Art:** [-1611] Hatfield House, Hertfordshire, built		
1608	Courts affirm common citizenship for those born after James I's accession; New Book of Rates regulates customs duties [to Crown's advantage]; mutual defence treaty between England & Netherlands; Quebec fnd.d in 'New France' (Canada)	**P:** Donne	[c.1608–15] *Holy Sonnets* & other religious poems [wrtn]
		Pr/F: Dekker	*The Bellman of London & Lanthorn and Candlelight* [pamphlets about London vagabonds]
	Art: [-1610] Holland House, Kensington, built; El Greco, 'View of Toledo'. **Lit. 'Events':** The King's Men [Shakespeare's Co.] lease Blackfriars theatre; plague closes theatres [until Dec. 1609]	**Dr:** Anon	*A Yorkshire Tragedy* [prnt.d]
		Day	*Humour Out of Breath*
		Jonson	*The Masque of Beauty*
		John Fletcher (1579–1625)	*The Faithful Shepherdess*
1609	12-yr truce between Spain & United Provinces [Netherlands] – latter make alliance with England & France for 12 years	**Pr/F:** Dekker	*The Gull's Hornbook* [pamphlet about London gallants]
	Sir Robert Filmer, *Patriarcha* [extreme advocation of Divine Right of Kings]; Charterhouse School fnd.d; 1st regular newspapers pub.d in Germany; [c.] Galileo Galilei makes telescope & observes craters on moon – pubs scientific theories; Johann Kepler, *New Astronomy* [announces 1st 2 laws of planetary motion]. **Art:** [-1610] Peter Paul Rubens [pnt] 'Self-Portrait with his Wife Isabella [Brandt]'; Adam Elsheimer [pnt] 'The Flight into Egypt'	**Dr:** Jonson	*Epicoene, or The Silent Woman* [extant text in *Workes*, 1616] & *Masque of Queens*
		Shakespeare	[c.1609–13]: 'Last Plays': *Cymbeline, The Winter's Tale, The Tempest* [v.1613–14]
		Beaumont & Fletcher	[c.] *Philaster* [prnt.d 1620]
		Cyril Tourneur (c.1575–1626)	*The Atheist's Tragedy* [prnt.d 1611]
1610	Parliament refuses James substitution of annual grant for feudal dues – the 'Great Contract'; further vagrancy law passed; episcopacy restored in Scotland; Henry IV of France assassinated – Louis XIII, king; [-1611] Henry Hudson explores bay & river so named in Canada	**Pr/F:** Donne	*Pseudo-Martyr* [attack on Jesuits]
		Dr: Beaumont & Fletcher	[-1611] *The Maid's Tragedy* [prnt.d 1619]
	Tea 1st intro.d into Europe; [-1612] Wadham College, Oxford, fnd.d; Galileo records Saturn's rings & Jupiter's moons. **Music:** Campion, *Two Bookes of Ayres.* **Art:** Ham House, Surrey & Fountains Hall, Yorkshire, built; [c.] El Greco, 'Vision of the Apocalypse'; [c.] [attrib.] John Taylor [pnt] 'William Shakespeare' [NPG]	Jonson	*The Alchemist* [prnt.d 1612]
		Lit. 'Events':	[>] Stationers' Co. send a copy of every book pub.d in England to Bodleian Library; [-1611] George Chapman completes Eng. trans of Homer's *Iliad*
1611	Parliament dissolved; [-1623] tortuous negotiations begin over possible m. between Prince Charles & Sp. Infanta; [>] James I creates Order of Baronets – sold to raise money; 1st Eng. envoy visits Great Mogul [v.1614]; Dutch 1st trade with Japan	**P:** Donne	*An Anatomy of the World (The First Anniversary)* pub.d
		Aemilia Lanyer (1569–1645)	*Salve Deus Rex Judaeorum* [poems]
	The 'Authorised Version' of the Bible ('King James's Bible') pub.d – supersedes all previous edtns; Kepler invents astronomical telescope. **Art:** [c.] Guido Reni [pnt] 'Triumph of Samson'	**Pr/F:** Donne	*Ignatius His Conclave* [attack on RCism]
		Dr: Beaumont & Fletcher	*A King and No King*
		Jonson	*Catiline his Conspiracy* & *Oberon*
1612	Prince Henry dies, Prince Charles [later King Charles I] becomes heir apparent; last recorded burning of heretics; [c.] Lancashire witches hanged; Bermudas colonised from Virginia; [-1613] E. India Co. estab.s 'factory' [trading settlement] at Surat, Gujarat, India	**P:** Donne	*The Second Anniversary (The Progress of the Soul)* [with reprnt of 1st *Anniversary*, 1611]
		Drayton	*Poly-Olbion* [Pt 1 of long topographical patriotic poem; Pt II, 1622]
	John Smith, *A True Relation of Virginia since the First Planting of that Colony.* **Music:** Campion, *Third and Fourth Booke of Ayres.* **Art:** Rubens, 'Resurrection' [tryptych, Antwerp Cathedral] & [-1614] 'Descent from the Cross'. **Lit. 'Events':** T. Heywood, *An Apology for Actors*, pub.d	**Pr/F:** Bacon	*Essays* [2nd & enlarged edtn]
		Dr: Webster	*The White Devil* [prnt.d; wrtn c.1609–12]

PERIOD	YEAR	INTERNATIONAL AND POLITICAL CONTEXTS	SOCIAL AND CULTURAL CONTEXTS	AUTHORS	INDICATIVE TITLES
STUART/JACOBEAN	1613	Princess Elizabeth [James I's daughter] m. Frederick, Elector Palatine; Sir Thomas Overbury poisoned to death in Tower by Earl of Somerset & Countess of Essex; resevoir at Clerkenwell opens – new London river water supply; copper farthings 1st intro.d	Galileo's treatise supporting Copernican system pub.d. **Art:** Rubens, 'Susannah and the Elders' & 'Flight into Egypt'; Reni, 'Aurora' [fresco, Rome] **Lit. 'Events':** Globe Theatre burnt down; Sir Thomas Bodley leaves a fortune to rebuild Bodleian Library, Oxford [–1618]	**P:** Donne **Dr:** Middleton Shakespeare & Fletcher [?] Lady Elizabeth Cary (1585/6–1639)	'Good Friday, 1613, Riding Westward' & *Epithalamion* ('On Lady Elizabeth and Count Palatine') [wrtn] [c.] *A Chaste Maid in Cheapside* *Henry VIII* & [–1614] *The Two Noble Kinsmen* [uncertain] *The Tragedy of Mariam* [1st extant original Eng. drama by a woman]
	1614	'Added Parliament' refuses to discuss finance until its grievances are met; [–1617] crisis in cloth trade; James I writes in English to the Mogul Emperor to promote trade with E. Indies – embassy visits Agra in 1615; Virginian colonists prevent Fr. settlements in Maine & Nova Scotia; John Smith explores coast of 'New England'	Sir Walter Raleigh, *History of the World* [1st & only vol.]; John Napier discv.s logarithms. **Art:** Blickling Hall, Norfolk, built; Domenichino [pnt] 'Last Communion of St Jerome'	**Dr:** Jonson Webster **Lit. 'Events':**	*Bartholomew Fair* [prnt.d 1631] [c.] *The Duchess of Malfi* [prnt.d 1623] [–1616] Chapman, Eng. trans of Homer's *Odyssey*; 2nd Globe Theatre built; Hope theatre built [from 1617 mainly used for bull- and bear-baiting]
	1615	Overbury murder rumours become public – Somerset loses royal protection as George Villiers becomes James I's [& then Charles I's] favourite – Somerset & Countess of Essex arraigned	Camden, *Annals of the Reign of Elizabeth I* [& 1625 – Elizabeth's 1593 'dissolution' speech pub.d in it]; Joseph Swetnam, *Arraignment of Lewd, Idle, Froward and Unconstant Women* pub.d. **Int. Lit.:** Cervantes, *Don Quixote* – Pt II completed. **Art:** Inigo Jones becomes Surveyor of the King's Works	**Dr:** Jonson **Lit. 'Events':**	*The Golden Age Restored* Donne ordained – 1st surviving sermon delivered
	1616	Sir Walter Raleigh released from Tower to lead 2nd expedition [1617] to Guiana in search of the gold of 'El Dorado' [v.1595]; Princess Pocahontas arrives in England; 1st rounding of Cape Horn	[>] William Harvey lectures on circulation of the blood [treatise pub.d 1628]; Galileo accused by RC Church of heresy; John Smith, *A Description of New England*. **Art:** I. Jones builds Queen's House, Greenwich; Rubens, 'The Last Judgement' & [–1617] 'Descent from the Cross'	**Dr:** Jonson **Lit. 'Events':**	*The Devil is an Ass & Workes* [pub.d; incls revised 'London' version of *Everyman in His Humour* & non-dramatic poems – e.g. 'To Penshurst'] Shakespeare & Cervantes die; Cockpit (Phoenix) theatre opens
	1617	James I revists Scotland for 1st time since accession; Villiers becomes Earl of Buckingham; Eng. hostility to Dutch settlement at Surat	Rachel Speght, *A Muzzle for Melastomus*, Ester Sowernam, *Ester Hath Hang'd Haman* & Constantia Munda, *A Sop for Cerberus* – ripostes to Swetnam, 1615. **Art:** [–1620] Rubens, 'The Lion Hunt' [& other 'Hunt' paintings]	**Dr:** Jonson **Lit. 'Events':**	*The Vision of Delight* & *Christmas His Masque* [c.] James appoints Ben Jonson as poet to royal family [in effect, Poet Laureate]
	1618	James tries to modify Scots Presbyterianism; Francis Bacon, Lord Chancellor; Raleigh's expedition fails [v.1616] – executed for treason on return; English W. Africa Co. fnd.d – occupies Gambia & Gold Coast; Bohemian Protestant revolt against Hapsburg rule [Defenestration of Prague': Emperor's governors thrown out of a window] begins Thirty Years War [–1648] – Britain supports Protestant powers but does not fight; Charter of Liberties granted to Virginia	1st burning of gas from coal; James I issues *Book of Sports* permitting traditional Sunday pastimes [e.g. dancing] – disliked by Puritans; Johann Kepler, 3rd law of planetary motion. **Music:** Byrd composes setting for 'Non Nobis Domine'. **Art:** Aston Hall, Birmingham, built; [c.] Rubens, 'Rape of the Daughters of Leucippus'; Diego de Velázquez [pnt] 'Old Woman Frying Eggs' [SNG]; [c.] Daniel Mytens [pnt] 'Thomas Howard, Earl of Arundel' [NPG]	**Dr:** Jonson Philip Massinger (1583–1640) **Lit. 'Events':**	*Pleasure Reconciled to Virtue* [c.] *The Fatal Dowry* [–1619] William Drummond of Hawthornden's 'Conversations' with Ben Jonson [pub.d]
	1619	1st colonial representative Parliament meets in Jamestown, Virginia; [–1620] 1st African slaves	Dulwich College, London, fnd.d. **Art:** [–1622] I. Jones builds new Banqueting House, Whitehall;	**P:** Donne	[c.1619–23] late religious poems ('Hymns') [wrtn]

Year	History / Society	Science · Art · 'Events' (Int. Lit.)	Literature — Pr/F: & Dr:
1619	transported into Jamestown by Dutch; 1st attacks by Dutch on Eng. factories in E. Indies	[c.] Velázquez, 'Three Musicians' & 'Water Carrier of Seville' [Apsley House]	**Dr:** Fletcher — *The Humorous Lieutenant*
1620	Freedom of worship granted to RCs in England; [-c.1630] trade depression, esp.ly for clothworkers – much unemployment & misery; [Sept.] Pilgrim Fathers sail to America in *Mayflower* – settle at Plymouth in Massachusetts, 'New England'	[>] English competes with French, Spanish, Portuguese & Dutch as a language in colonial America; [-1642] *Corante* 1st Eng. periodical newsbooks [early newspapers] pub.d in London. **Art:** Rubens, 'Christ on the Cross'; [c.] Velázquez, 'Doña Jerónima de la Fuente' & 'St John in the Wilderness'; [-1621] Sir Anthony van Dyck 1st visits England & [c.] pnts 'The Three Graces'	**Pr/F:** Bacon — *Novum Organum* [phil.] **Dr:** Fletcher — *Women Pleased* Jonson — *News from the New World* Lady Mary Wroth, Countess of Montgomery (c.1587–1651) — *Love's Victory*
1621	Sir Francis Bacon impeached for taking bribes; 1st of 3 yrs of bad harvests; conflict between Eng. & Dutch E. India Cos; [>] British attempt to colonise Fr. Acadia (Nova Scotia); Sp./Dutch war resumes	Charter for Edinburgh University ratified [see 1583]; Oxford University botanical gardens 1st laid out; [>] Robert Burton, *The Anatomy of Melancholy* [final edtn 1651–2]. **Art:** [c.] van Dyck, 'St Martin'. **Lit. 'Events':** Donne becomes Dean of St Paul's; Fortune theatre burnt & rebuilt	**Pr/F:** Wroth — *[The Countess of Montgomery's] Urania* [1st Eng. prose romance by a woman – incls sonnet sequence, 'Pamphlia to Amphilanthus'] **Dr:** Dekker, William Rowley (c.1585–c.1626) & John Ford (1586–post-1639) — *The Witch of Edmonton* Jonson — *The Gypsies Metamorphosed* [masque; & prnt.d] Middleton — [c.] *Women Beware Women* [prnt.d 1657]
1622	Massacre at Jamestown, Virginia by Algonquian confederacy; 1st Eng. ambassador to Turkey	Slide-rule invented; Henry Peacham, *Compleat Gentleman*. **Int. Lit:** [c.] Charles Sorel, *Francion* [1st Fr. burlesque novel]. **Art:** Velázquez, 'Luis de Gongora' & [c.] 'Christ in the House of Mary and Martha' [NG]; [-1625] Gian Lorenzo Bernini [sculpt.] 'Apollo and Daphne'	**Pr/F:** Bacon — *History of Henry VII* **Dr:** Jonson — *The Masque of Augurs* Massinger — *The Duke of Milan* [prnt.d 1623] Middleton & Rowley — *The Changeling* [prnt.d 1653]
1623	Prince Charles's & Buckingham's final, failed visit to Madrid to negotiate m. with Infanta [v.1611] – return eager for war with Spain; Patents Law protects inventors; Dutch massacre Eng. colonists in Molucca Islands – E. India Co. driven from E. Indies – [>] concentrates on India; [c.] English settle in St Kitts, W. Indies	**Art:** I. Jones designs Marlborough House Chapel; Rubens, 'The Landing of the Médicis' [in series, 'History of Marie de Médicis', 1622–5]; [-1624] Bernini, 'David with his Sling'; Frans Hals [pnt] 'Young Man and Woman in an Inn (Yonker Ramp and His Sweetheart)'. **Lit. 'Events':** Shakespeare: 1st Folio pub.d	**Pr/F:** Bacon — *De Augmentis Scientiarum* [Lat. expansion of *The Advancement of Learning*, 1605] William Drummond of Hawthornden (1585–1649) — [c.] *The Cypresse Grove* [meditation on death] **Dr:** Dekker & Ford — *The Spanish Gypsy*
1624	James I & France allied against Spain – Parliament votes subsidies for war; proposed m. between Prince Charles & Fr. princess; Act passed forbidding monopolies; Cardinal Richelieu accedes to power in France; Virginia Co. hands Virginia to Eng. monarch – becomes 1st Crown Colony	[c.] Flemish chemist 1st invents the word 'gas'; Pembroke College, Oxford, fnd.d; John Smith, *The General History of Virginia, New England, and the Summer Isles*. **Art:** [-1633] Bernini's bronze canopy in St Peter's, Rome; [c.] van Dyck, 'Portrait of a Young Warrior'; Hals, 'The Laughing Cavalier' [Wallace Coll.]	**Pr/F:** Donne — *Devotions upon Emergent Occasions* [pub.d] **Dr:** Fletcher — *Rule a Wife and Have a Wife* Jonson — *Neptune's Triumph* & *The Masque of Owls* Middleton — *A Game at Chess* [prnt.d 1625]

Period	Year	International and Political Contexts	Social and Cultural Contexts	Authors	Indicative Titles
	1625	James I dies, King Charles I accedes; m. of Charles & Henrietta Maria of France; tension over revenues between king & 1st Parliament [largely landowners] – dissolved; John Pym begins parliamentary attacks on Arminian [anti-Calvinistic] doctrine; Charles I directs Scottish Act of Revocation against holders of former Church property; Colonial Office estab.d in London; plague kills 35,000–40,000 in London; war with Spain – Eng. expedition against Cadiz a disaster	1st Eng. fire-engines; 1st Hackney carriages in London. **Art:** [c.] Rubens, 'Adoration of the Magi'; Rembrandt van Rijn [pnt] 'Stoning of St Stephen'; [c.1720s] Francisco de Zurbarán [pnt] 'Christ on the Cross' **Lit. 'Events':** Plague closes theatres in London for several months; Donne delivers sermons on the plague & James I's death before Charles I	**Pr/F:** Bacon **Dr:** Heywood Massinger Webster & Rowley	*Essayes or Counsels, Civill and Morall* [3rd enlarged edtn] & *Of Masques and Triumphs* *The English Traveller* [prnt.d 1633] [c.] *A New Way to Pay Old Debts* [prnt.d 1633] *A Cure for a Cockold*
	1626	2nd Parliament persists in impeaching Duke of Buckingham for Cadiz debacle – again dismissed; [> thro'out reign] Charles I collects revenues without parliamentary consent; Dutch purchase Manhattan Island from Native Americans & fn.d New Amsterdam [becomes New York; v.1664]	**Art:** Rubens, 'Assumption of the Virgin' [Antwerp altarpiece], [c.] Velázquez, 'Infante Don Carlos' **Lit. 'Events':** George Sandys, Eng. verse trans of Ovid's *Metamorphoses* [1st literary work wrtn in American colonies]	**Dr:** Jonson Massinger James Shirley (1596–1666)	*The Staple of News* [prnt.d 1631] *The Roman Actor* *The Maid's Revenge*
	1627	'Five Knights' case: Habeas Corpus refused because they were 'Detained at his Majesty's Pleasure'; Bishop William Laud joins Privy Council; England & France at war – disastrous expedition to relieve Huguenot [Fr. Protestant] rebels besieged in La Rochelle; [–1628] Richelieu estab.s 'New France' [Canada] Co.; English colonise Barbados, W. Indies	Parian Chronicle discov.d [marble tablet outlining Grk history to 264 AD]. **Music:** Heinrich Schütz [comp] 'Daphne' [1st Ger. opera]. **Art:** [c.] Hals, 'Banquet of the Officers of the Company of St Hadrian' & '... of St George'; [–1628] Rembrandt, 'Simeon in the Temple'; Nicolas Poussin [pnt] 'Death of Germanicus'	**Pr/F:** Bacon	*New Atlantis* [pub. posthm.]
	1628	Parliament passes Petition of Right [against arbitrary imprisonment, martial law, forced loans, by king's Gvnmt]; Duke of Buckingham assassinated; Laud becomes Bishop of London; Oliver Cromwell, MP for Huntingdon; Wentworth, President of Council in the North; Richelieu starves La Rochelle into surrender; Dutch conquer Java	William Harvey, *On the Motion of the Heart and Blood*; *Alexandrian Codex* [5th C. ms.] presented to Charles I. **Art:** [–1629] Velázquez, 'The Drunkards (Merrymakers)'; Hals, 'Gypsy Girl (La Bohémienne)'; Zurbarán, 'St Serapion', 'St Bonaventure on his Bier' 'Charles I' [NPG]	**Pr/F:** John Earle (c.1601–65) **Dr:** Ford Shirley	*Microcosmographie* [character sketches & essays] *The Lover's Melancholy* *The Witty Fair One*
	1629	Parliament votes 'Three Resolutions' [against Arminianism & Charles I's collection of unauthorised revenues] – dissolved [does not meet again for 11 yrs] – [>] king's 'personal rule' – opponents imprisoned; peace with France; [–1631] trade slump; Huguenot wars end – Protestants have freedom to worship but political power broken; English capture Quebec from French; [>] English Puritans consolidate settlements in Massachusetts; English occupy the Bahamas [Crown Colony, 1729]	Charter granted to Guild of Spectacle Makers. **Int. Lit.:** Corneille, *Mélite*. **Art:** Rubens knighted by Charles I for artistic work undertaken on visit to London – pnts 'Thomas Howard. 2nd Earl of Arundel and Surrey' [NPG], [–1630] 'Allegory of War and Peace' [NG] & [–1630] 'Adam and Eve'; Velázquez, 'Triumph of Bacchus (Drunkards)'; Rembrandt, 'Self-Portrait'; Zurbarán, 'Life of St Peter Nolasco' [series] & 'St Bonaventure on his Bier'	**P:** John Milton (1608–74) **Dr:** Ford Richard Brome (c.1590–c.1652) Sir William D'Avenant (1606–68) **Lit. 'Events':**	'On the Morning of Christ's Nativity' [early ode] *The Broken Heart* [prnt.d 1633] *The Lovesick Maid* *The Tragedy of Albovine* Salisbury Court Theatre opens
	1630	Large fines collected from Eng. gentry by 'Distraint of Knighthood'; bad harvest – [>] large-scale emigration to New England ensues; peace treaties with France & Spain; Gustavus Adophus of Sweden	[c.] 1st pottery made at Lambeth; Pope dissolves order of Female Jesuits. **Int. Lit.:** Lope de Vega, *Laurel de Apolo* [Sp. play]. **Art:** I. Jones builds Stoke Park Pavilions, Towcester; Velázquez, 'Forge of	**Dr:** D'Avenant Dekker Brome	*The Cruel Brother* *The Honest Whore* [Pt II; v.1604] *The City Witt (or the Woman wears the Breeches)* [prnt.d 1653]

CAROLINE/STUART

	begins campaigns against Holy Roman Empire; 1st colonisation of Dutch Guiana	Vulcan'; [c.–1633] Hals, 'Malle Babbe'; Zurbarán, 'Apotheosis of St Thomas Aquinas'; [c.] Jusepe de Ribera [pnt] 'Martyrdom of St Bartholomew'	T. Heywood **Lit. 'Events':**	*The Fair Maid of the West* [Pt II]; v.1600] Plague closes theatres for 7 mths
1631	Charles I & Laud try to raise money for repairs to St Paul's; driven by Gustavus's intervention, war flares across Europe between Protestant & Catholic regimes; [c.] 1st Eng. settlements in Maryland; [>] English colonise Leeward Islands	1st Fr. newspaper, *Gazette de France*, pub.d. **Art:** I. Jones lays out Square of Covent Garden; New Palace, Kew, built; [c.] Rubens, 'The Artist with Hélène Fournier in Their Garden'; Velázquez, 'Infanta Maria, Queen of Hungary' & [c.–1632] 'Christ on the Cross'; Poussin, 'Kingdom of Flora' **Lit. 'Events':** John Donne dies	**Dr:** Brome Jonson Shirley Thomas May (1594–1650)	*The Queen's Exchange* *Chloridia* *Love's Cruelty* & *The Traitor* [prnt.d 1635] *The Tragedy of Antigone*
1632	Export of Eng. grain without royal licence banned; European wars continue – Gustavus Adolphus killed; Quebec returned to French; English settle in Antigua & Montserrat	1st London coffee shop opens; William Harvey becomes Charles I's physician; Galileo, *Dialogues on the Ptolemaic and Copernican Systems* [supports latter]. **Music:** Monteverdi [comp] 'Scherzi Musicali'. **Art:** van Dyck settles in England & becomes Court painter to Charles I; [c.–1643] Taj Mahal built by Mogul emperor, Shah Jahan, at Agra, India; [c.] Rubens, 'Garden of Love' & 'The Ildefonso Altar'; Rembrandt, 'The Anatomy Lesson of Dr Nicolaes Tulp'	**Dr:** Brome Ford Massinger Shirley	*The Northern Lass* *'Tis Pity She's a Whore* [prnt.d 1633] *The City Madam* *Hyde Park* [prnt.d 1637]
1633	Charles I crowned King of Scotland in Edinburgh; Thomas Wentworth becomes Lord Deputy in Ireland; Laud, Archbishop of Canterbury – begins harsh measures against Puritans; large fine imposed on City of London; Royal Scots estab.d – oldest regular regiment of British Army; [c.] Eng. Puritans fnd Colony at Connecticut; 1st Eng. 'factory' in Bengal [at Orissa]	*Book of Sports* reissued [v.1618]; Galileo forced to recant Copernican theories by Inquisition in Rome. **Art:** Velázquez, 'Prince Baltasar Carlos' [Wallace Coll.]; Van Dyck, 'Portrait of James Stuart, Duke of Lennox and Richmond' [after 1632; Kenwood] & 'Queen Henrietta with Dwarf Hudson and Monkey'; Rembrandt, 'Descent from the Cross'; Zurbará, 'Still Life with Oranges' **Lit. 'Events':** [–1634] William Prynne, *Histriomastix* [Puritan anti-theatre pamphlet implicitly critical of royal family – severly punished by Star Chamber, v.1637]	**P:** Donne Milton Abraham Cowley (1618–67) George Herbert (1593–1633) **Dr:** Jonson Shirley	*Poems* [1st collected edtn; pub. posthm.] *L'Allegro & Il Penseroso* *Poetical Blossoms* [incls *Pyramus and Thisbe* – verse romance wrtn in 1629 when 10-yrs-old] *The Temple* [pub. posthm.; incls 'The Collar', 'Virtue, 'Easter Wings'] *A Tale of a Tub* [rev.d version of c.1596 play] *The Gamester*
1634	To make himself financially independent of Parliament, Charles I levies 1st writ of 'Ship Money' – tax on maritime counties [to provide fleet against pirates]; [>] severe treatment of political & religious opposition by Star Chamber & Court of High Commission; [–1637] antiquated Tudor laws used to impose large fines on landowners for encroachments on Royal Forests; Lord Baltimore fnds colony in Maryland for RC settlers	Covent Garden Market opens; [–1652] Cornelius Vermuyden undertakes drainage of the Fens [v.1640]. **Int. Lit.:** 'Passion Play' 1st pf.d at Oberammergau, Germany [re-enacted every 10 yrs]. **Art:** Velázquez, 'Surrender of Breda' & 'Philip IV in Brown and Silver' [NG]; Rembrandt, 'Self Portrait' & 'Balshazzar's Feast'; Poussin, 'Adoration of the Golden Calf' [NG]; Ribera, 'Joseph with the Flock of Laban'	**Dr:** Brome & Heywood D'Avenant Ford Milton Shirley Thomas Carew (c.1595–1640)	*The Late Lancashire Witches* *Love and Honour* [prnt.d 1649] *Perkin Warbeck* [chronicle play] *Comus* [masque; 1st pf.d at Ludlow Castle] *The Triumph of Peace* [masque] *Coelum Brittanicum* [masque]

PERIOD	YEAR	INTERNATIONAL AND POLITICAL CONTEXTS	SOCIAL AND CULTURAL CONTEXTS	AUTHORS	INDICATIVE TITLES
	1635	2nd writ of 'Ship Money' extends to inland counties & towns; New Book of Rates levies increased customs duties	1st inland postal service estab.d between London & Edinburgh; Académie française fnd.d by Cardinal Richelieu; John Selden, *Mare Clausen* [outlines Eng. claims to sovereignty of the seas]. **Int. Lit.:** Pierre Corneille, *Médée* [Fr. tragedy]. **Art:** Rubens designs Baroque ceiling for Whitehall; [c.] Velázquez, 'Philip IV Hunting Wild Boar (La Tela Real)' [NG]; van Dyck, 'Charles I, King of England'; Rembrandt, 'Rape of Ganymede'; [c.] Poussin, 'Rape of the Sabines'; [c.] Guido Reni [pnt] 'St Jerome'	**P:** Francis Quarles (1592–1644) **Pr/F:** Sir Thomas Browne (1605–82) **Dr:** Shirley	*Emblemes, Divine and Morall* [c.] *Religio Medici* [wrtn; pub.d unauthorised, 1642; rev.d & authorised edtn, 1643] *The Lady of Pleasure*
	1636	Scottish Council orders new Prayer Book; 3rd writ of 'Ship Money'; plague kills 10,500 in London; Rhode Island colony fnd.d; [>] Dutch continue to extend trade & colonisation in Africa & Asia	1st university in American colonies fnd.d at Cambridge, Massachusetts [named Harvard after 1st benefactor, 1639]. **Int. Lit.:** Corneille, *Le Cid* [Fr. tragedy]. **Art:** Rubens, 'Judgment of Paris' & [c.–1640] 'The Three Graces'; Rembrandt, 'Danae' & 'Blinding of Samson'; [c.–1637] van Dyck, 'Three Sons of Charles I of England' & 'Charles I in Three Positions' [Royal Coll.]; Claude Lorraine [pnt] 'View of the Campo Vaccino' & 'View of a Seaport: Effect of the Rising Sun'	**Dr:** D'Avenant Massinger **Lit. 'Events':**	*The Platonick Lovers & The Wits* *The Bashful Lover* [May] plague closes theatres in London [–Oct. 1637]
	1637	John Hampden tried for refusing to pay 'Ship Money'; Scottish rebellion follows intro. of new Liturgy; Prynne again mutilated, fined & imprisoned for attacking Laud & Bishops [v.1633]; Eng. traders land on coast of China; E. India Co. sets up factories at Canton	Star Chamber imposes severe limits on Eng. press [only 3 typefounders allowed]; Descartes, *Discours de la Méthode*. **Music:** Venice Opera House opens. **Art:** [c.] Rembrandt, 'Angel Raphael leaving Tobias' & 'The Carpenter's Family'; [c.] Poussin, 'Bacchanal' [NG] & 'Triumph of Pan' [Sudeley]; [c.–1638] van Dyck, 'Charles I on Horseback' [NG]; Ribera, Pietà'	**P:** Milton **Dr:** T. Heywood Shirley **Lit. 'Events':**	*Lycidas* *The Royal King and the Loyal Subject* *The Royal Master* Ben Jonson dies
	1638	Judges declare 'Ship Money' a legal tax; Scottish Covenant drawn up – General Assembly in Glasgow restores Scottish Kirk to pre-1580 state – new Prayer Book revoked – Scottish Parliament called – Covenanters prepare for anti-C of E war; Thirty Years War continues to rage across Europe; Newhaven, Connecticut, fnd.d	Glaziers, Glovers & Distillers Cos, London, fnd.d; [–1639] 1st American printing press estab.d at Cambridge, Mass. **Art:** [–1640] Rubens, 'Nymphs and Satyrs: Peasant Dance'; Rembrandt, 'Marriage of Samson'; van Dyck, 'Thomas Killigrew and Thomas Carew' [Royal Coll.] & [c.] 'Lord George Stuart, Seigneur D'Aubigny' [NPG]	**P:** Quarles **Dr:** D'Avenant Ford **Lit. 'Events':**	*Hieroglyphicks of the Life of Man* *The Unfortunate Lovers* [prnt.d 1643] & *The Fair Favourite* *The Lady's Trial* Sir William D'Avenant, Poet Laureate
	1639	Scottish General Assembly abolishes episcopacy – Covenanters in arms against 'Popery' – seize Edinburgh & Dunfermline – Charles levies troops & advances to York & Berwick – 'First Bishops' War' ends with Pacification of Berwick – Scots Parliament prorogued for acting against bishops & royal power; last writ of 'Ship Money'; [–1640] 'taxpayers strike' – royal control of Eng. local gvnmt breaks down; 'Battle of the Downs' – Dutch defeat Sp. fleet in Eng. waters; Wentworth returns from Ireland – becomes Charles I's chief advisor; Maine & New Hampshire fnd.d – Connecticut has 1st written constitution in American colonies; [–1640] E. India Co. estab.s factory at Madras	**Art:** I. Jones & Christopher Wren design Greenwich Hospital [Royal Naval College]; Nicolas Poussin becomes painter to Fr. Court & [c.–1640] pnts 'Dance to the Music of Time' [Wallace Coll.]; Rubens, 'Self-Portrait'; [c.] Zurbarán, 'Adoration of the Shepherds', 'Angel with Censer' & 'Battle of El Sotillo'; van Dyck, 'Madagascar Portrait (Earl of Arundel and his wife)'; Ribera, 'Jacob's Dream'; [c.] Cornelius Johnson [pnt] 'The Capel Family' [NPG]	**Dr:** Brome D'Avenant Shirley	*The Lovesick Court* *The Spanish Lovers* *The Politician*

CAROLINE/STUART

1640	Wentworth created Earl of Strafford; 'Second Bishops' War' – Scots defeat king's forces – Treaty of Ripon; 'Short Parliament' summoned in April – dissolved in May; 'Long Parliament' in Nov. [sits until 1649] – attacks judges & monopolists – Strafford & Laud impeached – Commons challenge Church's right to bind clergy & laity without Parliament's consent; 'Root and Branch' Petition against episcopacy to Commons from London citizens; buccaneers settle in Barbados	Land below sea-level drained by wind-pumps in Holland – Bedford Levels drained in England [v.1634]; coke 1st made from coal; 8 postal lines & 1st stage-coaches in England; Thomas Hobbes, *Elements of Law, Natural and Politic* [pub.d 1650]; 'The Bay Psalm Book', 1st American book, prnt.d in Cambridge, Mass. [used until 1773]. **Int. Lit:** Corneille, *Horace*. **Art:** [c.] van Dyck, 'William II of Nassau and Orange'; Velázquez, 'Mars'; Fransisco de Zurbarán [pnt] 'Christ and the Virgin in the House at Nazareth'	**P:** Carew **Pr/F:** Donne Jonson **Dr:** Brome Day **Lit. 'Events':**	*Poems* [incls 'Elegy' on death of Donne & 'Ask me no more'] *LXXX Sermons* [pub. posthm.] *Timber; or Discoveries* [prose writings; pub. posthm.] *The Court Beggar* [prnt.d 1653] *The Parliament of Bees* [masque] King Charles I [attrib.], *Eikon basilike* [on Divine Right of Kings]
1641	Triennial Act against dissolving Long Parliament without its own consent; Courts of Star Chamber & High Commission abolished; Strafford executed; Commons pass [by 11 votes] the 'Grand Remonstrance' [list of Charles's acts of misrule] – also issue commission to deface images, altars & monuments; Parliamentarians gain control of gvnmt of London; RC rebellion in Ireland – Protestants massacred in Ulster; 1st Fr. settlement in Michigan	Press freedom follows demise of Star Chamber – *Diurnal Occurrences*, weekly periodical, issued; 1st mention of cotton goods made in Manchester; Descartes, *Meditationes de Prima Philosophia*. **Music:** Monteverdi [comp] 'The Holy Apostle'. **Art:** Lorraine, 'The Embarkation of St Paula'; Hals, 'Regents of the Company of St Elizabeth's Hospital at Haarlem'	**Dr:** Brome Shirley	*A Jovial Crew* [prnt.d 1653] *The Cardinal* [prnt.d 1652]
1642	Charles I fails in attempt to arrest the 'Five Members' & leaves London; Militia Ordinance takes control of militia & fortified places – navy declares for Parliament – Charles raises his standard at Nottingham – Parliamentary general, Essex, garrisons towns from Northampton to Worcester – Civil War begins [-1651] – battle of Edgehill [indecisive] – Royalist attack on London foiled at Turnham Green; 1st Income & Property Taxes intro.d; French fnd Montreal, N. America; Abel Tasman discovers Tasmania & New Zealand	Parliament proclamation against popular sports & pastimes; Hobbes, *De Cive*. **Int. Lit:** Corneille, *Polyeucte* & *Cinna*. **Art:** Velázquez, 'Prince Baltasar Carlos'; Rembrandt, 'Night Watch'; [c.] Dutch-born painter, Peter Lely, comes to England [v.1647]. **Lit. 'Events':** Parliament closes all Eng. theatres [reopen 1660]; regulation prohibits printing of author's work without their agreement – beginning of copyright	**P:** Sir John Denham (1615-69) **Pr/F:** Milton **Dr:** Shirley	*Cooper's Hill* [wrtn 1640; pastoral poem; rev.d edtn, 1655] *The Reason of Church Government* & *An Apology for Smectymnuus* [anti-episcopal tracts] *The Sisters*
1643	Tide of Civil War battles runs both ways: Prince Rupert sacks Bristol – Hampden defeated & killed at Chalgrove Field – Cromwell victorious at Gainsborough – Parliament agrees Solemn League & Covenant with Scots; new fiscal system intro.d – esp.ly excise duties; partial cessation of war in Ireland; [-1715] Louis XIV, king of France; [-1698] American colonies form 'New England Federation'; Tasman reaches Tonga, Fiji & New Guinea	Westminster Assembly set up to discuss religious settlement; Royalist newspaper, *Mercurius Aulicus*, issued; Charles issues 1st Eng. medals for bravery. **Int. Lit:** Corneille, *Le Menteur*. **Art:** [-1645] Rembrandt, 'Christ Healing the Sick (Hundred Guilders Print)' [etching]; David Teniers 'The Younger' [pnt] 'Village Fête with Cauldrons' [NG]	**Pr/F:** Browne **Lit. 'Events':**	*Religio Medici* [authorised edtn; v. 1635] Parliament revives censorship
1644	Royalist Parliament summoned at Oxford – Scots army takes Newcastle for Parliament – Committee of Both Kingdoms set up – both sides win & lose battles, but Cromwell's victory over Prince Rupert at Marston Moor is turning-point in Civil War – king loses control of the North; 'Self-denying Ordinance' passed by Long Parliament – deprives MPs of holding military or civil office; excise duties extended to food; Tasman charts parts of N. & W. coasts of 'New Holland' [Australia]; Ming dynasty ends in China – Manchu begins [-1912]	Westminster Assembly approves New Directory of Worship; [-1681] William Lily pubs annual astrological almanack; Descartes, *Principia Philosophiae*. **Int. Lit:** Corneille, *Rodogune*. **Art:** Rembrandt, 'Woman taken in Adultery' [NG]; Teniers, 'Boors' Carouse' [Wallace Coll.]	**Pr/F:** Milton	*Areopagitica* [against censorship] & *Tractate on Education*

Period	Year	International and Political Contexts	Social and Cultural Contexts	Authors	Indicative Titles
CIVIL WAR	1645	Laud beheaded; Parliament's New Model Army created - Fairfax commander - Cromwell & Thomas Fairfax defeat Charles I at Naseby – Royalists defeated in Scotland & at Langport & Bristol – [–1646] negotiations between king & Parliament break down over militia & Church; [–1662] Parliament approves New Directory of Worship & prohibits [Elizabeth I] Prayer Book; Dutch occupy St Helena	[c. >] regular meetings of scientists in London lead to founding of Royal Society [v.1662]. **Art:** Rembrandt, 'Holy Family with Angels'; Velazquez, 'Philip IV Hunting Wild Boar' [NG]; [–1652] Bernini [sculpt] 'The Ecstasy of St Theresa'; Lorraine, 'Cephalus and Procris Reunited by Diana' [NG]; [c.–1646] Bartolomé Estaban Murillo, 11 paintings in Convent of San Francisco, Seville [incls 'Angels' Kitchen']	**P:** Milton Edmund Waller (1606–87)	*Poems* [1st collected edtn] *Poems* [incls 'Go, lovely Rose']
	1646	Charles surrenders to Scots at Newark; Oxford surrenders to Parliament – 1st Civil War ends; Parliament orders Presbyterian Church system thro'out England – bishops abolished & lands sold; Catholic forces win a victory in Ireland; [–1650] successive bad harvests; [–1647] Eng. settlers from Bermuda colonise Bahamas	Earl of Clarendon, benefactor of University Press, Oxford, commences in exile his *History of the Rebellion and Civil Wars in England* [pub.d posthm. 1702]. **Int. Lit.:** [–1648, pub.d] *Le Roman Comique de Monsieur Scarron.* **Art:** Rembrandt, 'Winter Landscape'	**P:** Richard Crashaw (c.1612–49) Henry Vaughan (1621–95) Sir John Suckling (1609–42)	*Steps to the Temple: Sacred Poems* [expanded edtn 1648] *Poems, With the tenth Satyre of Juvenal Englished* [secular verse] *Fragmenta Aurea* [posthm.; coll. poems & other writings; incls 'A Ballad upon a Wedding']
	1647	Scots surrender Charles I to Parliament & withdraw over border for £400,000; disbanding of Army without arrears of pay ordered by Parliament – Army occupies London in direct action against this – Army seizes Charles – Charles escapes to Isle of Wight [Carisbrooke Castle] – signs 'Engagement' [treaty] with Scots; [–1649] Levellers become influential – 1st 'Agreement of the People' – Leveller-inspired mutiny in Army; Army defeats Irish at Dangan Hill	1st known advertisements appear in *Perfect Occurrences of Every Day*; Matthew Hopkins, *Discovery of Witches* [notorious witch-hunter]. **Art:** Rembrandt, 'Susanna and the Elders'; Lorraine, 'Flight to Egypt'; Sir Peter Lely [pnt] 'Charles I and the Duke of York' [Syon House Coll.] & 'Children of Charles I' [Petworth House]	**P:** Cowley **Lit. 'Events':**	*The Mistress* [love poems] Severe parliamentary ordinance on censorship
	1648	2nd Civil War: Scots invade England on Charles I's behalf – Cromwell defeats them at Preston; Royalist insurrections in Kent & Wales ends with Treaty of Newport; 'Pride's Purge' in Commons of Presbyterian majority; 2nd Leveller 'Agreement of the People'; Peace of Westphalia ends Thirty Years War in Europe	George Fox fnds Society of Friends; Cyrano de Bergerac, *Histoire comique des états de la lune et du soleil* [satirical science fantasy; pub.d 1656]. **Art:** Royal Academy of Arts, Paris, fnd.d; Rembrandt, 'Supper at Emmaus'; [c.] Velázquez, 'Lady with a Fan' [Wallace Coll.]; Poussin, 'Landscape with a Man Killed by a Snake' [NG], 'Landscape with the Body of Phocion Carried Out of Athens' [Oakly Park] & [>] 'The Holy Family' [series]; Lorraine, 'Embarkation of the Queen of Sheba' & 'Marriage of Isaac and Rebecca' [aka 'The Mill'; both NG]; Robert Walker [pnt] 'John Evelyn' [NPG]	**P:** Robert Herrick (1591–1674)	*Hesperides: or the Works both Humane and Divine of Robert Herrick Esq.* [secular poems; incls 'Gather ye rosebuds' & *His Noble Numbers* – separate section of religious poems]
INTERREGNUM/ COMMONWEALTH	1649	Long Parliament ends – 'Rump' of Commons assumes supreme power; Charles I tried & beheaded – Charles Stuart [later Charles II] proclaimed king in Edinburgh; monarchy & Lords abolished; England declared a Free Commonwealth; 3rd 'Agreement of the People' drawn up by Levellers [as basis for new constitution]; Leveller mutiny in Army – suppressed; Cromwell invades Ireland – sacks Wexford & Drogheda; 1st frigate, 'Constant Warrior', built for British Navy	'The Diggers' [or 'True Levellers': a co-operative community] begin to cultivate former Crown land in Surrey – Gerrard Winstanley defends action in a pamphlet, *A New-Yeers Gift Sent to the Parliament and Armie.* **Music:** Francesco Cavalli [comp] 'Jason' [It. opera]. **Art:** Parliament orders sale of Charles I's collection of paintings; [–1651] Velázquez, 'Toilet of Venus (Venus and Cupid)' [the 'Rokeby Venus'; NG] & [c.] 'St Anthony the Abbott and St Paul the Hermit'; Teniers, 'Village Merrymaking' [Royal Coll.]; [c.] Walker, 'Oliver Cromwell' [NPG]; Samuel Cooper [c.] 'Oliver Cromwell' [miniature; NPG]	**P:** Sir Richard Lovelace (1618-58) **Pr/F:** Donne Milton	*Lucasta; Epodes, Odes, Sonnets, Songs, etc.* [incls 'The Grasshopper', 'To Lucasta, Going to the Warres' & 'To Althea from Prison'] *Fifty Sermons* [pub. posthm.] *Eikonoklastes* [reply to Charles I's *Eikon Basilike* [v.1640] & *The Tenure of Kings and Magistrates* [defence of king's execution]

2 1650–1699

Commonwealth and Restoration

INTRODUCTION

This chapter covers a relatively short period of time, but one which is highly eventful in British history (e.g. the curtailing of royal power, the rise in importance of Parliament, the appearance of the British party political system [**Whigs*** and **Tories***]). Following **The English Civil War*** and the execution of Charles I in 1649 [see Chapter 1] is the period of 11 years known as the **Interregnum***. This includes the republican **Commonwealth***, which rapidly transmutes into the **Protectorate*** of Oliver Cromwell. After Cromwell's death in 1648 and the failure of his son's short-lived regime, the **Stuart*** monarchy [see also Chapter 1] is restored to the throne in 1660 with King Charles II (**The Restoration***). Charles's death in 1685 leads to the accession of his Roman Catholic brother, James II, and **The Glorious Revolution** of 1688 which deposed him and established the Protestant succession of William and Mary. The period also witnesses the beginnings of the **Neo-Classical*** or **Augustan*** movement in literature and the arts [see Chapter 3].

Chapter contents

2.1 INTERREGNUM

From the Latin 'inter' (between) and 'regnum' (rule or reign), literally: 'between two reigns'.

Although used more generally to define any period between two governments, the term in British history applies specifically to the period between the execution of Charles I in 1649 [see Chapter 1 under 1.5 **Stuart*** and 1.7 **Caroline***] and **The Restoration*** [2.7 below] of the monarchy in 1660 under Charles II. This 11-year period is also commonly referred to as that of *The English Revolution*, when Britain was governed first as a **Commonwealth*** and then as a **Protectorate***.

2.2 COMMONWEALTH

A 16th-Century word (originally 'commonweal') meaning the general or public good and echoing the Latin 'res publica', from which the notion of a 'republic' derives.

Commonwealth with an upper-case 'C' is used to define the nature of the British state during the **Interregnum*** [see above]: the republican Commonwealth of which Oliver Cromwell became Lord Protector [see 2.3 **Protectorate*** below]. While generally understood as covering the whole 11-year period, it refers more specifically to the period between 1649 (after the execution of Charles I) when Britain was declared 'a Commonwealth and free state by the supreme authority of this nation, the representatives of the people in parliament', with Cromwell as chair of the Council of State, and 1653 when the 'Rump' of the 'Long Parliament' (i.e. the remaining Commons) was forcibly dissolved by Cromwell. It is characterised by Parliament's abolition of the monarchy and House of Lords (the Anglican Church had effectively already been dismantled in 1646); Cromwell's brutal suppression of rebellion in Ireland, and the confiscation from 1652 onwards of Irish lands; the crushing by Cromwell of the Scots under Charles Stuart (already proclaimed King of Scotland; King Charles II to be); continuing conflicts with the Dutch over trade and British claims to sovereignty of British seas; and the height of activities by the radical dissenting groups, **The Fifth Monarchists, Ranters, Levellers** and **Diggers***.

2.3 PROTECTORATE

'Protectorate' is the noun applying to a region or period when the office of Protector of a kingdom or state is instituted.

In 1653, Cromwell dissolved both the 'Rump' Parliament and the Puritan Convention he had summoned (nicknamed the 'Barebones Parliament' [see timeline table for explanation of this). The council of army officers then appointed him Lord Protector of the Commonwealth under a new constitution, the 'Instrument of Government' (Britain's only written constitution), which was to create a balance between Army and Parliament. Under Cromwell's dictatorship (he ruled by decree and ordinance), the Union of England, Scotland and Ireland was recognised in the representation of MPs from all three countries in the first Protectorate Parliament; peace was made with Holland, commercial and/or treaties of friendship signed with Portugal, Sweden, Denmark and France, and in alliance with France, Spain defeated on sea and land; the Anglican Church was reorganised and Puritanism established, but Cromwell upheld religious tolerance; there were a number of Royalist risings against Cromwell and his relations with Parliament were continuously strained, but when offered the title of king in 1657, he refused it. He died in 1658, and his son, Richard, succeeded him as Lord Protector; but within months, Richard Cromwell, in conflict with the Army, had resigned, and the way was open for the restoration of the monarchy under Charles Stuart as Charles II.

2.4 FIFTH MONARCHISTS, RANTERS, LEVELLERS AND DIGGERS

These are all names of dissenting Puritan sects during The English Revolution, whose activities and publications concerning both religious and political freedom were so radical that Cromwell and his government had to suppress them.

The Fifth Monarchy Men were a fanatical millenarian group during the Commonwealth* who advocated forcibly establishing Christ's kingdom on earth as the last of the five monarchies prophesied in the Book of Daniel. Their rebellion in 1653, as Cromwell became Lord Protector, was rapidly put down. *The Ranters* were an antinomian sect during the same period who believed that Christians were justified by faith alone and were absolved by the gospel from the obligation to obey the moral law. *The Levellers* (the name has both religious – Christ the 'Great Leveller' – and constitutional connotations), who saw the execution of Charles I as finally ending the line of descent from the Norman Conquest, and hence the oppression of a Norman aristocracy and feudal system, promoted notions of a return to native liberties and a root-and-branch reform of English society.

In the second half of the 1640s, the Leveller's rigorous defence of the freedom of the press as a defence against tyranny (e.g. the pamphlet, *England's Birth-Right Justified*, attributed to John Lilburne; see below) had caused their religious and political ideas to spread widely throughout the Army, culminating in a series of debates at Putney in the autumn of 1647. Their documents, *England's Misery and Remedy* (1645) and *An Agreement of the People for a firme and present Peace, upon grounds of common right* (1647–9), written in plain and forceful English, began to foster radical ideas amongst the common people about a popular sovereignty which could create a society based on equality. The latter pamphlet, for example, propounded wide-ranging parliamentary and executive reform, the need to protect the 'native rights' of the 'Free-born People of England', and the enfranchising of all male commoners by abandoning the property qualification to vote. This was not at all what Cromwell's largely land-owning generals had in mind. A prominent Leveller in the late-1640s and 1650s was John Lilburne, who had been imprisoned and otherwise punished by Charles I's Star Chamber on several occasions for distributing Puritan literature, and who was then imprisoned for publishing attacks on Cromwell's government as too aristocratic and for failing to protect the ancient rights and liberties of the English people.

The Diggers, or *True Levellers* as they regarded themselves, were a sect who, in the spring of 1649, took Leveller notions of individual freedom and equality in religious and social matters to their logical conclusion by setting up a co-operative community on former royal land at St George's Hill in Surrey. This they began to cultivate (hence 'Diggers'), claiming they were taking back land originally stolen from the English common people by Charles I's Norman forebears. This again was deeply disturbing, even for Parliamentarian land-owners, and the sect was forced to defend itself later the same year in front of the ruling generals. One of the most prominent Diggers, Gerrard Winstanley, was central to this defence with his pamphlet, *A New-Yeers Gift Sent to the Parliament and Armie* (1649), which, in the rhetorical language of Christian communism, accused the government of perpetuating the monarchical system and failing to establish Christ's Kingdom on English soil as a second Eden. However, by the mid-1650s, the Diggers, along with other radical sectarian movements, had largely been suppressed, although something of the Digger ideology can be seen to inform James Harrington's influential republican utopia, *The Common-Wealth of Oceana* (1656), and their egalitarian and libertarian thinking on behalf of 'the free-born Englishman' became a point of reference for later radicals in the English political tradition.

2.5 STUART [continued]

The family name of the line of monarchs – The Stuarts – who occupied the British throne from the accession of King James I in 1603 to the deposition and execution of King Charles I in 1649; and from the Restoration of King Charles II in 1660 to the death of Queen Anne in 1714.

The Stuart line was restored to the throne in 1660 with Charles II [for more detail, see 2.7 **Restoration***]. Because his marriage remained childless, his brother, James, Duke of York, succeeded to the throne on Charles's death in 1685. King James II was a declared Roman Catholic who had also married a Catholic, and his undisguised attempts to return Britain to Catholicism led to *The Glorious (or 'Bloodless') Revolution* of 1688. When James fled to France, Mary, James's Protestant daughter, with her Dutch Protestant husband, William of Orange, were summoned back to Britain to become joint monarchs, William III and Mary II, in 1689 (the royal House until William's death in 1702 is described as that of 'Stuart and Orange'). The marriage was again childless; Mary died in 1694, and William in 1702. A year earlier, Parliament had passed the Act of Settlement which ensured that only a Protestant could accede to the British throne, amongst other constitutional constraints on the royal prerogative. On William's death, the staunchly Protestant Anne, Mary II's sister, all of whose children had died very young, became queen. Anne had accepted the Act of Settlement which meant that when she died in 1714, the succession automatically went to George of Hanover, Anne's nearest Protestant cousin, who became George I of Great Britain [see Chapter 3: **Hanoverian***].

2.6 JACOBITE

'Jacobus' is Latin for James, but 'Jacobite' should not be confused with Jacobean [see Chapter 1] or with jacobin [see Chapter 4].

After the deposition of James II in 1688, his death in exile in 1701, and the deaths without issue of William and Mary, the Jacobites – supporters of his line of succession – claimed the right to the throne for his son, James Francis Edward Stuart (the 'Old Pretender'), who made a failed expedition to Scotland from France in 1708. After the death without heir of Queen Anne in 1714 – when the British throne passed to the house of Hanover [see above and **Hanoverian*** in Chapter 3] – further attempts were made to incite rebellion in Scotland (and Ireland), the most significant being in 1715. This process was continued by the 'Old Pretender's' son, Charles Edward Stuart (the 'Young Pretender', aka 'Bonnie Prince Charlie'), who led the rebellion in 1745 known as 'the '45' which was crushed by George I's army at the Battle of Culloden in 1746. This effectively spelt the end of the Stuart claim to the British throne (the male line became extinct in 1807).

2.7 (THE) RESTORATION

With the direct article, the noun defines the period in British history from the restoration of the monarchy in 1660 when Charles II regained the throne, following the Interregnum of the Commonwealth* and Cromwellian Protectorate*, until his death in 1685.*

Charles II married Catherine of Braganza in 1662, but the union remained childless. Much of his reign was therefore bedevilled by questions of the succession to the throne on his death without heir, which would pass to his Catholic brother, James, and which therefore acted as a focus for continuing religious strife in the country. Charles was a cunning politician who never clarified his own religious beliefs (although indicatively tolerant of Roman Catholics; see, for example, his attempts to introduce 'Declarations of Indulgence' in 1662 and 1672), but he was constantly at odds with Parliament over its attempts at severe repression of religious dissenters. The Great Fire of London (1666 – widely held at the time to be the result of a Catholic plot), unsuccessful wars with Protestant Holland, and dubious dealings with the the increasingly powerful Louis XIV of Catholic France (including the sale of Dunkirk for £400,000 in 1662) caused intense Protestant hostility and anti-Catholic feeling.

The future James II married a Catholic in 1673, and Charles tried unsuccessfully to introduce a Declaration of Indulgence (1672) which would annul the penal laws against Catholics and other dissenters. In return, Parliament passed the Test Act, which prohibited Roman Catholics from sitting in Parliament or holding government office, and made repeated attempts to pass a bill preventing James from acceding to the throne (the 'Exclusion Crisis' of the 1770s and early 1780s). In 1678, anti-Catholic sentiment reached boiling-point with the 'Popish Plot' to kill the king, spuriously revealed by Titus Oates and exploited by the Earl of Shaftesbury [see **Whigs*** below]. For three years, the Stuart monarchy seemed doomed, and the crisis helped to create the political party divisions between **Whigs*** (favouring James's exclusion) and **Tories*** (refusing to alter the succession) [see below for these terms]. From 1681, Charles ruled without Parliament, and despite another unmasked conspiracy to kill him and James (the Rye House Plot, 1683), which intensified the repression of dissenters, the king died in his bed in 1685 with the succession intact.

The period of The Restoration* is often extended to include the reign of King James II (1685–88). 1685 saw the Duke of Monmouth's abortive rebellion in the West Country against James's accession, the 'Bloody Assize' of Judge Jeffries which followed it, and James's use of royal prerogative to overrule Parliament and introduce pro-Catholic policies. 1688, the year of the 'Glorious Revolution', therefore witnessed the forced removal of James and the riotous welcome to, and joint accession to the throne of, the securely Protestant monarchs, William III (Prince of Orange, Holland) and Mary II (James's daughter and Charles II's niece). With French aid, James's **Jacobite*** supporters held out in Scotland and Ireland, where French and Catholic Irish troops were besieging Londonderry, but William of Orange's Protestant army defeated them in Scotland in 1689, was victorious at the Battle of the Boyne in 1690 (with repercussions which are still being felt today), and forced the surrender of Limerick in 1691. This was effectively the end of Jacobite resistence [but see Jacobite* above]. William was now free to return to the continental war between Louis XIV's France and the League of Augsburg (the 'Grand Alliance') which Britain had joined in 1689. This was concluded by the Treaty of Ryswick in 1697, when Louis XIV recognised William as King of Great Britain, but the anti-French alliance (especially with the German House of **Hanover*** [see Chapter 3]) was renewed in 1701 at the start of what became the War of the Spanish Succession (1702–14). The 1689–97 war caused the introduction of a system of National Debt and other significant financial developments [see 'Government and Finance' below], and the settlement between King and Parliament of 1698–9 saw control of the nation's standing army now vested in Parliament.

Key Timeline Narratives 1660–1699

⮑ **Naval, Trade and Colonial Expansion**   The assumption of absolute power in France by King Louis XIV in 1661, and his expansionist policies in Europe and the rest of the world, which produced resentment and fear in Britain; but at the same time Charles II's secret pro-French sympathies and negotiations with the French king; and the rapid development of British sea power in this period, with Parliament willing to grant funds to support the navy and new shipyards built at Sheerness and Devonport.

Related to this is Britain's mercantile and colonial expansion, especially in North America and India (the East India Company, for example, founded Calcutta in 1690), but also in Africa (trading in gold, ivory and slaves), which led to conflicts with the French and Dutch in particular (there were Anglo-Dutch naval wars for much of the 1660s and again in 1672–4 over maritime power and trade); and the founding throughout the period of new British colonies on the eastern seaboard of North America (e.g. North and South Carolina, the seizing of New Amsterdam [New York] from the Dutch, New Hampshire, Pennsylvania and the establishing of Philadelphia); but also, by the early 1680s, of a French colonial empire there which stretched from Louisiana in the south to Quebec in the north.

➲ *Government and Finance*   Throughout the period, further extreme tensions between king and Parliament resulted from the former's chronic shortage of money and the latter's resistance to voting him funds, especially without the right to scrutinise public spending. But towards the end of the period, under William III, a system of National Debt had been put in place (1693); the Bank of England was founded (1694), as was the Bank of Scotland (1695); financial reforms were introduced (overseen by Sir Isaac Newton and John Locke, who became Master of the Mint in 1696); the Royal Board of Trade was established (with Locke as one of its commissioners); and Lloyds' coffee-house became the headquarters of marine insurance (1692). Such financial innovations were central to the stabilising of the British economy and to the expansion of Britain's mercantile activities at home and abroad.

➲ *Law*   As noted earlier, both Stuart monarchs and Parliamentarians had used censorship to control opposition, and this remained a feature of The Restoration, too, with Licensing Acts in 1662 and 1685 introducing strict pre-printing censorship for all English publications. However, the lapsing of this Act in 1695 laid the foundations for the freedom of the press in Britain.

➲ *Cultural Developments*   Two of the best-known disasters of the early part of the period were the Great Plague of London in 1665 and the Great Fire of London the following year. However, as a result, Sir Christopher Wren was appointed 'Surveyor-General and principal architect' for the rebuilding of the capital city. Wren's architectural work in London and elsewhere (including St Paul's Cathedral, parts of Westminster Abbey, Buckingham House and Marlborough House) is one of the great cultural achievements of the age. But so, too, are the founding of the Royal Society (1662) and of the Clarendon Press, Oxford (1672); the mathematical and scientific work of Sir Isaac Newton and Edmund Halley; the philosophical writings of John Locke; the diaries of John Evelyn and Samuel Pepys; the carving of Grinling Gibbons; the music of Henry Purcell; and the paintings of Sir Peter Lely and Sir Godfrey Kneller.

➲ *Literature and Theatre*   The commonest usage of the adjective 'Restoration' in literary studies is in 'Restoration Comedy', the drama which followed Charles's reopening of the theatres in 1660 – a bawdy but urbane reaction to the austere morality of the preceding Puritan culture. The problems of strict periodisation can be appreciated, however, if we note that one of the most admired Restoration Comedies is William Congreve's *The Way of the World*, first produced in 1700, and that George Farquhar's cognate comedies, *The Recruiting Officer* and *The Beaux Strategem*, date from 1706 and 1707 respectively. It is worth remembering, too, that other examples of 'Restoration literature' include John Milton's epic poems, Andrew Marvell's poetry, the prose of John Bunyan, the many plays and novels of the prolific woman writer, Aphra Behn, and the extraordinary flowering of drama by women playwrights which continues into the 18th Century.

Finally, there are the plays and poems of John Dryden, who is usually regarded as the harbinger of the **Augustan*** period in his deployment of **Neo-Classical*** forms and genres [see Chapter 3], and who therefore also indicates the impossibility of precise periodisation (he died in 1700). In this context, too, we might register that the French poet and critic, Nicolas Boileau, published his critical essay, *L'Art poétique*, which outlines the principles of French classicism, in 1674 – a work imitated by Alexander Pope in his poem, *An Essay on Criticism*, written in 1709 and published in 1711.

2.8 HABEAS CORPUS

Latin: literally, 'have the body [brought into court before a judge]'.

In English and US law, this is a writ issued by a judge requiring an imprisoned person to be brought physically into court in order to state the reasons for, and examine the legality of, their detention. It was made enforceable by the Habeas Corpus Act of 1679 in England, and is guaranteed in the US Constitution. In both countries, the right of Habeas Corpus can only be suspended during a period of emergency.

2.9 WHIGS

Although its etymology remains doubtful, 'Whig' probably derives from the Scottish word 'whiggamore', a supporter in the 16th and 17th Centuries of the Covenanters, the Scottish Presbyterians who fought for the belief that the Church should be governed by elected elders rather than bishops, and more generally for civil and religious liberties [see 1643, for example, in the timelines].

Whig and Tory were the terms for the major British political parties for the next century and a half. By 1679, Whig was applied to the political group, led by the Earl of Shaftesbury, opposed to the succession of James, Duke of York, Charles II's brother, and more generally to those upholding popular rights and opposed to the king. The Whigs were instrumental in bringing about the 'Glorious Revolution'; were in power in Britain from 1714 to 1760, most notably under the ministry of Sir Robert Walpole (1721–42); were finally ousted by the Tories (1783–4) who held power until 1830 (many Whigs sided with the Tory Party during the French Revolution in defence of the landed interest); they secured the passage of the Reform Bill of 1832 and other measures of reform; but by the late 1860s had merged with the new **Liberal***** Party [see glosses in Chapter 5]. Unlike 'Tory', the word no longer has currency in present-day politics.

2.10 TORIES

Etymologically, 'Tory' is again uncertain. It probably derives from the Irish word 'toraidhe', 'outlaw', 'highwayman', and was originally used for dispossessed Irish people who lived as robbers and attacked English settlers.

Tory also came to refer to marauders in the Scottish Highlands, and was then adopted around 1679 as a term of abuse for the political supporters of the succession of the future James II. After the 'Glorious Revolution' of 1688, the word gradually lost its abusive connotations and became the accepted name for the political party which supported the Anglican Church, the hereditary right to the throne, and the established political order. The Tories were briefly in power between 1710 and 1714, but their Jacobite* sympathies and negotiations with the 'Old Pretender' [see under **Stuart (continued)*** in this chapter] discredited them, and they were out of power until the accession of King George III in 1760, when many of them joined the 'King's friends'. After being ousted by the Whigs in 1830, the party was refashioned by Sir Robert Peel, and during the 1830s became the **Conservative Party** [see gloss on **Conservatives and Liberals** in Chapter 5]. The word is still in use as an informal term for the Conservatives.

Timelines: 1650–1699

PERIOD	YEAR	INTERNATIONAL AND POLITICAL CONTEXTS	SOCIAL AND CULTURAL CONTEXTS	AUTHORS	INDICATIVE TITLES
INTERREGNUM/COMMONWEALTH	1650	Cromwell returns from Ireland [although conquest continues]; succeeds Fairfax as Lord General [of all forces in Commonwealth]; Charles Stuart lands in Scotland – Cromwell invades & defeats Scots at Dunbar – Edinburgh Castle surrendered; Rump Parliament decides all court proceedings should now be in English; height of the Ranter & Digger movements; frontier between Eng. & Dutch colonies in N. America defined; [–1652] civil war in Barbados	Parliamentary journal, *Mercurius Publicus*, estab.d; tea 1st imported into England – coffee-house opens in Oxford; Hobbes, *Human Nature* [1st work of modern psychology]; Jeremy Taylor, *Holy Living*. **Int. Lit.:** Corneille, *Nicomède*; Anne Bradstreet, *The Tenth Muse, lately sprung up in America* [1st American woman poet; pub.d in London without her knowledge]. **Music:** [c.] development of modern harmonic divisions. **Art:** Velázquez, 'Pope Innocent X'; Rembrandt, 'Man with a Golden Helmet'; Walker, 'Self-Portrait' [NPG]	**P:** Vaughan Andrew Marvell (1621–78) **Pr/F:** Donne	*Silex Scintillans; or Sacred Poems and Private Ejaculations* [enlarged edtn with 'Preface', 1655] 'An Horation Ode upon Cromwell's Return from Ireland' [best-known poems pub. posthm.; v.1681] *Letters & Essays in Divinity* [pub. posthm.]
	1651	Charles Stuart crowned King of Scots at Scone – invades England – defeated by Cromwell at Worcester – flees to France; Eng. Army under Gen. Monck sacks Dundee; Navigation Act [hostile to Dutch] – promotes Eng. monopoly in merchant shipping; English annexe St Helena; [–1652] Dutch 1st settle at Cape of Good Hope	Hobbes, *Leviathan* [on metaphysics, psychology & political philosophy]; Taylor, *Holy Dying*. **Music:** John Playford, *English Dancing Master* [describes country dances]. **Art:** Rembrandt, 'Young Woman with a Broom'	**P:** D'Avenant Vaughan John Cleveland (1613–58)	*Gondibert* [romantic epic poem] *Olor Iscanus* [secular poems] *Poems*
	1652	Act of Pardon & Oblivion to reconcile Royalists; Perpetuation Bill to secure all existing MPs as members – Army rejects it; Act 'for the Settling of Ireland' begins Cromwell's land confiscations; [–1654] 1st Anglo-Dutch [United Provinces] war [over trade disputes & Eng. claims to sovereignty in British seas] – Dutch defeated in the Channel by Admiral Blake – Eng. defeated off Dungeness; Sp. take Dunkirk; American colonies accept Parliamentary authority; Dutch fnd.d Cape Town	Blaise Pascal makes 1st calculating machine [from 1647]; Gerrard Winstanley, *Law of Freedom* [communistic theory]. **Music:** Giovanni Lully popularises the Minuet at Fr. Court. **Arts:** Carel Fabritius [pnt] 'A View of Delft' [NG]	**P:** Marvell	[c.] 'Upon Appleton House' & 'The Garden' [wrtn]
PROTECTORATE	1653	Long Parliament expelled by Cromwell – 'Short Parliament' instituted, aka 'Parliament of Saints' or 'Barebone's' Parliament [after member Praise-God Barebone (or Barbon), Anabaptist & 'Fifth Monarchy' preacher [v. next column] – members were selected from lists of nominations of 'godly men'] – soon dismissed; Cromwell appointed Lord Protector of England, Scotland and Ireland by Instrument of Government [only written constitution Britain has ever had], with New Council of State; Eng. defeat Dutch fleet off Texel – shatters Dutch maritime supremacy; commercial treaty with Portugal	Height of 'Fifth Monarchist Men' [extreme Puritan sect advocating establishment of Christ's kingdom on earth by force as the final monarchy prophesied in the Book of Daniel following the four monarchies of Antichrist]. **Art:** Rembrandt, 'The Three Crosses'; [c.] Lely, 'Capel Sisters', 'Nymphs by a Fountain' & [undated] 'Abraham Cowley' [last two, Dulwich]; [c.] Jacob van Ruïsdael [pnt] 'Castle of Bentheim'	**P:** Margaret Cavendish (Duchess of Newcastle; 1623–73) **Pr/F:** Izzak Walton (1593–1683) **Dr:** Shirley	*Poems and Fancies* *The Compleat Angler, or the Contemplative Man's Recreation* [expanded 5th edtn, 1676] *Cupid and Death* [masque]
	1654	1st Protectorate Parliament – MPs from all 3 kingdoms – Union of England, Scotland & Ireland recognised; Cromwell excludes republicans for	Anna Trapnel, Fifth Monarchist supporter, preaches & prophesies; Timothy Pont's maps of Scottish counties pub.d [drawn earlier]. **Int. Lit.:** de	**P:** Marvell	'The First Anniversary' [pub.d]

Year	History & Politics	Arts, Science & Culture	English Literature (Author — Work)
(cont. from previous page)	attacking 'government by a single person'; Board of Triers appointed to vet ministers given livings by patrons & 'Ejectors' to remove incapable clergy; Anglo-Dutch Peace of Westminster – recognises Navigation Act [v.1651]; commercial treaties with Sweden, Portugal & Denmark; Nova Scotia taken from France	Bergerac, *Le Pédant Joué*; Mme de Scudéry, *Clélie* [Fr. chivalric novel]. **Art:** Rembrandt, 'Portrait of Jan Six', 'Bathsheba' & 'Woman Bathing in a Stream' [NG]; Fabritius, 'Soldier' & 'Goldfinch'	
1655	Parliament dissolved by Cromwell; Penruddock's Royalist rising in Wiltshire suppressed; Cromwell divides Britain into 11 administrative districts under major-generals; Anglican services banned; Anglo-Fr. treaty against Spain & commercial treaty – also excludes Charles Stuart from France; war with Spain in Sp. colonies – English take Jamaica; Blake defeats Barbary Coast pirate fleet off Tunis – asserts Eng. seapower in Mediterranean	[–1660] the periodical, *Publick Intelligencer*, pub.d; 1st Berlin newspaper pub.d; [–1757] Cristian Huyghens invents 1st pendulum clock; Hobbes, *De Corpore*. **Art:** [–1777], St Surplice, Paris [classical-style church], built; Rembrandt, 'The Artist's Son, Titus' [> often uses son as model]; [c.] Jan Vermeer [pnt] 'Christ at the House of Mary and Martha' [SNG]	
1656	2nd Protectorate Parliament – over 90 republicans & Presbyterians excluded; regiment of Grenadier Guards formed; Spain declares war on England; Blake intercepts & despoils Sp. treasure fleet; treaty between Spain & exiled Charles Stuart; Anglo-Fr. treaty of friendship; Dutch commence trade with China	[–1657] Pascal, *Lettres Provinciales* [against Jesuits]. **Music:** D'Avenant evades ban on stage plays by claiming his were 'music & instruction' – opens opera house in London – stages 'The Siege of Rhodes' [sometimes claimed as 1st Eng. opera – with actress in cast]. **Art:** [–1667] Bernini builds colonnade of St Peter's, Rome; Velázquez, 'Las Meninas' & [–1657] 'Infanta Margarita'; Rembrandt, 'Jacob blessing the Sons of Joseph'; Murillo, 'Vision of St Anthony' [Seville Cathedral]; Vermeer, 'The Procuress'	**P:** Cowley — *Poems* [incls series of 'Pindaric Odes', 'Davideis' (unfinished epic) & 'On the Death of Mr William Hervey'] **Pr/F:** James Harrington (1611–77) — *The Common-Wealth of Oceana* [political utopia]
1657	Cromwell refuses title of king offered by 'Humble Petition & Advice' from Parliament; further 'Petitions' create new House of Lords & increase both Cromwell's & Parliament's power; great ceremony at Westminster for 2nd inauguration of Cromwell; [–1661] 5 successive bad harvests – trade depression begins; Treaty of Paris – Anglo-Fr. alliance against Spain; Blake destroys Sp. treasure fleet at Santa Cruz off Tenerife	Cromwell fnds new university college at Durham [dissolved 1660; v.1832]; 1st fountain pen made in Paris. **Art:** [c.] Velázquez, 'The Spinners'; [c.] Rembrandt, 'The Apostle Paul', 'Old Man of Padua' & 'Self-Portrait' [SNG]; [c.] Vermeer, 'Girl Asleep at a Table' & 'Soldier and a Laughing Girl'	**P:** (Bishop) Henry King (1592–1669) — *Poems* [pub. anon. & unauthorised; incls 'The Exequy' – elegy to his wife, wrtn 1624]
1658	Cromwell dies – son, Richard, succeeds as Lord Protector; New Parliament [incl. Lords] meets – 2 houses in conflict – soon dissolved; English & French defeat Spanish at Battle of the Dunes – England gains Dunkirk; French explore Minnesota; Dutch take last Portug. possession in Ceylon	1st Eng. spring pendulum clock; John Evelyn, Eng. trans of *The French Gardener*; [–1659] Hobbes, *De Homine*. **Music:** D'Avenant, 'The Spaniards in Peru' ['music & instruction']. **Art:** [c.] Vermeer, 'Lady Reading a Letter at an Open Window' & 'Kitchen Maid'; Poussin, 'Landscape with Orion'; Pieter de Hooch [pnt] 'Courtyard in Delft with a Woman and Child' [NG] & 'Card Players in a Sunlit Room' [Royal Coll.]	**P:** Marvell — 'A Poem upon the Death of his late Highness the Lord Protector' **Pr/F:** Browne — *Hydriotaphia: Urn Burial* & *The Garden of Cyrus*
1659	Richard Cromwell in conflict with Army – resigns; 'Rump Parliament' [v.1649] recalled & then expelled by John Lambert & Army; Royalist rising in Cheshire suppressed by Lambert; [–1660] Gen. Monck marches into England with Army of Scotland – Lambert sent against him	**Int. Lit.:** Corneille, *Oedipe*; Molière, *Les Précieuses ridicules* [Fr. comedy]. **Music:** D'Avenant, 'Sir Francis Drake' ['music & instruction']	**P:** John Dryden (1631–1700) — *Heroique Stanzas* [on Cromwell's death]

Period	Year	International and Political Contexts	Social and Cultural Contexts	Authors	Indicative Titles
	1660	Gen. Monck marches S. – Fairfax persuades Lambert & Army not to oppose him – Monck reaches London & readmits to Rump Parliament members excluded by 'Pride's Purge' [v.1648] – Long Parliament dissolves itself; Declaration of Breda by Charles Stuart sets out conciliatory terms for Restoration of the monarchy – invited to return to England as king by Convention Parliament – proclaimed Charles II – Earl of Clarendon, Chief Minister; Act of General Pardon, Indemnity & Oblivion; disbanding of New Model Army begins; [–1661] Navigation Law of 1651 re-enacted – transportation of goods to America only by Eng. ships [repeated 1662]; export of wool from Britain banned – seriously harmed trade [repeated 1662; in force until 1825]	Estab.mnt of Royal Society mooted [v.1662]; glass mirror factory at Vauxhall estab.d. **Music:** Master of the King's Musick created. **Art:** Kingston Lacy, Dorset, built; Prince Rupert intro.s mezzotint process in England; [c.] Lely, 'Self Portrait' [NPG] & 'Two Ladies of the Lake Family [NG]; [c.] Vermeer 'Street in Delft'; 'Four Seasons' [series]; [c.] van Ruisdael, 'The Jewish Cemetary' & 'The Inn'; Albert Cuyp [pnt] 'River Landscape with Horseman and Peasants' [from 1655; NG]; [c.–1663] Jan Steen [pnt] 'Skittle Players Outside an Inn' [NG] **Lit. 'Events':** Charles II grants patents to D'Avenant [Duke's House, Lincoln Inn Fields; moves to Covent Garden, 1732/3] & Thomas Killigrew [Drury Lane; v.1663] for 2 theatres to reopen in London – 1st actresses permitted on Eng. stage	**P:** Dryden **Pr/F:** John Evelyn (1620–1706) Samuel Pepys (1633–1703)	*Astraea Redux* [poetic panegyric on Charles II – to offset *Heroic Stanzas* on Cromwell, v.1659] [–1706] *Diary* [1st Pt covers period from birth in 1620, wrtn 1660; 2nd Pt, 1684–1706, contemporary account; pub.d 1818] [1/1/1660–31/5/69] *Diary* [wrtn in code; deciphered & partially pub.d 1825; fully pub.d 1970–83]
	1661	Charles II crowned; Cavalier Parliament meets – confirms Acts of Convention Parliament; Corporation Act requires all holders of municipal office to take oath of allegiance; Act of Settlement restores some Ir. lands; episcopacy restored in Scotland; Lambert tried & executed for treason; New Model Army paid off – Charles II's army estab.d – Militia Act gives him supreme control of all armed forces; Louis XIV assumes absolute power in France	Evelyn attacks air pollution in London; Robert Boyle, *The Sceptical Chymist* – fnds modern chemistry; 1st banknotes issued in Sweden. **Int. Lit.:** Molière, *L'Ecole des Maris* & *Les Fâcheux*. **Art:** [–1786] Palace of Versailles built for Louis XIV; Lely becomes portrait painter to Charles II; [–1662] Rembrandt, 'Conspiracy of Julius Civilis' & 'Head of Christ'; van Ruisdael, 'Landscape with Watermill'	**P:** Dryden **Pr/F:** Donne	*To His Sacred Majesty* [panegyric on Restoration] *XXVI Sermons* [pub. posthm.]
	1662	Charles II m. Catherine of Braganza – Tangier & Bombay [v.1674] ceded to Britain by Portugal as part of dowry – Dunkirk sold to France; Restoration of C of E – final revision of Prayer Book; Act of Uniformity [ministers must consent to use revised Prayer Book] – non-conformist clergy ejected from livings; Charles's '1st Declaration of Indulgence' for dissenters; Law of Settlement moves people chargeable under Poor Law from parish of residence to that of birth; 'Hearth Tax' of 2s. p.a. imposed on every home in Britain	Charles II's Charter estab.s Royal Society; Robert Boyle [founder member of Royal Soc.] formulates 'Boyle's Law' on expansion of gas. **Int. Lit.:** Molière, *L'Ecole des femmes*; Michael Wigglesworth, *The Day of Doom* [1st American epic poem]. **Art:** Rembrandt, 'Syndics of the Amsterdam Cloth Hall'; [c.] Vermeer, 'View of Delft' & [c.–1664] 'Young Woman with a Water Jug'	**Dr:** Lady Cavendish **Lit. 'Events':**	*Plays* Licensing Act intro.s strict pre-printing censorship for all Eng. publications & bans import of anti-Xian literature; Act of Parliament bans male actors from playing women's parts
	1663	1st attempt by Parliament to scrutinise public spending; republican rebellions in Ireland, Yorkshire & Durham; 1st Turnpike Act intro.s tolls; Charles II estabs. Sheerness Dockyard; Royal Africa Co. fnd.d to trade in ivory, gold & [–1698] slaves [reformed 1672]; colony of Carolina fnd.d [v.1691]	1st Eng. guinea minted. **Art:** [–1665] Sir Christopher Wren builds Pembroke College Chapel, Cambridge; Steen, 'Morning Toilette' [Royal Coll.] & [c.] 'Merry Company' **Lit. 'Events':** Killigrew's 1st Theatre Royal, Drury Lane, built – King's Co. of actors perform there	**P:** Samuel Butler (1612–80) **Dr:** Katherine Philips ('the matchless Orinda'; 1631–64)	*Hudibras* Pt. I [Pt I of satirical poem; Pt. II, 1664; Pt. III, 1678] *Pompey* [trans of Corneille, *La Mort de Pompée*; pf.d in Dublin & London]
	1664	Treason trials in N. of England – 24 executions; Triennial Act [v.1641] repealed – no automatic summons of Parliament after 3 yrs; Conventicle Act bans religious assemblies other than C of E; Anglo-	Royal Society sets up committee to make English a better language for science; periwig style intro.d from France; Descartes, *De l'homme*. **Int. Lit.:** Molière, *Tartuffe* [pf.d; final revised version pf.d	**P:** Philips **Dr:** Dryden	*Olor Iscanus. The Poems. By the Incomparable, Mrs K.P.* [pirated edtn prnt.d 6 mths before her death] *The Rival Ladies* [tragic-comedy] & *The Indian*

Year	History	Int. Lit. / Art / Music	Author	Works
	Dutch naval skirmishes in W. Indies & Africa – Eng. seize New Amsterdam from Dutch & rename it New York – Parliament votes £2.5 million for war; 1st Royal Marine Regiment fnd.d; French fnd E. & W. India Cos to rival Eng. colonisation	1669]. **Art:** Burlington House, London, 1st built; [–1669] Wren builds Sheldonian Theatre, Oxford; Rembrandt, 'Jewish Bride'	Sir George Etherege (1635–91)	*Queen* [heroic drama; with Sir Robert Howard] *The Comical Revenge, or Love in a Tub*
1665	The Great Plague of London kills c.100,000 people; Cavalier Parliament meets in Oxford; Five Mile Act bans ejected ministers [v.1662] from living near corporate towns or teaching in schools; Parliament votes more funds for 2nd Anglo-Dutch naval war – Dutch fleet heavily defeated by Duke of York off Lowestoft – reconstituted Dutch fleet blockades Thames for 3 weeks; Eng. colony of New Jersey fnd.d [ceded by Dutch, 1664]	1st publication of proceedings of Royal Society; Isaac Newton experiments with gravitation; Duc de La Rochefoucauld, *Maximes*. **Int. Lit.:** Jean de La Fontaine, *Contes et nouvelles en vers*. **Art:** Bernini completes High Altar of St Peter's, Rome [from 1657] & 'Bust of Louis XIV' [marble]; [c.] Rembrandt, 'Self-Portrait'; [c.] Vermeer, 'Woman Reading a Letter', 'Maid Handing a Letter to her Mistress', 'Head of a Girl', 'Woman Weighing Pearls', [c.–1668] 'Lace Maker', [c.–1670] 'Girl with a Flute' & 'Woman in a Red Hat'; [c.] van Ruisdael, 'Windmill at Wijk'; [–1688] Murillo, 'S. Thomas of Villanueva Giving Alms'; Hobbema, 'The Watermill' [Wallace Coll.]	**Dr:** Dryden	*The Indian Emperor*
1666	The Great Fire of London destroys c.13,000 homes & 'old' St Paul's Cathedral; bitter tension between King & Parliament over war funding & inspection of naval accounts; France declares war on England – sea battles between English & Dutch – Prince Rupert & Monck [now Duke of Albemarle] finally victorious – 'Holmes' Bonfire': 250 Dutch trading ships burnt; French take Eng. possessions in Leeward Islands – [–1667] Dutch capture Surinam [Dutch Guiana] – exchanged by English for Dutch possessions in NE America	[> present] *London Gazette* estab.d as official gvnmt paper; Newton discovers integral calculus & prism of colours in rainbows. **Int. Lit.:** Molière, *Le Misanthrope* & *Le Médecin malgré lui*; Antoine Furetière, *Roman Bourgeois* [Fr. realist novel satirising lawyers]. **Music:** [–1737] Antonio Stradivarius begins making & labelling his violins. **Art:** [>] Wren appnt.d 'Surveyor-General & principal architect' for rebuilding of London after Great Fire – St Paul's Cathedral [v.1675] & 51 parish churches result [incls St James's, Picadilly; St Bride's; St Stephen, Walbrook; St Mary-le-Bow; St Magnus the Martyr]; Lely, 'The Greenwich Flagmen' [portrait series of Duke of York & admirals who defeated Dutch fleet, 1665; NMM], 'Lady Byron' & 'Comtesse de Grammont' [both Hampton Court]; John Hayls [pnt] 'Samuel Pepys' [NPG]	**P:** Cavendish **Pr/F:** John Bunyan (1628–88)	*The Blazing World* *Grace Abounding to the Chief of Sinners* [spiritual autobiog.]
1667	Dutch fleet enters Thames at Medway – burns laid-up Eng. battleships & captures the 'Royal Charles' – Earl of Clarendon, architect of Restoration settlement, banished by Charles II; [–1673] 'Cabal Ministry' [Clifford, Arlington, Buckingham, Ashley, Lauderdale] in power; 1st parliamentary Accounts Commission; [–1759] Act bans importation of Ir. livestock to England – later extended to other produce – severe damage to Ir. economy; English defeat French off Martinique & save Eng. W. Indies from annexation; French open tariff war against England; Treaty of Breda – Anglo-Dutch peace	Systematic weather recordings begun. **Int. Lit.:** Bradstreet, *Works in Prose and Verse* [early American writings; v.1650, 1678]; Jean Racine, *Andromaque* [Fr. Neo-Classical drama]. **Art:** [c.>] Murillo, several series of paintings for religious buildings in Seville; Bernini, 'Angel with the Crown of Thorns' [marble]; [late-1660s] Lely, 'Windsor Beauties' [portrait series of royal maids of honour; Hampton Court]; [c.] Steen, 'Feast of St Nicholas'; [c.] John Michael Wright [pnt] 'Thomas Chiffinch' [NPG]	**P:** Dryden Marvell Milton Philips **Dr:** Dryden	*Annus Mirabilis, The Year of Wonders, 1666* 'The Last Instructions to a Painter' [poem on gvnmt's mismanagement of Dutch war] *Paradise Lost* [10 Bks; 2nd rev.d edtn, 12 Bks, 1674] *Poems* [pub. posthm.; incls *Pompey* & her trans of the greater part of Corneille's *Horace* – v.1663–4] *Secret Love, or the Maiden Queen* & *Sir Martin Mar-All; or the Feigned Innocence* [comedies]

Period	Year	International and Political Contexts	Social and Cultural Contexts	Authors	Indicative Titles
	1668	Mutual acrimony between Houses of Parliament; [>] France [contra Spain] extends power in Europe – esp.ly in the Netherlands; Anglo-Dutch-Swedish alliance against France; 1st Fr. trading post in India	Newton constructs efficient reflecting telescope [& 1671]. **Int. Lit.:** Molière, *L'Avare*; Racine, *Les Plaideurs*; [–1694] La Fontaine, *Fables*. **Art:** [–1669] Rembrandt, 'Prodigal Son'; Lorraine, 'Landscape with Hagar and the Angel' [NG]; Vermeer, 'Astronomer' & [c.–1670] 'Lady at the Virginals with a Gentlemen Listening' [Royal Coll.]; Steen, 'Twelfth Night'; Wright, 'Mrs Claypole' [NPG]. **Lit. 'Events':** D'Avenant dies – John Dryden, Poet Laureate	**P:** Thomas Traherne (1637–74) **Dr:** Cavendish Etherege Thomas Shadwell (c.1642–92) **Theory/crit:** John Dryden	*Centuries of Meditations* [c: religious prose poems wrtn; mss of these & other poems discv.d in 1896; 1st pub.d 1903 & 1908] *Plays, Never Before Printed* *She Wou'd if She Cou'd* *The Sullen Lovers: or the Impertinents* *An Essay of Dramatick Poesy* [wrtn 1666]
	1669	James, Duke of York [later King James II], proclaims his conversion to RCism; Charles II nurtures secret RC, pro-Fr. sympathies – recalcitrant Parliament reinforces these – begins clandestine negotiations with France leading to secret treaty of 1670	[–1701] Newton, Professor of Maths at Cambridge; William Penn [founder of Pennsylvania – v.1681–2] pub.s *No Cross, No Crown* [Quaker writings]. **Art:** [c.] Rembrandt, 'Self-Portrait' [Kenwood House]; [c.] Vermeer, 'Lady Standing at the Virginal' [NG]. **Lit. 'Events':** Dryden becomes Royal Historiographer	**Dr:** Frances Boothby (dates unknown) **Theory/crit:** Dryden	*Marcelia* [1st original play by a woman pf.d on London stage; prnt.d 1670] *Defence of the Epilogue*
	1670	Secret Anglo-Fr. Treaty of Dover – French given free hand in Holland – English receive Fr. subsidies; Duke of Monmouth [Charles II's illegitimate son], Captain General of Army; Hudson's Bay Co. estab.d for fur trading in N. America	John Ray, *Catalogue of English Plants*; Pascal, *Pensées*; Spinoza, *Tractatus theologico-politicus*. **Int. Lit.:** Molière, *Le Bourgeois gentilhomme*; Racine, *Bérénice*; Mme de La Fayette, *Zaÿde* [early novel]. **Art:** [c.] Vermeer, 'Allegory of the Art of Painting' & 'The Letter'; [c.] van Ruisdael, 'The Wheat Field' & 'View of Haarlem with Bleaching Grounds'	**Dr:** Dryden (Mrs) Aphra Behn (1640–89)	[–1671] *The Conquest of Granada*; heroic drama in 2 Pts] *The Forc'd Marriage: or, the Jealous Bridegroom* [tragi-comedy]
	1671	Commons & Lords in conflict over Bill to ban RCs from office; Customs & Excise processes tightened; Charles II makes Henry Morgan [ex-pirate] Deputy Governor of Jamaica; pirates wreak destruction in Panama; [by now] great increase in Fr. naval power	**Int. Lit.:** Molière, *Les Fourberies de Scapin*; [c.] Mme de Sévigné begins her 25 yrs of letters to her daughter. **Art:** Wren begins the Monument, London, commemorating the Great Fire & rebuilds Royal Exchange; [–1673] Murillo, 'St John of God Carrying an Invalid', 'Moses Striking Water from the Rock', 'Miracle of the Loaves and Fishes' & 'Plague-Stricken' [for chapel in Seville]; Meindert Hobbema [pnt] 'Ruins of Brederode Castle' [NG]	**P:** Milton **Dr:** Dryden William Wycherley (c.1641–1715) George Villiers (Duke of Buckingham; 1627–87)	*Paradise Regained* [4 Bks] & *Samson Agonistes* [verse drama] *Marriage à-la-Mode* [comedy] *Love in a Wood, or, St James Park* [comedy] *The Rehearsal* [satirical comedy on Dryden's heroic drama]
	1672	Charles's 2nd Declaration of Indulgence [v.1662] allows toleration to both Puritan & RC dissenters; 'Stop of Exchequer' – no capital repayments on government loans for 1 yr – many made bankrupt; Ashley [now Earl of Shaftesbury], Lord Chancellor – reorganises Economic Council; 3rd Anglo-Dutch war – Eng. & Fr. fleets defeated in Sole Bay – Prince William of Orange [later m. to Charles II's niece, Mary – v.1677] leads Dutch troops [v. late-1680s]; Baltic trade thrown open to all Eng. merchants	Clarendon Press fnd.d – official press of Oxford University. **Int. Lit.:** Molière, *Les Femmes savantes*; Racine, *Bajazet*. **Music:** John Banister starts 1st regular series in Europe of public concerts at Whitefriars, London	**Pr/F:** Marvell **Dr:** Shadwell Wycherley	*The Rehearsal Transpros'd* [satire against religious intolerance; Pt I pub.d anon.; Pt II, 1673, under his name] *Epsom Wells* *The Gentleman Dancing-Master*
	1673	Conflict of interest leads Charles II to withdraw Declaration of Indulgence – assents to 1st Test Act: excludes all non-Anglicans from public office under	**Int. Lit.:** Racine, *Mithridate*; Molière, *Le Malade imaginaire*. **Music:** John Playford, *Musical Companion*. **Art:** Wright, 'Sir Robert Vyner and His	**P:** Milton **Dr:** Dryden	*Poems* [2nd collected edtn] *Amboyna*

STUART (CONT.)/RESTORATION

Year	History / Politics	Science / Culture	Authors	Works / 'Events'
1674	Crown; violent anti-RC, anti-war & anti-Court feeling in Parliament; Cabal disintegrates – Shaftesbury dismissed as Chancellor; Dutch defeat Eng. & Fr. fleets; French fnd factory in India	Family' [NPG]; Edward Pierce [sculpt] 'Sir Christopher Wren' [marble bust; Ashmolean] **Int. Lit.:** Racine, *Iphigénie*. **Music:** Lully [comp] 'Alceste' [Fr. opera]; Matthew Locke [comp] incidental music to Shadwell's operatic adaptation of *The Tempest* as 'The Enchanted Island'	**Lit. 'Events':** **Theory/Crit:** **Lit. 'Events':**	John Bunyan, imprisoned in Bedford gaol, begins writing *The Pilgrim's Progress* [v.1678] Nicolas Boileau, *L'Art poétique* [principles of Fr. literary Neo-Classicism – imitated by Alexander Pope, v.1711] Milton dies; Theatre Royal, Drury Lane, rebuilt
1675	Buckingham dismissed; Earl of Danby, Lord Treasurer – reorganises Eng. finances; Parliament clamours for peace – 3rd Anglo-Dutch war ends; many Bills hostile to Court [incl. agitation to exclude James, Duke of York, from Succession] – Charles prorogues Parliament; Charles II gives Bombay [v.1662] to E. India Co. which fnds Fort William [Calcutta]	[c.] Gottfried Leibniz & Newton simultaneously develop theory of calculus. **Music:** Locke, music for Shadwell's *Psyche* [early Eng. opera]. **Art:** Wren builds Royal Observatory, Greenwich & [–1711] present St Paul's Cathedral; Murillo, 'Girl and her Duenna' & 'Self-Portrait' [NG]	**P:** John Wilmot (Earl of Rochester, 1647–80) **Dr:** Dryden Wycherley Thomas Otway (1652–85)	'A Satyr against Reason and Mankind' *Aureng-Zebe* *The Country Wife* *Alcibiades* [tragedy]
1676	Danby cements his power; Parliament & King in conflict over finances; Charles II given 500,000 crowns by Louis XIV – prorogues Parliament for 15 months; [–1676] war against Native Americans in New England	Edmund Halley catalogues southern stars. **Int. Lit.:** [c.] Matsuo Basho develops Japanese haiku poetry. **Art:** [–1784] Wren builds Trinity College Library, Cambridge	**P:** Dryden **Dr:** Etherege Otway Wycherley	[c.] *MacFlecknoe* [wrtn; v.1682, 1684] *The Man of Mode, or, Sir Fopling Flutter* *Don Carlos, Prince of Spain* & *Titus and Berenice* *The Plain Dealer*
1677	Secret treaty between Charles II & Louis XIV; further anxiety over Duke of York's religious stance; Fr. successes against Dutch alarm England	Co. of Masons fnd'd; Halley observes transit of Venus; Spinoza, *Ethics* [pub. posthm.]. **Int. Lit.:** Racine, *Phèdre*. **Music:** Henry Purcell becomes Court composer. **Art:** Sir Godfrey Kneller [pnt] 'James Vernon' [NPG] & 'Duke of Monmouth'	**Pr/F:** Marvell **Dr:** Behn Dryden Nathaniel Lee (c.1650–92)	An Account of the Growth of Popery and Arbitrary Government in England [pub.d anon. – £100 reward offered for discovery of author] *The Rover* [1st Pt of comedy; 2nd Pt, 1681] *All for Love: or, The World well Lost* [based on *Anthony and Cleopatra*; prnt.d 1678] *The Rival Queens; or, the Death of Alexander* [tragedy]
1678	Charles II ratifies treaty with Dutch, but enters further secret subsidy agreements with Louis XIV; war with France urged & royal army raised, but Dutch make separate peace [of Nijmegen] – fears of an Eng. standing army result; Titus Oates 'reveals' [spurious] 'Popish Plot' [RC uprising to kill Charles & destroy Eng. Protestantism] – panic in London – many RCs prosecuted [incl. Viscount Stafford] – [–1679] RCs excluded from either House of Parliament by 2nd Test Act – Shaftesbury leads attempts to exclude James, Duke of York, from Succession in favour of Duke of Monmouth; secret treaty of 1676 with Louis XIV revealed – Danby impeached – bitter conflict between King & Commons [incl. refusal to vote revenue] – Parliament prorogued; [–1685] importation of all Fr. goods into England banned	**Int. Lit.:** Bradstreet, *Several Poems* [pub. posthm.; v.1650, 1667]. **Music:** Thomas Britton's weekly concerts begin in Clekenwell; 1st Ger. opera house opens at Hamburg; Henry Purcell [comp] music for *Timon of Athens*. **Art:** Murillo, 'Immaculate Conception'	**P:** Vaughan **Pr/F:** Bunyan **Dr:** Behn Otway	*Thalia Rediviva* [pub. unauthorised] *The Pilgrim's Progress* [Pt I; enlarged edtn 1679; Pt II, 1684] *The Feign'd Curtezans* [dedicated to Nell Gwynne] *Friendship in Fashion* [comedy]

(The following note appears under the 1677 row:) Princess Mary [James, Duke of York's daughter] m. William III of Orange – public rejoicing in London; Anglo-Dutch treaty for peace with France; Charles given 2m. Fr. livres to keep Parliament prorogued till April 1678; [–1688] Eng. trade greatly prospers. Parliament recalled – Shaftesbury & Buckingham sent to the Tower for questioning its legality; Commons & Danby urge Charles II to assume anti-Fr. policy & alliance with Dutch – Navy supply increased.

Period	Year	International and Political Contexts	Social and Cultural Contexts	Authors	Indicative Titles
	1679	Cavalier Parliament dissolved; James, Duke of York, exiled to Brussels as precaution; 1st 'Exclusion' Parliament – passes Habeus Corpus Act & Bill to exclude James from Succession – dissolved, killing Bill; Shaftesbury back in Privy Council [later again dismissed]; 2nd 'Exclusion' Parliament called & prorogued & [–1680] 6 more times – 'Whigs' begin petitioning campaign to ensure Parliament meets – [c.] political party names, 'Whig' & 'Tory', 1st used to identify sides in Succession/Exclusion conflict [v. chapter glosses for definitions]; revolt of Scottish Covenanters crushed at Bothwell Bridge by Monmouth	Halley, aged 23, elected Fellow of Royal Society (FRS); [c.] Niagara Falls discovered; [–1714] In Mauritius, the Dodo [bird] becomes extinct; [–1714] Sir William Petty, *A Treatise on Taxes and Contributions*; [–1681] Bishop Gilbert Burnet, *History of the Reformation in England* [vols I & II; vol. III, 1714]. **Music:** Purcell becomes Westminster Abbey organist; Alessandro Scarlatti, 'Gli Equivoci nell' Amore' [It. opera]. **Art:** [>] Wren builds Ashmolean Museum, Oxford	**Dr:** Dryden & Lee	*Oedipus King of Thebes*
	1680	'Petitioners' [Whigs] demand that Charles II assemble 1679 Parliament – 'Abhorrers' [Tories] oppose; [–1882] Monmouth's semi-royal progresses through W. & NW England strengthen his case to be Protestant successor; Commons pass Exclusion Bill – Lords reject it; Stafford executed as suspect in 1678 'Popish Plot'; [c.] buccaneers seize Sp. ships at Panama & scourge S. Seas	[c.] penny postage system unsuccessfully proposed for London [v.1840]; Newton sketches a steam-propelled vehicle; Sir Robert Filmer, *Patriarcha* pub.d [wrtn during Charles I's 'personal rule'; extreme advocation of Divine Right of Kings based on patriarch as natural head of family; demolished by John Locke in 1st of *Two Treatises*, v.1681]. **Int. Lit.:** Comédie-Française [theatre] fnd.d. **Art:** Ragley Hall, Warwicks, built; Wright, 'Sir Neil O'Neill' [Tate]; [c.–1885] Edward Hawker [pnt] 'Charles II' [NPG]	**P:** Otway Rochester **Pr/F:** Bunyan Dryden **Dr:** Dryden Otway	*The Poet's Complaint of His Muse Poems* [pub. posthm.] *The Life and Death of Mr Badman* [allegory] *Ovid's Epistles* [trans] *The Spanish Friar* *The History and Fall of Caius Marius, The Orphan, or, the Unhappy Marriage* [tragedies] & *The Soldier's Fortune* [comedy]
	1681	Charles II refuses Exclusion Bill – Parliament withholds supplies – dissolved; new Parliament called to Oxford – 3rd Exclusion Bill – Parliament refuses Charles's offer of Regency of William of Orange for James, Duke of York – dissolved – James in exile; William Penn granted royal patent for land at Pennsylvania; [–1682] French explore entire Mississippi – claim territory as Louisiana – colonial empire now stretches from there to Quebec	[c.] 1st [oil] street lamps in London; Wren becomes President of Royal Society; John Locke, *Two Treatises of Government* [largely wrtn; pub.d anon., 1689–90]; Thomas Burnet, *Telluris Theoria Sacra, or, Sacred Theory of the Earth* [imaginary account of evolution]. **Music:** Purcell [comp] 'Swifter, Isis, swifter flow' [musical ode]. **Art:** Wren builds Tom Tower, Christ Church, Oxford	**P:** Dryden Marvell **Dr:** Behn Otway	*Absalom & Achitophel* [Pt I] *Miscellaneous Poems* [pub. posthm.; incls 'To His Coy Mistress', 'The Garden', 'Upon Appleton House', 'Bermudas', 'On a Drop of Dew'] *The Roundheads; or the Good Old Cause* *Venus Preserv'd, or, A Plot Discover'd* [prmt.d 1682]
	1682	Plot of radical Whigs under Shaftesbury – again faces trial for treason – flees country; Crown campaign against Whiggery begins – Charters of 65 boroughs remodelled – political power in London wrested from Whigs; James, Duke of York, returns – increases power; French fnd St Louis; Pennsylvania fnd.d [incls Delaware] – elected assembly issues Great Charter [constitution] – Penn's Treaty of Peace with Native Americans – plans city of Philadelphia	Halley observes eponymous Comet; Advocates Library, Edinburgh, fnd.d [later Scottish National Library]. **Music:** Lully, 'Persée' [opera]. **Art:** [–1692] Wren builds Chelsea Hospital for disabled soldiers; Badminton [Palladian mansion] built	**P:** Dryden **Pr/F:** Bunyan **Dr:** Behn	*The Medall, a Satyre against Sedition, Absalom and Achitophel* [Pt II – largely wrtn by Nahum Tate], *Religio Laici* [religious poem] & *MacFlecknoe* [pirated edtn] *The Holy War* [allegory] *The City Heiress*
	1683	London's Charter declared forfeit; Rye House plot to kill Charles II & brother James – Whigs Lord William Russell & Algernon Sidney executed – Duke of Monmouth, implicated by Shaftesbury, flees to Holland – John Locke, after Shaftesbury's fall & death, does the same; severe repression begins of Covenanters in Scotland	Sadler's Wells 'pleasure garden' [with 'Musick House'] opens on site of mineral water spring in N. London [proper theatre built, 1765 – entirely devoted to opera & ballet from 1934]; Haley's 1st full map of winds; Newton's gravitational theory of tides; Penn, *General Description of Pennsylvania*		

Year	History / Culture	Lit.	Author	Works
1684	Charles ignores Triennial Act & omits to call Parliament; James restored to all offices [incl. Privy Council in defiance of Test Act]; 'killing times' in Scotland: c.100 Covenanters executed – 'Great Persecution' of Eng. dissenters; number of Fr. Huguenot churches reduced by c.75%; Hudson Bay Co. dividend 50%; Massachusetts Charter annulled – hostile reaction starts in American colonies; Bermudas become Crown Colony	**P:** Dryden **Pr/F:** Bunyan		*Miscellany Poems* [1st in series (–1704); incls authorised version of *MacFlecknoe*] *The Pilgrim's Progress* [Pt II]
1685	Charles II dies, King James II accedes; RCs appointed as Army officers in spite of Test Act – Parliament protests – prorogued; Earl of Argyle's rebellion in Scotland quashed – Argyle executed; Monmouth lands at Lyme – W. Country rebellion at Sedgemoor crushed – Monmouth executed – Judge Jeffreys's 'Bloody Assize' follows; Louis XIV revokes Edict of Nantes [v.1598] – large-scale Huguenot migration to England – increases alarm in England at having an RC king; French settle in Texas; all Chinese ports opened to foreign trade; E. India Co. at war with Mogul Emperor	Press Licensing Act [censorship] renewed; Huguenots begin silk manufacture in Britain; Sir Henry Wotton, *Reliquiae Wottonianae* [posthm. pmt.d]. **Art:** 508-foot-long Orangery erected at Versailles; [>] Wren builds Belton House, Lincs. – carvings by Grinling Gibbons; Kneller, 'Self-Portrait' [NPG] & 'Philip, Earl of Leicester'	**P:** Waller		*Divine Poems*
1686	James claims & uses prerogative to dispense with Parliamentary laws – 'Godden v. Hales' case supports Crown's right to ignore Test Act & give army commission to an RC – other pro-RC measures intro.d [e.g. RC appointed Dean of Christ Church, Oxford]; all but one of Hudson Bay Co.'s trading forts captured by French	Halley explains trade winds, monsoons & salinity of sea; Newton presents 1st book of *Principia* [v. 1687] to Royal Society. **Art:** [–1696] Petworth House, Sussex, rebuilt	**Dr:** Behn		*The Lucky Chance* [comedy]
1687	Earl of Tyrconnel [RC] becomes Lord Deputy of Ireland & other RCs given high office; James II issues Declaration of Indulgence – suspends law in all ecclesiastical matters; lists of RCs & Nonconformists suitable for election [to pack Parliament] demanded of Lords Lieutenants – many resign – Parliament dissolved; William [of Orange] & Mary declare for both Tests & toleration in pub.d letter; E. India Co. transfers its HQ to Bombay; Connecticut's Charter annulled; Huguenots settle at Cape of Good Hope	Continuing attempts by James II to break Anglican monopoly in Oxford; Newton, *Philosophiae Naturalis Principia Mathematica* [3 books in Latin – pub.d in English, 1727]; Marquis of Halifax, *Letter to a Dissenter*; François Fénelon, *Traité de l'éducation des filles*. **Art:** [–1707] Chatsworth House, Derbyshire, built	**P:** Dryden Matthew Prior (1664–1721)		*The Hind and the Panther* [religious poem] & 'A Song for St Cecilia's Day, 1687'; *The Hind and the Panther Transvers'd to the Story of the Country Mouse and the City Mouse* [with Charles Montagu, Earl of Halifax; satirical poem on Dryden]
1688	James II orders clergy to read 2nd Declaration of Indulgence – 'Seven Bishops' refuse – tried & acquitted; 'The Glorious Revolution': 7 opposition lords invite William & Mary to restore liberties of England – land at Torbay with powerful army – march on London – welcomed everywhere – anti-RC riots in London [word 'mob' 1st used] – James, deserted by ministers & troops, flees to France; William summons members of Charles II's Parliaments – calls a Convention Parliament; William Dampier, Eng. buccaneer, reaches Australia	RC made President of Magdalen College, Oxford; Jean de La Bruyère, *Caractères* [Fr. moral & satirical pen portraits]. **Lit. 'Events':** John Bunyan dies; [–1689] loyalty to James II causes Dryden to lose Poet Laureateship & other public posts at the 'Glorious Revolution'	**Pr/F:** Behn **Dr:** Shadwell		*Oroonoko, or the History of the Royal Slave* [early Eng. novel by woman novelist] *The Squire of Alsatia* [comedy]

PERIOD	YEAR	INTERNATIONAL AND POLITICAL CONTEXTS	SOCIAL AND CULTURAL CONTEXTS	AUTHORS	INDICATIVE TITLES
	1689	Convention Parliament – Declaration [later Bill] of Rights [completes work of Magna Carta]; William III & Mary II proclaimed king & queen; James II lands in Ireland – Fr. & Ir. RC troops besiege Londonderry; Scots Jacobites' victory at Killiecrankie – defeated at Dunkeld; Scottish Convention Parliament accepts William & Mary – abolishes episcopacy; Toleration Act gives religious freedom to all who accept 36 of 39 Articles; Mutiny Act – Army legalised annually; export duty on Eng. corn abolished; William III builds 1st naval dockyard at Devonport; old Charters of colonies recognised by monarchs; [–1697] England joins League of Augsburg ['Grand Alliance'] in war against France; [–1725] Peter I ('the Great'), Tsar of Russia	[–1690] Locke, Two Treatises ... [pub.d anon.; v.1681] & 1st Letter on Toleration. Int. Lit.: Racine, Esther. Music: [c.] Purcell [comp] 'Dido and Aeneas' [early Eng. opera with libretto by Nahum Tate]. Art: [–1702] Wren builds Kensington Palace; Hobbema, 'The Avenue, Middleharnis' [NG] Lit. 'Events': Thomas Shadwell, Poet Laureate	**Dr:** Behn Shadwell	*The Widow Ranter* [pub. 1690] *Bury Fair*
	1690	General Election shifts influence from Whigs to Tories; Fr. fleet victorious at Beachy Head – burns Teignmouth – dominates Channel – fear of invasion – Parliament votes large sums for army & navy; [–1691] war in Ireland – William III's Protestant army victorious at Battle of the Boyne; E. India Co. sets up factory at Calcutta	1st weekly Eng. provincial paper issued in Worcester; Locke, *Essay Concerning Human Understanding* & *Second Letter Concerning Toleration*. **Music:** Purcell, 'Diocletian' [opera; adaptn from Beaumont & Fletcher]. **Art:** Stamford Hall, Leicestershire, begun	**Dr:** Lee **Theory/Crit:**	*Massacre of St Bartholomew* Sir William Temple, *Essay upon the Ancient and Modern Learning* [cites (spurious) *Epistles of Phalaris* (ed. Charles Boyle) as evidence that ancient works are best; begins 'the Battle of the Books' – v.1694 & Swift, 1704]
	1691	Public Accounts Act passed; Battle of Aughrim – Ir. Jacobites [v. chapter glosses] defeated – siege of Limerick successful – Treaty of Limerick ends Ir. rebellion; Eng. parishes made responsible for upkeep of highways; Massachusetts absorbs Plymouth Colony & receives new Charter; Carolina divides into N. & S. – constitutions modelled on Virginia's	Sir William Petty, *Political Survey, or Anatomy of Ireland*. **Int. Lit.:** Racine, *Athalie*. **Music:** Purcell, 'King Arthur, or the British Worthy' [opera; libretto by Dryden]. **Art:** [–1694] Andrea (Fra) Pozzo [pnt] 'Allegory of the Missionary Work of the Jesuits/ Triumph of St Ignatius of Loyola' [frescoes, Rome]	Lit. 'Events':	*Compleat Library*, early Eng. periodical, 1st pub.d
	1692	Duke of Marlborough dismissed on suspicion of Jacobite intrigues; Macdonald highlanders massacred at Glencoe; Louis XIV & James II plan invasion of England – Fr. fleet destroyed off La Hogue; [–1693] British suffer land & sea defeats as Grand Alliance's war against Louis continues; Salem wichcraft trials in Massachusetts, New England	Lloyd's coffee-house estab.d as HQ of marine insurance; bank [later Coutts & Co.] opens in Strand; 1st auction house opens in London. **Music:** Purcell, 'Nymphs and Shepherds' [song for Shadwell's *The Libertine*] & 'The Fairy Queen' [opera; adaptn of *A Midsummer Night's Dream*]. **Art:** Dyrham Park, Gloucestershire, begun	**Pr/F:** Dryden William Congreve (1670–1729)	*The Satires of Juvenal and Persius* [trans] *Incognita, or Love and Duty Reconciled* [novel; pub.d under name 'Cleophil']
	1693	Tontine Loan Act inaugurates 'National Debt'; Old E. India Co. obtains new Charter by bribery; Kingston, Jamaica, fnd.d	Locke, *Some Thoughts concerning Education* [advocates use of 'direct method' in learning foreign languages]	**Dr:** Congreve	*The Old Bachelor* & [–1694] *The Double Dealer* [comedies]
	1694	Mary II dies childless [v.1700] – William III remains king; Triennial Act limits Parliament to 3 yrs duration; 'Lancashire Plot' [Jacobite] uncovered; Bank of England fnd.d to finance loans to gvnmt;	Chelsea Royal Hospital opens; Mary Astell, *A Serious Proposal to Ladies for the advancement of their true and great interest* [advocates fn.ding all-female Anglican academy of learning; Pt II, 1697];	**Dr:** Dryden **Theory/Crit:** William Wotton	*Love Triumphant* [last play; wrtn 1693] *Reflections upon Ancient and Modern Learning* [with appendix by Richard Bentley]

STUART (CONT.)/RESTORATION

Year	History & Politics	Science, Society & Culture	Authors	Literary Works
(1694 cont.)	proving *Epistles of Phalaris* a forgery; central to 'Ancients v. Moderns' controversy – v.1690 & Swift, 1704] scandal of E. India Co.'s Charter exposed – India trade opened to all Eng. subjects	*Dictionnaire de L'Académie française* pub.d **Music:** Purcell, 'Jubilate' & 'Te Deum'	**Dr:** Congreve 'Ariadne' (dates unknown) Catherine Trotter (1679–1749) **Lit. 'Events':**	*Love for Love* [comedy] *She Ventures and He Wins* [comedy; 1st play pf.d at new theatre – see below] *Agnes de Castro* [tragedy] Freedom of press estab.d in England by non-renewal of Licensing Act [v.1685]; 2nd theatre opens at Lincoln's Inn Fields, London – co. led by Thomas Betterton – many plays by new women dramatists pf.d there – see below]
1695	New Parliament passes Recoinage Bill, prompted by devaluation of silver coinage through 'clipping' – Locke & Newton instrumental in directing it; Bank of Scotland estab.d; [–1699] so-called 'King William's III Years' in Scotland – succession of bad harvests leads to great suffering; William retakes Namur from French	Leibniz, *Système nouveau de la nature*. **Music:** 1st public concert in Edinburgh; Bishop Ken, 'Awake, my Soul' [hymn]; Purcell, *The Indian Queen* [opera; adaptn of Dryden & Howard's play – v.1664; incls song 'I Attempt from Love's Sickness'] & 'The Tempest' [opera; adaptn by Shadwell; incls song 'Arise, ye Subterranean Winds']		*Love's Last Shift* [comedy]
1696	Act regulates treason trials in England; Jacobite plot to assassinate William III uncovered – Whigs pledge to defend king; Royal Board of Trade estab.d – Locke one of 1st commissioners; Newton, Master of the Mint; Window Tax intro.d in England [until 1851]; [c.] British & Fr. settlers in open conflict in N. America; Fort William, Calcutta, built	1st Eng. insurance company [for property] estab.d; [–1698] 1st Eddystone Lighthouse built; John Aubrey, *Miscellanies* [folklore/anthropology; only work pub.d in lifetime; *Brief Lives* pub.d as *Letters by Eminent Persons*, 1813; edited, 1898]. **Art:** [–1702] Wren builds Greenwich Hospital; [–1704] Carshalton House, Surrey, built	**Dr:** Colley Cibber (1671–1757) Delariviere Manley (1663–1724) Mary Pix (1666–1709) Sir John Vanbrugh (1664–1726)	*The Lost Lover, or, the Jealous Husband* [comedy] & *The Royal Mischief* [tragedy] *Ibrahim, Thirteenth Emperor of the Turks* [tragedy] & *The Spanish Wives* [comedy] *The Relapse* [continuation & parody of Cibber's play above]
1697	Figures of National Debt 1st known; [–1699] high wheat prices & 2nd failure of Scottish harvest cause serious famine in Britain; France & Grand Alliance sign Treaty of Ryswick – end of war – Louis XIV recognises William III as king – French restore only Fort Albany to Hudson Bay Co. – retain Acadia; [–1698] Royal Africa Co.'s monopoly of Africa trade withdrawn; Carribean buccaneers capture Cartagena – activities decline thereafter	Britannia standard intro.d for silverware; [c.] Cotton Mather uses the term 'American' for English-speaking colonists. **Int. Lit.:** Charles Perrault, *Histoires ou Contes du Temps Passé* [fairy stories; incls 'Sleeping Beauty', 'Little Red Riding Hood', 'Bluebeard', 'Tom Thumb', 'Cinderella']. **Art:** [>] Grinling Gibbons's carvings in St Paul's Cathedral **Theory/Crit:** [–1699] dispute conts between Bentley & Boyle over *Epistles of Phalaris* in 'Battle of Books' [v.1690, 1694, 1704]	**P:** Dryden **Dr:** Congreve Pix Vanbrugh	'Alexander's Feast; or the Power of Musique. An Ode, in Honour of St Cecilia's Day' & *The Works of Virgil* [trans] *The Mourning Bride* [tragedy] *The Deceiver Deceived* & *The Innocent Mistress* [comedies] *The Provoked Wife*
1698	Conflict between King & Parliament over size & role of standing army; 3rd failure of Scottish harvest causes deaths from starvation & widespread depopulation; 1st Partition Treaty: England agrees with other European powers on Sp. Succession & partition of Sp. Empire; 'New' E. India Trading Co. fnd.d [v.1693–4]	Society for Promoting Christian Knowledge (SPCK) fnd.d; Mrs White's Chocolate House opens [later 'White's' Club]; Newton calculates speed of sound **Theory/Crit:** Jeremy Collier, *Short View of the Immorality and Profaneness of the English Stage* [Dryden attacked amongst others; fierce debate ensues]	**Dr:** Pix Trotter George Farquhar (c.1677–1707)	*Queen Catherine, or, The Ruins of Love* [tragedy] *Fatal Friendship* [tragedy] *Love and a Bottle* [comedy]
1699	Disbanding Bill passed – William III's regiments of Dutch Guards returned to Holland – naval estimates also reduced; final bad harvest in Scotland – c. 33% of population has left or is dead; [–1700] Dampier, in HMS Roebuck, sent to SW Pacific to explore NW coast of New Holland [Australia], New Guinea & New Britain	Billingsgate becomes a market; Fénelon, *Adventures of Télémaque* [satirical novel – suppressed – pub.d 1717]	**Dr:** Farquhar Pix	*The Constant Couple, or, a Trip to the Jubilee* [comedy] *The False Friend; or, The Fate of Disobedience* [tragedy]

3

1700–1789

The Augustan Period

INTRODUCTION

The problem of exact periodicity is sharply apparent in the present chapter. The first 14 years of this new 'period' are ruled by the last of the **Stuart*** line [see glosses in Chapter 2], while the **Hanoverian*** succession lasts from 1714, with the accession of King George I, to the death of Queen Victoria in 1901 (see Chapters 4 and 5). However, because literary history tends to see Queen Anne's reign (1702–14) – if not the last two decades of the 17th Century – as part of the **Neo-Classical*** or **Augustan*** period, the start-date for this chapter goes back to 1700. Furthermore, modern historians often use the concept of the 'Long 18th Century' when dealing with the period under consideration, a period of political change and consolidation which stretches roughly from **The Glorious Revolution** of 1688 [see Chapter 2] to the passing of the First Reform Bill in 1832 [see Chapter 5]. While this prevents the period being broken up into artificial/arbitrary segments, for the purposes of literary history it includes too diverse a range of movements and tendencies – although, as we shall see, there are also overlaps and continuities between the Augustan* and **Romantic*** movements [for the latter, see Chapter 4]. The chapter ends with the year of **The French Revolution** in 1789 [see Chapter 4 for more on this and its aftermath].

Chapter contents

3.1 HANOVER / HANOVERIAN

*The family name of the line of monarchs – **The Hanoverians** – who occupied the British throne from the accession of King George I in 1714 to the death of Queen Victoria in 1901.*

On the death of Queen Anne in 1714, the provisions of the Act of Settlement (1701) came into force [see Chapter 2, **Stuart (continued)***], and Anne's Protestant cousin, George Louis, Elector of Hanover (Germany), became George I of Great Britain. His descendants ruled both Hanover and Britain until the accession of Queen Victoria in 1837, when the two thrones were separated. Victoria married Prince Albert of Saxe-Coburg-Gotha in 1840, and on her death and the accession of King Edward VII in 1901, the name of the royal house was changed to 'Saxe-Coburg and Gotha'.

The reigns of later Hanoverians will be glossed in subsequent chapters. Here, the reigns of King George I, King George II and part of the reign of King George III will be considered. Having divorced his wife in 1694 for adultery, George I brought no queen consort to Britain with him, and he never learnt English. The Hanoverian succession was deeply unpopular among sections of the public, and there were widespread demonstrations against the new king, who did little to court British favour. However, the unsuccessful **Jacobite*** uprising of 1715 [see Chapter 2, Stuart (continued)*] strengthened Whig* [see Chapter 2] support for him, and the king's preference for the Whigs helped to give them a monopoly of power for the next 50 years. George's ignorance of English and his lack of attendance at Cabinet meetings, combined with the Septennial Act of 1716 which extended the life of a parliament for seven years, meant that government largely rested in the hands of the ruling Whig oligarchy, especially during Sir Robert Walpole's ministry (1721–42). This reduced popular participation in the political process, and increased constitutional control over the Crown, whilst giving the so-called 'Court Party' unprecedented dominance over Parliament. By becoming both First Lord of the Treasury and Chancellor of the Exchequer in 1721 (after the bursting of the 'South Sea Bubble' in 1720, the first great financial scandal of modern times), Walpole was effectively Britain's first 'Prime Minister'.

On his father's death in 1727, George II became king. He had opposed George I's government, but rapidly found himself maintaining Walpole as the Chief Minister, until his first son, Frederick, Prince of Wales (d. 1751), became the centre of opposition to Walpole in the late 1730s and forced the latter's resignation (1742). George II was then obliged to accept William Pitt 'the Elder' (Earl of Chatham), leader of the younger 'patriotic' Whigs opposed to Walpole, to enter his government. Walpole's policy of peace with Britain's European neighbours was broken in 1739 by war with Spain and by the king's support for the Austrian cause in the War of the Austrian Succession (1740–8). George was the last British monarch to fight in battle – at Dettingen (1743) where he was victorious. In 1745, the most serious of the Jacobite* uprisings began when Charles Edward Stuart, the 'Young Pretender' [see Chapter 2, Stuart (continued)*], landed in Scotland and invaded England as far south as Derby before retreating back to Scotland. Without the expected assistance from France, the rising was doomed, and the Duke of Cumberland, George II's second son, brutally suppressed it at the Battle of Culloden Moor in 1746.

George reluctantly made Pitt his first minister in 1756, who then took charge of the conduct of the Seven Years War (1756–63) in which Britain sided with Prussia (in defence of Hanover) against France and her allies (the North American dimension of this, the French and Indian War, had begun earlier in 1754). Reverses in Europe were offset by victories elsewhere: pre-eminently, Clive's victories in India (Plassey and Chinsura, 1757–8), which effectively began Britain's conquest of India; Wolfe's victory over the French to take Quebec in 1759, which consolidated British power in North America; and the Royal Navy's supremacy in maritime power by the same year. George died suddenly the following year, 1760.

The eldest son of George II, Frederick, Prince of Wales, had predeceased his father by dying in 1751, hence Frederick's eldest son, George (1738–1820), succeeded his grandfather in 1760 as King George III of Great Britain and Elector of Hanover (then King, 1815–20). George was initially popular with his people, but he was keen to govern as well as reign, and in 1761, he forced William Pitt the Elder, whom he disliked, to resign over Pitt's conduct of the Seven Years War. A succession of first ministers followed, largely in post through the king's patronage, the one most to George's taste being Lord North, who was his chief minister from 1770–82 (when the American War of Independence ended [see below]). In effect, therefore, George III governed by personal rule for 20 years, in the process breaking the supremacy of the old Whig* [see Chapter 2] oligarchy. From 1765, with the imposition of Stamp Duty on the American colonies, then other forms of taxation which infuriated the colonists, and the inept handling of the situation during Lord North's administration (he was easily swayed by the king's views which saw the colonists simply as rebels), the process was underway that would lead to the American War of Independence (1775–83), the Declaration of Independence (1776), and the final recognition of the United States of America as fully independent of British rule at the Peace of Versailles (1783).

The loss of the American colonies was deeply unpopular in Britain, North resigned, and George III had to look elsewhere for his Prime Minister. After months of political upheaval in 1782–3, George compelled his existing ministers to resign, called on William Pitt ('the Younger') to form a ministry, and dissolved Parliament. At the general election in 1784, Pitt's **Tories*** won a large majority; at 24, Pitt became Britain's youngest Prime Minister; his ministry lasted for 17 years; and Whig* power was in abeyance until Earl Grey's reforming ministry was returned in 1830 (see Chapter 2 for Whigs and Tories).

From 1784 onwards, George took a much less active role in politics and government (in 1788, he suffered his first attack of mental illness; see Chapter 4, Hanoverian (continued) I* and **(The) Regency***), allowing Pitt to introduce his own programme of policies. Despite fierce opposition from the liberal Whig, Charles James Fox, by the end of the period under consideration in this chapter (1789, and the start of *The French Revolution* – given more detailed treatment in the glosses to Chapter 4), Pitt had created a 'Sinking Fund' to reduce the National Debt; passed the Government of India Act in 1784, which effectively put the East India Company under government control; advocated reform of the slave trade; and attempted to reform Parliament [for the later years of Pitt's ministry and George III's reign, see the glosses in Chapter 4].

Key Timeline Narratives 1700–1789

➲ **International Events**   Other international issues involving Great Britain: from the 1700s onwards, the institutional promotion of the slave trade between Africa and the Americas, but by the late 1780s the beginnings of movements to reform it; the continuing settlement, especially in the first half of the period, of North America by the British and French in particular; the struggle for power in India between France and Britain/Britain and the Nawab of Bengal, and the consolidation of British dominion there by c.1760; the voyages of Captain Cook from 1768 into the 1770s exploring the east coast of Australia and claiming it for Britain (in 1770, he 'discovered' Botany Bay; by 1788, the first convicts were arriving there); the periodic but devastating famines that beset Ireland in the mid-18th Century.

➲ **Science and Industry**   In Britain, perhaps the single most formative process, outside the political arena, was the rapid progress in science and engineering, hence inaugurating *The Industrial Revolution*. For example, in the mid-1760s, Joseph Priestley investigated electricity, while Henry Cavendish identified hydrogen and analysed air; in 1772, Daniel Rutherford isolated nitrogen; two years later, Priestley did the same for oxygen and also discovered ammonia. As early as 1709, coke was first used to smelt iron ore; in 1759 the Carron Iron Works was established; the Bridgewater Canal opened in 1761; in 1779 the first iron bridge was completed over the River Severn at Coalbrookdale; and in 1786, the first attempts were made to use coal-gas for lighting.

From the 1730s onwards, James Hargreaves, Richard Arkwright, Samuel Crompton, Edmund Cartwright and others invented spinning and weaving machines, looms and then power mills which transformed the cloth-making industries (causing great social distress and unrest), with the first steam-driven cotton factory opening in Manchester in 1789. In the 1760s and 1770s, James Watt, Matthew Boulton and others developed steam engines, which were then used to smelt iron and drive looms; in 1720, salt-glazed pottery was first made in Staffordshire; from the 1750s, porcelain factories were established at Worcester and Burslem (Wedgwood); and in 1742, the silver-plating process was discovered in Sheffield. At the end of the period, the first flight in a hot-air balloon was made by the French Montgolfier brothers (1783) and Blanchard and Jeffries made the first Channel crossing in one two years later.

➲ **Health**   Related to developments in science was a noticeable increase in concern about health: early in the period, Fahrenheit invented the mercury thermometer, and in 1742 Celsius proposed the Centigrade scale; around 1717, Lady Mary Wortley Montagu introduced innoculation against smallpox into Britain, and by 1740 it was in general use; Guy's Hospital was founded in 1722, the Royal Infirmary, Edinburgh, in 1730, Queen Charlotte's (Maternity) Hospital in 1739, the Middlesex Hospital in 1745, and the first mental hospital opened in London in 1751.

➲ **North American Culture**   Supplementing the accelerating dissidence of the American colonies, and evidence of a growing sense of independence and self-identity, was the development of an indigenous cultural infrastructure, especially the founding of libraries and universities (Pennsylvania, Yale, Princeton, Columbia).

➲ **Society and Culture**   In Europe, the period witnessed the high point of **The Enlightenment*** [see below] in the writings of Voltaire, Diderot and the French Encyclopaedists, and the flowering of classical music and opera in the work of Handel, Bach, Haydn and Mozart. By the later part of the period, however, the proto-Romantic work of Jean-Jacques Rousseau was in reaction to it in France, as was that of the 'Sturm und Drang' movement in Germany, most particularly in the writing of Goethe, Schiller and Herder.

In Britain, social and cultural narratives would include: from the late-1720s, the growth of Methodism, especially under the leadership of John Wesley; the first appearance of daily newspapers (in 1702, *The Daily Courant* was published in London; *The Times* in 1788); the widespread publication of periodicals, journals and magazines like Daniel Defoe's *Review*, Richard Steele's *The Tatler*, Steele and Joseph Addison's *The Spectator*, Eliza Haywood's *The Female Spectator* and Dr Johnson's *The Rambler*.

The production of major reference works: for example, early English dictionaries appeared in 1702 and 1721, whilst Dr Johnson's was published in 1755; Ephraim Chambers' *Cyclopaedia* (not to be confused with the more famous 19th-Century *Chambers Encyclopaedia*) appeared in 1728, and early versions of the *Encyclopaedia Britannica* in Edinburgh in 1768 and 1771; the founding, in the 1750s, of the British Museum (opens 1759); the production of new editions of Shakespeare's works.

In 1709–10, the first English Copyright Act to protect writers was introduced, while in 1737, the Theatres Licensing Act established the Lord Chamberlain's right to censor all plays. The period also witnessed, especially in the second half of it, the rapid rise of 'Grub Street', of a new kind of professional writer or 'hack' who wrote for money and therefore directly for the market, and who heralded a different kind of literary culture to the older aristocratic one based on patronage.

➲ **Arts**   In the arts, Handel – based in London from c.1712 – was the principal composer of the first half of the century. In painting, Willam Hogarth, Thomas Gainsborough, Sir Joshua Reynolds and George Romney were the dominant figures, while the second half of the century saw the caricatures of James Gillray; the production of furniture by Thomas Chippendale and George Hepplewhite; and the **Neo-Classical*** designs of Thomas Sheraton.

The architectural achievements of the period include: Sir John Vanbrugh's Blenheim Palace and Castle Howard, Yorkshire; James Gibbs's St Mary-le-Strand, St Martins-in-the-Fields, the Radcliffe Library, Oxford, and the Senate House, Cambridge; the 'Palladian' designs (i.e. based on the Classical work of the the Italian Renaissance architect, Andreas Palladio) of William Kent (Kensington Palace; Horse Guards Parade, Whitehall), Lord Burlington (Burlington House), and Kent and Burlington (Chiswick House; Holkham Hall, Norfolk). The Neo-Classical* work of John Wood the Elder (the North and South Parades, Queen Square, the Circus, and Prior Park, all in Bath), John Wood the Younger (Royal Crescent and the Assembly Rooms, Bath), Robert Adam (Kedleston Hall), and Robert and William Adam (Portland Place and Lansdowne House, London; the 'Old Quad', Edinburgh University). A rather different style of architecture appeared in 1784, as work began on the orientalist Brighton Pavilion for George, Prince of Wales (later Prince Regent and then George IV; see Chapter 4 under Regency*).

➲ **Literature**   In literature, the early part of the period was dominated by the **Augustan*** writers and the members of the Tory* (see Chapter 2) 'Scriblerus Club' (founded in 1713) which included Alexander Pope, Jonathan Swift, John Arbuthnot, John Gay and Viscount Bolingbroke, while the middle of it witnessed the immense achievement of Dr Johnson, poet, novelist, lexicographer, biographer and foundational English critic. But it also saw the so-called 'Rise of the [Realist] Novel'

(Daniel Defoe, Samuel Richardson, Henry Fielding, Tobias Smollett, Laurence Sterne) – despite the presence of Aphra Behn's 30 fictional works written some 30 years before Defoe's. However, the period presently under consideration did witness the increasing prominence of women writers, and they, like the male novelists, do not always or easily fit the Augustan* or Neo-Classical* labels (Lady Mary Wortley Montagu, Anne Finch, Eliza Haywood, Sarah Fielding, Clara Reeve, Anna Barbauld, Fanny Burney, Charlotte Smith, Elizabeth Inchbald, Mary Wollstonecraft).

Furthermore, and once again to illustrate just how precarious any notion of exact periodisation is, it is also worth noting how early in the period the work of writers began to appear whose concern with 'Sensibility' and 'Nature' foreshadowed the **Romantic*** movement around the turn of the 18th Century [see Chapter 4]. James Thomson and John Dyer published poems with 'transitional' elements in the late 1720s; Thomas Gray, Edward Young, Mark Akenside and William Collins were all active in the mid-1740s; James Macpherson's 'Ossian' poems appeared in the early 1760s; Horace Walpole's 'Gothic' novel, *The Castle of Otranto*, was published in 1764, and Thomas Chatterton's 'Rowley' forgeries were written later in the same decade; by the 1770s, the poetry of George Crabbe and William Cowper was being published, as was Henry Mackenzie's novel, *The Man of Feeling*; and by 1789, when the present 'period' ends, unmistakably Romantic works by Robert Burns, William Blake and William Beckford (the Gothic fantasy, *Vathek*) had been produced.

3.2 GEORGIAN I

An adjective used to define the period of the reigns of the Hanoverian* monarchs of Great Britain from the accession of George I in 1714 to the death of George IV in 1830.

Note that this should not be confused with **Georgian II***, which is the descriptor for the early years (*c*.1910–14) of the reign of King George V, and especially for a poetic movement, *Georgian Poetry*, which flourished shortly before the outbreak of the First World War [see Chapter 6.]

'Georgian' is seldom used these days to describe the literature of the Hanoverian period (perhaps because of the potential confusion noted above), but it is still widely used to describe the silverware, furniture and neo-classical architecture of the period.

3.3 THE ENLIGHTENMENT

The name given to an intellectual movement in Europe originating during the late 17th Century, which reached its apogee by the mid-18th Century and was a fundamental influence on the American and French Revolutions.

The movement was critical of traditional beliefs, superstitions and prejudices, and placed its central faith in human reason and strict scientific method. At its heart, therefore, Enlightenment thinking embraced notions of human progress, the rational perfectibility of humankind, and the universe as governed by observable laws and systematic principles. Such rationalism led, in the religious context, to anti-clericalism, deism and atheism, but it was also applied to ethical, social and political matters, seeing the state as the principal guardian of order and believing in tolerance, individualism and equality before the law.

It is represented in Germany by Gotthold Lessing; in France by Voltaire, Diderot, d'Alembert and other contributors to that symptomatic monument of the French Enlightenment, the *Encyclopédie, ou Dictionnaire Raisonné des Sciences, des Arts et des Métiers* (35 vols; 1751–76); and in Britain by the empirical philosopher, John Locke, the scientist and mathematician, Sir Isaac Newton, the Scottish atheist and sceptical philosopher, David Hume, the historian Edward Gibbon, and later in the century, by the economist and philosopher, Adam Smith, the political philosophers, William Godwin and Thomas Paine, and the radical feminist, Mary Wollstonecraft.

Aspects of the Enlightenment cast of mind are to be found in Augustan* literature, although never comprehensively or unproblematically, but the rejection of the irrational and the distrust of feelings and the imagination common to both certainly led to the Romantic* reaction at the end of the century [see Chapter 4]. While many Enlightenment ideas (e.g. reason, progress, equality, scientific truth) became the accepted foundations ('grand narratives') of Western thinking over the following two centuries, by the late 20th Century, poststructuralism, postmodernism and postcolonialism had challenged both the credibility of such 'universal' ideas and their Eurocentric partiality.

3.4 AUGUSTAN / AUGUSTANISM

'Augustan' is an adjective borrowed from the name given to the reign of Augustus Caesar, the first Roman Emperor (27 BC to AD 14).

Augustus Caesar restored Rome to peace, power and glory in the aftermath of a disastrous civil war and the assassination of Julius Caesar which ended the Roman republic. He beautified the city and patronised the arts, the period being exemplified in literature by the work of Virgil, Horace, Ovid, Propertius, Tibullus and Livy. In it most general sense, therefore, the term implies the height of classical artistic taste and refinement.

In British literary history, its application is somewhat various in terms of the length of period it covers. The OED gives its earliest usage as 1712 in reference to Jonathan Swift: 'King Charles the Second's Reign, which may be the Augustan Age of English Poetry'; hence one version of the period would see the years following the **Restoration*** of the monarchy under Charles II [see Chapter 2] as parallelling that of Augustus Caesar – relative peace restored to the nation after the Civil War and **Interregnum*** [see Chapter 2] and a monarch who patronised the arts and sciences. This was certainly a contemporary view amongst the supporters of the Restoration, and many literary historians still see the Augustan period as stretching from the the advent of John Dryden as a major literary figure to the death of Alexander Pope (1744) and Jonathan Swift (1745). A rather more limited conception of it is signalled by Oliver Goldsmith's 'Account of the Augustan Age in England' (1759) which sees the term as applying to the literature of Queen Anne's reign (1702–14), a view sustained by Matthew Arnold in 1861, who refers to 'the Augustan [Age] of Queen Anne'.

Further complications can be discerned in Horace Walpole's reference in 1772 to 'this our Augustan Age'; and when the term 'Augustanism' is first used (pejoratively) in 1903–4, we find the following period limits laid out: 'The period of Augustanism in English Literature – that age of acceptance which began after Milton and ended with Gray and Collins' (i.e. by the 1760s/1770s). But we should also accept, in our ongoing contest with periodisation, that Augustan principles underlie the work of Dr Johnson, that Jane Austen (1775–1817) is sometimes considered to be a 'late Augustan', and that, as noted in timeline 'narrative' **Literature** above, the transition from Neo-Classical* literature to that which promotes 'Sensibility' and evinces proto-Romantic* tendencies is apparent relatively early in the 18th Century.

Despite the above variations, the terms 'Augustan' and 'Augustanism' (in non-pejorative usage, those features of form, content and stance which are commonly found in the arts so defined) may be understood to include literary work from the later decades of the 17th Century through to the mid-18th Century, but exemplified most typically by the writings of such 'Augustans' as Dryden, Pope, Addison, Steele, Gay and Swift. The aesthetic characteristics of Augustan literature are outlined in the following gloss on the adjective Neo-Classical*.

3.5 NEO-CLASSICAL / NEO-CLASSICISM

In the arts, the terms used to describe work which displays a revival of interest in and veneration for the classical attitudes and styles of ancient Greece and Rome, and which is influenced by and/or imitates such models in seeking to emulate their pursuit of order, clarity, harmony, grace, humanity, self-discipline and rational beauty.

In British literary history, 18th-century Neo-Classicism is effectively coterminous with Augustanism*, which drew its inspiration from such works as the poems of Homer and Virgil, and the critical theory of Aristotle's *Poetics* and Horace's *Ars Poetica*. Symptomatically, John Dryden translated Virgil and Juvenal, and Alexander Pope, Homer, whilst legislative criticism became an important strategy in promoting literary theory and practice: Dryden, Pope, Jonathan Swift, Thomas Rhymer and John Dennis are significant names in this context, with Pope laying out the main tenets of English Neo-Classicism in his poem, *Essay on Criticism* (itself drawing heavily on the French critic Nicolas Boileau's *L'Art poétique* of 1674). Augustan Neo-Classicism is characterised by: a tendency to be conservative in its view that contemporary culture was necessarily inferior to that of the classical past (witness the fierce debate between the 'Ancients' and the 'Moderns' throughout the 1690s and 1700s, of which Swift's satirical essay *The Battle of the Books* is the best-known contribution in English); by valuing and admiring the 'proprieties': regularity and simplicity of form, order and proportion, elegance and polished wit; by encouraging emotional restraint and rating most highly art which displayed technical mastery.

Notions of 'decorum' lie at the heart of this, since the strict observation of formal conventions implies that the concept of what is fitting – both in art and in life – is premised on a sense of established or accepted values (as articulated in Pope's synoptic line from the *Essay on Man*, 'One truth is clear, WHATEVER IS, IS RIGHT'). In literary practice, decorum regulated distinctions between genres and determined which kinds of style and subject were in keeping with each other: for example, epic required an elevated style to match the heroic proportions of character and action, while a low style was suitable for comedy, in which ignoble vices and follies were ridiculed (Shakespeare's mingling of genres thus produced problems for Neo-Classical editors and critics; and it is also to the point here that Henry Fielding, in wryly claiming some status for the new, 'low' genre of the novel form, described his own *Joseph Andrews* as 'a comic epic poem in prose'). Such attitudes also explain the prevalence of Augustan 'poetic diction' (the use of stylised and stock epithets, classical references, artificial tropes, etc. to 'heighten' the language of poetry), and Augustanism's appropriation of classical genres and forms such as epic, tragedy, comedy, satire, polemic, the eclogue, the elegy, the epistle, the fable, the alexandrine, the heroic couplet and the ode. Satire, in particular, is a characteristic mode in high Augustan literature, with its ferocious ridiculing of deviation from accepted norms, of human folly and pretension; its deployment of parody (in, for example, Swift's *A Tale of a Tub* and *A Modest Proposal*) and mock-epic (especially in Dryden's and Pope's deflationary heroic couplets, but also in Fielding's use of bathos in *Tom Jones*). In addition, neo-classical principles, first exemplified in the work of the 17th-century French dramatists, Racine and Corneille, also underpin the dramatic criticism and heroic tragedies of Dryden, Thomas Otway's tragedies, *Alcibiades* (1675) and *Titus and Berenice* (1676; based on Racine), and Joseph Addison's tragedy, *Cato* (1713).

Timelines: 1700–1789

PERIOD	YEAR	INTERNATIONAL AND POLITICAL CONTEXTS	SOCIAL AND CULTURAL CONTEXTS	AUTHORS	INDICATIVE TITLES
	1700	Death of only surviving son of Princess Anne [Mary II's staunchly Protestant sister] creates Succession problem [v.1694]; Resumption Act [restoring all forfeited Ir. lands to public] finally passed; 2nd Partition Treaty between William III & Louis XIV on Sp. issue; Rotherhithe wet dock begun in London; Dampier visits New Guinea; administrative organisation of Bengal by Sir George Eyre	[c.] 1st bonded warehouses in Britain; Astell, *Some Reflections on Marriage* [warns women of the potential tyranny of the institution]; Francis Moore, *Vox Stellarum* [later pub.d as *Old Moore's Almanack*]; Samuel Sewall, *Selling of Joseph* [1st American protest against slavery]. **Art:** [−1712] Sir John Vanbrugh's Castle Howard, Yorkshire, built **Lit. 'Events':** John Dryden dies; Cotton Collection of early mss, books & coins given to the nation	**P:** Dryden Thomas Brown (1663–1704) **Dr:** Cibber Congreve Farquhar Susanna Centlivre (c. 1667–1723)	*Fables, Ancient and Modern* [paraphrases of Chaucer, Ovid & Boccaccio] *Amusements Serious and Comical* [misc. satires, epigrams, etc.] *Love Makes a Man* [comedy] & adaptn of Shakespeare's *Richard III* [1st pf.d] *The Way of the World* [comedy] *Sir Harry Wildair* [comedy] *The Perjured Husband; or, The Adventures in Venice* [tragi-comedy]
	1701	James II dies – Louis XIV recognises son, James Edward Stuart [the 'Old Pretender'] as 'James III'; Britain joins German House of Hanover in Grand Alliance against France – leads to Act of Settlement: estab.s that Protestant Hanoverians have constitutional right to British throne [v.1714] – many new constraints on royal prerogative – French impose embargo on British goods; Tory ministers impeach Whig ministers over Partition Treaties – acquitted	Jethro Tull invents horse-drawn seed-drill; Collegiate School of America fnd.d [later Yale University – Library also estab.d]; Antoine Cadillac fnds Fr. settlement at Detroit	**Pr/F:** Daniel Defoe (1660–1731) Sir Richard Steele (1672–1729) **Dr:** Pix Steele Trotter	*The True-Born Englishman* [pamphlet] *The Christian Hero* [religious treatise] *The Double Distress & The Czar of Muscovy* [tragedies] *The Funeral, or grief à la mode* [comedy] *The Unhappy Penitent* [tragedy]
	1702	William III dies, Queen Anne succeeds; [−1713] War of Spanish Succession – Eng. attack on Cadiz fails, but Fr-Sp. fleet routed at Vigo Bay; Assiento Guinea Co. fnd.d to promote slave trade from Africa to America [v.1713]; [c.] French settle in Alabama	*The Daily Courant* – 1st regular daily paper – pub.d in London; John Kersey, *A New English Dictionary* [1st to include ordinary Eng. words]; [−1703] Edward Hyde, Earl of Clarendon, *History of the Rebellion and Civil Wars in England* [pub.d posthm.] **Lit. 'Events':** early Eng. pantomime pf.d at Drury Lane	**Pr/F:** Defoe **Dr:** Cibber Nicholas Rowe (1674–1718)	*The Shortest Way with Dissenters* [satirical religious polemic – leads to imprisonment for seditious libel] *She Would and She Would Not* *Tamerlane* [tragedy]
	1703	Parliament increases size of army & navy; 'The Great Storm' devastates S. England & Channel shipping – 1st Eddystone lighthouse destroyed [v.1686]; Anglo-Portuguese Methuen Treaties – secure naval bases, but commit English to Peninsula campaigns & preferential markets for port, madeira & Eng. cloth; Peter the Great fnds St Petersburg; Delaware becomes separate colony [v.1682]	[−1727] Newton, President of Royal Society. **Art:** Buckingham Palace begun for Duke [purchased by George III in 1762]; [−1713] Kneller, 42 portraits of the 'Kit-Cat Club' [Whig drinking/intellectual artistic club] – incls portrait of 'Sir John Vanbrugh', c.1705, NPG] **Lit. 'Events':** [>] Defoe recruited by Robert Harley to secret service for Tory gvnmt	**P:** Defoe **Dr:** Centlivre Rowe Steele	*Hymn to the Pillory* [mock-pindaric ode re. imprisonment in 1702] *The Beau's Duel & The Stolen Heiress* [comedies] *The Fair Penitent* *The Lying Lover*
	1704	Scottish Act of Security reserves right to choose own successor after Q. Anne; 'Queen Anne's Bounty' for relief of poor clergy; Marlborough & Prince Eugene's victory over French at Blenheim [celebrated in Wren's new St Paul's, 1705]; British fleet captures Gibralta	[>] Beau Nash influential in Bath; Newton, *Opticks* [in English]; Leibnitz, *New Essays on Human Understanding* [pub.d 1765]. **Int. Lit.:** Jean François Regnard, *Les Folies amoureuses* [Fr. comic play]. **Music:** George Frederick Handel [compl] 'St John Passion' **Lit. 'Events':** [−1712] Defoe single-handedly writes & edits thrice-weekly *Review*	**Pr/F:** Jonathan Swift (1667–1745) **Dr:** Cibber	*The Battle of the Books* [satire; v.1690s for 'Ancients v. Moderns' controversy] & *A Tale of a Tub* [satire] *The Careless Husband* [sentimental comedy]

STUART (CONT.)/AUGUSTAN

1705	Constitutional & party conflict between Lords & Commons at its height; Commissioners meet to negotiate Union between England & Scotland; English take Barcelona	Halley predicts return of his comet in 1758; Newcomen builds improved steam engine. **Music:** Handel, 'Almira' [opera]. **Art:** [–1722] Vanbrugh designs & builds Blenheim Palace – presented to Duke of Marlborough by Queen Anne	**P:** Bernard Mandeville (1670–1733)	The Grumbling Hive [satirical poem; rev.d edtns, 1714, 1723, as The Fable of the Bees: or Private Vices, Public Benefits]
			John Philips (1676–1709)	The Splendid Shilling [burlesque in Miltonic blank verse] & Blenheim [celebratory poem]
			Pr/F: Defoe	The Apparition of Mrs Veal [ghost story]
			Manley	The Secret History of Queen Zarah [satirical novel]
			Dr: Centlivre	The Basset Table [comedy]
			Steele	The Tender Husband
1706	Articles of Union have rough passage in Scots Parliament – anxiety about securing Presbyterianism – Eng. troops posted on border; Marlborough routs French at Ramillies – French open peace talks; successful defence of Charleston, S. Carolina, against French & Spanish	[–1709] 2nd Eddystone lighthouse built **Lit. 'Events':** Evelyn's Diary ends [v.1660]	**P:** Congreve	'A Pindaric Ode to the Queen' [with 'A Discourse on the Pindaric Ode']
			Dr: Farquhar	The Recruiting Officer
			Manley	Almyna; or, The Arabian Vow [tragedy]
			Pix	The Adventures in Madrid [comedy]
1707	Act of Union [of Eng. & Scots Parliaments] creates United Kingdom of Great Britain [UK; religion, education & laws remain separate]; English defeated at Almanza – allies' siege of Toulon fails	Edward Lhuyd, Archaeologica Britannica [re. Celtic languages]. **Int. Lit.:** Alain-René Le Sage, Diable boiteux & Crispin rival de son Maître [Fr. plays]. **Music:** Isaac Watts, Hymns and Spiritual Songs (incls 'When I survey the wondrous cross'). **Art:** [–1717] Sir James Thornhill creates Painted Hall, Greenwich	**Dr:** Farquhar	The Beaux Stratagem
1708	Whig Ministry attacked for conduct of war in Spain; Marlborough & Eugene rout French at Oudenarde; 'Old Pretender' [v.1701] makes failed expedition to Scotland; [–1709] 2 successive appalling harvests	[c.] early excavations of Pompeii & Herculaneum. **Int. Lit.:** Regnard, Le Légataire universal [Fr. comedy]; 1st Ger. theatre estab.d at Vienna. **Art:** New figures of Gog & Magog replace those destroyed in Great Fire at Guildhall	**P:** Philips	Cyder. A Poem. In Two Books [political imitation of Virgil's Georgics]
			Pr/F: Swift	The Bickerstaff Papers
1709	[Jan.] Thames freezes – savage winter thro'out Europe – famine in France; Marlborough & Eugene capture Tournai & defeat French at Malplaquet, but with high cost to Allies – war increasingly unpopular at home – French sue for peace – talks at the Hague fail; 1st Ger. mass emigration to Pennsylvania	1st coke in England used to smelt iron; George Berkeley, New Theory of Vision. **Int. Lit.:** Le Sage, Turcaret [satirical play]. **Music:** [c.–1710] Bartolommeo Cristofori produces 1st piano in Italy. **Art:** 1st European porcelain made at Dresden. **Lit. 'Events':** [–1710] 1st Eng. Copyright Act [protects rights of writers & publishers]; [–1711] Richard Steele's periodical, The Tatler, pub.d; Nicholas Rowe, early edtn of Shakespeare's works	**P:** Alexander Pope (1688–1744)	Pastorals [poems; wrtn 1704–7]
			Pr/F: Defoe	History of the Union of Great Britain
			Manley	The New Atalantis [sic; anti-Whig satirical fiction]
			Dr: Centlivre	The Busy Body [2nd Pt, Mar-Plot, 1710] & The Man's Bewitched [comedies]
1710	'Sacheverell riots': High Church supporters attack Dissenters' meeting houses [& v.1715]; Whig Ministry dismissed – replaced by Tories with large majority [led by Harley & Bolingbroke]; Allied victories at Almenara & Saragossa – English defeated at Brihuega; English & New England militia take Acadia [Nova Scotia]	3-colour printing invented; Berkeley, Treatise on the Principles of Human Knowledge. **Music:** Handel becomes Kapellmeister to Elector of Hanover [future King George I of Great Britain]	**Pr/F:** Swift	Meditation up on a Broomstick [parody of pious essay], [c.–1713] Journal to Stella [letters wrtn; pub. posthm. as J to S, 1766] & [–1711] writes 33 issues of Tory periodical, The Examiner
			Dr: Congreve	Works

Period	Year	International and Political Contexts	Social and Cultural Contexts	Authors	Indicative Titles
	1711	Q. Anne creates 12 Tory peers to ensure approval of peace with France – dismissal of Marlborough as C. in C. [replaced by Duke of Ormonde, a Jacobite]; Occasional Conformity Bill passed [against Dissenters' strategy for gaining public office]; South Sea Trading Co. formed & 'buys' from gvnmt a portion of the National Debt to 'float' as Co. shares [v.1713 & 1720]; Eng. attack on Quebec fails	Birmingham Cathedral begun; Queen Anne estab.s Ascot races; 3rd Earl of Shaftesbury, *Characteristicks* [philosophical writings]. **Music:** tuning fork invented; Handel, 'Rinaldo' [opera]. **Art:** present St Paul's Cathedral finally completed by Wren [v.1675]; Kneller opens London Academy of Arts & pnts 'Sir Christopher Wren' [NPG]. **Lit. 'Events':** [–1712] Joseph Addison & Steele's periodical, *The Spectator*, pub.d; Delariviere Manley succeeds Swift as editor of *The Examiner*	**P:** Pope Lady Mary Wortley Montagu (1689–1762) **Pr/F:** Swift	*An Essay on Criticism* [wrtn 1709; **Theory/Crit.**] Pope's autographed ms. of her poems & *Court Eclogues* [cause of celebrated row with Pope] *The Conduct of the Allies* [pamphlet attacking Whig war policy]
	1712	Sir Robert Walpole in Tower for alleged peculation; Peace Congress, Utrecht – Parliament make separate peace policy – English & French truce – French-Dutch truce; last Eng. judicial trial for witchcraft; Moghul Empire in India starts to decline	Newspaper Stamp Act – 'censorship by price'. **Music:** Arcangelo Corelli's 12 'Concerti Grossi' estab. the concerto in classic form; Handel returns to England – 'Il pastor fido' & 'Teseo' [operas]	**P:** Pope **Pr/F:** John Arbuthnot (1667–1735) **Dr:** Centlivre	*The Rape of the Lock* [2 cantos; enlarged to 5 cantos, 1714] *The History of John Bull* [5 satirical pamphlets against Marlborough – originates stereotype of Englishman] *The Perplexed Lovers* [comedy]
	1713	Peace of Utrecht ends European War of Spanish Succession – French cede Acadia, Hudson's Bay & Newfoundland to Britain & recognise Protestant Succession – Gibraltar ceded by Spain & 'Assiento' contract [to supply slaves to Sp. colonies in Americas]; South Sea Co. takes over whole National Debt & continues to sell inflated shares [v.1720]	**Music:** Handel, 'Te Deum' [for Peace of Utrecht]; Alessandro Scarlatti, 'St Francis Neri' [oratorio]. **Art:** [c.–1720] Sir James Thornhill executes decorative paintings on walls & ceilings at Hampton Court, All Souls College, Oxford, Blenheim Palace & St Paul's Cathedral. **Lit. 'Events':** Tory 'Scriblerus Club' formed [incls Pope, Swift, Arbuthnot, Gay]; Addison & Steele edit *The Guardian*	**P:** Pope Anne Finch, Countess of Winchilsea (1661–1720) **Dr:** Joseph Addison (1672–1719)	*Windsor Forest* *Miscellany Poems on Several Occasions, Written by a Lady* *Cato* [tragedy]
	1714	Q. Anne's illness promotes Succession anxieties – Tory ministers negotiate with Old Pretender – Anne dies [end of Stuart line], King George I [Elector of Hanover] accedes [v.1701]; Whig ministry formed; Schism Act prevents Dissenters from school-teaching in England without bishop's licence; Parliament offers £20k reward for discovery of NW Passage	Worcester College, Oxford, fnd.d; [–1715] Gabriel Daniel Fahrenheit invents mercury thermometer. **Art:** Gibbons, master wood-carver to George I; [c.–1729] Nicholas Hawksmoor builds 6 London churches [e.g. St Anne's, Limehouse, St Mary Woolnoth & Christchurch, Spitalfields]	**P:** John Gay (1685–1732) **Pr/F:** Manley **Dr:** Rowe	*The Fan* & *The Shepherd's Week* *The Adventures of Rivella* [autobiog. fiction] *The Tragedy of Jane Shore*
	1715	Gen. Elec: large Whig majority; pro-Jacobite High Church riots in London – Tory ministers impeached – Bolingbroke flees to France – Old Pretender – Habeas Corpus Act suspended; Riot Act passed – Scotland – Jacobite rebellion – defeated at Preston; Walpole, Chancellor of Exchequer; 1st Liverpool dock opens; Louis XIV dies; E. India Co. sets up trading post at Canton	Total eclipse of sun – accurately predicted by Halley. **Int. Lit.:** [–1735] Le Sage, *Gil Blas* [picaresque novel]. **Music:** Watts's hymns, *Divine Songs for Children*; Handel, 'Amadigi' [opera]; A. Scarlatti, 'Tigrane' [opera]. **Art:** [–1720] Wanstead House, Essex, built [early Palladian designs by Colin Campbell]; [–1740] Hawksmoor designs quadrangle at All Soul's College Oxford	**P:** Pope Prior **Dr:** Rowe Gay **Lit. 'Events':**	[c.–1726] edits & trans Homer's *Iliad* & *Odyssey* [c.] *Solomon on the Vanity of the World* [soliloquy in couplets] *The Tragedy of Lady Jane Grey* *The What D'Ye Call It: A Tragi-Comi-Pastoral Farce* Nicholas Rowe, Poet Laureate; [–1716] Addison launches periodical, *The Freeholder*
	1716	[–1911] Septennial Act extends duration of Parliament to 7 yrs; leaders of 1715 revolt in England executed; Old Pretender leaves Scotland; Royal Regiment of Artillery fnd.d; Mogul Empire awards E. India Co. trade concessions	Mineral waters discv.d at Cheltenham. **Art:** [c.] rebuilding of Burlington House in Palladian style begins [designed by Campbell]; Studley Royal Gardens, Yorkshire, laid out; Antoine Watteau [pnt] 'The Conversation'	**P:** Gay **Dr:** Centlivre	*Trivia: or, The Art of Walking the Streets of London* *The Cruel Gift* [tragedy]

STUART (CONT.)/AUGUSTAN   HANOVERIAN

	History/Politics	Science/Art/Music	Authors	Works
1717	'Whig schism' – Walpole & others forced out of office; Triple Alliance of Britain, France & Holland; [>] Russia enters general European system; [–1719] Fr. Mississippi Co. fnd.d – acquires monopoly of trade in Louisiana; Prussian colonies in Africa sold to Dutch	Value of gold guinea fixed at 21s; [c.] Lady Mary Wortley Montagu intro.s smallpox inoculation in England; Downing College, Cambridge, endowed [Charter, 1800]. **Music:** Handel, 'Water Music' [pub.d, 1740]; Johann Sebastian Bach, 'Little Organ Book' [46 preludes/chorales]. **Art:** James Gibbs builds St Mary-le-Strand; Sir John Vanbrugh's house at Greenwich, built; Kneller, 'Jacob Tonson' [NPG]; Watteau, 'Pilgrimage on the Isle of Cythera'	**P:** Pope **Dr:** Gay, Arbuthnot & Pope Manley	*Works* [incls 'Elegy to the Memory of an Unfortunate Lady' & 'Eloisa to Ebelard'] *Three Hours after Marriage* [satirical play] *Lucius, the First Christian King of Britain* [tragedy]
1718	Secret gvnmt talks with South Sea Co. over settlement of National Debt; Quadruple Alliance [Triple & Austria] against Spain – Byng destroys Sp. fleet off Cap Passaro; Fr. Mississippi Co. fnds New Orleans; Bahamas pirates suppressed	1st bank-notes appear – Bank of England appoints a paper-maker; London Society of Antiquaries fnd.d; 'Yale University' moves to New Haven & is so named [v.1701]. **Int. Lit.:** Voltaire, *Oedipe* [Fr. play pf.d]. **Art:** Ebberston Hall, Yorkshire [Palladian style], designed; Elysée Palace, Paris, built; [c.] Watteau, 'Fêtes galantes' [series of paintings]	**P:** Allan Ramsay (1686–1758) **Dr:** Centlivre Cibber	*Christ's Kirk on the Green* [adds 2 new cantos to old Scots poem] *A Bold Stroke for a Wife* [comedy] *The Nonjuror* [adaptn of Molière's *Tartuffe*]
1719	Occasional Conformity & Schism Acts repealed; Peerage Bill [to restrict Crown's right to create peers] passed by Lords – rejected by Commons; Statute enables Eng. Parliament to legislate for Ireland; Spanish [pro-Jacobite] invasion of Scotland defeated at Glenshiel	Sterling silver standard resumed [v.1697]; water-powered silk factory estab.d on River Derwent, Derbyshire; Westminster Hospital fnd.d; [–1723] radical Whig 'Cato's Letters' appear in *London Journal*. **Music:** Watts, *The Psalms of David Imitated* [incls 'Time Like an Ever Rolling Stream']; Handel completes 'Chandos Anthems'	**P:** Thomas D'Urfey (1653–1723) **Pr/F:** Defoe	[–1720] *Wit and Mirth, or Pills to Purge Melancholy* [6 vols; songs] (*Serious Reflections of Robinson Crusoe*)
1720	'South Sea Bubble' inflates & bursts – widespread losses & bankruptcies – gvnmt again responsible for 'liquidised' National Debt; peace between Quadruple Alliance & Spain; national bankruptcy in France; [c.] 1st colonial settlements in Vermont	[–1726] William Stukeley pubs pioneering fieldwork at Stonehenge & Avebury. **Int. Lit.:** Voltaire, *Artémise* [play]. **Music:** Handel, 'Acis and Galatea' & 'Esther'. **Art:** [>] salt-glazed pottery made in Staffordshire; Cavendish Square, London, built. **Lit. 'Events':** 1st Haymarket Theatre, London, built	**Pr/F:** Defoe	*Adventures of Captain Singleton*
1721	S. Sea Co. directors condemned; Walpole becomes 1st Lord of the Treasury & Chancellor of the Exchequer [in effect, Britain's 1st PM] – 'restores Public Credit'; Act to protect wool & silk manufacture from competition by painted calicoes; Dutch buy last Ger. factories in Africa	Regular postal servive estab.d between London & the North; Nathan Bailey, *An Universal Etymological English Dictionary* [& 1727: used by Dr Johnson – v.1755]. **Int. Lit.:** Montesquieu, *Lettres persanes* [Fr. social satire]. **Music:** J.S. Bach, 'Brandenburg Concertos'. **Art:** [–1727] Gibbs builds St Martin's-in-the-Fields; Stourhead, Wiltshire, built [Palladian house by Campbell]	**P:** Ramsay **Dr:** Eliza Haywood (c.1693–1756)	*Poems* *The Fair Captive* [tragedy]
1722	Gen. Elec: Whigs gain increased majority; Jacobite ['Atterbury'] plot revealed – Habeas Corpus Act suspended; William Wood contracted to mint Ir. copper coinage ['Wood's Half-Pence'] – [–1725] 'patriotic' protest in Ireland	Guy's Hospital fnd.d. **Int. Lit.:** Pietro Metastasio, *The Garden of Hesperides* [It. masque]. **Music:** J.S. Bach, *The Well-tempered Clavier* [piano preludes & fugues; vol. 2, 1744] & 'Anna Magdalena' suites. **Art:** [–1727] Houghton Hall, Norfolk, built for Sir Robert Walpole [Palladian designs by Campbell]	**P:** Ramsay **Pr/F:** Defoe **Dr:** Centlivre Steele	*Fables and Tales* *A Journal of the Plague Year, Moll Flanders & Captain Jack* *The Artifice* [comedy] *The Conscious Lovers* [sentimental comedy]
1723	Bolingbroke pardoned – returns from exile; Walpole reduces duty on tea; Workhouse Test Act to aid the poor	**Music:** J.S. Bach, 'St John Passion'. **Art:** Wren dies; [–1727] William Kent designs Kensington Palace	**Dr:** Haywood	*A Wife to Be Let* [comedy]

PERIOD	YEAR	INTERNATIONAL AND POLITICAL CONTEXTS	SOCIAL AND CULTURAL CONTEXTS	AUTHORS	INDICATIVE TITLES
	1724	Earl Granville, Lord Lieutenant, sent to pacify Ireland; [>] gin-drinking becomes popular in England	Burnet, *History of My Own Times* [pub. posthm. & 1734]. **Music:** Three Choirs Festival begins [oldest Eng. music festival] **Lit. 'Events':** Longman, publishers, fnd.d	**P:** Ramsay **Pr/F:** Defoe Swift	[–1737] *Tea-Table Miscellany* [4 vols; coll. of Scots songs] *Roxana* & [–1727] *A Tour through the Whole Island of Great Britain* [–1725] *The Drapier's Letters* [re. 'Wood's Half-Pence' – v.1722]
	1725	1st Treaty of Vienna [Spain & Empire] arouses anti-Jacobite fears in England, also about trade & balance of power; new Book of Rates [customs duties] undertaken; Malt Tax riots in Scotland	**Int. Lit.:** [–1726] Mme de Sevigné's letters pub.d [v.1671]. **Art:** [–1729] Earl of Burlington & William Kent build Chiswick House; [c.] Antonio Canaletto [pnt] 'The Grand Canal seen from the Ca'Foscari'	**Pr/F:** Haywood **Dr:** Ramsay **Lit. 'Events':**	*Memoirs of a Certain Island adjacent to Utopia* [pub.d anon.] *The Gentle Shepherd, a Pastoral Comedy* [pub.d; pf.d, 1729] Pope's edtn of Shakespeare pub.d
	1726	War with Spain imminent – navy deployed; poor Ir. harvest – onset of famine	1st issue of new opposition [Tory] journal, *The Craftsman*. **Lit. 'Events':** 1st circulating library opened in Edinburgh by Allan Ramsay	**P:** John Dyer (1699–1757) James Thomson (1700–48) **Pr/F:** Swift	'Grongar Hill' & 'The Country Walk' *Winter* [with *Summer*, 1727; *Spring*, 1728; *Autumn*, 1730 – pub.d as *The Seasons*] *Gulliver's Travels*
	1727	George I dies, King George II accedes – Walpole remains PM; Gen. Elec. – Tory strength lowest since 1679; 1st Annual Act to remove disabilities from Eng. Dissenters; [–1729] epidemics & high mortality in England & Wales; Spanish blockade Gibraltar	**Art:** [c.] Canaletto, 'The Mole and the Ducal Palace' **Lit. 'Events':** [–1732] Pope, Swift, Gay, Arbuthnot & Bolingbroke pub. periodical vols of *Miscellanies* [satires & poems]	**P:** Thomson **Pr/F:** Defoe Gay Haywood	'To the Memory of Sir Isaac Newton' *The Complete English Tradesman* [1st ser.] *The Secret History of the Present Intrigues of the Court of Caramania* [pub.d anon.]
	1728	Walpole's majorities in Commons huge & impregnable; publication of parliamentary debates declared a breach of privilege; poor harvest in Ireland; Spain ceases hostilities; Vitus Bering discovers 'his' Straits between Asia & America	Ephraim Chambers pubs *Cyclopaedia, A Universal Dictionary of Arts and Sciences* [2 vols; 1st encyclopaedia]. **Int. Lit.:** Voltaire, *La Henriade* [Fr. epic poem]. **Art:** [–1736] John Wood 'the Elder' builds Queen's Square, Bath [Palladian]. **Lit. 'Events':** [>] Sir Robert Walpole & regime subjected to literary-political satire by Gay, Pope, Fielding & others	**P:** Pope **Pr/F:** Haywood **Dr:** Cibber Gay	[–1729] *The Dunciad* [1st versions; v.1742–3] *The Disguised Prince, or, The Beautiful Parisian* *The Provoked Husband* [completes Vanbrugh's unfinished play, *A Journey to London*] *The Beggar's Opera* [music by J.C. Pepusch]
	1729	Public & gin houses subject to high duties to curb public drunkenness; worst killer epidemics of 18C sweep England & Wales; Treaty of Seville ends war in Europe; Bahamas become a Crown Colony; N. & S. Carolina estab.d as Crown Colonies; Baltimore fnd.d	John Wesley becomes leader of small 'methodist' society in Oxford. **Music:** [–1757] Domenico Scarlatti [compl] harpsichord music; J.S. Bach, 'St Matthew Passion'. **Art:** [>] Gibbs rebuilds St Bartholomew's Hospital; William Hogarth [pnt] 'Wedding of Stephen Beckingham and Mary Cox'	**P:** Thomson **Pr/F:** Swift **Dr:** Cibber Gay Haywood Thomson	'Britannia' [jingoistic poem attacking Walpole's war policy] 'A Modest Proposal' [satirical pamphlet] *Love in a Riddle* [ballad opera] *Polly* [sequel to *The Beggar's Opera* – banned but pub.d – 1st pf.d, 1777] *Frederick, Duke of Brunswick-Lunenburgh* [tragedy] [–1730] *Sophonisba* [tragedy]
	1730	Parliamentary storm over French refortification of Dunkirk; duties on salt abolished; Walpole opens secret negotiations with Empire in Vienna to resolve British problems in Europe	John & Charles Wesley fnd Methodist Society at Oxford; Royal Infirmary, Edinburgh, fnd.d; [>] 'Turnip' Townshend intros 4-year rotation of crops in Norfolk; Matthew Tindal, *Christianity as Old as the Creation* ['Deist's Bible']. **Int. Lit.:** Pierre Marivaux, *Le Jeu de l'amour et du hasard* [Fr. comedy]. **Art:** Gibbs builds Senate House,	**Dr:** Henry Fielding (1707–54) **Lit. 'Events':**	*Tom Thumb: A Tragedy* [rev.d as *The Tragedy of Tragedies*, 1731] Colley Cibber, Poet Laureate; [–1737] *The Grub Street Journal* pub.d

HANOVERIAN/AUGUSTAN

Year	History & Politics	Science, Society & the Arts	Literature
1731	PM 1st resides at 10 Downing Street; 2nd Treaty of Vienna – Spain partly satisfied, but hostilities between Spanish & British mercantile shipping in Central America continue – Spanish seize the 'Rebecca' – Captain Jenkins loses an ear [v.1739]; [–1732] Georgia, last British colony in America, fnd.d	Cambridge; Burlington builds [Palladian] Assembly Rooms, York; [c.] Canaletto, 'The Bucintoro Returning to the Molo on Ascension Day'. [–1914] The Gentleman's Magazine 1st pub.d; French abolished as legal language in England; Benjamin Franklin fnds Philadelphia free library & [–1751] State House [later Independence Hall] built; Voltaire, Histoire de Charles XII [of Sweden]. **Int. Lit.:** [–1741] Marivaux, La Vie de Marianne [unfinished novel]; L'Abbé Prévost, Manon Lescaut [Fr. psychological novel]. **Art:** [1730–1] Hogarth, 'A Harlot's Progress' [paintings destroyed by fire, 1755; engravings made, 1732]	**P:** Pope — [1731–5] Moral Essays [4 'Epistles' to Burlington (1731), Bathurst (1733), Cobham (1734), a Lady (Martha Blount; 1735)]. **Dr:** George Lillo (1693–1739) — The London Merchant [domestic tragedy]. **Lit. 'Events':** Daniel Defoe dies
1732	Parliamentary rows over Salt Tax – Act passed – duties reimposed; massive frauds revealed in tobacco/wine trades & Customs – 'Excise Scheme' proposed – The Craftsman [v.1726] furiously attacks both actions	Linnaeus visits Lapland & starts botany collection; Benjamin Franklin, Poor Richard's Almanack. **Int. Lit.:** Voltaire, Zaïre [drama]; Carlo Goldoni, Belisario [It. tragedy].	**Lit. 'Events':** 1st theatre ['Royal'] opens at Covent Garden
1733	Extensive Parliamentary & public opposition to Excise scheme; Molasses Act imposes duties on imports to American colonies from [mainly French] W. Indies – [>] widespread evasion of them; [–1738] War of Polish Succession begins: France, Spain & Sardinia v. Austria & Russia [over rival candidates for Polish throne]	John Kay invents the 'flying shuttle' for weaving. **Music:** Handel, 'Athalea' & 'Deborah' [operas]; J.S. Bach, 'B-minor Mass'. **Art:** Hogarth, 'A Modern Midnight Conversation', 'Southwark Fair' & [–1735] [pnt & engrv.] 'A Rake's Progress' [series of 8 paintings; Sloane Museum]; [c.–1734] Canaletto, 'Venice: A Regatta on the Grand Canal' [Royal Coll.]; Jean-Baptiste Chardin [pnt] 'Lady Sealing a Letter' & 'Washerwoman'	**P:** Pope — [–1734] An Essay on Man & [–1738] Imitations of Horace [prefaced by 'An Epistle from Mr Pope to Dr Arbuthnot', 1735]. Lord Hervey (1696–1743) [with Lady Mary Wortley Montagu] — Verses Addressed to the Imitator of Horace [satire on Pope; Hervey is 'Sporus' in 'Epistle to Arbuthnot'; Lady WM is 'Sappho' in 'Epistle to a Lady' & elsewhere]
1734	Gen. Elec: stormy campaign around Excise issue – greatly reduced majority for Walpole's ministry; [–1786] Anglo-Russian trade treaty; 8000 Protestants expelled from Salzburg emigrate to Georgia	Lloyd's List [later Lloyd's Register of Shipping] 1st issued – oldest daily paper; Voltaire, Lettres sur les Anglais; Emanuel Swedenborg, Opera philisophica et mineralia [metaphysics & metallurgy]. **Int. Lit.:** Marivaux, Le Paysan parvenu [novel]. **Music:** J.S. Bach, 'Christmas Oratorio'. **Art:** Holkham Hall, Norfolk, begun [Palladian designs by Kent & Burlington]	**Lit. 'Events':** Lewis Theobald's edtn of The Plays of Shakespeare pub.d
1735	Parliament votes large increases for Army & Navy in view of war in Europe; William Pitt becomes MP for Old Sarum [family 'Rotten Borough']; 'Hogarth's (Copyright) Act' passed to protect engravers from piracy; Fr. E. India Co. estab.s sugar industry in Mauritius & Réunion	Freedom of press estab.d in New England; Russian Imperial Ballet School fnd.d at St Petersburg; Bolingbroke, A Dissertation upon Parties [attacks Walpole & Whigs]; Linnaeus, Systema Natura. **Art:** Trevi Fountain, Rome, built; [–1748] Wood the Elder builds Prior Park, near Bath; Hogarth, 'The Pool of Bethesda' & 'The Good Samaritan' [St Bart's]	**P:** Thomson — [–1736] Liberty. William Somerville (1675–1742) — The Chase [4 Bks; in praise of hunting]
1736	London weavers, fearful of losing their livelihood, attack Ir. workers' property in Shoreditch & Spitalfields; Act passed to raise money by lottery for stone bridge over Thames at Westminster; all statutes against witchcraft repealed in England & Scotland; Gin Act passed to control drinking epidemic; Porteous Riots in Edinburgh – Captain of Guard lynched after firing on a crowd watching a hanging	The chronometer invented; india-rubber brought to Europe; [–1738] J. Wesley goes to Georgia as missionary & [c.] begins Journal [–1790; 1st printed 1739]; Joseph Butler, The Analogy of Religion. **Music:** Handel, 'Alexander's Feast' [oratorio; based on Dryden's 'Ode on St Cecilia's Day' – v.1697]	**Pr/F:** H. Fielding — Pasquin, a Dramatic Satire on the Times [attacking Walpole]. **Dr:** Lillo — The Fatal Curiosity [domestic tragedy]

PERIOD	YEAR	INTERNATIONAL AND POLITICAL CONTEXTS	SOCIAL AND CULTURAL CONTEXTS	AUTHORS	INDICATIVE TITLES
	1737	Long quarrel between George II & Frederick, Prince of Wales, culminates in latter becoming permanent focus of opposition to king's ministers – Queen Caroline [Walpole's main supporter] dies; Bill to punish Edinburgh for Porteous riots alienates Scottish members at Westminster; Richmond, Virginia, fnd.d	Linnaeus, *Genera Platarum & Critica Botanica* [origins of modern botany]. **Int. Lit.**. Marivaux, *Les Fausses confidences* [comedy]. **Music:** J. Wesley pub.s *Collection of Psalms and Hymns*. **Art:** [–1749] Gibbs builds Radcliffe Library, Oxford; [c.] Jonathan Richardson [pnt] 'Alexander Pope' [NPG] **Lit. 'Events':** Theatres Licensing Act estab.s Lord Chamberlain's censorship of all plays [partly prompted by Fielding's satires of 1736–37]	**P:** William Shenstone (1714–63) Charlotte Lennox (1720–1804) **Pr/F:** Wortley Montagu **Dr:** H. Fielding	*The Schoolmistress* [in Spenserian stanzas] *Poems on Several Occasions* *The Nonsense of Common Sense* *The Historical Register for 1736* [satire on Walpole]
	1738	Merchants petition Commons over Sp. attacks on British shipping – esp.ly in Americas; 3rd Treaty of Vienna ends War of Polish Succession	Spinning machines using rollers 1st invented; Bolingbroke, in France, writes *The Idea of a Patriot King* [pub. 1749]. **Music:** Handel, 'Saul' [oratorio]. **Art:** Chardin, 'The Cellar Boy' [Glasgow Univ.]; Richardson, 'George Vertue' [NPG]	**P:** (Dr) Samuel Johnson (1709–84) **Pr/F:** Gay **Dr:** Thomson	*London: A Poem* [pub.d anon., 'imitation' of Juvenal's 3rd satire] *Fables* [2nd ser.; pub. posthm.] *Agamemnon* [tragedy]
	1739	Walpole yields to demand for war with Spain – 'War of Jenkins's Ear' [v.1731] – merges into War of Austrian Succession [v.1740] – Puerto Bello, base of Sp. revenue ships on Isthmus of Panama, captured; Dick Turpin, highwayman, hanged; severe frost in Ireland for 7 wks – much damage to livestock & crops; French reach Colorado	George Whitefield & J. Wesley begin open-air preaching near Bristol – 1st Methodist chapel fnd.d & meeting place at Moorfields, London estab.d; Philosophical Society fnd.d; Royal Society of Edinburgh fnd.d; [–1740] David Hume, *A Treatise of Human Nature*. **Music:** Charles Wesley [comp] 'Hark the Herald Angels Sing'; Handel, 'Israel in Egypt'. **Art:** [–1740] Chardin, 'Le Bénédicité' & 'Industrious Mother'	**P:** Swift	*Verses on the Death of Dr Swift* [wrtn c.1731]
	1740	Opposition to Walpole mounts; Ir. harvest fails – most severe nationwide famine prior to 1840s; famine in Paris; War of Austrian Succession begins – Britain supports Maria Theresa of Austria [threatened by Prussia, Bavaria & France]; [–1786] Frederick II ('the Great') rules Prussia – lays foundations of later Prussian power	Smallpox inoculation now in general use in England; [–1741] Thomas Coram estab.s Foundling Hospital, London. **Music:** James Thomson & Thomas Arne, *Alfred, a Masque* [incls song 'Rule Britannia']. **Art:** Hogarth, 'Captain Thomas Coram' [Foundling Hospital]; [c.] Canaletto, 'The Square of St Marks' & 'The Quay of the Piazzetta'; François Boucher [pnt] 'The Triumph of Venus'	**Pr/F:** Cibber Samuel Richardson (1689–1761) **Lit. 'Events':**	*Apology for the Life of Mr Colley Cibber, Comedian* [autobiog.] *Pamela: or Virtue Rewarded* [novel; vols I–II; 1741; III–IV] Debut of Peg Woffington at Covent Garden [Irish actress famous for her male roles]
	1741	Motion for dismissal of Walpole defeated; Gen. Elec: Ministry's majority precarious; Highway Act to improve Eng. roads; drought ruins Ir. harvest – mortality from famine around 15% of population; British attacks on Carthagena & Sp. Cuba fail	Royal Military Academy, Woolwich, fnd.d; [–1742] Hume, *Essays Moral and Political*. **Int. Lit.:** Voltaire, *Mahomet* [drama]. **Music:** Handel, 'Samson' & 'Deidamia' [last opera]; Christoph Gluck [comp] 'Artaxerxes' [Ger. opera]. **Art:** Pietro Longhi [pnt] 'The Concert'	**Pr/F:** H. Fielding **Dr:** David Garrick (1717–79) **Lit. 'Events':**	*Shamela* [parody of *Pamela*] *The Lying Valet* [farce] David Garrick 1st appears on London stage as Richard III; 1st Ger. trans of a Shakespeare play [*Julius Caesar*]
	1742	Walpole resigns – Commons attempt to investigate the conduct of his ministry over past 10 yrs; Parliament agrees to continue paying Hanoverian troops in British service; peace between Prussia & Austria	Trinity College, Dublin, becomes a university; Sheffield silver-plating process discv.d; Anders Celsius proposes Centigrade scale. **Music:** Handel 'The Messiah' [1st pf.d Dublin – London, 1743]; J.S. Bach, 'Goldberg Variations'. **Art:** Kent designs 44 Berkley Square, London; [–1746] Hogarth, 'Marriage à la Mode' [6 paintings; NG; engravings, BM]; Boucher, 'Bath of Diana'	**P:** Pope Thomas Gray (1716–71) Edward Young (1683–1765) **Pr/F:** H. Fielding	[–1743] *The Dunciad* [final versions; in 4 Bks] 'Ode on a Distant Prospect of Eton College' [pub.d 1747] & 'Ode on the Spring' [–1745] *The Complaint, or Night Thoughts on Life, Death and Immortality* [blank verse poem pub.d serially] *Joseph Andrews*

HANOVERIAN/AUGUSTAN

Year		Culture / Arts	Authors	Works
1743	George II defeats French at Dettingen – Treaty of Worms [Britain, Austria & Sardinia] pushes France into further alliance with Spain; French reach Rocky Mountains; 1st settlements in Dakota	E. India yarns imported into Lancashire. **Int. Lit.:** Voltaire, *Mérope* [drama]. **Music:** Handel, 'Samson' & 'Dettingen Te Deum'. **Art:** Wood the Elder begins South Parade, Bath [completed (& The Circus & North Parade) by son, John Wood 'the Younger' (v.1767)]	**P:** Robert Blair (1699–1746) **Pr/F:** H. Fielding	*The Grave* [blank verse poem; 1808 edtn illustrated by William Blake] *The Life of Jonathan Wild the Great* [pub.d as vol. 3 of his *Miscellanies*]
1744	France threatens invasion of Britain – threat recedes; French & Native Americans invade Nova Scotia – fail to take Annapolis; Robert Clive arrives in Madras as E. India Co. clerk	1st Methodist coference held; [c.] rules of cricket 1st codified. **Music:** Madrigal Society fnd.d in London; tune of 'God Save the King' appears [pub.d 1745, with 'The Cambells are Coming']. **Art:** Longhi, 'The Rhinoceros' **Lit. 'Events':** Alexander Pope dies; [–1746] Eliza Haywood pub.s & edits *The Female Spectator*	**P:** Dyer Mark Akenside (1721–70) **Pr/F:** Johnson Sarah Fielding (1710–68)	*The Ruins of Rome* [long poem] *The Pleasures of Imagination* [rev.d edtn 1772 as *The Ps of the Imag.*] *Account of the Life of Mr Richard Savage* [biog.] *The Adventures of David Simple* [novel; sequel, *Volume the Last*, 1753]
1745	Walpole dies; 'The '45' – 2nd Jacobite Rebellion: Prince Charles Edward Stuart ['the Young Pretender'/'Bonnie Prince Charlie'] lands in Scotland & invades England [as far as Derby], then retreats back to Scotland; French defeat British at Fontenoy & control most of Flanders; Britain & Prussia make peace; colonial force from Massachusetts captures Louisberg & Cape Breton Island [in St Lawrence river] from French; [>] E. India Co. in conflict with French in India	Last native Cornish speaker dies; Royal Navy seamen's ration of grog intro.d; Middlesex Hospital fnd.d; case of 'The Man in the Iron Mask' [Bastille prisoner] becomes known; 'Leyden Jar' invented in Germany; Philadelphia Academy fnd.d [University of Pennsylvania, 1791]. **Art:** Wordsworth House, Cumberland, built; [c.–1750] Giambattista Tiepolo [pnt] 'Antony and Cleopatra' [series of frescoes, Palazzo Labia, Venice]; Giovanni Piranesi pubs *Carceri d'Invenzioni* ['Prisons'; book of etchings]	**Pr/F:** James Hervey (1714–58) **Dr:** Thomson **Lit. 'Events':**	[–1747] *Meditations among the Tombs* *Tancred and Sigismunda* [tragedy] Jonathan Swift dies
1746	William Pitt 'the Elder' [Earl of Chatham] joins gvnmnt – made Paymaster-General; Duke of ('Butcher') Cumberland crushes Jacobite Rebellion at Culloden Moor – Highlanders ruthlessly suppressed & clan system dismantled – Charles Stuart escapes disguised as Flora Macdonald's maid – wearing of tartan banned; Wales & Berwick Act assumes both to be included in England; French capture Madras from E. India Co.	Princeton University & Library fnd.d at Elizabethville [moved to Newark, 1748 & to Princeton, 1756]; Denis Diderot, *Pensées philosophiques* [burned by Paris Parliament]. **Music:** Handel, 'Judas Maccabaeus' & 'Occasional Oratorio'. **Art:** [–1751] Canaletto in England; Boucher, 'Madame Bergeret'; [c.–1750] Francesco Guardi [pnt] 'The Convent Parlour' & 'The Ridotto (Gaming Room) Venice'; Allan Ramsay [pnt] 'Dr. Mead' [Foundling Hospital]; Richard Wilson [pnt] 'Admiral Thomas Smith' [NMM]	**P:** Gray William Collins (1721–59) Joseph Warton (1722–1800)	[c.] 'Ode on the Death of a Favourite Cat, Drowned in a Tub of Gold Fishes' [wrtn; pub. 1748] [dated 1747] *Odes* [incls '… to Evening', '… to Liberty' & '… on the Poetical Character' *Odes* [1st vol. pub.d 1744; reaction away from Pope]
1747	Gen. Elec: Tories again sustain losses; Scottish lords executed for part in 'the '45'; French defeat British at Lauffeldt, but British naval victories off W. coast of France; Anglo-Russian Treaty of St Petersburg – leads to Aix-la-Chapelle [1748]	Hannah Glasse, *The Art of Cookery Made Plain and Easy*. **Int. Lit.:** Voltaire, *Zadig* [oriental tale]. **Music:** Handel, 'Joshua' & 'Alexander Balus'. **Art:** Woburn Abbey redesigned in style of Inigo Jones; Hogarth, 'Industry and Idleness' [satirical prints]; [c.] Sir Joshua Reynolds [pnt] 'Self-Portrait' [NPG] & 'Lieutenant Roberts' [NMM]	**Pr/F:** Richardson **Dr:** Garrick **Lit. 'Events':**	[–1748] *Clarissa, or, the History of a Young Lady* [7 vols] *Miss in her Teens* [farce] Dr Johnson pub.s his *Plan for a Dictionary of the English Language* [v.1755]; Haywood issues *The Parrot* [periodical]
1748	Peace of Aix-la-Chapelle ends War of Austrian Succession – France & Britain relinquish conquests – Prussia retains Silesia; Ohio Co. fnd.d in Virginia & Maryland [Royal Charter, 1749]	Roller-spinning & wool-carding machines invented; fuller excavations of Pompeii commence [v.1708]; Hume, *Philosophical Essays concerning Human Understanding* [repub. 1758 as *Enquiry* …]; Montesquieu, *L'Esprit des Lois* [on the nature of the state & its laws]. **Music:** Holwell Music Room, Oxford, opens; Handel, 'Royal Firework Suite' [pf.d in Green Park, London, to celebrate peace]; 'Susanna' & [–1749] 'Solomon' [oratorios]. **Art:**	**P:** Thomson **Pr/F:** Tobias Smollett (1721–71) John Cleland (1709–89) **Dr:** Thomson	*The Castle of Indolence* [patriotic 'Spenserian' allegory] *The Adventures of Roderick Random* [novel] [–1749] *Memoirs of a Woman of Pleasure* [or *Fanny Hill*; 2 vols; novel] *Coriolanus* [tragedy; prnt.d 1749]

PERIOD	YEAR	INTERNATIONAL AND POLITICAL CONTEXTS	SOCIAL AND CULTURAL CONTEXTS	AUTHORS	INDICATIVE TITLES
HANOVERIAN/AUGUSTAN	1749	Act passed to reduce the interest charged on National Debt [now £57m.]; Jacobite demonstrations in Oxford; Treaty with Spain confirms British commercial rights; Georgia becomes a Crown Colony; British estab. Halifax, Nova Scotia, with 3000 gvnmt-sponsored settlers	The Monthly Review pub.d; [–1788] George de Buffon, Histoire naturelle [36 vols]. Music: Handel, 'Theodora'; J.S. Bach, 'The Art of the Fugue'. Art: [c.] Tiepolo, 'Procurator Giovanni Querini'. Hogarth, 'Calais Gate' [Tate]; Ramsay, 'Norman, 22nd Chief of MacLeod' [Dunvegan Castle]; [c.–1749] Thomas Gainsborough [pnt] 'Mr and Mrs Andrews' [NG] & 'The Charterhouse' [Foundling Hospital]	**P:** Johnson **Pr/F:** H. Fielding S. Fielding Smollett **Dr:** Johnson	The Vanity of Human Wishes ['imitation' of Juvenal's 10th satire] The History of Tom Jones The Governess, or the little female academy Le Sage, Gil Blas [Eng. trans] Irene [tragedy]
	1750	'Chiltern Hundreds' [Crown sinecure allowing MPs to vacate their seat without resigning] 1st granted by Parliament; commercial treaty with Spain – favourable to Britain – Britain renounces 'Assiento' of African slaves [v.1702 & 1713]; Franco-British Commission to settle boundaries in N. America fails; [c.] Labrador colonised	1st Westminster Bridge completed; Hume, Enquiry concerning the Principles of Morals; Jean-Jacques Rousseau, Discours sur les arts et sciences. Art: [–1770] Horace Walpole designs & builds Strawberry Hill [Gothic house]; [c.–1755] Tiepolo, 'Rinaldo and Armida'; Hogarth, 'Six Servants' [Tate]; Joseph Highmore [pnt] 'Samuel Richardson' [NPG]	**Pr/F:** Lennox **Lit. 'Events':**	The Life of Harriet Stuart [novel] [–1752] Johnson single-handedly writes & edits The Rambler twice-weekly [208 issues]
	1751	Prince of Wales dies – his son, Prince George [later King George III], becomes heir apparent under a Regency; most effective of 18thC Gin Acts comes into force; Clive captures & defends Arcot from French – turning-point in British power in India	1st mental asylum in London; [–1772] the Encyclopédie [35 vols – Voltaire, Diderot, d'Alembert, Montesquieu & Rousseau collaborate]; Voltaire, Le Siècle de Louis XIV; Linnaeus, Philosophica botanica. Art: [–1758] Horse Guards Parade, Whitehall, built [posthm. designs by William Kent]; Royal Worcester porcelain factory estab.d; Hogarth, 'Four Stages of Cruelty', 'Gin Lane' & 'Beer Street' [satirical prints]; Boucher, 'The Toilet of Venus'	**P:** Gray **Pr/F:** Haywood H. Fielding Smollett	'Elegy Written in a Country Churchyard' The History of Betsy Thoughtless Amelia The Adventures of Peregrine Pickle
	1752	Lawrence & Clive capture Trichinopoly from French	Britain finally joins rest of Europe in adopting the Gregorian calendar [v.1582] – 3rd Sept. becomes 14th –'give us back our 11 days!' riots; Benjamin Franklin invents lightning conductor; Manchester Infirmary estab.d; Hume, Political Discourses; Bolingbroke, Letters on the Study and Use of History [pub. posthm.]; 1st 2 vols of Fr. Encyclopédie suppressed for attacks on clergy. Art: Boucher, 'Young Girl Resting (Louise Murphy)'	**Pr/F:** Lennox **Lit. 'Events':**	The Female Quixote: or, the Adventures of Arabella H. Fielding pub.s ferocious satires in twice-weekly The Covent Garden Journal
	1753	Mass destruction of turnpikes [tollgates] on W. Yorks roads – militia kill rioters; Clandestine Marriages Act to prevent abuse of marriage, esp.ly of minors; Jewish Naturalisation Act causes widespread hostility; last British Jacobite plot to restore the Pretender foiled; France bankrupt for 2nd time in the century; Duquesne, Fr. Governor of Canada, seizes Ohio valley & builds Fort Duquesne, threatening Virginia; truce attempted at Sadras between warring Fr. & Eng. E. India Cos	Parliamentary grant to purchase private collections for the nation – origin of British Museum [v.1757 & 1759]; Linnaeus, Species plantarum. Int. Lit.: [c.] Carlo Goldoni, La Locandiera [It. comedy]. Art: Hogarth, The Analysis of Beauty [art theory]; Thomas Chippendale sets up furniture business in St Martin's Lane; Tiepolo, 'The Four Continents with Apollo' [ceiling fresco, Würzburg]; [–1754] Reynolds, 'Commodore Augustus Keppel' [NMM]; [–1754] Wilson, 'Rome: S. Peter's and the Vatican from the Janiculum', [Tate]	**Pr/F:** Haywood Richardson Smollett	The History of Jemmy and Jenny Hessamy [–1754] The History of Sir Charles Grandison [7 vols] The Adventures of Ferdinand Count Fathom

Year	Events		Literature
1754	'Jew Act' repealed; Albany Congress of New England colonies rejects Benjamin Franklin's scheme for union & common policy towards Native Americans; George Washington's Virginian militia fails to expel French from Fort Duquesne; 1000 Brit. troops ordered to N. America; [>] French abandon conquests in India	George II fnds King's College, NY [later Columbia University]; Society for the Encouragement of Arts fnd.d; [−1762] Hume, *History of England* [5 vols]. **Art:** Chippendale, *The Gentleman and Cabinet Maker's Directory* [influential trade catalogue]; Boucher, 'The Sunrise' & 'The Sunset' [Wallace Coll.]; Ramsay, 'Hew Dalrymple, Lord Drunmore' [Colston, E. Lothian]	**P:** Gray **Theory/Crit:** Thomas Warton 'The Progress of Poesy' ['Pindaric Ode'] *Observations on the Faerie Queene*
1755	Pitt out of favour with George II for opposing treaty with Hesse for mercenaries to defend Hanover; Admiralty takes over & estab.s Royal Marines; British defeated by French near Fort Duquesne − British deport Fr. settlers ['Acadians'] from Nova Scotia; Frederick II of Prussia refuses to defend Fr. territory in N. America; earthquake at Lisbon − 30,000 killed	[−1835; re-estab-d, 1936] carpets made at Axminster; Rousseau, *Discours sur l'origine et les fondements de l'inégalité parmi les hommes*. **Int. Lit.:** Gotthold Lessing, *Miss Sara Sampson* [Ger. tragedy on Eng. model]; Voltaire, 'La Pucelle d'Orléans' [poem on Joan of Arc]. **Art:** [c.−1760] Tiepolo, 'Aurora Dispersing the Clouds of Night'; [−1760] Ramsay, 'Margaret Lindsay, the Artist's Second Wife' [SNG]; [c.] Gainsborough, 'Joseph Gibbs'; Wilson, 'Et in Arcadia Ego' [Wrotham Park]	**P:** Shenstone **Pr/F:** H. Fielding Johnson Smollett Thomas Amory (c.1691–1788) *Pastoral Ballad* *Journal of a Voyage to Lisbon* [posthm.] *Dictionary of the English Language* [1st standard Eng. dictionary] & 'Letter to Lord Chesterfield' [denouncing patronage; pub posthm. 1790] Cervantes, *Don Quixote* [Eng. trans] *Memoirs of Several Ladies of Great Britain* [misc. writings]
1756	Devonshire & Pitt form ministry − latter's Militia Bill passed − raises Highland regiments; acute grain shortages lead to serious rioting in Midlands & W. Country; Treaty of Westminster − Anglo-Prussian alliance; Prussia invades Saxony − British declare war on France − Seven Years War begins − French prepare to invade Britain; Admiral Byng loses Minorca to French − [1757] court-martialled & executed; the flag-ship 'Royal George' launched [v.1782]; Nawab of Bengal captures Fort William at Eng. factory, Calcutta − confines 146 prisoners in 'Black Hole' − 23 survivors next day	Cotton velvets 1st made at Bolton; Princeton University moves to Princeton [v.1746]; Edmund Burke, *A Vindication of Natural Society* [anon. satire on Bolingbroke] & *A Philosophical Enquiry into the Origin of our Ideas of the Sublime and the Beautiful*. **Int. Lit.:** Voltaire, 'Poème sur le désastre de Lisbonne'; Salomon Gessner, *Idyls* [Swiss pastoral poems]. **Music:** C.P.E. Bach [comp] 'Easter cantata'. **Art:** Sèvres porcelain factory fnd.d	**P:** Clara Reeve (1729–1807) **Pr/F:** Amory **Lit. 'Events':** *An Argument in Favour of the Natural Equality of Both the Sexes* *The Life of John Buncle, Esq.* [vol. I; vol. II, 1766; misc. writings] *The Critical Review* fnd.d
1757	Pitt resigns & is reinstated − vigorously directs Seven Years War; widespread food rioting & popular protests at Militia Act sweep Britain; Russia & Sweden join France & Austria against England & Prussia; Calcutta retaken − Clive crushes Nawab's forces at Plassey − becomes Governor of Bengal − effectively begins conquest of India	1st British canal constructed in Lancashire; Lord Mayor of London's coach made; old Royal Library given to British Museum; Hume, *Four Dissertations: the Natural History of Religion; of the Passions; of Tragedy; of the Standard of Taste*; Diderot, *Le fils naturel*. **Music:** Handel, 'The Triumph of Time and Truth'. **Art:** [−1765] Robert Adam builds Kedleston Hall; [c.] Hogarth, 'Self-Portrait' [NPG]; Reynolds, 'Countess of Albemarle' [NG]	**P:** Dyer Gray **Pr/F:** Smollett **Theory/crit:** Thomas Warton **Lit. 'Events':** *The Fleece* [long poem] 'The Bard' ['Pindaric Ode'] [−1758] *Complete History of England* [4 vols] *Essay on the Genius and Writings of Pope* [2nd vol. 1782] *Nibelungenlied* 1st edited
1758	London Convention grants Frederick II annual subsidy of £670,000; Frederick indecisively defeats Russians at Zorndorf [terrible losses]; British take back Louisbourg on Cape Breton Island from French − British forces take Fort Duquesne; British naval victories off Cartagena, Basque Roads & Cherbourg [forts destroyed]; British capture Fr. Senegal; Dutch capitulate to Clive at Chinsura	Halley's Comet returns as predicted; Hume, *An Enquiry concerning Human Understanding* [v.1748]; Helvétius, *De l'esprit* [publicly burnt in Paris]; Diderot, *Le Père de famille*. **Art:** [c.] Tiepolo, 'Merit Between Nobility and Virtue'; Boucher, 'Madame de Pompadour'; Hogarth, 'Parliamentary Elections' [begun 1755]; [c.−1763] Ramsay, 'Dr William Hunter' [Hunterian]; [c.] Gainsborough, 'Mary and Margaret, the Artist's Daughters' [V&A]; Wilson, 'Hadrian's Villa' [MAG]; 'Snowdon' [Walker AG], 'Cader Idris' [NG] & [−1759] 'View of Croome Court, near Worcester' [BAG]; [−1759] Jean Baptiste Greuze [pnt] 'The Wool Winder'	**P:** Gray **Pr/F:** Lennox **Lit. 'Events':** *Pindaric Odes* *The History of Henrietta* [−1760] Johnson's 'Idler' papers in the *Universal Chronicle*

PERIOD	YEAR	INTERNATIONAL AND POLITICAL CONTEXTS	SOCIAL AND CULTURAL CONTEXTS	AUTHORS	INDICATIVE TITLES
HANOVERIAN/ AUGUSTAN	1759	French revive plan to invade England – Fr. fleets routed at Lagos & Quiberon Bay – Royal Navy has complete command of sea; British maritime policy forces Spain to ally with France; varied fortunes in land war in Europe; Gen. Wolfe takes Quebec [killed – >] British begin to consolidate power in N. America; further British victories in India; French surrender Guadeloupe	[–1788] Burke fnds & writes Annual Register [of political & literary events]; British Museum opens at Montagu House [v.1823]; Carron Iron Works estab.d; Josiah Wedgwood leases a factory in Burslem, Staffs & Arthur Guinness a brewery in Dublin; Bridgewater Canal built [opens 1761]; 3rd Eddystone lighthouse opens. Int. Lit.: Voltaire, Candide. Music: William Boyce [comp] 'Harlequin's Invasion' [incl.s song 'Hearts of Oak']; Franz Joseph Haydn [comp] 'First Symphony'. Art: Adam begins Harewood House, Yorkshire; [–1790] Panthéon, Paris, built [pseudo-Grecian style]; [c.] Gainsborough, 'Self-Portrait' [NPG]	**P:** Christopher Smart (1722–71) **Pr/F:** S. Fielding Johnson Laurence Sterne (1713–68) **Theory/Crit:** Oliver Goldsmith (c.1730–74)	[c.1759–61] Jubilate Agno [wrtn; pub.d 1939] The History of the Countess of Dellwyn The History of Rasselas, Prince of Abyssinia [oriental tale] [–1767] The Life and Opinions of Tristram Shandy, Gentleman [novel; 9 vols] Enquiry into the Present State of Polite Learning in Europe [essays]
HANOVERIAN	1760	George II dies – his grandson, King George III, accedes; Earl Ferrers hanged for murder at Tyburn – last Eng. peer executed as a felon; Montreal capitulates to British; Fr. invasion force defeated at Kinsale, Ireland; Sir Eyre Coote defeats French at Wandiwash & [1761] captures Pondicherry – completes downfall of French in India	1st bankers' cheques printed; Kew Botanical Gardens [private] 1st opened. Int. Lit.: [c.–1785] Sturm und Drang movement in Germany [v.1773, 1776]. Art: [c.] Hogarth, 'The Shrimp Girl' [NG]; Gainsborough, 'Earl Nugent'; [c.] Canaletto, 'Piazza San Marco seen through an archway'; Guardi, 'View from Mira over the Brenta Canal'; Longhi, 'Masked Figure with a Fruit Seller'	**P:** James Macpherson ('Ossian'; 1736–96) **Pr/F:** S. Fielding Smollett	Fragments of Ancient Poetry Collected in the Highlands of Scotland [purported 'translations' of Gaelic poet 'Ossian' – v.1762 & 1763] History of Ophelia [–1761] The Life and Adventures of Sir Launcelot Greaves [serialised; as book, 1762]
	1761	5000 Northumberland miners march to Hexham – 42 killed by Yorkshire militia; Pitt resigns over opposition to war policy; British capture Belle Isle (off Brittany); Portugal refuses to close ports to British ships – Spain declares war on Britain – reciprocated; British take Dominica, Cuba & Antilles	Int. Lit.: Rousseau, Julie, ou la Nouvelle Héloïse [novel]. Music: Thomas Arne [comp] 'Judith' [1st Eng. oratorio to require women singers]. Art: Jean-Baptiste Greuze [pnt] 'The Marriage Contract/Village Bride'	**P:** Gray **Pr/F:** Smollett	[c.] The Fatal Sisters & The Descent of Odin [imitations of ancient Scandanavian myths] [–1774] The Works of Voltaire [trans; 37 vols]
	1762	Earl of Bute, PM; subsidies to Frederick II withdrawn [v.1758]; British take St Vincent, Grenada, Martinique, Havana & Manila [Philippines]; Spanish invade Portugal – suffer defeats; negotiations for peace opened with France; Catherine II ('the Great') rules Russia	John Wilkes fnds North Briton [radical newspaper]. Int. Lit.: Rousseau, Du Contrat social & Emile, ou Traité de l'éducation [novel]. Music: [–1763] young Mozart begins tour of Europe; Arne, 'Artaxerxes' [opera]; Christoph Gluck [comp] 'Orfeo' [opera]. Art: Gainsborough, 'Mr William Poyntz' [Spencer Coll.]; George Stubbs [pnt] 'Molly Longlegs with a Jockey' [Walker AG]	**P:** Macpherson **Pr/F:** Lennox Goldsmith **Lit. 'Events':**	Fingal, an ancient Epic Poem in Six Books ['Ossian' poems; v.1760] Sophia The Citizen of the World [repub. of 'Chinese Letters'; begun 1760 – pub.d in The Public Ledger] [–1766] Christoph Wieland, 1st Ger. trans of Shakespeare
	1763	John Wilkes arrested on a 'General Warrant' for attack on gvnmt in North Briton – freed under Habeus Corpus; 'Oakboy' & 'Whiteboy' agrarian unrest in Ireland; Peace of Paris ends Seven Years War – British regain Minorca, secure territories in W. Indies & Canada, Nova Scotia. Cape Breton & Florida – increase power in N. America, proclamation estab.s new N. American colonies & fixes westward boundaries of older ones – George III promises administrative reforms in New England; [–1767] Eng. surveyors Mason & Dixon begin to mark boundary between Maryland & Pennsylvania [free & slave regions: 'Mason & Dixon Line']; Native	[–1783] Catherine Macaulay, History of England [8 vols]; Rousseau's Social Contract publicly burnt in Geneva; Voltaire, Traité sur la Tolérance. Art: [c.] Chardin, 'The Breakfast Table'; [c.–1764] Gainsborough, 'Mary, Countess Howe' [Kenwood]; Johann Zoffany [pnt] 'Garrick and Mrs Cibber as Jaffier and Belvidera'	**P:** Macpherson Smart **Pr/F:** Wortley Montagu **Lit. 'Events'**	Temora, an Epic Poem in Eight Books ['Ossian' poems] A Song to David [religious poem] Letters from the East [pub. posthm.] Boswell meets Dr Johnson

1764	American rebellion under Pontiac on western frontier of Virginia & Pensylvania – all British outposts taken & Fort Pitt besieged – British begin counter-attack; 1st Eng. Chambers of Commerce in NY & NJ	James Hargreaves invents 1st 'Spinning Jenny'; Voltaire, *Dictionnaire philosophique.* **Music:** Haydn, 'The Philosopher' [symphony]; 8-year-old Mozart [comp] 1st symphony. **Art:** J.J. Winckelmann [archeologist of Pompeii], *History of Ancient Art* [Eng. trans by Henry Fuseli]; Jean-Honoré Fragonard [pnt] 'Rinaldo and Armida'	**P:** Goldsmith **Pr/F:** Horace Walpole (1717–97) **Lit. 'Events':**	*The Traveller, or, A Prospect of Society* *The Castle of Otranto* [novella] [>] Johnson fnds the '[Literary] Club' at Turk's Head, Soho [incls Burke, Gibbon, Boswell, Garrick, Goldsmith, Bishop Percy, Joshua Reynolds, Adam Smith]
1765	Stamp Act [duty on stamps] imposed on N. American colonies & American Mutiny Act – Virginia Assembly resolves to resist it, followed by other 13 colonies – riots in Boston spread across the colonies – boycott of all British goods instituted – London merchants clamour for measures to end it; Clive reforms Indian administration; HMS 'Victory' launched [later Horatio Nelson's flagship]	James Watt invents steam engine condenser; [–1769] Sir William Blackstone, *Commentaries on the Laws of England.* **Art:** Adam designs Lansdowne House; Chardin, 'Attributes of the Arts ' & 'Attributes of Music'; [c.] Zoffany, 'Parsons, Bransby, and Watkyns in "Lethe"' [BAG]	**P:** (Bishop) Thomas Percy (1729–1811) **Pr/F:** Johnson	[ed.] *The Reliques of Ancient English Poetry* [3-vol. collection of balladry; incls 'Sir Patrick Spens' & 'Chevy Chase'] [ed.] *The Plays of Shakespeare* [incls 'Preface to Shakespeare'– **Theory/Crit.**]
1766	Pitt [as Earl of Chatham] forms ministry; Parliament, after Wilkes case, declares General Warrants illegal; Stamp Act repealed – replaced by Declaratory Bill [asserts right to tax Amer. colonies]; 'Old Pretender' dies – all RC powers refuse to recognise 'Young Pretender' as 'Charles III' – demise of Jacobite cause; [–1767] food riots at price of grain in W. Country, Midlands, Thames Valley & E. Anglia; Anglo-Russian treaty of friendship & commerce	Henry Cavendish identifies hydrogen & analyses air. **Music:** Haydn, 'Great Mass with Organ'. **Art:** Gotthold Lessing, *Laokoon* [theory]; George Stubbs pubs illustr.d book, *Anatomy of the Horse* [begun 1756]; Fragonard, 'The Swing' [Wallace Coll.]; [–1768] Reynolds, 'Warren Hastings' [NPG]; Ramsay, 'Jean-Jacques Rousseau in Armenian Costume' [SNG]; [–1767] Zoffany, 'Queen Charlotte with the Two Elder Princes' [Royal Coll.]; [c.] Joseph Nollekens [sculpt] 'David Garrick' [marble bust] & 'Laurence Sterne' [ditto; NPG]	**Pr/F:** Goldsmith Smollett Swift **Theory/Crit:** Johann Herder **Lit. 'Events':**	*The Vicar of Wakefield* *Travels in France and Italy* *Journal to Stella* [pub. posthm.] *Fragmente über die neuere deutsche Litteratur* [pub. posthm., 1778]
1767	American Import Duties Act [on tea, glass, paper & dye-stuffs] – infuriates American colonists – Boston urges resistance – trade boycott reintro.d	Joseph Priestley, *The History and Present State of Electricity.* **Int. Lit.:** Lessing, *Minna von Barnhelm* [1st major Ger. comedy]. **Music:** Haydn, 'Stabat Mater'; Gluck, 'Alcestis' [Ger. opera]. **Art:** [–1775] John Wood 'the Younger' builds Royal Crescent, Bath; Gainsborough, 'Harvest Wagon' [Barber Inst.]; [c.] Benjamin West [USA; pnt] 'Departure of Regulus from Rome' [Kensington Palace]	**Pr/F:** Henry Brooke (c.1703–83) **Theory/Crit:** Gotthold Lessing	[–1770] *The Fool of Quality* [novel in 5 vols] *Hamburgische Dramaturgie* [rejects dominance of Fr. classical drama]
1768	Wilkes [now popular focus of 'English Liberty'] elected MP for Middlesex – imprisoned – widespread rioting in London – 'St George's Fields Massacre' [troops kill 7 rioters]; Earl of Chatham [Pitt] resigns; Boston disturbances against duties provoke occupation by British troops; [–1771] Captain Cook's 1st voyage to the South Pacific in the 'Endeavour'	*Encyclopaedia Britannica* 1st pub.d in parts in Edinburgh [v.1771]; [–1790] Forth-Clyde Canal built; Linnaeus, *Systema naturae.* **Music:** 1st piano solo played in England [of J.S. Bach]; Haydn, 'La Passione' [symphony]. **Art:** Royal Academy of Arts [RA] fnd.d in London [Sir Joshua Reynolds 1st President]; Adam brothers build Adelphi Terrace; [c.] Guardi, 'The Bucentaur leaving the Lido'; (Joseph) Wright of Derby [pnt] 'Experiment with the Air-Pump' [Tate]	**P:** Gray Thomas Chatterton (1752–70) **Pr/F:** Sterne **Dr:** Goldsmith Walpole	*Poems* [–1770] writes poems supposedly by 15thC Bristol monk, Thomas Rowley – soon exposed as forgeries; coll. edtn pub. posthm. 1777] *A Sentimental Journey through France and Italy* [travel parody] *The Good-Natur'd Man* [comedy] *The Mysterious Mother* [tragedy]

PERIOD	YEAR	INTERNATIONAL AND POLITICAL CONTEXTS	SOCIAL AND CULTURAL CONTEXTS	AUTHORS	INDICATIVE TITLES
	1769	Wilkes expelled by Parliament & re-elected 3 times; 1st Secretary for the Colonies appointed; [~1770] American duties repealed – except on tea; Austria, Prussia & Russia begin partition of Poland; Cook circumnavigates & charts New Zealand – explores E. coast of Australia & claims it for England	Richard Arkwright operates 1st [water-powered] spinning mill – [~>] factory system begins to displace domestic labour; [~1772] Anon. [Sir Philip Francis?], Letters of Junius [pub.d in Public Advertiser – trenchant exposés of corruption in political life]; Burke, Observations on ... 'The Present State of the Nation'; **Int. Lit.:** Johann Wolfgan von Goethe, Neue Lieder [early poems]. **Art:** [~1790] Reynolds's 15 Discourses [on Art] delivered to RA [v.1794] & pnts 'Dr Johnson' [Knole, Kent]; [~1771] Wood the Younger builds Assembly Rooms, Bath [Palladian]; Wedgwood's early pottery made at 'Etruria', Staffordshire; [c.] Wright of Derby, 'Academy by Lamplight' [R. Coll. Surgeons]	**Pr/F:** Smollett **Theory/Crit:** Elizabeth Montagu	The Adventures of an Atom [satire] & The Present State of All Nations [begun 1768; a history of the 'known world'] Essay on the Writings and Genius of Shakespeare
	1770	Lord North, PM – resigns – personal rule by George III; Horne Tooke fnds Constitutional Society for Parliamentary Reform; 'Boston Massacre': British troops fire on rioters; Sp. troops expel British settlers from Falklands – nearly leads to war; Captain Cook discovers Botany Bay & claims E. coast of Australia for Britain; famine in Bengal	1st edtn of the Bible in Welsh pub.d; Burke, Thoughts on the Cause of the Present Discontents [re. Wilkes controversy; v.1763–9]; Diderot, Essai sur la peinture; Baron d'Holbach, Systeme de la nature. **Music:** Mozart [comp] 'Mitridate' [opera]. **Art:** [c.] Guardi, 'Regattas on the Grand Canal, Venice' & [~1775] 'Doge Embarking on a Bucintoro'; Gainsborough, 'Blue Boy'; Stubbs, 'Horse Attacked by a Lion' [Walker AG; enamel version, Tate]; West, 'Death of Wolfe'	**P:** Goldsmith **Lit. 'Events':**	The Deserted Village Chatterton commits suicide [v.1769]
	1771	Right to report Parliamentary debates acquired; Wilkes elected High Sheriff of London; war averted – Spain cedes Falkland Islands to Britain [unoccupied till 1833]; Russia & Prussia agree to partition Poland [effected 1772]	1st 3-vol. edtn of Encyclopaedia Britannica pub.d; [~1774] John Wesley, Works [32 vols]; Assembly Rooms, Bath, open; New York Hospital fnd.d. **Art:** [1772] Fragonard, 'Pursuit', 'Meeting', 'Love Letters' & 'Lover Crowned' [4 panels]; [~1795] Wright of Derby, 'Alchemist in Search of the Philosopher's Stone Discovers Phosphorus' [Derby AG]; Zoffany, 'The Academicians of the Royal Academy' & 'George III' [both Royal Coll.]	**P:** James Beattie (1735–1803) **Pr/F:** Goldsmith Smollett Henry Mackenzie (1745–1831)	The Minstrel [Spenserian poem; Pt I; Pt II, 1774] The History of England The Expedition of Humphrey Clinker The Man of Feeling [novel]
	1772	Royal Marriages Act [to prevent undesirable ones]; [& 1773] widespread food rioting at price of grain thro'out summer; 'Steelboy' agrarian disturbances in Ulster; Boston Assembly threatens secession from Britain if colonies' rights not protected – revenue schooner 'Gaspee' burnt by American mob; [~1775] Cook's 2nd voyage of discovery to Antarctic; Warren Hastings, Governor of Bengal	[~1937] The Morning Post pub.d; Priestley pub.s findings – beginnings of modern chemistry; Daniel Rutherford isolates nitrogen. **Int. Lit.:** Lessing, Emilia Galotti [Ger. tragedy]; Pierre-Augustin de Beaumarchais, The Barber of Seville [Fr. comedy wrtn; pf.d 1775]. **Music:** Mozart, 'Lucio Silla' [opera]. **Art:** Reynolds, 'Dr Samuel Johnson' [NG]		
	1773	[New Corn Laws passed; purpose-built home erected for 'The Stock Exchange'; legislation gives E. India Co. monopoly of American tea trade – North's Regulating Act controls E. India Co.'s conduct of affairs; hatred of tea duties [& colonial rule from London] sparks 'Boston Tea Party';	Sheet glass into.d from France; Hester Chapone, Letters on the Improvement of the Mind. **Int. Lit.:** Goethe, Götz von Berlichingen ['Sturm und Drang' drama]; Gottfried Bürger, 'Lenore' [Ger. ballad]; Friedrich Klopstock, The Messiah [Ger. poem, complt.d]. **Music:** Muzio Clemente [comp] 3 piano	**P:** Anna Laetitia Barbauld (1743–1825) **Pr/F:** Barbauld Mackenzie	Poems Miscellaneous Pieces in Prose [with her brother] The Man of the World

HANOVERIAN

Year	History / Politics	Science, Philosophy, Art, Music	Author	Literary Works
	Hastings becomes Govenor General in India; Cook sights 'his' islands & becomes 1st person to cross Antarctic Circle	sonatas. **Art:** [–1778] Wood the Younger builds Hot Baths, Bath [Palladian]; Reynolds, 'Lady Cockburn and her Children'	**Dr:** Goldsmith **Theory/Crit:** Goldsmith Johann Herder	*She Stoops to Conquer* / 'Essay on the Theatre' / *Von deutscher Art und Kunst* [manifesto of 'Sturm und Drang' movement]
1774	Quebec Act extends British province to include area S. of the Great Lakes – estab.s tolerance to Canadian RCs & Fr. forms of law – angers New England Puritans; 'Intolerable Acts': Boston harbour closed until E. India Co. recompensed for 'Tea Party' losses – charter of Massachusetts revoked; 1st Congress of 13 Colonies [minus Georgia] at Philadelphia; Bombay & Madras placed under control of Bengal – E. India Co. now in effect a 'state'	Burke, speech on 'American Taxation'; Priestley isolates oxygen & discovers ammonia; Earl of Chesterfield, *Letters to his Son* [1737–68; pub posthm.]. **Int. Lit.:** Goethe, *The Sorrows of Young Werther*, Voltaire, *Sophonisbe*. **Art:** Radcliffe Camera, Oxford, completed; [c.] Nollekens, 'George III' & 'Dr Samuel Johnson' [portrait busts]; Wright of Derby, 'The Old Man and Death'	**P:** Mary Scott (1751–93) **Theory/Crit:** Thomas Warton **Lit. 'Events':**	*The Female Advocate: A Poem* / [–1781] *History of English Poetry* [3 vols; up to end of 16th C] / [–1782] John Bell pub.s *Poets of Great Britain* [109 vols] & *Shakespeare* & *The British Theatre* [21 vols]
1775	Massachusetts [& later all colonies] deemed to be in rebellion – American access to all foreign trade ended; [–1783] War of Independence begins – Britain hires 29,000 Ger. mercenaries – colonists' 'Olive Branch' petition rejected – Paul Revere's ride from Boston to Lexington to warn of British movements – British sortie from Boston routed at battle of Lexington-Concord – siege of Boston begins – British victory over Massachusetts militia at battle of Bunker's Hill – 2nd Congress of colonies meets – Washington, C. in C. of American forces; British take over Indo-Chinese opium trade from Portuguese	Burke, speech on 'Conciliation with America'; 1st Thames Regatta; Watt & Matthew Boulton begin to produce 1st commercial steam engines; Thomas Jeffreys, *The American Atlas*. **Int. Lit.:** Goethe arrives in Weimar – begins *Faust* [v.1808 & 1832]; Pierre-Augustin Beaumarchais, *The Barber of Seville* [Fr. comedy; v. Rossini, 1816]; Vittori Alfieri, *Cleopatra* [It. tragedy]. **Music:** Mozart, 5 violin concertos; C.P.E. Bach [comp] 'The Israelites in the Wilderness' [oratorio]; Augustus Toplady [comp] 'Rock of Ages'; **Art:** Adam brothers build Portland Place; Reynolds, 'Miss Bowles and her Dog' [Wallace Coll.]; Gainsborough, 'Honourable Mrs Graham' [SNG]; Fragonard, 'Fête at St-Cloud'; George Romney [pnt] 'Lady Louisa Stormont'	**P:** George Crabbe (1754–1832) **Pr/F:** Johnson **Dr:** Richard Sheridan (1751–1816) **Lit. 'Events':**	*Inebriety: A Poem* / *A Journey to the Western Isles of Scotland* [account of expedition with Boswell] / *The Rivals* [comedy], *St Patrick's Day* [farce] & *The Duenna* [comic opera] / Sarah Siddons 1st acts at Drury Lane as Portia
1776	Embargo proclaimed on Ir. export of provisions to anywhere but Britain & non-rebellious colonies; [4 July] Declaration of Independence at Philadelphia – 13 'United Colonies of America' henceforth to be the 'United States of America' – British forces evacuated from Boston to Nova Scotia – British land on Long Island – rout Washington's forces at battle of Brooklyn Heights – capture NY & NJ – recaptured by Colonists – Colonists abandon attack on Canada & capture of Montreal [late 1775]; [–1779] Cook begins 3rd voyage of discovery [from Pacific to W. & N. coast of America]	John Wilkinson, iron-master, uses a Watt steam-engine to pump bellows in blast-furnace; 1st St Leger horse race at Doncaster; Adam Smith, *An Enquiry into the Nature and the Causes of the Wealth of Nations*; Thomas Paine, *Common Sense* [best-selling pamphlet advocating complete American independence from Britain]; Jeremy Bentham, *A Fragment on Government*. **Int. Lit.:** Friedrich von Klinger, *Der Wirwarr, oder Sturm und Drang* [Ger. tragedy – gives name to 'Storm and Stress' school; v.1760, 1773]. **Music:** [–1789] Charles Burney, *A General History of Music* [4 vols]. **Art:** [–1786] Sir William Chambers builds Somerset House; [c.] Gainsborough, 'Lady Margaret Fordyce' [Rosebery Coll.]; Romney, 'Mrs. Carwardine and Son'	**Pr/F:** Edward Gibbon (1737–94) **Lit. 'Events':**	[–1788] *The History of the Decline and Fall of the Roman Empire* [6 vols] / Garrick retires from stage [v.1741]
1777	Habeas Corpus Act suspended; Washington defeated at Brandywine Creek – British capture Philadelphia – Gen. Burgoyne surrenders to	Burke, *Letter to the Sheriffs of Bristol on the Affairs of America*; Antoine Lavoisier shows air mainly composed of oxygen & nitrogen; John Howard, *The*	**Pr/F:** Mackenzie Reeve	*Julia de Roubigné* / *The Old English Baron* [novel; 1st pub.d as *The Champion of Virtue, a Gothic Story*, 1776]

Period	Year	International and Political Contexts	Social and Cultural Contexts	Authors	Indicative Titles
		Colonists at Saratoga – Confederation Articles drawn up [1st US constitution – ratified 1781] – American Continental Congress Flag adopted: 13 stars & 13 stripes; [–1778] Cook discovers & names the Sandwich Islands	State of the Prisons in England and Wales; Johann Georg Förster, A Voyage Round the World [1st-hand account of Cook's 2nd voyage of 1772–5]. **Music:** Haydn, 'La Roxelane Symphony'. **Art:** Gainsborough, 'The Watering Place' [Tate]	**Dr:** Sheridan Hannah More (1745–1833)	A Trip to Scarborough [adapted from Vanbrugh's The Relapse – v.1696] & The School for Scandal Percy [tragedy]
	1778	RC Relief Act passed; War of Independence: British abandon Philadelphia & retreat to NY – defeat Washington at battle of Monmouth, NJ – British subdue Georgia – John Paul Jones, American privateer, sails into Ir. Sea & raids Solway Firth, Scotland – 1st Company Irish Volunteers formed in Belfast – movement spreads across Ireland; France allies with Colonists against Britain & declares war – Fr.–American commercial treaty; British take St Lucia – French take Dominica; Cook discovers Hawaii [murdered there, 1779]	Thomas Coke begins experiments in farming methods at Holkham, Norfolk. **Int. Lit.:** [–1779] Herder, Stimmen der Völker in Liedern [coll. of folk-songs]. **Music:** 'Les Petits Riens' [1st pf.d – music by Mozart]. **Art:** Reynolds, 'Family of George, Duke of Marlborough' [Blenheim]; West, 'Penn's Treaty with the Indians'; John Copley [pnt] 'Brook Watson and the Shark' [Christ's Hospital]; Jean-Antoine Houdon [sculpt] 'Voltaire' & 'Benjamin Franklin' [busts]; [c.] Stubbs, 'Mares and Foals' [Tate]	**Pr/F:** Frances [Fanny] Burney (1752–1840) **Lit. 'Events':**	Evelina, or The History of a Young Lady's Entrance into the World [novel; pub.d anon.] Voltaire & Rousseau die; [–1783] J.J. Eschenburg, 1st complete Ger. trans of Shakespeare
	1779	Regulation of framework-knitting trade rejected – riots & machine-breaking in Nottingham – Arkwright's mill destroyed; Dissenting ministers & schoolmasters no longer have to subscribe to 39 Articles; Irish begin boycott of English goods; Anglo-Fr./American battles in S. Carolina, Florida & Savannah; Fr./American naval squadron led by Jones engages British off Flamborough Head; Spain allies with Colonists & French against Britain – declares war – [–1783] lays siege to Gibralta; 1st war with Mahrattas in India	Samuel Crompton invents 'Spinning Mule'; [>] 1st steam mills in operation; 1st iron bridge completed – over R. Severn at Coalbrookdale [now Ironbridge]; Hume, Dialogues Concerning Natural Religion [pub.d posthm.]. **Int. Lit.:** Lessing, Nathan der Weise [Ger. dramatic poem]. **Music:** Imperial Ballet School fnd.d at St Petersburg; Gluck, 'Iphigénie en Tauride' [opera]. **Art:** [–1780] Copley, 'Death of the Earl of Chatham' [Tate]; Houdon, 'Jean-Jacques Rousseau' & 'Benjamin Franklin' [busts]; Thomas Bewick [illustr.] John Gay's Fables [wood engrvs]	**P:** William Cowper (1731–1800) **Dr:** Sheridan More **Theory/Crit:** Johnson	Olney Hymns [with John Newton; 68 by Cowper, incl. 'God moves in a mysterious way' & 'Oh! For a closer walk with God'] The Critic, or, A Tragedy Rehearsed [burlesque based on Buckingham's The Rehearsal; v.1671] The Fatal Secret [tragedy] [–1781] The Lives of the [Most Eminent English] Poets [originally: The Works of the English Poets, with Prefaces, Biographical and Critical, 52 essays]
	1780	William Pitt the Younger enters Parliament; [–1781] widespread petitioning for economic & parliamentary reform – John Cartwright ['Father of Reform'] fnds Constitutional Society [advocates annual parliaments, the ballot, manhood suffrage]; demonstrations against RC Relief Act [1778] lead to 'No Popery'/Gordon Riots in London [Bank of England attacked – Newgate prison burned & plundered – prisoners freed]; Ireland admitted to equal trade with colonies; British take Charleston – S. Carolina 'pacified' by Cornwallis – American defeat at Camden; Sp. fleet defeated off Cape St Vincent; Russia, Denmark, Sweden & then Holland form 'League of Armed Neutrality' [in protest at RN searching neutral ships at sea]; 2nd war with Mahrattas in India – all British ports under siege – Madras threatened	Watt invents a letter-copying press; Robert Raikes opens 1st Sunday School in Gloucester; 'the Derby' horse race 1st run. **Int. Lit.:** Christoph Wieland, Oberon [Ger. heroic poem]. **Music:** Haydn, 'The Toy Symphony'. **Art:** Thomas Turner intro.s 'Willow Pattern' for china; [–1781] Gainsborough, 'George III' & 'Queen Charlotte' [both Royal Coll.] & 'Cottage Door'; [c.] Wright of Derby, 'Moonlight Landscape' [Alfreton Hall]; Houdon, 'Diana' [marble]; Romney, 'Self-Portrait' [NPG]; Jacques-Louis David [pnt] 'Belisarius Begging for Alms'; John Trumbull [USA, pnt] 'Portrait of George Washington'; [c.–1785] Thomas Rowlandson, 'A Coffee House' [w/c drawing; Aberdeen AG]	**Pr/F:** Thomas Holcroft (1745–1809)	Alwyn, or the Gentleman Comedian [novel]

HANOVERIAN

HANOVERIAN/ROMANTIC

Year	History / Politics	Science, Art, Music, Int. Lit.	Authors	Works
1781	American War campaigns turn against British – Cornwallis surrenders to Washington at Yorktown; Articles of Confederation & Perpetual Union ratified by all States of N. America; French attack on Jersey fails; Prussia joins 'Armed Neutrality' [as does Portugal in 1782]; Fr./Sp. force besieges Minorca [garrison surrenders, 1782]; Eyre Coote raises siege of British ports in India & defeats combined Indian & Fr. forces	1st Building Society fnd.d in Birmingham; Jonathan Hornblower patents 2-cylinder steam-engine; Immanuel Kant, *Critique of Pure Reason*. **Int. Lit.:** J.C.F. Schiller, *Die Räuber* [revolutionary political Ger. play – pf.d 1782]. **Music:** Haydn, 'La Chasse Symphony'; Mozart, 'Idomeneo' [opera] & 6 'Russian String Quartets'. **Art:** Gainsborough, 'Cattle Crossing a Bridge'; Houdon, 'Voltaire with Antique Drapery' [statue, Comédie-Française, Paris]; Wright of Derby, 'Sir Brooke Boothby' [Tate]; Henry Fuseli [pnt] 'The Nightmare'	**P:** Crabbe **Dr:** Holcroft	*The Library* *Duplicity*
1782	Act passed allowing Eng. & Welsh parishes to administer Poor Law; Burke's Civil Establishment Act [for economic reform]; congress of Ir. Volunteers at Dungannon wins repeal of 'Poynning's Law' [of 1495 extending Eng. jurisdiction to Ireland & requiring Eng. approval to call Ir. Parliament]– Ir. Parliament gains legislative independence – some RC disabilities removed – Henry Grattan's Free Irish Parliament meets; peace preliminaries agreed with Americans; Bank of N. America estab.d at Philadelphia; Fr. fleet defeated at Isle of Saints– British dominance in W. Indies & naval power restored; siege of Gibralta raised	HMS 'Royal George' sinks in Portsmouth harbour; Watt & Boulton invent double-acting rotary steam-engine; Evangelical Movement launched at Cambridge University; [–1789] Rousseau, *Confessions* pub.d. **Int. Lit.:** Choderlos de Laclos, *Les Liaisons dangereuses*. **Music:** Haydn, 'Il Seraglio' [opera]; Mozart, 'Haffner Symphony'. **Art:** Reynolds, 'William Beckford' [NPG] & [c.] 'Mrs. Thomas Meyrick' [Ashmolean]; Romney, 'Portrait of Mrs Davenport' & 'Prayer (Lady Hamilton)' [Kenwood]	**P:** Cowper John Wolcot ('Peter Pindar'; 1738–1819) **Pr/F:** Burney **Dr:** H. More	*Poems* [8 moral satires; incls 'Table Talk' & 'The Progress of Error'] *Lyrical Odes to the Royal Academicians* [satires] *Cecilia, or Memoirs of an Heiress* *Sacred Dramas* [pub.d]
1783	[Dec.] Pitt the Younger, PM ['Mince Pie' ministry]; troops put down riots by framework-knitters in Nottingham; Irish Renunciation Act frees Ireland from all legislative subordination to Westminster; Bank of Ireland fnd.d; American War formally ends with Peace of Versailles [Britain, France, Spain, USA] – American colonies' independence recognised by Britain – NW Territory [from Mississippi & Ohio rivers to Great Lakes] acquired by USA; British restore Minorca & Florida to Spain – retain Gibraltar & recover W. Indian possessions; [c.–1800] United Empire Loyalists [supported Britain in American War] forced to migrate to Canada from USA	Montgolfier brothers make 1st aerial voyage in hot-air balloon; Order of St Patrick fnd.d by George III in Ireland; oldest British Chamber of Commerce incorporated in Glasgow. **Int. Lit.:** Schiller, *Fiesco* & *Kabale und Liebe* [plays]. **Music:** John Broadwood patents piano pedal; [c.] Mozart, 'Mass in C'. **Art:** Reynolds, 'Captain Bligh'; Houdon, 'Winter' & [1785] 'Summer' [sculpt. figures]; David, 'Andromache Mourning Hector'; Copley, 'Death of Major Pearson' [NG]; Francisco de Goya [pnt] 'Family of the Infante Don Luis'; [c.–1785] John Opie [pnt] 'Peasant's Family' [Tate]	**P:** Cowper Crabbe William Blake (1757–1827) **Pr/F:** Thomas Day (1748–89)	'John Gilpin' [wrtn; comic ballad] *The Village* [narrative poem in couplets] *Poetical Sketches* [prnt.d not pub.d] [–1789] *The History of Sandford and Merton* [children's story; 3 vols]
1784	Gen. Elec: Pitt & Tories win large majority – end of old Whig families' domination – Pitt's ministry lasts 17 yrs; Pitt reduces customs duties & attacks smuggling; food riots in Edinburgh; Government of India Act puts E. India Co. under Government control; United Empire Loyalists [v.1783] estab. New Brunswick & Ontario as separate provinces; 1st Anglican colonial bishop appointed; hostilities cease in India	1st official mail coach – between London & Bristol; 1st air balloon ascent in England; [–1809] Arthur Young edits *Annals of Agriculture* [farming journal]; Cook, *Voyages of Discovery* [pub. posthm.]; [–1791] Herder, *Ideas toward a Philosophy of a History of Mankind*. **Int. Lit.:** Marquis de Sade, *Les 120 Journées de Sodome* [Fr. novel]; Beaumarchais, *The Marriage of Figaro* [comedy; v. Mozart, 1786]. **Music:** Haydn, ' Six ['Paris''] Symphonies'. **Art:** [–1827] Brighton Pavilion begun for Prince of Wales [later Prince Regent & George IV]; Romney, 'Self-Portrait' [NPG]; [–1785] David, 'The Oath of the Horatii'; Rowlandson, 'Vauxhall Gardens'; Sir Henry Raeburn [pnt] 'Reverend Robert Walker Skating on Duddingston Loch' [SNG]	**P:** Charlotte Smith (1749–1806) **Dr:** Holcroft **Lit. 'Events':**	*Elegaic Sonnets, and Other Essays* [incls 'Written at the Close of Spring'; 3rd edtn, 1786, has 20 additional sonnets] *The Follies of a Day* [Eng. adptn of Beaumarchais's *The Marriage of Figaro*; v. preceding column] Samuel Johnson dies

Period	Year	International and Political Contexts	Social and Cultural Contexts	Authors	Indicative Titles
	1785	Pitt intro.s Bill to reform Parliament – defeated; clash between RCs & Protestants in Armagh leads to fnd.tn of Orange Order [v.1795]; Warren Hastings resigns as Governor General of India	1st Channel crossing by balloon [Blanchard & Jeffries]; Edmund Cartwright invents the power-loom. **Art:** Prado Museum fnd.d by Charles III of Spain; Gainsborough, [c.] 'The Morning Walk' [NG], 'Mrs Siddons' & 'Country Girl with Dog and Pitcher' [Bott Coll.]; Romney, 'Ariadne (Lady Hamilton)' [NMM] & [c.] 'Lady Hamilton' [NPG]; [~1796] Houdon, 'George Washington' [statue] **Theory/Crit:** Clara Reeve, *The Progress of Romance* [account of contemporary fiction] **Lit. 'Events':** Thomas Warton, Poet Laureate	**P:** Cowper Wolcot Ann Yearsley ('the Bristol Milkwoman'; 1756–1806) **Pr/F:** James Boswell (1740–95) **Dr:** Elizabeth Inchbald (1753–1821)	*The Task* [narrative poem] *The Lousiad, a Heroi-Comic Poem* *Poems, on Several Occasions* *A Journal of a Tour to the Hebrides with Dr Johnson, LLD, 1773* *I'll Tell You What* [comedy; prnt.d 1786]
	1786	Pitt intro.s financial reforms: excise scheme, reconstructs Board of Trade, creates Sinking Fund [revenue set aside to reduce National Debt]; Anglo-Fr. commercial treaty [lowers duties on Eng. clothes, cotton & iron goods & Fr. wines, soap & olive oil]; [~1793] Lord Cornwallis, Governor General of India – fnds Indian Civil Service	[c.] 1st attempts to use coal-gas for lighting. **Music:** Mozart, 'Marriage of Figaro' [opera] & 'Prague Symphony'. **Art:** [c.] Gainsborough, 'Miss Linley' & 'The Market Cart'; Goya, 'Charles III'; Reynolds, 'Lady Anne Bingham' [Spencer Coll.] & 'The Duchess of Devonshire and her small Daughter'; [c.] Romney, 'Study of Lady Hamilton' [NG]; Opie, 'A Gentleman and a Miner with a Specimen of Copper Ore'; Trumbull, 'Battle of Bunker's Hill'; [c.] Rowlandson, 'Skaters on the Serpentine' [London Mus.] **Lit. 'Events':** [~1788] Goethe travels to Italy	**P:** H. More Robert Burns (1759–96) Helen Williams (1761–1827) **Pr/F:** William Beckford (1759–1844)	*Florio, A Tale, and the Bas-Bleu; or, Conversation* *Poems, Chiefly in the Scottish Dialect* ['Kilmarnock' edtn; incls 'The Cotter's Saturday Night', 'The Jolly Beggars', 'To a Mouse'; expanded edtns, 1787, 1794] *Poems* *Vathek: An Arabian Tale* [Gothic fantasy; unauthorised Eng. edtn; Fr. version pub.d 1787]
	1787	Impeachment of Warren Hastings, ex-governor of India, for corruption [trial: 1788 – famous opening speech by Edmund Burke & orations by Richard Sheridan – acquitted 1795]; Philadelphia Convention draws up US Constitution – Federal gvnmt estab.d in USA – Delaware, Pennsylvania & New Jersey become 1st, 2nd & 3rd States of the Union – dollar currency 1st intro.d; [1788] William Wilberforce, supported by Quakers, forms society for the abolition of the slave trade [v.1807 & 1833] – society fnds Freetown in Sierra Leone as settlement for freed slaves; [>] political & financial problems accelerate in France	1st steam-boat invented in America; Marylebone Cricket Club fnd.d at Thomas Lord's new London cricket ground. **Int. Lit.:** Schiller, *Don Carlos* [blank-verse drama]; Goethe, *Iphigenie auf Tauris* [verse play]; [~1788] Bernardin de Saint-Pierre, *Paul et Virginie* [tragic love-story]; Johann Heinse, *Ardinghello* [Ger. novel]. **Music:** C.P.E. Bach, 'The Resurrection and Ascension of Jesus' [oratorio]; Mozart, two String Quintets, 'Don Giovanni' [1st pf.d Prague] & 'Eine Kleine Nachtmusik'. **Art:** [c.] Reynolds, 'Heads of Angels'; David, 'Death of Socrates'; Stubbs, 'Phaeton' [NG]; Trumbull, 'Thomas Jefferson'; Wright of Derby, 'The Dead Soldier' [Meir Coll.]	**P:** Burns Yearsley **Pr/F:** Mary Wollstonecraft (1759–97)	*Poems on Various Subjects* *Thoughts on the Education of Daughters*
	1788	George III's 1st attack of mental illness; Triple Alliance between Britain, Holland & Prussia to secure European peace; US Constitution comes into force – 1st US Federal Congress in NY – declared Federal capital & seat of Congress – Georgia (4th), Connecticut (5th), Massachusetts (6th), Maryland (7th), S. Carolina (8th), New Hampshire (9th), Virginia (10th) & New York (11th) become States; food shortages & bread riots in France; New South Wales, Australia, fnd.d as penal settlement – 1st convicts arrive in Botany Bay	*The Times* 1st pub.d [fnd.d by John Walter as *The Daily Universal Register*, a scandal sheet, in 1785]; Roman baths found at Bath; Kant, *Critique of Practical Reason*. **Int. Lit.:** Goethe, *Egmont* [tragedy]. **Music:** Haydn, 'Oxford Symphony'; Mozart, 'Jupiter Symphony'. **Art:** George Hepplewhite, *The Cabinet-Maker and Upholsterer's Guide* [pub. posthm.]; David, 'Love of Paris and Helen'; Goya, 'Don Manuel de Zuniga'; Reynolds, 'Master Francis George Hare'	**P:** H. More H. Williams Yearsley **Pr/F:** C. Smith Wollstonecraft	*Slavery: A Poem* *A Poem on the Bill Lately Passed for Regulating the Slave Trade* *A Poem on the Inhumanity of Slavery* *Emmeline* *Mary*

HANOVERIAN/ROMANTIC

1789

Pitt advocates reform of slave trade; 1st National Election in USA – George Washington 1st President – USA declared an economic & customs union – US Post Office estab.d – N. Carolina becomes 12th State; French Estates General meet at Versailles – 3rd Estate declares itself National Assembly – Union of 3 Estates – [July] storming of the Bastille – French Revolution begins – Declaration of the Rights of Man adopted by National Assembly [also use of the guillotine] – feudal system abolished – Louis XVI forced to return to Paris from Versailles – National Guard formed under Lafayette – risings in Fr. provinces; Tippo Sahib of Mysore attacks Travancore [state protected by Britain; v.1790–92]; mutiny on HMS 'Bounty' in S. Seas – Captain Bligh & 18 seamen cast adrift in open boat – sail 4000 miles to Timor, E. Indies – mutineers settle in Pitcairn Islands

1st steam-driven cotton factory in Manchester; Henry Greathead patents design for life-boat; Gilbert White, *Natural History and Antiquites of Selborne*; Bentham, *Introduction to the Principles of Morals and Legislation* [central text of Utilitarianism: 'greatest happiness of greatest number']. **Int. Lit.:** Goethe, *Tasso*. **Music:** [–1790] Mozart, 3 'Prussian Quartets'; Charles Dibdin [compl] 'Tom Bowling'. **Art:** Reynolds, 'Lord Heathfield, Governor of Gibraltar' [NG]; [–1791] Fragonard, 'Boy as Pierrot' [Wallace Coll.]; David, 'Lictors bringing Brutus the Bodies of his Sons'; [c.] Antonio Canova [sculpt] 'Cupid and Psyche'; Sir Thomas Lawrence [pnt] 'Lady Cremorne'

P: Blake

Songs of Innocence [v.1794], *The Book of Thel* [long poem; both prnt.d & illustr.d by Blake; BM] & [c.] *Tiriel* [only in ms.]

4

1790–1829

The Romantic Period

INTRODUCTION

Another short but eventful period, the years 1790 to 1829 see the continuation of the **Hanoverian*** monarchy: first by George III, then – as George's insanity becomes permanent – by his son as Prince Regent (**The Regency***, 1811–20), who accedes to the throne as George IV in 1820 (his death in 1830, and the ensuing succession, is dealt with in Chapter 5). But the period is most emphatically marked by a Europe ripped apart by the **French Revolutionary Wars**, the rise to pan-European power of Napoleon Bonaparte, and the subsequent Napoleonic Wars, ending only with Napoleon's final defeat at the Battle of Waterloo in 1815. It also witnesses the high point of the European **Romantic*** movement in the arts. In the British context, the later part of the period experiences developments in political, religious and social reform which will become one of the hallmarks of the **Victorian*** period to follow [see Chapter 5].

Chapter contents

4.1 HANOVERIAN (continued) I

The family name of the line of monarchs – The Hanoverians – who occupied the British throne from the accession of King George I in 1714 to the death of Queen Victoria in 1901.

The central event in the earlier part of this period had begun in 1789 with the inception of the *French Revolution*, the series of violent political and social upheavals in France which ended with the establishment of the Consulate (1799) and the rise to power of Napoleon Bonaparte (he crowned himself Emperor in 1804). It had widespread repercussions throughout Europe – miltary, political and cultural – especially the example it offered of overthrowing an old and corrupt feudal regime, freeing the peasantry and enfranchising the bourgeoisie; its ideals of liberty, equality and fraternity acted as an inspiration to European liberationists throughout the 19th Century. However, from 1792 to 1802, Europe was embroiled in the *French Revolutionary Wars*, in which France fought two coalitions of other European powers: the first was composed of Austria, Prussia, Sardinia, and then Britain, Spain and the Netherlands, and lasted until 1798; the second, instituted the same year by Willam Pitt the Younger [see Chapter 3, and below], initially involved Britain, Russia, Austria, Naples, Portugal and Turkey, but Napoleon's military supremacy meant that, by 1801, Britain was isolated and had to agree the Peace of Amiens with France in 1802.

In 1803, Britain again declared war on France, and thus commenced the *Napoleonic Wars* (1803–15). Another coalition was formed against France in 1805 (Britain, Austria, Russia, Sweden, with Prussia joining in 1806), but Napoleon defeated all his enemies except Britain, and by 1809 controlled most of Continental Europe: the Holy Roman Empire had been dissolved in 1806; the German states were reorganised as the Confederation of the Rhine; the Helvetic Confederation and the Grand Duchy of Warsaw were bound to France by alliances; and Napoleon made his brothers and other close associates kings of Westphalia, Spain, Italy, Holland and Naples. He then attempted to force Britain into submission by economic blockade ('the Continental System'), but Britain's naval supremacy had been established at the Battle of Trafalgar (1805), and the blockade proved impossible to enforce. The Peninsula War (1808–14) – in which Britain assisted Spain and Portugal in resisting Napoleon by keeping 200,000 of his troops tied up there and finally pushing France out of the Iberian Peninsular – became Napoleon's 'running sore'; Russia left the Continental System and was invaded in 1812, but Moscow never fell, and Napoleon's retreat was a disaster for his army. A new coalition was formed in 1813 (Britain, Russia, Prussia, Sweden and Austria) which this time defeated Napoleon at the Battle of the Nations; Napoleon abdicated and was exiled to Elba; the Congress of Vienna assembled (1814); Napoleon returned to Paris in 1815; the Congress of Vienna dispersed; after his 'Hundred Days', Napoleon was finally defeated at Waterloo, and exiled to St Helena where he died in 1821. The Congress of Vienna (1815) reassembled to put in place a European settlement.

As will be seen from the timeline narratives for this period indicated below [towards the end of the gloss on **Hanoverian (continued) (II*)**], the French Revolution and the ensuing wars in many ways dominate the domestic context, too. The **Tory*** [see Chapter 2] Prime Minister, William Pitt continued to govern for George III. He introduced Income Tax in 1799 (as a temporary wartime measure, but which, except for two short intervals, has remained in force ever since); but he also passed the Canada Act of 1791, which divided Canada into two provinces, one English and one French, each with its own representative government; and the Act of Union of Britain and Ireland in 1800 which united the two Parliaments, allowing Irish MPs to sit at

Westminster, and creating 'The United Kingdom of Great Britain and Ireland'. However, in 1801, when Pitt attempted to fulfil his pledges about Catholic emancipation, George III refused his assent, causing a political crisis in which Pitt resigned. But in 1804, with Napoleon beginning to dominate the whole of mainland Europe and planning to invade Britain, Pitt returned as Prime Minister, and as noted above, formed a European alliance in 1805 which disastrously failed to halt Napoleon's progress. He witnessed Nelson's victory over the French fleet at Trafalgar in 1805, but also the defeat of the the Russians and Austrians at Austerlitz the same year. Pitt died in 1806. Five years later, King George became hopelessly insane, and from 1811 to 1820, when he died, Great Britain was governed by **The Regency*** of the Prince of Wales (later George IV).

4.2 (THE) REGENCY

As a noun with the direct article, 'The Regency' defines the period in British history from 1811 to 1820 when George III's insanity became so severe that his eldest son, George, the Prince of Wales (afterwards George IV), was appointed Prince Regent.

It was an era of international and national turbulence: the final years of the *Napoleonic Wars* [see above], which bankrupted the British economy, ended with the Battle of Waterloo in 1815, while the 'Peterloo' massacre of demonstrators for political reform occurred in Manchester in 1819. Accelerating enclosure (from 1801) dispossessed land workers, and this source of cheap labour, which began to migrate to the growing urban centres, was increasingly exploited by the wealthy new entrepreneurs of the *Industrial Revolution.* But opposition was developing, too: in 1811–12, Nottingham weavers founded the 'Luddite' movement, which smashed industrial machinery, and as the timeline narratives below show, industrial unrest and the beginnings of the trade union movement are important features of the period.

Nevertheless, The Regency is also associated with a witty and civilised, if somewhat febrile, culture inspired in part by George himself: Beau Brummell, the exquisite Regency dandy, was a close friend and protégé until they quarrelled in 1813; Jane Austen (albeit reluctantly) dedicated *Emma* to the Prince Regent in 1816; the painters J. M. W. Turner and John Constable were producing mature work at this time, and the caricaturist Thomas Rowlandson was also highly popular (George himself was the butt of some of the most savage drawings). A patron of the arts who bequeathed a valuable collection of books and paintings to the nation, the Prince Regent was responsible, *inter alia,* for major refurbishment at Windsor Palace and especially for the rebuilding of the Brighton Pavilion with its ornate oriental style and chinoiserie interior. The Pavilion was undertaken by John Nash, whose talents as architect and town planner George recognised. Nash was charged by him to plan the new Regent's Park in London, together with the curved Regency terraces around it (1811–25), and to design Regent Street to connect the Park with Westminster. He also built Carlton House Terrace; laid out Trafalgar Square and St James's Park; reconstituted Buckingham Palace from the old Buckingham House; and designed Marble Arch, which stood in front of the former until it was moved in 1851.

As an adjective, 'Regency' denotes the English furniture, clothing, architecture, and so on of the period, the latter characterised by fine proportions, **Neo-Classical*** (see Chapter 3) elements, the use of stucco on buildings and the decorative use of ironwork. In addition to John Nash's work above, Regency Brighton and Cheltenham were two of the fastest growing towns of this period, and offer excellent examples of such architectural features.

4.3 HANOVERIAN (continued) II

In 1820, on the death of George III, the Prince Regent became King George IV. Although a professed **Whig*** [see Chapter 2], who had close association with Charles James Fox, Edmund Burke and the politician/playwright, Richard Brinsley Sheridan during his father's reign (and thus the source of much antagonism between them), as Prince Regent and then King, George governed with the support of the Tories* [see Chapter 2], Spencer Perceval (the only British Premier to be assassinated), Lord Liverpool, George Canning, Viscount Goderich (later Earl of Ripon) and the Duke of Wellington all forming ministries during his reign. George's personal extravagance and dissipation caused the monarchy to lose power and prestige during the period, reaching an all-time low in 1820–1, when the king brought an unsuccessful divorce action against Queen Caroline, who was popular with the people, and barred her from attending his coronation in 1821 – a scandal only resolved by her death a few days later. George IV died without heir in 1830, and was succeeded by his younger brother as William IV, George III's third son. [See Chapter 5, for glosses on his reign and the **'Early Victorian'*** period more generally].

Key Timeline Narratives 1790–1829

⮑ ***International Events***   In the international context, it is possible to track such narratives as: the expansion of the original United States by the gradual creation of new states, the purchase of Louisiana from France (1803 – which effectively doubled the size of the USA), the purchase of Florida from Spain (1819), and the appropriation of Texas from Mexico (after 1821); the continued acquisition of new colonies by Britain, and the consolidation of the British Government's supreme power in India; the exploration and settlement by Britain of Australia, Tasmania and New Zealand; the settlement of Cape Colony and other parts of South Africa by the Boers and the British; and the struggle of Greece for independence from Turkey throughout the 1820s (during which Lord Byron joined the insurgents and died [1824]).

⮑ ***French Revolution***   In Britain, the political fall-out from the French Revolution, especially during the 1790s, was extensive. Many Whigs supported the Tories' hostility to it, and only a small group led by Charles James Fox remained in opposition; Burke produced his famous *Reflections*, and Tom Paine responded with his equally famous *The Rights of Man*; in 1793–5, severe curbs were imposed on the freedom of the press (and again in 1798), **Habeas Corpus*** [see Chapter 2] was suspended, and repressive legislation was passed by Parliament to prevent treason and sedition; France attempted to support a rebellion in Ireland by invading it, but both failed; however, there was much radical support for the Revolution and much extra-parliamentary opposition to the Government (hence the term 'English **Jacobins***, see below).

➲ *Politics*   The pressure for political reform ran throughout the period: in 1792, the reform movement was instigated by dissident Whigs and the London Corresponding Societies; a Bribery Act of 1809 prohibited the sale of parliamentary seats. In 1816, provincial Hampden Clubs were set up to press for reform and there was a pro-reform riot in London; in 1817, Habeas Corpus was again suspended and an anti-sedition Act introduced as popular support for reform intensified; 1819 witnessed the 'Peterloo' massacre in Manchester, when an 80,000-strong reform meeting was attacked by troops, and the Six Acts (or 'Gag Laws') were introduced to curb public and press freedoms and suppress public disorder. The General Election of 1830 showed pro-reform attitudes predominating with the election of the Whigs under Earl Grey, and 1831–2 witnessed the first reform stuggle resolved by the Reform Act of 1832 [see Chapter 5, 'Early Victorian'*].

➲ *Economics*   From c.1795, high food prices caused by the war gave rise to great distress amongst the poor, and the 'Speenhamland System' of poor relief was introduced to supplement wages with doles; in 1812, wheat prices rose to their highest point in the whole 19th Century causing further economic distress; in 1815, a Corn Law prohibited foreign imports until British corn was 80 shillings a quarter (of somewhat less than a ton); there was acute post-war depression, unemployment and unrest in 1816; a Select Committee was set up in 1817 to investigate the high cost of relieving the poor; protective duties were reduced between 1823 and 1827; a revised Corn Law of 1828 introduced a sliding scale of duties on imports [for further developments regarding poverty and the Corn Laws, see Chapter 5].

➲ *Unions*   Related both to political reform and to poverty/high food prices was the development of workers' institutions to challenge and resist government and employers: the Combination Acts of 1799 and 1800 prohibited political associations (e.g. to press for better pay and conditions), and effectively made trade unions illegal. However, strikes by Durham miners against Government economic policy broke out in 1810, followed by the 'Luddite' riots of 1811–12. The Combination Acts of 1799–1800 were repealed in 1824, thus making trades unions legal, but a rash of strikes caused the repeal to be amended in 1825; the same year saw the founding of the Northumberland and Durham Miners Union. In 1829, the National Association for the Protection of Labour was founded, and the Grand General Union of Cotton Spinners held its first national conference.

➲ *Reform*   Other reform movements in this period include: that instigated by William Wilberforce in 1788 [and see 1791] to abolish the slave trade (banned in the British Empire, 1807) and then slavery itself (prohibited throughout the British Empire from 1834); the gradual introduction from 1802 onwards of legislation to regulate the use of child labour in industry (e.g. Factory Acts in 1819 and 1825), accelerating under the reformed Commons in the 1830s and beyond [see Chapter 5]; those of Sir Robert Peel in the 1820s of the legal and penal systems, including introducing a professional police force in London; the beginnings of local government reform from 1835; and the continuing struggle for religious freedom. Pitt's attempt to grant Catholic emancipation failed in 1801, but the issue became hot again in the mid-1820s with the repeal of the Test and Corporation Acts in 1828, which gave religious liberty to Non-Conformists and split the Tory Party, and the Roman Catholic

Relief Act of 1829 which made discrimination against Catholics illegal, splitting the Tories even further.

⮕ **Science and Engineering**   In respect of developments in science, we may notice: John Dalton's pioneering experiments in chemistry throughout the 1800s; Sir Humphrey Davy's investigations in electro-chemistry and his invention of the miner's safety lamp in 1815; the first publication of *The Lancet* in 1823. In British engineering, key developments comprise: from 1802, the extensive building of docks in London; from 1801, the opening of major canals across the country; from 1803, the construction of thousands of miles of roads in Scotland by Thomas Telford, and of his Menai suspension bridge (1819–26). The development in the 1810s of John Macadam's road-building techniques and his appointment in 1815 as Surveyor-General of British roads; the first successful experiments with gas-lighting for buildings and streets in the course of the period; and perhaps most strikingly, from 1800, the building, refinement and successful deployment of steam locomotives and the construction of the first railways by Richard Trevithick, William Hedley and George and Robert Stephenson [see, for example, 1800, 1813 and 1814, 1821]. In 1825, the first steam passenger line opened with the Stockton and Darlington railway; Stephenson's 'Rocket' reached 29 mph in the trials for the Liverpool–Manchester railway in 1829, which opened in 1830 [for further developments in steam power, see Chapter 5, 'Early Victorian'*]

⮕ **European Culture**   European cultural achievements in the period include: in philosophy, the work of Kant, Hegel, Schopenhauer and Comte; in literature, the writings of Goethe, Schiller, Schlegel, Herder, Hölderlin, Heine, Novalis, de Staël, Dumas Père, Hugo, de Vigny, Balzac and Pushkin; in music, the continuing compositions of Haydn and Mozart, but also those of Beethoven, Schubert, Rossini, Schumann, Mendelssohn and Berlioz; in painting, the work of David, Ingres, Géricault, Delacroix, Goya and Caspar David Friedrich. It is also worth noting that an indigenous literature was developing in America with the writings of Washington Irving and James Fenimore Cooper, and that Noam Webster's *An American Dictionary of the English Language* was first published in 1828.

⮕ **British Culture**   In Britain, cultural developments include: the founding of Sunday newspapers (the *Observer*, 1791; *The Sunday Times*, 1822), and the first publication of the *Scotsman* (1817) and the *Manchester Guardian* (1821); the founding of literary/political periodicals such as the *Edinburgh Review* (1802), the *Quarterly Review* (1809), *Blackwood's Magazine* (1817, which in 1818 attacked Keats and 'The Cockney School' of poets), the *Westminster Review* (1824), *The Spectator* (1828) and *Fraser's Magazine* (1830); the founding of the colleges which were to become the constituent parts of London University (Birkbeck, 1823; University and King's, 1827–8); the work of philosophers and economists (Thomas Malthus, Jeremy Bentham, James Mill, David Ricardo, Thomas Carlyle) and social reformers (William Godwin, Mary Wollstonecraft, Robert Owen and William Cobbett); in the visual arts, the colour-printed drawings of William Blake, the portraits of Sir Henry Raeburn and Sir Thomas Lawrence, the paintings of J. M. W. Turner, the landscapes of John Constable, John Cotman and the 'Norwich School', and the water-colours of Samuel Palmer. [For British literature in this period, see the gloss on Romanticism* below.]

4.4 JACOBIN

Although also derived, like Jacobean* and Jacobite* [see Chapters 1 and 2] from the Latin for James ('Jacobus'), Jacobin should not be confused with either. Originally the name given to French Dominican monks whose establishment was the church and then convent of St Jacques in Paris, it was taken over by a radically democratic political club of the French Revolution, formed in May 1789, which began meeting in the hall of the Jacobin convent the following October.

Led by Robespierre, the Jacobin club became increasingly extreme, overthrew the Girondins in 1793, instigated the Reign of Terror, and was closed down after the coup of Thermidor in 1794 (Robespierre was executed).

'Jacobin' is still used occasionally to describe any extreme political radical, but in British cultural history, the term 'English Jacobins' is most commonly applied to the English supporters of the French Revolution in the 1790s. The full title of Edmund Burke's critique of the Revolution was *Reflections on the Revolution in France and on the Proceedings in Certain Societies in London Relative to that Event*, the later part of which was directed at the Constitutional and Revolutionary Societies, largely made up of religious non-conformists who traced their descent back to the English Revolution in the mid-17th Century [see Chapter 2] and who considered themselves oppressed and discriminated against by unjust laws. Amongst these were the Unitarian radicals, Richard Price and Joseph Priestley, but the best-known revolutionaries of the time are Tom Paine (*The Rights of Man*, 1791 and 1792; *The Age of Reason*, 1794–6) and William Godwin (*Enquiry Concerning Political Justice*, 1793; *Things as They Are or, the Adventures of Caleb Williams*, 1794). Godwin's circle of political reformers and writers included Mary Wollstonecraft (later his wife and mother of Mary [who married Shelley and wrote *Frankenstein*]: *Vindication of the Rights of Man*, 1790; *A Vindication of the Rights of Women*, 1792; *Maria, or the Wrongs of Woman*, 1798); Mary Hays (*Memoirs of Emma Courtney*, 1796); Elizabeth Inchbald (*A Simple Story*, 1791); Thomas Holcroft (*Anna St Ives*, 1792; *The Adventures of Hugh Trevor*, 1794); and Robert Bage (*Man as He Is*, 1792; *Hermsprong; or, Man as He is Not*, 1796).

4.5 ROMANTICISM / ROMANTIC

The terms 'Romanticism' and 'Romantic' apply to the anti-Neo-Classicist movements in the arts which developed in Europe during this period.

In many respects, these are the terms in literary history and criticism which are the most controversial and difficult to define with any precision (a critic apparently counted 11,396 definitions of them in 1948). Derived from the Old French word for '[a] romance' ('romanz'), then from the French 'romantique', the word 'romantic' in English still holds several meanings, the commonest – apart from the literary-period descriptor outlined below – being that which suggests an inclination to love and romance (as in 'a romantic dinner for two'). But 'romantic' is also used to describe a person who is idealistic and fanciful ('he's incorrigibly romantic – he romanticises everything'), and to suggest an account or project which is fictitious, exaggerated, far-fetched, wild or fantastic ('a romantic version of events'). The noun 'a romance' was used originally for a medieval tale of chivalry and ideal love – often in combination with magic and the marvellous – of the kind written in the 'Romance languages' (the vernaculars of French, Italian, Spanish, etc.); then (in earlier periods, sometimes pejoratively) for those freely imaginative literary fictions, especially of a historical variety (a 'historical romance'), which do not fit the category of 'the realist novel'; but it also remains the term used to describe a literary work which is clearly fictitious and wonderful (again, in contemporary usage, often to do with love/love-affairs: 'a Mills and Boon romance').

Although it is possible to perceive vestigial connections between the above usages and the terms under consideration here, 'Romantic' and 'Romanticism' (usually with the initial letter capitalised) apply to the movements in philosophy, literature and the other arts which developed in Europe during the late-18th Century and the first quarter of the 19th Century [but see the caveat in Chapter 3, timeline narrative under **European Culture**, and the final paragraph of the present gloss].

In Germany, Romanticism was driven by the 'Sturm und Drang' ('Storm and Stress') movement which began in the 1770s, exemplified in the work of Johann Herder and the emotional turmoil depicted in the earlier writings of Goethe and Schiller, and then by August Wilhelm von Schlegel and his brother, Friedrich, who developed its literary application (the latter is credited with the earliest formulation of the term 'Romantic poetry' [1798], although Madame de Staël in France gave it widespread currency in 1810 with her book *De l'Allemagne*).

In France, the work of Jean-Jacques Rousseau prefigures many of the characteristics of Romanticism in its celebration of nature and the natural goodness of human nature, its valuing of feeling and emotion over reason, and its propagation of an educational method in which a pupil would develop freely in accordance with the inclinations of their own innate nature. Rousseau's *The Social Contract* (1762), which opens with the famous paradox, 'Man is born free; and everywhere he is in chains', and which has as its catchwords 'Liberty, Equality, Fraternity', was a prime influence on the French Revolution (see above) and on other progressive and liberationist movements in the 19th Century.

In the British context, the *OED* gives the first usage of the word 'Romantic' as 1812, when H.C. Robinson comments in a journal entry: 'Coleridge's first lecture … . He spoke of … a classification of poetry into ancient and romantic'; and in 1814, a reviewer in the *Monthly Review* writes of a 'chapter [which] divides European poetry into two schools, the classical, and the romantic'. In the *New Monthly Review* in 1823, appears the first listed (albeit pejorative) use of the word 'Romanticism': 'the dramatic heresy of romanticism'; and in 1827, Thomas Carlyle speaks of the 'grand controversy … between the Classicists and Romanticists'.

Romanticism, then, represents a reaction to Classicism and Neo-Classicism* [see Chapter 3], which were held to have dominated art and thought from the 17th Century, and which denied expression to the emotional and irrational depths of the human psyche (Romanticism's exploration of such experience opened the way for psychology and psychoanalysis to develop in the course of the 19th Century). Although Romanticism is differently inflected in different countries and periods, the following generalisations (orientated towards the literary) hold good for the period under consideration:

- It exalts individual aspirations and values above those of society, and is personal and subjective in inclination.
- It turns for inspiration to the Middle Ages (regarded by the Augustans as barbaric), to earlier forms of language (e.g. in Old English poetry), to folklore and folk-tales, to the supernatural as a means of expressing 'strange states of mind', and to Nature, celebrating both its specificity and the spiritual and moral bond between humanity and the natural world.
- It generally follows Rousseau's belief in human goodness and the innocence of children and 'primitive' peoples ('the noble savage'), and is optimistic about human progress, whilst also registering the potential anomie involved in sustaining a Romantic sensibility in modern urbanising and industrialising societies.
- Aesthetically, it is characterised by the privileging of the Imagination rather than canonic models (as the Neo-Classicists had done), by freedom of subject, form and style, by the elevation of feeling ('Sensibility') over reason ('Sense'), and in poetry – arguably the dominant literary genre in the British context at least – by rejecting **Augustan*** poetic diction [see Chapter 3], by the use of traditional forms (e.g. lyrics, songs and ballads) and by the quest for a simpler, more direct style (see, for example, Wordsworth's comments about 'the real language of men in a state of vivid sensation' in the Preface to the second edition of [the symptomatically titled] *Lyrical Ballads*, 1800).

British literature in the period includes the work of the first- and second-generation Romantic poets (first: William Blake, Robert Burns, William Wordsworth, Samuel Taylor Coleridge; second: Lord Byron, Percy Bysshe Shelley, John Keats), but also the later poetry of George Crabbe, the poems of John Clare, James Hogg and Robert Bloomfield; the work of such Romantic women poets as Anna Barbauld, Letitia Landon, Ann Yearsley, Felicia Hemans, Anna Seward, Charlotte Dacre and Anne Grant; and, by the late-1820s, the earlier poetry of Alfred, Lord Tennyson, and Elizabeth Barrett Browning.

The period also contains the 'Gothic' fiction of Ann Radcliffe, Matthew Lewis and Charles Maturin; the essays of Charles Lamb, William Hazlitt, Leigh Hunt and Thomas de Quincey; and the fiction of Fanny Burney, Maria Edgeworth, Jane Austen, Sir Walter Scott, Mary Shelley, John Galt and Thomas Love Peacock, but also again, in its later years, novels by Edward Bulwer-Lytton and Benjamin Disraeli. As proof once again that literary periodisation can only ever be approximate is the fact that the Romantic period slides so imperceptibly into the **Victorian*** age [see Chapter 5].

Timelines: 1790–1829

Period	Year	International and Political Contexts	Social and Cultural Contexts	Authors	Indicative Titles
HANOVERIAN/ROMANTIC	1790	Whigs Burke & Charles James Fox in direct opposition over French Revolution; rebellion of Austrian Netherlands suppressed [declared independence as 'Belgium', 1789]; Supreme Court of USA 1st meets; [–1791] Washington fnd.d [1800>] capital of USA – Rhode Island becomes 13th State	Oxford-Birmingham Canal opens; Lavoisier lists 1st table of [31] chemical elements; Burke, *Reflections on the Revolution in France*; Kant, *Critique of Judgment*. **Music:** [–1791] Haydn, 'London Symphonies'; Mozart 'Cosi fan tutti'. **Art:** Bewick, *A General History of Quadrupeds* [wood engrv.s]; [c.] Raeburn, 'Sir John Sinclair of Ulster' [SNG]; Lawrence, 'Queen Charlotte' [NG] & 'Miss Eliza Farren'	**P:** Blake **Pr/F:** Lennox H. Willams Wollstonecraft (Mrs) Ann Radcliffe (1764–1823)	[c.–1793] *The Marriage of Heaven and Hell* [prnt.d & illustr.d by Blake] *Euphemia* *Julia, A Novel* *Vindication of the Rights of Man* [riposte to Burke's *Reflections*; v. preceding column] *A Sicilian Romance* [gothic novel]
	1791	Pro-Church & King anti-French Revolution riots in Birmingham – Dissenter & scientist, Joseph Priestley's laboratory & library destroyed; Wilberforce's 'Motion for Abolition of Slave Trade passed thro' Parliament; pro-French group formed in Ireland by Wolfe Tone & Edward Fitzgerald; Pitt's Canada Act creates 2 separate provinces: Ontario [Upper Canada – British] & Quebec [Lower Canada – French] – each has representative government; Louis XVI accepts new French Constitution – flees Paris – captured at Varennes – brought back as prisoner; US Congress ratifies Bill of Rights – 1st amendments to the Constitution intro.d – 1st US bank estab.d – Vermont becomes 14th State; uprising of black population in San Domingo [Haiti]	The *Observer*, oldest UK Sunday newspaper, fnd.d; 1st institution for the blind opens in Liverpool; University of Pennsylvania fnd.d; Thomas Paine, *The Rights of Man* [Pt I; Pt II, 1792 – reply to Burke's *Reflections*]; Sir James Mackintosh, *Vindiciae Gallicae* [reply to Burke by secretary to 'Friends of the People']; Burke, *Appeal from the New to the Old Whigs*; Bentham, *Panopticon* [on the ideal prison]. **Int. Lit.:** de Sade, *Justine*. **Music:** the waltz intro.d into England; Mozart, 'The Magic Flute' & 'Requiem' [wrtn on deathbed]. **Art:** [–1794] Thomas Sheraton, *Cabinet Makers' and Upholsterers' Drawing Book*; George Morland [pnt] 'Interior of a Stable' [NG] **Lit. 'Events':** [–1792] William Wordsworth's 2nd visit to France [revolutionary sympathies & affair with Annette Villon]	**P:** Blake Burns H. Williams **Pr/F:** Boswell Inchbald Radcliffe Wollstonecraft **Theory/Crit:** William Gilpin	*The French Revolution* [prnt.d; not pub.d] [c.] *Tam o'Shanter* [verse tale] & [c.] 'Auld Lang Syne' [wrtn; pub.d 1794] *A Farewell, for Two Years, to England. A Poem* *The Life of Samuel Johnson* [biog.] *A Simple Story* [novel] *The Romance of the Forest* *Original Stories from Real Life* *Essays on Picturesque Beauty*
	1792	Indictment of Tom Paine – flees to France; Manchester radicals attacked by loyalist crowd; Paris Commune estab.d & Revolutionary Tribunal – guillotine erected in Paris – Paris mob invades the Tuileries – September Massacres of royalists – France declared a Republic – national bankrupcy; Prussia & Austria at war with & invade France – Revolutionary Wars begin; US mint estab.d – dollar currency developed [v.1787] – White House, Washington, built & [–1830] the Capitol – Kentucky becomes 15th State; Tippoo Sahib defeated by British at Seringapatam – cedes half his territory; [c.] 1st Europeans settle in New Zealand; slave trade abolished in Danish colonies	[22 Sept.] French revolutionary calendar intro.d [abolished, 1804]; British parliamentary reform movement revived by Whig 'Friends of the People' Society & the London Corresponding Society; [c.] Missionary Society fnd.d in London; 1st Eng. home lit by coal-gas; Arthur Young, *Travels in France*. **Music:** Haydn, 'The Creation' [oratorio]; Rouget de l'Isle [comp] 'La Marseillaise'. **Art:** Boydells' edtn of Shakespeare illustr.d by Opie; Romney, 'William Cowper' [NPG]; Lawrence, 'Julius Angerstein and His Wife'; Morland, 'Tavern Door' [SNG]; Trumbull, 'George Washington Before the Battle of Trenton'; Antoio Canova [sculpt] 'Cupid and Psyche'	**P:** Burns Samuel Rogers (1763–1855) **Pr/F:** Holcroft Wollstonecraft Robert Bage (1728–1801) **Dr:** Holcroft	'Ye Banks and Braes' [song] *The Pleasures of Memory* *Anna St Ives* [novel] *A Vindication of the Rights of Woman* [feminist treatise] *Man as He Is* [novel] *The Road to Ruin*
	1793	Pitt estab.s Board of Agriculture; Aliens Act restricts liberty of foreign visitors to Britain; Scottish Treason Trials – 2 radicals transported for advocating reform; Ir. RCs restored right to vote; Louis XVI & Marie Antoinette executed – fall of Girondins –	Seditious Publications Act restricts liberty of press; [c.] 1st legal recognition of Friendly Societies; Kant, *Religion within the Boundaries of Pure Reason*; [–1795] de Sade, *La Philosophie dans le boudoir*. **Int. Lit.:** Goethe, *Reineke Fuchs* [epic poem satirising Ger. Romantics]. **Music:** [–1841] George	**P:** Blake Burns	[all prnt.d & illustr.d by Blake] *Visions of the Daughters of Albion, America: a Prophecy* [early 'Prophetic Book'] & *The Gates of Paradise* [for children; *The Gates of Paradise* 'for the sexes', c.1820] 'Scots wha hae' [song]

History	Arts / Science / Literature	Authors	Works
Reign of Terror lasts 15 mths – 2596 victims in Paris – Revolutionary Army formed – Charlotte Corday executed for assassinating Marat – Xianity abolished; France at war with 1st Coalition [incls Austria, Prussia, Britain, Holland, Spain] – USA declares neutrality; 'Jay's Treaty' settles outstanding problems between USA & Britain [regulates navigation & commerce] – Democrats see it as betrayal of France; British seize Fr. possessions in India – permanent settlement of Bengal – Cornwallis reorganises justice, police & revenue	Thomson, *A Select Collection of Original Scottish Airs* [6 vols; incls songs by Burns]; [c.] 'The Girl I left behind me' 1st sung. **Art:** David, 'Death of Marat'; [–1798] Goya, 'Los Caprichos (The Caprices)' [series of satirical etchings] & [c.] 'Fire'; Stubbs, 'Prince of Wales' Phaeton' [Royal Coll.]	C. Smith William Wordsworth (1770–1850) **Pr/F:** C. Smith Wordsworth William Godwin (1756–1836)	*The Emigrants, A Poem, in Two Books* [on disenchantment with Fr. Revolution] *An Evening Walk & Descriptive Sketches* *The Old Manor House* [novel] *A Letter to the Bishop of Llandaff, by a Republican* [wrtn; pub.d 1875] *Enquiry Concerning Political Justice* [treatise]

1794

History	Arts / Science / Literature	Authors	Works
[–1801] Habeas Corpus suspended in Britain & curbs imposed on press; Thomas Holcroft, Hardy, Horne Tooke & other radicals tried for high treason – acquitted; Whig Party split: most join Pitt – small opposition group with Fox; Danton & Robespierre executed – Jacobin Club closed – Commune replaced by Commissioners – policy of Terror reversed; British naval victory in Channel at Battle of 1st June – British capture St Lucia & Corsica from French; US Navy estab.d; slavery abolished in Fr. colonies	Manchester Chamber of Commerce estab.d; John Dalton 1st describes colour-blindness ['Daltonism']; Paine, *The Age of Reason* [Pt I; Pt II 1796]; [–1796] Erasmus Darwin, *Zoönomia, or the Laws of Organic Life* [C. Darwin's grandfather]. **Music:** Haydn, 'The Clock' & 'The Military' symphonies; James Hewitt [comp] 'Tammany' [1st US opera]. **Art:** Reynolds's complete *Discourses* [on Art] pub.d [v.1769]; Blake [engrv.] 'The Ancient of Days' [frontispiece for *Europe: a Prophecy*; BM]; [c.] Raeburn, 'Doctor Nathaniel Spens' [Royal Co. of Archers] **Lit. 'Events':** Goethe & Schiller's friendship begins.	**P:** Blake **Pr/F:** Godwin Holcroft Radcliffe Mary Robinson ('Perdita'; 1758–1800) **Dr:** Holcroft Samuel Taylor Coleridge (1772–1834) & Robert Southey (1774–1843)	[all prnt.d & illustr.d by Blake] *Songs of Experience* [combined vol. with *Songs of Innocence*; v.1789], *The Book of Urizen* & *Europe: a Prophecy* *Things as They Are or, the Adventures of Caleb Williams* [novel] *The Adventures of Hugh Trevor* *The Mysteries of Udolpho* *The Widow, or, A Picture of Modern Times* [novel] *Love's Frailties* *The Fall of Robespierre*

1795

History	Arts / Science / Literature	Authors	Works
Treasonable Practices & Seditious Meetings Act – against public meetings & political organisations; high prices cause food riots & widespread economic distress; [–1834] Speenhamland system of poor relief in Britain [doles to supplement wages]; Protestant Orange Order fnd.d in Ireland [1st demonstration, 1796]; British take Cape of Good Hope & Ceylon from Dutch – French retake St Lucia; White Terror in France – National Guard reorganised – 2nd uprising in Paris – dispersed by Napoleon Bonaparte [becomes C. in C. in Italy] – Directory replaces Convention – Fr. empire in Europe grows – civil war in Brittany aided by Britain – RN attack on Quiberon Bay fails; Prussia & Spain make peace with France; Mungo Park explores W. Africa	[>] Stamp Duty on newspapers increased; metric system adopted in France; [–1797] Burke, *Letters on a Regicide Peace*; Lindley Murray, *English Grammar*; G. White, *A Naturalist's Calendar* [pub. posthm.]; John Playfair, *Elements of Geometry*. **Int. Lit:** Johann Paul Richter ('Jean Paul'), *Hesperus* [Ger. fiction]; Schiller, *Letters concerning the aesthetic education of mankind*. **Music:** Conservatoire de Musique, Paris, fnd.d; Haydn, 'Drum-Roll' & 'London Symphony' [pf.d; wrtn 1791]; Ludvig van Beethoven [compl] early works for piano. **Art:** Blake, 'God Creating Adam', 'Newton' & 'Nebuchadnezzar' [colour-printed drawings; Tate]; [c.] Raeburn, 'Mrs Eleanor Urquhart'	**P:** Blake Ann Cristall (c.1769–[date unknown]) Southey Erasmus Darwin (1731–1802) **Pr/F:** H. More H. Williams Maria Edgeworth (1768–1849)	[all prnt.d & illustr.d by Blake] *The Song of Los*, *The Book of Los* & *The Book of Ahania* *Poetical Sketches, in Irregular Verse* *Poems & Joan of Arc* [epic poem] *The Botanic Garden* [long poem composed of 2 earlier ones, 1789, 1791–2] *Cheap Repository Tracts* [moral tales; incls 'The Shepherd of Salisbury Plain'] *Paul and Virginia* [Eng. trans of Fr. novel, 1787] *Letters to Literary Ladies* [on female education]

PERIOD	YEAR	INTERNATIONAL AND POLITICAL CONTEXTS	SOCIAL AND CULTURAL CONTEXTS	AUTHORS	INDICATIVE TITLES
	1796	British peace talks with Fr. Directory fail – Fr. invasion attempt at Bantry Bay, Ireland, fails – British capture Guiana & St Lucia – return Corsica to France; Napoleon's Italian campaign begins – defeats Austrians at Lodi & Arcola – Fr/Sp. alliance – Spain declares war on Britain; Paris divided into 12 municipalities; Tennessee becomes 16th State; Teheran becomes capital of Persia (Iran); British take Ceylon from Dutch – annexed by E. India Co. until 1802 when it becomes a Crown Colony; China bans importation of opium	Royal Technical College, Glasgow, fnd.d; Edward Jenner 1st uses smallpox vaccine [derived from cows]; Burke, A Letter to a Noble Lord; [–1799] Joseph Strutt, Dresses and Habits of the English People. Int. Lit.: Schiller, Über naive und sentimentalische Dichtung [begun 1795; on ancient & modern poetry]; Goethe, Wilhelm Meisters Lehrjahre. Music: Haydn, 'Holy Mass', 'Kettledrum Mass' & 'Emperor Quartet'. Art: [–1813] James Wyatt builds Fonthill Abbey, Wiltshire, for William Beckford [18thC Gothic]; Thomas Jefferson designs Monticello, Virginia [classical style]; [c.] 'The Washington Family'; Antoine-Jean Gros [pnt] 'Napoleon on the Bridge at Arcola' Lit. 'Events': Robert Burns dies	P: Coleridge Robinson Yearsley Anna Seward (1742–1809) Pr/F: Bage Burney Edgeworth Gibbon Inchbald Emma Hays (1760–1821) M.[atthew] G. Lewis (1775–1818) Dr: Wordsworth Thomas Morton (1764–1838)	Poems on Various Subjects & 'Ode to the Departing Year' Sappho and Phaon [sonnet series] The Rural Lyre Llangollen Vale, with Other Poems Hermsprong; or, Man as He is Not Camilla; or, a Picture of Youth [–1800] The Parent's Assistant [essays on education] Miscellaneous Works [posthm.; incls Memoirs of my Life and Writings] Nature and Art [novel] Memoirs of Emma Courtney [novel] The Monk [gothic novel] [–1797] The Borderers [in 5 acts; wrtn; pub.d 1842] The Way to Get Married [comedy]
	1797	Financial crisis – cash payments suspended by Bank of England [restored 1817–21]; RN mutinies at Spithead & Nore – suppressed; Fr. invasion of Fishguard repulsed; British naval victories at St Vincent [Spanish] & Camperdown [Dutch] – Texel blockaded; British take Trinidad from Spain; further religious prohibitions in France – Royalist revolt put down; Napoleon defeats Austria at Rivoli – occupies Venice & controls Genoa & Lombardy; Fr./Aust. peace leaves Britain isolated; John Adams, US President; [–1805] Lord Wellesley [later Duke of Wellington], Governor General of India [Britain becomes supreme power]; final treaty between Russia, Prussia & Austria partitions Poland – removes it from the map; French make Toussaint l'Ouverture C. in C. in Haiti – drives out Spanish & British	1st copper pennies minted & £ notes issued by Bank of England; Wilberforce, A Practical View of Christianity; Vicomte de Chateaubriand, Essai sur les révolutions anciennes et modernes. Int. Lit.: Goethe, Hermann und Dorothea [pastoral poem]; [–1799] Friedrich Hölderlin, Hyperion [Ger. novel]. Music: Haydn, 'Emperor Quartet'. Art: Goya, 'Duchess of Alba' [also 1795]; Blake completes 537 colour illustr.ns to Edward Young's Night Thoughts [v.1742]; Bewick, History of British Birds [vol. I; vol. II, 1804; wood engr.s] Lit. 'Events': William & Dorothy Wordsworth (sister) move to Somerset to be near Coleridge; August W. von Schlegel begins Ger. trans of 17 Shakespeare plays	P: Blake Coleridge Wordsworth Pr/F: Radcliffe Robinson Dr: Morton	[c.] The Four Zoas, or Vala [completed 1803, but unrevised ms.] 'Kubla Khan' [wrtn; pub. 1816] 'The Ruined Cottage' [completed; rev.d version appears as Bk I of The Excursion, 1814] The Italian Walsingham, or, the Pupil of Nature [story] A Cure for the Heart-Ache [comedy]
	1798	French attempt to invade Ireland during rebellion led by Wolfe Tone & Robert Emmet fails; [>] Ir. emigration to Canada underway; British capture Minorca & take Honduras from Spain; Horatio Nelson victorious at Battle of the Nile [Aboukir Bay]; French invade Switzerland – occupy & loot Rome, Piedmont, Naples – Napoleon's Egyptian campaign: captures Malta – occupies Alexandria – victorious at Battle of Pyramids; [–1799] Tippoo Sahib of Mysore renews war	[>] Luke Hansard prnts Parliamentary Reports; Joseph Lancaster opens school in London based on monitorial system; 1st weaving mill opens in Bradford; Thomas Malthus, Essay on the Principle of Population [enlarged & rev.d edtn, 1807]. Music: Haydn, 'The Creation' [oratorio]. Art: Sir John Soane, Sketches in Architecture; François Gerard [pnt] 'Psyche Receiving the First Kiss from Cupid'; J.M.W. Turner [pnt] 'Morning on Coniston Edge' & [c.] 'Aeneas and the Sibyl' [both Tate] Lit. 'Events': [–1799] Wordsworths & Coleridge visit Germany; A.W. & Friedrich von Schlegel fnd Das Athenäum [Ger. Romantic literary journal]	P: Coleridge Coleridge & Wordsworth Charles Lamb (1775–1834) Pr/F: Edgeworth Lamb	'Ode to France', 'Fears in Solitude' & 'Frost at Midnight' [pub.d anon; wrts 'Christabel' Pt I; v.1800, 1816] Lyrical Ballads [pub.d anon.; opens with 'The Rime of the Ancient Mariner'; closes with 'Lines Written a few miles above Tintern Abbey'] 'The Old Familiar Faces' [in vol. entitled Blank Verse] Practical Education The Tale of Rosamund Gray and Old Blind Margaret [prose romance]

HANOVERIAN/ROMANTIC

	Author	Literature
	Wollstonecraft	Maria, or the Wrongs of Woman [pub. posthm.; unfinished novel]
	Dr: Inchbald	Lovers' Vows [comedy; features in Jane Austen's Mansfield Park]
	Morton	Speed the Plough [comedy; incls 'Mrs Grundy', a character who never appears; prnt.d 1800]

1799

Events (political/historical): Pitt 1st introduces Income Tax as wartime measure [>; except 1803 & 1817–42]; Combination Act prohibits political associations [e.g. trade unions working for better pay & conditions]; London Corresponding Society, Ulster Irishmen & other named societies proscribed; Napoleon defeats Turks at Aboukir – returns from Egypt – seizes power from Directory in Paris coup d'état [18th Brumaire] & is declared 1st Consul; 2nd Coalition [Austria, Britain, Russia, Portugal & Savoy] at war with France; British capture Seringapatam – Tippoo Sahib killed – Mysore war ends; Russo/American Co. obtains monopoly for Alaska

Events (culture/science): Newspaper Act restricts freedom of press; 3rd Earl Stanhope builds 1st iron printing-press; machine making paper in continuous sheets invented; [c.] Missionary Society [v.1792] begins work in S. Africa; Fr. troops in Egypt discover Rosetta Stone [made trans. of hieroglyphics possible]; Murray, *English Reader*; Mungo Park, *Travels in the Interior of Africa*. **Int. Lit.:** Schiller, *Wallenstein* [trilogy of history plays, begun 1796]. **Music:** Beethoven, 'First Symphony' & 'Pathétique Sonata'. **Art:** David, '(The Rape of the) Sabine Women'

Author	Literature
P: Cowper / Wordsworth	'The Castaway' [–1800] *The Prelude* [wrts Bks I & II; v.1805, 1850]
Mary Alcock (c.1742–98)	*Poems* [pub. posthm.; incls 'The Chimney Sweeper's Complaint']
Thomas Campbell (1777–1844)	*The Pleasures of Hope*
Pr/F: H. More	*Strictures on Modern Female Education*
Lit. 'Events':	Wordsworths move to Grasmere in Lake District

1800

Events (political/historical): Act of Union of Britain & Ireland unites Parliaments [Ir. MPs to sit at Westminster] & creates 'UK of Great Britain & Ireland' [effective 1/1/1801]; 2nd Combination Act extended to employers [completes illegality of trade unions – v.1799]; French reoccupy Cairo & defeat Austrians at Marengo & Hohenlinden – British capture Malta; Napoleon's lawyers begin to draw up Civil Code; Russia leaves Coalition & revives League of Armed Neutrality against Britain [v.1780–1]; Spain cedes Louisiana to France; Penang, Malaya, ceded to Britain

Events (culture/science): Royal College of Surgeons fnd.d; Robert Owen estab.s New Lanark 'model' factory & community; [–1815] Richard Trevithick builds steam road carriages & [1803 in Wales] 1st steam railway locomotive; Friedrich von Schelling, *System des transzendentalen Idealismus* [Ger. idealist philosophy]. **Int. Lit.:** Schiller, *Mary Stuart* [drama]; Mme De Staël, *Littérature et ses rapports avec les institutions sociales*. **Music:** Beethoven, '3rd piano concerto' (in C minor); François Boieldieu [comp] 'The Caliph of Baghdad' [Fr. opera]. **Art:** Josiah Spode begins making fine Eng. porcelain [using bone in china]; David, 'Madame Récamier'; Thomas Girtin [pnt] 'Village of Jedburgh' & 'White House at Chelsea' [Tate]. **Lit. 'Events':** Thomas Moore, Eng. trans. of Anacreon's poetry

Author	Literature
P: Burns / Coleridge & Wordsworth	*Works* [coll. edtn pub. posthm.] / 'Christabel' [Pt II wrtn; pub.d 1816] *Lyrical Ballads* [2nd edtn, 2 vols, dated 1800, pub.d 1801; incls *Michael* & 4 'Lucy' poems; reprnt.d 1802, 1805]
Robinson	*Lyrical Tales* [pub. posthm.; incls 'The Haunted Beach']
Robert Bloomfield (1766–1823)	*The Farmer's Boy* [b-s. poem by 'peasant poet'; with wood-engr.v by Thomas Bewick]
Pr/F: Edgeworth	*Castle Rackrent, an Hibernian Tale Taken from Fact, and from the Manners of the Irish Squires before the Year 1782* [novel]
Theory/Crit: Wordsworth	'Preface' to *Lyrical Ballads*

1801

Events (political/historical): George III refuses RC emancipation – Pitt resigns; Habeas Corpus suspended; General Enclosure Act: private estates enclose ancient common land – 1000s forced into cities; economic distress & high food prices; 'Horne Tooke Act' [Tooke elected to Old Sarum] bars C of E clergy from sitting in Commons; British troops land at Aboukir – defeat French at Alexandria – British occupy Madeira – Nelson destroys Dan. fleet off Copenhagen – Danes exclude British ships from the Elbe – French sign peace treaties with Austria, Spain, Portugal & Naples – Concordat between Napoleon & Pope restores RC Church in France – Russia reconciled to Britain; Toussaint l'Ouverture becomes ruler of Haiti & works towards independence from France; Thomas Jefferson, US President; [–1803] Matthew Flinders circumnavigates Australia & names whole continent

Events (culture/science): Union Jack becomes flag of UK; 1st full census of England & Wales [> every 10 yrs]; Grand Union Canal opens; Dalton outlines his laws on gases; Surrey Iron Railway [Wandsworth to Croyden] opens [horse-drawn freight trucks]; Strutt, *Sports and Pastimes of the People of England*; Johan Pestalozzi, *How Gertrude Teaches her Children* [Swiss education treatise]. **Int. Lit.:** Schiller, *The Maid of Orleans* [drama]; Vicomte de Chateaubriand, *Atala* [unfinished Fr. romantic epic of Native American life]. **Music:** Beethoven, 'Moonlight Sonata'; Haydn, 'The Creation Mass' & 'The Seasons' [oratorio]. **Art:** David, 'Napoleon Crossing the Alps'; Jean-Dominique Ingres [pnt] 'Envoys from Agamemnon'; James Gillray, 'Dido in Despair' [BM; e.g. of satirical prints, c.1775–1807]

Author	Literature
P: Southey	*Thalaba: the Destroyer* [narrative poem]
James Hogg (the 'Ettrick Shepherd'; 1770–1835)	*Scottish Pastorals, Poems, and Songs*
Thomas Moore (1779–1852)	*Poems by Thomas Little*
Edgeworth	*Belinda* & *Moral Tales* [for children]

Period	Year	International and Political Contexts	Social and Cultural Contexts	Authors	Indicative Titles
	1802	Health & Morals of Apprentices Act [1st law to regulate child labour – pauper children in textile mills to work no more than 12 hrs]; W. India Docks, London, built; Peace of Amiens ends 1st stage of war with France – British retain Ceylon & Trinidad as colonies; Napoleon appointed 1st Consul for life – institutes Legion of Honour; Peshawa surrenders independence to E. India Co.	Dalton compiles Table of Atomic Weights [in chemistry]; *Debrett's Peerage* 1st pub.d; [–1835] William Cobbett begins [weekly] *Political Register*. Bentham, *Discourse on Civil and Penal Legislation*. **Int. Lit.:** Hölderlin, *Hymnen* [poems]. **Music:** Beethoven, '2nd Symphony' & 'Moonlight Sonata'. **Art:** Gérard, 'Madame Récamier'; Lawrence, 'Elizabeth, Lady Conyngham, as Diana the Huntress' [Londesborough Estates]. **Lit. 'Events':** Whig *Edinburgh Review* fnd.d [1st literary review]	**P:** Bloomfield Coleridge Amelia Opie (1769–1853) Sir Walter Scott (1771–1832) **Dr:** Holcroft Lamb	*Rural Tales, Ballads and Songs* 'Dejection: an Ode' *Poems* [–1803] *Minstrelsy of the Scottish Border* [3 vols; collection of old ballads & verse by Scott] *A Tale of Mystery* [intros melodrama to Eng. stage] *John Woodvil* [pastiche of Elizabethan/Jacobean drama]
	1803	Poaching made a capital offence if resisting arrest; rebellion in Ireland suppressed– patriot Robert Emmet executed; [–1815] war with France renewed ['Napoleonic Wars'] – British capture St Lucia & Tobago, restore Cape Colony to Holland; USA doubles its size by buying all remaining Fr. territories in N. America ['Louisiana Purchase'] – Ohio (17th) becomes a State; French suppress rebellion & recover Haiti – Toussant l'Ouverture dies in prison in France; 2nd Mahratta war – Wellesley defeats Sindhia at Assaye – all lands ceded to Britain	[c.] Sunday School Union fnd.d; [–1823] Thomas Telford begins building 1000 miles of roads in Scotland & Caledonian Canal; Lancaster, *Improvements in Education* [–1870, helps to estab. voluntary elementary schools]. **Int. Lit.:** de Staël, *Delphine* [feminist novel]; Schiller, *Die Braut von Messina* [verse drama]. **Music:** 'Prix de Rome' 1st awarded for music; Beethoven, 'Christ on the Mountain of Olives' [oratorio] & 'Kreutzer Sonata'. **Art:** Turner, 'Calais Pier' [NG]; John ('Old') Crome fnds 'Norwich School' of [mainly landscape] artists	**P:** Chatterton **Pr/F:** Jane Porter (1776–1850) **Lit. 'Events':**	*Works* [pub. posthm.] *Thaddeus of Warsaw* [historical romance] Blake tried for sedition – acquitted
	1804	Pitt returns as PM; Napoleon assumes title 'Emperor of France' – coronation [begins to dominate whole of mainland Europe] – Civil Code comes into force; Russia allies with Britain & Austria against France – Spain declares war on Britain – [–1814] British take Dutch Guiana; further British conquests in India; 1st British settlement fnd.d at Hobart, Van Dieman's Land (Tasmania); Haiti declared an independent republic	British & Foreign Bible Society fnd.d; Royal Horticultural Society's 1st flower show; Oliver Evans runs 1st US steam carriage on roads. **Int. Lit.:** Schiller, *William Tell* [popular play]; [–1805] 'Jean Paul' (Richter), *Wild Oats* [Ger. romantic fiction]. **Music:** Beethoven, 'Eroica Symphony' (No. 3). **Art:** [c.] Goya, 'The Naked Maja' & 'The Clothed Maja'; Ingres, 'Bonaparte as First Consul'; Antoine-Jean Gros [pnt] 'Napoleon Visiting the Plague House at Jaffa'	**P:** Blake Ann & Jane Taylor (1782–1866; 1783–1824) **Pr/F:** Edgeworth Jane Austen (1775–1817)	[prnt.d & illustr.d by Blake] [c.] *Milton* – 'Preface' incls 'And did those feet in ancient times' [later titled 'Jerusalem' & set to music] & [c.–1820] *Jerusalem* [last of 'Prophetic Books'] [–1805] *Original Poems for Infant Minds* [children's poems] *Popular Tales* [for children] [c.] 'The Watsons' [unfinished fragment; pub.d in J.E. Austen-Leigh, *A Memoir of Jane Austen*, 2nd edtn, 1871]
	1805	London Docks open; Napoleon crowns himself king of Italy – deposes king of Naples – adds Venice to Italy; 3rd Coalition against France – Nelson defeats Fr./Sp. fleet at Battle of Trafalgar – killed [Britain now has total control of seas] – French defeat Austrians at Ulm & Austr.-Russ. armies at Austerlitz – Austro/Fr. peace; Wellesley recalled from India – Lord Cornwallis, Governor-General; Mungo Park explores River Niger	1st factory lit by gas in Manchester; Royal Military Canal built. **Music:** Beethoven, 'Fidelio' [opera – final version 1814] & 'Kreutzer Violin Sonata'. **Art:** British Institution for Development of Fine Arts fnd.d; David, 'Pope Pius VII' & [–1807] 'Coronation of Josephine (Le Sacre)'; [c.–1810] Raeburn, 'The MacNab' [Dewar Coll] & [c.–1812] 'Mrs James Campbell' [SNG]; Turner, 'Shipwreck' [Tate]. **Lit. 'Events':** [–1806] Thomas Holcroft edits monthly *Theatrical Recorder*	**P:** Scott Wordsworth 'Charlotte Dacre' (Charlotte Byrne; c.1771–1825) Mary Tighe (1772–1810) **Pr/F:** Austen	*The Lay of the Last Minstrel* [narrative poem] *The Prelude, or Growth of a Poet's Mind* [early version in 13 Bks completed; v.1850] *Hours of Solitude* *Psyche; or, the Legend of Love* [3rd edtn, with other poems, 1811] [c.] 'Lady Susan' [fragment; pub.d in *Memoir* 1871; v.1804]
	1806	Pitt dies – Baron Grenville, PM; E. India Docks, London, open; Napoleon abolishes Holy Roman Empire – all Hapsburg estates become Austrian Empire [German, official language] – conquers S. Italy – makes brother Joseph Bonaparte king of Naples & brother Louis king of Holland – Franco-Prussian war –	Building of Dartmoor Prison begins [opens 1809]; E. India Co. fnds Haileybury College [boy's public school]; Sir Humphrey Davy lectures on electro-chemistry. **Music:** Arnim & Brentano, *Des Knaben Wunderhorn* [Ger. folk-song collection]; Beethoven, '4th Symphony' & 'Violin Concerto in D'. **Art:**	**P:** Bloomfield Moore Robinson A. J. Taylor George Gordon	*Wild Flowers* *Epistles, Odes, and other Poems* *Poetical Works* [pub. posthm.] *Rhymes for the Nursery* [incls 'Twinkle, Twinkle, Little Star'] *Fugitive Pieces* [early poems: rev.d twice in

Year	History	Science / Art / Music / Int. Lit.	Authors	Works & Lit. 'Events'
	Prussians defeated at Jena & Auerstädt – French enter Berlin – Federation of Rhine estab.d by Napoleon – occupies Warsaw – Napoleon's Berlin Decree to close ports to British trade ['Continental System']; British take control of Cape Colony from Dutch; Aaron Burr conspires to make Texas an independent republic [tried for treason, 1807]	[–1836] Arc de Triomphe, Paris, built; Goya, 'Doña Isabel Cobos de Porcel' [NG]; [–1808] Turner, 'Death of Nelson' [Tate]; John Cotman joins 'Norwich School' [v.1803]; Sir David Wilkie [pnt] 'The Village Politicians'; John Constable [pnt] 'Borrowdale' [w/c; V&A]	Lord Byron (1788–1824) Pr/F: 'C. Dacre' Edgeworth Lit. 'Events':	1807] Zofloya, or the Moor [gothic novel] Leonora [–1809] Elizabeth Inchbald (ed.) The British Theatre [24 vols; old & new plays]; [–1808] Walter Scott (ed.), coll. works of Dryden Lit. 'Events':
1807	Abolition of slave trade in British Empire [v.1833]; Orders In Council declare reciprocal British blockade of all Fr. & allied ports – British bombard Copenhagen & seize Dan. Fleet – preparations for Fr. invasion along Eng. coast – Napoleon routs Russians at Friedland – Treaty of Tilsit between Napoleon & Tsar Alexander I & with Prussia [loses lands W. of Elbel – Jerome Bonaparte [brother], king of Westphalia – France & Portugal at war – Braganza dynasty dethroned by Napoleon – Russia & Denmark ally with France against Britain – Napoleon's Milan Decree reinforces trade war – Russia & Prussia join Continental System – Britain now isolated in war	Drainage of Fens completed; Robert Fulton launches 1st successful paddle-steamer 'Clermont' on the Hudson River; G.W.F. Hegel, The Phenomenology of Spirit; [–1808] Johann Fichte, Sermons Addressed to the German Nation [nationalist lectures]. Int. Lit.: de Staël, Corinne [romance]. Music: I.G. Pleyel begins making pianos; Beethoven, 'Appassionata Sonata' & '5th Symphony'. Art: Thomas Hope, Household Furniture and Interior Decoration [pioneers Regency Neo-Classical style]; [–1819] Turner, 'Liber Studiorum' [landscape engravings]; Wilkie, 'Blind Fidler' [NG]; John Cotman [pnt] 'Window Between St Andrew's Hall and the Dutch Church, Norwich'; Caspar David Friedrich [pnt] 'Cross on the Mountain'	P: Byron Crabbe Hogg Moore C. Smith Wordsworth Sydney Owenson (Lady Morgan; 1777–1859) Pr/F: Charles & Mary Lamb (1764–1847)	Poems on Various Occasions & Hours of Idleness The Parish Register [verse sketches of village life] The Mountain Bard [–1834] Irish Melodies [coll. of songs set to Ir. tunes] Beachy Head: with Other Poems Poems in Two Volumes [incls 'Resolution and Independence', 'Ode to Duty', 'Intimations of Immortality', 'The Solitary Reaper'] The Lay of an Irish Harp; or Metrical Fragments Tales from Shakespeare & Mrs Leicester's School [stories]
1808	Sweden under Fr. domination – Charles IV of Spain abdicates – Joseph Bonaparte, king of Spain – Madrid revolt against Fr. occupation begins Peninsular War – British force lands in Portugal – Prussian army limited in size by Napoleon [to little effect by 1812]; Russians invade Finland – Czar Alexander I becomes Grand Duke; Federal gvnmt bans importation of slaves into USA; Sierra Leone becomes British colony	Trevithick exhibits locomotive on circular track at Euston; Dalton develops theory of atomic structure of matter [v.1810]; Bentham & James Mill begin collaboration. Int. Lit.: Goethe, Faust, Pt I [v.1775 & 1832]; Heinrich von Kleist, Der zerbrochene Krug [Ger. comedy]. Music: Théâtre St Philippe, New Orleans [early US opera house]; Beethoven, 'The Pastoral Symphony' (No. 6). Art: Blake, 12 illustr.ns to Robert Blair's The Grave [v.1743]; Ingres, 'Oedipus and the Sphinx' & 'Bather of Valpinçon (La Grande Baigneuse)'; Gros, 'Napoleon on the Battlefield at Eylau'; Friedrich, 'Morning Light'; [–1810] John Crome [pnt] 'Moonrise on the Marshes of the Yare' [NG]	P: Opie Scott (Mrs) Felicia Dorothea Hemans (1793–1835) Pr/F: C. Lamb Lit. 'Events':	The Warrior's Return, and Other Poems Marmion; A Tale of Flodden Field Poems [ed.] Specimens of English Dramatic Poets who lived about the time of Shakespeare [anthol.] & [with Mary Lamb] The Adventures of Ulysses [stories] [–1821] Leigh Hunt edits The Examiner; Edinburgh Review attacks Byron's Hours of Idleness, 1807 [v.1809]; Covent Garden Theatre burns down [Handel's organ & many ms. opera scores lost]
1809	Curwen's Bribery Act prohibits sale of Parliamentary seats; Fr. invade Papal States – Rome added to Fr. Empire – Napoleon excommunicated by Pope – latter imprisoned at Savona – further Austro-Fr. warfare – French enter Vienna – Austrians defeated at Wagram – peace – Metternich, chief minister in Austria, joins Continental System – death of Sir John Moore at Battle of Corunna, Portugal – succeeded by Wellesley – defeats French at Talavera [made Duke of Wellington] – peace between Russia & Sweden – Russia takes Finland; British take Martinique & Guadaloupe; US Non-Intercourse Act against British commerce [renewed 1811]; treaty of friendship between British & Sikhs	Bristol harbour built; [c.] Thomas Heathcote invents lace-making machine; 2000 Guineas 1st run at Newmarket. Int. Lit.: Chateaubriand, Les Martyrs [prose epic]. Music: Beethoven, 'The Emperor Concerto'. Art: exhibition of Blake's paintings in London fails; Turner, 'London Seen from Greenwich' [Tate]; Raeburn, 'Mrs Spiers'; Constable, 'Malvern Hall, Warwickshire' [NG]. Theory/Crit: A.W. von Schlegel, Dramatic Art and Literature [Ger. lectures; Eng. trans 1815]	P: Byron Campbell Pr/F: Edgeworth H. More Lit. 'Events':	English Bards and Scottish Reviewers [verse satire riposte to Edinburgh Review attack, 1808] Gertrude of Wyoming [long poem] Tales of Fashionable Life [stories; incls 'The Absentee'; also 1812] Coelebs in Search of a Wife [didactic novel] Tory Quarterly Review fnd.d [assisted by Scott]; [–1810] Coleridge pubs periodical, The Friend; 2nd Drury Lane Theatre burns down; Sir Robert Smirke rebuilds Covent Garden Theatre

PERIOD	YEAR	INTERNATIONAL AND POLITICAL CONTEXTS	SOCIAL AND CULTURAL CONTEXTS	AUTHORS	INDICATIVE TITLES
HANOVERIAN/ ROMANTIC	1810	Strikes begin in reaction to gvnmt's economic policy [eg. Durham miners]; Napoleon m. Marie Louise, Austrian Emperor's daughter – Penal Code of 'Code Napoléon' decreed – France annexes Holland – Louis Bonaparte abdicates – Wellington holds the line at Battle of Torres Vedras, Portugal; Trianon Tariff permits smuggling of British & colonial goods into Europe – Fontainbleau Decrees to confiscate & burn all British-made goods on Fr. territory; Spain's American colonies reject Joseph Bonaparte's rule; Mauritius & Seychelles annexed by Britain	Dalton, New System of Chemical Philosophy [explains atomic theory]; [c.]Sir Humphrey Davy discv.s electric arc; John Macadam begins to build roads in England – 1st 'macadamised' surfaces laid from c.1816; Krupp ironworks fnd.d at Essen, Germany. Int. Lit.: de Staël, De l'Allemagne [completed; pub.d London, 1813 – promotes Ger. Romanticism outside Germany (de Staël 1st to use word 'Romanticism')]; Kleist, Michael Kohlhaas [Ger. story] & Prinz Friedrich von Hamburg [play; 1st pf.d posthm. 1821]. Art: [–c.1820] Goya, 'The Disasters of War' [etchings]; David, 'Distribution of the Eagles' & [–1814] 'Leonidas at Thermopylae'; Fuseli, 'Succubus'; [c.–1811] Crome, 'New Mills, Norwich' & Cotman, 'Greta Bridge' [both Norwich] Lit. 'Events': Anna Barbauld [ed.] The British Novelists [50 vols, with prefatory essay]	P: Crabbe Hogg Scott A. & J. Taylor Anne Grant (1755–1838) Pr/F: Porter Wordsworth	The Borough [24 verse 'letters'; incls 'Peter Grimes'] The Forest Minstrel The Lady of the Lake [verse tale] Hymns for Infant Minds The Highlanders, and Other Poems The Scottish Chiefs [historical romance] Description of the Scenery of the Lakes in the North of England [intro. to Joseph Wilkinson, Select Views in Cumberland, Westmoreland and Lancashire; pub.d separately, 1822; & v.1835]
REGENCY/ROMANTIC	1811	George III now permanently insane – Regency Act makes Prince of Wales [future George IV] Prince Regent [–1820]; 1st Luddite riots in Nottingham – [–c.1815] exploited workers [led by 'Ned Ludd', mythical commander] smash new industrial machinery – handloom weavers estab. HQ in Glasgow to co-odinate protection of apprenticeships; Wellington drives French out of Portugal – invades Spain – victories at Fuentes d'Onoro & Albuera; Paraguay & Venezuela declare independence from Spain; Hudson Bay Co. fnd settlements in Manitoba [under its control until 1869–70]; [–1816] British occupy Java	National Schools Society fnd.d; [–1817] John Rennie builds Waterloo Bridge [replaced 1945]; [–1812] Barthold Niebuhr lectures on Roman history in Berlin. Int. Lit.: Goethe, Dichtung und Wahrheit [autobiog.]; Friedrich Fouqué, Undine [Ger. fairy-tale]. Art: [–1814] Soane builds Dulwich College Art Gallery – 1st collection open to public; [–1827] Prince Regent engages John Nash to design layout of Regent's Park, Regent St & adjacent terraces; Ingres, 'Jupiter and Thetis'	P: Bloomfield Southey Pr/F: Austen Percy Bysshe Shelley (1792–1822)	The Banks of the Wye The Curse of Kehama, a Poem Sense and Sensibility ['Elinor and Marianne' wrtn 1795; rev.d as S and S, 1797–8; rev.d again, 1810] The Necessity of Atheism [pamphlet – causes him to be sent down from Oxford]
	1812	Spencer Percival, PM, assassinated – [–1827] Lord Liverpool [Tory], PM – Viscount Castlereagh, Foreign Sec.; widespread economic distress – wheat price rises to 126s. [19thC peak] – worst year of Luddite rioting – frame-breaking made a capital offence; British Orders In Council [1807] revoked to help trade; new Toleration Act repeals Five Mile & Conventicle Acts [v.1664–5]; alliance of Sweden, Russia & Britain – Napoleon invades Russia – Russ. defeat at Battles of Smolensk & Borodino – Napoleon enters Moscow – Fr. army retreats [20,000 out of 550,000 survive]; Peninsular War: British victory at Battle of Salamanca – Wellington advances to Madrid – forced to retreat; [–1814] USA & Britain at war over trade embargos, rivalry in NW America & British maritime policy – US invasion of Canada fails; Louisiana becomes 18th State	Baptist Union of Great Britain fnd.d; Henry Bell launches 1st European passenger-carrying steam-boat on Clyde; Hegel, Science of Logic [vol. I; vol. II, 1816: 'thesis', antithesis', synthesis']. Int. Lit.: Grimm Brothers pub. Kinderhund Haus-Märchen coll. ['Grimm's Fairy Tales']; Goethe, Gedichte [poems]. Music: Beethoven, '7th & 8th Symphonies'; Boïeldieu, 'Jean de Paris' [opera]. Art: Turner, 'Snow Storm: Hannibal and His Army Crossing the Alps' [Tate]; Wilkie, 'Blind Man's Bluff' [Royal Coll.]; Canova, 'Venus Leaving the Bath' [marble]; Théodore Géricault [pnt] 'Light Cavalry Officer Charging'	P: Barbauld Byron Crabbe Hemans Pr/F: Edgeworth William Hazlitt (1778–1830) Lit. 'Events':	Eighteen Hundred and Eleven [poem envisioning decline of Britain & progress of USA] Childe Harold's Pilgrimmage [Cantos I & II] Tales in Verse [21 tales] The Domestic Affections, and Other Poems The Absentee [in 2nd ser. of Tales of Fashionable Life; v.1809] [begins writing for Morning Chronicle & The Examiner] Present Drury Lane Theatre built; [–1815] John Nichols pub.s Literary Anecdotes of the Eighteenth Century

1813

[–1814] Apprentices Statute (1563) repealed [ends wage-regulation & compulsory apprenticeships – free trade in labour – causes much resentment]; people of Prussia start war of independence – alliance of Russia & Prussia for war with France – Sweden joins – Austria declares war – 'Battle of Nations' at Leizig – Napoleon defeated – refuses terms of peace at Conditions of Frankfort – Dutch throne returned to House of Orange – Wellington defeats French at Vittoria – drives French from Spain; [–1823] Lord Hastings, Governor General of India – E. India Co.'s monopoly of Indian trade abolished; Macquarie River, Australia, discovered & Murray Basin explored; 2 British ships enter Nagasaki harbour, Japan, by force to eject Dutch traders

Last gold guineas issued in England; William Hedley's 'Puffing Billy' steam locomotive 1st runs on smooth rails; [c.] 'shoddy' 1st made in W. Riding, Yorkshire; McGill University, Montreal, fnd.d [Charter, 1821]; Robert Owen forms New Lanark into new Co. with Bentham & others – pub.s *A New View of Society*. **Int. Lit.:** Adalbert von Chamisso, *Peter Schlemihl* [Ger. story of man who lost his shadow]. **Music:** London [later Royal] Philharmonic Society fnd.d; Franz Schubert [comp] 1st symphony. **Art:** [c.–1818] Goya, 'The Follies' [etchings]; Turner, 'Frosty Morning' [Tate]; Blake, 'The Day of Judgment'; Thomas Phillips [pnt] 'George Gordon, 6th Baron Byron' [NPG; copy]

P: Byron — *The Giaour & The Bride of Abydos* [narrative poems]
Hogg — *The Queen's Wake*
Scott — *Rokeby & The Bride of Triermain* [narrative poems]
Shelley — *Queen Mab: A Philosophical Poem*
Pr/F: Austen — *Pride and Prejudice* [1st version, *First Impressions*, completed 1797]
Southey — *Life of Nelson* [biog.]
Dr: Coleridge — *Remorse* [verse play pf.d; wrtn 1797 as *Orsorio*]
Lit. 'Events': Robert Southey, Poet Laureate [Walter Scott having declined]

1814

French restore Papal authority – Pope returns to Rome – Allied powers invade France – capture Paris – Napoleon abdicates – keeps title & sovereignty of island of Elba – Bourbons restored with Louis XVIII [unpopular] – 1st Treaty of Paris – France keeps frontiers of 1792 – cedes Malta, Mauritius, St Lucia & Tobago to Britain – Congress of Vienna to finalise peace terms; British restore Madeira to Portugal & annex Cape Colony; British troops sack Washington, DC – Treaty ends Anglo-American war; [–1816] war with Gurkhas of Nepal; Civil Courts estab.d in NSW; Cape Colony, SA, ceded to Britain; [>] Sp. colonies in S. America cont. their struggle to break away from Spain

George Stephenson uses 1st effective steam locomotive, 'Blucher', at Killingsworth Colliery, Newcastle; 1st steam-cylinder press used in printing; [c.] Westminster streets 1st to have gas-lighting; British & Foreign Schools Society fnd.d; MCC moves to present Lord's cricket ground. **Int. Lit.:** Ernst Hoffman, *Phantasiestücke in Callots Manier* [coll. of stories – some used for Offenbach's *Tales of Hoffman* (1881) & Delibes's *Coppelia* (1870)]. **Music:** Schubert [comp] an opera, the Mass in F & songs [incls 'Gretchen and her Spinning Wheel' from Goethe's *Faust*]. **Art:** West, 'Death on a Pale Horse' & 'Christ Rejected by Caiaphus'; Goya, '(Shooting of) May the Third, 1808'; Ingres, 'The Great Odalisque'; [c.] Lawrence, 'George IV' [NPG]; [–1819] Katsushika Hokusai [draws] 'Mangwa' [10 vols; sketches of Jap. Life]

P: Byron — *The Corsair & Lara* [narrative poems]
Southey — *Roderick, the Last of the Goths* [verse narrative]
Wordsworth — *The Excursion*
Pr/F: Austen — *Mansfield Park*
Burney — *The Wanderer; or, Female Difficulties*
Edgeworth — *Patronage*
Scott — *Waverley; Or, 'Tis Sixty Years Since* [pub.d anon.; 1st in sequence of historical 'Waverley' novels]
Hazlitt — [–1830] contributes to *Edinburgh Review*
Swift — *Works* [19 vols; ed. Walter Scott; 2nd enlarged edtn, 1824]

1815

Corn Law prohibits foreign imports until British price is 80s. per quarter; trial by jury estab.d in Scotland; Davy invents coal-miners' safety lamp; Macadam appointed Surveyor-General of British roads; Napoleon escapes from Elba – lands in France – enters Paris – Louis XVIII flees – Congress of Vienna dispersed – Wellington defeats Ney at Quatre Bras – Napoleon finally defeated at Battle of Waterloo [his '100 days' end] – abdicates – Louis XVIII restored – 2nd Treaty of Paris – Napoleon banished to St Helena [from 1816] – Congress of Vienna reassembles & reconstructs post-war Europe & its colonies – Holy Alliance of Russia, Austria, Prussia & other European states [not Britain]; [>] British occupy Ascension Island; war against king of Kandy, Ceylon

University of NY fnd.d; Malthus, *Enquiry into the Nature and Progress of Rent* [anticipates Ricardo's economics]; Nichols, *The History and Antiquities of Leicestershire* [from 1795]. **Int. Lit.:** Johann Uhland, *Gedichte* ['Swabian School' poems]. **Music:** Schubert [comp] 'The Wanderer Symphony' (3rd) & songs 'The Erl King' (pf.d 1819) & 'Heidenröslein'. **Art:** [–1821] Nash rebuilds Brighton Pavilion for Prince Regent in oriental style; [c.–1820] Rowlandson, 'The Mall, St James's Park' [London Mus.]; [c.] Crome, 'View on Mousehold Heath' [V&A]; [c.] Constable, 'View of Dedham (Stour Valley and Dedham Village)'; Turner 'Dido building Carthage' & 'Crossing the Stream' [Tate]; Goya, 'Bull-Fighting' [etchings]; [–1817] Canova, 'Three Graces' [sculp.]

P: Scott — *The Lord of the Isles* [narrative poem]
Wordsworth — *Poems* [2 vols] & *The White Doe of Rylstone*
Pr/F: Scott — *Guy Mannering*
(Mrs) Mary M. Sherwood (1775–1851) — *Little Henry and his Beaver* [children's story]
Dr: James Sheridan Knowles (1784–1862) — *Caius Gracchus* [tragedy]

PERIOD	YEAR	INTERNATIONAL AND POLITICAL CONTEXTS	SOCIAL AND CULTURAL CONTEXTS	AUTHORS	INDICATIVE TITLES
	1816	Income Tax abolished in peacetime [effective 1817–42]; [–1817] acute post-war trade depression, unemployment & unrest in England; provincial Hampden Clubs for Parliamenary reform fnd.d – Spa Fields Riot of crowds listening to reform speeches; Game Law offenders face transportation for 7 yrs; USA imposes 1st protective tariff against British imports – Indiana becomes 19th State; Argentina declares independence from Spain; [c.] Barbary Coast pirates finally suppressed; [–1817] king of Kandy deposed in Ceylon – revolt against British rule finally suppressed; Java restored to Holland; British fnd colony at Bathurst, Gambia	Cobbett's *Political Register* reduced to 2*d*. to attract wide readership; Viscount Fitzwilliam's bequest of 17thC music to Cambridge University fnds Fitzwilliam Museum [v.1837]; [c.] transatlantic packet service begins; American Bible Society fnd.d. **Int. Lit.:** Benjamin Constant, *Adolphe* [Fr. psychological novel]. **Music:** quadrille [dance] intro.d to England from France; Giacchino Rossini, 'The Barber of Seville' [It. comic opera; 1st pf.d, Rome]; Schubert, 'The Tragic Symphony' (4th) & '5th Symphony'; 'Hoffman [comp] 'Undine' [opera]. **Art:** Elgin Marbles purchased for the nation & later housed in BM [sculpts from the Parthenon, Athens, brought to UK by Lord Elgin, c.1800–2]; Constable, 'Wivenhoe Park, Essex'; [–1824] Trumbull decorates rotunda of US Capitol, Washington, with paintings representing the Revolution. **Lit. 'Events':** Jane Austen's *Emma* praised by Scott in the *Quarterly Review*	**P:** Byron Coleridge Shelley John Keats (1795–1821) **Pr/F:** Austen Holcroft Scott Lady Caroline Lamb (1785–1828) Thomas Love Peacock (1785–1866)	*Childe Harold* [Canto III], *The Prisoner of Chillon, Parisina & The Siege of Corinth* *Christabel and Other Poems* [incls 'Kubla Khan', 'Pains of Sleep', 'The Lime-Tree Bower my Prison'] *Alastor [or, The Spirit of Solitude] and Other Poems* 'O Solitude …' & 'On First Looking into Chapman's Homer' [early sonnets pub.d in *The Examiner*] *Emma* [pub.d, Dec. 1815] *Memoirs* [ed. Hazlitt; pub. posthm.] *The Antiquary, Old Mortality & The Black Dwarf* *Glenarvon* [novel – incls caricature of Byron] *Headlong Hall* [satirical novel]
	1817	[–1821] Bank of England begins to resume cash payments; [&1818] Habeas Corpus suspended – Act against seditious meetings passed – 'Derbyshire Insurrection' at Pentrich – march of 'Manchester Blanketeers' to press for reform; Select Committee set up to consider high cost of relieving the poor; Princess Charlotte, heir to British throne, dies; Anglo-Sp. treaty opens up W. Indian trade to Britain; James Monroe, US President; Mississippi becomes 20th State; Greeks revolt against Turkish rule	William Hone tried & acquitted of treasonable publishing [landmark in freedom of British press]; [–1824] T.J. Wooler pubs *Black Dwarf* [radical journal]; David Ricardo, *Principles of Political Economy and Taxation*; Hegel, *Encyclopaedia of the Philosophical Sciences*. **Int. Lit.:** Franz Grillparzer, *Die Ahnfrau* [Austr. tragedy]. **Music:** Muzio Clementi wrts *Gradus ad Parnassum* [influential piano studies]. **Art:** [–1819] Thomas Jefferson designs University of Virginia [Neo-Classical style]; [–1821] Crome, 'Poringland Oak' [NG]; Constable, 'Flatford Mill' [Tate]; Géricault, 'Race of the Riderless Horses' & [c.] 'Capture of a Wild Horse'. **Lit. 'Events':** Jane Austen dies; *The Scotsman & Blackwood's Magazine* [Tory rival to *Edinburgh Review*] fnd.d in Edinburgh; Covent Garden Theatre 1st lit by gas	**P:** Byron Keats T. Moore Scott **Pr/F:** Austen Edgeworth Peacock Scott **Dr:** Byron **Theory/Crit:** Coleridge Hazlitt	*The Lament of Tasso* *Poems* [incls 'Sleep and Poetry' & 'I stood tip-toe …'] *Lalla Rookh* [4 oriental verse tales – hugely popular] *Harold the Dauntless* [narrative poem] *Sanditon* [fragment, wrtn; 1st pub. 1925] *Ormond* *Melincourt* *Rob Roy* *Manfred* *Biographia Literaria* *The Round Table & Characters of Shakespeare's Plays* [essays]
	1818	Commons reject Sir Francis Burdett's resolution on Annual Parliaments & universal suffrage; Congress of Aix-la-Chapelle – Allied army of occupation leaves France – France reincluded amongst European powers; frontier between USA & Canada defined; Illinois becomes 21st State; India: Peshwa's dominions annexed & Rajputana States under British protection; Bernadotte [ex-Napoleonic Marshall] accedes to Swed. throne as Charles XIV	[c.] 1st iron passenger ship on the Clyde; [c.] Institute of Civil Engineers fnd.d; Jeremiah Chubb patents 'detector' lock; James Mill, *History of British India* [completed]. **Int. Lit.:** Grillparzer, *Sappho* [drama]. **Music:** Rossini, 'Moses in Egypt' [opera]; Gaetano Donizetti [comp] 'Enrico, Conte di Borgogna' [It. opera]. **Art:** Wilkie, 'Penny Wedding' [Royal Coll.]; [c.–1826] Blake, *Illustrations to the Book of Job* [21 plates]; Bewick, *Aesop's Fables* [wood engrv.s]; [–1819] Géricault, 'Raft of the Medusa'; [c.] Friedrich, 'Wanderer above the Mists'. **Theory/Crit:** Hazlitt, *On The English Poets* [lectures]. **Lit. 'Events':** London Theatre fnd.d [later named the Old Vic]; attack on Keats, Leigh Hunt &	**P:** Byron Keats Shelley **Pr/F:** Austen Lamb Peacock Scott Sherwood Susan Ferrier (1782–1854)	*Childe Harold* [Canto IV] & *Beppo* *Endymion* & [–1819] *Hyperion* [Bks I–III wrtn & abandoned] *The Revolt of Islam, Julian and Maddalo* [wrtn; pub. 1824] & 'Ozymandias' [wrtn] *Northanger Abbey* [wrtn 1797–8] & *Persuasion* [wrtn. 1815; both pub. posthm.] *The Works of Charles Lamb* *Nightmare Abbey* *The Heart of Midlothian* *The History of the Fairchild Family* Pt I [Pts II & III, 1842, 1845; children's classic] *Marriage* [novel of Scottish life]

Year	History / Political Events	Cultural & Literary Context	Authors	Works
1819	'Peterloo Massacre', Manchester: 80,000-strong reform meeting attacked by troops – 11 killed; Six Acts ['Gag Acts'] passed to curb public & press freedoms & suppress public disorder; Factory Act [Peel & Owen]: 12-hour day for children in cotton mills; Stamford Raffles fnds unauthorised British settlement at Singapore [ceded to E. India Co., 1824]; Alabama becomes 22nd State – USA buys Florida from Spain; Simón Bolívar, President of new Republic of Greater Columbia [Venezuela & New Granada; Ecuador added, 1822]	Burlington Arcade, London, opens; Cleopatra's Needle presented to Britain by Egypt [v.1878]; [–1826] Telford builds Menai suspension bridge linking N. Wales to Anglesey; [–1822] St Pancras Church, London, built; S.S. 'Savannah', 1st transatlantic steamship [takes 26 days]; Arthur Schopenhauer, *The World as Will and Idea* [Ger. philosophy]. **Int. Lit.:** [–1820] Washington Irving, *The Sketch Book of Geoffrey Crayon, Gent* [US stories; incls 'Rip van Winkle' & 'The Legend of Sleepy Hollow']. **Music:** Schubert, 'Trout Quintet'. **Art:** Constable, 'White Horse'. **Theory/Crit:** Hazlitt, *On the English Comic Writers* [lectures]; Thomas Campbell [ed.], *Specimens of the British Poets* [prefaced by critical essay]	Mary Wollstonecraft Shelley (1797–1851) **P:** Byron Crabbe Keats Shelley Wordsworth **PrF:** Scott **Dr:** Shelley	*Frankenstein* [novel] [–1824] *Don Juan* [Cantos I, II] & *Mazeppa Tales of the Hall* [verse narratives] 'Ode to a Nightingale' [pub.d] & *The Fall of Hyperion. A Dream* [begun; unfinished fragment pub.d 1856/7] *The Masque of Anarchy* [inspired by 'Peterloo Massacre'; 1st edtn 1832] & 'Ode to the West Wind' [wrtn; pub. 1820] *The Waggoner* [wrtn 1805] & *Peter Bell* *The Bride of Lammermoor* & *Ivanhoe* *The Cenci* [wrtn; pub.d 1820; pf.d 1886] & [–1820] *Prometheus Unbound* [poetic drama]
1820	George III dies, King George IV [Prince Regent] accedes – [–1821] divorce action against Queen Caroline fails; Cato St. conspiracy to murder Cabinet foiled – leaders later executed; [>] movement for Free Trade gets underway; Duc de Berri dies – sole hope of Bourbon succession in France; [>1820s] Liberal revolutions spread across Europe & S. America – Congress of Troppau considers concerted action against this tendency – Austria crushes revolts in Italy; American Colonising Society fnds Liberian Republic for freed slaves [1st settlement, 1822]; [–1821] 'Missouri Compromise' on slavery allows Maine to join the Union as a free State (23rd) & Missouri as a slave State (24th; 1821) – rest of 'Louisiana Purchase' territories divided into south (slave) & north (free) areas; [>] British immigrants settle in Cape Colony – Port Elizabeth fnd.d	Regent's Canal, London, opens; *John Bull* magazine fnd.d; Malthus, *Principles of Political Economy*; Friedrich Accum, *Treatise on Adulterations of Food* [against unclean food & dishonest trading]. **Int. Lit.:** Alphonse de Lamartine, *Méditations poétiques* [tragic love poems]; Alexander Pushkin, *Ruslan and Lyudmilla* [Russ. poems]. **Art:** [>] Nash designs & builds Cumberland Terrace, Regent's Park; classical statue of 'Venus de Milo' discv.d; [–1824] Ingres, 'Vow of Louis XIII'; Constable, 'Stratford Mill' [NG]. **Theory/Crit:** Thomas Love Peacock, *The Four Ages of Poetry*; William Hazlitt, *The Dramatic Literature of the Age of Elizabeth* [lectures]. **Lit. 'Events':** *London Magazine* fnd.d – Lamb's *Essays of Elia* 1st pub.d there [v.1823, 1833]	**P:** Keats Shelley Wordsworth John Clare (1793–1864) **PrF:** Scott John Galt (1779–1839) Charles Maturin (1782–1824) **Dr:** Knowles	*Lamia, Isabella, The Eve of St Agnes and Other Poems* [incls 'Hyperion' (v.1818–19) & the 'Odes'] & 'La Belle Dame Sans Merci' *Oedipus Tyrannus, or Swellfoot the Tyrant* [satire on George IV's divorce], 'The Cloud', 'Ode to Liberty' & 'To a Skylark' [wrtn] *The River Duddon: A Series of Sonnets, Vaudracour and Julia, and Other Poems* & *Miscellaneous Poems* [4 vols] *Poems Descriptive of Rural Life and Scenery* *The Monastery* & *The Abbot* [–1821] *The Ayrshire Legatees* [novel] *Melmoth the Wanderer* [gothic novel] *Virginius* [pf.d in Glasgow]
1821	Queen Caroline granted annuity – turned away from George IV's coronation & dies a few days later – her unpopular treatment causes disturbances in London; some reduction in tariffs heralds move towards Free Trade; Congress of Laibach [Russia, Austria, Prussia & UK] seeks measures to counter revolution in Naples – UK refuses to agree; [–1829/30] Greek War of Independence against Turkey – most European Powers support it; US settlers move into Mexican territory of Texas; Mexico & Peru declare independence from Spain; Republic of Santo Domingo (Dominica) declared independent of Spain; the Gold Coast (Ghana) becomes a Crown Colony	*Manchester Guardian* 1st pub.d; London Co-operative Society fnd.d; Stephenson appointed to construct Stockton & Darlington railway [v.1825] – [1823] builds world's 1st iron bridge for it; James Mill, *Elements of Political Economy*; Owen, *Report to County of Lanark*; Hegel, *Philosophy of Right*. **Int. Lit.:** Heinrich Heine, *Gedichte* [Ger. poems]; James Fenimore Cooper, *The Spy* [US novel]. **Art:** Constable, 'The Hay Wain' [NG; creates sensation at Paris Salon, 1824] & [–1823] 'View on the Stour Near Dedham'; Géricault, 'Epsom Derby'; Friedrich, 'Wreck of the "Hoffnung"'; [–1823] Joseph Severn [pnt] 'John Keats'. **Theory/Crit:** Percy Bysshe Shelley, *The Defence of Poetry* [wrtn; riposte to Peacock, 1820; pub. posthm. 1840]. **Lit. 'Events':** John Keats dies in Rome	**P:** Byron Clare Shelley Southey **PrF:** Galt Hazlitt Scott Thomas de Quincey (1785–1859) **Dr:** Byron	*Don Juan* [Cantos III–V] *The Village Minstrel and Other Poems* *Adonais* [on Keats's death] & *Epipsychidion* *A Vision of Judgment* [attacks Byron] *The Steam Boat & Annals of the Parish* *Table Talk* [London Magazine essays] *Kenilworth & The Pirate* *The Confessions of an English Opium Eater* [in London Magazine; book edtn 1822; rev.d & expanded, 1856] *Marino Faliero* [verse drama, pf.d]; *The Two Foscari, Sardanapalus & Cain* [verse dramas pub.d]

HANOVERIAN (REGENCY ENDS)/ROMANTIC

1816–1821

PERIOD	YEAR	INTERNATIONAL AND POLITICAL CONTEXTS	SOCIAL AND CULTURAL CONTEXTS	AUTHORS	INDICATIVE TITLES
	1822	Castlereagh commits suicide – George Canning, Foreign Sec.; 1815 Corn Law slightly amended; 30,000 Greeks massacred at Chios [entire population]; Congress of Verona discusses Grk & Sp. issues – rifts appear in European alliance system; Brazil declares independence from Portugal; Costa Rica declares independence from Spain	Sunday Times fnd.d; 1st British railway uses locomotives for haulage, Hetton, County Durham; Louis Daguerre invents 'diorama' [illuminated pictures in dark room]. **Int. Lit.:** Alexander Pushkin, The Prisoner of the Caucasus [Russ. poems]; Charles Nodier, Trilby [Fr. novel]; Alfred de Vigny, Poems [pub.d anon.]; Victor Hugo, Odes et Ballades [Fr. poems; 2nd coll, 1826]; Adam Mickiewicz, Ballads and Romances [initiates Pol. Romantic movement]. **Music:** Royal Academy of Music fnd.d; Beethoven, 'Missa Solemnis'; Schubert, 'The Unfinished Symphony' (8th). **Art:** [–1825] Nash builds All Souls' Church, London; Wilkie, 'Chelsea Pensioners Reading the Gazette of the Battle of Waterloo' [Apsley House]; Eugène Delacroix [pnt] 'Bark of Dante'; Richard Bonington [pnt] 'Market Tower at Bergues' [Wallace Coll.] & 'Interior of Senlis Cathedral'. **Lit. 'Events':** P.B. Shelley drowns in Italy; Allan Cunningham, Traditional Tales of the English and Scottish Peasantry	**P:** Byron Shelley Wordsworth **Pr/F:** Edgeworth Galt Lady C. Lamb Peacock Scott Wordsworth Thomas Carlyle (1795–1881) John Lockhart (1794–1854)	The Vision of Judgement [satirical parody of Southey's 1821 poem] Hellas [poetic drama] & The Triumph of Life [wrtn; unfinished] Ecclesiastical Sketches [sonnets] Frank [for children] Sir Andrew Wylie & The Provost Graham Hamilton [novel] Maid Marian [historical romance] The Fortunes of Nigel A Description of the Scenery of the Lakes in the North of England [wrtn & 1st pub.d, 1810; as A Guide through the District of ..., 1835] Essay on Goethe's Faust [in New Edinburgh Review] Adam Blair [novel]
	1823	[–1827] William Huskisson & Earl of Ripon reduce protective duties & reform British fiscal policy; Sir Robert Peel, Home Sec., begins legal & penal reforms; Daniel O'Connell ('the liberator') fnds Catholic Association in Ireland to fight for rights of RCs; in USA, 'Monroe Doctrine' 1st spelt out [closing the American continents to external colonialisation & warning European powers not to interfere in the political affairs of American republics]; British gvnmt acknowledges legitimacy of Grk War of Independence & S. American Republics	Mechanics Institutes fnd.d in London & Glasgow; rugby football originates at Rugby School; Birkbeck College, London, fnd.d; [–1847] Sir Robert Smirke builds present British Museum; Charles Babbage starts to make a calculating machine [unfinished]; The Lancet 1st pub.d. **Int. Lit.:** Heine, Lyrisches Intermezzo [poems]. **Music:** Sir Henry Bishop [comp] 'Home, Sweet Home' [song]; Schubert, music to 'Rosamunde' & song-cycle 'Die Schöne Müllerin' [incls 'Das Wandern']; Carl Weber, 'Euryanthe' [Ger. opera]. **Art:** Cotman, 'Dieppe Harbour'; Lawrence, 'The Calmady Children'; Bonington, 'Abbey of St Bertin, Saint-Omer' [NAG]	**P:** Byron **Pr/F:** Carlyle Galt Hazlitt Lamb Lady C. Lamb Lockhart Scott	Don Juan [Cantos VI–XIV] [–1824] Life of Schiller [in London Magazine; as book, 1825] The Entail Liber Amoris [autobiog. essay] Essays of Elia [coll. edtn; 1st pub.d London Magazine, 1820; & v.1833] Ada Reis Reginald Dalton Quentin Durward, Peveril of the Peak & St Ronan's Well
	1824	Repeal of 1662 Settlement (Poor Law) Act; Combination Acts of 1799–1800 repealed – legalises trade unions; Act estab.s Imperial gallon as standard liquid measure; Allied Conference fails to agree over Grk Question; British fleet rescues Portuguese Liberals arrested by king's son in plot to overthrow constition; Canning recognises independence of Mexico & Columbia; [–1826] 1st Burmese War – British capture Rangoon [v.1852, 1885–6]; Frontier Treaty between USA & Russia; last Sp. army in S. America capitulates; Murray River, Australia, discv.d; Port Natal (Durban), S. Africa, fnd.d; [–1827] 1st Ashanti War [independent kingdom in W. Africa resists British rule; v. 1873, 1893, 1895, 1901]; Malacca ceded to Britain	Benthamite radical Westminster Review fnd.d; Athenaeum Club fnd.d; RSPCA fnd.d; [–1827] Telford builds St Katherine's Docks, London; Charles Macintosh produces 1st rubberised waterproofs [patent 1823]. **Int. Lit.:** [c.] Hugo, Bug-Jargal [Fr. novel of black revolt in W. Indies]; [–1827] Adolphe Thiers, Histoire de la revolution française. **Music:** Beethoven, 'Choral Symphony' (9th). **Art:** National Gallery (NG) fnd.d to collect pictures for British people [v.1838]; [–1827] Blake illustr.s Dante's Divine Comedy [Tate]; Constable, 'Brighton Beach'; Lawrence, 'Master (Charles William) Lambton'; Delacroix, 'Massacre at Chios' [v.1822]; [c.] Samuel Palmer [pnt] 'Repose of the Holy Family' [Ashmolean]. **Lit. 'Events':** Byron dies helping Greek struggle for independence	**P:** Byron Letitia Elizabeth Landon ('L.E.L.'; 1802–38) **Pr/F:** Carlyle Ferrier Hogg Lockhart Scott Mary Mitford (1787–1855) Walter Savage Landor (1775–1864)	Don Juan (Cantos XV–XVI) The Improvisatrice; and Other Poems Wilhelm Meister's Apprenticeship [Eng. trans of Goethe 1796] The Inheritance The Private Memoirs and Confessions of a Justified Sinner Matthew Wald Redgauntlet [–1832] Our Village [country sketches; 5 vols] [–1829] Imaginary Conversations [I & II; historical biog.]

HANOVERIAN (REGENCY ENDS)/ROMANTIC

			P: / Pr/F: / Dr:	Works
1825	Financial & commercial crisis in England; repeal of Combination Acts amended after rash of strikes; Irish Catholic Association declared illegal; Northumberland & Durham Miner's Union fnd.d; Levant Co.'s Turkish trade opened to all Eng. merchants; British declare neutrality in Grk War of Independence; New Zealand Colonisation Co. formed; Portugal recognises Brazil's independence; Bolivar liberates Upper Peru – declared independent as Bolivia	Stockton & Darlington railway opens [1st steam-train passenger line – Stephenson's Locomotive No. 1 reaches 16 mph]; Edinburgh Royal High School built; tea-rose intro.d to Europe from China; Augustin Thierry, *Histoire de la Conquête de l'Angleterre* [on Norman Conquest]. **Int. Lit.:** Pushkin, *Boris Godunov* [historical verse drama]. **Music:** Beethoven, 'Great Fugue' [1st pf.d in England]; Boïeldieu, 'La Dame blanche' [opera]. **Art:** [–1830] Nash commissioned by George IV to rebuild Buckingham House as Palace & designs Marble Arch [later moved to present site]; Bonington, 'View of the Parterre d'Eau at Versailles'; Constable, 'Leaping Horse'; Lawrence, 'King Charles X' [Royal Coll.]; Jean-Baptiste Corot [pnt] 'Corot at His Easel'	**P:** Barbauld Landon Allan Cunningham (1784–1842) **Pr/F:** Coleridge Edgeworth Hazlitt Scott **Dr:** Knowles **Theory/Crit:** Scott **Lit. 'Events':**	*Works* [pub. posthm.; incls 'Corsica', 'The Rights of Woman' & other radical poems wrtn in 1790s] *The Troubadour* *Songs of Scotland, Ancient and Modern* *Aids to Reflection* [religious essays] *Harry and Lucy* [for children] *The Spirit of the Age, or Contemporary Portraits* *The Talisman & The Betrothed* *William Tell* *Lives of the Novelists* [biog.] Pepys's diary 1st pub.d [v.1660]
1826	Gen. Elec. improves Tory majority – RC issue important; anti-power-loom riots in Manchester; 1st Temperance Society fnd.d; Protocol of St Petersburg between Russia & Britain re. Greece – France accedes; Liberal constitution in Portugal – British troops sent to Tagus against threat from Spain; Bolivar convenes 1st pan-American Congress at Panama; Straits Settlements estab.d by E. India Co. on Malay Peninsula	Burke's Peerage 1st pub.d; Joseph Niepce produces 1st photo-engraving [photograph on a metal plate]. **Int. Lit.:** Fenimore Cooper, *The Last of the Mohicans & The Prairie*; [–1827] Heine, *Reisebilder* [prose, 2 vols; & 2 vols, 1830–1]; de Vigny, *Poèmes antiques et modernes*; Hölderlin, *Gedichte* [poems]; Joseph von Eichendorff, *Aus dem Leben eines Taugenichts & Das Marmorbild* [Ger. novels]. **Music:** Carl Weber, 'Oberon' [Ger. opera, 1st pf.d Covent Garden Theatre]; Schubert, 'String Quartets' & songs 'Who is Sylvia?' & 'Hark, Hark the Lark'; Hector Berlioz [comp] 'Symphonie Fantastique'; Felix Mendelssohn-Bartholdy [comp] overture to 'A Midsummer Night's Dream'. **Art:** Lawrence, 'Miss Murray' [Kenwood]; Constable, 'The Cornfield' [NG]; Palmer, 'The Hilly Scene'; Bonington, 'View of the Piazzetta and Ducal Palace, Venice' [Tate]	**P:** Elizabeth Barrett Browning (1806–61) **Pr/F:** Hazlitt Radcliffe Scott M. Shelley Benjamin Disraeli (1804–81) **Lit. 'Events':**	*Essay on Mind and Other Poems* *The Plain Speaker* [coll. of *London Magazine* essays] *Gaston de Blondeville … with Some Poetical Pieces* [romance & poems] *Woodstock* *The Last Man* [futuristic novel] *Vivian Grey* [novel] Karl Lachmann, critical edtn of *Nibelungenlied*
1827	Liverpool resigns – Canning, PM – dies – Viscount Goderich (Ripon), PM; Peel reforms criminal law – number of capital offences reduced & redefinition of law of property; sand-filters intro.d to purify London's water supply; Turks capture Acropolis, Athens – Greeks destroy Turkish fleet at Salona – Fr./Russ./British fleets destroy Turkish fleet at Navarino – Treaty of London between Allies to secure independence of Greece – Count Capodistrias, President of Greek National Assembly	Henry Brougham fnds Society for the Diffusion of Useful Knowledge; Karl Baedeker 1st pubs travel guides. **Int. Lit.:** Fenimore Cooper, *The Red Rover*; Heine, *Das Buch der Lieder* [poems]; Pushkin, *Tzigani* [poems]; Hugo, *Cromwell* [drama; preface becomes Fr. Romantic creed]; François Guizot, *Mémoires relatifs à la Révolution d'Angleterre* [Fr. history of Eng. Revolution]; Alessandro Manzoni, *I Promessi Sposi* (*The Betrothed*) [It. novel]. **Art:** Nash designs Carlton House Terrace; 1st of J.J. Audubon's illustrated portfolios, *Birds of America* pub.d [–1838]; Ingres, 'Apotheosis of Homer'; Delacroix, 'Death of Sardanapalus' & 'Combat of the Giaour and the Pasha'; [c.] Constable, 'Salisbury Cathedral' [NG]; Bonington, 'Piazza San Marco, Venice' [Wallace Coll.] & 'Institut, Paris, from the Quais' [BM]; William Etty [pnt] 'Hero's Farewell to Leander' [Tate]. **Lit. 'Events':** William Blake dies	**P:** Clare Landon Wordsworth Thomas Keble (1792–1866) Alfred, Lord Tennyson (1809–1892) **Pr/F:** De Quincey Scott **Dr:** Douglas Jerrold (1803–57)	*The Shepherd's Calendar, with Village Stories and Other Poems & The Parish* [satirical poem; mainly wrtn 1820–4; pub. posthm.] *The Golden Violet, with its Tales of Romance and Chivalry: and Other Poems* *Poetical Works* [5 vols; incls *The Excursion*; 1 vol. edtn, 1828, Paris] *The Christian Year* [religious poems & meditations] *Poems by Two Brothers* [with brother Charles] 'On Murder Considered as one of the Fine Arts' [essay] [–1828] *Napoleon* [biog; 9 vols] *Paul Pry* [farce]

PERIOD	YEAR	INTERNATIONAL AND POLITICAL CONTEXTS	SOCIAL AND CULTURAL CONTEXTS	AUTHORS	INDICATIVE TITLES
	1828	Duke of Wellington [Tory], PM; repeal of Test & Corporation Acts gives religious liberty to Nonconformists – seriously splits Tory party; revised Corn Law intros sliding scale of duties; O'Connell elected MP for County Clare – as an RC, cannot take up seat [v.1829]; Portug. constitution revoked by new king; Turks evacuate Greece – Allied Powers guarantee Grk independence; Uruguay recognised as independent republic; [>] peasant discontent & uprisings increase in Russia	University College & King's College, London, fnd.d [v.1836]; Royal Menagerie moves to Zoological Gardens, Regent's Park, under control of Royal Zoological Society [fnd.d 1826]; Thomas Arnold appointed headmaster of Rugby School; *The Spectator* fnd.d; Webster's, *American Dictionary of the English Language* 1st pub.d. **Int. Lit.:** [–1838] Casanova, *Mémoires écrit par lui-même* [12 vols]; Adam Mickiewicz, *Konrad Wallenrod* [Polish epic patriotic poem]. **Music:** Schubert, 'The Great Symphony' (7th in C major). **Art:** Wilkie, 'Defense of Saragossa' [Royal Coll.]; Goya, 'Milkmaid of Bordeaux'; Constable, 'Dedham Vale' [SNG]; Lawrence, 'William Wilberforce' [NPG]; Palmer, 'Self-Portrait' [Ashmolean]; Bonington, 'English Landscape with a Timber Wagon' [Wallace Coll.]; Ingres, 'La Petite Baigneuse'	**P:** Coleridge Hemans Rogers **Pr/F:** Lockhart Scott Lord Edward Bulwer-Lytton (1803–73) **Dr:** Jerrold **Theory/Crit:** Charles-Augustin Sainte-Beuve	*Poetical Works* [so dated; pub.d 1829] *Records of Women* [incls 'The (Stately) Homes of England'] *Italy* [long poem, begun 1822; edtn with 114 illustr.s by J.M.W. Turner & Thomas Stothard, 1830–4] *Life of Burns* [biog.] *The Fair Maid of Perth* *Pelham* ['silver fork' novel] *Fifteen Years of a Drunkard's Life* [melodrama] *Tableau historique et critique de la poésie française au seizième siècle*
	1829	Catholic Emancipation Act places RCs on equal footing with Nonconformists [v.1828] & allows RCs to sit in Parliament – further splits Tories – O'Connell re-elected for County Clare – can now take up seat in Parliament; Robert Peel intros professional police force ['Peelers' or 'Bobbies'] in London; Grand General Union of Cotton Spinners holds 1st national conference; Andrew Jackson, US President; British colonisation of W. Australia commences with Swan River Settlement; suttee [widow burning herself to death on husband's pyre] declared illegal in British India; Treaty of Adrianople: Turkey acknowledges Grk independence – Russia gains concessions on navigation in Bosphorous & Dardenelles from Turkey [v.1833–4]	1st horse-drawn buses in London [22 passengers from Marylebone to Bank]; Stephenson's 'Rocket' [29 mph] wins Rainham trial of engines for Liverpool-Manchester Railway; 1st Oxford & Cambridge boat race at Henley [v.1845]; [>] Niepce joins Daguerre to advance research on photography; Louis Braille completes reading system for the blind. **Int. Lit.:** W. Irving, *A Chronicle of the Conquest of Grenada*; Lamartine, *Harmonies poétiques et religieuses*; [–1831] Honoré de Balzac, *Les Derniers Chouans & La Peau de chagrin*; Alexandre Dumas ('Père'), *Henry III et sa Cour* [Fr. historical drama]; Prosper Mérimée, *Chronique du Règne de Charles IX* [Fr. historical novel] & *Mateo Falcone* [stories]; [–1830] Alfred de Musset, *Contes d'Espagne et d'Italie* [poems]. **Music:** Mendelssohn, 'Hebrides' overture & 'Scotch Symphony'; Rossini, 'William Tell' [It. opera]. **Art:** Constable, 'Hadleigh Castle' [Tate]; Turner, 'Ulysses Mocking Polyphemus' [NG] & 'Park at Petworth' [Tate]; [c.] Palmer, 'In a Shoreham Garden' [V&A]	**P:** Hemans Hogg Tennyson Thomas Hood (1799–1845) **Pr/F:** Carlyle Coleridge Peacock Scott Frederick ('Captain') Marryat (1792–1848) **Dr:** Jerrold	*The Forest Sanctuary* [2nd edtn (1st, 1825) – incls 'Casabianca' ('The boy stood on the burning deck')] *The Shepherd's Calendar* *Timbuctoo* [won Cambridge University poetry medal] 'The Dream of Eugene Aram' [poem; pub.d in *The Gem*] 'Signs of the Times' [essay pub.d anon. in *Edinburgh Review*] *On the Constitution of the Church and State* [essay; pub. 1830] *The Misfortunes of Elphin* [historical romance] *Anne of Geierstein & Count Robert of Paris* *Frank Mildmay* [novel of sea life] *Black-Eyed Susan; or, All in the Downs* [nautical drama]

HANOVERIAN (REGENCY ENDS)/ROMANTIC

5

1830–1899

The Victorian Period

INTRODUCTION

King William IV, who had acceded to the throne on the death of George IV in 1830, died without legitimate heir in 1837, and was succeeded by his neice, Victoria, the only child of George III's fourth son, Edward, Duke of Kent. Victoria was crowned Queen in 1838, and died in 1901. However, because of the difficulties with precise periodisation, and the contiguity of events in the earlier 1830s with those that follow in Victoria's reign, historians often include William IV's monarchy in their conception of **The Victorian Age***. The present chapter follows suit, while the last two years of the queen's reign (1900–1) slip over into the period dealt with in Chapter 6. Historians also commonly divide the period into **'Early Victorian'** (1830s–*c*.1850: accelerating political and social reform; establishing the economic and infrastructural foundations on which later developments would build); **'Mid-Victorian'** (1850s–*c*.1880: 'Free Trade' in full operation; many of the main social and cultural achievements of the period; imperial power in dynamic phase); and **'Late Victorian'** (1880s–1901: proliferation of tensions and anxieties, decline in confidence; increase in imperial and economic competition from the United States and other European nation states; growth of industrial unrest and extra-parliamentary opposition; the exigence of the 'Irish Question'). The present chapter again follows suit.

Chapter contents

5.1 VICTORIAN

The adjective 'Victorian' (itself dating from the mid-1870s) is strictly used to describe the period of the reign of Queen Victoria of the United Kingdom of Great Britain and Ireland, 1837–1901 [but see Introduction above for slippages].

However, whilst 'Victorian' is an accurate and useful period descriptor, it is also commonly employed in ways which are more problematical and should be regarded with suspicion. For example, most dictionaries give as the word's secondary meaning such definitions as: 'having stiff or prim habits of thought or manner'; 'strict but somewhat conventional in morals, inclining to prudery and solemnity'; and for the noun, 'a Victorian': 'a contemporary of Queen Victoria: a person of Victorian morality or outlook'. Even the most up-to-date dictionary consulted (published 2001) defines its second sense of 'Victorian' as: 'relating to the attitudes and values associated with the Victorian period, especially those of prudishness and high moral tone'. There can be no argument that the word (especially when transmuted into the noun 'Victorianism') carries these meanings in contemporary usage, but when one considers the chronological extent and the social, political, religious and cultural diversity of the period, the problem of the unitary notion implied by 'Victorian' becomes sharply apparent. When the British ex-Prime Minister, Margaret Thatcher, famously referred in the 1980s to 'Victorian values' (in a positive sense), the assumption was that she was invoking the 'high moral tone' and domestic virtues associated with the 19th-Century British middle class, rather than the double standard of middle-class husbands preying on child prostitutes, the exploitation of workers by industrialists and entrepreneurs, or the oppression of native peoples throughout the British Empire. A quotation from the entry on 'Victorian' in *The Oxford Guide to the English Language* (1992) may be helpful here in pointing up the problematics of the term:

> Some [views of the era] have looked back on the period as a time of unsurpassed visionary optimism and admirable moral rectitude; others ... have seen it as a time of strict, stifling,

bigoted, and often hypocritical narrow-mindedness; still others have focused on the struggle between social reformers and liberal thinkers and an entrenched élite regarded as self-serving exploiters of the people and the natural world (both at home and in the colonies).

But the problem of a spurious inclusiveness implied by the term 'Victorian' is never more apparent than in the literary context, where phrases like 'Victorian poetry' and 'the Victorian novel' (with that symptomatic definite article) assume a homogeneity which can only serve to over-simplify and distort. It is probably safer, therefore, to use the term 'Victorian' simply to define the temporal limits of the period, both in historical and literary terms. So we may then say that 'Victorian literature' (i.e. that produced within the period so designated) witnesses the novel becoming the dominant literary genre – especially as widening literacy expanded the reading public – and the vehicle of both social comment and popular entertainment. As evidence of the diverse range of British fiction published between 1837 and 1901, we may cite the work of, *inter alia*, Harrison Ainsworth, Bulwer Lytton, Benjamin Disraeli, Charles Dickens, Elizabeth Gaskell, W. M. Thackeray, the Brontë sisters, Charles Kingsley, Charles Reade, Charlotte Yonge, Anthony Trollope, George Eliot, Wilkie Collins, George Meredith, Thomas Hardy, R. L. Stevenson, George Gissing, Henry James, Samuel Butler and Joseph Conrad.

Non-fictional prose – but often deploying literary language of equivalent imaginative range and inventiveness – is a feature of the period, too; for example, that written by the so-called 'Victorian Prophets' or 'Sages': Thomas Carlyle, John Stuart Mill, John Ruskin, Matthew Arnold, J. H. Newman and William Morris.

Poetry may not have retained quite the position it held during the **Romantic*** era [see Chapter 4], but the Victorian period again sees enormous diversity of range and register (from public utterance to private doubt) in the work of the later William Wordsworth, Alfred Tennyson, Robert Browning, Elizabeth Barrett Browning, Matthew Arnold, Arthur Clough, Dante Gabriel and Christina Rossetti, Coventry Patmore, William Morris, Algernon Swinburne, Robert Bridges, William Barnes, Gerard Manley Hopkins, W. B. Yeats and Thomas Hardy.

While the Victorian age is not greatly esteemed today for its drama, we may notice that the popular theatre flourished (for instance, with the plays of Dion Boucicault, Arthur Pinero, H. A. Jones, James Barrie, and in Victorian melodrama), while the last two decades of the century saw the innovative work of George Bernard Shaw and Oscar Wilde first produced on stage.

5.2 THE VICTORIAN AGE

As noted above, the reign of King William IV (1830–7) is here included in the general concept of 'The Victorian Age'.

William had seen some service in the Navy and was formally promoted through the ranks, becoming admiral of the fleet in 1811 and lord high admiral in 1827, hence his soubriquet 'the sailor king'. A Whig until his accession in 1830, William, like his father and brother before him, governed through the **Tories*** [see Chapter 2] and did much to obstruct the passing of the first Reform Bill; however, during 1831–2, with a reforming **Whig*** [see Chapter 2] government in power and widespread rioting against the Lords' rejection of the Bill, the king threatened to create enough Whig peers to ensure its passing, and the First Reform Act finally became law in 1832 (one in five male citizens with property could now vote).

On his death in 1837, William IV was succeeded by his neice, Victoria. Queen Victoria in fact continued the **Hanoverian*** succession in Britain [see Chapters 3 and 4], although an ancient Germanic law which limited the line of succession to males excluded her from also ruling Hanover, so that from 1837 the thrones of Britain and Hanover separated, and 'Hanoverian' is hence seldom used to describe Victoria's reign.

As a young woman, she had been carefully tutored by her uncle, King Leopold I of Belgium, and thereafter, during her early years as monarch, was mentored by Lord Melbourne, her Prime Minister and chief advisor, and later by her husband, Prince Albert of Saxe-Coburg & Gotha (from 1857, the Prince Consort), whom she married in 1840. Victoria quickly demonstrated an acute grasp of constitutional principles and the extent of her own prerogative [e.g. see the entry on the 'Bedchamber Crisis' in the timeline for 1839], and showed an active interest in the policy of her ministers. Her relations were particularly good with those of **conservative*** persuasion, Melbourne, Sir Robert Peel and Benjamin Disraeli, but rather more tense with the **Liberals***, Lord Palmerston and William Gladstone. Her conscientious performance of official duties helped to raise the reputation of the monarchy, although her long retirement from public view after the untimely death of Prince Albert in 1861 was unpopular. However, during the Disraeli administration of 1874–80, she was declared Empress of India (1876), and again rose high in public favour, most clearly witnessed by the celebrations for her golden jubilee in 1887 and the diamond jubilee in 1897.

From the Battle of Waterloo in 1815 to 4th August 1914, there was no major international war, although there were numerous smaller-scale ones (the Crimean War, the Franco–Prussian War, the Boer War, the Russo–Japanese War, scores of colonial wars throughout the various European empires – and especially the British). The presumptuously entitled 'Pax Britannica' (a peace policed by British power) was sustained until the complex network of alliances and secret treaties between the European powers unravelled into the First World War, and the ensuing relative stability and prosperity was the matrix in which Victorian Britain developed.

As the 'Industrial Revolution' gathered momentum [see Chapter 4 for its earlier stages], the Victorian period saw the rapid industrialisation of Britain, hence its common appellation as 'the first industrial nation'. This was combined with strenuous commercial, technological and financial development, underpinned by the new economic ideology of unrestricted 'Free Trade', and resulted in immense growth in the national wealth (from the 1870s, Britain was fundamental to the global economy).

In addition, the period witnessed the fullest extension of the British Empire and of British influence throughout the world (especially as English became a global language and British models of education were exported worldwide). The exponential growth of London and other major cities is also evidence that a modern urban economy based on manufacturing, international trade, financial institutions and communications systems was displacing older modes of British life, as do the further development of steam power (railways, ships, printing presses, industrial and agricultural machinery – we may recall the steam threshing-machine in Thomas Hardy's novel, *Tess of the d'Urbervilles*), the establishing of a nationwide postal service and the invention of telegraphy and the telephone.

Accompanying such social and economic innovations – at least in the earlier decades of the period, and amongst those who most benefited from them – was a sense of optimism and progress, perhaps encapsulated in the following quotations – all from the early 1840s: 'God's in his heaven / All's right with the world!' (Robert Browning, 'Pippa Passes', 1841); 'The History of England is emphatically the history of progress' (Thomas Macaulay, *Essays*, 1843); '["The Hero as Man of Letters" is] our most important modern person. He … is the soul of all. What he teaches, the whole world will do and make' (Thomas Carlyle, *Heroes and Hero Worship*, 1840); and

> Forward, forward let us range,
> Let the great world spin for ever down the ringing grooves of change.

Thro' the shadow of the globe we sweep into the younger day:
Better fifty years of Europe than a cycle of Cathay.
  (Alfred Tennyson, 'Locksley Hall', 1842, with its erroneous railway image in line 2)

But the period is also marked by tensions between such confidence and what Tennyson was later to call 'honest doubt': the result of a growing scepticism about Christianity, the religious reforms of 1828–32 which undermined the central status of the Church of England, the increase in politico/religious dissent – for example Anglo-Catholicism [the 'Oxford Movement'; see 1833 and 1845] and Christian Socialism [see 1848] – and the fall-out from the 'Evolution' debate, especially after the publication of Charles Darwin's *The Origin of the Species* in 1859. Tensions also developed between the repression of social unrest and reform and tolerance; and between the pressure to introduce universal literacy and numeracy and the fear of 'educating our [future] masters' (i.e. of mass democratic 'anarchy', in Matthew Arnold's word). Such fault-lines traverse the Victorian period, as the timeline narratives below will indicate.

In order to make the following timeline narratives less unwieldy, and despite potentially creating even more artificial periodisations, the narratives have been split into the three rough periodisations outlined in the introductory paragraph to this chapter: 'Early', 'Mid', 'Late'.

Key 'Early Victorian' Timeline Narratives 1830s–c.1849

➲ ***Parliamentary Reform***   The General Election of 1830 showed pro-reform attitudes predominating with the election of the Whigs under Earl Grey, and 1831–2 witnessed a bitter struggle between Lords and Commons, during which three Reform Bills were brought before Parliament. The Lords' rejection of the first two resulted in widespread rioting, but the final passing of the third Bill resulted in the [First] Reform Act of 1832. From 1836, however, the **Chartist*** movement [see below] and the

London Working Men's Association were pressing for further reform and greatly increased enfranchisement [for later developments, see '**Mid-Victorian**' below].

⮑ *Social Reform*   1833 saw an Act banning slavery throughout British territories; from 1831 onwards, there were a series of factory and coal mine Acts principally to regulate the conditions of women and children employed in industry [see, for example, 1831,1833, 1842, 1844, 1845, 1847]; from 1835, local government reform for urban areas began to be introduced, and with cholera epidemics in 1831 and 1848, legislation on public health also got underway, with a Royal Commission on Health in Towns set up in 1844 and the first Public Health Act becoming law in 1848 (Edwin Chadwick's *Report on the Sanitary Condition of the Labouring Poor* had been published in 1842); less humanitarian was the passing of the Poor Law Amendment Act in 1834, which replaced the 'Speenhamland System'of poor relief [see 1795] with workhouses for the poor and elderly segregated by gender.

⮑ *Corn-Law Reform and Free Trade*   The Corn Laws were ancient English laws which limited the import and export of corn, and were used effectively to protect the interests of landowners. In 1815 [see Chapter 4], a Corn Law prohibited the import of foreign corn until the British price was 80 shillings for a little less than a quarter of a ton, making bread prohibitively expensive; in the years following, this was the cause of widespread severe povery and suffering. During the 1820s, agitation for repeal grew, and in 1838, seven Manchester businessmen founded the Anti-Corn Law League (led by the apostles of 'Free Trade' Richard Cobden and John Bright).

Sir Robert Peel held out against repeal, and fierce agitation continued; but finally, after the threat of mass starvation in 1845 in Britain and the Irish famine of 1845–6, Peel repealed the Corn Laws in 1846, thus splitting the Tories* and allowing the Whigs* to form a government under Lord John Russell [for both party names, see Chapter 2; Russell's period in office, 1846–52, is sometimes considered the first Liberal* ministry – see below]. During the 1840s, the Free Trade movement (i.e. that pressing for the abolition of protective tariffs in international trade) gathered increasing momentum more generally – again inspired by Cobden and Bright – and Liberal governments throughout the middle decades of the century introduced Free Trade legislation and budgets [see 'Mid-Victorian' below].

⮑ *Education*   In 1833, the Education Grant Act gave the first state aid to religious societies to build schools; by 1839, a Privy Council Committee was set up to oversee the disbursement of public money for education, and the first H. M. Inspectors of Schools appointed; and in 1846, the first state-supported provision for teacher training was introduced. The founding colleges of the University of London [see Chapter 4: 1823 and 1827–8] were amalgamated and the University received its Charter in 1836; London University Library opened in 1839–40; Queen's College in 1848; and Bedford College, London, the first for women, was founded in 1849.

⮑ *Industrial Relations*   In 1830, the 'Captain Swing' riots of agricultural workers in southern England were brutally suppressed, with 10 executed and 450 transported; the Operative Builders Union was founded in 1832; in 1834, Robert Owen founded the Grand National Consolidated Trades Union to co-ordinate labour activity, but it soon failed, and in the same year, the 'Tolpuddle Martyrs' were sentenced to seven years' transportation for swearing an illegal oath to join a trades union; in 1837, Glasgow cotton-spinners went on a three-month strike; from 1836, Chartism* was becoming a mass working-class movement [see below]; and in 1844, the 'Rochdale Pioneers' founded the first working-people's Co-operative Society.

⊃ **Ireland** In the 1840s especially, the 'Irish Question' acquired a new dynamic: in 1840, Daniel O'Connell founded his Repeal Association (to repeal the Union of England and Ireland) and massive meetings were held thereafter (a huge meeting planned at Clontarf was abandoned in 1843 after the British government proclaimed it); O'Connell himself was tried and sentenced for sedition, and the 'Young Ireland' movement gradually displaced him, although an attempted national rebellion led by Smith O'Brien in 1848 was a complete failure. The agitation was compounded by the onset of famine (1845–50), especially after the failure of the potato crop in 1845.

⊃ **The Railways** In 1830, the Liverpool–Manchester railway opened (when William Huskisson, MP, an ex-president of the Board of Trade, was killed by a train); the first train in London ran to Greenwich in 1836; Euston Station was designed and built in the late-1830s (which Dickens wrote about in *Dombey and Son*); in 1838, the London–Birmingham railway opened; the Great Western Railway (London–Bristol; with Isambard Kingdom Brunel as main engineer) was completed in 1841; railway speculation was at its height in the mid-1840s; and in 1846, the introduction of the British standard gauge for track facilitated the rapid and pervasive expansion of the railway system in Britain.

We might also notice that during this period, steam-ship crossings of the Atlantic were becoming more common and faster: the first was in 1833, followed by Brunel's SS 'Great Western' in 1838 and his SS 'Great Britain' in 1845, the first ocean-going screw-steamer. (Brunel's SS 'Great Eastern' was launched in 1858, and for the next 40 years was the largest ship ever built; during the present period, Brunel also erected the Hungerford Suspension Bridge over the Thames at Charing Cross and helped design the Wapping–Rotherhithe Thames Tunnel which opened in in 1843).

⊃ **The European Context** In 1831–3, Belgium rebelled against Dutch rule and declared its independence; the European powers agreed to guarantee it; and in 1839, the powers signed the Treaty of London which guaranteed the perpetual neutrality of Belgium (this was the 'scrap of paper' which Germany was deemed to have torn up in 1914, and the immediate reason for Britian's declaration of war). The early 1830s saw the beginnings of the 'Young Germany' and 'Young Italy' nationalist movements. The Italians, Guiseppe Mazzini, Camillo Cavour and Giuseppe Garibaldi, in particular, helped to spread the seeds of militant nationalism and the struggle for independence throughout Europe, which resulted in 'The Year of Revolutions' in 1848. Britain managed to remain insulated from this (despite a mass Chartist* rally in London [see below]), and the revolutions were gradually suppressed during 1849. However, independence and unification movements achieved success later in the century.

In philosophical, economic and political thought, work was published by Auguste Comte, D. F. Strauss, Ludvig Feuerbach, P. J. Proudhon, Vicomte de Chateaubriand, Frederick Engels and Karl Marx (their *Communist Manifesto* appeared in 1848); in music, the principal European composers of the period were: Mendelssohn, Schumann, Chopin, Donizetti, Verdi, Puccini, Liszt and Wagner; in the fine arts, the major painters were: Delacroix, Ingres, Corot, Daumier and Millet; while in literature, significant names were: Heine, Balzac, Hugo, Gogol, Musset, Stendhal, Dumas, George Sand and Dostoevsky.

⊃ **The US Context** From 1830 onwards, Native Americans were gradually dispossessed of their tribal lands and 'Indian Territories' constituted; in the early 1830s, the US Anti-Slavery/Abolitionist movement began; more new states were founded (eg. Texas seceded from Mexico in 1836 as an independent republic and became a US state in 1848, along with Florida; the war with Mexico over border disputes resulted in the USA acquiring Arizona, New Mexico, Utah, Nevada, California, and parts of Colorado and Wyoming between 1845 and 1848). In literature, this period saw the flowering of 'American Romanticism' (Ralph Waldo Emerson, Edgar Allen Poe, Nathaniel Hawthorne, Henry W. Longfellow, and in the 1850s, Henry Thoreau).

⊃ **The British Empire**

- **Australia**   The Murray River was discovered and explored (1830); a settlement at what would become Melbourne began the colony of Victoria (1835); South Australia became a British province and Adelaide was founded (1835–6; Crown Colony, 1842); the transportation of convicts to New South Wales was ended (1840), but continued to Tasmania and Western Australia; in the 1840s, emigration from Britain to Australia was being encouraged.

- **New Zealand**   In 1839, New Zealand was proclaimed a British colony and incorporated with New South Wales; a year later, Maori chiefs ceded sovereignty to Britain, and in 1841, New Zealand became an autonomous British colony; the 1840s also saw conflict between settlers and Maoris.

- **Canada**   A constitutional crisis developed in 1837 when a Canada Bill was introduced in Parliament to unify Upper (British) and Lower (French) Canada, and rebellions broke out against this and against imperial government. Lord Durham was sent to Canada to resolve the issue, and he reported to Parliament in 1839. The Canada Act of Union was passed in 1840–1, but the 'Durham Report' had recommended responsible government (i.e. internal self-government) for the colonies, and this was granted to Canada in 1848, with the maritime provinces becoming self-governing, 1848–51. In this recommendation, the Report had far-reaching effects in radically changing the British conception of empire.

- **South Africa**   In 1835–6, the Boers made the 'Great Trek' from Cape Colony to found Natal, the Transvaal and the Orange Free State, defeating the Zulus at Blood River in 1838. Britain annexed Natal in 1843, but recognised the independence of the Transvaal (1852) and the Orange Free State (1854), although relations between British and Boers later deteriorated [see **Imperialism** under **'Late Victorian'**, vii) below]. The very end of this period also saw the beginning of David Livingstone's explorations of Central and Southern Africa.

- **India**   In 1833, an Act of Parliament ended the East India Company's trade monopoly in the Far East, it ceased trading and became solely involved with the government of India [see also 1858 and 1874]; in 1853, Lord Macaulay delivered his 'Minute on Education' which established that English should be the medium of education in British India; in 1842, Sindh was annexed by Britain; an Anglo-Sikh war broke out in 1845–6, when the Sikhs were defeated and the Punjab placed under British control; the Sikhs revolted again in 1848–9 when they were finally defeated, thus ending the Sikh state and the annexing of the Punjab by Britain.

- **Other Colonies**   In the course of the period, Britain continued to acquire colonies throughout the world (e.g. the Falkland Islands and St Helena, 1832–3; Hong Kong was ceded to Britain in 1842, following the first 'Opium War' with China, 1839).

⊃ **Science and Technology**   The period saw many new inventions and discoveries in Great Britain and the wider world; the following are amongst them: from 1830–3, Charles Lyall's *Principles of Geology*; Michael Faraday's work on electricity from the 1830s onwards; the voyage round the world of Charles Darwin as a naturalist aboard HMS 'Beagle' (1831–6), and the publication of his account of it (1839); Thomas Hodgkin's identification of 'Hodgkin's Disease' (1832); the invention in 1834 by Joseph Hansom of his 'Patent Safety Cab', which then appeared on London's streets; the discovery of magnetic and electric telegraphy in the USA and Britain in 1837; the early inventions in photography of Louis Daguerre (1822 and 1839) and William Fox Talbot (1839), and then in the 1840s, the development of photographic portraiture by David Octavius Hill and Robert Adamson; in 1844, in the USA, Samuel Morse transmitted the first telegraph message, while Charles Goodyear invented vulcanised rubber; and in 1848, Linus Yale invented the cylinder lock.

⊃ **British Cultural Developments**   The old Houses of Parliament burnt down in 1834, and in 1840 Sir Charles Barry began rebuilding the present ones (employing the designs of Augustus Pugin [see below] for the elevations, decoration and sculpture); 1840 was also the year that Rowland Hill introduced the 'Penny Post' (first British postage stamps), Nelson's Column was erected in Trafalgar Square, and Kew Botanical Gardens were opened to the public. Augustus Pugin had published his *Contrasts: or a Parallel Between the Noble Edifices of the Fourteenth and Fifteenth Centuries, and Similar Buildings of the Present Day: Showing the Present Decay of Taste* in 1836, thus inaugurating the 'Gothic Revival' in Victorian architecture, witnessed by further publications (e.g. 1841) and his own buildings [see, e.g., 1839–41, 1848, 1851].

The second half of the 1830s saw the opening of 'Madame Tussaud's' waxworks exhibition in London, the opening of the present National Gallery in Trafalgar Square, the foundation of the Public Record Office, the first Royal Agricultural Show, the first Henley Regatta and the first Grand National run at Aintree. In the early 1840s, Thomas Cook opened his travel agency (1841), the Royal Botanical Gardens were presented to the nation (1842), and the Theatre Regulations Act of 1843 abolished the monopoly of Covent Garden and Drury Lane, thus encouraging the development of more diverse kinds of theatre.

In the earlier part of the period, legislation to protect writers' copyright began to be introduced [see 1833, 1839, 1842], and stamp duty on newspapers was reduced to one penny (1836), thus making them available to a wider readership; J. S. Mill founded and edited the *London and Westminster Review* (1835–40), and Charles Dickens co-founded and edited *Bentley's Miscellany* (1837–9); *Punch*, the *Illustrated London News*, the *News of the World* and *Who's Who* were all first published in the 1840s; in 1842, Chambers brought out *The Cyclopaedia of English Literature*, and Mudie's Circulating Library was founded.

John Constable and Sir David Wilkie were still painting in the early years of the period, and J. M. W. Turner was immensely productive throughout; 1848 saw the founding of the 'Pre-Raphaelite Brotherhood' (of poets and painters), and the early paintings of John Everett Millais and Dante Gabriel Rossetti [for much of the work of the PRB, see the timeline narratives for 'Mid-Victorian' and **(The) Pre-Raphaelite(s)***, 5.7 below].

5.3 CHARTISM

A mass working-class oppositional movement principally of the late 1830s and early 1840s. It arose as a response to the 1832 Reform Act [see above], which, while extending the franchise to some degree, nevertheless retained the property qualification to vote and thus continued to disenfranchise the vast majority of people.

Chartism's cause was popularly advanced by Fergus O'Connor's newspaper, the *Northern Star* (founded in 1837 in Leeds), but it takes its name from the publication in 1838 of 'The People's

Charter', which listed six demands for political reform: universal manhood suffrage; vote by ballot; payment of MPs; equal electoral districts; the abolition of the property qualification for MPs; and annual parliaments.

In 1839, the Chartist National Convention opened, and the first Chartist Petition, with around one-and-a-quarter-million signatures was presented to Parliament. It was rejected, and serious rioting commenced. In 1841, during a period of deep trade depression, acute industrial crisis and economic distress, Chartism revived, and a second Petition was rejected by Parliament. Rioting broke out once more, especially in the cotton areas of Lancashire and in Staffordshire. The last major upsurge of Chartist activity occurred in 1848 with the presentation of a massive third Petition to Parliament, which again failed; **Habeas Corpus*** [see Chapter 2] was suspended, but on this occasion, a mass demonstration in London dispersed peacefully, and thereafter Chartism as an active movement went into decline.

At its most successful, Chartism mobilised the working class in a way which indicated its potential political strength, and offered its class-base self-confident social, educational and cultural experience (for example, much Chartist poetry was written and published in papers like the *Northern Star*). But it was a regionally and politically diverse movement (despite all the radical language of political reform and the identification of the enemy as 'Old Corruption', in 1845 the Chartists adopted Fergus O'Connor's scheme for land settlement as the economic solution to the plight of the masses); and it drew on many different traditions and solidarities, witnessed most sharply perhaps in the division between 'moral force' Chartism (which advocated peaceful radical-democratic action) and 'physical force' Chartism (which was steeped in a more insurrectionary tradition of popular protest). Paradoxically, despite its short life and sudden demise, all the aims articulated in the original 'People's Charter' – except the last one – were later achieved.

5.4 CONSERVATIVES

The British political party which succeeded the Tories during the first half of the 19th Century. The party tends to uphold traditional values and institutions, and to favour free enterprise, private ownership and socially conservative ideas.

After the General Election of 1830, the Wellington-Peel Tory* ministry was succeeded by a Whig* government under Earl Grey [see Chapter 2 for glosses on both party names]. In 1834, Grey and then Melbourne resigned, and Sir Robert Peel became Prime Minister (until 1835). His 'Tamworth Manifesto' speech during the election of 1834 rallied the Tory cause in support of the recent Whig reforms and so laid the foundations for what became during the 1830s the **Conservative Party**, which returned to power under Peel after the General Election of 1841. Although based on maintaining existing institutions, it promoted less reactionary, more reformist policies, so that it was Peel who finally abolished the Corn Laws in 1846 [see above, timeline narrative under **Corn-Law Reform** and **Free Trade**], and Benjamin Disraeli [see below] as

Chancellor of the Exchequer of a Conservative government who brought in the Second Reform Bill of 1867 and much other social legislation (1874–80).

However, Peel's repeal of the Corn Laws split the new party into two factions – the 'Peelites' and the 'No Surrender' Tories (including Disraeli) – which weakened it during the 1840s and 1850s. Nevertheless, Disraeli, too, was central to a new brand of Tory radicalism. He entered Parliament in 1837, and by 1842 had become leader of the 'Young England' movement, a group of Tories who, while believing staunchly in the aristocracy, the Queen and the Church, also saw their responsibilty as protecting the working class. These views were given fictional form in Disraeli's trilogy of socio-political novels, *Coningsby* (1844), *Sybil* (1845, with its famous synoptic sub-title, *or The Two Nations*, [i.e. of rich and poor in Victorian Britain]), and *Tancred* (1847). Later in the period, when Gladstone's Irish Home Rule Bill split the Liberals* [see below] into Liberals and Liberal Unionists (led by Joseph Chamberlain from 1895), the Conservatives allied with the latter, and were in power – except for 1886 and 1892–5 – until the party again split over tariff reform in 1905 [see **'Late-Victorian'** below, for more detailed treatment of domestic politics, and **Edwardian*** in Chapter 6].

5.5 LIBERALS

The British political party which superseded the Whigs in the mid-19th Century. The party favoured free trade, gradual democratic reform, individual liberty and other moderately progressive social, religious, economic and cultural programmes.

Although the name 'Liberal' was only adopted formally by the Whig Party in 1868 (when William Ewart Gladstone formed his first ministry), the term 'Liberals' had been in use since the 1830s to describe reforming Whigs, and as noted above [see timeline narrative under Corn Law Reform and Free Trade. See also **Liberalism** below], Lord John Russell's ministry between 1846 and 1852 is often considered to be the first Liberal government. Unlike 'Tory', however, 'Whig' never thereafter had currency as a familiar term for the Liberals.

The Liberal Party was associated throughout much of the century with Free Trade, and was led from 1868 to 1894 by Gladstone, who had himself started his political life as a Conservative and been a 'Peelite' during the repeal of the Corn Laws [see above].

The party was instrumental during Gladstone's leadership in introducing an extensive programme of political, social and educational reform [see 'Mid-' and 'Late Victorian' below for more detail]. However, it split in 1886 over Irish Home Rule [see under **Conservatives** above], and again over the Boer War (1899–1902), but returned to power with a landslide victory in the General Election of 1906. It was then beset by constitutional, social and economic problems in the period immediately before the First World War; entered a wartime coalition government in 1915; and was effectively effaced as the party of progressive policies in the post-war period by **Labour*** [see Chapter 6]. In 1958, and for the next 30 years, the Liberals had a small-scale renaissance as a free-standing party; and then in 1988 merged with the Social Democratic Party (founded by ex-Labour Party members in 1981) to form the present Liberal Democrat Party [see Chapters 7, 8 and 9].

'Liberalism' is both the term for the policies of the Liberal Party and more generally for a set of progressive social, political, religious, economic and cultural doctrines. As a political philosophy, Liberalism can first be identified in the early part of the 19th Century and, certainly in Britain, is the dominant informing ideology behind much of the social and cultural achievement of the Victorian period, regardless of political party affiliations (reform of all kinds is an example of this, as is the socially concerned writing of the time: for instance, that of Dickens, Gaskell, Disraeli, Kingsley, John Stuart Mill, Matthew Arnold and William Morris). Liberalism tends to be critical of institutions, whether political or religious, which restrict individual liberty; is marked by its faith in progress and human goodness and rationality; expresses itself in demands for freedom of expression, equality of opportunity and education for all; and is distinguished from more radical progressive movements by its insistence on gradual democratic reform rather than by direct revolutionary action.

'Economic liberalism' derives from the *laissez-faire* doctrines of Adam Smith, Thomas Malthus and David Ricardo [see Chapter 4], and developed in 19th-Century economics, commerce and industry as favouring free trade, market regulation of wages and prices, and opposition to state intervention. However, in late 19th-Century Britain, such attitudes were relaxed somewhat to allow the state to intervene to a limited degree in the provision of welfare services and social security, although such Liberalism still marks itself off from Socialism by remaining a centrally individualistic philosophy. A much later version of economic liberalism appears in the extreme free-market ideology of Reaganite (USA) and Thatcherite (UK) economics in the 1980s and 1990s [see Chapters 8 and 9].

Key 'Mid-Victorian' Timeline Narratives 1850s–c.1880

➲ **Parliamentary Reform**   Continues with the property qualification for MPs abolished (1858) and the legislation which introduces the Second Reform Bill (1866–7), enfranchising a million urban artisans. It is worth noting, too, that the beginnings of the Labour movement in British politics are apparent in this period (e.g. 1869, 1874 [first two Trade Union-sponsored MPs elected]; for a gloss on (The) Labour (Party)*, see Chapter 6).

➲ **Social Reform**   Included a series of measures to reform working conditions in industry (e.g. 1850, 1860, 1864, 1867, 1872, 1874, 1878); the development of an active trade unionism, and its gradual legalisation (e.g. 1851, 1852, 1853, 1858, 1859, 1864, 1869, 1871 [Trade Union Act legalises unions], 1872, 1874 [Women's Trade Union League founded], 1876). Prompted by a series of cholera epidemics in London in the early 1850s and Florence Nightingale's work during the Crimean War (1854–6; see **The European Context** below), public health improvements were initated, including new Public Health legislation (e.g. 1854, 1875), nurse training (1856–60), and slum clearance (e.g. 1864, 1874); women's campaigns for fairer divorce laws led to the (First) Married Women's Property Act of 1870. Henry Mayhew's four-volume work of social investigation, *London Labour and the London Poor*, was published in 1861–2 after ten years' research.

◗ **Free Trade**   Led by Gladstone, Cobden and Bright in particular, by 1860–1, very few imported items were any longer subject to duty.

◗ **Education**   The debate on the right to primary education for all (e.g. the Newcastle Commission Report of 1861) produced Forster's Elementary Education Act of 1870, which made free public education available to all 5–13-year-old children, and then Sandon's Act of 1876 which made it compulsory.

In higher education, the Universities Tests Act of 1871 finally allowed non-Anglicans to enter Oxford and Cambridge; Owens College – later to become Manchester University – opened in 1851; a Working Men's College was founded in London in 1854 (Ruskin lectured there) and University Extension Classes were established at Cambridge (1873); the period also saw a significant number of colleges for women open in London (1860, 1875–6), Cambridge (1869, 1871) and Oxford (1878, 1879).

◗ **Ireland**   The late-1850s saw the founding of the **Fenian*** movement in the USA and Ireland. It was particularly active in challenging the British Government and drawing attention to the 'Irish Question' in the mid-1860s. But the main 19th- and 20th-Century narrative of 'Home Rule for Ireland' begins in earnest with the obstructing of House of Commons business by Irish Nationalist MPs led by Charles Parnell in 1877–8 [see 'Late Victorian', below, for further developments].

◗ **The European Context**   1852 saw Louis Napoleon confirmed as Napoleon III of the restored (Second) Empire in France until 1870–1, when the Franco–Prussian War resulted in the seige of Paris, the revolutionary uprising of the Paris Commune (suppressed), the defeat of the French, the fall of Napoleon III and the end of the Second Empire. In 1853, Russia invaded Turkey causing Britain and France to come to the latter's aid, and thus triggering the Crimean War (1854–6) – the only European conflict Britain was involved in between 1815 and 1914, the mismangement of which caused grave concern over the condition of the Armed Forces. The Peace of Paris in 1856 ended the war and guaranteed the integrity of Turkey, but from then until 1914 the Turkish Empire was the 'Sick Man of Europe' (i.e. the potential source of imperial collapse and further conflict; see e.g. 1877–8).

The nationalist movement for independence and unification noted in the earlier part of this period continued in Italy with the gradual ejection of the Austrians (e.g. 1857–9), partial unification in 1860 (involving Garibaldi's 1000 'Red Shirts'), and the crowning of Victor Emmanuel of Savoy as first king of a united Italy in 1861 (Venice joined in 1866; Rome, as a result of the Franco–Prussian War, in 1871). After a sustained strategy by Bismarck from 1862, the unification of Germany was proclaimed at the end of the Franco–Prussian War in 1871, with William I of Prussia Emperor of Germany and Bismarck Imperial German Chancellor.

◗ **The US Context**   During the 1850s, a number of new states joined the union, but the single dominating event of the mid-19th Century was the American Civil War (1861–5) and its aftermath in the 'post-bellum' period: President Lincoln's 'Gettysburg Address' (1863), his Inaugural Address' and assassination (1865), the passing of the 13th and 14th amendments to the Constitution (1865–6; abolishing slavery and enfranchising black Americans), the gradual erosion of 'Reconstruction' in the 1870s and the repossession of the South by white 'Democrats'.

◗ **The British Empire**   Prominent 'narratives' here are: the continuing, apparently random, accrual of territories to the British Crown (hence the disingenuous proposition that 'the British Empire was acquired in a fit of absent-mindedness'); the move to self-governing Dominion status of Australia and Canada (e.g. 1850, 1855, 1858, 1867), but tensions in the latter in respect of its French-speaking citizens (1869); the relative stability of British India after the 'Indian Mutiny' and its suppression (1857–8); British wars in South Africa with the Kaffirs (1853) and the Zulus (1879), and growing tension with the Boers over their claim for a 'Free State' or Republic (e.g. 1879).

⮑ *Science and Technology*   Major examples here would include: the Great Exhibition in London in 1851 (sometimes seen as symbolising the acme of Victorian power and accomplishment); the building of the Suez Canal (opened 1869); the launching of Brunel's SS 'Great Eastern' (1858); the development of Charles Siemens's open-hearth furnaces in steel-making (1861); the commencement of the first underground railway line in London (1863); the laying of a transatlantic telegraph cable (1866); Joseph Lister's pioneering antiseptic surgery (1867); Alexander Bell's telephone (1876); Thomas Edison's phonograph (1877) and electric light bulb (1879). However, perhaps the most significant scientific and cultural event of the mid-Victorian period was the publication in 1859 of Charles Darwin's *The Origin of the Species* and the bitterly controversial 'Evolution' debate which followed.

⮑ *Cultural Developments*   In Britain, aside from the Great Exhibition of 1851, this part of the period witnesses the first Public Libraries Act (1850), the opening of the South Kensington Museum (1857; became the Victoria and Albert Museum, 1909), the founding of the National Portrait Gallery (1857; opens 1896), the opening of the new Royal Opera House in Covent Garden (1858) and of the Scottish National Gallery (1859), the building of the Albert Hall (1867–71), the founding of the Guildhall Library, London (1872), and the first Shakespeare Memorial Theatre in Stratford-upon-Avon.

The abolition of Stamp Duty on newspapers in 1855 (the year the *Daily Telegraph* – Britain's first mass-circulation daily – was founded, along with the *Daily Chronicle*) was followed in 1861 by the removal of duty on paper, and opened the way for the rapid development of the print industry [see 'Late Victorian' below] and of a mass readership. Also of note is the inception in 1858 of what was to become the *Oxford English Dictionary* (*OED*) and from 1879 [–1928] Sir James Murray's editing of it, while in Edinburgh, from 1859 to 1868, Robert Chambers edited *Chambers Encyclopaedia*.

Sport saw the founding in 1862 of Notts County, the oldest club in the Football League, the establishing of both the FA Cup and the Rugby Union in 1871, and the first All-England Tennis Championships played at Wimbledon in 1877.

In Britain, Pre-Raphaelitism* [see below] was the most significant art movement, while in the later part of the period the experimental paintings of James McNeill Whistler began to appear. In France, the period witnessed the dominance of such realist 'plein air' painters as Gustave Courbet and Jean François Millet, but by the 1860s, significant work by painters such as Degas, Manet, Monet, Renoir, Sisley, Pissarro, Morisot and Cézanne was being produced, with the first Impressionist Exhibition held in Paris in 1874 and seven more during the late 1870s and early 1880s.

In philosophy and political thought, the mid-19th Century was the main period of production of Comte, Schopenhauer, Spencer, J. S. Mill, Carlyle, Ruskin, Nietzsche and Marx, while in literature, the roll-call of significant European names includes: Hugo, Zola, Flaubert, Dumas, Verne, Tolstoy, Turgenev, Dostoevsky, Ibsen, Strindberg and, towards the end of the period, the Symbolist poets in France; and in the USA: Hawthorne, Melville, Emerson, Longfellow, Whitman, Twain and Alcott. [For the major British Victorian writers, see the 'Authors' and 'Indicative Titles' columns in the timeline tables.]

5.6 FENIAN

The popular name (based on the Old Irish word, 'Fène', for the Irish people) for members of the Irish Republican Brotherhood.

The Irish Republican Brotherhood was a secret society founded in 1857–8 in the USA and Ireland by John O'Mahony and James Stephens and dedicated to the overthrow of the British Government in Ireland. It was active in North America, the UK and Ireland in the mid-1860s, and drew attention to the 'Irish Question', but went into decline thereafter. The word is still used offensively by Protestants in Ulster for Roman Catholics.

5.7 (THE) PRE-RAPHAELITE(S)

As noun or adjective, the term coined by Dante Gabriel Rossetti to describe a group of anti-establishment British painters founded in 1848: 'The Pre-Raphaelite Brotherhood' ('PRB').

The central members of the PRB were Rossetti, William Holman Hunt and John Everett Millais, but Ford Madox Brown was a kindred spirit and Edward Burne-Jones, William Morris, Arthur Hughes and Henry Wallis were also closely associated with the movement, as was the poet, Christina Rossetti – the term being just as appropriately used for the poetry of both Rossettis and the early Morris (a literary magazine, *The Germ*, was edited by William Michael Rossetti for four issues in 1850, and Morris and Burne-Jones set up *The Oxford and Cambridge Magazine* in 1856 which published poems by Rossetti and Morris).

The visual artists sought to return to the spirit and manner of painting before the time of the Italian High Renaissance painter, Raphael (1483–1520), advocating and practising an adherence to natural forms and effects, a precise concern with minute detail, a preference for outdoor settings, the use of bright colour, and subjects commonly of a religious or medieval-literary kind. The high point of the movement was the five years or so after 1848, but its influence can be felt in much later 19th-Century British painting, in Morris's founding of his Arts and Crafts business [see 1861], and in the poetry, for example, of Algernon Charles Swinburne. John Ruskin defended the group's ideas in the pamphlet, 'Pre-Raphaelitism' (1851), but Robert Buchanan (as 'Thomas Maitland') fiercely attacked their poetry (and especially D. G. Rossetti's) in an essay in the *Contemporary Review*, 'The Fleshly School of Poetry' (1871); Rossetti replied with 'The Stealthy School of Criticism'.

Key 'Late Victorian' Timeline Narratives 1880s–c.1901

➲ ***Parliamentary Reform***   This continued with legislation (1883) to curb corrupt and illegal practices in electioneering; the Third Reform Act (1884) which enfranchised most men in rural areas and thus achieved almost universal male suffrage; and the Redistribution Act of 1885 which introduced the modern pattern of single-member constituencies for the Commons. In addition, legislation was introduced to transfer devolved local government powers to elected County Councils rather than JPs as in the past (1888), so that in 1899 the London County Council (LCC; to 1965) and other Borough Councils were established, and to set up Parish, Rural and District Councils (1894). One social effect of this were Acts of 1887 and 1891 which allowed local councils to buy land compulsorily to let as Allotments and Small Holdings.

A significant further development – one of several which began to dominate the period up to the First World War – is flagged by Emmeline [Mrs] Pankhurst's founding of the Women's Franchise League in 1889, and the inauguration of the National Union of Women's Suffrage Societies in 1897 (with Millicent Fawcett as President).

⊃ **Social Reform**   The Employers' Liability Acts of 1880 and 1897 established compensation for workers injured through employer negligence; Acts of 1887 and 1891 respectively prohibited boys under 13 years of age from working underground and under 12 at the surface, and no child under 11 to work in factories; a Royal Commission was set up to report on the housing of the working classes (1884); the Housing of the Working Classes Act (1890) began slum clearance; and the Second Married Women's Property Act (1882) established the right to separate ownership of property.

East London, the first volume of Charles Booth's 17-volume work of social exploration, *Life and Labour of the People of London* (to 1903), was published in 1889, and William Booth's *In Darkest England and the Way Out* the following year.

⊃ **Education**   The Mundella Education Act of 1880 made elementary education compulsory for all children up to the age of 13 [raised to 14 in 1900]; Regent Street Polytechnic and the Guildhall School of Music were founded in London in the same year; Liverpool University was founded in 1882; in 1889, the Technical Education Act allowed Local Councils to levy a 1*d.* rate to provide technical and manual instruction; the Federal University of Wales was founded in 1893; a Royal Commission on Secondary Education reported in 1895, and in the same year, Sidney Webb helped to found the London School of Economics (and Political Science).

The University of London Act of 1898 reorganised the university as a teaching institution; a Board of Education was established in 1899; in the same year, Ruskin College, Oxford, was founded to offer education based on socialist principles; and by 1897, it was established that only trained nurses could work in hospitals. Higher Education opportunites for (some) women also improved in the course of the period: in 1880, the University of London began to admit women for degrees; and St Hughes College, Oxford, was founded in 1886, followed by St Hilda's and St Anne's Colleges in 1893.

⊃ **The Labour Movement**   [For a fuller gloss on (The) Labour (Party)*, see Chapter 6.] Throughout the period, and indeed up to the First World War [see glosses in Chapter 6], industrial and social unrest was endemic (from 1896–1914, in particular, the UK saw a period of rising prices and falling wages). In 1885, the Socialist League (founded by William Morris in 1884) demonstrated against unemployment in London; it was again involved in the 'Bloody Sunday' demonstration of unemployed workers in Trafalgar Square, which was brutally suppressed by police and troops. In 1888, the Miners Federation of Great Britain was founded, and demanded a minimum wage, and in the same year there was the 'London Matchgirls' strike of Bryant and May's female workforce; 1889 saw the 'Great London Dock Strike, and the growth thereafter of unskilled workers unions; a London omnibus strike in 1890 was only settled by a 12-hour-day agreement; the National Free Labour Association was formed in 1893, the same year as there was a national mining strike; an anarchist bomb exploded at Greenwich in 1894; and in 1899, the General Federation of Trades Unions was founded.

⊃ **Ireland**   The 'Irish Question' comes very high up the political agenda from the beginning of this period onwards (and indeed remains so at least until the 1920s). In 1880, in response to thousands of evictions, the Irish National Land League began a policy of withholding rents; Gladstone's Second Irish Land Act of 1881 attempted to give tenant farmers greater rights, with courts to establish fair rents, but Parnell rejected it; Habeas Corpus* [see Chapter 2] was suspended in Ireland, the Irish MPs at Westminster again obstructed Commons business, and Parnell was imprisoned in Ireland till 1882.

The murders in Phoenix Park, Dublin, of two Secretaries for Ireland in 1882 exacerbated the situation, with further agitation and repression ensuing; in 1886, Gladstone introduced his first Irish Home Rule Bill which split the Liberal Party [see 'Early Victorian', Conservatives and Liberals*, above], was thus defeated and Gladstone resigned. In 1887, Parnell was falsely accused of complicity in the Phoenix Park murders, was cleared but weakened, and his citing as co-respondent in the Captain O'Shea divorce case of 1890 – with all its resonances for Catholic Ireland – effectively ended his political career (he died suddenly in 1891).

Gladstone's second Home Rule Bill was rejected by the Lords in 1893, the same year as the Gaelic League was founded in Ireland, and he resigned and retired in 1894 – thus the two most committed politicians who might have resolved the Irish issue before the end of the 19th Century were defeated.

⊃ **The European Context**   A significant 'narrative' to track in this period and the following one is the complex concatenation of events, alliances and policies which determine the outbreak of war in 1914 [this should be considered in combination with the cognate narrative of *Imperialism* outlined below]. In 1882, the Triple Alliance of Italy, Germany and Austria was formed (renewed 1887, 1891, 1902); a Franco–Russian Entente was signed in 1891; from 1894 to 1906, the Dreyfus Affair dragged on in France, with its sub-text of militarism and anti-semitism; in 1897, there was war between Greece and Turkey, Greece was defeated, but the European Powers intervened; the German Navy League was founded in 1898, and the Reichstad passed the first Navy Law (to increase German naval power) – a second Act to double the size of the German fleet by 1920 was passed in 1900, the year Kaiser Wilhelm II made his 'Hun' speech.

⊃ **Imperialism**   This period is marked by frenetic European empire-building, most especially the 'Scramble for Africa' which was legitimised by the Berlin Conference of 1884–5, during which Germany, France, Belgium, Italy, Portugal and Great Britain carved up areas of control, principally in Africa. The years following in the timeline tables indicate the continuation of this process, the tensions thereby created between the European Powers themselves, and the 'agreements' and 'exchanges' over areas of control which sought to resolve them (see, e.g., the Colonial Conferences of 1887 and 1897, and almost every year throughout the 1890s).

More specifically regarding the British Empire, the notable events are: the establishing of British control over territories throughout Africa and Asia (often as 'protectorates' or 'annexations'; but also see Cecil Rhodes's quasi-commercial ventures in Africa in the late-1880s and early 1890s).

In South Africa: the first Anglo–Boer War of 1880–1 which results in partial independence for a Boer Republic based on the Transvaal; the election of Paul Kruger as its President in 1883 (and several times thereafter); a treaty of friendship between the Republic and Germany (1885); the ill-fated 'Jameson Raid' of 1895–6 when British troops invaded the Transvaal and were forced to surrender to the Boers; Kaiser Wilhelm's 'Kruger Telegram' (1896) congratulating the Republic on the defeat of the raid; and the outbreak of the second 'Boer War' in 1899 (to 1902), in which the effectiveness of the British Army was called to account.

In the Sudan: the routing of British forces in the Mahdi's rebellion of 1883–4; the besieging of Khartoum in which General Gordon and the garrison were trapped and then killed (1884–5; in 1896–8, Lord Kitchener launched a campaign against the Khalifa in revenge and the Sudan was conquered).

In China, Britain gained a 99-year lease on the New Territories adjacent to Hong Kong (1896), but there were 'Boxer Rebellions' (members of anti-foreign secret societies) in 1896 and 1900, the latter involving the besieging of legations in Peking and its suppression by an international force.

➲ **Science and Technology**   Notable developments here include: the invention of the pedal and chain bicycle around 1880 (on the market, 1885), the beginning of the construction of the Panama Canal (but see also 1889); Daimler and Benz both developed the internal combustion engine and began to build motor cars between 1885 and 1887; Hertz identified electromagnetic waves [radio, etc.] in 1887; the Eiffel Tower was erected in Paris from 1887–9; in 1888, Dunlop made the first pneumatic tyres, The Pasteur Institute in Paris was founded, and Eastman invented the 'Kodak' box camera (the Kodak 'Brownie' followed in 1900); 1889 saw the first skyscraper built in Chicago; in 1890, the Forth Bridge was completed in Scotland; the Blackwall Tunnel under the Thames in London was begun in 1892.

Henry Ford made his first petrol-driven car in 1893; the Manchester Ship Canal was begun a year later, and Blackpool Tower opened; in 1895–6, Marconi experimented successfully with 'wireless' telegraph and Röntgen discovered X-rays; the 'Red Flag Act' of Parliament (1896) increased the maximum speed for road vehicles to 14 mph; Rudolf Diesel demonstrated his internal combustion engine in 1897–8; between 1898 and 1899, Marconi sent wireless signals across the Channel and formed the Marconi Telegraph Co.; and during 1898–1900, London Underground lines were electrified.

➲ **Cultural Developments**   [For British literature, see the 'Authors' and 'Indicative Title' columns in the timeline tables.] The print trade and publishing continued to develop rapidly: wood-pulp was first used to produce cheap paper around 1880, and Newnes first published the popular magazine, *Tit-Bits*, the same year [he also published *The Strand Magazine* in 1891 and *Country Life* in 1897]; in 1896, the Harmsworth brothers founded the *Daily Mail* and revolutionised Fleet Street; and monotype typesetting was in use by 1897.

Serious attempts to enforce copyright law were a feature of this period, and in 1883, Walter Besant founded the Society of Authors and its journal, *The Author*; in 1884, the first part (*A-Ant*) of Murray's *OED* [see Cultural Developments under 'Mid-Victorian'), above] was published, and the first issue of the *English Historical Review* appeared in 1886; in 1890, William Morris founded the Kelmscott Press [the 'Kelmscott Chaucer' was published in 1896]; 1895 saw the trial and imprisonment of Oscar Wilde for homosexuality, the founding of the National Trust, and the showing of one of the earliest 'movie' films by the Lumière brothers in Paris; the Natural History Museum, Kensington, opened in 1881; Sir Henry Tate gave the Tate Gallery to the nation in 1897, when it opened, and the Wallace Collection was given to the nation [opened 1900].

In sport; 'The Ashes' first featured in Anglo–Australian cricket in 1882, and the Davis Cup was first presented for tennis in 1900.

In philosohy and the arts, many of the 'names' from the 'Mid-Victorian' period – especially, for example, Nietzsche, Tchaikovsky, Brahms, Flaubert, Ibsen, Strindberg and the Impressionist painters – continue to dominate. But as the **Fin de Siècle*** approaches, new forms of artistic production start to emerge: fiction by Maupassant, Huysmans, Anatole France, D'Annunzio; plays by Hauptmann, Wedekind, Maeterlinck, Hoffmansthal, Chekhov, Rostand; the 'Symbolist' poetry of Rimbaud, Mallarmé, Verlaine, Stefan George; music by Rimsky-Korsakov, Offenbach, Debussy, Puccini, Richard Strauss, Elgar, Sibelius; the paintings and posters of Toulouse-Lautrec, the sculpture of Rodin, and the 'Post-Impressionist' work of Cézanne, Van Gogh, Gauguin and Seurat.

5.8 (THE) *FIN DE SIÈCLE*

The French term (literally 'the end of the century') used specifically to designate the period at the end of the 19th Century in Britain and France especially, and as an adjective, to characterise certain attitudes and styles associated with it, especially 'Aestheticism' and 'Decadence' in the arts.

However, although chronologically more or less coterminous with the 1890s, '*fin de siècle*' is seldom used to describe the artistic production of the period as a whole (which, of course, contains a diverse variety of work by writers and artists that would not normally be considered 'Aestheticist' or 'Decadent': for example, the 'New Woman' novel of the 1880s and 1890s). Rather, it tends to imply the prominence of works which promote the cult of the morbidly over-sensitive, socially alienated 'Artist' ('poète maudit', in Verlaine's phrase), and the pursuit of 'art for art's sake' without social, moral or political purpose or reference. The characteristic attitude of refined abstraction is well represented by Arthur O'Shaughnessy's 'Ode':

> We are the music-makers,
> And we are the dreamers of dreams,
> Wandering by lone sea-breakers,
> And sitting by desloate streams,
> World-losers and world-forsakers,
> On whom the pale moon gleams ...

A life-style pose of debauched bohemianism intensified the sense of 'decadence' and helped to associate the poets and artists with 'degeneration', a late 19th-Century obsession which found many contemporary symptoms of the degeneration of the human race. In the British literary context, therefore, the term is principally associated with Oscar Wilde ('all art is quite useless'; and hence the significance of his trial and conviction for homosexuality in 1895); the Rhymers Club (W. B. Yeats's 'companions of the Cheshire Cheese' [the pub where they met]: Ernest Dowson, Lionel Johnson, Arthur Symons, John Davidson); Yeats's own conception of 'The Celtic Twilight' (essay of 1893) and his early poems; Aubrey Beardsley and the *Yellow Book*.

Timelines: 1830–1899

PERIOD	YEAR	INTERNATIONAL AND POLITICAL CONTEXTS	SOCIAL AND CULTURAL CONTEXTS	AUTHORS	INDICATIVE TITLES
HANOVERIAN	1830	George IV dies without heir, King William IV [Duke of Clarence, George III's 3rd son] accedes; Gen. Elec. indicates pro-reform attitudes; Wellington resigns – Earl Grey [Whig], PM; Birmingham Political Union formed; Metropolitan Police fnd.d; 'July Revolution' in Paris – Louis Philippe of Orleans elected king [–1848]; revolution in Belgium – independence declared from Dutch; Protocol of London declares Greece an independent kingdom [guaranteed by France, Russia & Britain]; in USA, Indian Removal Act forces Native Americans W. of Mississippi; Venezuela becomes an independent republic – Bolivar abdicates [Columbian union of 1819 dissolved in 1831]; E. India Co. annexes Mysore; Richard Landers explores River Niger; Charles Sturt discovers lower Murray River, Australia	Liverpool-Manchester railway opens – William Huskisson, MP, killed by train; Royal Geographic Society fnd.d; Rev. John Darby fnds Plymouth Brethren; *Fraser's Magazine* fnd.d; Richard Oastler, *Letters on Yorkshire Slavery* [on factory reform]; [–1833] Charles Lyell, *Principles of Geology*; [–1842] Auguste Comte, *Cours de Philosophie positive*. **Int. Lit.:** Hugo, *Hernani* ['lyric' drama]; Lamartine, *Harmonies poétiques et religieuses*; Stendhal, *Le Rouge et le Noir*; Théophile Gautier, *Albertus* [Fr. long poem]. **Music:** Thomas Rice [original Negro minstrel] sings 'John Crow'; Donizetti, 'Anna Bolena' [opera]; Mendelssohn, 'Reformation Symphony'; Hector Berlioz [comp] 'Symphonie fantastique'. **Art:** Wilkie, 'George IV in Highland Dress' [Royal Coll.]; Delacroix, 'Liberty Leading the People'; Palmer, 'Magic Apple Tree' [Fitzwilliam] & [c.] 'Cornfield by Moonlight with the Evening Star' [Clark Coll.]; Corot, 'Cathedral, Chartres'	**P:** Hemans Tennyson **Pr/F:** Galt William Cobbett (1763–1835)	*Songs of the Affections, with Other Poems* *Poems, Chiefly Lyrical* [incls 'Mariana'] *Lawrie Todd* *Rural Rides* [reprinted from *Political Register*; 1st appeared 1821]
	1831	1st Reform Bill in Commons – defeated – Gen. Elec. strengthens reform majority – 2nd Reform Bill passes Commons – rejected by Lords – widespread rioting, esp.ly in Bristol, Nottingham & Derby; Cotton Mills Act limits those under 18 to 12-hr day; Sadler's Committee on child employment in factories [v.1833]; [–1832] 'Captain Swing' riots sweep through S. England – 10 agricultural labourers executed, [c.] 450 transported; 1st cholera epidemic in England; London Conference agrees on separation of independent Belgium from Holland – Leopold of Saxe-Coburg elected 1st king of Belgium – Dutch invade; Giuseppe Mazzini makes appeal for It. independence & fnds 'Young Italy' movement – sentenced to perpetual banishment – Congress to estab. It. unity crushed by Austria; Capodistrias assassinated in Greece	London Bridge opens [re-erected over Colorado River, USA, 1968]; [–1836] Charles Darwin circumnavigates globe as naturalist on HMS 'Beagle' expedition to southern oceans [v.1839]; Michael Faraday discovers electro-magnetism; Sir James Ross locates magnetic north pole; [–1865] William Lloyd Garrison pubs *The Liberator* [US abolitionist periodical]; 1st Mormon Church in Ohio, USA. **Int. Lit.:** Fenimore Cooper, *The Bravo*; Hugo, *Nôtre Dame de Paris* [aka *The Hunchback of …*], *Les Feuilles d'automne* [poems] & *Marion Delorme* [play]; Giacomo Leopardi, *I Canti* [It. lyric poems]. **Music:** Louis Hérold [comp] 'Zampa' [Fr. comic opera]; Giacomo Meyerbeer [comp] 'Robert le Diable' [Ger. opera]. **Art:** Constable, 'Wateroo Bridge'; Corot, 'View of the Forest of Fontainebleau'	**P:** Ebenezer Elliott (the 'Corn Law Rhymer'; 1781–1849) **Pr/F:** Disraeli Ferrier Peacock **Lit. 'Events':**	*Corn-Law Rhymes* [anti-'bread tax' poems] *The Young Duke* *Destiny* [Scottish romance] *Crotchet Castle* [–1841] John Keble lectures on theory of poetry at Oxford [pub.d in the *British Critic*, 1838]
	1832	3rd Reform Bill passes Commons & [after a struggle] the Lords – 1st Reform Act [1 in 5 adult men – with property – could now vote] – Scots. & Ir. Reform Acts passed; Gen. Elec. produces huge Whig victory; Operative Builders Union fnd.d; 30 London services amalgamated to form Fire Engines Establishment; Royal Commission to assess Eng. Poor Law; France, Britain, Austria, Prussia & Russia guarantee Belgium's independence; National Assembly elects Prince Otto of Bavaria 1st king of Greece; [–1833] Anti-Slavery Abolitionist Party	Durham University re-fnd.d [Charter, 1837; v.1657]; Thomas Hodgkin describes 'his' disease; Robert Chambers [with brother] fnds *Chambers's Edinburgh Journal* & [–1834] writes *A Biographical Dictionary of Eminent Scotsmen*. **Int. Lit.:** Balzac, *La Femme de trente ans* & [–1837] *Contes drolatiques* [100 stories]; Hugo, *Le Roi s'amuse* [drama – becomes 'Rigoletto']; Mérimée, *Contes et Nouvelles*; Nikolaus Lenau, *Gedichte* [Ger. lyric poems]; Alfred de Musset, *Le Spectacle dans un Fauteuil* [Fr. dramas]; 'George Sand', *Indiana* & *Valentine* [early erotic novels by Fr.	**P:** Tennyson **Pr/F:** Bulwer-Lytton Disraeli Galt Scott Harriet Martineau (1802–76) Frances Trollope (1780–1863)	*Poems* [dated 1833; incls 'The Lady of Shalott' & 'The Lotus-eaters' (much rev.d by 1842)] *Eugene Aram* ['Newgate' novel] *Contarini Fleming* *The Member* *Castle Dangerous* *Illustrations of Political Economy* [didactic stories; incls 'A Manchester Strike'] *The Domestic Manners of the Americans* [graphic account of visit

1833

formed in Boston, USA; [c.] 1st US railway built; Poland becomes province of Russia; [–1833] British re-occupy & claim sovereignty over Falkland Islands [v.1770]; Mazzini expelled from France

1st session of reformed Commons – Lord Althorp's 1st Factory Act [creates inspectors to regulate child labour – 1st Report, 1839] – Abolition of Slavery Act [thro'out British territories – effective 1834]; Education Grant Act gives religious societies 1st state aid to build schools; 1st meeting of Judicial Committee of Privy Council; Act reduces Ir. bishoprics from 22 to 12; marriages allowed in non-conformist chapels; after defeat by French in 1832, Dutch accept Belgian independence; Russ./Aust./ Pruss. League [opposed to British & Fr. liberalism]; Indian Civil Service opened to Indians; Act deprives E. India Co. of India & China trade monopoly – ceases trading & becomes solely involved with gvnmt of India; Kandy & Ceylon amalgamated; [–1834] St Helena becomes a Crown Colony]

SS 'Royal William' makes 1st full steam crossing of Atlantic; Keble's assize sermon, 'National Apostasy Considered', launches the Oxford (Tractarian) Movement – [–1841] intermittent publication of Tracts for the Times; [–1867] Michelet, Histoire de France [26 vols]. **Int. Lit.:** Pushkin, Eugene Onegin [novel in verse]; Balzac, Eugénie Grandet [early vol. in 'La Comédie Humaine' sequence]; Hugo, Lucrèce Borgia & Marie Tudor [plays]; Musset, Les Caprices de Marianne [tragi-comedy]. **Music:** [c.–1844] Robert Schumann edits Neue Zeitschrift für Musik; Donizetti, 'Lucrezia Borgia' [opera]; Mendelssohn, 'Italian Symphony'; Frédéric Chopin [comp] early pieces for piano. **Art:** Turner exhibits 1st Venetian paintings; Wilkie, 'William IV in the Uniform of the Grenadier Guards' [Royal Coll.]; Branwell Brontë [pnt] 'The Brontë Sisters' [NPG]

woman of letters]. **Music:** Donizetti, 'L'Elisir d'Amour' [opera]; Mendelssohn, 'Fingal's Cave' [1st pf.d, London]. **Art:** Ingres, 'Monsieur Bertin'; Etty, 'Youth on the Prow and Pleasure at the Helm' [Tate]

Dr: Knowles — The Hunchback
Lit. 'Events': George Crabbe & Sir Walter Scott die; Goethe dies – Faust Pt II pub.d

P: Robert Browning (1812–89) — Pauline [early poem pub.d anon.]
Pr/F: Carlyle — [–1834] Sartor Resartus [in Fraser's Magazine; as book in USA, with intro. by Emerson, 1836]

Disraeli — Alroy
Lamb — The Last Essays of Elia [2nd coll.]
Martineau — [–1834] Poor Law and Paupers Illustrated [stories]

Charles Dickens (1812–70) — [–1836] early stories & Sketches by Boz [pub.d in Monthly Magazine & other papers; coll. edtn 1836–7 – illust., George Cruikshank]

Lit. 'Events': Dramatic Copyright ['Bulwer-Lytton's'] Act gave authors' rights for limited period

1834

Ir. Church problems cause Grey to resign – Melbourne, PM – resigns – Peel, PM – 'Tamworth Manifesto' to rally Tory cause; Robert Owen fnds Grand National Consolidated Trades Union to co-ordinate labour activity – rapidly collapses; 6 Dorchester agricultural workers ['Tolpuddle Martyrs'] sentenced to 7 yrs transportation for taking illegal oath to join a trades union; Old Houses of Parliament burn down; Central Criminal Court estab.d; Poor Law Amendment Act consigns poor & elderly to segregated workhouses; Mazzini organises abortive invasion of Savoy; [>] 'Young Germany' movement created; 'Straits Question': Turkey agrees to close the Bosporus & Dardanelles to foreign warships, except those of Russia [v.1841]; [c.] US Indian Territory designated

Faraday announces laws of electrolysis; Joseph Hansom invents the 'Patent Safety (Hansom) Cab' – appears on London streets; [–1837] Leopold von Ranke, History of the Popes in the 16th and 17th Centuries. **Int. Lit.:** Balzac, La Père Goriot; Mickiewicz, Pan Tadeusz [Thaddeus] [novel of Lithuanian society]; Grillparzer, Der Traum ein Leben [Austr. play]. **Music:** Schumann, 'Carnaval' [20 piano pieces]; Konradin Kreutzer [comp] 'Das Nachtlager von Granada' [Ger. opera]. **Art:** Institute of British Architects fnd.d ['Royal' in 1837]; Corot, 'View of Santa Maria della Salute'; Turner, 'Venice, Dogana and San Giorgio Maggiore'; Delacroix, 'Women of Algiers'; [c.] Hokusai, 'Hundred Views of Mount Fuji'; Honoré Daumier, 'Rue Transnonain, le 15 Avril, 1834' [lithograph]

P: Crabbe — Posthumous Tales [in verse]
Pr/F:
Bulwer-Lytton — The Last Days of Pompeii [historical novel]
Marryat — Peter Simple & Jacob Faithful
De Quincey — [>] Reminiscences of the English Lake Poets [in Tait's Magazine; later coll.]

William Harrison Ainsworth (1805–82) — Rookwood [novel about Dick Turpin]

Lit. 'Events': Samuel Taylor Coleridge dies

1835

Gen. Elec. brings Tory gains, but Peel resigns after defeat over Ir. Church issue – Melbourne, PM; Municipal Corporation Act for England & Wales begins local gvnmt reform in urban areas; Lord Macaulay's 'Minute on Education': English to be language of education in British India, civil war in Spain – Britain, France Spain & Portugal form alliance favouring liberal gvnmts in Spain & Portugal; Giuseppe Mazzini leads 'Young Italy' movement from Switzerland; [–1836] 'Great Trek' of Boers from Cape Colony, SA; settlement at Port Phillip Bay (Melbourne) begins colony of Victoria – S. Australia Act

Mme Tussaud opens London Waxworks; Goldsmiths' Co.'s Hall, London, built; D.F. Strauss, Das Leben Jesu, kritisch bearbeitet [Eng. trans by George Eliot, 1846]. **Int. Lit.:** Hugo, Les Chants du Crépuscule [poems]; de Vigny, Chatterton [drama]; Musset, Nuit de mai & Nuit de décembre [love poems]; Gautier, Mademoiselle de Maupin [novel]; Nikolai Gogol, Mirgorod & Arabesques [Russ. stories]; Georg Büchner, Dantons tod [Ger. drama]. **Music:** Maria Luigi Cherubino, Counterpoint and Fugue [lt. music theory]; Donizetti, 'Lucia di Lammermoor' [opera]; Jacques Halévy [comp] 'Le Juive' & 'L'Éclair' [Fr. operas]. **Art:** Turner, [c.] 'View of the Piazzetta' [Tate] & 'Burning of the Houses of Parliament'; Etty, 'Venus and Her Satellites'

P: Browning — Paracelsus [long poem]
Clare — The Rural Muse
Wordsworth — Yarrow Revisited and Other Poems & A Guide through the District of the Lakes in the North of England [enlarged version; v.1810]

Lit. 'Events': [–1840] John Stuart Mill finds & edits London and Westminster Review [incls essays on 'Bentham' (1838) & 'Coleridge' (1840)]

Period	Year	International and Political Contexts	Social and Cultural Contexts	Authors	Indicative Titles
	1836	Financial crisis in England & Ireland; [–c.1848] Chartist Movement for political reform fnd.d; Stamp Duty on newspapers reduced to 1d; Tithe Commutation Act: ends payment in kind – now collected as rent; Act for civil registration of births, deaths & marriages [begins 1837]; [>] London Working Men's Association fnd.d to press for further reform; Arkansas becomes 25th State; [–1845] Texas separates from Mexico & declares itself an independent republic – siege of El Alamo; S. Australia becomes British province – Adelaide fnd.d	London University receives Charter [supersedes autonomous Colleges of 1828]; Philip Hardwick designs Euston Station [reconstructed, 1960s]; 1st train in London [to Greenwich]. **Int. Lit.:** Lamartine, *Jocelyn* [narrative poem]; de Musset, *Confession d'un Enfant du Siècle* [accounts of early 19thC 'mal du siècle']; *Nuit d'Août & Il ne faut jurer de rien* ['armchair' play]; Gogol, *The Government Inspector* [comedy]; Ralph Waldo Emerson, *Nature* [US prose poem]. **Music:** Mendelssohn, 'St Paul' [oratorio]; Giacomo Meyerbeer, [comp] 'Les Huguenots' [Ger. opera]; Mikhail Glinka [comp] 'A Life for the Tsar' [1st Russ. opera]. **Art:** Augustus Pugin, *Contrasts between the Architecture of the 15th and 19th Centuries* [estabs Victorian Gothic]; Daumier, 'Robert Macaire' [lithograph]	**P:** Browning Wordsworth **Pr/F:** Dickens Hazlitt Marryat Samuel Lover (1797–1868)	'Porphyria's Lover' [1st of dramatic monologues] [–1837] *Poetical Works* [6 vols; v.1842] [–1837] *The Posthumous Papers of the Pickwick Club* ['Pickwick Papers'] *Literary Remains* [essays] *Mr Midshipman Easy* *Rory O'More* [Irish novel]
	1837	William IV dies, Queen Victoria accedes – 1st monarch to reside in Buckingham Palace; Hanover separates from British Crown; cotton-spinners in Glasgow on 3-mth strike; [c.] last use of pillory in England; constitutional crisis in Canada – Lord John Russell intros Canada Bill – rebellions led by Papineau [Montreal] & Mackenzie [Toronto] against union of Upper & Lower Canada [v.1791] & imperial gvnmt; Michigan becomes 26th State; Mazzini banished from Switzerland – settles in London; Dutch fnd Orange Free State Republic & [–1840] settle in Natal	F.E. O'Connor fnds Chartist *Northern Star* newspaper in Leeds; Sir Isaac Pitman, *Stenographic Sound Hand* [1st intros shorthand]; [–1838] Samuel Morse exhibits magnetic telegraph in USA – Charles Wheatstone & William Cooke patent electric telegraph in UK; Fizwilliam Museum, Cambridge, built to house bequest [v.1816]. **Int. Lit.:** Nathaniel Hawthorne, *Twice-Told Tales* [enlarged edtn, 1842]; Sand, *Mauprat* [novel]; Hugo, *Les Voix intérieures* [poems]; de Musset, *La Nuit d'Octobre*; Büchner, *Woyzeck* [drama]. **Music:** Berlioz, 'Benvenuto Cellini' [opera] & 'Grand Messe des morts' [requiem]. **Art:** Delacroix, 'Battle of Taillebourg'; Constable, 'Arundel Castle' [unfinished]; Sir Edwin Landseer [pnt] 'Old Shepherd's Chief Mourner' [V&A]	**Pr/F:** Carlyle Dickens Disraeli Landon Lockhart F. Trollope **Dr:** Browning Knowles Lit. **'Events':**	*The French Revolution* [history; begun 1834; 3 vols] [–1838] *Oliver Twist: or The Parish Boy's Progress* [illustr., Cruikshank] *Henrietta Temple* *Ethel Churchill* [–1838] *Memoirs of the Life of Scott* [7 vols] *The Vicar of Wrexhill* *Strafford* *The Love Chase* [–1839] Dickens [with Samuel Lover] fnds & edits *Bentley's Miscellany*
	1838	Lord Durham, Governor-in-Chief of Canada – rebels defeated at Toronto; People's Charter with 6 democratic points demanding suffrage pub.d by Chartists; Anti-Corn Law League fnd.d by Manchester businessmen; Ir. Poor Law Amendment Act passed; Parliament estabs prison sentences for juvenile offenders; Public Record Office fnd.d; 'Dingaan's Day': Boers massacre Dingaan & Zulu followers at Blood River; British occupy Aden; treaty estab.s British free trading rights in Turkey & Egypt; [–1842] 1st Opium War between Britain & China [to end Chinese restrictions on foreign trade, esp.ly on import of opium from British India]; [–1842] Anglo-Russ. rivalry causes 1st Afghan War; 1st of regular transatlantic crossings – Brunel's SS 'Great Western' [14½ days]	London–Birmingham railway opens; Royal Agricultural Society fnd.d; St George's Hall, Liverpool, built; Daguerre invents the 'daguerrotype' [1st practicable photographic plate]; Charles Hennell, *An Inquiry into the Origins of Christianity*. **Int. Lit.:** Hugo, *Ruy Blas* [drama]; Lamartine, *La Chute d'un Ange* [poems]; de Vigny, *La Mort du Loup* [pessimistic poem]; Gautier, *Comédie de la mort* [Fr. play]; Eduard Mörike, *Gedichte* [Ger. lyric poems]; Edgar Allen Poe, *The Narrative of Arthur Gordon Pym* [US story]. **Music:** Lady John Scott [comp] 'Annie Laurie' [song]; Berlioz,'Roméo et Juliette' [dramatic symphony]. **Art:** present National Gallery opens in Trafalgar Square [built by William Wilkins from 1832]; Turner, 'The Fighting Téméraire' [NG]; Wilkie, 'Bride's Toilet' [SNG]	**P:** Barrett Browning Landon Wordsworth Martin Tupper (1810–89) **Pr/F:** Dickens **Dr:** Bulwer-Lytton Lit. **'Events':**	*The Seraphim and Other Poems* *The Works of L. E. Landon* [posthm.] *Sonnets* [pub.d in 1 vol.] *Proverbial Philosophy* [popular moral commonplaces in free verse] [–1839] *Nicholas Nickleby* *The Lady of Lyons; or, Love and Pride* [historical drama] [–1849] Lady Charlotte Guest, Eng. trans of *Mabinogion* [old Welsh tales]

(HANOVERIAN ENDS)/VICTORIAN

1839

Deep trade depression – Chartist National Convention opens – 1st Chartist Petition of c.1¼ m. signatures presented to Parliament – rejected – attempted rising in Newport suppressed; Melbourne resigns – Peel summoned – 'Bedchamber Crisis' over Queen's refusal to accept the dismissal of her ladies-in-waiting – Peel resigns – Melbourne resumes as PM; Privy Council Committee to organise disbursement of public money for education – HM Inspectors of Schools app.ntd; Durham Report on Canada presented to Parliament – recommends responsible gvnmt for colonies [v.1848]; Treaty of London: European powers guarantee perpetual neutrality of Belgium ['Scrap of Paper' of 1914] – Luxemburg becomes independent grand duchy; NZ proclaimed [v.1840–1]; Aden annexed to British India; British occupy Kabul; Opium War: British take Hong Kong

Penny Postage Act [v.1840]; 1st Royal Agricultural Show; 1st Henley Regatta; 1st Grand National run at Aintree; William Fox Talbot announces invention of 'photogenic drawing' [photography; v.1838]; Samuel Cunard fnds Steamship Co; C. Darwin [with Robert Fitzroy], Narrative of the Surveying Voyages of HMS 'Adventure' and 'Beagle' [v.1831]. **Int. Lit.:** Balzac, Le Curé de Village; Stendhal, La Chartreuse de Parme; Sand, Spiridion [socialist writings]; Karl Immermann, Münchhausen [Ger. satirical novel]. **Music:** Giuseppi Verdi [comp] 'Oberto' [It. opera; pf.d La Scala]. **Art:** [–1840] Ingres, 'Oedalisque with Slave'; Delacroix, 'Hamlet and Horatio in the Graveyard' [also 1859]; Landseer, 'Queen Victoria' [Royal Coll.]; Daniel Maclise [pnt] 'Charles Dickens' [NPG]

P: Hemans / Shelley
- Collected Works [posthm.]
- Poetical Works [posthm.]

Pr/F: Ainsworth / Carlyle / Marryat / Martineau / F. Trollope
- Jack Sheppard [illust., Cruikshank]
- Chartism [essay; dated 1840]
- The Phantom Ship
- Deerbrook [novel]
- [–1840] The Life and Adventures of Michael Armstrong, the Factory Boy & The Widow Barnaby

Dr: Bulwer-Lytton / Philip Bailey (1816–1902) / **Lit. 'Events':**
- Richelieu; or, the Conspiracy [tragedy]
- Festus: a Poem [popular poetic drama imitating Goethe's Faust]
- Wordsworth pubs open letter in Morning Post supporting Talfourd's Copyright Bill [v.1842]; London University Library opens

1840

Queen Victoria m. Prince Albert of Saxe-Coburg [Prince Consort, 1857]; O'Connell fnds Repeal Association in Ireland [to repeal the Union]; famine in Ireland begins [v.1845]; Treaty of Waitangi: Maori chiefs cede sovereignty of NZ to Britain – Auckland fnd.d; transportation of convicts to NSW ends [continues to Tasmania & W. Australia]; Canada Act of Union reunites Upper & Lower provinces [v.1791; proclaimed 1841]; China severs all trade with Britain; Captain Charles Wilkes [USA] explores Antarctic coast

Rowland Hill intros 'Penny Post' [1st stamps: 1d. black & 2d. blue]; Nelson's Column erected in Trafalgar Square; Kew Botanical Gardens open; P.J. Proudhon, Qu'est-ce que la propriété? ('C'est le vol!') [Fr. socialism: 'Property is Theft']. **Int. Lit.:** Fenimore Cooper, The Pathfinder; Hugo, Les Rayons et les ombres [poems]; Eugène Scribe, Verre d'eau [Fr. play]; Juljusz Slowacki, Lilla Weneda [Pol. tragedy]. **Music:** [c.] Adolphe Sax invents the saxophone; Donizetti, 'La Favorita' [opera]; Max Schreckenburger [comp] 'Die Wacht am Rhine' [Ger. national song]. **Art:** [–1860] Sir Charles Barry rebuilds [present] Houses of Parliament [d.1860; completed later; Pugin assisted with designs]; Delacroix, 'The Justice of Trajan' & 'Shipwreck of Don Juan'; Turner, 'Slave Ship'; Cotman, 'World Afloat' [drawing; BM]. **Lit. 'Events':** London Library opens

P: Browning
- Sordello [narrative poem]

Pr/F: Ainsworth / Dickens
- The Tower of London [illustr., Cruikshank]
- [–1841] The Old Curiosity Shop [begun as story in D's periodical, Master Humphrey's Clock]

F. Trollope
- The Widow Married

Thomas Babington, Lord Macaulay (1800–59)
- Essay on Clive

William Makepeace Thackeray (1811–63)
- The Paris Sketch-Book & [c.–1844] other pieces, mainly for Fraser's Magazine, under the pseudonyms 'Yellowplush', 'Fitz-Boodle', 'Titmarsh', 'Wagstaff', 'Snob'

Dr: Bulwer-Lytton
- Money [comedy]

1841

Gen. Elec: Tory victory – Melbourne resigns – Peel, PM; deep economic distress, esp.ly in cotton areas – Chartism revives; massive Repeal Meetings in Ireland; Miners' Association of GB fnd.d; Great Western Railway [London-Bristol] completed [begun 1835] – [–1845] Brunel builds Hungerford Suspension Bridge over Thames at Charing Cross; European Powers guarantee Turkish independence – Dardanelles & Bosphorus closed to all nations' battleships; NZ becomes separate British colony; Sultan of Brunei makes Sir James Brooke rajah of Sarawak; [c.] Royal Mail Steam Packet Co. begins service to W. Indies; British refugees from Canton settle at Hong Kong

Punch 1st pub.d; Thomas Cook begins his travel agency; Royal Botanical Gardens given to the nation; Cardinal J.H. Newman, Tract XC [most famous & controversial of 'Oxford Movement' tracts]; Ludwig Feuerbach, Das Wesen des Christentums [Eng. trans, G. Eliot, 1854]; New York (Herald) Tribune 1st pub.d. **Int. Lit.:** Fenimore Cooper, The Deerslayer; Emerson, Essays [coll. lectures; 2nd ser., 1844]; Henry W. Longfellow, Ballads [US poems; incls 'The Wreck of the Hesperus' & 'The Village Blacksmith']. **Music:** Schumann, 'Spring Symphony'; 'Hoffman von Fallersleben' [comp] 'Deutschland, Deutschland, über Alles' [became Ger. national anthem, 1922]. **Art:** Pugin, True Principles of Christian Architecture; George Gilbert Scott designs Martyrs Memorial, Oxford [Gothic Revival]; [–1842] Turner, 'Peace – Burial at Sea of Sir David Wilkie' [Tate]

P: Browning
- Pippa Passes [poetic drama; 1st in Bells and Pomegranates (B&P) series of pamphlets of plays & poems (–1846)]

Pr/F: Ainsworth / Carlyle / Dickens / Marryat / Martineau
- Old St Paul's & Guy Fawkes
- On Heroes and Hero Worship and the Heroic in History [lectures pub.d]
- Barnaby Rudge [in Master Humphrey's Clock]
- Masterman Ready
- The Hour and the Man [novel about Toussaint L'Ouverture; v.1797–1803]

Dr: Dion Boucicault (c.1820–90)
- London Assurance [comedy]

Period	Year	International and Political Contexts	Social and Cultural Contexts	Authors	Indicative Titles
EARLY VICTORIAN	1842	Parliament rejects 2nd Chartist Petition – riots, esp.ly in Staffs & Lancs; revenue deficit forces Peel to reintroduce Income Tax [v. 1816] – modifies sliding-scale of Corn Laws & reduces general tariffs; Shaftesbury's Coal Mines Act bans employment of women & children underground [boys until 10]; Disraeli leads 'Young England' group of Tories; Webster-Ashburton Treaty settles British/US boundary dispute – frontier between Maine & Canada defined; S. Australia becomes a Crown Colony – British emigration encouraged; China defeated in Opium War – Treaty of Nanking opens 5 ports to Western trade – Hong Kong ceded to Britain [becomes Crown Colony; but v. 1984, 1997]; Afghan War: Kabul evacuated – massacre of British troops in Khyber Pass	Philological Society fnd.d in London; *Illustrated London News* 1st pub.d; Sir Edwin Chadwick, *Report on the Sanitary Condition of the Labouring Poor*. **Int. Lit.:** Gogol, *Dead Souls* [Russ. novel]; [–1843] Sand, *Consuelo* [socialistic novel]; [c.] Friedrich Hebbel, *Maria Magdalena* [Ger. play]; Eugène Sue, *Les Mystères de Paris* [1st Fr. novel to be pub.d in a newspaper]. **Music:** Guiseppe Verdi, 'Nabucco' [It. opera]; Mikhail Glinka, 'Russlam and Ludmilla' [pioneering Russ. opera based on poem by Pushkin]; Richard Wagner [comp] 'Rienzi' [Ger. opera]. **Art:** Turner, 'Snowstorm at Sea' [NG]; Benjamin Robert Haydon [pnt] 'William Wordsworth' [NPG]. **Lit. 'Events':** Sir Thomas Talfourd's Literary Copyright Act consolidates authors' rights; Mudie's Circulating Library fnd.d; Chambers [ed.], *The Cyclopaedia of English Literature*	**P:** Browning Macaulay Tennyson Wordsworth Susanna Blamire (1747–94) **Pr/F:** Bulwer-Lytton Dickens Thackeray F. Trollope Lover	*Dramatic Lyrics [B&P;* incls 'Porphyria's Lover', 'My Last Duchess' & 'The Pied Piper of Hamelin'] *The Lays of Ancient Rome* [narrative poems & ballads] *Poems* [2 vols; incls 'Locksley Hall', 'Ulysses', 'The Epic (Morte d'Arthur)' & 'Break, break, break'] *Poems Chiefly of Early and Late Years* [as vol. 7 of *Poetical Works*; v.1836–7; incls 'The Borderers' & 'Guilt and Sorrow'] *Poems* [posthm. coll.; known as 'The Muse of Cumberland'] *Zanoni* [fantasy] *American Notes* [on visit to USA] [>] contributes to *Punch* [e.g. 'The Book of Snobs', 'Punch's Prize Novelists' & 'Jeames's Diary'] [–1843] *Jessie Phillips* *Handy Andy*
	1843	Free Trade movement gathers momentum [*The Economist* fnd.d to promote it]; Thames Tunnel opens [Wapping-Rotherhithe; designed by Brunel; begun 1825]; 1st public telegraph line [Paddington-Slough]; Ir. gvnmt bans Clontarf meeting in support of O'Connell's Repeal of Union agitation; 'Rebecca Riots' against Turnpike Tolls in S. Wales; United Free Church of Scotland estab.d; British annexe Natal to Cape Colony, SA; British annexe Sindh in India; Anglo-Chinese commercial treaties set up	*News of the World* 1st pub.d; Royal Hunt Cup 1st run at Ascot; Royal Hunt public school fnd.d; John Stuart Mill, *A System of Logic*. **Int. Lit.:** Berthold Auerbach, *Schwarzwälder Dorfgeschichten* [sketches of Black Forest life]. **Music:** John Curwen, *Grammar of Vocal Music* [advocates Tonic Sol-fa system]; Berlioz, 'Le Carnival romain' [overture]; Donizetti, 'Don Pascale' [comic opera]; Wagner, 'The Flying Dutchman' [opera]. **Art:** [–1848] David Octavius Hill & Robert Adamson develop photographic portraiture, Turner, 'The "Sun of Venice" Leaving Port' [NG]. **Lit. 'Events':** Robert Southey dies – William Wordsworth, Poet Laureate; Theatre Regulations Act removes monopoly of Covent Garden & Drury Lane & encourages musical entertainments	**P:** Hood **Pr/F:** Ainsworth Carlyle Dickens Macaulay Thackeray John Ruskin (1819–1900) George Borrow (1803–81)	'The Song of the Shirt' [in *Punch* – against sweated labour] *Windsor Castle* [about Herne the Hunter] *Past and Present* 'A Christmas Carol' [1st of Christmas Books] & [–1844] *Martin Chuzzlewit* *Critical and Historical Essays* [3 vols; from *Edinburgh Review*] *The Irish Sketch-Book* [in *Fraser's*] [–1860] *Modern Painters* [5 vols] *The Bible in Spain* [travel writing]
	1844	O'Connell tried & sentenced for sedition – Lords reverse verdict, but his influence declines; Royal Commission on Health of Towns; Factory Act regulates working hrs of women and children in textile mills; 'Rochdale Pioneers' fnd 1st workmen's Co-operative Society; Bank Charter Act modernises note-issuing function of Bank of England); state visit of Tsar Nicholas I to England; Mazzini charges British gvnmt with opening his letters & passing contents to It. rulers – huge national outcry	Morse transmits 1st telegraph message in USA; [c.] Charles Goodyear in USA invents vulcanised rubber [tyre named after him]; Chambers, *Vestiges of the Natural History of Creation* [pub.d anon.; precursor of Darwinism]; J.S. Mill, *Essays on Some Unsettled Questions of Political Economy*. **Int. Lit.:** [–1846] Dumas, *Le Comte de Monte-Cristo* & *Les Trois Mousquetaires*; Heine, *Neue Gedichte* & *Deutschland* [satirical poem]; [–1845] Sue, *Le Juif errant* [novel]. **Music:** polka dance intro.d to Britain from Bohemia; Berlioz, *Traité de l'Instrumentation* [on orchestration]; Mendelssohn, 'Violin Concerto in	**P:** Barrett Browning Hood **Pr/F:** Dickens Disraeli Thackeray Alexander Kinglake (1809–91)	*Poems* [2 vols; incls 'The Cry of the Children' – against child labour] [–1845] 'The Haunted House', 'The Lay of the Labourer' & 'The Bridge of Sighs' [pub.d in *Hood's Monthly Magazine*] 'The Chimes' [Christmas Book] *Coningsby* [1st in trilogy of political novels*] *The Luck of Barry Lyndon* [novel pub.d in *Fraser's*; later rev.d as *The Memoirs of Barry Lyndon*] *Eöthen* [travel: about the East]

Year	History / Events	Arts & Literature Context	Author	Works
1845	Budget abolishes export duties & reduces number of import duties; Peel refuses to abolish Corn Laws despite mass starvation – Cabinet split – Peel resigns – Lord John Russell [Whig] cannot form ministry – Peel returns; Factory Acts extended to print works; [c.–1851] railway speculation at its height; [c.–1851] 1st cable laid under Channel; potato blight in Ireland – crop fails – [–1850] Ir. famine; Chartists adopt F.E. O'Connor's Land Scheme [mass settlement on land to assist poor]; Peel's Maynooth Act estab.s non-sectarian Queen's Colleges in Ireland; Florida becomes 27th State – USA annexes Texas from Mexico – becomes 28th State; [–1846] 1st Sikh War [Kashmir ceded to Britain & indemnity paid]; [–1853] Sir George Grey, 1st Governor of NZ – [–1848] Maori uprising as NZ settlers infringe Treaty of Waitangi	E minor'; [–1848] Schumann, 'Scenes from Goethe's Faust'. **Art:** Turner, 'Rain, Steam and Speed' [NG] **Lit. Events':** [–1845] Dickens visits Italy Brunel builds 'Great Britain' [1st ocean-going screw-steamer]; all-Protestant Evangelical Alliance fnd.d to oppose RCism; Cardinal Newman converts to Rome – pubs *Essay on the Development of Christian Doctrine*; Oxford & Cambridge boat race transfers to Putney [v.1829]; [–1847 & 1849–51] Sir A.M. Layard excavates Nineveh; Friedrich Engels, *The Condition of the Working-Class in England* [in Ger; Eng. edtn with preface by Engels, 1892]. **Int. Lit.:** Hoffmann, *Struwwelpeter* [Eng. trans 1846]; Poe, *Tales of Mystery and Imagination* & 'The Raven' [poem]; Dumas, *Vingt Ans Après*. **Music:** Wagner, 'Tannhäuser' [opera]; Franz Liszt [comp] 'Preludes'; W.H. Fry [comp] 'Leonora' [early US opera]. **Art:** Delacriox, 'Sultan of Morocco and His Entourage'	**P:** Browning Wordsworth **Pr/F:** Carlyle Dickens Disraeli	*Dramatic Romances and Lyrics* [B&P], incls 'How They Brought the Good News from Ghent to Aix', 'The Lost Leader', 'The Bishop Orders His Tomb …' & 'Home Thoughts from Abroad'] *Poems* [in 1 vol.] [ed.] *Oliver Cromwell's Letters and Speeches, with Elucidations* 'The Cricket on the Hearth' [*Christmas Book*] *Sybil, or The Two Nations* [*]
1846	Peel repeals Corn Laws protecting landowners – Tories split – Peel resigns after defeat on an Ir. issue – [–1852] Russell, PM [last 'Whig'/1st 'Liberal' ministry] – Lord Palmerston, Foreign Sec.; Liverpool Sanitary Act makes local council its own health authority – appoints town medical officer of health; Kay-Shuttleworth's Minute of Education intros state-supported teacher-training provision; famine conts in Ireland [prompts mass emigration to USA]; treaty defines frontier between Canada & USA [extends from Rocky Mountains to Pacific coast along 49th parallel – USA gains Idaho, Washington & Oregon – Britain obtains Vancouver Island] – [–1848] US/Mexican war over annexation of Texas – Iowa becomes 29th State	G.J. Holyoake fnds Secularism [social ethics free of religion]; British standard gauge intro.d – facilitates railway expansion; Smithsonian Institute, Washington, fnd.d; G. Eliot, Eng. trans of D.F. Strauss, *The Life of Jesus, critically examined* [3 vols, from 1844; v.1835]; Karl Marx, *The German Ideology*; [–1856] George Grote, *History of Greece*. **Int. Lit.:** Hawthorne, *Mosses from an Old Manse*; Balzac, *La Cousine Bette*; Sand, *La Mare au Diable* [rural novel]; Fyodor Dostoyevsky, 'Poor Folk' [1st story]. **Music:** Mendelssohn, 'Elijah' [oratorio]; Schumann '2nd Symphony'; Berlioz, 'The Damnation of Faust' [cantata]; Liszt, 1st 'Hungarian Rhapsody'; César Franck [comp] 'Ruth' [Fr. oratorio]. **Art:** Turner, 'Angel Standing in the Sun' [Tate]	**P:** Wordsworth Brontë sisters [under pseudonyms – for details, v.1847] Edward Lear (1812–88) **Pr/F:** Bulwer-Lytton Dickens	*Poetical Works* [7 vols] *Poems, by Currer, Ellis and Acton Bell* *A Book of Nonsense* *Lucretia* [about Thomas Wainewright, artist & poisoner] *Pictures from Italy*, 'The Battle of Life, a Love Story' ['with a Selection of Christmas Carols'] & [–1848] *Dombey and Son*
1847	Gen. Elec. increases Liberal majority; wheat prices rise sharply – last food riots in Britain; Factory Act (Ten Hours Act) regulates working day for women & children of 13–18; [–1848] 'Young Ireland' movement active; Cavour fnds *Il Risorgimento* newspaper in Sardinia seeking a constitution; [>] Mormons begin to emigrate to Utah; Liberian Republic declared independent – constitution as negro state estab.d 1848; Kaffir province estab.d in Cape Colony under British protection; [c.>] David Livingstone explores C. & S. Africa	Manchester Cathedral estab.d; Sir James Ross, *Voyage of Discovery* [account of exploration of Antartica, 1839–43]. **Int. Lit.:** Longfellow, *Evangeline* [US poem]; Heine, *Atta Troll* [polemic against political poetry – 'swansong of Romanticism']; Balzac, *Le Cousin Pons* [as bk, 1848]; Mérimée, *Carmen* [novel]; [–1848] Sand, *François le Champi* [rural novel]; [–1854] János Arany, *Toldi* [Hung. trilogy]. **Music:** Chopin, 'Minute Waltz'; Verdi, 'Macbeth' [opera]. **Art:** [–1849] Delacroix, 'Othello and Desdemona'; Ford Madox Brown [pnt] 'Wickliffe Reading His Translation of the Bible to John of Gaunt' [Bradford AG]	**P:** Tennyson **Pr/F:** Disraeli Marryat Thackeray Anne Brontë ('Acton Bell'; 1820–49) Charlotte Brontë ('Currer Bell'; 1816–55) Emily Brontë ('Ellis Bell'; 1818–48)	*The Princess* [narrative poem] *Tancred** *Children of the New Forest* [–1848] *Vanity Fair* *Agnes Grey* [novel; wrtn 1845] *Jane Eyre* [novel; v.1857] *Wuthering Heights* [novel]

PERIOD	YEAR	INTERNATIONAL AND POLITICAL CONTEXTS	SOCIAL AND CULTURAL CONTEXTS	AUTHORS	INDICATIVE TITLES
	1848	Habeas Corpus suspended – presentation of 3rd Chartist Petition fails – mass demonstration in London disperses peacefully [> Chartism declines]; 2nd cholera epidemic in England – 1st Public Health Act estab.s General Board of Health; Smith O'Brien's 'Young Ireland' rebellion fails; 'Year of Revolutions' in Europe: in France, Louis Philippe abdicates – workers riot in Paris – Louis Napoleon elected President of 2nd Republic; nationalist revolutions in Venice, Parma, Rome [Pope flees], Milan, Sicily, Sardinia [king grants liberal constitution], Berlin, Vienna, Warsaw, Cracow, Prague, Budapest; Mexican War ends [v.1846] – Mexico cedes Arizona, New Mexico, Utah, Nevada, California, Colorado & Wyoming to USA – Wisconsin becomes 30th State – gold discv.d in California – [–1849] gold rush begins; self-gvnmt estab.d in Canada; [–1856] Lord Dalhousie, Governor General of India – [–1849] 2nd revolt of Sikhs leads to invasion of Punjab; Boers defeated at Boomplatz – retreat across the Vaal – British annexe Orange River area; [c.] 1st British settlers at Dunedin, NZ	Queen's College, London, opens; [c.] F.D. Maurice & Charles Kingsley fnd Christian Socialist movement; 1st women's rights conventions [beginnings of suffrage movement] held in USA; Linus Yale invents cylinder lock in USA; Karl Marx & Frederick Engels, *Communist Manifesto*; J.S. Mill, *Principles of Political Economy*; Chateaubriand, *Mémoires d'Outre-Tombe* [autobiog; parts pub.d before death in 1848; pub.d posthm. complete in 6 vols, 1902]; **Int. Lit.:** James R. Lowell, *A Fable for Critics* & the *Biglow Papers* [US poems]; Balzac completes 'La Comédie Humaine' sequence [c. 90 novels]; [c.] Henri Murger, *Scènes de la vie de Bohème* [Fr. novel – basis for Puccini's opera]. **Art:** Pre-Raphaelite Brotherhood (PRB) of artists & writers fnd.d [incls William Holman Hunt, Edward Burne-Jones, John Everett Millais, Dante Gabriel Rossetti & William Morris]; August Pugin designs Southwark Cathedral (RC); Ingres, 'Venus Anadyomene'; Jean-François Millet [pnt] 'The Winnower'; [c.] Alfred Stevens [pnt] 'King Alfred and his Mother' [Tate]	**P:** Bulwer-Lytton Arthur Hugh Clough (1819–61) **Pr/F:** Ainsworth A. Brontë Bulwer-Lytton Dickens Macaulay Ruskin Thackeray (Mrs) Elizabeth Gaskell (1810–65) J.[ohn] H.[enry] [Cardinal] Newman (1801–90)	[–1849] *King Alfred* [epic poem] 'The Bothie of Toper-na- Fuosich' *The Lancashire Witches* *The Tenant of Wildfell Hall* *Harold, the Last of the Saxons* 'The Haunted Man' *History of England from the Accession of James II* [vols I & II; vols III & IV 1855; unfinished vol. V pub. posthm. 1861] [–1849] *The Seven Lamps of Architecture* [–1850] *Pendennis* *Mary Barton* [novel; pub.d anon.] *Loss and Gain* [religious novel]
	1849	Liberals reduce duties on W. Indian sugar; Encumbered Estates Act facilitates sale of Ir. land; Society to promote Working-Men's Associations fnd.d; Navigation Laws of 1651 & 1660–2 repealed; Mazzini greeted with wild enthusiasm at Leghorn – Rome proclaimed a Republic– Garibaldi enters Rome – French retake Rome & restore Pope – revolutions across Europe gradually suppressed – Universal Peace Congress in Paris; Sikhs defeated at Gujarat & Rawal Pindi – end of Sikh state – Treaty of Lahore places Punjab under British control	*Who's Who?* 1st pub.d; Bedford College, London, for women fnd.d [incorporated in University of London, 1869]; [–1855] Amelia Bloomer fnd.s & edits *The Lily* in USA [champions women's rights, equality & dress reform – hence 'bloomers']; Proudhon, *Confessions d'un révolutionnaire & Actes de la Révolution*. **Int. Lit.:** Sand, *La Petite Fadette* [rural novel]; Augustin Scribe, *Adrienne Lecouveur* [Fr. play]. **Art:** [–1850] Gustave Courbet [pnt] 'Burial at Ornans'; Dante Gabriel Rossetti [pnt] 'Girlhood of Mary Virgin' [with 'PRB' after signature – v.1848; Tate]; Sir John Everett Millais [pnt] 'Lorenzo and Isabella' [Walker AG]	**P:** Wordsworth Matthew Arnold (1822–88) **Pr/F:** Bulwer-Lytton C. Brontë Dickens J.A. Froude (1818–94)	[–1850] *Poetical Works* [6 vols] *The Strayed Reveller and Other Poems* [incls 'The Forsaken Merman'] *The Caxtons* *Shirley* [–1850] *David Copperfield* *The Nemesis of Faith* [about religious doubt]
	1850	Palmerstone's abrasive foreign policy censured; Factory Act: those covered by 1847 Act not to work before 6 am. or after 6 pm. (2 pm. Saturdays); Pope appnt.s new RC bishops to Britain; 1st Public Libraries Act; Australia Constitution Act separates Victoria from NSW [effective 1851] – S. Australia & Van Dieman's Land granted responsible gvnmt; Denmark sells Britain settlements on the Gold Coast; Clayton-Bulwer agreement between USA & UK for a Central American canal; California becomes 31st State	Oxford offers degrees in science; *Harper's Magazine* fnd.d in USA; University of Sydney fnd.d; [>] Levi Strauss begins to make jeans in USA; Spencer, *Social Statics*. **Int. Lit.:** Emerson, *Representative Men*; Hawthorne, *The Scarlet Letter*; Ivan Turgenev, *A Month in the Country* [Russ. play]. **Music:** Schumann, 'Rhenish Symphony' (3rd); Wagner, 'Lohengrin' [opera, 1st prod. by Liszt at Weimar; complt.d 1848]. **Art:** Daumier, 'Ratapoil' [sculpture]; Millet, 'The Sower'; Rossetti, 'Ecce Ancilla Domini' [Tate]; Millais, 'Christ in the House of His Parents/in the Carpenter's Shop' [Tate] & 'William Wilkie	**P:** Barrett Browning Tennyson Wordsworth Christina Rossetti (1830–94) Dante Gabriel Rossetti (1828–82) **Pr/F:** Bulwer-Lytton Carlyle	*Poems* [incls 'Sonnets from the Portuguese'] *In Memoriam AHH* *The Prelude, or Growth of a Poet's Mind* [final rev.d version in 14 bks; pub. posthm.; v.1799, 1805] 'An End' & 'Dream Lane' [in *The Germ*, as by 'Ellen Alleyne'] 'The Blessed Damozel' [in *The Germ*] *Paul Clifford* [penal reform novel] *Latter-Day Pamphlets*

EARLY VICTORIAN

MID-VICTORIAN

Year	History / Events	Literature & Cultural Events	Authors: Works
		Collins' [NPG]; **Lit. 'Events':** William Wordsworth dies – Alfred Tennyson, Poet Laureate; [–1859] Dickens pubs weekly magazine, *Household Words*; Pre-Raphaelite magazine, *The Germ*, fnd.d	Gaskell: 'The Moorland Cottage' [story] Charles Kingsley (1819–75): *Alton Locke: Tailor and Poet* [social novel]
1851	The Great Exhibition in London [under patronage of Prince Albert] – Sir Joseph Paxton builds the 'Crystal Palace', Hyde Park, for it [re-erected at Sydenham, SE London, 1852; burnt down, 1936]; Palmerston acts without consulting Crown or PM – forced to resign; Window Tax repealed – houses taxed instead; Amalgamated Society of Engineers fnd.d; *coup d'état* in France by Louis Napoleon – all opposition ruthlessly suppressed – supported by huge popular vote; gold discovered in NSW, Australia; Cuba declares independence – suppressed by Spain	William Cubitt builds King's Cross Station; Owens College, Manchester, opens [later M/c University]; H.E. Manning [later Cardinal] converts to RC; [–1863] the Capitol, Washinton DC, erected; *The New York Times* 1st pub.d; [–1854] Comte, *Système de politique positive*; Artur Schopenhauer, *Parerga und Paralipomena* [Ger. phil. writings]. **Int. Lit.:** Hawthorne, *The House of the Seven Gables*; Herman Melville, *Moby Dick*; Eugène Labiche, *Le Chapeau de Paille d'Italie* [Fr. comedy]. **Music:** Verdi, 'Rigoletto' [opera]; [–1886] Liszt comps 20 'Hungarian Rhapsodies'; Charles Gounod [comp] 'Sapho' [Fr. opera]. **Art:** Millais, 'Bridesmaid' [Fitzwilliam]; F.M. Brown, 'Pretty Baa-Lambs' [BAG]; Landseer, 'The Monarch of the Glen'; Stevens, 'Mrs Young Mitchell and Her Baby, Mary' [Tate]; [–1852] William Holman Hunt [pnt] 'The Hireling Shepherd' [MAG]	**Pr/F:** Borrow: *Lavengro* [novel of gypsy life] Gaskell: [–1853] *Cranford* [1st pub.d in *Household Words*] Kingsley: *Yeast* Ruskin: [–1853] *The Stones of Venice* [3 vols; incls 'On the nature of the Gothic'] & *Pre-Raphaelitism* [pamphlet defending movement] Mrs (Dinah Maria) Craik 1826–87): *The Head of the Family* [novel] **Theory/Crit:** W.M. Thackeray: *The English Humorists of the Eighteenth Century* [lectures; pub.d 1853] Charles-Augustin Sainte-Beuve: [–1862] *Causeries de Lundi* [Fr. lit. crit. in weekly periodical]
1852	Tory ministry under Earl of Derby – Disraeli's 1st Budget defeated – resigns – Coalition Ministry under Aberdeen – Gladstone, Chancellor; Bribery Act allows enquiries into corrupt elections; 3rd cholera epidemic – London Water Act to safeguard purity of supply [fully implemented by 1880s]; 1st Congress of Co-op. Societies in London; Treaty of London (Britain, France, Russia, Austria, Prussia, Sweden) guarantees integrity of Denmark; Louis Napoleon issues new constitution – plebiscite confirms him as Napoleon III of restored [2nd] Empire; [–1854] US naval expedition forces Japan into diplomatic negotiations & 1st trade treaty with a Western state; Britain recognises independence of Transvaal; NZ granted self-gvnmt; [–1853] 2nd Burma War	Morse develops telegraph code for alphabet; Wells Fargo Co. fnd.d in USA; *Roget's Thesaurus* 1st pub.d. **Int. Lit.:** Hawthorne, *The Blithedale Romance*; Harriet Beecher Stowe, *Uncle Tom's Cabin* [serialised, 1851]; Gautier, *Émaux et Cammés* [poems]; Hebbel, *Herodes und Marianne* [Ger. play]; 1st Turgenev, *A Sportsman's Sketches*/'Notes of a Hunter'; [–1856] Leo Tolstoy, *Childhood, Boyhood, Youth*; Alexandre Dumas ('fils'), *La Dame aux Camélias* [play; as novel, 1848]. **Music:** Johannes Brahms [comp] 7 early piano sonatas. **Art:** Millais, 'Ophelia' [Tate]; F.M. Brown, [–1855] 'The Last of England' [BAG] & [–c.1863] 'Work' [MAG]	**P:** Arnold: *Empedocles on Etna, and Other Poems* [incls 'Tristram and Iseult'] Tennyson: 'Ode on the Death of the Duke of Wellington' **Pr/F:** Dickens: [–1853] *Bleak House* Newman: *Discourses on the Scope and Nature of University Education* Thackeray: *Henry Esmond* **Lit. 'Events':** [–1854] George Eliot edits *Westminster Review*
1853	Gladstone's 1st budget approaches complete Free Trade – duty on 123 items abolished – death duty intro.d; Report on Civil Service criticises patronage as method of appointment [v.1855]; [–1854] Preston cotton spinners' strike; smallpox vaccination compulsory in England; Russia invades Turkey – Turkey declares war – Anglo-Fr. fleet enters Black Sea; transportation of convicts to Van Dieman's Land ends – ceases to be convict settlement – renamed Tasmania; Cape Colony granted responsible gvnmt; Kaffir war – British annexe Kaffraria	Q. Victoria is administered chloroform during childbirth; [>] reaping machines come into common use; Wellington College & [–1854] Cheltenham Ladies College fnd.d; Martineau trans Comte (1830) as *Positive Philosophy*. **Int. Lit.:** Hawthorne, *Tanglewood Tales*; Hugo, *Les Châtiments* [poems]; Heine, *Neueste Gedichte*; Gustav Freytag, *Die Journalisten* [Ger. social comedy]. **Music:** [c.] Heinrich Steinway fnds piano-makers in NY; Verdi, 'Il Trovatore' & 'La Traviata' [operas]. **Art:** Millet, 'Harvesters Resting'; Courbet, 'Bathers'; Rossetti, 'Found' [unfinished]; Holman Hunt, 'Claudio and Isabella' [from 1850; Tate] & [–1854] 'The Awakening Conscience' [Tate]; Gustav Doré [illustr.] edtn of Rabelais	**P:** Arnold: *Poems. A New Edition* [excludes 'Empedocles' – incls 'The Scholar Gypsy', 'Sohrab and Rustum' & critical 'Preface'] **Pr/F:** Bulwer-Lytton: *My Novel* [of contemporary life] Thackeray: [–1855] *The Newcomes* C. Brontë: *Villette* Gaskell: *Ruth* Kingsley: *Hypatia* Charles Reade (1814–84): *Peg Woffington* [novel] Charlotte Yonge (1823–1901): *The Heir of Redclyffe* [novel]

Period	Year	International and Political Contexts	Social and Cultural Contexts	Authors	Indicative Titles
	1854	Separate Secs of State for War & Colonies created; Act to commit juvenile offenders to reformatories; Chadwick dismissed – new Public Health Board appointed; cholera in London kills 10,000 people – [c.] doctors first discover it is water-borne; Millwall Docks open; Eng. coastal trade opened to ships of all nations; [–1856] Crimean War: Britain & France declare war on Russia [to protect Turkey] – Battles of Alma, Balaclava [Charge of the Light Brigade] & Inkerman – siege of Sebastopol begins – Florence Nightingale advances nursing profession in Crimea; Kansas & Nebraska become US territories – Kansas-Nebraska Act allows settlers to decide whether to have slavery or not [cancels 'Missouri Compromise', v.1820] – US Republican Party fnd.d by anti-slavery groups opposed to it; Orange Free State becomes independent Boer province; British annexe Nagpur, India; gold rush in Australia	Working Men's College, London, fnd.d – Ruskin 1st lectures there; Trinity & University Colleges, Dublin, fnd.d; [c.] Ur of the Chaldees, Sumeria, excavated; Elisha Otis exhibits hydraulic lift in NY; [–1856] Theodore Mommsen, *Römische Geschichte* [3 vols; Ger. history of Rome]. **Int. Lit.:** Henry Thoreau, *Walden, or Life in the Woods* [US account of solitary life]; Guillaume Augier, *Le Gendre de M. Poirier* [Fr. social comedy]; Josef von Scheffel, *Der Trompeter von Säkkingen* [Ger. comic verse romance]. **Music:** Wagner, 'Das Rheingold' [1st Pt of 'Der Ring des Nibelungen' cycle of operas]; Berlioz, 'Childhood of Christ' [oratorio]. **Art:** Courbet, 'The Meeting ("Bonjour, Monsieur Courbet")'; Stevens, 'Mrs Mary Ann Collman' [Tate]; Holman Hunt, 'The Scapegoat' [Lady Lever AG], 'The Light of the World' [Keble College] & [–1860] 'Finding of Christ in the Temple' [BAG]; William Frith [pnt] 'Ramsgate Sands' [Royal Coll.]	**P:** Arnold Tennyson Coventry Patmore (1823–96) **Pr/F:** Dickens Yonge **Lit. 'Events':**	*Poems: Second Series* [selection from 2 previous vols & 'Balder Dead' & further 'Preface'] 'The Charge of the Light Brigade' [–1862] *The Angel in the House* [poetic celebration of married love – Pt. I 'The Betrothal'] *Hard Times* & *A Child's History of England* *The Little Duke* G. Eliot trans Feuerbach (1841) as *The Essence of Christianity* & [–1856] writes for *Westminster Review*
	1855	Aberdeen ministry falls – Palmerston, PM; Stamp Duty on newspapers abolished; *Daily Telegraph* fnd.d [1st mass-circulation daily] & *The Daily Chronicle*; William Russell, *Times* correspondent, reveals mismanagement of British troops in Crimea – Committee of Enquiry set up – fall of Sebastopol – Sardinia under Cavour joins Allies; Metropolitan Board of Works fnd.d – London sewers modernised after cholera epidemic; Civil Service Commission appointed – entry exam. instituted; Royal Victoria Docks open; Livingstone discovers Victoria Falls; representative government of NSW estab.d	Universal Exposition in Paris [& 1867]; [c.] Melbourne University fnd.d; Herbert Spencer, *Principles of Psychology* [evolutionary theory]; Harriet Martineau, *Autobiography* [pub.d posthm. 1877]; Joseph Gobineau, *Essai sur l'inégalité des races humaines* [Fr. phil. of the 'super-man']. **Int. Lit.:** Walt Whitman, *Leaves of Grass*; Longfellow, *Hiawatha*; [–1862] Hebbel, *Nibelungen* trilogy [plays]; Freytag, *Debit and Credit* [realist novel]; Gottfried Keller, *Der grüne Heinrich* [Swiss autobiog. novel]. **Music:** Berlioz, 'Te Deum'; Liszt, 'Faust Symphony'. **Art:** Ruskin helps to design Museum of Natural Science, Oxford; [>] Delacroix pnts 'Lion Hunt' series; Courbet, 'The Atelier (Allegory of Realism)'; Doré [illustr.] Balzac's *Droll Stories*; Sir Frederic Leighton [pnt] 'Ciambue's Madonna Carried in Procession Through the Streets of Florence' [bought by Q. Victoria]	**P:** Browning Tennyson **Pr/F:** Dickens Gaskell Kingsley Sir Richard Burton (1821–90) George Meredith (1828–1909) Anthony Trollope (1815–82) **Theory/Crit:** G.H. Lewes	*Men and Women* [dramatic monologues] *Maud and Other Poems* [–1857] *Little Dorrit* *North and South* *Westward Ho!* *A Personal Narrative of a Pilgrimage to Mecca* [travel] *The Shaving of Shagpat* [burlesque oriental fantasy] *The Warden* [1st 'Barchester' novel] *Life of Goethe*
	1856	Victoria Cross (VC) instituted; [>] police forces estab.d nationwide; feminist campaign for Married Women's Property Act; Florence Nightingale finds nurse-training institution at St Thomas's & King's College Hospitals, London [courses begin, 1860]; Sir Henry Bessemer's converter transforms steel industry; Peace Congress of Paris ends Crimean War – Black Sea to be neutral – integrity of Turkey guaranteed – Cavour puts 'Italian Question' on the agenda; Declaration of Paris bans privateering – recognises principle of 'free ships, free goods'; 'representative	Skull of Neanderthal Man discv.d; [–1869] J.A. Froude, *History of England from the Fall of Wolsey to the Spanish Armada* [12 vols]. **Int. Lit.:** Emerson, *English Traits*; Alexis de Tocqueville, *L'Ancien Régime et la Révolution* [vol. I]; Hugo, *Les Contemplations* [poems]; Keller, 'A Village Romeo and Juliet' [Swiss story]. **Music:** Karl Bechstein fnds piano-making Co. in Berlin; Wagner, 'Die Walküre' [2nd pt of 'Ring' cycle]. **Art:** [–1857] National Portrait Gallery (NPG) fnd.d; Ingres, 'La Source' & 'Madame Moitessier' [NG]; Courbet, 'Girls on the Banks of the Seine'; [–1875] Stevens [sculpt.]	**P:** Patmore George MacDonald (1824–1905) **Pr/F:** Carlyle Craik Kingsley Reade R.M. Ballantyne (1825–94) **Lit. 'Events':**	*The Angel in the House Pt II* ['The Espousals'] *Within and Without* [narrative poem] *Collected Works* *John Halifax, Gentleman* *The Heroes* [Grk myths for children] *It is Never Too Late to Mend* *The Young Fur Traders* [adventure novel] William Morris & Edward Burne-Jones fnd *The Oxford and Cambridge Magazine* [pubs poems by Morris & Rossetti]

MID-VICTORIAN

1857

Events: gvnmt in Tasmania & Victoria set up; British & French at war with China over trading disagreements; Transvaal becomes independent republic – Natal becomes separate colony; British annexe Oudh – tension rises in India

Prince Albert is made Prince Consort; Palmerston defeated over China policy – resigns – Gen. Elec.: Palmerston returned with larger majority; over-speculation in US railways causes financial panic in Britain; Matrimonial Causes Act estab.s divorce courts; [c.] British transportation of convicts ends; lt. National Association fnd.d & [–1859] Sardinia under Cavour seeks to drive Austria out of Italy; [–1858] 'Indian Mutiny' [rebellion of Sepoys] – siege of Lucknow – Cawnpore massacre – Delhi taken & recaptured – relief of Lucknow; British destroy Chinese fleet & with French take Canton

S. Kensington Museum opened with profits from Great Exhibition [becomes V&A, 1909]; *Birmingham Post* fnd.d; [c.] Bombay University fnd.d; David Livingstone, *Missionary Travels in South Africa*; [–1858] Marx, *Grundrisse* [pub.d 1939–41]. **Int. Lit.:** Gustave Flaubert, *Madame Bovary* [Fr. novel]; Charles Baudelaire, *Les Fleurs du Mal* [Fr. poems]. **Music:** Sir Charles Hallé fnds concerts in Manchester; Wagner, 'Siegfried' [Acts 1 & 2 – 3rd Pt of 'Ring' cycle]; Liszt, 'Dante Symphony' pf.d; Georges Bizet [comp] 'Chloris et Clotilde'. **Art:** Ruskin rescues Turner coll. of paintings from decay in NG cellars & pubs *Catalogue*; Millet, 'The Gleaners'; Landseer, 'Dignity and Impudence' [Tate]; Rossetti, 'The Blue Closet' & 'Wedding of St George and the Princess Sabra' [w/cs; both Tate]; Wallis, 'The Stonebreaker' [BAG]; [–1858] John Brett [pnt] 'The Stonebreaker' [Walker AG]; Robert Howlett, 'Isambard Kingdom Brunel' [photo. in front of SS 'Great Eastern's' chains; NPG]

P: Barrett Browning — *Aurora Leigh* [blank-verse 'novel']
MacDonald — *Poems*
Pr/F: Borrow — *The Romany Rye*
C. Brontë — *The Professor* [1st novel, wrtn 1846; pub. posthm.]

Gaskell — *The Life of Charlotte Brontë* [biog.]
Kingsley — *Two Years Ago*
Thackeray — [–1859] *The Virginians* [sequel to *Henry Esmond*]

A. Trollope — *Barchester Towers*
'George Eliot' (Mary Ann Evans; 1819–80) — 'The Sad Fortunes of the Rev. Amos Barton' pub.d in *Blackwood's Magazine* – 1st of *Scenes of Clerical Life*, 1858]
Thomas Hughes (1822–96) — *Tom Brown's Schooldays* [novel]

Lit. 'Events': [–1867] Matthew Arnold, Professor of Poetry at Oxford: inaugural lecture, 'On the Modern Element in Literature' [in English, not Latin]

1858

Events: Palmerston defeated on Conspiracy to Murder Bill – resigns – Derby's 2nd minority Tory ministry; Property Qualification for MPs abolished; Jewish Disabilities Act removes political restrictions from Jews; National Miners' Association fnd.d; Banking Cos Act extends limited liability to banks; Public Health Board dissolved – new Public Health Act; General Medical Council 1st meets in London; Irish Republican Brotherhood ('Fenians') fnd.d in USA by John O'Mahony & James Stephens; unsuccessful Orsini Plot to assassinate Napoleon III in France; Napoleon & Cavour meet to prepare for unification of Italy against Austria; Indian Mutiny suppressed – gvnmt of British India transferred from E. India Co. to Crown; Treaty of Tientsin – China opens ports & admits European ambassadors; Minnesota becomes 32nd State; Speke & Burton discover Lake Tanganyika – [–1860] Speke discovers Lake Victoria & identifies it as source of the Nile

'Big Ben' bell cast for Westminster clock-tower; Brunel's SS 'Great Eastern' launched [largest vessel ever built until 1899]; [c.] 1st transatlantic cable laid; Keble College, Oxford, fnd.d [designed by William Butterfield, Gothic architect]; Battersea Park designed; [>] Louis Pasteur's research on bacteria underway. **Int. Lit.:** Longfellow, *The Courtship of Miles Standish* [US narrative poem]; Oliver Wendell Holmes, *The Autocrat at the Breakfast-Table* & [–1860] *The Professor at the B-T* [US essays]; Charles Leconte de l'Isle, *Poésies Complètes* [Fr. 'Parnassian' poems]. **Music:** 3rd Royal Opera House, Covent Garden, opens [designed by Barry]; Gounod, 'Le Médecin malgré lui' [comic opera]; Jacques Offenbach [comp] 'Orpheus in the Underworld' [Fr. light opera]; Peter Cornelius [comp] 'The Barber of Baghdad' [Ger. comic opera]. **Art:** [–1859] Millet, 'The Angelus'; Rossetti, 'Mary Magdalene at the House of Simon the Pharisee' [Fitzwilliam]; William Morris [pnt] 'La Belle Iseult (Queen Guinevere)' [Tate]; [–1859] Edouard Manet [pnt] 'Absinthe Drinker'

P: Clough — *Amours de Voyage* [wrtn 1849; pub. posthm.]
William Morris (1834–96) — *The Defence of Guenevere and Other Poems*
Pr/F: Ballantyne — *The Coral Island*
Bulwer-Lytton — *What will He Do with It?* [novel]
Carlyle — [–1865] *Frederick the Great* [biog; 6 vols]
Eliot — *Scenes of Clerical Life* [2 vols]
MacDonald — *Phantastes: a Faerie Romance*
A. Trollope — *Dr Thorne* ['Barchester' novel]
William Farrar (1831–1903) — *Eric, or Little by Little* [school story]

[Dean] Edward Bannerman Ramsay (1793–1872) — *Reminiscences of Scottish Life and Character* [memoirs]

Lit. 'Events': Philological Society calls for new Eng. dictionary based on historical principles [becomes *OED*]; Eng. trans of Goethe's *Poems and Ballads*

Period	Year	International and Political Contexts	Social and Cultural Contexts	Authors	Indicative Titles
MID-VICTORIAN	1859	Disraeli's Reform Bill defeated & Derby's ministry falls – Palmerston forms Liberal government – Gladstone, Chancellor; peaceful picketing in strikes legalised; Fenians active in Ireland & Britain; Monaco becomes independent from France; Sardinia & France at war with Austria – Austrians defeated – Treaty of Zurich gives Sardinia more It. territories; [c.–1869] Ferdinand de Lesseps builds Suez Canal [92 miles long] – Port Said, Egypt, fnd.d; Queensland becomes separate colony [from NSW]; Oregon becomes 33rd State; 1st US oil-wells drilled in Pennsylvania [1st refinery, 1860]; 3rd Anglo-Chinese war; Livingstone discovers Lake Nyasa [Malawi]	Charles Darwin, *The Origin of Species by Means of Natural Selection*; J.S. Mill, *On Liberty*; Samuel Smiles, *Self-Help*; [–1868] *Chambers* edits *Chambers Encyclopaedia*; Marx, *Zur Kritik der politischen Ökonomie*; [–1860] Mrs Beeton, *Book of Household Management* [1st pub.d in parts]. **Int. Lit.:** Sand, *Elle et lui* [her affair with de Musset]; Hugo, *La Légende des siècles* [epic poem]; Frédéric Mistral, *Mirèio* [Provençal poems]; Ivan Goncharov, *Oblomov* [Russ. realist novel]. **Music:** 'John Brown's Body' [song] comp.d in USA; Wagner completes 'Tristan and Isolde'; Gounod, 'Faust' [opera]. **Art:** Scottish National Gallery (SNG) opens; William Butterfield builds All Saints' Church, Margaret St, London ['Gothic Revival']; frescoes by William Dyce]; Philip Webb builds The Red House, Bexley, Kent, for William Morris]; [–1863] Ingres, 'The Turkish Bath'; Courbet, 'La Toilette'; [–1866] Landseer sculpt. lions for Nelson's Column, Trafalgar Square [unveiled, 1867]; James McNeill Whistler [pnt] 'At the Piano'	**P:** Tennyson Edward FitzGerald (1809–83) **Pr/F:** Dickens Eliot Meredith Ruskin **Dr:** Boucicault **Lit. 'Events':**	[>] *Idylls of the King* [1st Pts pub.d; last Pt pub.d 1885] *Rubáiyát of Omar Khayyám* [Eng. trans of Persian poem] *A Tale of Two Cities* [1st serialised in *All the Year Round*] *Adam Bede* [3 vols] & 'The Lifted Veil' [in *Blackwood's*] *The Ordeal of Richard Feverel* *The Two Paths* [lectures] [c.] *The Octoroon; or, Life in Louisiana* [about US Negroes] Dickens ends *Household Words* & begins new weekly, *All the Year Round*
	1860	Gladstone's Free Trade budget leaves only a few items subject to duty; 'Cobden's Treaty' estab.s free trade with France; Mines Regulation Act intros safety measures; London Trades Council estab.d; [–1861] 'HMS Warrior', 1st Brit. 'ironclad' [battleship] built; plebiscites thro'out Italy [except Nice & Savoy] favour Italian unification – Cavour unites Sardinia with other It. states – 1st It. National Parliament at Turin – Garibaldi & his 1000 'Red Shirts' invade & capture Naples and Sicily – united with Sardinia – Sardinia invades Papal States – British public & gvnmt support It. unification; Abraham Lincoln, US President – S. Carolina secedes from Union; British capture Peking – 3rd Chinese war ends; Maori uprising in NZ to resist British land-ownership – [–1872] Maori Wars	[>] Bishop Wilberforce/ T.H. Huxley debate over Darwinian theory engenders bitter controversy; [c.] Sir George Gilbert Scott builds Government Offices; the *National Reformer* [free-thinking journal]; J.S. Mill, treatise on *Representative Government*. **Int. Lit.:** Hawthorne, *The Marble Faun*; Eugène Labiche, *Le Voyage do M. Perrichon* [Fr. comedy]. **Music:** Gounod, 'Philémon et Baucis' [opera]; Daniel Emmett ('The Negro Minstrel') 'I wish I was in Dixie's Land' [estabs name 'Dixieland']. **Art:** Jacob Burckhardt, *Civilization of the Renaissance in Italy*; Manet, 'Spanish Singer (La Guitarrero)'; Edgar Degas [pnt] 'Spartans Exercising' [NG]	**P:** Barrett Browning Patmore **Pr/F:** Dickens Eliot Peacock Reade Thackeray (William) Wilkie Collins (1824–89) **Dr:** Boucicault Charles Algernon Swinburne (1837–1909)	*Poems before Congress* *The Angel in the House* Pt III, 'Faithful for Ever' [–1861] *Great Expectations* [1st serialised in *All the Year Round*] & *The Uncommercial Traveller* [misc. writings] *The Mill on the Floss* [3 vols] [–1861] *Gryll Grange* *The Cloister and the Hearth* *The Four Georges* [history lectures] *The Woman in White* [mystery novel] *The Colleen Bawn* [–1861] *The Queen Mother & Rosamund*
	1861	Prince Albert dies of typhoid – Victoria retires from public duties; Gladstone abolishes duty on paper – makes 'knowledge' cheaper for the working class; Royal Commission Report on 'Popular Education in England'; Post Office Savings Bank estab.d; Victor Emanuel of Savoy, 1st king of a united Italy [except Rome & Venice]; in USA, 7 Southern States form the Confederacy under Pres. Jefferson Davis – Pres. Lincoln's inaugural address declares the Union perpetual & that laws apply in all states – Confederates attack Fort Sumter in Charleston harbour – [–1865] US Civil War begins – battles of Bull Run, Virginia & Lexington – Britain stays	[–1870] Sandringham House built for Q. Victoria; 1st horse-drawn trams in London; Charles Siemens' open-hearth furnace advances steel manufacture; [–1875] Garnier's Opera House & [–1869] Lambrouste's Bibliothèque Nationale built in Paris; [–1862] J.S. Mill, *Utilitarianism* [in *Fraser's Magazine*; as bk, 1863]; [–1862] Henry Mayhew, *London Labour and the London Poor* [4 vols; from 1851]. **Int. Lit.:** Sand, *Le Marquis de Villemer* [novel]; [–1862] Fyodor Dostoevsky, *Memoirs from the House of the Dead*; Hans Christian Andersen, *Fairy Tales* [begun in 1830s]. **Music:** [c.] *Hymns Ancient and Modern* 1st pub.d. **Art:** William Morris starts	**P:** D.G. Rossetti **Pr/F:** Arnold Eliot Meredith Reade A. Trollope Mrs Henry Wood (1814–87) **Lit. 'Events':**	*The Early Italian Poets* [trans of c.60 poets, incl. Dante & Cavalcanti; rev.d as *Dante and his Circle*, 1874] *On Translating Homer* & *The Popular Education of France* *Silas Marner* *Evan Harrington* *The Cloister and the Hearth* [historical novel] *Framley Parsonage* ['Barset' novel] *East Lynne* [popular novel] Francis T. Palgrave's *Golden Treasury of English Verse* 1st pub.d

1862

neutral – 'Cotton Famine' begins in Lancashire – Kansas becomes 34th State; Alexander II abolishes serfdom in Russia; Lagos [later Nigeria] ceded to Britain to stamp out slave trade

Arts & Crafts business [1st wallpapers, 1862]; Doré [illustr.] Dante's Inferno; Leighton, 'Paola and Francesca'

P: Barrett Browning — Last Poems
Meredith — Modern Love [novel in sonnets] & Poems of the English Roadside
Patmore — The Angel in the House Pt IV, 'The Victories of Love'
C. Rossetti — Goblin Market and Other Poems
Pr/F: Borrow — Wild Wales
Collins — No Name
Eliot — [–1863] Romola [historical novel, in Cornhill; 3 vols, 1863]
Ruskin — Unto This Last [4 essays on political economy; 1st pub.d Cornhill, 1860]
A. Trollope — [–1864] The Small House at Allington ['Barset' novel]
Wood — Mrs Halliburton's Troubles & The Channings [popular novels]
Mary Elizabeth Braddon (1837–1915) — Lady Audley's Secret [popular novel]
George Whyte-Melville (1821–78) — The Queen's Maries [historical novel]

Gladstone's tours of N. increase popular reputation as reformer; Ironworkers' Association fnd.d; Industrial Provident Societies Act to encourage co-operative developments; Act requires 2 shafts to be sunk in new coal-mines; Companies Act intros limited liability to businesses [Ltd. Co.]; Highways Act: parishes compulsorily combined to maintain roads; Garibaldi [unsuccessfully] invades Papal States to eject Pope from Rome – Ir. RCs fight his supporters in Hyde Park; Ger. Reform Union advocates pan-German state – Bismarck becomes Prussian Premier ['man of blood and iron' speech]; US Civil War: Lincoln makes 'Emancipation Proclamation' that all slaves in rebel states should be free on or after 1 Jan. 1863 – battles of Mill Springs & Williamsburg – British-built Confederate battleship 'Alabama' damages Unionist fleet – diplomatic tension; Lincoln issues 1st legal US paper money ('greenbacks'); [–1867] Fr. war in Mexico against liberal regime of Benito Juarez; Speke is 1st European in Uganda; British Honduras becomes a Crown Colony

[–1863] Gilbert Scott erects Albert Memorial; Clifton College, Bristol, fnd.d; 1st Eng. cricket team tours Australia; Notts County fnd.d – oldest club in Football League; Spencer, First Principles; [–1879] Bishop Colenso, The Pentateuch and the Book of Joshua Critically Examined [controvertibly questions accuracy of Bible]. **Int. Lit.:** [–1873] Hugo, Les Misérables [epic social novel]; Flaubert, Salammbô; Leconte de l'Isle, Poèmes barbares; Turgenev, Fathers and Sons [Russ. novel]; Henrik Ibsen, Love's Comedy [Norw. satirical comedy]. **Music:** Henry Richards [comp] 'God Bless the Prince of Wales' [song]; Julia Ward Howe [comp] 'Battle Hymn of the Republic' [pub.d in Atlantic Monthly – sung by Union forces in US Civil War]; Berlioz, 'Béatrice et Bénédict' [comic opera]; Gounod, 'La Reine de Saba' [opera]; Liszt, 'The Legend of St Elizabeth' [oratorio]; Verdi, 'La Forza del Destino' [opera]. **Art:** John Gould, Birds of Great Britain [5 vols, illustr.d]; Frith, 'Railway Station' [Royal Holloway]; Manet, 'Musique aux Tuileries' [NG]; [c.] Daumier, 'Third-Class Carriage'; Whistler, 'Symphony in White No. 1: the White Girl'

1863

Pr/F: Gaskell — Sylvia's Lovers
Kingsley — The Water Babies
Whyte-Melville — The Gladiators
Joseph Sheridan Le Fanu (1814–73) — The House by the Churchyard [novel of the supernatural]
Margaret [Mrs] Oliphant (1828–97) — The Rector and the Doctor's Family & Salem Chapel [1st novels in The Chronicles of Carlingford* (–1876)]
'Ouida' (Marie Louise de la Ramée; 1839–1908) — Held in Bondage [popular fiction]
Theory/Crit: Hippolyte Taine — Histoire de la littérature anglaise

'Cotton Famine' distress in Lancashire at its height; Co-op Wholesale Society fnd.d; [–1890] 1st underground railway begun in London [7-station Metropolitan Line between Paddington & Farringdon St]; Broadmoor Prison opens; Britain agrees to return Ionian Islands to Greece; succession crisis in Duchies of Schleswig-Holstein – dispute with Denmark incorporates Schleswig – dispute with Prussia; [1/1/63] emancipation of US slaves proclaimed – Confederate defeats at Gettysburg, Vicksburg & Chattanooga – Lincoln's 'Gettysburg Address' ['government of the people, by the people, for the people']; W. Virginia becomes 35th State; Fr. troops enter Mexico City

Football Association fnd.d – codifies rules of sport; Cambridge Overseas Examinations estab.d; J.S. Mill, Utilitarianism; Thomas Huxley, Man's Place in Nature; Lyell, The Geological Evidence of the Antiquity of Man; Ernest Renan, La Vie de Jésus. **Int. Lit.:** Hawthorne, Our Old Home [essays on England]; Longfellow, Tales of a Wayside Inn [incls 'Paul Revere's Ride']; Gautier, Le Capitaine Fracasse [novel]; Eugène Fromentin, Dominique [Fr. novel]. **Music:** Bizet, 'The Pearl Fishers' [opera]. **Art:** Millais, 'My First Sermon' [Guildhall]; Manet, 'Déjeuner sur l'Herbe' & 'Olympia' [exhib.d, 1865]; Doré [illustr.] Cervantes's Don Quixote; Eugène Boudin [pnt] 'Beach at Trouville'; Sir Edward Burne-Jones [pnt] 'Merciful Knight'. **Lit. 'Events':** W.M. Thackeray dies

1864

P: Browning — Dramatis Personae
Tennyson — Enoch Arden [narrative poem]
Pr/F: Arnold — A French Eton [on education]
Dickens — [–1865] Our Mutual Friend
Gaskell — [–1866] Wives and Daughters [in Cornhill – unfinished; 2 vols, 1866]
Le Fanu — Uncle Silas [mystery novel]
Newman — Apologia pro Vita Sua [autobiog.]
Oliphant — The Perpetual Curate*

Manchester Reform Union fnd.d [largely middle class]; '1st International' ('International Workingmen's Association') set up by Karl Marx [dissolved, 1876]; Chimney Sweeps Act forbids use of children – ineffective; Dale Dyke resevoir, Sheffield, collapses – great loss of life; Octavia Hill begins housing improvement scheme in London slums; Franco-It. Convention: France will withdraw troops from Rome – Italy will renounce claim to it –

Int. Lit.: John G. Whittier, In War Time [US poems; incls 'Barbara Frietchie']; Vigny, Les Destinées [phil. poems; posthm.]; Brothers Goncourt, Renée Mauperin [Fr. novel]; Jules Verne, Voyage au centre de la terre [Fr. sci. fi.]. **Music:** Gounod, 'Mireille' [Fr. opera]; Offenbach, 'La Belle Hélène' [Ger. opera bouffe]; Anton Bruckner [comp] 'Mass No. 1'. **Art:** [–1867] Gilbert Scott builds Albert Memorial, London; Corot, 'Souvenir of Mortefontaine';

Period	Year	International and Political Contexts	Social and Cultural Contexts	Authors	Indicative Titles
		Florence made It. capital; Denmark at war with Austria & Prussia over Schleswig/Holstein – defeated – cedes S/H by Treaty of Vienna ; US Civil War: battles of Petersburg, Cedar Creek, Farmville – Nevada becomes 36th State; [–1867] French proclaim Archduke Maximilian of Austria Emperor of Mexico	Maclise, 'Death of Nelson' & [–1861] 'Meeting of Wellington and Blücher' [House of Lords]; Rossetti, 'Beata Beatrix' [Tate]; Whistler, 'Little White Girl' [Tate] & 'Rose and Silver: La Princesse du Pays de la Porcelaine'; Claude Monet [pnt] 'The Breakwater at Honfleur' – [>] Fr. Impressionism developing [v.1874]; George Frederic Watts [pnt] 'Ellen Terry' [NPG]	A. Trollope **Dr:** Boucicault **Lit. 'Events':**	[–1865] *Can You Forgive Her?* [1st 'Palliser' political novel] *Arrah-na-Pogue* John Clare dies
1865		Palmerston dies – Russell, PM; Reform League fnd.d [middle class & skilled working class]; Metropolitan Fire Service estab.d; Bismarck & Napoleon III meet – France to be neutral in event of Austro-Pruss. War; US Civil War ends – Confederate army under Lee capitulates at Appomattox Court House – Lincoln re-elected President – 'Inaugural Address' on moral sigficance of the war – Lincoln assassinated – 13th Amendment to US Constitution passed abolishing slavery – [–1877] period of 'Reconstruction' in USA; Governor Eyre suppresses rebellion in Jamaica [becomes Crown Colony, 1866]	J.S. Mill elected to parliament – [–1866] urges extension of suffrage to women; *Fortnightly Review* fnd.d; William Booth fnds 'Christian Mission' in London's E. End [precursor of Salvation Army, 1878]; Massachusetts Institute of Technology fnd.d; William Lecky, *History of the Rise and Influence of the Spirit of Rationalism in Europe.* **Int. Lit.:** Hugo, *Les Chansons des rues et des bois* [poems]; [–1869] Tolstoy, *War and Peace* [begun 1863]; Ibsen, *Brand* [verse play]. **Music:** Wagner's 'Tristram and Isolde' 1st pf.d. **Art:** [c.] Boudin, 'Beach Scene', 'Deauville' [Tate] & 'Harbour of Trouville' [NG]; Sir Edward Poynter [pnt] 'Faithful Unto Death' [Walker AG]; Julia Margaret Cameron, 'Alfred, Lord Tennyson' [photo; NPG]. **Lit. 'Events':** Elizabeth Gaskell dies	**P:** Newman **Pr/F:** Meredith Ouida Ruskin Yonge 'Lewis Carroll' (Charles Dodgson; 1832–98) **Dr:** Swinburne **Theory/Crit:** Matthew Arnold	'The Dream of Gerontius' [wrtn; pub.d 1874] *Rhoda Fleming* *Strathmore* *Sesame and Lilies* [lectures] *The Clever Woman of the Family* *Alice's Adventures in Wonderland* [illustr.d by Sir John Tenniel] *Atalanta in Calydon* [poetic drama; incls 'Hymn to Artemis'] & *Chastelard* [1st in 'Mary, Queen of Scots' trilogy*] *Essays in Criticism* [1st ser.; incls 'The Function of Criticism at the Present Time']
1866		Gladstone's Reform Bill defeated – resigns – Derby, PM – Disraeli leads in Commons – Reform riots in Hyde Park [railings pulled down] & elsewhere; banks' over-speculation in new joint-stock Cos creates financial crisis; Fenian unrest in Ireland – Habeas Corpus suspended there; 'Seven Weeks War': Austria & Prussia fight over Schleswig-Holstein – Austria defeated at Sadowa – Prussia gains many Ger. territories; Italy declares war on Austria – defeated – Austria cedes Venice to France – plebiscite in favour of Italy – Venice joins Italy; [c.] Crete seeks independence from Turkey; US Senate passes Civil Rights Bill & 14th Amendment giving blacks the rights & privileges of full citizenship; transatlantic telegraph cable completed [from Ireland to Newfoundland]	[–1880] St David's Cathedral, Bangor, restored; Ernst Siemens invents dynamo; Alfred Nobel invents dynamite. **Int. Lit.:** Whittier, *Snow-Bound* [US poems]; Dostoevsky, *Crime and Punishment*; François Coppée, *Le Reliquaire* & [1867] *Intimités* [Fr. 'Parnassian' poems]; Emile Gaboriau, *L'Affair Lerouge* [Fr. detective novel with M. Lecoq]; Paul Verlaine, *Poèmes saturniens.* **Music:** Liszt, 'Deux Légendes' [for piano] & 'Christus' [oratorio]; Offenbach, 'La Vie Parisienne' [light opera]; Bedřich Smetana [comp] 'The Bartered Bride' [Czech opera]; Ambroise Thomas [comp] 'Mignon' [Fr. light opera]. **Art:** Courbet, 'Sleepers' (aka 'Slumber'); Manet, 'The Fifer'; [–1867] Monet, 'Women in a Garden'; Winslow Homer [pnt] 'Prisoners from the Front' [US Civil War]	**P:** Arnold C. Rossetti Swinburne Robert Buchanan (1841–1901) **Pr/F:** Collins Eliot Kingsley Oliphant Ruskin Yonge **Lit. 'Events':**	'Thyrsis' [in *Macmillan's Magazine*] *The Prince's Progress and Other Poems* *Poems and Ballads* [incls 'The Garden of Prosepine' & 'Hesperia'] *London Poems* *Armadale* *Felix Holt* [3 vols] *Hereward the Wake* *Miss Marjoribanks** *The Crown of Wild Olive* [lectures] *A Dove in the Eagle's Nest* Gerard Manley Hopkins converts to Rome
1867		Disraeli's Representation of the People Act [2nd Reform Act] enfranchises 1m. urban male artisans; 'Hornby v. Close' case: trades unions declared outside the law; Factory Extension Act regulates hours beyond textile industry & to workshops [no child under 8 to work; those 8–13 must have 10 hrs education a week]; Agricultural Gangs Act bans children under 8 from farm-work & women & children from working in field-gangs with men; Fenian disturbances in England – anti-Catholic	[>] University Extension courses begin to be organised; [–1871] Francis Fowke builds the Albert Hall, London; Joseph Lister pioneers antiseptic surgery; Thomas Barnado opens 1st children's home in Stepney; Marquis of Queensbury codifies rules for boxing; Marx, *Das Capital* [vol. I, wrtn in London]; Walter Bagehot, *The English Constitution.* **Int. Lit.:** Mark Twain, *The Celebrated Jumping Frog of Calaveras County* [pub.d; wrtn 1865]; Ibsen, *Peer Gynt* [poetic drama]; Emile Zola, *Thérèse Raquin* [Fr.	**P:** Arnold Morris Swinburne **Pr/F:** Meredith Ouida Ruskin A. Trollope **Theory/Crit:** Arnold	*New Poems* [incls 'Dover Beach' & 'Thyrsis'] *The Life and Death of Jason* [narrative poem] *Song of Italy* *Vittoria* *Under Two Flags* *Time and Tide by Weare and Tyne* ['25 Letters to a Working Man of Sunderland'] *The Last Chronicle of Barset* & [–1869] *Phineas Finn* ['Palliser' novel] *On the Study of Celtic literature*

History: Federation fnd.d [27 members led by Prussia]; Garibaldi invades Papal States – defeated by French; British North America Act estab.s [1st self-governing] Dominion of Canada [New Brunswick, Quebec, Nova Scotia, Ontario] – Ottawa becomes capital; Nebraska becomes 37th State – 'Alaska Purchase': USA buys Alaska from Russia for $7,200,000; Fr. troops leave Mexico – Juarez's forces regain control & execute Emperor Maximilian; [–1873] Livingstone explores Congo; [c.] S. African diamond fields discv.d

Arts: Tyl Ulenspiegel [Belg. prose epic]. **Music:** Bizet, 'La Jolie Fille de Perth' [opera]; Gounod, 'Roméo et Juliette' [opera]; Liszt, 'Hungarian Coronation Mass'; Wagner, 'Der Meistersinger von Nürnberg' [opera]; Johann Strauss [comp] 'The Blue Danube' [Viennese waltz]. **Art:** [–1868] Holman Hunt, 'Isabella and the Pot of Basil' [Laing AG]; Doré [illustr.] La Fontaine's Fables; Watts, 'Algernon Charles Swinburne' [NPG]; Cameron, 'Thomas Carlyle' [photo; NPG]; Manet, 'The Execution of Maximilian'; [c.] Monet, 'Terrace at Sainte-Adresse'; Auguste Renoir [pnt] 'Diane Chasseresse'

P: Browning — [–1869] *The Ring and the Book* [4 vols; 'verse-novel' of dramatic monologues]
Eliot — *The Spanish Gypsy*
Morris — [–1870] *The Earthly Paradise* [3 vols; verse narratives]

Pr/F: Collins — *The Moonstone*

1868

History: Derby resigns – Disraeli, PM for 1st time – Lib. victory in Gen. Elec. – [–1874] Gladstone, PM for 1st time; [c.] further anti-Irish/Catholic riots in Lancashire towns; Scottish Co-op Wholesale Society fnd.d; Press Association fnd.d; [c.] Ku Klux Klan fnd.d in S. States to ensure white supremacy after US Civil War [declared illegal, 1871]; Basutoland (Lesotho) becomes a British protectorate

Arts: Whitaker's Almanac 1st pub.d; 1st successful typewriter patented in USA; [–1869] Q. Victoria pubs Leaves from a Journal of our Life in the Highlands [More Leaves, 1883–4]. **Int. Lit.:** [–1869] Louise M. Alcott, *Little Women*; [–1869] Dostoevsky, *The Idiot*; Alphonse Daudet, *Le Petit Chose* [Fr. semi-autobiog. novel]. **Music:** Brahms, 'A German Requiem' [pf.d]; Johann Strauss, 'Tales from the Vienna Woods' [waltz]; Modest Moussorgsky [comp] 'Boris Gudunov' [Russ. opera; pf.d 1874]; Nikolai Rimsky-Korsakov [comp] 'The Maid of Pskov' [opera – later staged by Diaghilev as 'Ivan the Terrible']. **Art:** [–1874] Gilbert Scott builds St Pancras Station Hotel [Gothic Revival]; [c.] Watts [sculpt.] 'Clyte' [Tate]; Manet, 'The Balcony' & 'Émile Zola'; Monet, 'The River'; [c.–1869] Degas, 'Interior (The Rape)'; Renoir, 'The Sisley Family'; Sir Laurence Alma-Tadema [pnt] 'The Visit' [V&A]

1869

History: Trade Union (Protection of Funds) Act; wages in iron industry regulated to sale price; Ir. Church Disestablishment Act – its revenues to aid poverty & social causes; Endowed Schools Act reforms grammar schools; National Education League & Union fnd.d; Royal Commission on Sanitation; Contagious Diseases Act [prostitutes in garrison towns forced to have medicals]; [–1879] Pope Pius IX summons Vatican Council to Rome – Papal Infallibility declared; Napoleon III liberalises Fr. Constitution – Parliamentary Empire – [1870] approved by huge vote in plebiscite; Suez Canal completed [opens 1870]; Union Pacific, 1st US transcontinental railway, completed; Britain buys Hudson Bay Co. territories – ceded to Canada [1870; incls province of Manitoba] – [–1870] Red River uprising: the Métis [Fr. half-breeds] oppose incorporation of NW Territories in dominion of Canada & set up provisional gvnmt under Louis Riel – suppressed

Arts: Blackfriars Bridge, London, built; Girton College for women fnd.d [moves to Cambridge, 1873]; 'Cutty Sark' sailing-ship launched; J.S. Mill, On the Subjection of Women [advocates female emancipation]; Lecky, History of European Morals. **Int. Lit.:** Twain, *Innocents Abroad* [US humour]; Alcott, *Good Wives* [UK 1871]; Hugo, *L'Homme qui rit* [historical novel]; Goncourt Bros, *Madame Gervais* [novel]; Flaubert, *L'Éducation sentimentale*; Verlaine, *Fêtes galantes* [poems]; Daudet, *Lettres de mon moulin* [stories of Provençal life]. **Music:** Alexander Borodin, '1st Symphony' [pf.d; comp 1862–7]. **Art:** Ruskin appointed 1st Slade Professor of Art at Oxford University [resigns 1878; resumes 1883]; Courbet, 'Woman of Munich'; Monet, 'La Grenouillère'; Renoir, 'La Grenouillère'; [–1872] Degas, 'At the Races – Before the Stands'; Homer, 'Long Branch, New Jersey'; Alma-Tadema, 'Pyrrhic Dance' [Guildhall]; Henri Fantin-Latour [pnt] 'Engagement Still Life'; Berthe Morisot [pnt] 'Port of Lorient' & [–1870] 'La Lecture'

P: Arnold — *Poems* [coll. edtn, 2 vols]
Tennyson — *The Holy Grail and Other Poems* [in Idylls sequence]

Pr/F: Arnold — *Culture and Anarchy* [as bk; 1st pub.d in Cornhill, 1867–8]
Oliphant — *The Minister's Wife*
R.D. Blackmore (1825–1900) — *Lorna Doone* [historical novel of Devon]

Lit. 'Events': William Morris pubs Eng. trans of 2 Icelandic sagas

PERIOD	YEAR	INTERNATIONAL AND POLITICAL CONTEXTS	SOCIAL AND CULTURAL CONTEXTS	AUTHORS	INDICATIVE TITLES
	1870	[1st] Married Women's Property Act grants some independent protection over property; Forster's Elementary Education Act – free public education in Board Schools available for 5–13 yr-olds [not yet compulsory; v.1876, 1880]; Ir. Land Act to provide protection against eviction & compensation; Civil Service opened to competitive exams [except Foreign Office]; [–1871] Franco-Prussian War – French declare war – Prussia & allies invade – French defeated at Sedan – Napoleon III capitulates – revolution in Paris – Republic declared – siege of Paris – fall of Napoleon – end of 2nd Empire; Fr. troops leave Rome – Italians enter – Papal States elect to join Kingdom of Italy; 15th Amendment to US Constitution [enforces civil & political rights regardless of race]; W. Australia granted representative gvnmt; diamonds found in Orange Free State – Kimberley fnd.d	½d. stamp intro.d; Pasteur devises process for destroying bacteria in milk; [–1872] Heinrich Schliemann excavates Troy. **Int. Lit.:** Alcott, *An Old Fashioned Girl*; Francis Brett Harte, 'The Luck of Roaring Camp' & 'The Outcasts of Poker Flat' [US stories; wrtn 1868–9]; Verne, *Vingt mille lieues sous les mers* [Fr. sci. fi. novel]. **Music:** Léo Delibes [comp] 'Coppélia' [Fr. ballet]. **Art:** Metropolitan Museum of Art fnd.d in NY; Courbet, 'Cliffs at Étretat After a Storm'; Watts, 'Sir Edward Burne-Jones' [BAG] & 'William Morris' [NPG]; Millais, 'Boyhood of Raleigh' [Tate]; Monet, 'On the Beach, Trouville' [Tate]; Renoir, 'The Bather' & 'Odalisque'; Fantin-Latour, 'L'Atelier aux Batignolles' [group portrait of Impressionist friends]; Pissarro, 'Lower Norwood, London' [NG] & 'Diligence at Louveciennes'; Alfred Sisley [pnt] 'Canal St Martin, Paris'	**P:** Lear D.G. Rossetti Disraeli Morris Ruskin **Lit. 'Events':**	*Nonsense Songs, Stories, Botany, and Alphabets* [incls 'The Owl and the Pussycat' & 'The Jumblies'] *Poems* [incls 'Dante's Dream'] *The Mystery of Edwin Drood* [unfinished] *Lothair* *The Story of the Volsungs and Niblungs* [trans from Icelandic] *Lectures on Art* [Slade lectures, 1st ser.] Charles Dickens dies
	1871	Trade Union Act legalises unions – 'Parliamentary committee' of TUC formed]; Universities Tests Act allows non-Anglicans to enter Oxford & Cambridge; Local Government Act sets up Local Government Board; Railway Act empowers Board of Trade to investigate accidents; purchase of commissions in British Army abolished; fall of Paris after 4-mth siege – Paris Commune uprising – suppressed – Treaty of Frankfurt ends war – France cedes Alsace-Lorraine & pays 5 milliard francs; unification of Germany completed: William I of Prussia proclaimed Emperor of Germany at Versailles – 1st Reichstag meets in Berlin – [–1890] Bismarck, Imperial Ger. Chancellor – anti-RC Church 'Kulturkampf' begins; Papal States & Rome [as capital] become part of united Italy – Pope loses temporal power – 'Prisoner in the Vatican'; 'Great Fire' at Chicago; [c.] liberal intelligentsia under attack in Russia; British Columbia [incls Vancouver] becomes a province of Canada; Britain annexes Kimberley diamond fields; Stanley rediscovers Livingstone at Lake Tanganyika	Bank holidays intro.d in England & Wales; [c.] Newnham College, Cambridge, [for women] fnd.d; English FA Cup estab.d; Rugby Union fnd.d to regulate sport; Ruskin gives financial support to Octavia Hill's housing scheme in Marylebone [v.1864]; Darwin, *The Descent of Man and Selection in Relation to Sex*; Mikhail Bakunin, *Dieu et l'état* [anarchist work]. **Int. Lit.:** Alcott, *Little Men*; Hugo, *L'Année terrible* [poems of the Franco-Prussian War]; [–1893] Zola begins 20-vol. ser. of novels, *Les Rougon-Macquart*; [–1872] Dostoevsky, *The Possessed*; Arthur Rimbaud, *Le Bateau ivre* [Fr. poems]. **Music:** Verdi, 'Aïda' [opera, 1st pf.d]; Camille Saint-Saëns [comp] 'Le Rouet d'Omphale' [Fr. symphonic poem]. **Art:** Corot, 'Belfry of Douai'; Monet, 'Westminster Bridge' [Astor Coll.]; Camille Pissarro [pnt] 'Upper Norwood, London' & 'Crystal Palace'; [–1872] Whistler, 'Arrangement in Grey and Black No. 1: the Artist's Mother' & 'Miss Cicely Alexander' [Tate]; [c.] Paul Cézanne [pnt] 'L'Homme au chapeau de paille'	**P:** Swinburne Lear **Pr/F:** Arnold Eliot MacDonald Meredith Ruskin A. Trollope Thomas Hardy (1840–1928) **Lit. 'Events':**	*Songs before Sunrise* *More Nonsense Rhymes* *Friendship's Garland* [essays] [–1872] *Middlemarch* *At the Back of the North Wind* [as bk] & [–1872] *The Princess and the Goblin* [both children's stories] *The Adventures of Harry Richmond* [–1877] *Fors Clavigera* ['Letters to the Working Men of England', 1st ser., 1–84, pub.d monthly] [–1873] *The Eustace Diamonds* ['Palliser' novel] *Desperate Remedies* [1st pub.d novel] [–1882] Sir Leslie Stephen edits *Cornhill Magazine*; Robert Buchanan ['Thomas Maitland'] attacks Pre-Raphaelites in 'The Fleshly School of Poetry' in *Contemporary Review* – Rossetti replies with 'The Stealthy School of Criticism'; Benjamin Jowett trans *Dialogues of Plato*
MID-VICTORIAN	1872	Ballot Act intros secret voting; Bruce's Licensing Act closes 1000s of beer-shops & restricts pub opening hours; Metalliferous Mines Act bans employment of women & children; Joseph Arch fnds National Agricultural Labourers Union; Disraeli gives pro-Empire speech at Crystal Palace; Ulysses S. Grant, US President – General Amnesty Act pardons most Confederates; Germany expels Jesuits; Emperors of	[c.] Penny-farthing bicycles in general use; Guildhall Library, London, fnd.d; Aberystwyth UC fnd.d; Friedrich Nietzsche, *The Birth of Tragedy* [Ger. phil: 'Apollonian' v. 'Dionysian' values]. **Int. Lit.:** Daudet, *Tartarin de Tarascon* [comic novel]; Coppée, *Les Humbles* [poems]; Rimbaud, *Les Illuminations* [c. wrtn; pub.d 1886]. **Music:** Bizet, 'L'Arlésienne' [incidental music to Daudet's play]; Antonín Dvořák	**P:** Browning Tennyson **Pr/F:** Carroll Hardy Ruskin	*Fifine at the Fair* *Gareth and Lynette* ['Idylls' poem] *Through the Looking Glass and What Alice Found There* [illstr.ns by John Tenniel] *Under the Greenwood Tree* & [–1873] *A Pair of Blue Eyes* *Munera Pulveris* [4 essays on political economy in *Fraser's*, 1862]

	Germany, Austria & Russia meet – 'Dreikaiserbund' estab.d, 1873; Cape Colony granted responsible gvnmt; [–1882] St Gotthard Tunnel built	[comp] 'Hymnus' [Czech cantata; pf.d]. **Art:** [–1875] Leighton, 'Sir Richard Burton' [NPG]; [c.–1875] Whistler, 'Nocturne in Blue and Gold: Old Battersea Bridge' [Tate] & [–1873] 'Thomas Carlyle' [Glasgow AG]; Monet, 'Impression: Sunrise' [gives name to Impressionist movement]; Pissarro, 'Entrance to the Village of Voisins'; Renoir, 'Pont-Neuf'	Samuel Butler (1835–1902)	*Erewhon* [Utopian satire; pub.d anon.]
1873	Supreme Court of Judicature Act reforms English legal system & law courts [& 1875]; severe economic crisis in Europe, USA & Australia – industrial & agrarian depression in Britain begins; Co-op Wholesale Society begins to manufacture its own goods; Railway Commissioners appointed to administer railways & canals; [–1886] Severn Tunnel built; Ger. forces leave France; [–1874] attempts to restore monarchy in France defeated – Napoleon III dies in exile in England; 'May Laws' in Germany restrict power of RC Church; [–1874] Ashanti War leads to creation of Gold Coast Crown Colony, W. Africa [now Ghana]; Prince Edward Island becomes province of Canada	George Newnes fnds *The Westminster Gazette*; 1st University Extension Classes estab.d at Cambridge; J.S. Mill, *Autobiography* [pub. posthm.]. **Int. Lit.:** [–1876] Tolstoy, *Anna Karenina*; Daudet, *Contes de Lundi* [stories]; Verne, *La Tour du Monde en 80 jours* [sci. fi. novel]; Rimbaud, *Une Saison en Enfer* [visionary prose]. **Music:** Carl Rosa Opera Co., London, fnd.d. **Art:** Millais, 'Mrs Bischoffsheim' [NG]; Manet, 'Le Bon Bock' & 'Masked Ball at the Opera'; Monet, 'Boulevard des Capucines'; Degas, 'The Cotton Exchange, New Orleans'; Renoir, 'Monet Working in his Garden in Argenteuil'; Morisot, 'The Cradle' & 'Madame Pontillon Seated on the Grass'; Cézanne, 'House of the Hanged Man' & 'Dr Gachet's House, Auvers' [exhib.d, 1st Impressionist Exhibition, 1874]	**P:** Robert Bridges (1844–1930) **Pr/F:** Arnold Newman A. Trollope **Theory/Crit.:** Walter Pater	*Poems* *Literature and Dogma* [essays] *The Idea of a University Defined and Illustrated* [–1874] *Phineas Redux* ['Palliser' novel] *Studies in the History of the Renaissance*
1874	Tory victory in Gen. Elec. – Disraeli, PM – 1st 2 Trade Union ['Labour'] MPs elected; Women's Trade Union League fnd.d; new gvnmt promotes slum clearance & public health – Factory Act limits working-week to 56 hrs – minimum age raised to 9 [10 after 1875]; Public Worship Act attempts to restrict ritualism in C of E; sliding scale of wages in coal-mining linked to sale price; E. India Co. dissolved; [>] Britain begins to make treaties with local rulers in Malay States; Fiji Islands become a British colony	1st commercial typewriters sold in USA; J.R. Green, *Short History of the English People*; [–1878] William Stubbs, *Constitutional History of England*. **Int. Lit.:** Hugo, *Quatre-vingt-treize* [romance]; Flaubert, *La Tentation de St Antoine*; Verlaine, *Romances sans paroles* [poems]. **Music:** Verdi, 'Requiem'; Saint-Saëns, 'Danse macabre' [symphonic poem]; Johann Strauss, 'Die Fledermaus' [operetta]; M.P. Musorgsky [comp] 'Boris Gudunov' [Russ. opera] & 'Pictures in an Exhibition'; B. Smetana, 'My Country' [Czech symphonic poem]. **Art:** 1st Fr. Impressionist Exhibition, Paris [7 more follow: '76, '77, '79, '80, '81, '82, '86]; Corot, 'Gypsy with a Mandolin'; [c.] Whistler, 'Nocturne in Black and Gold: Falling Rocket' [exhib.d, 1877]; Manet, 'River at Argenteuil' [Aberconway Coll.]; Degas, 'Ballet Rehearsal' & 'Two Dancers on the Stage' [Courtauld]; Renoir, 'La Loge (The Opera Box)' [Courtauld]; Sisley, 'Misty Morning'	**P:** G. Eliot Newman James Thomson (aka 'B.V.'; 1834–82) **Pr/F:** Hardy A. Trollope **Dr:** Boucicault Swinburne **Theory/Crit.:** Sir Leslie Stephen	*The Legend of Jubal and Other Poems* *Verses on Various Occasions* [v.1865] *The City of Dreadful Night* [long poem] *Far from the Madding Crowd* [–1875] *The Way We Live Now* *The Shaughraun* *Bothwell, a Tragedy* [*; v.1865, 1881] *Hours in a Library* [2nd & 3rd ser., 1876, 1879]
1875	Disraeli's social reform Acts incl: Public Health [legislates for proper control by local authorities of sanitation & general health] – Artisans' Dwellings [1st public housing legislation] – Sale of Food & Drugs [regulates] – Climbing Boys [chimney sweeps] – Enclosure of Commons; London drainage system completed; agricultural depression in UK; British gvnmt buys Khedive of Egypt's shares in Suez Canal; 3rd Republic constituted in France –	London Medical School for Women fnd.d; Mme Blavatsky fnds Theosophical Society in NY [psychic movement]; Octavia Hill, *Homes of the London Poor*; Taine, *Les Origines de la France contemporaine*; Mary Baker Eddy, *Science and Health with a Key to the Scriptures* [teachings of Xian Science movement]. **Music:** Bizet, 'Carmen' [opera, 1st pf.d]; Piotr Tchaikovsky [comp] 'Swan Lake' [ballet, 1st pf.d 1877]; William Gilbert &	**P:** Morris Gerard Manley Hopkins (1844–89) **Pr/F:** Hardy Meredith Ruskin	*Three Northern Love Stories* [inspired by Icelandic culture] & *The Aeneids of Virgil* [trans] [–1876] 'The Wreck of the Deutschland' [1st major poem wrtn; pub. posthm. by Bridges – v.1918] *The Hand of Ethelberta* *Beauchamp's Career* [–1877] *Mornings in Florence* [essays]

PERIOD	YEAR	INTERNATIONAL AND POLITICAL CONTEXTS	SOCIAL AND CULTURAL CONTEXTS	AUTHORS	INDICATIVE TITLES
		law strengthening army causes crisis with Germany – Anglo-Russ. intervention averts war; Prussia abolishes all RC institutions; German Socialist Labour Party fnd.d [incls Marxists]; Central Parliament estab.d in NZ [new Constitution, 1876]; Universal Postal Union fnd.d in Berne	Arthur Sullivan [comp] 'Trial by Jury' [1st light opera produced by Richard D'Oyly Carte]. **Art:** Manet, 'Grand Canal, Venice'; Morisot, 'Women with a Mirror'; Renoir, 'Portrait of Claude Monet' & 'Victor Choquet'; [–1876] Degas, 'In a Café (The Absinthe Drinker)'; [c.–1877] Cézanne, 'Victor Choquet' [Rothschild Coll.]	Henry James (1843–1916)	*Transatlantic Sketches, A Passionate Pilgrim* [stories] & *Roderick Hudson* [novel]
	1876	Royal Titles Act proclaims Q. Victoria 'Empress of India'; Sandon's Education Act makes schooling compulsory for all children of 5–10 & selectively to 14; [>] university entrance & medical education opened to women; peaceful picketing during strikes legalised; Royal Albert Docks, London, opened; [>] Franco-British dual control of Suez Canal & its finances estab.d; Democrats in USA regain control of S. States – blacks disenfranchised – 'Reconstruction' waning; Colorado becomes 38th State; Battle of Little Big Horn: Sioux defeat US cavalry – 'Custer's Last Stand'; revolts against Ottoman Empire [Turkish rule] in Balkans – 'Bulgarian Atrocities': Xians massacred by Turk. irregulars [Gladstone pubs pamphlet, *The Bulgarian Horrors*] – 'Dreikaiserbund' insists on Turkish reforms; Socialist People's Party fnd.d in Russia	Alexander Graham Bell patents telephone in USA [Co. fnd.d, 1877]; [–1878] Schliemann 1st excavates Mycenae; [–1896] H. Spencer, *Principles of Sociology*. **Int. Lit.:** Twain, *The Adventures of Tom Sawyer*; Stéphane Mallarmé, *L'Après-midi d'un faun* [Fr. 'Symbolist' poem; illustr. by Manet; inspires Debussy's musical 'Prelude']. **Music:** Wagner, 'Siegfried' – his theatre at Bayreuth opens with 1st complete production of 'Ring' cycle; Brahms, 'Symphony No. 1'; Edvard Grieg [compl] 'Peer Gynt' suite [Norw. music based on Ibsen's play]. **Art:** [–1880] Burne-Jones, 'Golden Staircase' [Tate]; Renoir, 'Le Moulin de la Galette', 'The Swing' & 'La Balançoire'; [–1878] Degas, 'The Laundresses' & [c.] 'At the Seaside' [NG]; Sisley, 'Floods at Port-Marly'; Auguste Rodin [sculpt] 'The Age of Bronze' [controversy at Salon, 1877; V&A]	**P:** Bridges Carroll Lear Morris Eliot Oliphant **Theory/Crit:** Stephen	*The Growth of Love* [sonnet sequence] *The Hunting of the Snark* [nonsense poem] [–1877] *Laughable Lyrics* *The Story of Sigurd the Volsung and the Fall of the Nibelungs* [4-vol. epic] *Daniel Deronda* [pub.d in 8 Bks] *Phoebe, junior* [*] *The History of English Thought in the Eighteenth Century*
	1877	[–1878] Irish Nationalist MPs led by Charles Stewart Parnell begin obstructing Commons' business; Prisons Act brings all local prisons under control of Home Office; Rivers Pollution Act; US railway strike – 1st major industrial dispute in USA; conflicts continue in Turkish Balkans – London Protocol of Great Powers demands Turk. reforms – Sultan refuses – Russia invades Turkey – Serbia declares war on Turkey; Britain annexes Transvaal – leads to 1st Boer War [1880–1]; [>] Portugal develops its African colonies; [–1880] Porfirio Díaz, President of Mexico – Columbus statue erected in Mexico City	Gilbert Scott & William Morris fnd Society for the Preservation of Ancient Buildings; Thomas Edison patents the phonograph [gramophone]; All-England Lawn Tennis Championship 1st played at Wimbledon. **Int. Lit.:** Hugo, *L'Histoire d'un crime* & *L'Art d'être grand-père* [poems]; Flaubert, *Trois contes* [stories]; Daudet, *My Brother Jack* [social novel; as *Jack*, 1880]; Zola, *L'Assommoir* [novel about drunkenness]; [c.] Keller, *Züricher Novellen* [Swiss stories]; Ibsen, *The Pillars of Society* [realist social drama]; Turgenev, *Virgin Soil*; Giosuè Carducci, *Odi barbare* [It. poems]; Jens Jacobsen, *Fru Marie Grubbe* [Dan. novel]. **Music:** Brahms, 'Symphony No. 2'. **Art:** Praxiteles' statue of Hermes discv.d at Olympus; [c.] Rossetti, 'Christina Rossetti and her Mother, Frances' [NPG] & 'Proserpina' [Tate]; [–1878] Manet, 'The Road-menders in the Rue de Berne' & 'Nana'; Monet, 'Gare St-Lazare'; Degas, 'At the Seaside' [NG]; Pissarro, 'The Côte des Bœufs at l'Hermitage, near Pontoise' [NG]; Homer, 'The New Novel'; Cézanne enters 16 pictures in 3rd Impressionist Exhibition	**P:** Hopkins **Pr/F:** Arnold James MacDonald Martineau Morris W.H. Mallock (1849–1923) Anna Sewell (1820–78) **Dr:** Arthur Pinero (1855–1934) **Lit. 'Events':**	[wrtn, *inter alia*] 'God's Grandeur', 'Spring', 'The Windhover', 'Pied Beauty', 'Hurrahing in Harvest' [pub. posthm. by Bridges – v.1918] *Last Essays on Church and Religion* *The American* *The Princess and the Curdie* *Autobiography* [pub. posthm.] *To the Working Men of England* [manifesto] *The New Republic: Culture, Faith and Philosophy in an English Country House* [pub. anon. as bk; (1st pub.d in periodical, 1876); part roman à clef, part autobiog.] *Black Beauty, the Autobiography of a Horse* [novel] *£200 a Year* Gerard Manley Hopkins becomes a Jesuit priest
	1878	English wheat prices begin to fall; Factories & Workshops Act extends regulation of hrs &	Cleopatra's Needle brought to Thames Embankment from Alexandria [v.1819]; Lady Margaret Hall,	**P:** Arnold Swinburne	*Selected Poems* ['Golden Treasury' ser.] *Poems and Ballads* [2nd ser.]

MID-VICTORIAN

Year	History	Arts & Culture	Authors	Works
	conditions; Red Flag Act: mechanical road vehicles have max. speed of 4mph & a man with a red flag in front; CID estab.d at New Scotland Yard; attempted assassination of Emperor William I of Germany – laws outlawing Socialists intro.d; Turkey defeated – Russo-Turk. Armistice – European Powers summon Congress of Berlin to resolve Eastern Question/Balkan crisis: Russian gains in Turkey lost – Austria occupies Bosnia-Herzegovenia – Romania & Serbia gain independence – Britain administers Cyprus – some autonomy for Crete – Russ. Slavophiles now engage in terrorism; Zulu territory incorporated in Transvaal – [-1879] Zulu War; [–1880] 2nd Afghan War	Oxford, fnd.d for women; Octavia Hill, *Our Common Land*; Stanley, *Through the Dark Continent*. **Int. Lit.:** Theodore Fontane, *Vor den Sturm* [Ger. realist novel]. **Music:** Brahms, '4th Symphony'; Gilbert & Sullivan, 'HMS Pinafore' [operetta]. **Art:** Whistler's libel action against Ruskin [who criticised him in 1877 for 'flinging a pot of paint in the public's face' awarded 1 farthing damages]; Manet, 'La Servante de Bocks'; [c.] Degas, 'Dancer Lacing her Shoe'; Monet, 'Rue Montorgueil Decked out with Flags'; Sisley, 'Snow at Louveciennes'; Morisot, 'Young Woman Behind a Blind'; [c.] Cézanne, 'Madame Cézanne in a Red Armchair'; [–1880] Rodin, 'John the Baptist' [V&A]. **Lit. 'Events':** Stephen launches *English Men of Letters* ser.; [–1902] Henry Irving, actor-manager of Lyceum Theatre, in partnership with Ellen Terry as leading lady	**Pr/F:** Hardy James Robert Louis Stevenson (1850–94) Richard Jefferies (1848–87) **Theory/Crit:** Walter Bagehot Henry James	*The Return of the Native* [begun 1876; incls 1st map of 'Wessex'] 'Daisy Miller' [story; estabs reputation; dated 1879] & *The Europeans* *An Inland Voyage* [account of canal journey in Belgium/N. France] *The Gamekeeper at Home* [on rural life] *Literary Studies* *French Poets and Novelists*
1879	Gladstone's Midlothian electoral campaign intros mass political rallies; Irish Land League fnd.d with Charles Stewart Parnell as president; City of Glasgow Bank fails – leads to Ltd Liability Act; Bismarck abandons free trade – intros protection; [–1918] Austro-Ger. Dual Alliance; British defeated by Zulus at Isandhlwana – Zulus at Rourke's Drift & Ulundi – peace; Boers in revolt – Transvaal Republic proclaimed; British envoy murdered at Kabul – troops enter Kabul & Kandahar; [–1880] 4 attempts to murder Tsar Alexander II by Russ. extremists; Stanley explores Upper Congo with Belgians & fnds Congo Free State for King Leopold II	*Boy's Own Paper* 1st pub.d; Somerville College, Oxford fnd.d for women; Edison patents the incandescent light bulb [early use of electicity]; [–1928] Sir James Murray edits the Philological Society's *New English Dictionary on Historical Principles* [becomes the *Oxford English Dictionary* (OED)]; Heinrich von Treitschke, *History of Germany in the 19th Century*. **Int. Lit.:** [–1880] Dostoevsky, *The Brothers Karamazov*; Ibsen, *A Doll's House*; August Strindberg, *The Red Room* [Swed. satirical novel]; Gabriele d'Annunzio, *Primo vere* [It. poems]. **Music:** Tchaikovsky, 'Eugene Onegin' [opera]; Gilbert & Sullivan, 'The Pirates of Penzance' [light opera]. **Art:** [c.] Renoir, 'The Skiff' [Abberconway Coll.]; Degas, 'Duranty' [portrait; Glasgow AG]; Cézanne, 'Three Bathers'; Sir Hubert von Herkomer [pnt] 'John Ruskin' [NPG]; Mary Cassatt [pnt] 'The Cup of Tea'	**P:** Browning William Barnes (1801–86) **Pr/F:** Arnold Eliot Jefferies Meredith Stevenson **Lit. 'Events':**	*Dramatic Idyls* *Poems of Rural Life in the Dorset Dialect* *Mixed Essays* & ed. [with intro.] *Poems of Wordsworth* *The Impressions of Theophrastus Such* [coll. misc. essays] *The Amateur Poacher & Wild Life in a Southern County* *The Egoist* *Travels with a Donkey in the Cévennes* 1st Shakespeare Memorial Theatre opens in Stratford-upon-Avon [v.1926 & 1932]; Andrew Lang & Samuel Butcher, prose trans of Homer's *Odyssey*
1880	Disraeli loses Gen. Elec. – Gladstone, PM; Charles Bradlaugh elected MP for Northampton – as atheist, refused to take oath – expelled from Commons [–1886, re-elected regularly; takes seat in 1886]; Mundella's Education Act makes elementary schooling compulsory to 13; University of London admits women for degrees; Employers Liability Act: compensation for injured workers from negligent employers; Irish National Land League policy of 'boycotting' [rents] begins; 'Kulturkampf' relaxed in Germany; [–1881] 1st Anglo-Boer War in SA – British routed at Majuba – Transvaal declared independent; France annexes Tahiti	Wood-pulp used to produce cheap paper; London Telephone Co. issues 1st directory [c.250 names]; Manchester University, Regent St Polytechnic & Guildhall School of Music fnd.d. **Int. Lit.:** Twain, *A Tramp Abroad*; Joel Chandler Harris, *Uncle Remus: His Songs and Sayings* [US stories: Brer Rabbit, Brer Fox, et al]; Lew Wallace, *Ben Hur* [US historical novel]; Zola, *Nana*; Guy de Maupassant, 'Boule de suif' [Fr. story]; 'Pierre Loti', *Rarahu* [as *Le Mariage de Loti*, 1882 – love-story set in Tahiti]; Jens Jacobsen, *Neils Lhyne* [Dan. novel]. **Music:** Tchaikovsky '1812 Overture' & 'Italian Capriccio' [tone poem]. **Art:** Poynter, 'A Visit to Aesculapius' [Tate]; Pissarro, 'La Mère Larchevêque'; Renoir, 'Mont St-Victoire'; [c.–1881] Degas [sculpt.] 'Little Dancer Aged Fourteen'; Paul Gauguin [pnt] 'Nursemaid'; [–1917] Rodin, 'Gate of Hell' [huge project composed of individual sculptures – e.g. 'The Thinker' [Burrell Coll.]	**P:** Arnold Browning Tennyson **Pr/F:** Disraeli Hardy Jefferies Ouida Ruskin George Gissing (1857–1903) **Dr:** Pinero **Theory/Crit:** Arnold Emile Zola **Lit. 'Events':**	[ed. & intro.] *Poems of Byron* *Dramatic Idyls* (2nd ser.) *Ballads and Other Poems* *Endymion* *The Trumpet-Major* *Hodge and His Masters* *Moths* *A Joy for Ever* [1857 lectures on 'The Political Economy of Art'] *Workers in the Dawn* [novel] *The Money-Spinner* 'The Study of Poetry' [essay] *The Experimental Novel* George Eliot dies

LATE
VICTORIAN 1876–1880

Period	Year	International and Political Contexts	Social and Cultural Contexts	Authors	Indicative Titles
	1881	Disraeli dies – Earl of Salisbury, Cons. leader; Royal Commission on agricultural depression reports; H.M. Hyndman estabs Social Democratic Federation (SDF); Gladstone's 2nd Irish Land Act gives tenant farmers greater rights – courts to set fair rents – Parnell rejects it – Habeas Corpus suspended in Ireland – Ir. MPs again obstruct Commons business – Parnell imprisoned in Kilmainham gaol [released 1882]; flogging abolished in British Army & Navy; Fr.-British intervention against Turkey secures Thessaly & Epirus for Greece; US Pres. Garfield shot & later dies; Tsar Alexander II of Russia assassinated – Alexander III succeeds; Boers defeat British forces at Laing's Neck & Majuba Hill – Britain concedes independence to Transvaal republic [under British suzerainty]; Egyptian revolt under Arabi Pasha; Stanley fnds Leopoldville in Belgian Congo; [–1889] de Lesseps & Eiffel attempt to build Panama Canal [ends in bankruptcy]	Rev.d version of New Testament; George Newnes fnds *Tit-Bits* [popular magazine]; Natural History Museum, Kensington, opens; [c.] mosquitoes discv.d to carry malaria; [c.] pedal & chain bicycle invented; [–1888] Leopold von Ranke, *Weltgeschichte* ['history of the world']. **Int. Lit.:** Flaubert, *Bouvard et Pécuchet* [pub.d posthm.]; Maupassant, 'La Maison Tellier'; Ibsen, *Ghosts* [drama]. Anatole France, *Le Crime de Sylvestre Bonnard* [Fr. novel]. **Music:** D'Oyly Carte opens Savoy Theatre [1st to have electric lighting] with Gilbert & Sullivan's 'Patience' [light opera]; Boston Symphony Orchestra fnd.d; Offenbach, 'Tales of Hoffman' [pf.d posthm.]. **Art:** Millais, 'Benjamin Disraeli' [NPG]; [–1882] Manet, 'Bar at the Folies-Bergère' [Courtauld] & 'Spring: Jeanne de Marsy'; Monet, 'Sunshine and Snow, Lavacourt' [NG]; Renoir, 'Boating Party'	**P:** C. Rossetti D.G. Rossetti Oscar Wilde (1854–1900) **Pr/F:** Hardy James Jefferies Stevenson Talbot Baines Reed (1852–93) 'Mark Rutherford' (William Hale White; 1831–1913) **Dr:** Pinero Swinburne Lit. **'Events':**	*A Pageant and Other Poems* *Ballads and Sonnets* [incls 'The House of Life' sonnet sequence] *Poems* *A Laodicean* *The Portrait of a Lady* *Wood Magic* 'Thrawn Janet' [story in *Cornhill* & *Virginibus Puerisque* [essays] *The Fifth Form at St Dominic's* [1st pub.d in *Boy's Own Paper*] *The Autobiography of Mark Rutherford: Dissenting Minister* [novel] *The Squire* *Mary Stuart* [*: v. 1865, 1874] Thomas Carlyle dies; Benjamin Jowett trans works of Thucydides
	1882	2nd Married Women's Property Act [England & Wales] – right to separate ownership of property; Extension of Allotments Act [parish lands can be let as such]; Conservative Primrose League fnd.d [Q. Victoria had sent a primrose to Disraeli's funeral]; Ir. 'No Rent' manifesto pub.d; Phoenix Park murders of Cavendish & Burke [under-secretaries for Ireland] in Dublin – further repression ensues; British fleet bombards Alexandria – Arabi Pasha defeated at Tel-el-Kabir – [–1914] British occupy Egypt & Sudan & estab. Protectorate; [–1914] Triple Alliance of Italy, Germany & Austria; Italy estabs colony of Eritrea; Lord Ripon grants freedom of press in India	Darwin dies; Q. Victoria gives Epping Forest to the nation; Selwyn College, Cambridge & UC Liverpool [University, 1903] fnd.d; 3rd Eddystone lighthouse built; the 'Ashes' 1st feature in Anglo-Australian cricket; [–1891] Stephen 1st editor of *Dictionary of National Biography* – begins publication; Nietzsche, *The Joyous Science*. **Int. Lit.:** Fontane, *L'Adultera* [Ger. realist novel]; Ibsen, *An Enemy of the People*; Henry Becque, *Les Corbeaux* [Fr. naturalist social drama]. **Music:** Berlin Philharmonic Orchestra fnd.d; Gounod, 'The Redemption' [oratorio, pf.d at Birmingham Festival]; Wagner, 'Parsifal' [opera]; Gilbert & Sullivan, 'Iolanthe' [opera]. **Art:** J.K. Huysmans, *Art Moderne* [on Impressionist painting]; Manet, 'Autumn: Méry'; Monet, 'Fishermen's Nets at Pourville'; [–1883] Degas, 'Milliners'; Napoleon Sarony, 'Oscar Wilde' [photo; NPG]. Lit. **'Events':** D.G. Rossetti & Anthony Trollope die. **Theory/Crit:** George Saintsbury, *A Short History of French Literature*	**P:** Swinburne **Pr/F:** Arnold Hardy Jefferies Stevenson 'F. Anstey' (Thomas Anstey Guthrie; 1856–1934) Sir Walter Besant (1836–1901) G.[eorge] B.[ernard] Shaw (1856–1950) **Dr:** H.[enry] A.[rthur] Jones (1851–1929)	*Tristram of Lyonesse* [medieval romance in verse] *Irish Essays* *Two on a Tower* *Bevis: The Story of a Boy* [autobiog. novel] *The New Arabian Nghts & Familiar Studies of Men and Books* [essays] *Vice Versa* [humorous fantasy novel] *All Sorts and Conditions of Men* [social novel] *Cashel Byron's Profession* [novel] *The Silver King* [realist social drama]
LATE VICTORIAN	1883	World economic depression; Corrupt & Illegal Practices Act reforms electioneering; Railway Act intros linked signals & points system; SDF [v. 1881] pubs 1st Socialist pamphlet; [–1884] Fabian Society fnd.d [to promote Socialism]; Q. Victoria fnds Royal Red Cross Order; the Mahdi's rebellion in Sudan British/Egyptian forces routed – Sudan evacuated; Ger. protectorate declared over part of W. African coast; Ripon seeks equality for British & Indian magistrates; Paul Kruger elected President of	Karl Marx dies; parcel post begins in Britain; [–1890] Forth (Rail) Bridge built; Cardiff University fnd.d; Boys' Brigade fnd.d in Glasgow; Sir John Seeley, *The Expansion of England* [history]; Andrew Mearns, *The Bitter Cry of Outcast London*; [–1893] Nietzsche, *Thus Spake Zarathustra*. **Int. Lit.:** Maupassant, *Une Vie* [novel]; Emile Verhaeren, *Les Flammandes* [Belg. poems]. **Music:** Royal College of Music fnd.d; Metropolitan Opera House, NY, opens; Brahms, 'Symphony No. 3'; Dvořák, 'Stabat Mater' [1st pf.d,	**P:** Edward Carpenter (1844–1929) **Pr/F:** Jefferies Stevenson George Moore (1852–1933) Olive Schreiner (1855–1920)	[–1888] *Towards Democracy* [long poem] *The Story of My Heart* [autobiog.] *Treasure Island* *A Modern Lover* [naturalist novel] *The Story of an African Farm* [novel; 1st pub.d as by 'Ralph Iron']

1884

Transvaal Republic [& in '88, '93, '98]; [c.>] Greenwich 'Mean Time' generally accepted; Brooklyn Bridge, NY, opens

3rd Reform Act enfranchises many rural inhabitants – achieves almost universal male suffrage; Royal Commission on Technical Instruction reports; Royal Commission on housing of the working classes set up; William Morris leaves SDF & [–1885] fnds Socialist League; Co-operative Women's Guild fnd.d; Ger. left-wing hostility to Bismarck grows; [>] European Powers begin 'Scramble for Africa': Berlin Conference oversees its partition – agrees to 'Congo Free State' with Leopold II of Belgium as its independent king [estab.d 1885] – Germany annexes part of SW Africa, Togoland, Cameroons & N. New Guinea – Britain acquires Somaliland, Nigeria & rest of New Guinea – Cecil Rhodes annexes Bechuanaland [later Rhodesia]; Mahdi takes Omdurman – Gen. Gordon sent to relieve besieged garrison in Khartoum – trapped; Convention of London restores Transvaal's autonomy; USA gains Pearl Harbour, Hawaii, as Pacific naval base

London]; Emmanuel Chabrier [comp] 'España' [orchestral rhapsody]. **Art:** Monet, 'Rough Sea, Etretat'; Pissarro, 'River Banks, Rouen' [Courtauld]; [–1887] Cézanne, 'Blue Vase'; [–1884 & 1887] Georges Seurat [pnt] 'Bathing at Asnières' ['Pointillism'; NG]

[c.] Maxim machine gun invented; 1st deep underground railway begun in London; rev.d version of Old Testament; 1st part [A-Ant] of Murray's OED pub.d; UC Bangor fnd.d; George Eastman makes photographic roll-film. **Int. Lit.:** [–1885] Twain, The Adventures of Huckleberry Finn; Daudet, Sapho [novel]; Huysmans, A rebours [novel]; Maupassant, 'The Necklace'; Jean Moréas, Les Syrtes [Fr. 'Symbolist' poems]; Ibsen, The Wild Duck. **Music:** Gilbert & Sullivan, 'Princess Ida'; Anton Bruckner [comp] '7th Symphony'. **Art:** Antonio Gaudi begins Sagrada Familia Church, Barcelona [d.1926; still unfinished]; Fabergé makes 1st jewelled Easter egg for Tsar Alexander III; Burne-Jones, 'King Cophetua and the Beggar Maid' [Tate]; [c.] Renoir, 'Les Parapluies' [NG]; [–1886] Seurat, 'Sunday Afternoon on the Island of the Grande Jatte'; [–1886] Rodin, 'Burghers of Calais' [erected, 1895]; Sargent, 'Mme Gautreau (Madame X)'

Lit. 'Events':
[–1884] Sir Walter Besant fnds Society of Authors & its journal, The Author

Pr/F: Braddon — Ishmael
Gissing — The Unclassed
Ruskin — The Old Road [lectures & essays] & 'The Storm-Cloud of the Nineteenth Century' [lecture]
Dr: Jones — Saints and Sinners
Pinero — The Profligate
Theory/Crit: James — 'On the Art of Fiction' [essay]
Paul Verlaine — Poètes maudits [critical studies]

1885

Gladstone resigns over budget – Lord Salisbury briefly PM; office of Sec. of State for Scotland created; Redistribution Act intros modern pattern of single-member constituencies for Commons; W.T. Stead, editor of Pall Mall Gazette, exposes extent of child prostitution in article, 'The Maiden Tribute of Modern Babylon' – leads to Criminal Amendment Act – age of sexual consent raised to 16; Socialist League 'Free Speech' demonstration in London; Mahdi takes Khartoum – Gen. Gordon & troops killed; Anglo-Russ. crisis over Afghan border – resolved; Berlin Conference continues: Bechuanaland becomes a British protectorate – French extend influence along Senegal River – Germany annexes Zanzibar & Tanganyika – the 3 powers agree on spheres of influence in Pacific; treaty of friendship between Germany & SA Republic (Transvaal); 2nd Métis insurrection in Canada (v.1869) – leader, Louis Riel, hanged; Indian National Congress fnd.d; 3rd Burmese War begins

The Rover Co. market safety bicycle [chain-drive to back-wheel]; Gottlieb Daimler invents internal combustion engine [builds 4-wheel motor car, 1887] & Karl Benz builds his 1st petrol-driven car. **Int. Lit.:** Zola, Germinal ['Naturalist' novel of Fr. mine-workers]; Maupassant, Bel-Ami [novel]; Daudet, Tartarin sur les Alpes; Becque, La Parisienne [novel]; A. France, Le Livre de mon ami [portrays childhood happiness]. **Music:** Brahms, 'Symphony No. 4' (in E minor]; Gilbert & Sullivan, 'The Mikado'. **Art:** Watts, 'Mammon' [Tate]; [–1886] Renoir, 'Mother and Child'; [c.] Cézanne, 'L'Estaque' & [–1887] 'Mont St Victoire' [Courtauld]; Degas, 'Woman Bathing'; [–1887] Gauguin, 'Landscape, Pont-Aven'; Vincent Van Gogh [pnt] 'Potato Eaters'
Lit. 'Events': [–1888] Sir R. Burton trans Arabian Nights [16 vols]; Jowett trans Aristotle, Politics; [–1890] Morris finances & edits Commonweal for Socialist League

P: Arnold — Poems [3-vol. coll. 'library' edtn]
Morris — The Pilgrims of Hope [long poem pub.d in Commonweal]
Stevenson — A Child's Garden of Verses
Tennyson — Tiresias and Other Poems
Pr/F: Jefferies — After London, or Wild England
Meredith — Diana of the Crossways
Moore — A Mummer's Wife
Ruskin — [–1889] Praeterita [unfinished autobiog. pub.d in monthly parts]
Rutherford — Mark Rutherford's Deliverance [2nd Pt of Autobiography]
Sir [T.H.] Hall Caine (1853–1931) — The Shadow of a Crime [popular novel]
Walter Pater (1839–94) — Marius the Epicurean [phil. romance]
Sir Henry Rider Haggard (1856–1925) — King Solomon's Mines [popular novel]
Dr: Pinero — The Magistrate

1886

Salisbury falls – Gladstone, PM – intros 1st Irish Home Rule Bill – Liberal Party splits into Liberals & Unionists – defeated – Gladstone resigns – Tory victory in Gen. Elec. – Salisbury, PM [–1892];

St Hughes Coll, Oxford, [for women] fnd.d; Colonial & India Exhibition at S. Kensington; [c.] Olympia, Hammersmith, erected; English Historical Review 1st pub.d; Huxley, Science and Morals; Froude, Oceana

P: Tennyson — Locksley Hall, Sixty Years After
Rudyard Kipling (1865–1936) — Departmental Ditties [satirical verses of Anglo-India]
Pr/F: Besant — Children of Gibeon

Period	Year	International and Political Contexts	Social and Cultural Contexts	Authors	Indicative Titles
		political radicals demonstrate in Pall Mall & Trafalgar Square against gvnmt policies; Tilbury Docks open for Eastern trade; Socialist-driven strikes in Belgium suppressed by troops; Georges Boulanger popular Minister of War in France; Greece forced to keep peace with Turkey by Allied blockade; Statue of Liberty, gift to USA by France, unveiled & dedicated on Bedloe's Island, NY; Zanzibar under British protection; Anglo-Ger. agreement over E. Africa; gold discv.d in Transvaal – influx of 'Uitlanders' [immigrants] – Kruger refuses them the franchise [helps to provoke Boer War – v.1899] – growth of Johannesburg; Upper Burma annexed – Burma absorbed into British India; 1st meeting of Indian National Congress	[travel in Australasia]; Nietzsche, *Beyond Good and Evil*. **Int. Lit.:** Alcott, *Jo's Boys*; Frances Hodgson Burnett, *Little Lord Fauntleroy* [US novel]; Loti, *Pêcheur d'Islande* [novel]; Rimbaud, *Les Illuminations* [pub.d]; Ibsen, *Rosmersholm*. **Music:** Saint-Saëns, 'La Carnival des animaux'. **Art:** New English Art Club (NEAC) fnd.d by Whistler, Steer & Sickert; last Impressionist Exhibition – [>] Post-Impressionism begins to develop; Millais, 'Bubbles' [owned by Pears Soap & used in famous advert]; Watts, 'Hope' [Tate]; Degas, 'The Tub'; Homer, 'Eight Bells'; Gauguin, 'Breton Seascape'; Van Gogh, 'Le Moulin de la Galette, Montmartre' [Glasgow AG] & [–1887] 'Fishing in Spring'; Rodin, 'The Kiss'	Gissing Hardy James Oliphant Stevenson 'Marie Corelli' (Mary Mackay; 1855–1924) **Theory/Crit:** Andrew Lang	*Demos: A Story of English Socialism & Isobel Clarendon* *The Mayor of Casterbridge* *The Princess Casamassima & The Bostonians* *Effie Ogilvie* *Kidnapped & The Strange Case of Dr Jekyll and Mr Hyde* *A Romance of Two Worlds* [popular novel] *Books and Bookmen & Letters to Dead Authors* [essays]
	1887	Q. Victoria's Golden Jubilee – ends retirement at Windsor [v.1861] – opens People's Palace [for popular recreation]; 'Bloody Sunday' demonstration supporting striking miners in Trafalgar Square [incls Morris's Socialist League] – brutally suppressed by police; Parnell falsely accused of complicity in Phoenix Park murders [v.1882] – cleared but damaged, 1889; Coal Mines Regulation Act prohibits boys under 13 underground or under 12 at surface; Allotments Act empowers local authorities to acquire land for such compulsorily; Ger. Reichstag dissolved – Bismarck has majority in new one; 1st Colonial Conference held in London; Triple Alliance renewed – 'Dreikaiserbund' ends; [–1888] Russia disallowed from raising loans in Berlin – France advances 350 m. francs; Baluchistan [incl. Quetta] united with British India	[–1889] Eiffel Tower erected in Paris; L.L. Zamenhof invents 'Esperanto' [international lang.]; [–1888] Heinrich Hertz identifies electro-magnetic waves; Carpenter, *England's Ideal*; Nietzsche, *On the Genealogy of Morals*. **Int. Lit.:** Zola, *La Terre* [as bk – serial 1886; 'naturalist' novel of Fr. peasants]; Strindberg, *The People of Hemsö* [novel] & *The Father* [drama]; Hermann Sudermann, *Frau Sorge* [Ger. realist novel]. **Music:** Verdi, 'Othello' [opera]; Claude Debussy [comp] 'Le Printemps' [symphonic suite]; Sir John Stainer [comp] 'The Crucifixion' [oratorio]. **Art:** Gauguin, 'Martinique Landscape'; Renoir, 'Les Grandes Baigneuses' [begun 1884]; [c.] Cézanne, 'Aix: Paysage rocheux' [Tate]; Van Gogh, 'The Yellow Books, Parisian Novels'; Seurat, 'Café-concert' & [–1888] 'The Parade'	**P:** Morris **Pr/F:** Corelli Gissing Hall Caine Hardy Rider Haggard Rutherford Sir Arthur Conan Doyle (1859–1930) Margaret Harkness (1854–1920; as 'John Law') **Lit. 'Events':**	*Homer's Odyssey* [trans] *Thelma* *Thyrza* *The Deemster* [b-s. novel] *The Woodlanders* [bk; serial, 1886–7] *She & Allan Quatermain* *The Revolution in Tanner's Lane* 'A Study in Scarlet' [1st Sherlock Holmes story; but v.1891] *A City Girl: A Realistic Story* [novel] International Copyright Act passed; [–1897] Sir Herbert Beerbohm Tree manages Haymarket Theatre
	1888	James Keir Hardie, 1st ever 'Labour' candidate, defeated at Mid-Lanark; Local Government Act: elected County Councils take over administrative duties of JPs; Miners Federation of GB formed – demands minimum wage; 'London Matchgirls' Strike [of Bryant & May women match makers]; Scottish Labour Party fnd.d; London General Omnibus Co. fnd.d; 'Jack the Ripper' murders 6 women in Whitechapel; London's E. End; [–1889] Boulanger's popularity supported by monarchists threatens 3rd Republic in France; Kaiser Wilhelm II becomes Emperor of Germany; [–1889] Convention of Constantinople declares Suez Canal open to all ships & free of blockade; British E. Africa Co. fnd.d with Royal Charter – controls Kenya; Cecil Rhodes gains monopoly of SA mineral rights [incls diamonds & gold]; Sarawak, N. Borneo & Brunei	[–1889] John Dunlop manufactures 1st pneumatic tyres; Institut Pasteur fnd.d in Paris; Eastman invents 'Kodak' box camera [Eastman Kodak Co fnd.d, 1892]; Emile Berliner invents flat disc gramophone record; Havelock Ellis, *Women and Marriage*; Charles Doughty, *Travels in Arabia Deserta*; Nietzsche, *Ecce Homo* [autobiog. completed; pub. 1908]; [–1896] Goncourt Brothers, *Journals* pub.d [9 vols]. **Int. Lit.:** Edward Bellamy, *Looking Backward* [US Utopian romance]; Strindberg, *Miss Julie* [play]; Iannis Psichari, *My Journey* [in modern demotic Greek]. **Music:** Rimsky-Korsakov, 'Capriccio Espagnol', 'Easter Festival' & 'Scheherazade' [symphonic suites]; Tchaikovsky, '5th Symphony'; Gilbert & Sullivan, 'The Yeomen of the Guard'. **Art:** 1st exhibition of Arts & Crafts Movement, London; Leighton, 'Captive Andromache' [MAG]; Pissarro,	**P:** W.E. Henley (1849–1903) **Pr/F:** Gissing Hardy Harkness Kipling Moore Morris Stevenson Wilde Constance Howell (c.1860–1910)	*A Book of Verses* *A Life's Morning* *Wessex Tales* [stories; 2 vols] *Out of Work* *Plain Tales from the Hills & Soldiers Three* [stories of India] *Confessions of a Young Man* [autobiog.] *A Dream of John Ball* [prose romance; 1st serialised in *Commonweal*, 1886–7] *The Black Arrow* *The Happy Prince and Other Stories* [fairy-tales] *The Excellent Way* [novel]

[1888]

Works:
Robert Elsmere [popular religious romance]

Essays in Criticism [2nd ser.; coll. & pub. posthm.]

'The Profitable Reading of Fiction' [essay]

Matthew Arnold dies; W.B. Yeats edits & contributes to Fairy and Folk Tales of the Irish Peasantry

Authors:
Mrs Humphrey Ward (1851–1920)
Theory/Crit: Arnold
Hardy
Lit. 'Events':

Arts:
'L'Île Lacroix, Rouen'; Degas, 'After the Bath'; Cézanne, 'Mardi Gras'; Gauguin, 'Vision after the Sermon or Jacob Wrestling with the Angel' [SNG] & 'Van Gogh Painting Sunflowers'; [–1889] Van Gogh's most prolific period [incls: 'Sunflowers', 'Cornfield', 'Drawbridge at Arles', 'Café at Evening', 'Madame Ginoux (La Arlésienne)']; Henri Toulouse-Lautrec [pnt] 'Bare-Back Rider at the Circus Fernando'; John Singer Sargent [pnt] 'Claude Monet Painting at the Edge of a Wood' [Tate]

Political:
become British protectorates – also [–1894] Kenya, Uganda & Zanzibar

1889

[>] 'New Unionism': growth of unskilled workers' unions [e.g. dockers & transport workers] – 'Great London Dock Strike': the 'Dockers' Tanner' – Gas Workers Union fnd.d – gas strike wins 8-hr day; Board of Agriculture becomes full ministerial gvnmt department; Technical Education Act: Councils can levy 1d. rate to provide technical & manual instruction; Act to prevent cruelty to children; Naval Defence Act; [Mrs] Emmeline Pankhurst fnds the Women's Franchise League; London County Council formed; '2nd International' fnd.d; Boulanger prosecuted – flees France; N. & S. Dakota, Montana & Washington become 39th, 40th, 41st + 42nd States respectively; Royal Charter for British S. Africa Co. to conquer Mashonaland & develop mining in region [–1896, Rhodes, director]; Ethiopia becomes It. protectorate; Anglo-Portug. crisis over boundaries in Zambesi Valley; Eiffel Tower completed for World Exhibition in Paris; [c.] 1st skyscraper built in Chicago [13 storeys]

Carpenter, Civilisation: Its Cause and Cure; Charles Booth, East London [1st vol. of Life and Labour of the People of London (–1902/3), 17 vols]; Henri Bergson, Time and Freewill [Fr. phil.]; Bertha von Suttner, Lay Down Your Arms [Ger. pacifist work]. Int. Lit.: Twain, A Connecticut Yankee in King Arthur's Court; Tolstoy, The Kreutzer Sonata; Strindberg, The Creditors [play]; Gerhart Hauptmann, Vor Sonnenaufgang [Ger. realist social drama]. Music: 'Keep the Red Flag Flying High' wrtn for Dockers strike [v. preceding column]; Gilbert & Sullivan, 'The Gondoliers'; Tchaikovsky, 'The Sleeping Beauty' [ballet]; R. Strauss, 'Death and Transfiguration' [symphonic poem]. Art: [–1890] Seurat, 'Woman Powdering Herself' [Courtauld]; Van Gogh, 'Self-Portrait with a Severed Ear' & 'Yellow Cornstalks with Cypress Trees' [both Courtauld], 'Starry Night', 'Old Willow Trees' [Lefevre Coll.], 'Field of Irises' & 'Vincent's Room'; Gauguin, 'Yellow Christ'; Toulouse-Lautrec, 'Ball at the Moulin de la Galette'

P: Browning
W.[illiam] B.[utler] Yeats (1865–1939)
Pr/F: Conan Doyle
Gissing
Stevenson
Sir James Barrie (1860–1937)
Jerome K. Jerome (1859–1927)
'Somerville & Ross' (Edith Somerville 1858–1949 & Violet Martin 1865–1915)
Dr: Pinero
Lit. 'Events':

Asolando
The Wanderings of Oisin and Other Poems
The Sign of Four [Sherlock Holmes novel]
The Nether World
The Master of Ballantrae
A Window in Thrums [autobiog. novel]
Idle Thoughts of an Idle Fellow & Three Men in a Boat [comic novel]
An Irish Cousin [novel]

The Profligate
Robert Browning, G.M. Hopkins & Wilkie Collins die; [>] Shaw edits Fabian Essays; [>] William Archer trans. Ibsen's plays – 1st Eng. production of A Doll's House

1890

O'Shea divorce case ends Parnell's career as leader of Irish Nationalist party [dies 1891]; all Eng. elementary education to be free; London omnibus strike settled by 12-hr-day agreement; Housing of the Working Classes Act begins slum clearance; Lunacy Act: visiting committees to manage asylums; financial panic in London & Paris; Bismarck falls from power – [>] personal rule of Kaiser Wilhelm II; Idaho & Wyoming become 43rd & 44th States; Treaty of Busah improves Fr./British relations in W. Africa – Anglo-Portug. Agreement on Congo & Zambesi – Tanganyika a Ger. protectorate – Anglo-Ger. Convention: Britain exchanges Heligoland for Zanzibar & Pemba; W. Australia granted responsible gvnmt; Rhodes, PM of Cape Colony – seeks federal dominion of Southern Africa

1st underground railway opens [City & S. London line; v.1863]; Sidney Webb, Socialism in England; [–1915] Sir James Frazer, The Golden Bough: A Study in Comparative Religion [12 vols; anthropology]; William James [H. James's brother], Principles of Psychology; H.M Stanley, In Darkest Africa; William Booth, In Darkest England and the Way Out. Int. Lit.: Emily Dickinson, Poems [US; posthm.; & 1891, 1896]; Zola, La Bête humaine; Ibsen, Hedda Gabler; Stefan George, Hymnen [Ger. poems]; Knut Hamsun, Hunger [Norw. novel]. Music: Tchaikovsky, 'Queen of Spades' [opera]; Borodin, 'Prince Igor' [opera; posthm.]; Pietro Mascagni, 'Cavalleria Rusticana' [It. operal. Art: Whistler, The Gentle Art of Making Enemies [re. 1878 libel case against Ruskin]; [–1891] Monet, 'Haystacks' ser.; Renoir, 'Gabrielle Reading'; [c.] Degas, 'The Bath'; [–1892] Cézanne, 'Card Players' [Courtauld], [–1894] 'Still Life with Basket of Fruit', [–1895] 'Boy in the Red Waistcoat' & [c.] 'Dish with Apples'; Gauguin, 'Portrait of a Woman with a

P: Sir William Watson (1858–1935)
Pr/F: Gissing
Hall Caine
Harkness ('John Law')
James
Morris
Oliphant
Rutherford
Wilde
Theory/Crit: Hardy
Lit. 'Events':

Wordsworth's Grave
The Emancipated
The Bondman
A Manchester Shirtmaker
The Tragic Muse
News from Nowhere [Utopian romance; 1st serialised in Commonweal & as book, USA; 1st Eng. edtn, 1891, Kelmscott Press edtn, 1892]
Kirsteen
Miriam's Schooling
The Picture of Dorian Gray [in magazine; bk, 1891]
'Candour in English Fiction' [essay]
William Morris fnds Kelmscott Press – 1st book his The Story of the Glittering Plain, 1891

PERIOD	YEAR	INTERNATIONAL AND POLITICAL CONTEXTS	SOCIAL AND CULTURAL CONTEXTS	AUTHORS	INDICATIVE TITLES
			Cézanne Still Life'; [–1891] Seurat, 'Circus'; Van Gogh, 'At the Foot of the Alpilles', 'Church at Auvers' & 'Cornfield with Crows'; Toulouse-Lautrec, 'Dance at the Moulin Rouge'; [c.] Aubrey Beardsley, 'Isolde' [coloured drawing]		
	1891	Gladstone endorses National Liberal Federation programme of widespread social & political reforms; Factory Act: no child under 11 to work in factories; free primary education in England; Small Holdings Act: County Councils can buy land to let as such; Brooklands Agreement estabs wage negotiations in cotton industry; [c.] Ferranti builds Deptford power station to supply electricity for London; Franco-Russ. Entente; Triple Alliance renewed to 1902; Anglo-It. agreement on NE. Africa; British S. Africa Co. charter extended N. of Zambesi – Nyasaland becomes a British protectorate; Young Turk Movement fnd.d for liberal reforms; [–1893] widespread famine in Russia; [–1915] trans-Siberian Railway built	[c.] ILP newspaper, *The Clarion*, pub.d; Newnes fnds *The Strand Magazine*; Beatrice Webb, *The Co-operative Movement in Great Britain*. **Int. Lit.:** Huysmans, *Là-bas* ['decadent' novel]; Hauptmann, *Einsame Menschen* [novel]; Franck Wedekind, *Frühlings Erwachen* [Ger. drama; pf.d 1906]; Selma Lagerlöf, *Gösta Berlings saga* [Swed. novel]. **Music:** Tchaikovsky, 'The Nutcracker Suite' [ballet]. **Art:** Leighton, 'Return of Proserpina' [Leeds AG]; [–1892] Monet, 'Poplars' series ['Poplars on the Epte'; Tate]; Cassatt, 'Young Women Picking Fruit', 'The Toilet' & [c.] 'The Bath' [coloured etching influenced by Jap. prints]; Toulouse-Lautrec, 'Moulin-Rouge: La Goulue' [poster]; Gauguin [–1893, in Tahiti], 'Two Women on the Beach' & 'Vahine no te Tiare (Woman with a Gardenia)'; Philip Wilson Steer [pnt] 'Mrs Cyprian Williams and Her Daughters' [Tate]. **Lit. 'Events':** Yeats, Ernest Dowson & Lionel Johnson form 'The Rhymers' Club'; [–1892] Yeats fnds Ir. Literary Society; 1st British Actors' Association fnd.d	**P:** Morris **Pr/F:** Barrie Conan Doyle Gissing Hardy Harkness ('John Law') Kipling Wilde Ménie Muriel Dowie (1867–1945) **Dr:** Jones **Theory/Crit:** Hardy Shaw	*Poems by the Way* *The Little Minister* [novel; popular drama, 1897] [>] *The Adventures of Sherlock Holmes* [stories pub.d in Strand Magazine & later coll. as vols] *New Grub Street* *Tess of the d'Urbervilles* & *A Group of Noble Dames* [stories] *In Darkest London* [1st pub.d as *Captain Lobe*, 1889] *The Light that Failed* [in magazine] *Lord Arthur Savile's Crime and Other Stories* *A Girl in the Karpathians* [travel] *The Dancing Girl* 'The Science of Fiction' [essay] *The Quintessence of Ibsenism*
	1892	Salisbury resigns – Gladstone, PM for 4th time; Keir Hardie, 1st elected 'Labour' (ILP) MP [for West Ham S.]; Blackwall Tunnel, London, begun; Franco-Russ. military convention; anarchist attacks in Paris; Brit. S. Africa Co. takes over N. Rhodesia; Anglo-Ger. agreement on Cameroons; gold discv.d in W. Australia	**Int. Lit.:** Whittier, *At Sundown* [US poems]; Zola, *La Débâcle* [novel about 1870]; Ibsen, *The Master Builder*; Hauptmann, *Die Weber* [play about weavers' revolt]; Paul Claudel, *L'Annonce fait à Marie* [Fr. play]; Hugo von Hoffmansthal, *Der Tod der Tizian* [Austr. 'lyrical drama']; Maurice Maeterlinck, *Pelléas et Mélisande* [Belg. play]. **Music:** Ruggiero Leoncavallo [comp] 'I Pagliacci' [It. opera]. **Art:** [–1894] Monet, 'Rouen Cathedral' ser. [20 exhibited, 1895]; Renoir, 'Young Girls at the Piano'; Gauguin, 'Manao Tupapau (The Spirit of the Dead is Watching)'; Toulouse-Lautrec, 'Jeanne Avril Dancing', 'Jeanne Avril Leaving the Moulin Rouge', 'Aristide Bruant dans son cabaret' [poster], 'At the Moulin Rouge' & 'Englishman at the Moulin Rouge' [litho.]; Rodin, 'Orpheus'; Wilson Steer, 'Sands of Boulogne' [Tate]; Edvard Munch [pnt] 'Karl Johans Gate'	**P:** Henley Kipling Yeats **Pr/F:** Gissing George Grossmith (1847–1912) Israel Zangwill (1864–1926) **Dr:** Barrie Shaw Wilde Brandon Thomas (1849–1914) **Theory/Crit:** Samuel Butler **Lit. 'Events':**	*The Song of the Sword* *Barrack-Room Ballads* *The Countess Kathleen* [verse play] *Denzil Quarrier* & *Born in Exile* *The Diary of a Nobody* [wrtn with brother Weedon] *Children of the Ghetto* [novel] *Walker, London* *Widowers' Houses* [1st of 'Plays Unpleasant'] *Lady Windemere's Fan* *Charley's Aunt* [farce] 'The Humour of Homer' [essay] Alfred Tennyson dies
	1893	Gladstone's 2nd Home Rule Bill rejected by Lords; 1st meeting in Bradford of Independent Labour Party (ILP) under Keir Hardie – William Morris, G.B. Shaw & Sidney Webb draft *Manifesto of English Socialists*; National Free Labour Association formed; national mining strike in Britain; Gaelic League	St Hilda's & St Anne's Colleges, Oxford [for women] & Federal University of Wales fnd.d; Henry Ford makes his 1st petrol-driven motor car. **Int. Lit.:** Stephen Crane, *Maggie: A Girl of the Streets* [US novel]; Mallarmé, *Vers et prose*; Ricarda Huch, *Ludolph Ursleu* [Ger. novel]. **Music:** Tchaikovsky,	**P:** Henley Yeats Francis Thompson (1859–1907) **Pr/F:** Corelli Gissing	*London Voluntaries* *The Rose* *Poems* [incls 'The Hound of Heaven'] *Barabbas* *The Odd Women*

Events	Arts / Music / Lit.	Author	Work
fnd.d in Ireland; [–1914] Franco-Russ. Alliance [& secret military convention]; Ivory Coast becomes Fr. colony – French take Dahomey; Franco-British agreement on Siam; US troops overthrow local government in Hawaii; frontier between India & Afghanistan defined; Britain gains Gilbert & Solomon Islands; Matabele rising in S. Rhodesia [again in 1896] – British troops occupy Buluwayo; [–1894] 3rd Ashanti War	'Pathétique Symphony' (No. 6 in B minor); Verdi, 'Falstaff' [opera]; Dvořák, 'From the New World' (symphony); Engelbert Humperdinck [comp] 'Hansel and Gretel' [opera]; Giacomo Puccini [comp] 'Manon Lescaut' [opera]. **Art:** Pissarro, 'Washerwoman at Eragny'; Toulouse-Lautrec, 'Jeanne Avril at the Jardin de Paris' & 'M. Boileau in a Café'; [–1894] Cassatt, 'The Boating Party'; Rodin, 'Victor Hugo' [bust]; Gauguin, 'Annah the Javanese'; Munch, 'The Scream' [painting & litho.] & [c.] 'Jealousy'; William Strang [pnt] 'Thomas Hardy' [NPG]. **Film:** [>] Thomas Edison's Co. making early 'movies'	Rutherford Stevenson Yeats Zangwill E. F. Benson (1867–1940) 'George Egerton' (Mary Chavelita Bright; 1860–1945) Sarah Grand (1854–1943) **Dr:** Pinero Shaw Wilde	Catharine Furze Catriona [sequel to Kidnapped] The Celtic Twilight [essays] Tragedies of the Ghetto Dodo [novel] Keynotes [novel] The Heavenly Twins [novel] The Second Mrs. Tanqueray Mrs. Warren's Profession [censored] & The Philanderer ['Plays Unpleasant'; pf.d privately in 1900s] A Woman of No Importance & Salome [wrtn & pub.d in French]
1894 Gladstone resigns over Irish Home Rule & retires – Lord Rosebery, PM; budget intros death duties; Act estabs Parish, Rural & Urban District Councils; naval building programme begins; Merchant Shipping Act requires officers to have Board of Trade certificate; anarchist explosion at Greenwich; Captain Dreyfus unjustly convicted of treason in France [led to years of militarism & anti-semitism; freed, 1899; original verdict reversed, 1906]; Anglo-It. agreement over E. Africa, [–1896] Uganda becomes a British protectorate; Women's Suffrage Act passed in NZ; Kurds massacre Armenians at Sassoun; [–1917] accession of Nicholas II of Russia, last Romanov Tsar; [–1896] war between China & Japan	Manchester Ship Canal opens [begun 1881]; [c.] Blackpool Tower opens; Sidney & Beatrice Webb, The History of Trade Unionism; Robert Blatchford, Merrie England [social comment]. **Int. Lit.:** Ibsen, Little Eyolf; [c.] Wedekind, Earth Spirit. **Music:** Debussy, 'L'Après-midi d'un faune'; [–1895] R. Strauss, 'Till Eulenspiegel's Merry Pranks' [symphonic poem]. **Art:** Monet, 'Rouen Cathedral: Full Sunlight'; [c.–1896] Renoir, 'Gabrielle and Her Children'; [–1895] Cézanne, 'Still Life with Plaster Cupid' [Courtauld]; Toulouse-Lautrec, studies of 'Yvette Guilbert', 'Au salon de la rue des Moulins' & 'Two Friends' [Tate]; Sargent, 'Coventry Patmore' [NPG]; Wilson Steer, 'Girls Running: Walberswick Pier' [Tate]; Munch, 'Anxiety'; Paul Signac [pnt] 'Port of St-Tropez' [Pointillism']; Frederick Evans, 'Aubrey Beardsley' [photo; NPG]. **Lit. 'Events':** R.L. Stevenson dies; [c.] demise of triple-decker novel; [–1897] John Lane & Aubrey Beardsley's 'Art Nouveau' periodical, The Yellow Book, pub.d; Jowett trans Plato, The Republic	**Pr/F:** Gissing Hardy Kipling Moore Stevenson Wilde Zangwill 'Anthony Hope' (Sir 'A.H.' Hawkins; 1863–1933) George du Maurier (1834–96) Arthur Morrison (1863–1945) **Dr:** Jones Shaw Yeats Sydney Grundy (1848–1914)	In the Year of the Jubilee Life's Little Ironies [stories] [–1895] The Jungle Books [1 & 2] Esther Waters The Ebb-Tide Salome [Eng. trans, Lord Alfred Douglas; illustr., Aubrey Beardsley] Ghetto Tragedies The Prisoner of Zenda [popular novel of 'Ruritania'; dramatised, 1896] Trilby [popular novel of 'Svengali'] Tales of Mean Streets [stories & sketches] The Case of Rebellious Susan Arms and the Man [1st of 'Plays Pleasant'] The Land of Heart's Desire The New Woman, an original comedy
1895 Liberals defeated in Gen. Elec.: Salisbury, PM – Joseph Chamberlain, Colonial Sec.; Royal Commission on 2ndary Education reports; completion of Kiel Canal makes Germany a N. Sea power [begun 1887; enlarged 1909–14]; [>] Anglo-Fr. interests in Nile Valley start to conflict; [–1896] 'Jameson Raid' in S. Africa: British force enters Transvaal Republic from Bechuanaland led by L.S. Jameson to help Uitlanders [v.1886] overthrow Kruger gvnmt – forced to surrender to Boers [helps to provoke Boer War – v.1899] – Rhodes resigns as premier of Cape Colony; Kenya becomes a British protectorate; [–1896] 4th Ashanti War; National League set up in Poland – seeks limited autonomy	Engels dies; Sidney Webb helps fnd London School of Economics and Political Science; National Trust fnd.d [incorporated, 1907]; Marconi's 1st successful experiments with 'wireless' telegraph at Bologna; William Röntgen discvs X-rays; Sigmund Freud, Studien über Hysterie [1st work of psychoanalysis]. **Int. Lit.:** Crane, The Red Badge of Courage; Fontane, Effie Briest [novel]; [c.] Henryk Sienkiewicz, Quo Vadis [Pol. novel]. **Music:** Sir Henry Wood starts Queen's Hall Promenade Concerts; Frederick Delius [comp] 'Over the Hills and Far Away' [choral work]. **Art:** Leighton, 'Flaming June'; [c.] Cézanne, 'Bathers' & [–1900] 'The Clockmaker'; Renoir, 'Caillebotte Children'; Toulouse-Lautrec, 'May	**P:** Yeats **Pr/F:** Corelli Dowie Hardy Grant Allen (1848–99) Joseph Conrad (1857–1924) H.[erbert] G.[eorge] Wells (1866–1946) **Dr:** Jones Shaw	Poems [incls 'Lake Isle of Inisfree' & 'When You are Old'] The Sorrows of Satan [b-s. novel] Gallia Jude the Obscure [last novel, but v.1897] The Woman who Did [novel] Almayer's Folly [novel] The Time Machine & The Wonderful Visit [sci. fi. novels] The Triumph of the Philistines Candida ['Plays Pleasant']

Period	Year	International and Political Contexts	Social and Cultural Contexts	Authors	Indicative Titles
		from Russia; USA protests at brutal suppression of revolt by Spain in Cuba; 50,000 Armenians massacred in Constantinople	Belfort' [poster] & 'Marcelle Lender Dancing the Bolero'; [c.] Degas, 'Dancers at the Practice Bar'. **Film:** Lumière Bros launch Cinématographe – 1st public film show of 'motion pictures' in Paris ('Arrival of a Train', 'Workers Leaving the Lumière Factory', 'L'Arroseur arosé')	Wilde **Lit. 'Events':**	*The Importance of Being Earnest & An Ideal Husband* Trial of Oscar Wilde for homosexuality – 2-yr sentence in Reading Gaol
	1896	[–1914] period of rising prices & falling wages in Britain; Truck Act: to suppress payment in goods as wages not money; Conciliation Act: boards to settle industrial disputes if both parties agree; Locomotives Act repeals 'Red Flag Act' [v.1878] – max. speed for road vehicles now 14 mph; 'Kruger Telegram' – Kaiser Wilhelm congratulates Transvaal premier on defeat of 'Jameson Raid' [v.1895]; Utah becomes 45th State; French annexe Madagascar; insurrection in Crete against Turk. rule [becomes independent state, 1898]; Sierra Leone becomes a British protectorate; [–1898] Kitchener's campaign against Khalifa in Sudan to avenge Gordon's death; [–1897 & 1899] widespread famine in India; Britain has 99-yr lease on New Territories adjacent to Hong Kong – 1st 'Boxer Rebellion' in China [anti-foreigner secret society]; gold discv.d in Yukon, Canada – [1897–8] Klondyke gold rush	Alfred & Harold Harmsworth fnd *The Daily Mail* [revolutionises Fleet Street]; museums open on Sundays; [–1897] Marconi demonstrates successful wireless telegraphy on Salisbury Plain; 1st modern Olympics held in Athens; [–1906] Simplon Tunnel built; Carpenter, *Love's Coming of Age*; Bergson, *Matter and Memory* [phil.]. **Int. Lit.:** Ibsen, *John Gabriel Borkman*; Hauptmann, *Die Versunken Glocke* [Ger. play]; Anton Chekhov, *The Seagull* [Russ. play – failed; revived by Stanislavski, 1898]; Alfred Jarry, *Ubu roi* [Fr. play]; Pierre Louÿs, *Aphrodite* [Fr. novel]. **Music:** R. Strauss, 'Also Sprach Zarathustra' [symphonic poem]; Giacomo Puccini [comp] 'La Bohème' [It. opera]. **Art:** National Portrait Gallery (NPG) opens; Degas, 'La Coiffure' [NG]; Toulouse-Lautrec, 'Maxime Dethomas at the Opera Ball' & 'Circus' ser.; Beardsley [illustr.] Pope's *The Rape of the Lock*; Pissarro, 'The Great Bridge at Rouen'; Munch, 'Frieze of Life'. **Film:** Edison, 'The Kiss'. **Lit. 'Events':** Alfred Austin – Poet Laureate; Kelmscott Chaucer pub.d by William Morris [dies same year]	**P:** Hilaire Belloc (1870–1953) A.E. Housman (1859–1936) **Pr/F:** Conrad Corelli Morris Morrison Rutherford Stevenson Wells Sir Max Beerbohm (1872–1956) **Dr:** Jones Shaw Wilde **Theory/Crit:** George Saintsbury	*The Bad Child's Book of Beasts* [nonsense verse] *A Shropshire Lad* *An Outcast of the Islands* *The Mighty Atom* *The Well at the World's End* [prose romance] *A Child of the Jago* *Clara Hopgood* *Weir of Hermiston* [unfinished; posthm.] *The Island of Dr Moreau* [sci. fi.] *The Works of Max Beerbohm* [essays] *Michael and his Lost Angel* *You Never Can Tell* ['Plays Pleasant'] *Salome* [produced in Paris by Sarah Bernhardt] *A History of 19th-Century Literature*
	1897	Q. Victoria's Diamond Jubilee; Royal Commission on agricultural depression reports; Employers' Liability Act: responsible for injuries at work & Workmen's Compensation Act; Scottish TUC fnd.d; [>] only trained nurses to work in hospitals; [–1919] Millicent Fawcett, President of National Union of Women's Suffrage Societies; 2nd Colonial Conference: agreements over Tunisia [Anglo-Fr.], Albania [It.-Austr.] & Macedonia [Austr.-Russ.]; Crete proclaims union with Greece – war between Greece & Turkey – Greeks defeated – European Powers intervene – Peace of Constantinople; revolt on Indian NW Frontier; 2 Ger. missionaries murdered in China	Newnes fnds *Country Life* magazine; [c.] monotype typesetting comes into use; 1st Women's Institute estab.d at Stoney Creek, Canada [in UK, 1915]; [–1928] Henry Havelock Ellis, *Studies in the Psychology of Sex* [7 vols]. **Int. Lit.:** Edmond Rostand, *Cyrano de Bergerac* [Fr. play]. **Music:** R. Strauss, *Don Quixote* [symphonic poem]; Paul Dukas [comp] 'The Sorcerer's Apprentice' [Fr. symphonic poem]. **Art:** Sir Henry Tate gives Tate Gallery to the nation – opens in London; Wallace Collection donated to the nation [opens 1900]; Pissarro, 'Woman in an Orchard'; [c.–1898] Cézanne, 'La Vielle au chapelet' [NG]; Renoir, 'Sleeping Bather'; Gauguin, 'Nevermore' [Courtauld] & 'Where Do We Come From? What Are We? Where Are We Going?'; Henri ('Le Douanier') Rousseau [pnt] 'Sleeping Gypsy'; Charles Shannon [pnt] 'Self-Portrait' [NPG]; [c.] Walter Sickert [pnt] 'The Old Bedford: A Corner of the Gallery' [Walker AG]	**P:** Sir Henry Newbolt (1862–1938) **Pr/F:** Conrad Hardy James Kipling Wells Bram Stoker (1847–1912) **Dr:** Jones Shaw **Theory/Crit:** George Meredith **Lit. 'Events':**	*Admirals All and Other Verses* [incls 'Drake's Drum'] *The Nigger of the 'Narcissus'* *The Well-Beloved* [as bk; extensive revision of 1892 serial] *What Maisie Knew & The Spoils of Poynton* *Captains Courageous* [sea story] *The Invisible Man* *Dracula* [popular horror story] *The Liars* [c.] *The Devil's Disciple* [1st of '3 Plays for Puritans'; pub.d 1901] 'The Idea of Comedy …' [lecture] Her Majesty's Theatre opens under Beerbohm Tree

Year	History/Events		Authors	Works
1898	Chamberlain proposes Anglo-Ger. alliance; Irish Local Government Act follows Eng. pattern; German Navy League fnd.d – Reichstad passes 1st Navy Act; Anglo-Fr. agreement over Nigeria & Gold Coast – Anglo-Ger. over Portug. African colonies; Sp.-Amer. War: US battleship blown up in Havana harbour – Spain defeated – cedes Cuba, Porto Rico, Guam & Philippines to USA; USA annexes Hawaii [becomes a US territory, 1900]; Yukon becomes a Canadian territory; Kitchener's victory over Mahdi's forces at Omdurman – conquest of Sudan – Fr.-Brit. tension after French occupy Fashoda on Upper Nile; [–1902] Aswan Dam, Egypt, built	London Underground electrified from Mansion House to Waterloo; Marconi sends wireless signals across the Channel & [1899] fnds Marconi Telegraph Co. in London; Pierre & Marie Curie discv. radium; [c.] Rudolph Diesel demonstrates 1st internal combustion engine. **Int. Lit.:** Stanislavsky helps fnd Moscow Art Theatre; Zola, *J'accuse* [wrtn in support of Dreyfus; v.1894]; [–1904] Strindberg, *To Damascus* [trilogy of plays]. **Music:** [–1900] Samuel Coleridge-Taylor [comp] series of 'Hiawatha' cantatas. **Art:** [–1909] Charles Rennie Mackintosh builds Glasgow School of Art ['Art Nouveau' architecture]; Pissarro, 'Place du Théâtre Français' & 'Avenue de l'Opéra'; [–1905] Cézanne, 'Women Bathers'; Shannon, 'Charles Ricketts' [NPG]; Rodin, 'Balzac' [controversial sculpt; only erected in public in 1939]; Toulouse-Lautrec, 'At the Bar: the Chlorotic Cashier'; Beardsley [illustr.] Jonson's *Volpone*. **Theory/Crit:** Saintsbury, *A Short History of English Literature*	**P:** Hardy Newbolt Wilde **Pr/F:** Butler Conrad Grand Hope James Kipling Wells Arnold Bennett (1867–1931) Maurice Hewlett (1861–1923) **Dr:** Pinero Shaw	*Wessex Poems* [1st vol. of poetry – illustr. by himself] *The Island Race* *The Ballad of Reading Gaol* *The Iliad* [trans of Homer] *Tales of Unrest* [stories] *The Beth Book* *Rupert of Hentzau* [set in 'Ruritania'] *The Turn of the Screw* [novella] *The Day's Work* [stories] *The War of the Worlds* *A Man from the North* [novel] *The Forest Lovers* [historical romance] *Trelawney of the 'Wells'* *Plays Pleasant and Unpleasant* [pub.d]
1899	Kaiser Wilhelm II in London to discuss Anglo-Ger. alliance; [–1965] London County Council & Borough Councils estab.d; [>] 1st Garden City to be estab.d at Letchworth; Board of Education estab.d; General Federation of Trade Unions fnd.d in England; International Women's Conference in London; [–1902] 2nd Anglo-Boer War in S. Africa – Boers invade Natal – British defeats at Magersfontein, Stormberg, Colenso – siege of Ladysmith – [–1900] Lords Roberts & Kitchener put in charge of army; Hague Court of Arbitration set up; Anglo-Fr. agreement over areas of influence in W. Africa; [–1914] Samoa under Ger. control	Ruskin College, Oxford, fnd.d to provide socialist education; T. Huxley, *Science and Education* [posthm.]. **Int. Lit.:** Tolstoy, *Resurrection*; Ibsen, *When We Dead Awaken*; Chekhov, *Uncle Vanya* [pf.d at Moscow Arts Theatre]; D'Annunzio, *Romances of the Rose* [trilogy of novels]; Mallarmé, *Poésies*. **Music:** Sir Edward Elgar [comp] 'Enigma Variations'; Jean Sibelius [comp] 'Finlandia' [overture]. **Art:** Monet, 'Water Lilies' [NG; 1st in ser. cont.d to his death in 1926]; Gauguin, 'Tahitian Women with Mango Blossoms'; Toulouse-Lautrec, 'At the Races' ser. [incs 'The Jockey' (litho.)] & 'In a Private Room at the Rat Mort' [Courtauld]; Homer, 'In the Bermudas'; [c.] Gwen John [pnt] 'Self-Portrait' [NPG]. **Film:** George Méliès [Fr.], 'The Dreyfus Affair' & 'Cendrillon' **Lit. 'Events':** Wyndham's Theatre opens; Incorporated Stage Society fnd.d – 1st production, Shaw's *You Never Can Tell*; Irish Literary Theatre in Dublin fnd.d by Yeats, Lady Gregory & George Moore – 1st production, Yeats's *The Countess Kathleen*	**P:** Yeats **Pr/F:** Conrad James Kipling Morrison Somerville & Ross Wells Ernest Hornung (1866–1921) **Dr:** Pinero Shaw	*The Wind Among the Reeds* 'Heart of Darkness' [serial; pub.d in *Youth* vol., 1902] & *Lord Jim* [serial] *The Awkward Age* *Stalky and Co.* [school story] *To London Town* *Some Experiences of an Irish R.M.* [novel; sequel, 1908] *When the Sleeper Wakes* [rev.d as *The Sleeper Awakes*, 1910] *The Amateur Cracksman* [1st 'Raffles' story] *The Gay Lord Quex* *Caesar and Cleopatra* ['Plays for Puritans'; pub. 1901]

6

1900–1939

World War I and the Modernist Period

INTRODUCTION

The period covered runs from the year before the death of Queen Victoria in 1901 to the outbreak of the Second World War in 1939. It therefore includes the **Edwardian*** and **Georgian*** periods, the **Great War/First World War/World War I***, and the **Inter-War Period*** (the 1920s and 1930s). In terms of literature and the other arts, it is also the period which witnesses the high point of **Modernism***.

[**NB**: the extrapolated narratives for the period 1900–19 are run together at the end of the gloss on The Great War/First World War/World War I*.]

Chapter contents

6.1 EDWARDIAN

The adjective which describes the period of the reign (1901–10) of King Edward VII of Great Britain and Ireland, Queen Victoria's eldest son (Albert Edward).

Edward VII was heir to the throne for 60 years; on his father Prince Albert's death in 1861, he took his seat in the House of Lords as the Duke of Cornwall and married Princess Alexandria of Denmark in 1863. However, 'Bertie' was a *bon viveur* who travelled widely (he was the first royal prince to tour the United States and Canada [1860]), was deeply interested in the theatre, horse-racing and yachting, and had several mistresses (he caused a scandal in 1870 by being cited as a witness in a divorce suit). Hence his mother regarded him as too frivolous for public responsibility. Nevertheless, in the later years of her reign, he was much in the public eye and his accession to the throne in 1901 was widely popular (he compounded this regard by undergoing one of the earliest appendicitis operations). Edward VII took an active interest in foreign affairs and endeavoured to promote international good relations by visiting other European capitals, for example, helping to pave the way for the Anglo-French Entente Cordiale of 1904 and the Anglo-Russian Agreement of 1907, which effectively established the Triple Entente (opposing the Triple Alliance of 1882 [see Chapter 5]). In effect, of course, this contributed to the complex network of alliances and 'agreements' noted in Chapter 5 which made the battle lines of the conflict in 1914 almost inevitable.

The style and vitality of Edward's monarchy, coinciding as it did with the beginning of the new century, was perceived as a welcome reaction against the austerity of Victoria's reign, and for the upper classes at least it was a time of extravagant pleasure, often being seen in retrospect (from the other side of the **First World War***) as an 'Indian Summer' of the old order (cf. Osbert Sitwell's autobiographical volume, *Great Morning*, and Vita-Sackville-West's novel, *The Edwardians*). Indeed, some historians have seen the end of the 19th Century occurring effectively in 1914 rather than 1900, with the the appalling experience of **World War I*** finally ushering in the recognisably 20th-century world. But the Edwardian and Georgian periods also witnessed the beginning of what George Dangerfield was to call 'The Strange Death of Liberal England' – the embattlement on many political, social and cultural fronts of 19th-Century English **Liberalism*** [see Chapter 5, **'Early Victorian'**], and its accelerating demise.

6.2 GEORGIAN II

The adjective used to define the period of four years or so (1910–14) at the beginning of the reign of King George V of Great Britain and Ireland (1910–36), Edward VII's eldest surviving son.

[**NB:** see the gloss on **Georgian I*** in Chapter 3.]

The term is seldom, if ever, used to describe George V's reign as a whole, the First World War seeming to terminate the society so described (see preceding gloss), and is most commonly employed in literary history, where it is derived from the title of the series of five *Georgian Poetry* anthologies launched by Sir Edward Marsh in 1912 (–1922), The Preface to the first one of these claimed that it would 'help the lovers of poetry to realise that we are at the beginning of another "Georgian period" which may take rank in due time with the several great poetic ages of the past' – a prediction nullified by, amongst other things, the First World War and the advent of **Modernist*** poetics. Central 'Georgian' poets were Rupert Brooke, Lascelles Abercrombie, Wilfrid Gibson and John Drinkwater, although the anthologies printed a wide range of contemporary poets, including Edward Thomas, D.H. Lawrence and Siegfried Sassoon.

While the pre-war 'Georgian' years of George V's reign saw the Union of South Africa established and the king's visit to India for the Coronation Durbar (1911), they were also marked by a series of political, social and constitutional crises (bitter strikes, reform of the House of Lords, Irish Home Rule and the rise of Ulster Unionism, and international tensions as a prelude to World War I). Thereafter came the outbreak of **The Great War*** in 1914 (in 1917, to signal the break with even a nominal link to Germany, George changed the name of the British royal family from Saxe-Coburg and Gotha to the House of Windsor); the Easter Rising in Dublin in 1916, and the inception of the Irish Free State (1922); the first (minority) **Labour*** governments of 1924–5 and 1929–31, and the General Strike of 1926; the world economic crisis (1929–31), 'National Government' (1931) and the Depression of the 1930s; the rise to power of the Fascist regimes in Germany and Italy and the rearming of those countries; the Government of India Act (1935; which gave a measure of power to provincial legislatures).

George V also inaugurated the annual Christmas Day radio broadcasts by the reigning monarch in 1932; he died early in 1936 and was succeeded on 20th January by his eldest son, King Edward VIII, who abdicated on 11 December the same year [see **Inter-War Period*** below].

6.3 THE FIRST WORLD WAR / WORLD WAR I (WWI) / 'THE GREAT WAR'

'The Great War' was the contemporary name given to the First World War/World War I (1914–18) in the early years of the conflict, and although retrospectively discarded in favour of less grimly ironic descriptors, the term is still current – but only in respect of that particular war: it is not used of World War II (1939–45; see Chapter 7).

The war was the result of political, economic and colonial rivalries between the European Powers during the last decades of the 19th Century, as outlined in Chapter 5: Pan-Slavism, backed by Russia, endangered the stability of the Austro-Hungarian Empire; the loss of Alsace-Lorraine to Germany after the Franco–Prussian War aggrieved France; rampant colonialism, especially in Africa, backed by an armaments race based on the rapid development of German heavy industry increased tensions (e.g. the campaign in the UK to build increasing numbers of 'Dreadnought' battleships in the period 1905–14); the web of secret diplomacy throughout Europe meant that many nations would be automatically involved if one strand was damaged.

The assassination of Archduke Franz Ferdinand of Austria by Serb nationalists at Serajevo on 28 June 1914 was that strand: Austria issued an unacceptable ultimatum to Serbia and declared war a month later; Russia mobilised on Serbia's behalf; Germany declared war on Russia (1 August) and on France (3 August), then invaded Belgium, the protection of whose neutrality had been a principle of European diplomacy since 1839; Britain then declared war on Germany (4 August) and Austria on Russia (6 August). The Central Powers (Germany et al) were later joined by Turkey and Bulgaria (October 1914); the Allies (Britain et al) by Japan (1914), Italy (1915–16) and the USA (1917).

The War was fought on many fronts: the Western Front (which stretched from Flanders to the Swiss border) where, after some fierce early battles, for the next three years the war settled into the impasse of deadlocked trench warfare punctuated only by largely futile and extremely costly attempts to break it (Verdun, the Somme, Passchendaele); the Eastern Front, where a sequence of heavy defeats for Russia led finally to the Bolshevik Revolution of 1917, the abdication of the Tsar and an armistice with Germany, which released thousands of German troops on to the Western Front; the Allies, in order to attack Turkey and relieve the pressure on Russia, made an ill-fated attack on the Dardanelles (1915–16); the Turks were finally defeated by the Allies in Palestine and Iraq (1917–18), and the German colonies in Africa and the Pacific captured.

The main sea battle was fought off Jutland (1916), after which the German fleet remained in harbour for the rest of the war; however, unrestricted submarine warfare intended to starve Britain into submission had the effect finally of bringing the United States into the war in 1917. With the help of US troops, the Allies were therefore able to withstand the German offensives of March–July 1918 (fuelled by troops from the Eastern Front), and counter-attack during the summer and autumn. Bulgaria, Turkey and Austria capitulated to the Allies between Sepember and November, and German opposition finally collapsed, the armistice being signed on 11 November 1918.

The war was ended by a series of treaties (e.g. Versailles, St Germain and Neuilly), and out of it came the League of Nations (1920–46) to promote international peace and co-operation, but, as it transpired, without the means to enforce its decisions (apropos, 1919–20 also saw Adolph Hitler found the National Socialist German Workers Party [NAZI] and Benito Mussolini the Fascist movement in Italy). Chemical weapons, tanks, submarines and aircraft were all first used in World War I, evidence of a now thoroughly mechanised warfare which caused many millions of casualties throughout the combatant nations.

Key Timeline Narratives 1900–1919

⊃ **International Context** [excluding the run-up to World War I and the war itself]   The continuation and conclusion of the Boer War (1900–2); the Russo–Japanese War (1904–5); the Italian–Turkish War of 1911–12; the Balkan Wars of 1912–13; the first (unsuccessful) Russian Revolution of 1905, the second successful Revolution of 1917 (the Tsar and his family were assassinated in 1918), and the establishing of the Soviet Republic (1919); the USA's acquiring of the right to build the Panama Canal (1901–13); the granting of dominion stautus to Australia (1900–1) and to the Union of South Africa (1911).

⊃ **The UK Political and Social Context**   The rise of (The) Labour (Party)*; the Liberal landslide victory in the General Election of 1906, the political and social agitation which undermined the Liberal Government, and the gradual demise of the party as a force in British politics thereafter; Liberal legislation (1908–11) to provide Old Age Pensions and a National Insurance Scheme; the ensuing Constitutional Crisis (1909–11) in which the Lords blocked David Lloyd-George's 'People's Budget' and then had their powers reduced by the Parliament Bill (1910–11); industrial agitation, especially amongst miners, dockers and railwaymen during 1910–12; the increasing militancy of the Women's Suffrage Movement (see **Women's Movement/Feminism*** below); the Representation of the People Act of 1918 which enfranchised all men over 21 and women over 30; the first election to Parliament of women MPs (1918–19); the introduction, in 1919, of the 48-hour working week and Acts to provide 'homes fit for heroes' to ex-servicemen and their families.

⊃ **Ireland**   Continuing attempts to find a solution to the 'Irish Question'; the founding of Sinn Fein and the Ulster Unionist Council in 1905; from 1910, the Liberal Governnment's reliance on Irish Nationalist MPs (and on Labour) for a majority in the Commons; the Government's attempts, in 1912–13, to introduce a (limited) Home Rule Bill for Ireland, the ensuing opposition of the Unionists and the rejection of it twice by the Lords; the intense hostility of both Nationalists and Unionists which left the UK in 1914 on the brink of civil war; the 'Easter Rising' in Dublin (1916) and its suppression; the victory of Eamon De Valera's Sinn Fein party in the General Election of 1918 (it won every Irish seat outside Ulster), and the refusal of the Irish MPs to take up their seats at Westminster; and in 1919, the founding of the Dáil Éireann (assembly of Irish MPs), a declaration of Irish independence by Sinn Fein, the forming of the Irish Republican Army (IRA), and (to 1921), guerrilla warfare between the IRA and British troops, police and government irregulars (the 'Black and Tans'). [See **Inter-War Period*** below for the Irish Civil War and the founding of the Irish Republic.]

⊃ **Education**   The period witnessed provision of secondary education to be funded by Town and County Councils out of the rates (1902); the establishing of the Workers' Educational Association (WEA) in 1903, the English Association (1906), and the English-Speaking Union (1918); and throughout the 1900s, many of the civic universities (aka 'provincial', 'red-brick') were founded in the UK.

⊃ **Science and Technology**   Telegraphy continued to develop with messges being transmitted across the Atlantic (1901; for the arrest of the wife-murderer, Dr Crippen, see 1910) and the Pacific (1903). The age of the motor car fully dawned – with Henry Ford founding his company in 1903 and pioneering 'assembly-line' mass-production techniques (the first Model T Ford was produced in 1908–9); Henry Royce making his first car in 1904 (C. S. Rolls joined him in 1906 to found Rolls-Royce Ltd.); and in 1905, Herbert Austin opened his first car factory in Birmingham.

The age of flight also dawned in this period – with Count von Zeppelin flying his first airship in 1900; the Wright Brothers making the first powered air-flight in the USA (1903); A. V. Roe building his first biplane in 1907; Louis Blériot, the first person to fly across the Channel in 1909; Italy first using planes in offence during the war with Turkey (1911–12); the extensive use of aircraft for observation and air raids during World War I; the first non-stop flight across the Atlantic by Alcock and Brown in 1919, and the first flight from England to Australia (it took 28 days).

In the sciences, Albert Einstein first proposed his 'special' theory of relativity in 1905 and his 'general' theory in 1916; Marie Curie isolated pure radium in 1910; Ernest Rutherford and Niels Bihr announced their theory of atomic structure in 1911 and hence founded nuclear physics; and major works in psychology were published by Sigmund Freud and Karl Jung [see, e.g., 1900, 1904, 1911, 1913, 1919].

➲ **The Cultural Context**   In the earlier part of the period, the newspaper industry continued to expand: in 1900, Sir Cyril Pearson's the *Daily Express* was first published; Alfred Harmsworth (Lord Northcliffe) published the *Daily Mirror* in 1903 (the first paper principally aimed at women and with illustrations), and in 1908, he took over *The Times* (reducing its price to 1*d*. in 1914); Horatio Bottomley's weekly, *John Bull*, first appeared in 1906; and the Labour newspaper, the *Daily Herald*, in 1912.

While the Lumière Brothers had publicly shown 'moving pictures' in Paris in 1895, the rapid development of cinematography and the film industry is one of the most striking features of the period: early 'movies' were produced throughout the 1900s; by 1914, Charlie Chaplin was making his first films in Hollywood; D. W. Griffiths made 'The Birth of a Nation' (1915) and 'Intolerance' (1916); and in 1919, Mary Pickford (with Chaplin and Douglas Fairbanks) founded the United Artists Film Corporation.

Equally revolutionary were the new movements in the arts: in painting, Fauvism (Matisse, Derain), Cubism (Picasso, Braque), Expressionism (Kokoshka, Munch), Futurism (Boccioni, Severini) and Vorticism (Wyndham Lewis, Gaudier-Brzeska) were all initiated before World War I; Roger Fry brought the two Post-Impressionist exhibitions of 1910 and 1912 to London and caused an artistic furore; related movements in music are evidenced by the compositions of Stravinsky and the ballet of Diaghilev; in literature, the period saw the publication of works by Gide, Mann, Rilke, Rolland, Hesse, Stein, Pound, Proust, Apollinaire, Mayakovsky, Eliot, Joyce, and the Imagists (see **Modernism*** below).

6.4 THE WOMEN'S MOVEMENT / FEMINISM

One of the most significant developments in the period c.1890–1930 – and then for the 20th Century as a whole – was the rise of Feminism (the advocacy of women's rights, emancipation and advancement on the grounds of sexual equality) and of the Women's Movement.

Although the organised momentum for women's rights, equality, the vote and education had been building up since the mid-19th Century (see, e.g., 1848, 1849, 1856, 1869, 1870, 1874, 1880, 1882, 1886, 1893), the period under consideration saw the rapid mobilisation in the United States and Britain of the suffrage movement (sometimes called 'The First [or 'Old'] Wave' to distinguish it from 'The Second [or 'New'] Wave' of militant feminism from the late-1960s onwards; see Chapters 8 and 9). While much of the work of 19th-Century feminists was towards institutional political, legal and economic reform, that around the turn of the century and up to World War I became more organised, radical and militant.

In 1889, [Mrs] Emmeline Pankhurst founded the Women's Franchise League; 1897 saw the inauguration of the National Union of Women's Suffrage Societies, with Millicent Fawcett as president; an International Women's Conference was held in London in 1899; and in 1903, Emmeline and Christobel Pankhurst founded the Women's Social and Political Union (WSPU) to fight for female suffrage. From then on, until 1914, the campaign became increasingly militant and violent (see, e.g., 1907, 1908, 1912, 1913–14). In 1918, the Representation of the People Act enfranchised women over 30, while all women over 21 received the vote (hence equality with men) under the Women's Suffrage Bill of 1928 (effectively, the 5th Reform Act).

Running alongside this political struggle was a movement in literature by women which voiced the new feminist consciousness (and, amongst male writers, a not always positive consciousness of the new feminism). Examples from the pre-war period would include Olive Schreiner (1883); Margaret Harkness (1887); the first English production of Ibsen's *A Doll's House* (1889); Ménie Muriel Downie (1891); the 'New Woman' writers of the 1890s such as 'George Egerton', Sarah Grand and Sydney Grundy (1893–4); plays by G. B. Shaw (1892–3); novels by Grant Allen (1895), H. G. Wells (1909) and Elizabeth Robins (1907); and plays by Robins and Elizabeth Baker (1909).

The following two decades saw the first appearance of fiction by such Modernist* [see below] feminists as Katherine Mansfield (1911), May Sinclair (1914/15), Dorothy Richardson (1915), Virginia Woolf (1915), 'Rebecca West' (1918), Rose Macaulay (1921), Edith Sitwell (1922), Ivy Compton-Burnett (1925), Elizabeth Bowen, Rosamund Lehmann, 'Jean Rhys' (all 1927), and Radclyffe Hall (1928). Fittingly, the year after the Women's Suffrage Bill saw the publication of that classic of 20th-Century literary feminism, Virginia Woolf's *A Room of One's Own* (1929). The feminist project was not to be circumscribed by merely winning the vote.

6.5 THE INTER-WAR PERIOD

The period between 1918 and 1939; in other words, that between World War I and World War II (other more or less familiar phrases for it are 'Between the Wars' and 'The Long Weekend' [the title of a book by Robert Graves and Alan Hodge in 1940]).

In cultural history, as elsewhere, the inter-war period is often broken down into its two constituent decades – 'The Twenties' and 'The Thirties' – if only because they seem to evince such markedly different concerns, attitudes and characteristics (crudely flagged by their popular soubriquets, 'The Jazz Age' and 'The Red Decade'). Whatever the truth of these characterisations, the coincidence of the Wall Street Crash of 1929 with the end of the decade, the election of an all-Fascist parliament in Italy and a Nazi victory in elections in Bavaria the same year, do seem to legitimise a sense of changed priorities – a sense perhaps reflected in the very different ideological stances of the Modernist* intelligentsia [see below] and the politically committed intelligentsia of the 1930s.

At the very least, whilst the 1920s seemed to be trying to lay the ghost of the First World War (either by febrile hedonism – the world of Ernest Hemingway's *The Sun Also Rises* and Scott Fitzgerald's *The Great Gatsby*, of Evelyn Waugh's *Decline and Fall*, Aldous Huxley's *Antic Hay* and Wyndham Lewis's *The Apes of God* – or by the exorcism of personal trauma – C. E. Montague's *Disenchantment*, Richard Aldington's *Death of a Hero*, Robert Graves's *Gooodbye to All That*, Vera

Brittain's *Testament of Youth*), the 1930s were hag-ridden with fear about the approach of a second one (C. Day Lewis's poem 'Newsreel' and Louis McNeice's 'Bagpipe Music', George Orwell's *Coming Up for Air*, Graham Greene's *A Gun for Sale* and *The Confidential Agent*, Christopher Isherwood's *Goodbye to Berlin*).

Key Timeline Narratives 1918–1939

➲ **The International Context** Is dominated throughout by the international processes and events which lead to the **Second World War*** [see Chapter 7] and whose seeds are sown in the 'peace' which succeeds the war of 1914–18.

- **Germany** The terms of the Treaty of Versailles (1919; which the USA refused to ratify, nor would they join the League of Nations) were punitive to Germany (it was declared at the time that she should be 'squeezed till the pips squeak'), with the payment of huge financial reparations, the secession of Alsace-Lorraine to France, the occupation of the Saar by the French for 15 years and of the Rhineland by the Allies for the same period, the loss of other possessions to Poland, Belgium, Denmark and Japan, and the renunciation of German overseas colonies, which were put under League of Nations mandate.

  Such conditions (exacerbated by France building the Maginot Line of fortifications [1927–35] on the eastern border with Germany from Switzerland to Belgium) created great resentment and extreme inflation in Germany (the economic system collapsed in 1927), and this became the ground in which Adolph Hitler's Nazi party would thrive (a putsch at Munich in 1923 failed, Hitler was imprisoned, from whence he dictated *Mein Kampf* [published 1925, but not in English significantly until 1939]). By 1932, the Nazi Party had become the largest in Germany, and in 1933, Hitler was appointed Chancellor, began his programme of repression against all political opponents and especially the Communists (e.g. by way of the Reichstag fire), initiated anti-Jewish measures (concentration camps were first set up), and withdrew from both the World Disarmament Conference instituted the year before and the League of Nations (it had been admitted in 1926).

  By 1934, Allied troops finally left the Rhineland, German rearmament was underway, Hitler used the SS to purge the Nazi Party ('The Night of the Long Knives'), and after the death of President Hindenberg and a plebiscite became 'Reichsführer'. Thereafter, a plebiscite returned the Saar to Germaany (1935), the persecution of the Jews accelerated, as did German rearmament, the Rhineland was reoccupied without Allied protest in 1936, the construction of the defence system, the 'Siegfried Line', commenced together with Hitler's expansionist policies for a greater Germany ('lebenstraum'– more 'living room').

  In 1936-7, the Rome–Berlin Axis was established with Benito Mussolini [see below], and German aircraft bombed Guernica in support of General Franco's rebellion in Spain [see below]; in 1938, German troops entered Austria, which was declared part of the German Reich (the 'Anschluss'), and then the German part of Czechoslovakia, leading to the 'Munich Crisis', Neville Chamberlain's appeasement policy and the 'Munich Agreement'. But with the German invasion and occupation of Czechoslsovakia and Poland in 1939, the Allies were forced to declare war on the Axis Powers and **World War II*** began [see Chapter 7].

- **Italy** Preceding and then running alongside the rise of Nazism in Germany was that of Fascism in Italy, so that by 1922, Mussolini's march on Rome in effect established him as dictator, and in the course of the 1920s a Fascist state was established in Italy in which all opppositon had been suppressed. With the Rome–Berlin Axis Agreement (proclaimed by Mussolini in 1936), Italy entered its own expansionist phase with the invasion of Abyssinia (now Ethiopia) and the proclamation that the Italian king was Emperor of it; along with Germany in 1937, Italy withdrew from the European Powers non-intervention agreement over Spain and actively supported Franco; in 1939, she invaded and annexed Albania, and in 1940, declared war on Britain and France.

• **Spain**   Following a revolution which overthrew the monarchy in 1931, a Spanish Republic was declared, but in 1933, the Falange (Fascist Party) was founded, and in 1936 a revolt against the Popular Front Coalition Government by the Falangists led by Franco began the Spanish Civil War. The European Powers agreed to non-intervention, although Germany and Italy recognised Franco as 'Chief of the Spanish State', and over the next three years gave him extensive military support, while the Soviet Union and the 'International Brigades' of socialist volunteers supported the Republicans. In 1939, the war ended with victory for the Nationalists, Franco (whom Britain recognised) established a dictatorship which lasted until his death in 1975, Spain left the League of Nations, and remained neutral throughout World War II (although sympathetic to the Axis Powers).

• **Soviet Russia**   In the years immediately following the Russian Revolution of 1917, there was a civil war between the anti-Communist White Army (supported by the European Powers) and the Bolshevik Red Army, which was finally victorious in 1921. The apparatus of the Soviet state began to be put in place, the Union of the Soviet Socialist Republics (USSR) was formally established in 1922 under Lenin, a constitution based on public ownership was created in 1924, the year of Lenin's death, and Joseph Stalin effectively took power in the Soviet Union, purging opposition throughout the period (Leon Trotsky was ousted in 1927; the kulaks [prosperous land-owning peasants who opposed collectivisation] were liquidated as a class in 1929–30; political opponents were purged with the assistance of the secret police in Stalin's 'Show Trials' and executions in the mid-1930s).

The first 'Five-Year Plan' to reorganise the Soviets' resources was introduced in 1928, involving centralisation of legislative power, the collectivisation of agriculture, massive expansion of heavy industry, and state control over education and culture; non-aggression pacts were established with neighbouring states (including Poland; see below) and diplomatic relations with the USA (1933); the USSR was admitted to the League of Nations in 1934. In 1939, having signed a non-aggression pact with Germany, both the USSR and Germany invaded Poland, which was then partitioned, the Soviet Union also invaded Finland and annexed Estonia, Latvia and Lithuania, but with its own invasion by Germany in 1941 [see Second World War*, Chapter 7], it was drawn into the conflict against the Axis Powers.

• **China and Japan**   Between 1926 (when Hirohito also became Emperor of Japan) and 1928, General Chiang-Kai-shek became the Chinese leader, suppressing Communist influence in the Kuomintang (the Nationalist political party) and establishing a degree of unity in China. In 1931, Japan invaded Manchuria and began the 2nd Sino–Japanese War, which continued, in effect, until 1945 (Peking and other Chinese cities were attacked in 1937, and the civil strife between Chiang-Kai-shek and the Communist leaders, Mao Tse-tung and Chou-en-lai, was suspended until the end of World War II). In 1933, Japan withdrew from the League of Nations; Hirohito became increasingly militaristic in policy, capturing Canton and Hankow from the Chinese in 1938 and being declared the aggressor by the League of Nations, while Hitler recognised the Japanese puppet regime in the parts of China it controlled. In 1940, Japan joined the Axis Powers and invaded Indochina.

- **The Commonwealth and India** During the 1920s, Britain continued to acquire Crown Colonies, and responsibility for other territories under League of Nations mandates, in particular Palestine. Following the Balfour Declaration of 1917 which established Palestine as a site for a permanent home for the Jews, and which caused bitter Arab opposition, it became a British mandate in 1920. Hostlities broke out between Jews and Arabs, especially as Jewish immigration increased as a result of persecution in Europe during the 1930s and the Second World War. [For the continuation of this narrative, see Chapters 7, 8 and 9.] By 1931, the Statute of Westminster defined Britain and the British Dominions as equal independent sovereign states under the Crown, and from this point on the notion of the Commonwealth of Nations gained currency. In India, the pressure for independence grew: with the failure of the 1919 Government of India Act to transfer significant power to elected officials, Mahatma Gandhi began a civil disobedience campaign (1930–31) in the cause of Indian self-government, and a further Government of India Act (1935) set up provincial legislatures, although the rift between Muslims and Hindus over an all-India government continued to widen.
- **The United States** Despite the role of President Woodrow Wilson in helping to set up the League of Nations, the US Senate refused to join it, nor would it ratify the Treaty of Versailles, which it saw as illiberal (the USA signed separate peace treaties with the Central Powers in 1921), nor would it agree to the cancellation of war debts as proposed by Balfour in 1922. In fact, throughout the inter-war years, the USA adopted an isolationist foreign policy, except for promoting the Kellogg-Briand Pact of 1928–9, which outlawed war (and became the basis for the Nuremberg war criminal trials at the end of World War II).

  The Presidencies of W. G. Harding (1921–3) and Calvin Coolidge (1923–9), reinforced by US protectionist tariffs and a speculative boom, were marked by economic prosperity, but the Wall Street Crash of 1929 ushered in a period of deep depression. The earlier part of the period also saw 'Prohibition' in force with its attendant bootlegging trade (1920–33) and immigration quotas introduced. In 1932, Franklin D. Roosevelt became President, and in 1933 announced his 'New Deal' programme of interventionist financial and social measures to pull the USA out of its economic crisis (these included, in 1935, the Labour Relations Act and the Social Security Act). In 1937, Roosevelt signed the US Neutrality Act, and had his 'Peace Plan' rejected by Hitler in 1939 (although sympathetic to the Allies, the US government stayed out of World War II until the Japanese attack on Pearl Harbour in 1941).

- ⮑ **British Politics** In 1922, the Coalition Government led by Lloyd George fell, and the UK returned to party politics, with the Conservatives gaining a large majority under Bonar Law and **Labour*** becoming the main opposition party (from now on [until the 1960s], the Liberals* [see Chapter 5, **'Early Victorian'**] were in parliamentary decline). A second General Election in 1923 resulted in a minority Conservative government under Stanley Baldwin, and a third election in 1924 led to the first minority Labour government under Ramsay MacDonald, which only lasted from January to November when the Conservatives were again elected with a greatly increased majority. Britain returned to the Gold Standard in 1925, and 1926 (3–12 May) saw the only General Strike in British history, when troops and thousands of civilian volunteers were deployed to break it. The Women's Suffrage Bill became the 5th Reform Act in 1928, giving the vote to all women over 21, hence completing universal franchise in the UK [the voting age was finally lowered to 18 in 1969].

  With the resignation of the Baldwin government in 1929, the General Election returned the second minority Labour government under MacDonald (to 1931), in which a number of women MPs were elected and Margaret Bondfield, as Minister of Labour, became the first female cabinet minister in Britain. The world economic depression following the Wall Street Crash of 1929 created a financial crisis in the UK; the Labour Government resigned in 1931; a National Government took power led by MacDonald but dominated by the Conservatives; the Gold Standard was abandoned; and the National Government won the General Election in October with a majority of 558 seats to 56 in opposition, passed a National Economy Act which cut salaries by nearly 20 per cent, and faced unemployment of 2.5 million. The same year, Oswald Mosley left the Labour Party in order to form the British Union of Fascists (1932).

Free trade was abandoned in 1932, and full protection introduced, causing defections from the National Government. 1935 saw a General Election in which the National Government was again returned, this time under the Conservative Baldwin, and the Silver Jubilee of George V; but his death the following year and the accession of King Edward VIII caused a major constitutional crisis (the 'Abdication Crisis'). Edward made it clear to the Baldwin Government that he intended to marry the American divorcee, Mrs Simpson, even if it meant giving up the throne. In the event, he reigned from January to December 1936, when he abdicated in favour of his younger brother (King George VI), took the title of Duke of Windsor, and married Mrs Simpson in 1937.

That year also saw the resignation of Baldwin, who had been criticised for betraying the League of Nations by the Hoare-Laval pact with Italy over the latter's invasion of Abyssinia (1935) and non-intervention in Spain (1936); he was also criticised for not perceiving the Nazi threat and for his reluctance to rearm Britain (Winston Churchill was calling for this in 1936). Neville Chamberlain replaced him as Prime Minister of the National Government, and army reforms, air precautions and a rearmament policy were introduced. In 1938, the Foreign Secretary, Anthony Eden, resigned over Chamberlain's 'appeasement' policy towards fascist Italy, a policy extended to Germany the same year, but one leading only to the 'Munich Crisis' (when the British fleet was mobilised and civilian gas-masks distributed) and the 'Munich Agreement' with Hitler accepting Germany's occupation of Sudetenland (Chamberlain's 'piece of paper' denoting 'peace in our time') – an agreement rudely destroyed the following year, 1939, with the outbreak of World War II* [see Chapter 7, and Germany above].

↪ **The British Social Context**   Although the period opened with the government passing the Emergency Powers Act (1920; allowing the declaration of a state of emergency if necessary), the inter-war years also saw a rolling programme of social and industrial legislation, including unemployment insurance and the dole (1920–1; the Local Government Act of 1929 effectively abolished the Poor Law, but see also 1934), housing (1923, 1930, 1933), divorce (1923, 1937), pensions (1925), public health (1936), food and drugs (1938), the coal industry (1925, 1926, 1930), transport (1921, 1930, 1933, 1935), electricity (1926), steel (1934), town and country planning (1932) and secondary education (1926, 1938).

Despite this, social and industrial relations were fractious throughout the period, especially in the coal industry, and were most clearly exemplified by the General Strike of 1926 [see British Politics above]. This resulted in the Trades Disputes and Trade Unions Act of 1927 which outlawed general and sympathy strikes. The economic crisis following 1929 exacerbated unemployment, leading to hunger marches (1929, 1932, 1936) and unpopular government legislation like the founding of the Unemployment Assistance Board in 1934 which introduced means testing for poor relief.

◑ *Ireland*   The war between the IRA and British forces continued until 1921 [see Key Timeline Narrative 1900–19, under Ireland) for the start of this]. In 1920, the Government of Ireland Act (4th Home Rule Bill) partitioned the country and created the six counties of Ulster as Northern Ireland (the government of which first met in 1921); this Act was rejected by the IRA, but the Anglo-Irish Treaty of 1921 effectively gave independence to what became, in 1922, the Irish Free State. The IRA also rejected this as not securing full independence, and engaged in a bloody civil war with the new Irish government in the south (to 1923) but were finally suppressed, thereafter only being a marginal force in Irish affairs until the late-1960s (a bombing campaign in England in 1939, however, contributed to their being outlawed by Irish anti-partisan legislation).

The Irish government ratified the border between the Free State and Ulster in 1925, thus confirming partition. De Valera's Fianna Fáil party (founded in 1926, and in opposition in the Dáil in 1927) came to power in 1932, persuaded the British to recall the Governor-General, but set off an 'Economic War' (to 1938) by suspending the payment of land annuities from Irish farmers to the British government. The Executive Authority (External Relations) Act of 1936 limited the role of the Crown in the affairs of the Irish Free State to diplomatic formalities, and in 1937, after a referendum, a new constitution was introduced which removed the oath of allegiance to the Crown which MPs were required to take by the Anglo-Irish Treaty of 1921, and described what was now to be called Eire as a 'sovereign, independent, democratic state', with a directly elected President and in which Irish would be the first language. An Anglo-Eire agreement of 1938 ended the trade war begun in 1932, and transferred the control of Irish ports to Eire. The closing of the latter to Allied warships contributed to the problems for Britain of Irish neutrality during World War II.

◑ *Science and Technology*   The period contains a variety of advances in these areas (including Marie Stopes's first birth-control clinic in London [1921], the first demonstaration of radar [1935], the first test flight of the Hawker Hurricane plane [1935], the invention of photocopying and of nylon [1938] and Sikorsky's first functional helicopter [1939]). It also witnessed the publication of, and avid readerhip for, works of popular science (e.g. in the UK, by Sir Arthur Eddington and Sir James Jeans).

But perhaps the most striking development of this period was the rapidity with which communications technology advanced: photographs were first transmitted across the Atlantic by wireless telegraph in 1924; in 1920, Marconi opened the first British and American public broadcasting stations, and within a very few years, the radio ('wireless') was a central feature in the majority of homes; in 1922, the British Broadcasting Company was allowed to charge a 10s. licence fee and made its first transmissions (the British Broadcasting Corporation [BBC] was incorporated under Royal Charter in 1927), by 1925 it was broadcasting weekly to mainland Europe, and by 1930 had founded the BBC Symphony Orchestra.

In 1926, John Logie Baird first demonstrated a TV image, and in the following two years colour TV images, while the BBC first transmitted still TV pictures in 1928, began making experimental programmes in 1929, and broadcast the first TV programmes synchronising sight and sound in 1930. The first outside TV broadcast (the finish of the Derby horse race) was made in 1931, and in 1936, the BBC was broadcasting TV programmes from Alexandra Palace (these were discontinued from 1939–46).

◑ *The Cultural Context*   Narratives to look out for here would include: the acceleration from the 1920s to the 1930s of the technology and art of the film industry (from Buster Keaton comedies in 1920, through Chaplin's 'Gold Rush' and Eisenstein's 'Battleship Potemkin' in 1925, Lang's 'Metropolis' [1926], Al Jolson in 'The Jazz Singer' [1927; first 'talking picture'], Disney's 'Steamboat Willie' [1928; first Mickey Mouse cartoon with sound], to the famous Holywood and other movies of the 1930s culminating, perhaps, with 'Gone With the Wind' in 1939.

In the USA: the development and recording of jazz throughout the 1920s and 1930s, the main period of the 'Harlem Renaissance' of black culture (Langston Hughes, Zora Neale Hurston, Alain Locke, Countee Cullen, Claude Mckay, Jean Toomer); a roll-call of other US writers which includes Ezra Pound, Edith Wharton, Scott Fitzgerald, Sinclair Lewis, Eugene O'Neill, John Dos Passos, Robert Frost, Wallace Stevens, Elmer Rice, Ernest Hemingway, William Faulkner, Thornton Wilder, Clifford Odets, Erskine Caldwell, Damon Runyon, Nathaniel West, James Thurber, Gertrude Stein, John O'Hara, John Steinbeck., E. E. Cummings and Raymond Chandler.

In Europe: the rise of the Surrealist movement in the arts (Andre Breton's manifesto, 1924, the first Surrealist exhibition, 1925, films by Man Ray and by Dali and Buñuel, paintings by Magritte and Dali); the writing of Gide, Kafka, Pirandello, Brecht, Capek, Mann, Cocteau, Ortega y Gasset, Saint-Exupéry, Malraux, Silone, Lorca; the music of Prokofiev, Vaughan Williams, Gershwin, Berg, Shostakovitch, Lambert, Walton, Schoenberg and Britten.

6.6 (THE) LABOUR (PARTY)

The British socialist political party formed to represent the interests of working people through democratic process (Parliament) rather than by revolutionary action. It has its roots in 19th-Century trades unionism and the various socialist groupings of the later part of that century.

James Keir Hardie was the first 'Labour' candidate to stand for Parliament in 1888, when he was defeated at Mid-Lanark (the Scottish Labour Party was founded the same year). He then became the first such MP to be elected – in 1892, when he won West Ham South (to 1895) – and he founded the Independent Labour Party (ILP) in 1893 (its first meeting was in Bradford). In 1900, the ILP allied itself with the trades unions to form, first the Labour Representation Committee (which achieved modest success in the 'Khaki Election' that year), and then the Labour Party proper, with Keir Hardie sitting for Merthyr Tydfil from 1900–15. In the Liberal 'landslide victory' of 1906, Labour won some 29 seats, and was led in the House of Commons by Keir Hardie and then James Ramsay MacDonald until 1915.

The party participated in the wartime coalition government from 1915–18; rejected affiliation with the Communists in 1921; and became the main opposition party in 1922 led by Ramsay MacDonald. In January 1924, MacDonald became the first Labour Prime Minister of the first (minority) Labour Government, but was put out of office in the General Election of November the same year. He formed a second minority Government between 1929 and 1931, and then, in response to the economic crisis, led the coalition National Government until 1935 (dominated by the Conservatives, and with the bulk of the Labour Party in opposition).

Labour again participated in the wartime coalition Government (1940–5), with the

Conservative Winston Churchill as Prime Minister, but in the General Election of 1945 achieved a landslide victory to establish the first majority Labour Government, led by Clement Attlee (to 1951). This government (under 'Clause Four' of Labour's constitution: the commitment to state ownership of the means of production) nationalised the Bank of England, the coal mines, civil aviation, cable and wireless services, the railways, road transport and the steel industry; introduced the National Health Service (NHS) and other aspects of the Welfare State; and oversaw the independence of India (1947) and Burma (1948). However, foreign policy support for NATO in the face of Soviet hostility – especially over whether to rearm Germany – and the manufacture of British nuclear bombs precipitated long-term internal party strife, while Chancellor of the Exchequer Hugh Gaitskell's introduction of NHS charges in 1951 split the Labour Party (Aneurin Bevan and Harold Wilson resigned), which then lost the General Election of that year to the Conservatives.

Thereafter, Labour was out of power until 1964, and in the 1950s was riven by left-wing opposition to the party leadership, led by Aneurin Bevan (hence 'Bevanism'), which sought to make the party more socialist and less 'reformist'. In 1955, Hugh Gaitskell was elected party leader by a large majority over Bevan; he began a policy of modifying Labour from its policy of total nationalisation to one of the 'shareholder state', and rejected a narrow Party Conference motion in favour of unilateral disarmament in 1961. Gaitskell's 'centrism', aligned in the 1950s and early 1960s with the progressive stance of the Conservative minister, 'Rab' Butler, introduced the term 'Butskellism' to signify the apparently 'consensus politics' of the right and left wings of the two main parties.

Harold Wilson became party leader in 1963, and Prime Minister in the General Election of 1964 with a small majority. Labour was re-elected in 1966 with a greatly increased majority, but the progressive plans of the Wilson Government (to 1970) were seriously undermined by the balance of payments crisis, the declaration of unilateral independence by Ian Smith's Rhodesia, the continuing opposition of President General de Gaulle of France to the United Kingdom's entry into the European Common Market, and the problem of coming to terms with Britain's international status as no longer a world power. Wilson led the opposition to Edward Heath's Conservative Government from 1970 to 1974, when he returned Labour to power with, first a minority, then a small majority, and introduced the 'Social Contract' between the government and the TUC to restrain pay rises. But beset by industrial strife and massive inflation in the economy, he resigned in 1976.

James Callaghan became Prime Minister, witnessed the demise of the 'Social Contract', and saw his government only kept in power by a pact with a reinvigorated Liberal Party (the 'Lib-Lab Pact', 1977–8). On the collapse of the latter, the Callaghan Government struggled on, but 1978–9 was the 'Winter of Discontent', in which industrial strife and opposition to Labour was at its height. In the spring of 1979, the Government was defeated on a 'no confidence' motion, and in the ensuing General Election, Margaret Thatcher became the first woman Prime Minister of the UK as leader of the Conservative Party. She won further General Elections in 1983 and 1987, as did John Major in 1992, and Labour was out of power until May 1997.

The period in between was to see the Labour Party involved in bitter internecine strife as it tried to recreate itself as a party which stood some chance of being re-elected. In 1981, the Labour Conference voted for the re-selection of MPs (in order to vet their socialist credentials), Callaghan retired and Michael Foot became party leader. A year later, a special conference established an electoral college to select MPs; the 'Gang of Four' (Labour ministers Roy Jenkins, Shirley Williams, David Owen and William Rodgers) left the party because of what they saw as its leftward tendency, founded the Social Democratic Party (SDP) and formed an alliance with the Liberals. And in the deputy leadership contest of the same year, Tony Benn, the focus of the party's socialist left, was unsuccessful when Neil Kinnock led a group of left-wing MPs in refusing to support him.

In 1983, following the General Election defeat (partly the result of radical proposals on disarmament and withdrawal from Europe in the Labour manifesto, but also of the Liberals/SDP taking 25 per cent of the vote), Kinnock became party leader, and began a 'modernising' mission which, it was hoped, would make Labour a re-electable late 20th-Century party (he was himself re-elected as leader in 1988, defeating Tony Benn once more). During the 1980s, it was discovered that the Labour Party had been infiltrated by members of the Trotskyite 'Militant Tendency' (aka 'entryism'), and after a speech by Kinnock at the 1985 Conference denouncing them, moves were made for their expulsion.

In 1992, another reforming moderate, John Smith, succeeded Kinnock as party leader, but his sudden death in 1994 caused Tony Blair to be elected as his replacement. Over the following three years, Blair undertook the project of creating 'New Labour' ('Clause Four' on nationalisation was removed from Labour's constitution in 1995; it was promised in 1996 that a referendum would be held before joining the European single currency), and he won the General Election of 1997 with a landslide majority of 179. Despite this – and a sign perhaps that all would not run smoothly for 'New Labour' – in the 1999 elections for devolved government in Scotland and Wales, the party gained no overall majority in either of the new Assemblies.

6.7 MODERNISM / MODERNIST

The word's basic lexical sense means 'mental acceptance of modern values; to be of modern spirit or character'.

'Modernism' is one of the most difficult terms in cultural history to define with any precision or hope of consensus, so what follows is an attempt to offer some now more generally accepted characteristics associated with the term, while at the same time offering a definition which will necessarily contain elements that others would challenge. We have the word's basic lexical sense above; but in the later part of the 19th Century, 'modernism' also defined a movement which sought to combine traditional beliefs with modern scientific and philosophical thought (it was in this sense that Thomas Hardy used the word when he wrote of 'the ache of modernism' in *Tess of the d'Urbervilles*). Both these usages relate in certain ways to the Modernist movement under discussion here (it is useful to capitalise the word when referring to Modernism in literature and the other arts), but should not be conflated with it.

There follow some general points in helping to define the term and the movement described by it. First, Modernist is not a synonym for 'modern', although Modernism is both modern and evinces fundamental aspects of 'modernity'. Leaving aside the debate about when 'modernity' began (although now commonly associated with the Enlightenment in the 18th Century), the word 'modern' means simply 'of, or characteristic of, recent times', and in everyday parlance tends to refer broadly to the 20th Century onwards (as in phrases like 'the modern world', 'modern art', 'modern thinking', etc.). Used in this way, of course, it covers by now a period of over 100 years (hence the use of **Contemporary*** [see Chapter 9] to describe more recent events and cultural forms), but part of the point of distinguishing 'Modernist' from 'modern' lies precisely in this long timespan.

'Modern' – for instance, in respect of literature – can be used to describe anything written in the last 100 years, and this will include, even in the period of 'High Modernism' [see below], much that would not normally be characterised as 'Modernist' (for example, 1922 saw the publication of those central texts of literary Modernism, T. S. Eliot's *The Waste Land* and James Joyce's *Ulysses*, but also of Thomas Hardy's volume, *Late Lyrics and Earlier* – poems seldom if ever described as 'Modernist'; equally, British poetry and fiction in the 1950s was in strategic reaction to the dominance Modernism had achieved in literary history by that point, but it is nevertheless clearly 'modern').

Second, although Modernist tendencies were becoming apparent in the arts during the last two decades of the 19th Century, and continue well into the mid-20th Century, the principal period of Modernism was between *c.*1900 and *c.*1930, with that of 'High Modernism' – in literature in the British context at least – falling roughly between 1910 and 1930 and thus pivoting on the First World War. This period saw the early initiatives of T. E. Hulme, Ezra Pound and the Imagist poets [see below], and the production of major works by Henry James, Joseph Conrad, E. M. Forster, Pound, Eliot, W. B. Yeats, Joyce, Virginia Woolf, Dorothy Richardson, May Sinclair, D. H. Lawrence, Wyndham Lewis and Aldous Huxley (the ascription of 'Modernist' to some of these writers would nevertheless be as open to debate as the definition of the term itself).

Third, the Anglo-American and Anglo-Irish nature of literary Modernism as indicated by the list of names above suggests the international nature of the movement, but more importantly, Modernism in general was a movement which reached right across Europe and the United States, and had very different inflexions in its different locales (for example, the reactionary ideology informing Anglo-American Modernism [see below] *contra* the revolutionary dynamics of Soviet Modernism or the work of the Marxist playwright, Bertolt Brecht). A further feature of this internationalism was the transnational influences perceptible amongst many of the artists and writers.

Fourth, Modernism, as will already be apparent, was by no means restricted to literature: all the major art forms (including the new medium of film) were involved in the movement, and as with its international character, there was dynamic cross-fertilisation between the arts. Abstract painting, for example, was influenced by music, as was literary writing (e.g. Marcel Proust's use of the recurring motif in *Remembrance of Things Past*, or Eliot's use of a similar device and of musical structure in *The Waste Land*), whilst literature – most obviously in the cases of Virginia

Woolf and Wyndham Lewis – drew heavily on experiments in the visual arts. Although there were common elements to be perceived in all the Modernist arts [see below], it is clear that different media, like national provenance, created very different inflexions of the movement in form and effect. For this reason, and for those given above, it is becoming customary to refer, not to 'Modernism' (as though it were unitary), but to 'Modernism*s*' in order to recognise diversity and heterogeneity as themselves defining characteristics of the movement.

What common characteristics may, then, be extrapolated from the arts which allow them to be defined as 'Modernist'?

- At a particular historical moment, they seek to break with traditional forms and ideas, but are also hostile to the newly emerging 'mass' or 'popular' culture.
- In particular, they reject conventional forms of 'realism' (the long-standing mimetic tradition in European art which promotes verisimilitude [the appearance of being 'real', 'true', 'life-like'] in purporting to give an account of 'things as they really are').
- This leads to the disruption of conventionally accepted forms of representation (hence, for example, the Cubists' presentation of all sides of an object 'simultaneously'on the two-dimensional surface of a painting in attempting to convey the object's total visual reality in a moment of time, or the novelists' use of forms of 'stream of consciousness' [see below] to represent the workings of a character's conscious and subconscious thought processes).
- A concern, therefore, with subject-matter which conveys 'modern' experience (often of living in an 'alienating' urban, industrial society and in the problematic dimension of Time), and which gives form to the interiority of such experience (the work of Freud and Jung especially is a central influence on many Modernists).
- Paradoxically in light of the points above, Modernist artists in fact seek a fuller grasp and representation of 'reality' than that purportedly given by past art, and offer the art-object as some kind of talismanic device to ward off the destructive chaos of what Joyce called 'the nightmare of history' (this is reinforced by the experience of the First World War). In other words, while rejecting the past and its traditions, they neverthess concur in the notion that there is a 'reality' to be grasped and represented, and that art is the medium in which this can most valuably be achieved. Both tendencies, contorted and embattled as they may be, imply a humanistic sense of purpose and value which helps to distinguish Modernism from **Postmodernism*** [see Chapter 9].

Literary Modernism in the British Context

Modernist literature in Britain seems to be traversed by a major fault-line: in most cases, it was simultaneously highly innovative, not to say revolutionary, in its formal dimension, and reactionary in the ideology which underpinned it (this was not solely to do with the tendency of the male writers – Eliot, Pound, Yeats, Lawrence, Lewis – to hold right-wing political views). While there was little recognisably Modernist drama in Britain until the advent of Samuel Beckett in mid-century (although George Bernard Shaw's plays *Heartbreak House* [1919] and *Back to*

Methusela [1921] might be considered such), in poetry and fiction the kinds of experimental techniques outlined in the section above were pervasively present.

Influenced by the essays and lectures of T. E. Hulme (first published posthumously as *Speculations* in 1924), in which he proposed a new 'hard', 'dry', 'classical' kind of poetry to offset the 'emotional slither' of Romanticism, Ezra Pound, F. S. Flint, Richard Aldington, H. D. (Hilda Doolittle) and other Imagist poets in the years immediately preceding World War I promoted the idea of the 'image' ('which presents an intellectual and emotional complex in an instant of time') as the fundamental device in a poetry 'that is hard and clear, never blurred or indefinite', which seeks 'concentration', abjures 'abstractions' and 'superfluous words', and for the most part uses *vers libre* as its preferred verse form – tenets exemplified by Pound's haikku of the time and such two-line poems as 'In a Station of the Metro', 'Alba' and 'L'Art, 1910'. Pound, Eliot and Yeats, in their different ways, were to develop such techniques in the often apparently fragmentary images, symbols, motifs and uses of myth in their 'difficult', highly allusive poetry, a poetry in which the experience of the 'Modern City' and the spiritual plight of contemporary Europe featured prominently, but which also sought to give order and meaning to the 'ruins' of World War I and its aftermath.

In the fiction of Joyce, Woolf, Sinclair, Richardson and Lawrence, we see a reaction against the realist concern with behaviour, action, dialogue and temporal narrative in attempting, in Lawrence's phrase, to get below 'the old stable ego of the character' – hence the extensive use of forms of 'stream of consciouness', 'interior monologue' and 'free indirect speech' in order at once to access characters' mental processes and to give shape to their impressions and emotions. As with the poets, the principal focus was on the individual's negotiations with a usually inimical social reality.

It is, perhaps, that last phrase above which signals the seemingly contradictory ideology that informs the experimental and innovative work of 'British' Modernists, an ideology which may be described as one of 'cultural despair' or 'cultural pessimism'. In this, the individual (and, more especially, the figure of 'the Artist' as the highest form of the individual) is profoundly alienated by and from the society to which s/he nevertheless is indissolubly tied: an impasse at the heart of the crisis of liberal-humanism (where the individual as a social being pardoxically identifies society as its real enemy, but is unable to do anything about it). Henry James in 1896 wrote: 'I have the imagination of disaster – and see life as ferocious and sinister'; Conrad thought in terms of the 'darkness' at the 'heart' of European civilisation and of modern life as 'the destructive element'; Forster wrote of a world dominated by 'panic and emptiness', 'telegrams and anger'; Lewis could conceive of the artist only as 'the Enemy', and Lawrence as an exile who had to 'fire his bombs' into a corrupt world; Eliot presented post-war society as a sterile 'Waste Land' peopled by 'Hollow Men', while Pound regarded it as 'an old bitch gone in the teeth' and 'a botched civilization'; Joyce had his artist-hero attempting to 'fly by the nets' which society 'flings at his soul' and to 'escape the nightmare of history'; Woolf pivoted *To the Lighthouse* on a section in which human achievements were destroyed as 'Time Passes'; and in Yeats's grotesque vision of 'The Second Coming', 'Things fall apart; the centre cannot hold; / Mere anarchy is loosed upon the world' and a 'rough beast' with 'slow thighs' 'Slouches towards Bethlehem to be born'.

Such a world-view amongst the Modernist writers was the result of many factors: among them, the deepening doubts about human progress in the second half of the 19th Century; the development of a mass reading-public increasingly catered to by 'lowbrow' media and 'popular' publishing, which left the 'serious' writer bereft of an audience (cf. George Gissing's *New Grub Street*, 1891); the roots of a number of Modernists in the *weltschmerz* and aestheticism of the **Fin de Siècle*** [see Chapter 5]; growing anomie in regard to an urban, industrialised, materialistic mass civilisation; and an overpowering sense of the impotence of the individual to resist these tendencies – so that, in Raymond Williams's words, 'there is the acceptance, reluctant at first but strengthening and darkening, of failure and breakdown as common and inevitable'.

What Modernism of the kind discussed here was to offer in response to this bleak vision was itself: its values and its aesthetic culture as a defensive bulwark against the depredations of modern life, in order, as Forster memorably put it, to 'keep open a few breathing holes for the human spirit'. Woolf had Lily Briscoe complete her painting as the novelist herself completes *To the Lighthouse*; Eliot famously closed *The Waste Land* with the Fisher King 'shoring against his ruins' 'these fragments' of past cultures and religions; and Forster himself – at least before the First World War in *Howards End* – praised Beethoven for blowing away the 'goblin footfall' of 'panic and emptiness' in the finale to the Fifth Symphony even though the composer knew it would return as a fundamental reality (after the war, in *A Passage to India*, he had the Marabar Caves announce 'everything exists, nothing has value'). Although Forster was only tangential to Modernism in formal terms, in many ways he spoke most eloquently for its ideology when he wrote: '[Art] is valuable because it has to do with order, and creates little worlds of its own, possessing internal harmony, in the bosom of this disordered planet. It is needed at once and now.'

As a footnote to this partial account of literary Modernism, it is worth remembering that its high point coincided in the 1920s with the rise of professional academic criticism in British universities (and especially Cambridge); that its formal complexity placed it in a kind of symbiotic relationship with the new criticism's promotion of close textual analysis – one became the ideal text for the other; and that its most influential propagandist as *the* truly modern literature was the literary and cultural critic, F. R. Leavis. It was Leavis, throughout the middle decades of the last century and throughout the secondary and tertiary educational system, who, in the tradition of Arnold and Eliot, proselytised for the (Modernist) values of a 'Minority Culture' in the face of a 'Mass Civilisation'.

Timelines: 1900–1939

PERIOD	YEAR	INTERNATIONAL AND POLITICAL CONTEXTS	SOCIAL AND CULTURAL CONTEXTS	AUTHORS	INDICATIVE TITLES
LATE VICTORIAN	1900	Labour Representation Committee 1st meets [origin of Labour Party] – wins 2 seats in Oct. 'Khaki Election' [Keir Hardie, Merthyr Tydfil & Richard Bell, Derby] – Cons. Victory; Boer War: Bloemfontein captured – relief of Ladysmith, Mafeking, Kimberley – Boers surrender at Paardeberg – Britain annexes Transvaal & Orange Free State; Commonwealth of Australia Constitution Act estabs federalism; Germany passes 2nd Navy Act to double fleet by 1920; Yangtze Convention: Britain & Germany guarantee Chinese integrity & freedom of trade; Britain annexes Tonga; Nigeria becomes a Protectorate; Socialist Revolutionary Party fnd.d in Russia; Russia occupies Manchuria; 2nd 'Boxer Rebellion' in China [v. 1896] – international force enters Peking & suppresses it [peace protocol, 1901]	*Daily Express* 1st pub.d; Central London Tube opens – electrified; Birmingham University fnd.d; Max Planck 1st proposes quantum theory; Eastman invents Kodak 'Brownie' camera; Count von Zeppelin flies his 1st airship; D.F. Davis presents Davis Cup for tennis; Freud, *The Interpretation of Dreams*; Charles Péguy fnds *Cahiers de la quinzaine* [Fr. nationalist Catholic journal]. **Int. Lit.:** Theodore Dreiser, *Sister Carrie* [US novel]; Rostand, *L'Aiglon* [play]; Sidonie Colette ('Willy'), *Claudine à L'École* [Fr. novel]; Rainer Maria Rilke, *Geschichten vom lieben Gott* [Austr. poems]. **Music:** Puccini, 'Tosca' [opera]; Elgar, 'The Dream of Gerontius' [oratorio]. **Art:** [c.] G. John, 'Self-Portrait' [Tate]; William Orpen [pnt] 'The Mirror' [Tate]. **Film:** Méliès, 'Jeanne d'Arc'	**P:** Henley **Pr/F:** Conrad James Wells Beatrix Potter (1866–1943) **Dr:** Jones Shaw **Lit. 'Events':**	*For England's Sake* *Lord Jim* [as bk] *The Sacred Fount* *Love and Mr Lewisham* *The Tale of Peter Rabbit* [children's story] *Mrs Dane's Defence* *Three Plays for Puritans* [v. 1897/99; incls *Captain Brassbound's Conversion*] Oscar Wilde & John Ruskin die; Samuel Butler trans Homer's *Odyssey*
EDWARDIAN	1901	Q. Victoria dies – King Edward VII accedes; Salisbury, PM, notes British 'isolation' in world – Chamberlain makes hostile speech on Anglo-Ger. relations; 'Taff Vale judgment': trade unions liable for damages in respect of wrong actions made by their agents; Cockerton Judgment: illegal to provide 2ndary education from rate levied by Schools Board under 1870 Act; Commonwealth of Australia inaugurated as a Dominion of British Empire; Pres. McKinley assassinated in USA – Theodore Roosevelt, President; USA given power to build & police Panama Canal if open to shipping in peace or war; Britain annexes Ashanti Kingdom – incorporated in Gold Coast (Ghana); NW Frontier Province created in British India; [–1904] R.F. Scott commands the 'Discovery' on National Antarctic Expedition	British Academy fnd.d [Royal Charter, 1902]; Marconi sends 1st morse wireless messages across Atlantic; 1st electric tram in London; Wigmore Hall, London, opens; K.C. Gillette starts marketing safety razors; Nobel Prizes 1st awarded; B. Seebohm Rowntree, *Poverty: a Study of Town Life* [social investigation]. **Int. Lit.:** Frank Norris, *The Octopus* [US novel in unfinished 'wheat' trilogy]; René Bazin, *Les Oberlé* [Fr. provincial novel]; Thomas Mann, *Buddenbrooks* [Ger. novel]; Chekhov, *The Three Sisters*; Strindberg, *The Dance of Death & Easter*. **Music:** [–1907] Elgar, 'Pomp and Circumstance' [marches]. **Art:** Gauguin, 'And the Gold of Their Bodies'; Munch, 'The Frenchman'; Sargent, 'Betty Salaman'; [–1903] Sickert, 'Interior of St Mark's, Venice' [Tate]	**P:** Hardy **Pr/F:** Butler Kipling Wells 'George Douglas' [Brown] (1869–1902) **Dr:** Barrie **Lit. 'Events':**	*Poems of the Past and the Present* *Erewhon Revisited* *Kim* *The First Men in the Moon* *The House with the Green Shutters* [Scots realist novel] *Quality Street* Apollo Theatre opens
	1902	Salisbury retires – Arthur Balfour [Cons], PM – intros Education Act: abolishes School Board system – control by Town & County Councils – 2ndary education to be funded out of rates; Chamberlain advocates return to protection & imperial preference; Metropolitan Water Board estab.d [supplies London]; Peace of Vereeniging ends Boer War; [–1914] Triple Alliance renewed; Franco-It. agreement over N. Africa; [>] Krupp armaments & shipbuilding empire develops at Kiel, Germany; USA buys rights of Fr. Panama Co; white	Order of Merit instituted; Empire Day 1st celebrated [becomes Commonwealth Day, 1959]; C.F.G. Masterman, *From the Abyss* [social investigation; pub.d anon.]; J.A Hobson, *Imperialism* [economic theory]. **Int. Lit.:** T. Mann, *Tonio Kröger* [novella]; Strindberg, *A Dream Play*; Maeterlinck, *Monna Vanna* [play]; André Gide, *L'Immoraliste* [Eng. trans, 1930]; Maxim Gorky, *The Lower Depths* [Russ. play]; Sir Rabindranath Tagore, *Binodini* [Indian novel]. **Music:** Debussy, 'Pelléas et Mélisande' [opera, pf.d]; Sir Edward German [comp] 'Merrie England' [light	**P:** Newbolt Yeats Walter de la Mare (1873–1956) John Masefield (1878–1967) **Pr/F:** Belloc Bennett Conan Doyle Conrad	*The Sailing of the Long Ships and Other Poems* *Cathleen ni Houlihan* [verse drama] *Songs of Childhood* [children's verse] *Salt-Water Ballads* *The Path to Rome* [travel] *Anna of the Five Towns* & *The Grand Babylon Hotel* *The Hound of the Baskervilles* *Youth* [stories; incls 'Heart of Darkness']

Year	History / Politics	Science, Art & International	Authors	Works
(1902 cont.)	settlement of Kenya highlands begins; Anglo-Jap. treaty for defence & to maintain status quo in Far East; Russia agrees with Japan to evacuate Manchuria in 18 mths; trans-Pacific telegraph cable laid	opera]. **Art:** Gauguin, 'Riders on the Beach'; [–1903] Sickert, 'Piazza San Marco' [Laing AG]; Wilson Steer, 'The Golden Valley'; Sargent, 'Lord Ribblesdale' [Tate]; George Beresford, 'Virginia Woolf' [photo; NPG]. **Film:** Méliès, 'The Voyage to the Moon' & 'The Coronation of Edward VII'; Edwin S. Porter [US], 'The Life of an American Fireman'	James Kipling Morrison W.W. Jacobs (1863–1943) **Dr:** Barrie	The Wings of the Dove Just So Stories The Hole in the Wall 'The Monkey's Paw' [horror story] The Admirable Crichton
1903	Coronation Durbar for King-Emperor Edward VII at Delhi; Chamberlain resigns to promote Tariff Reform campaign; Emmeline & Christabel Pankhurst fnd the Women's Social & Political Union (WSPU) to fight for female suffrage; Wyndham's Land Act enables Ir. tenants to buy out landlords; road speed limit in England increased to 20 mph; Arbitration Treaty between France & Britain to settle disputes at the Hague – State visits to Paris & London; Alaska frontier between USA & Canada settled; USA signs treaty with Panama to build Canal & control 5-ml zone on either side; Russia refuses to evacuate Manchuria; Russ. Labour Party splits into Mensheviks [Plekhanov] & Bolsheviks [Lenin as leader & Trotsky]; Pacific Cable sends message from US Pres. Roosevelt round the world in minutes; Wright Brothers make 1st powered air-flight in USA	Workers' Educational Association (WEA) estab.d; Daily Mirror 1st pub.d; University of Liverpool fnd.d; Henry Ford fnds Ford Motor Co. in USA; G.E. Moore, Principia Ethica [phil; influences 'Bloomsbury Group']; Bertrand Russell, The Principles of Mathematics. **Int. Lit.:** Jack London, The Call of the Wild [US novel] & The People of the Abyss [study of London's E. End]; Hugo von Hofmannsthal, Electra [Austr. play; basis of R. Strauss's opera, 1909]. **Art:** Sir Giles Gilbert Scott wins design competition for new Anglican Cathedral, Liverpool [consecrated, 1924]; Monet, 'Waterloo Bridge, Grey Day' [1 of 'Banks of the Thames' ser.; begun 1899 – over 100 paintings by 1904]; Pablo Picasso [pnt] 'La Vie (Life)', 'The Old Jew (Blind Beggar with Boy)' & 'Célestine'. **Film:** Porter, 'The Great Train Robbery'	**P:** Henley Kipling Watson **Pr/F:** Butler Conrad Gissing James Eskine Childers (1870–1922) **Dr:** Shaw J.[ohn] M.[illington] Synge (1871–1909)	In Hospital [incls 'Invictus'] The Five Nations [incls 'Recessional'] For England The Way of All Flesh [pub. posthm.] Typhoon [stories] The Private Papers of Henry Ryecroft [mock autobiog.] The Ambassadors The Riddle in the Sand [popular novel about Ger. invasion of Britain] Man and Superman [wrtn; pf.d, 1905] In the Shadow of the Glen
1904	'Entente Cordiale' [Britain & France] estab.d [assisted by Edward VII] – accords over Morocco, Egypt, Siam & settlement of fishing rights in Newfoundland; Fr./Sp. agreement over Morocco; Kaiser Wilhelm II urges Russia to form bloc with France & Germany against Britain; [–1905] rebellion in Crete: demand for union with Greece refused by European Powers [v.1913]; [–1905] Russo-Jap. War: Japan besieges Port Arthur – Russia defeated; Tsar promises constitutional reform in Russia – not fulfilled; uprisings in Ger. SW Africa [suppressed], 1907]; Panama Canal begun	Leeds University fnd.d; Henry Royce makes his 1st car; Ladies Automobile Club fnd.d; Freud, The Psychopathology of Everyday Life. **Int. Lit.:** Hudson, Green Mansions; London, The Sea Wolf ; 'O. Henry', Cabbages and Kings [US stories]; [–1912] Romain Rolland, Jean-Christophe [Fr. novel sequence, 10 vols]; Hermann Hesse, Peter Camenzind [Swiss novel]; Chekhov, The Cherry Orchard. **Music:** 1st concert by London Symphony Orchestra; Puccini, 'Madam Butterfly' [opera]; Benedetto Croce, Aesthetics; Renoir, 'La Boulangère'; [–1906] Cézanne, 'Mont Sainte-Victoire'; Picasso, 'Frugal Repast' & 'Woman with a Crow'. **Lit. 'Events':** [–1907] Harley Granville-Barker & J.E. Vedrenne manage Court Theatre [intro. new European & British drama to London]; Yeats & Lady Gregory open the Abbey Theatre in Dublin [for Irish National Theatre, 1904–51]; Beerbohm Tree fnds Academy of Dramatic Art [later RADA]	**P:** Hardy Yeats **Pr/F:** Conrad James G.[ilbert] K.[eith] Chesterton (1874–1936) John Galsworthy (1867–1933) **Dr pf.d:** Barrie Shaw Synge **Theory/Crit:** A.C. Bradley	The Dynasts [verse drama; Pt I; Pt II, 1906; Pt III, 1908] In the Seven Woods Nostromo The Golden Bowl The Napoleon of Notting Hill [fiction] The Island Pharisees [novel] Peter Pan John Bull's Other Island Riders to the Sea Shakespearian Tragedy
1905	Balfour resigns – Sir Henry Campbell-Bannerman [Lib], PM – Sir Edward Grey, Foreign Sec. – Lord Haldane, Sec. for War; Royal Commission on Poor Law [reports 1909; no action results]; [>] suffragette agitation begins; proposal to construct 4 'Dreadnought' battleships each yr; Sinn Fein Party & Ulster Unionist Council fnd.d in Ireland; Anglo-Fr.	Sheffield University fnd.d; Albert Einstein 1st proposes 'special' theory of relativity ['general', 1916]; Herbert Austin opens car factory in Birmingham; motor-buses 1st used in London; [c.] 1st cartoon-strip pub.d in New York Herald. **Int. Lit.:** Edith Wharton, The House of Mirth [US novel]; Rilke, Das Stundenbuch [poems]; Wedekind, Die	**P:** Ernest Dowson (1867–1900) **Pr/F:** Wilde E.[dward] M.[organ] Forster (1879–1970)	Poems [posthm.] Kipps & A Modern Utopia De Profundis [testament; posthm.] Where Angels Fear to Tread [novel]

PERIOD	YEAR	INTERNATIONAL AND POLITICAL CONTEXTS	SOCIAL AND CULTURAL CONTEXTS	AUTHORS	INDICATIVE TITLES
		military convention; Kaiser Wilhelm II lands at Tangier to obstruct Fr. plans in Morocco; Alberta & Saskatchewan become provinces in Canadian federation; Roosevelt re-elected US President; 1st revolution in Russia after 'Bloody Sunday' in St Petersburg – Imperial troops massacre 1000s of people – naval mutiny on battleship 'Potemkin' at Odessa – St Petersburg Soviet estab.d under Trotsky – ''October Manifesto': Nicholas II promises a 'Duma' with full powers [meets 1906 – dismissed]; Russia surrenders to Japan & cedes Port Arthur – fleet destroyed – war ends; Anglo-Jap. Alliance; Bengal partitioned – [–1908] creates resistance movement in India	*Büchse der Pandora* [pf.d, 1918]; Heinrich Mann, *Professor Unrat* [Ger. novel; filmed as 'The Blue Angel', 1932]; [c.] Pio Baroja, *La lucha por la vida* [Sp. ser. of novels]. **Music:** R. Strauss, 'Salome' [opera of Wilde's play]; Debussy, 'La Mer' [orchestral music]; Franz Lehár [comp] 'The Merry Widow' [Hungarian light opera]. **Art:** 'Die Brücke' ('The Bridge') art movement fnd.d in Germany; Cézanne, 'Les Grandes Baigneuses' [begun 1894]; Signac, 'View of the Port of Marseilles'; Steer, 'Chepstow Castle' [Tate]; Picasso, 'Acrobat on a Ball', 'Family of Saltimbanques' & 'Mountebanks'; Henri Matisse [pnt] 'Luxe, calme, et volupté', 'Portrait of Madame Matisse (The Green Line)', 'Open Window, Collioure' & [–1906] 'The Happiness of Life'; Sir William Nicholson [pnt] 'Sir Max Beerbohm' [NPG]. **Film:** Cecil Hepworth [UK], 'Rescued by Rover'	Baroness [Emmuska] Orczy (1865–1947) Edgar Wallace (1875–1932) **Dr:** Shaw Synge Harley Granville-Barker (1877–1946) St John Hankin (1869–1909) **Theory/Crit:** Gordon Craig Holman Hunt Lit. 'Events':	*The Scarlet Pimpernel* [historical romance] *The Four Just Men* [crime novel] *Major Barbara* [banned in NY] & *The Philanderer* [wrtn, 1893] *The Well of the Saints* *The Voysey Inheritance* *The Return of the Prodigal* *The Art of the Theatre* [enlarged edtn, *On the Art of …, 1911*] *Pre-Raphaelitism and the Pre-Raphaelite Brotherhood* Aldwych Theatre opens; Actors' Union formed
	1906	Gen. Elect: Lib. landslide victory – supported by Labour Party [now so named, with 29 seats] & Irish Nationalists; Trades Disputes Act reverses Taff Vale judgment of 1901; Workmen's Compensation Act to include domestic servants; Education Act: local authorities may levy a compulsory rate to provide free school meals for poor children; [>] women's suffrage movement active; Women's Labour League fnd.d; HMS 'Dreadnought' 1st launched; liner 'Lusitania' launched [v.1915]; Algeciras Conference to resolve Franco-Ger. rivalry over Morocco; 3rd Ger. Navy Act; Franco-British loans to Russia after war with Japan; [–1911] Stolypin's agrarian reforms in Russia create land-owning 'kulak' class of peasants; Transvaal granted responsible gvnmt; San Francisco earthquake & severe fire; All-India Muslim League fnd.d; Roald Amundsen locates magnetic N. Pole while navigating NW Passage	Bakerloo & Piccadilly Tube lines open; Vauxhall Bridge opened; C.S. Rolls joins Royce to fnd Rolls-Royce Ltd; 1st Fr. Grand Prix; Horatio Bottomley fnds weekly *John Bull*; Henry & Frank Fowler, *The King's English* [pioneering work on Eng. usage]. **Int. Lit.:** Upton Sinclair, *The Jungle* [US novel]. **Music:** Dame Ethel M. Smythe [comp] 'The Wreckers' [opera]. **Art:** [c.] Cézanne, 'Le Jardinier' [Tate]; Wilson Steer, 'Richmond, Yorkshire' [Ashmolean]; Picasso, 'Toilette', 'Boy Leading a Horse', 'Two Nudes', 'Self-Portrait' & 'Gertrude Stein'; Matisse, 'Still Life with a Red Carpet' & 'Pink Onions' ['Fauvism']; André Derain [pnt] 'The Dancer' ['Fauvism']; [–1907] Maurice Utrillo [pnt] 'Roofs'. **Film:** Charles Tait [Austrl.], 'The Story of the Kelly Gang' [1st full-length 'feature' film]	**P:** Alfred Noyes (1880–1958) **Pr/F:** Conrad Galsworthy Kipling Edith Nesbit (1858–1924) **Dr:** Galsworthy Shaw Lit. 'Events':	*Forty Singing Seamen* & [–1908] *Drake* *The Mirror of the Sea* [memoirs] *The Man of Property* [1st vol. of *The Forsyte Saga*; v.1920–1*] *Puck of Pook's Hill* [Eng. history for children] *The Railway Children* [children's story] *The Silver Box* *The Doctor's Dilemma* [–1907] Granville-Barker produces 11 of Shaw's plays at the Court Theatre; The English Association fnd.d; [–1908] William Archer trans Ibsen's complete works [11 vols]
EDWARDIAN	1907	Labour bill to give votes to women defeated – suffragettes arrested in London; [–1912] Haldane's Act reforms British Army – intros Territorials & Expeditionary Force; [>] women allowed to serve on Local Gvnmt Councils; medical inspection of school-children intro.d; Companies Act: Ltd liability extended to private Cos; Channel Tunnel scheme rejected by Parliament; 1st airship flies over London; Edward VII visits Tsar Nicholas – Anglo-Russ. Entente [with France, becomes 'Triple	United Methodist Church estab.d; Oxford University forms Joint Committee with WEA; Imperial College, London, fnd.d; N. Line Tube opens; [c.] Sir A.V. Roe builds his 1st aeroplane; 1st regular studio-based radio broadcasts in USA; Bergson, *Creative Evolution* [phil.]. **Int. Lit.:** London, *White Fang*; Strindberg, *The Ghost Sonata*; Rilke, *Gedichte* [poems & 1908]; George, *Die Siebente Ring* [poems]; Jacinto Benavente, *Los intereses creados* [Sp. play]. **Music:** German, 'Tom Jones' [opera]; Frederick Delius	**P:** James Elroy Flecker (1884–1915) James Joyce (1882–1941) **Pr/F:** Beerbohm Belloc Conrad Forster Galsworthy	*The Bridge of Fire* *Chamber Music* *A Book of Caricatures* *Cautionary Tales for Children* *The Secret Agent* *The Longest Journey* *The Country House* [novel]

Year	History / Politics	Arts, Science & Culture	Authors	Works & Literary 'Events'
	Entente']; 2nd Hague Peace Conference fails to limit armaments & rejects ban on aerial bombing in war; Oklahoma becomes 46th State; [>] USA begins to restrict immigration; self-governing [i.e. white] colonies proclaimed Dominions [e.g. NZ]; responsible gvnmt for Orange Free State; 2nd Russ. 'Duma' dissolved – 3rd elected – allowed to discuss budget [1908]; SS 'Lusitania' crosses Atlantic in 5 days	[comp] 'A Village Romeo and Juliet' [Eng. opera]; [–1908] Maurice Ravel [comp] 'Spanish Rhapsody'. **Art:** Renoir, 'Gabrielle with an Open Blouse'; [c.] Sickert, 'The Mantlepiece' [Southampton AG]; Rousseau, 'Snake Charmer' & 'Virgin Forest at Sunset'; Picasso, 'Les Demoiselles d'Avignon' & 'Nude with Drapery'; Georges Braque [pnt] 'Large Nude' – Braque & Picasso initiate 'Cubism', 1908]; Matisse, 'Still Life with Blue Patterned Tablecloth' & 'Blue Nude: Memory of Biskra'; [–1908] Sir Jacob Epstein [sculpt.] 18 nude figures [for façade of BMA building, Strand]; Ernst Kirchner [pnt] 'Self-Portrait with Model' ['Expressionism']; Augustus John [pnt] 'W.B. Yeats' [Tate]. **Film:** [>] Hollywood becomes a film-making centre	Sir Edmund Gosse (1845–1928) Elizabeth Robins (1862–1952) **Dr:** Granville Barker Synge Yeats **Lit. 'Events':**	Father and Son [autobiog. novel] The Convert [feminist novel] Waste [privately pf.d; public, 1936] The Playboy of the Western World [riots at Abbey Theatre, Dublin] & The Aran Islands Deirdre Rudyard Kipling, Nobel Prize for Literature; Virginia Woolf occupies 29 Fitzroy Square, Bloomsbury; Miss A.E.F. Horniman fnds Manchester Repertory at the Gaiety Theatre [opens 1908]
1908	Campbell-Bannerman dies – Herbert Asquith [Lib], PM – David Lloyd-George, Chancellor of Exchequer – [–1909] intros Old Age Pensions Act: 1st state pensions [for anyone earning less than 10s. a week]; Children's Act: separate Juvenile Courts estab.d; Coal Mines Regulation Act estabs 8-hr day underground; National Farmers' Union fnd.d; feminist agitation – Mrs Pankhurst gaoled; Port of London Authority estab.d; 4th Ger. Navy Act; Austria annexes Bosnia – international crisis; Crete again proclaims union with Greece – revolt in Constantinople against it; Leopold II annexes Congo Free State to Belgium as colony [v.1885]; devastating earthquake in Sicily & Calabria; Sir Ernest Shackleton's expedition reaches a point 97 mls from S. Pole; fossilised Tyrannosaurus Rex discv.d in Montana	Harmsworth tales over The Times; Olympic Games held in London; Rotherhithe Tunnel, London, opens; Lord Baden-Powell pubs Scouting for Boys & fnds Boy Scout movement [1st Rally, Crystal Palace, 1909; Girl Guides fnd.d, 1910]; Ford intros moving production line in factory for 1st 'Model T' car; Carpenter, The Indeterminate Sex. **Int. Lit.:** Strindberg, The Ghost Sonata; France, L'île des pingouins [historical fable]. **Music:** Elgar, 'Symphony No. 1'; Ravel, 'Ma Mère l'Oye' & 'Gaspard de la nuit' [for piano]; Oskar Straus [comp] 'The Chocolate Soldier' [comic opera, from Shaw's play Arms and the Man]. **Art:** Monet, 'Views of Venice' ser.; Rousseau, 'The Jungle'; Picasso, 'Still Life with a Skull'; Matisse, 'Dessert, or Harmony in Red' & [sculpt.] 'Two Women (Two Negresses)'; Braque, 'Still Life with Musical Instruments'; [c.] Gwen Raverat [pnt] 'John Maynard Keynes' [NPG]	**P:** Newbolt **Pr/F:** Bennett Chesterton Forster Orczy W.H. Davies (1871–1940) Kenneth Grahame (1859–1932) **Dr:** Barrie Masefield Stanley Houghton (1881–1913) **Lit. 'Events':**	Clifton Chapel and Other School Poems The Old Wives' Tale The Man Who Was Thursday A Room with a View The Elusive Pimpernel The Autobiography of a Super-Tramp The Wind in the Willows [novel] What Every Woman Knows The Tragedy of Nan The Dear Departed [–1910] Ford Madox Ford edits The English Review; Granville-Barker & William Archer, A National Theatre: Scheme and Estimates [1st proposals for such]
1909	Lloyd George's 'People's Budget' [incls provision for Old Age Pensions] rejected by Lords – Parliament dissolved; Labour Exchanges intro.d; Town Planning Act to control use of rural land for building; Osborne Judgment: subscription to political levy by trade unionists illegal; women's suffrage movement increasingly militant; extreme naval rivalry between Britain & Germany; S. Africa Act proposes union of Cape Colony, Transvaal, Natal & Orange Free State [v.1910]; Franco-Ger. accord on Morocco; Morley-Minto administrative reforms in India [increase Indian representation in legislative councils]; Russian Land Law: peasants' conditions marginally improve; US expedition led by Robert Peary claims to be 1st to reach N. Pole	Louis Blériot makes 1st cross-Channel flight; Bristol & Belfast (Queen's) Universities fnd.d; South Kensington Museum becomes the V&A [v.1857]; 1st rugby match at Twickenham; Selfridge's store opens in Oxford St, London; Masterman, The Condition of England [social analysis]. **Int. Lit.:** Hodgson-Burnett, The Secret Garden; Gide, Strait is the Gate [novel; Eng. trans, 1924]; Maeterlinck, L'Oiseau bleu [play]; Ezra Pound, Personae & Exultations [US poems]; Maurice Barrès, Colette Baudouche [Fr. novel]. **Music:** Sergei Diaghilev's Russ. ballet co. in Paris [v.1911] & produces Fokine's 'Les Sylphides'; R. Strauss, 'Elektra' [opera]; Mahler, '9th Syphony'; Ralph Vaughan Williams [comp] 'Fantasia on a Theme of Tallis' [orchestral work]. **Art:** Picasso, 'Woman with a Fan'; [–1910] Matisse, 'The Dance', 'Music' & [sculpt.] 'La Serpentine'. **Film:** Mary Pickford makes her 1st film for D.W. Griffith at Biograph	**P:** Hardy Watson **Pr/F:** Galsworthy Wells **Dr:** Galsworthy Masefield Robins Synge Elizabeth Baker (1876–1962) **Lit. 'Events':** **Theory/Crit:** Marinetti	Time's Laughingstocks and Other Verses New Poems Fraternity Tono Bungay & Ann Veronica Strife The Tragedy of Nan and Other Plays [pub.d] Votes for Women [pub.d] The Tinker's Wedding [pf.d; wrtn, c.1902] Chains [feminist play; pub.d 1911] Charles Algernon Swinburne dies Manifesto of Futurist Poetry [in Le Figaro, Paris]

Period	Year	International and Political Contexts	Social and Cultural Contexts	Authors	Indicative Titles
GEORGIAN II/MODERNIST	1910	Edward VII dies – King George V accedes; Gen. Elec.: greatly reduced Lib. majority – gvnmt reliant on Ir. Nationalists & Lab. support – Parliament Bill to reduce power of Lords to block Commons legislation [v.1909 Budget] – [–1911] constitutonal crisis – 2nd Gen. Elect.: balance of parties equal; Tonypandy riots – miners & troops clash; Dr Crippen [US wife murderer] executed [arrested on Atlantic liner – 1st use of radio-telegraph to catch a criminal]; Union of S. Africa [v.1909] becomes a Dominion [Louis Botha, 1st Premier]; Japan annexes Korea	Westminster RC Cathedral consecrated; M. Curie isolates pure radium; 1st cheap radio receivers on sale in USA; Freud, Jung & Adler fnd Psychoanalytical Association in Vienna; [–1913] Russell & A.N. Whitehead, Principia Mathematica [3 vols]; Sir Norman Angell, The Great Illusion [proves economic futility of war even for victors]. **Music:** [>] the tango becomes a popular dance in USA & Europe; V. Williams, 'Sea Symphony' [choral]; Igor Stravinsky [comp] 'The Firebird' [ballet; produced by Diaghilev]. **Art:** Manifesto of Futurist Painting pub.d in Milan; Picasso, 'Girl with a Mandolin' & 'Daniel-Henri Kahnweiler'; Rousseau, 'The Dream'; Derain, 'Still Life with Pitcher' & 'Black Castle'; Orpen, 'Hommage à Manet' [MAG]; [–1911] A. John, 'Lyric Fantasy' [Tate]; Robert Delaunay [pnt] 'Tour Eiffel' & [–1912] 'Ville de Paris'; Oskar Kokoschka [pnt] 'Portrait of Herwarth Walden'	**P:** Yeats W.[ilfrid] W.[ilson] Gibson (1878–1962) **Pr/F:** Bennett Forster Wells John Buchan (1875–1940) **Dr:** Galsworthy Houghton Synge **Lit. 'Events':**	The Green Helmet and Other Poems Daily Bread [dramatic poems] Clayhanger [1st novel in eponymous trilogy*] Howards End The History of Mr Polly Prester John [adventure novel] Justice The Younger Generation Deirdre of the Sorrows [pub. posthm.] [–1915] May Morris (ed.), The Collected Works of William Morris [24 vols]
	1911	Population of England & Wales 36m. [doubled since 1851]; George V attends Imperial Durbar at Delhi as King-Emperor; after intervention by king, Lords pass Parliament Act: limits Lords' power of veto; MPs to be paid for 1st time [£400 p.a.]; Lloyd George's National Insurance Act intros sickness & unemployment benefits; Coal Mines Act: new safety regulations & no boy under 14 to work below ground/none under 12 to work at surface; Conciliation Act: board of bosses & workers to meet with permanent official to settle disputes; [–1912] widespread industrial discontent & strikes in docks, railway, mining & weaving; suffrage riots in London; gvnmt buys control of National Telephone Co; Agadir Crisis: France & Spain enter Morocco to aid Sultan – French to estab. protectorate [1912]; It.-Turk. war over Tripoli – Italy 1st to use aircraft in offence; 'Young Turks' refuse to open Dardanelles to Russ. warships; Stolypin, Russ. Premier, assassinated at Kiev; [Dec.] Amundsen reaches S. Pole 1 mth ahead of Scott	[–1913] Ernest Rutherford & Niels Bihr announce theory of atomic structure & fnd nuclear physics; [c.] 1st women admitted to Royal College of Surgeons; Fowler Brothers, Concise Oxford Dictionary; [–1912] Karl Jung, The Psychology of the Unconscious. **Int. Lit.:** Dreiser, Jennie Gerhardt [US novel]; Pound, Canzoni [poems]; Wharton, Ethan Frome [novel]. **Music:** Cecil Sharp fnds Eng. Folk-Dance Society; Diaghilev's permanent Ballets Russes Co. fnd.d in France; Elgar, 'Symphony No. 2'; Stravinsky, 'Petroushka' [ballet]; R. Strauss, 'Der Rosenkavalier' [opera; libretto by Hofmannsthal]; Ethel M. Smythe [comp] 'The March of the Women' [WSPU battle-song]; Irving Berlin [comp] 'Alexander's Ragtime Band' [song]. **Art:** 'Der Blaue Reiter' ('The Blue Rider') art movement fnd.d in Germany; Matisse, 'The Red Studio'; Braque, 'The Portuguese'; Epstein, Oscar Wilde's tomb, Paris; A. John, 'Dorelia in the Garden at Aldernay' [NMW] & 'The Blue Pool' [Aberdeen AG]; Kirchner, 'Nude with Hat'; [–1912] Utrillo, 'Place du Tertre' [NG] & [c.] 'Moulin de la Galette'; [–1912] Amedeo Modigliani [sculpt.] 'Head (of a Woman)' [Tate]; Umberto Boccioni [pnt] 'Elasticity' ['Futurism']; Marc Chagall [pnt] 'I and the Village' & 'Self-Portrait with Seven Fingers'	**P:** Masefield Rupert Brooke (1887–1915) **Pr/F:** Beerbohm Bennett Chesterton Conrad Wallace Wells D.[avid] H.[erbert] Lawrence (1885–1930) Katherine Mansfield (1888–1923; NZ) Hugh Walpole (1884–1941) **Dr:** Shaw **Lit. 'Events':**	The Everlasting Mercy [narrative poem] Poems Zuleika Dobson [novel] Hilda Lessways [*] & The Card The Innocence of Father Brown [detective stories] Under Western Eyes Sanders of the River [adventure story] The New Machiavelli & The Country of the Blind and Other Stories The White Peacock [novel] In a German Pension [stories] Mr Perrin and Mr Traill [novel] Fanny's First Play Liverpool Repertory Theatre [now 'The Playhouse'] fnd.d – oldest in UK; Copyright Act estabs modern law
	1912	Lib. gvnmt intros [limited] Home Rule Bill for Ireland; Ulster Covenant signed; Shops Act: ½-day holiday for assistants; strikes in mines & docks; County Hall, London, built; [>] 'Votes for Women'	[–1964] Lab. newspaper, Daily Herald 1st pub.d; 'Piltdown Man' skull discv.d [hoax exposed, 1953]; Russell, The Problems of Philosophy. **Int. Lit.:** Pound, Ripostes [poems]; A. France, Les Dieux ont	**P:** Bridges de la Mare Masefield	Poetical Works The Listeners The Widow in the Bye-Street [narrative poem]

[campaign becomes militant; Royal Flying Corps (RFC) fnd.d [becomes RAF, 1918]; *Titanic* sinks – 1500 drown; Fr.-British naval agreement shares areas of patrol – Fr.-Russ. naval convention; Ger. Navy Law to have 41 battleships & 20 cruisers by 1920; [–1913] army & navy bills passed thro'out Europe; [–1918] Triple Alliance renewed; Italy bombs Dardanelles – takes Rhodes – defeats Turkey – Tripoli & Cyrenaica ceded; Balkan League fnd.d – Turks massacre Bulgarians – [–1913] 1st Balkan War [Turkey cedes Crete to Greece, annexed 1913]; Albania declared independent; Woodrow Wilson, US President; New Mexico & Arizona become 47th & 48th States; S. African Natives National Council fnd.d [later African National Congress (ANC)]; China proclaimed a Republic; [Jan.] Scott's expedition reaches S. Pole, then perishes

soif [historical novel]; Tagore, *Gitanjali* [Indian poems]; 'Alain-Fournier', *Le Grand Meaulnes* [Fr. novel]; Ernst Barlach, *Der tote Tag* [Ger. play]. **Music:** Ravel, 'Daphnis and Chloë' [ballet for Diaghilev, pf.d]; R. Strauss, 'Ariadne auf Naxos' [opera]; Schoenberg, 'Pierre Lunaire' [song cycle]. **Art:** Futurists exhibit in Paris; 2nd Post-Impressionist Exhib. in London [incls Picasso, Braque, Matisse, Derain]; Matisse, 'Still Life with Basket of Oranges'; [–1914] Modigliani, 'Caryatid' [ser. in painted stone]; Chagall, 'Drinking Soldier' & [–1913] 'Pregnant Woman'; A. John, 'Llyn Treweryn', 'Robin' & 'Washing Day' [all Tate]; Delaunay, 'Windows' [ser.]; Marcel Duchamp [pnt] 'Nude Descending a Staircase, No. 2'; Giacomo Balla [pnt] 'Dog on a Leash' ['Futurism']; Gino Severini [pnt] 'Dynamic Hieroglyphic at the Bal Tamberin' & [–1914] 'Dancers' [ser.; 'Futurism']; Wassily Kandinsky [pnt] 'Black Arc'; Percy Wyndham Lewis, 'The Vorticist' [ink & wash; Southampton AG]. **Film:** [>] Mack Sennett makes 'Keystone Cops' comedies; Louis Mercanton [Fr.], 'Queen Elizabeth' [Sarah Bernhardt]]

Pr/F:	
Conan Doyle	*The Lost World*
Conrad	*'Twixt Land and Sea* [stories; incls 'The Secret Sharer'] & *Some Reminiscences* [aka *A Personal Record*]
Lawrence	*The Trespasser*
Wells	*Marriage*
Sir Compton Mackenzie (1883–1972)	*Carnival* [popular novel of theatre]
James Stephens (1882–1950)	*The Crock of Gold* [prose fantasy]
Dr: Houghton	*Hindle Wakes*
Shaw	*Androcles and the Lion* [pub. 1914]
Lit. 'Events':	Edward Marsh pubs 1st Georgian Poetry anthology

1913

Commons twice pass (Ir.) Home Rule Bill – Lords reject it twice; [–1914] Sir Edward Carson, Cons. leader of Ulster Unionists, fnds Ulster Volunteers to oppose integration with S. Ireland; Trade Union Act: members can opt out of political levy [v.'Osborne Judgment', 1909]; 'Marconi Scandal': Lloyd-George & others accused of corruption – acquitted; [c.] 1st woman magistrate in Britain; imprisoned suffragettes on hunger strikes – Emily Davison of WSPU trampled to death by King's horse on Derby Day; British telephone service nationalised – transferred to GPO; Britain & France oppose Ger.-Turk. military convention; [>] huge increase in Ger. standing army; 2nd & 3rd Balkan Wars – treaties partition Balkans – Turkey & Bulgaria settle differences – Turkey & Greece settle ownership of Aegean Islands; 4th & last elected Duma of Imperial Russia; Woolworth Building, NY, completed [792 ft]

In USA, Elmer McCollum identifies vitamins A & B [& D, 1920]; Freud, *Totem and Taboo*; Edmund Husserl, *Phenomenology* [Ger. phil.]. **Int. Lit.:** Robert Frost, *A Boy's Will* [US poems]; Tagore, *The Crescent Moon* [poems] & *Chitra* [play] – awarded Nobel Prize for Literature; T. Mann, *Death in Venice* [novella]; Marcel Proust, *Du côté de chez Swann* [1st in 8-Pt novel sequence (–1927), *À la Recherche du Temps Perdu*]; Guillaume Apollinaire, *Alcools* [Fr. 'Cubist' poems]. **Music:** Diaghilev ballet co. in London; Stravinsky, 'The Rite of Spring' [ballet]; Elgar, 'Falstaff' [orchestral work]; Alexander Scriabin [comp] 'Prometheus' [Russ. orchestral work]. **Art:** 'Armory Show' in NY intros modern art to USA; Apollinaire, *Les Peintres Cubistes* [art theory]; [c.] Sickert, 'Ennui' [Tate]; Sargent, 'Henry James' [NPG]; Picasso, 'Table with Violin and Glasses' & 'Guitar'; Braque, 'Still Life with Playing Card, Bottle, Newspaper, and Tobacco Packet: "Le Courrier"' [collage]; Matisse, 'Portrait of Madame Matisse'; Epstein, 'Rock Drill' [bronze head mounted on machine]; W. Lewis, 'Composition' ['Vorticism'; Tate]; Ferdnand Léger [pnt] 'Contrast of Forms'; [–1914] Matthew Smith [pnt] 'Lilies' [Leeds AG]; C.R.W. Nevinson [pnt] 'The Arrival' [Tate; Eng. 'Futurism' – v.1914]; Henri Gaudier-Brzeska [sculpt.] 'Red Stone Dancer' ['Vorticism'; Tate]. **Film:** Cecil B. de Mille [US], 'The Squaw Man' [1st Hollywood 'western']

P: Lawrence	*Love Poems and Others*
de la Mare	*Peacock Pie*
Flecker	*The Golden Journey to Samarkand*
Masefield	*Dauber* [narrative poem]
Pr/F: Lawrence	*Sons and Lovers*
Mackenzie	[–1914] *Sinister Street* [2 vols]
Walpole	*Fortitude* [novel]
E.C. Bentley (1875–1956)	*Trent's Last Case* [detective story]
Dr: Shaw	*Pygmalion* [in Berlin; v.1914]
Theory/Crit: Chesterton	*The Victorian Age in Literature*
Lit. 'Events':	Robert Bridges, Poet Laureate; Birmingham Repertory Theatre fnd.d

Period	Year	International and Political Contexts	Social and Cultural Contexts	Authors	Indicative Titles
	1914	Women's Suffrage riots in London; 3rd Ir. Home Rule Act restores Ir. Parliament – 42 MPs to sit at Westminster – mutiny at the Curragh – all-party conference on Ireland fails – Britain on brink of civil war; 1st single-seater fighter planes made in Britain; N. & S. Rhodesia united; Panama Canal opens to shipping; US fleet shells & takes Vera Cruz, Mexico; **1st World War begins**: [26 June] Archduke Franz-Ferdinand assassinated in Serajevo – Germany & Austria at war with Russia, France & Japan – Germany invades Belgium – [4 Aug.] Britain declares war on Germany & [10 Aug.] Austria-Hungary – British Expeditionary Force in France – battles of Mons, Marne & 1st Ypres – Russians defeated at Tannenberg – sea battles at Heligoland Bight, Coronel & Falklands – USA declares neutrality; on brink of war with Turkey, Egypt & Cyprus declared British protectorates	Russell, *Our Knowledge of the External World* [phil.]. **Int. Lit.:** Dickinson, *The Single Hound* [poems; posthm.]; Frost, *North of Boston* [poems]; Tagore, *The Post Office* [play]; Edgar Rice Burroughs, *Tarzan of the Apes* [US popular novel – 1st in ser. Gide, *Les Caves du Vatican* [novel; Eng. trans, 1952]. **Music:** V. Williams, 'London Symphony' & 'Hugh the Drover' [ballad opera]; Stravinsky, 'The Nightingale' [opera]; Diaghilev, 'Le Coq d'Or' [ballet] – [c.] Léonide Messine becomes Ballet Russe principal dancer; [–1917] Gustav Holst [comp] 'The Planets' [7-pt suite]. **Art:** [–1915] W. Lewis pubs *BLAST*: *Review of the Great English Vortex* [2 issues promoting 'Vorticism'] & 'Timon of Athens' [folio of drawings]; Nevinson pubs *Vital English Art* [manifesto of Eng. 'Futurism']; [c.] Renoir, 'Judgment of Paris'; Picasso, 'Portrait of a Young Girl' & 'Card Players'; Matisse, 'Goldfish and Palette'; Braque, 'Aria de Bach'; Delaunay, 'Homage to Blériot'; Balla, Mercury Passing Before the Sun'; Kandinsky, 'Fugue'; Kokoschka, 'Tempest'; Gaudier-Brzeska, 'Birds Erect' ['Vorticist' sculpture]; Giorgio de Chirico [pnt] 'The Song of Love' ['Metaphysical Surrealism']; Juan Gris [pnt] 'Breakfast' ['Cubism']; [–1915] Kasimir Malevich [pnt] 'Black Square' [Russ. 'Suprematism']; William Roberts [pnt] 'The Toe Dancer' ['Vorticism'; V&A]	**P:** Yeats **Pr/F:** Chesterton Conrad Forster Joyce Lawrence Walpole Wells Constance Holme (1880–1955) May Sinclair (1863–1946) 'Robert Tressell' (Robert Noonan; c.1870–1911) **Dr:** Shaw **Theory/Crit:** D.H. Lawrence **Lit. 'Events':**	*Responsibilities* *The Wisdom of Father Brown* *Chance* [as bk; serial, NY, 1912] *The Celestial Omnibus* [stories] *Dubliners* [stories] *The Prussian Officer* [stories] *The Duchess of Wrexe* *The War That Will End War* [pamphlet] *The Lonely Plough* [regional novel] *The Three Sisters* [novel] *The Ragged-Trousered Philanthropists* [novel; pub. posthm.; full edtn, 1955] *Pygmalion* [pf.d at His Majesty's Theatre; produced by Beerbohm Tree with Mrs Patrick Campbell as Eliza] & *Common Sense about the War* [controversial attack on gvnmt policy] 'Study of Thomas Hardy' [wrtn; pub. posthm. in *Phoenix*, 1936] *Des Imagistes* pub.d [Imagist poetry anthol.]
	1915	Asquith forms Coalition gvnmt – Lab. & Cons join Libs; Rent & Mortgages Interest Restrictions (war) Act regulates tenants' rights & payments; McKenna Duties on imported goods; Ministry of War Act – Ministry of Munitions formed under Lloyd-George; secret pact between Allies & Italy against Central Powers [joins war, 1916] – Gen. Haig replaces Gen. French as C. in C. of British forces – Nurse Edith Cavell executed by Germans – battles of Loos & 2nd Ypres [1st use of poison gas] – SS 'Lusitania' sunk by Ger. submarine [leads to USA entering war] – Ger. blockade of British Isles – Allied landings at Gallipoli & Salonika – Zeppelin raids on E. coast, S. counties & London; Botha takes Ger. SW Africa; Russia effectively ruled by Rasputin	[c.] Ford farm tractor developed; 1st Women's Institute set up in Britain. **Int. Lit.:** Pound, *Cathay* ('Chinese' poems). **Music:** 'Keep the Home Fires Burning' [wartime song] pub.d. **Art:** [–1922] 'Dadaism' flourishes in Zurich, Berlin & NY; Picasso, 'Harlequin'; [–1916] Modigliani, 'Head of a Woman'; Malevich, 'Suprematist Composition'; [–1923] Duchamp, 'The Bride Stripped Bare by Her Bachelors'; Nevinson [war paintings], 'The Doctor' [IWM], 'La Mitrailleuse (Machine Gun)' [Tate] & 'Column on the March'; Stanley Spencer [pnt] 'Swan Upping at Cookham'; Vanessa Bell [Virginia Woolf's sister] [pnt], 'Portrait of Iris Tree' [NPG]. **Film:** D. W. Griffith [US], 'The Birth of a Nation'; [>] Charlie Chaplin 1st makes films in Hollywood [incls 'The Champion']. **Lit. 'Events':** Rupert Brooke dies on the way to the Dardanelles; *Some Imagist Poets* anthology pub.d; T.S. Eliot settles in London	**P:** Brooke Flecker Gibson T.[homas] S.[tearns] Eliot (1888–1965) **Pr/F:** Buchan Conrad Lawrence Ford Madox Ford [Hueffer] (1873–1939) Dorothy Richardson (1873–1957) [William] Somerset Maugham (1874–1965) Virginia Woolf (1882–1941)	*1914 and Other Poems* [pub. posthm.; incls 'The Soldier'] 'The Soldier' *The Old Ships* *Battle* [war poems] 'The Love Song of J. Alfred Prufrock' [pub.d in *Poetry* magazine] *The Thirty-Nine Steps* [spy thriller] *Victory* *The Rainbow* [banned in UK] *The Good Soldier* [novel] *Pointed Roofs* [1st novel in 12-vol. sequence, *Pilgrimmage* (–1938)] *Of Human Bondage* [autobiog. novel] *The Voyage Out* [novel]
	1916	Asquith resigns – Lloyd-George, PM of Coalition gvnmt – War Cabinet formed; Germans try to land	Einstein's 'general' theory of relativity pub.d [v.1905]; Margaret Sanger fnds 1st birth-control	**P:** Bridges [ed.]	*The Spirit of Man* [anthol. of prose & verse for nation at war]

[1916]

arms in Ireland – Easter Rising in Dublin – armed rebellion suppressed – Sir Roger Casement executed; Federation of British Industries (FBI) fnd.d; Wheat Commission & Food Control estab.d; conscription intro.d for British Army; Brit. Summer Time (BST) intro.d; huge casualties in battles of Verdun, Somme [British 1st use tanks], Ancre & Jutland [naval] – Gallipoli evacuated – Germany steps up submarine warfare – HMS 'Hampshire' sunk – Kitchener drowned – British surrender Kut to Turks but repulse attack on Egypt – T.E. Lawrence joins Arab revolt against Turks – Ger. 'Peace Note' rejected by Allies – Allied economic conference, Paris, to pool resources – 1st British dirigible [airship 'R9'] built – British air raids over Germany; 1st ANZAC day parade in London; US troops invade Mexico; Wilson re-elected US President – makes plea for peace

clinic in NY – imprisoned; Lenin, *Imperialism: the Last Stage of Capitalism*. **Int. Lit.:** Pound, *Lustra* [incls 'Three Cantos']; Henri Barbusse, *Under Fire* [Fr. realist war novel]; Franz Kafka, 'Metamorphosis' [story]. **Music:** Elgar, 'The Spirit of England' [orchestral work]; Erich Korngold [comp] 'Violanta' [Ger./US opera]; *Chu Chin Chow* [musical comedy] begins run of over 2000 shows; George Robey stars in 'The Bing Boys Are Here' [musical revue]. **Art:** [–1918] 'Official War Artists' scheme set up by UK – artists sent to Front to record impressions; Renoir, 'Woman in White Reading' & 'Seated Nude'; Matisse, 'The Piano Lesson' & [–1917] 'The Studio, quai Saint-Michel'; [c.] Modigliani, 'The Waitress' & 'Leopold Zborowski'; [–1917] de Chirico, 'Disquieting Muses'; Gris, 'The Violin'; Nevinson, 'La Patrie' [Cadbury Coll.], 'Troops Resting' [IWM] & 'Returning to the Trenches' [Tate & IWM]; Man Ray [pnt] 'Rope Dancer Accompanies Herself with Her Shadows' ['Dadaism']; Naum Gabo [sculpt.] 'Female Head'. **Film:** Griffith, 'Intolerance' [early 'epic']; Chaplin, 'One A.M.', 'The Pawnshop' & 'The Count'

Charlotte Mew (1868–1928)
Robert Graves (1895–1985)
Pr/F: Bennett
Buchan
Joyce
Moore
Wells
Dr:
Harold Brighouse (1882–1958)
Lit. 'Events':

The Farmer's Bride
Over the Brazier
These Twain [*]
Greenmantle [spy thriller]
A Portrait of the Artist as a Young Man [Pts 1st pub.d in the *Egoist*, 1914–15]
The Brook Kerith [novel of Christ's life]
Mr Britling Sees it Through [war novel]

Hobson's Choice [in NY, 1915]

Henry James dies; [–1921] Edith Sitwell edits poetry magazine, *Wheels* [brothers Osbert & Sacheverell contribute]

1917

British royal family abandon Ger. name of Saxe-Coburg-Gotha & become the House of Windsor; gold sovereigns withdrawn from cirulation; Order of British Empire (OBE) fnd.d to recognise war service; Ministry of Labour estab.d; shipping, wool, cotton, food under gvnmt control – U-boat war causes large shipping losses & serious food problems – bread cards issued; Food Production Act encourages expansion of land under tillage & guarantees minimum prices to farmers – Agricultural Wages Board sets minimum wages for farm workers; new War Loan set up; Lord Lansdowne pubs letter in *Daily Telegraph* advocating negotiated peace; USA enters war on Allied side – sends troops to Europe – British Tank Corps formed – battles of Messines, Passchendaele, Cambrai [Germans use mustard gas] – Canadians take Vimy Ridge – mutinies in Fr. Army & Ger. fleet – Turks defeated at Gaza – Allenby captures Jerusalem –Zeppelins raid Britain – some destroyed; [Feb. & Oct.] Russian Revolutions – Tsar Nicholas II abdicates – Lenin & Bolsheviks take power – E. Front collapses – Armistice with Germany – Finland declares independence from Russia; 'Balfour Declaration' promises Jewish national state in Palestine; USA purchases part of Virgin Islands from Denmark

Int. Lit.: Sinclair, *King Coal* [US socialist novel]; Paul Valéry, *La Jeune Parque* [Fr. symbolist poem]; Georges Duhamel, *La Vie des martyrs* [Fr. war writing]; Luigi Pirandello, *Right You Are, If You Think You Are* [lt. play]. **Music:** [c.] Salzburg Festival fnd.d [1st event 1920]; 'Original Dixieland Jazz Band' [white New Orleans musicians] make earliest jazz records in NY; Holst, 'The Hymn of Jesus'; Sergei Prokofiev [comp] 'Classical Symphony'; Eric Satie [comp] music for Diaghilev's ballet 'Parade' [stage designs by Picasso]. **Art:** 'De Stijl' art movement fnd.d in Holland by Piet Mondrian; [–1920] modernist art movements fnd.d in Russia; Imperial War Museum (IWM) fnd.d [houses War Artists' work; moves to Lambeth, 1936]; Renoir [sculpt.] 'Kneeling Washerwoman'; Picasso, 'Italian Girl'; [–1918] Modigliani, 'Reclining Nude' ['Pink Nude'], 'Seated Nude' [Courtauld], 'Nude with Raised Arms' & portraits, 'Chaim Soutine', 'Girl in Blue', 'Madame Menier', 'Woman with a Black Scarf'; de Chirico, 'Grand Metaphysician'; Nevinson, 'Paths of Glory' [IWM]; John Nash [war paintings] ''Over the Top'' [1st Artists' Rifles at Marcoing, 30 December 1917' & 'Oppy Wood, 1917: Evening' [both IWM]. **Film:** Chaplin, 'The Cure' & 'The Immigrant'

P: Eliot
Graves
Lawrence
Yeats
Ivor Gurney (1890–1937)
Siegfried Sassoon (1886–1967)
Edward Thomas (1878–1917)
Pr/F: Conrad
Mansfield
Norman Douglas (1868–1952)
Alec Waugh (1898–1981)
Dr: Barrie
Lit. 'Events':

Prufrock and Other Observations
Fairies and Fusiliers
Look! We Have Come Through!
The Wild Swans at Coole
Severn and Somme
The Old Huntsman
Poems [pub. posthm.]

The Shadow Line
Prelude [stories]
South Wind [novel]
The Loom of Youth [autobiog. novel of school life]
Dear Brutus
Virginia & Leonard Woolf fnd The Hogarth Press; [–1919] T.S. Eliot edits the *Egoist* magazine

PERIOD	YEAR	INTERNATIONAL AND POLITICAL CONTEXTS	SOCIAL AND CULTURAL CONTEXTS	AUTHORS	INDICATIVE TITLES
WORLD WAR I ENDS	1918	Russo-Ger. Treaty of Brest-Litovsk – Ger. spring offensive collapses by July with huge losses – Ger. Navy mutinies – fleet surrenders to British Navy – allied offensive on W. Front leads to victory over Central Powers – [11 Nov.] Armistice signed – **WWI ends** – Kaiser Wilhelm II abdicates – Germany declared a Republic – Austria proclaims political union with Germany ('Anschluss') – [–1919] many now independent middle-European states declared republics – US Pres. Wilson announces '14 Points' for post-war peace; [–1919] world-wide influenza epidemic kills c.20 m. people; 'Coupon Election' renews British Coalition gvnmt mandate; Representation of the People Act gives vote to all men over 21 & women over 30; H.A.L. Fisher's Education Act raises school leaving age to 14 & abolishes elementary school fees; Labour Party constitution approved – incls 'Clause Four' ['common ownership of the means of production': nationalisation & state ownership of main industries; v.1995]; Eamon De Valera's Sinn Fein party win every Ir. seat outside Ulster – incls Countess Markiewicz, 1st woman MP ever elected – refuses to take her seat at Westminster like all other Ir. MPs; Tsar of Russia & family murdered – large Russ. industries nationalised by Bolshevik gvnmt – Moscow becomes capital of USSR	1st increase [to 1½d.] in postal letter-rate since 1840; English-Speaking Union fnd.d; [–1919] H.G. Wells active in promoting idea of a League of Nations; Oswald Spengler, *Decline of the West* [& 1922; Ger. phil; Eng. trans, 1926–9]; **Int. Lit.:** Apollinaire, *Calligrammes* [poems]; Duhamel, *Civilisation* [Fr. war writing]; André Maurois, *Les Silences du Colonel Bramble* [Fr. sketches of British soldiers]; V.V. Mayakovsky, *Mystery-Bouffe* [1st 'Soviet' play]. **Music:** [c.] 'Till We Meet Again' [song] pub.d; Stravinsky, 'The Soldier's Tale' [ballet]; Béla Bartok [comp] 'Bluebeard's Castle' [opera]. **Art:** [–1919] Modigliani, 'The Little Peasant', 'Anna Zborowska', 'Jeanne Hebuterne' & 'Reclining Nude' (Le Grand Nu)'; [c.] Malevich, 'Suprematist Composition: White on White'; Kirchner, 'Moonlit Winter Night'; Sargent, 'Gassed' [IWM]; A. John, 'A Canadian Soldier' [Tate] & [–1920] 'Ottoline Morrell' [NPG]; W. Lewis, 'A Battery Position in a Wood' [IWM]; [–1919] Roberts, 'A Shell Dump, France' [IWM]; Paul Nash [war paintings] 'We Are Making a New World' & 'The Mule Track' & 'The Ypres Salient at Night' [all IWM]. **Film:** Chaplin, 'Shoulder Arms' & 'A Dog's Life'; Abel Gance [Fr.], 'J'Accuse'	**P:** G.M. Hopkins Sassoon **Pr/F:** Wells Percy Wyndham Lewis (1882–1957) (Giles) Lytton Strachey (1880–1932) 'Rebecca West' (Cecily Isabel Fairfield; 1892–1983) P.G. Wodehouse (1881–1975) **Dr:** Joyce Maugham John D. Drinkwater (1882–1937)	*Poems* [pub. posthm. by R. Bridges] *Counter-Attack* *Joan and Peter* *Tarr* [novel; completed, 1914–15] *Eminent Victorians* [satirical biogs] *The Return of a Soldier* [novel] *Piccadilly Jim* [novel] *Exiles* [wrtn 1914; pub. 1918] *Caesar's Wife* *Abraham Lincoln*
INTER-WAR	1919	Lady Nancy Astor, 1st woman MP to take up a seat in the Commons; 48-hr working week becomes the norm; Ministries of Health & Transport created; Sankey Commission recommends coal mines be nationalised; Acts to supply cheap electricity, subsidise working-class houses & settle ex-servicemen on smallholdings; De Valera, President of 'Dáil Éireann' [assembly of Ir. MPs] – Sinn Fein congress declares Ireland independent – Ir. Republican Army (IRA) fnd.d – [–1921] guerrilla war between IRA & British troops, police & gvnmt irregulars ['Black & Tans']; Treaty of Versailles between Allies & Central Powers; Ger. fleet scuttled at Scapa Flow; Socialist uprising in Berlin suppressed – Rosa Luxemburg [left-wing revolutionary] murdered – Germany adopts Weimar Constitution; [–1920] Adolph Hitler fnds National Socialist German Workers Party (NAZI) – manifesto pub.d 1920; Benito Mussolini fnds Fascist movement in Italy; Soviet Republic estab.d – 3rd International' ('Comintern') formed [dissolved 1943] – [–1921] civil war between 'Red' & 'White' Russ. forces – Allied intervention against Bolsheviks	1st non-stop flight across Atlantic by Alcock & Brown, [16½ hrs] & 1st flight from England to Australia [28 days]; [–1920] Freud, *Beyond the Pleasure Principle*; Russell, *Theory and Practice of Bolshevism* [a critique]; John Maynard Keynes, *The Economic Consequences of the Peace* [critique of harsh terms imposed on Germany by Treaty of Versailles]. **Int. Lit.:** [–1929] major period of 'Harlem Renaissance' [black cultural movement] in USA [v.1925 'Culture' column]; Pound, 'Homage to Sextus Propertius'; Sherwood Anderson, *Winesburg, Ohio* [US stories]; Gide, *Two Symphonies*, [novel; Eng. trans, 1931]; Vincente Ibáñez, *The Four Horsemen of the Apocalypse* [Sp. novel of WWI]. **Music:** Holst, musical setting to Whitman's 'Ode to Death'; Manuel de Falla [comp] 'The Three-Cornered Hat' [Sp. ballet; sets designed by Picasso]. **Art:** Walter Gropius fnds Bauhaus architecture school in Germany; Modigliani, 'Boy with Blue Waistcoat', 'Léopold Zborowski', Seated', 'Marie, girl of the people' & 'The Yellow Sweater'; Duchamp, 'L.H.O.O.Q' ['Dada' drawing of moustache etc. on print of 'Mona Lisa' – Fr. phonetic letters for 'She's	**P:** Gurney Hardy Masefield **Pr/F:** Conrad Maugham Sinclair Walpole Wodehouse Woolf 'W.N.P. Barbellion' (Bruce Frederick Cummings; 1889–1919) Ronald Firbank (1886–1926) **Dr:** Shaw **Theory/Crit:** Virginia Woolf **Lit. 'Events':**	*War's Emblems* *The Collected Poems of Thomas Hardy* *Reynard the Fox* [narrative poem] *The Arrow of Gold & Victory* *The Moon and Sixpence* *Mary Olivier* *The Secret City & Jeremy* *My Man Jeeves* *Night and Day* *Journal of a Disappointed Man* [autobiog.] *Valmouth* [novel] *Heartbreak House* [pub.d; pf.d NY, 1920; London, 1921] *I'll Leave It to You* 'Modern Fiction' [essay] British Drama League fnd.d

	fails; Ger. colony of Tanganyika ceded to Britain; revolt against British rule in Egypt; Government of India Act intros some devolved responsibility – British troops massacre rioting civilians at Amritsar; [–1932] Zuider Zee drainage scheme in Holland undertaken	got a hot rump']; Wyndham Lewis, 'A Battery Shelled' [IWM]; P. Nash, 'The Menin Road' [IWM]; Spencer, 'Travoys Arriving with Wounded – Smol, Macedonia' [IWM]; A. John, 'Lady Ottiline Morrell' & 'T.E. Lawrence' [pencil drawing; NPG]; Matthew Smith, 'Apples in a Plate' [Tate]; [c.] Kurt Schwitters composes his 'Merz' pictures [misc. discarded objects & bits of print]. **Film:** Robert Weine [Ger.], 'The Cabinet of Dr Caligari'		
1920	George V unveils Cenotaph, Whitehall – the 'Unknown Soldier' buried in Westminster Abbey; Emergency Powers Act: gvnmt can declare state of emergency if necessary; unemployment insurance scheme extended; Court of Enquiry recommends national minimum wage & decasualisation of labour in docks; 'Council of Action' threatens general strike if Britain declares war on Russia; Communist Party of Great Britain fnd.d; Government of Ireland Act [4th Home Rule Bill]: Ireland to be partitioned – separate gvnmts in Belfast & Dublin – Sinn Fein rejects it – Terence MacSwiney, Ir. nationalist, dies on hunger strike in Brixton prison; France ratifies Treaty of Versailles – League of Nations fnd.d [–1946] – USA refuses to ratify Treaty or to join L of N – Britain to administer Palestine under L of N mandate; Spa Conference: Allies discuss Ger. war-reparations; US women receive the vote; [–1933] 'Prohibition' [of alcohol] in force in USA [intro.d by the Volstead Act, 1919]; political radicals Nicola Sacco & Bartolomeo Vanzetti accused of murder in USA – world-wide outcry [*v.*1927]; E. Africa protectorate becomes Kenya as British colony; Mahatma Gandhi begins civil disobedience campaign against British rule in India	Marconi Co. opens 1st British & US public radio broadcasting stations; 1st electrically recorded gramophone discs; Sir Arthur Eddington, *Space, Time and Gravitation* [popular science]. **Int. Lit.:** Pound, *Hugh Selwyn Mauberley*; Wharton, *The Age of Innocence*; F. Scott Fitzgerald, *This Side of Paradise* [US novel]; Sinclair Lewis, *Main Street* [US novel]; Eugene O'Neill, *The Emperor Jones* [US play]; [–1921] Čapek, *R.U.R. (Rossum's Universal Robots)* [Czech play; 1st use of word 'robot']; Ernst Toller, *Masse Mensch* [Ger. 'Expressionist' play]; [–1922] Sigrid Undset, *Kristin Lavransdatter* [Norw. historical novel; 3 vols]. **Music:** Ravel, 'La Valse' ['poème choréographique' – score for ballet]. **Art:** Roger Fry, *Vision and Design* [art theory]; Picasso, 'The Rape'; Duchamp [constr.] 'Revolving Glass Plates' [mixed media]; Léger, 'The Mechanic'; [–1921] W. Lewis, 'Mr Wyndham Lewis as a Tyro' [Hull AG]; Gabo, 'Kinetic Model' [moving sculpt.]; Spencer, 'Christ Carrying the Cross' [Tate]; Le Corbusier [pnt] 'Still Life with a Pile of Plates'; Otto Dix [pnt] 'Card-Playing War Cripples'; Piet Mondrian [pnt] 'Composition in Red, Yellow and Blue'. **Film:** British Board of Film Censors fnd.d; [>] Buster Keaton makes his comedies [incls 'One Week']	**P:** Eliot	*Poems* [incls 'Gerontion']
			Wilfred Owen (1893–1918)	*Poems* [pub. posthm.; ed. Sassoon]
			Pr/F: Conrad	*The Rescue*
			Agatha Christie (1890–1976)	*The Mysterious Affair at Styles* [1st detective novel with 'Hercule Poirot']
			Galsworthy	*In Chancery* [*'Forsyte Saga' – *v.*1906]
			Lawrence	*Women in Love* [NY; London, 1921] & *The Lost Girl*
			Mansfield	*Bliss and Other Stories*
			Wells	*The Outline of History*
			Wodehouse	*The Coming of Bill* [comic novel]
			Dr: Barrie	*Mary Rose*
			Galsworthy	*The Skin Game*
			Theory/Crit: T.S. Eliot	*The Sacred Wood* [incls 'Tradition and the Individual Talent' & 'Hamlet']
			Jessie L. Weston	*From Ritual to Romance* [on Grail legends – Eliot draws on it in *The Waste Land*]
1921	Education Act regulates conditions of work for children under 14; Railway Act amalgamates train companies into 4 groups (LMS, LNER, SR, GWR); Safeguarding of Industries Act: move against free trade; coal industry decontrolled – miners' strike; [c.] 'the dole' 1st intro.d; Lab. Party conference rejects affiliation with Communists; [c.] 1st British woman barrister; King George V Dock, London, opens; Michael Collins signs Anglo-Irish Treaty – narrow victory in Dáil – estabs Irish Free State (formally estab.d, 1922; still a dominion of British Empire) – De Valera resigns – 6 counties in North opt out; reparations crisis – French occupy Ruhr – Germany to pay £6600m. in 42 yrs – accepted; 1st 29 Fascists elected to It. parliament; USA signs peace treaties with Central Powers; widespread famine in Russia – anti-Bolshevik mutiny at Kronstadt naval base crushed – Red Army wins civil	Einstein, Nobel Prize for Physics; Earl Haig fnds British Legion; Sir Cyril Burt's standard educational aptitude tests pub.d; Marie Stopes opens 1st birth control clinic in London; [–1922] Herbert Austin produces 1st 'Baby Austin 7'; Frank Buchman fnds evangelist movement at Oxford [becomes 'Moral Rearmament' (MRA), 1938]; R.H. Tawney, *The Acquisitive Society*. **Int. Lit.:** John Dos Passos, *Three Soldiers* [US novel]; Pirandello, *Six Characters in Search of an Author* ['Absurd' play]; Paul Morand, *Ouvert la nuit* [Fr. novel of post-war Europe]; Grazia Deledda, *The Mother and the Priest* [It. novel]; Karel Čapek, *The Insect Play* [Czech drama predicting totalitarianism]. **Music:** Sergei Prokofiev [comp] 'The Love for Three Oranges' [Russ. opera]. **Art:** Picasso, 'Three Musicians' & 'Three Women at the Fountain'; Léger, 'Three Women (Le Grande Déjeuner)'; Max Ernst [pnt] 'The Elephant of Celebes' [Tate] &	**P:** de la Mare	*The Veil*
			Yeats	*Michael Robartes and the Dancer*
			Pr/F: de la Mare	*Memoirs of a Midget* [fantasy novel]
			Galsworthy	*To Let* [* 'Forsyte Saga' trilogy pub.d in 1 vol., 1922]
			Lawrence	*Psychoanalysis and The Unconscious* & [1922] *Fantasia of the Unconscious*
			Maugham	*The Trembling of a Leaf* [stories; incls 'Rain']
			Strachey	*Queen Victoria* [biog.]
			Aldous Huxley (1894–1963)	*Chrome Yellow* [novel]
			Rose Macaulay (1881–1958)	*Dangerous Acts* [novel]
			Dr: Shaw	*Back to Methusela* [5-Pt cycle; wrtn, 1917–20]
			Theory/Crit: Eliot	'The Metaphysical Poets' & 'Andrew Marvell'
			Percy Lubbock	*The Craft of Fiction*

Period	Year	International and Political Contexts	Social and Cultural Contexts	Authors	Indicative Titles
		war – Soviet Internal Affairs Commissariat & secret police estab.d	'Oedipus Rex'; Stuart Davis, 'Lucky Strike' [ser. of collages]; Constantin Brancusi, 'Adam and Eve' [wood carving]. **Film:** Chaplin, 'The Kid'; Keaton, 'The Goat', 'The Boat' & 'The Playhouse'; Fred Niblo, 'The Mark of Zorro' & 'The Three Musketeers' [D. Fairbanks Snr]; Rex Ingram, 'The Four Horsemen of the Apocalypse' [R. Valentino; also in 'The Sheik']		
	1922	'Geddes Axe' commission calls for extensive public spending cuts; Carlton Club meeting: junior Cons. ministers led by Baldwin revolt against leaders & Coalition gvnmt – Lloyd George resigns – return to party politics – Gen. Elec.: Cons. majority 344 [Lab. 138, Lib. 117] – Bonar Law, PM; Ir. election endorses terms of 1921 Treaty – Sinn Fein rejects them – [–1923] civil war between new Ir. gvnmt & IRA – Collins assassinated – last British troops leave Irish Free State – W.B. Yeats a member of the Ir. Senate [–1928]; Royal Ulster Constabulary (RUC) fnd.d; Austria renounces 'Anschluss' – receives loan; Balfour proposes cancellation of war debts – rejected by USA; Russia & Germany resume diplomatic & economic relations; Mussolini leads Fascist march on Rome – made PM of Italy & estabs dictatorship; British recognise independent kingdom of Egypt; Union of Soviet Socialist Republics (USSR) estab.d in Russia – Joseph Stalin, General Sec. of Communist Party; 9-Power treaty secures independence of China	British Broadcasting Company [private monopoly under charter] funded by 10s. licence fee – makes 1st transmissions [v. 1927]; *Reader's Digest* fnd.d in USA; Eng. trans of Einstein's *Theory of Relativity* pub.d; Tut'ankhamun's tomb discv.d in Valley of the Kings, Egypt; Ludwig Wittgenstein, *Tractatus Logico-Philosophicus* [Eng. trans, with intro. by Bertrand Russell; 1st pub.d in German, 1921]. **Int. Lit.:** Fitzgerald, *The Beautiful and the Damned & Tales of the Jazz Age*; Sinclair Lewis, *Babbitt* [US novel]; O'Neill, *The Hairy Ape* [play]; Valéry, *Charmes* [poems]; Bertolt Brecht, *Trommeln in der Nacht & Baal* [Ger. 'Expressionist' plays]. **Music:** Vaughan Williams, 'Pastoral Symphony (3rd)'; Arthur Bliss [comp] 'A Colour Symphony'. **Art:** [–1930] Frank Lloyd Wright [US architect] builds Imperial Hotel, Tokyo; Ernst, 'Reunion of Friends'; László Moholy-Nagy [constr.] 'Light-Display Machine (Light-Space Modulator)' [motorised mixed media]; [c.] Pierre Bonnard [pnt] 'La Toilette'; Frank Dobson, 'Osbert Sitwell' [pnt.d plaster cast; NPG]; Paul Klee [pnt] 'Twittering Machine'. **Film:** Gance, 'La Roue'; Ingram, 'The Prisoner of Zenda' [R. Navarro]; Robert Flaherty, 'Nanook of the North' **Lit. 'Events':** [–1939] T.S. Eliot fnds & edits *The Criterion* magazine; [–1924] Stanislavsky tours Europe & USA	**P:** Eliot Hardy Issac Rosenberg (1890–1918) Edith Sitwell (1887–1964) **Pr/F:** Joyce Lawrence Mansfield Sinclair Walpole Wells Woolf David Garnett (1892–1981) William Gerhardie (1895–1977) **Dr:** Flecker Galsworthy Maugham **Theory/crit:** John Middleton Murry	*The Waste Land* *Late Lyrics and Earlier* *Poems* [pub. posthm.; ed. G. Bottomley; *Collected Works*, 1937] *Façade* [poems; pf.d with music by William Walton, 1923] *Ulysses* [pub.d Paris; banned in UK until 1936] *Aaron's Rod* *The Garden Party and Other Stories* *The Life and Death of Harriet Frean* *The Cathedral* *A Short History of the World* *Jacob's Room* *Lady into Fox* [novel] *Futility: A Novel on Russian Themes* *Hassan* [pub. posthm.; pf.d, 1923] *Loyalties* *East of Suez* *Countries of the Mind* [2nd ser., 1931] & *The Problem of Style*
	1923	Bonar Law resigns – Baldwin, PM – Gen. Elec.: minority Cons. gvnmt [258; Lab., 191; Lib., 158; Independent, 8]; Housing Act: gvnmt subsidies over 20 yrs to assist local authorities [amount increased, 1924]; Matrimonial Causes Act gives women equality in divorce suits; 1st Local Records Office (Bradford); [–1925] French occupy Rühr as Germany defaults on reparations – Britain disapproves – hyper-inflation in Germany – currency stabilised – Hitler's Nazi putsch at Munich fails – imprisoned [dictates *Mein Kampf*; pub.d 1925; Eng. trans, 1939]; non-Fascist Pt. political parties dissolved; Interpol estab.d in Vienna; Anglo-US War Debt agreement; US protectionist tariff in force – Calvin Coolidge, US President; Britain	*The Radio Times* 1st pub.d; 'Big Ben's' chimes 1st broadcast; 1st Eng. FA Cup Final at Wembley; *Time* magazine fnd.d in USA; Le Mans 24-hr car race begins; [–1929] Winston Churchill, *The World Crisis* [4 vols]; Eddington, *Mathematical Theory of Relativity* [popular explanation of Einstein's theories]; Freud, *Ego and Id*. **Int. Lit.:** O'Neill, *All God's Chillun Got Wings*; Wallace Stevens, *Harmonium* [US poems]; Elmer Rice, *The Adding Machine* [US play]; Rilke, *Die Sonnette an Orpheus & Duineser Elegien* [poems]; Colette, *La Maison de Claudine* [Fr. novel – 1st in sequence]. **Music:** Holst, *The Perfect Fool* [comic opera]; Poulenc, 'Les Biches' [ballet music for Diaghilev]; Arthur Honegger [comp] 'Pacific 231'	**P:** Hardy Lawrence Mansfield **F &Pr:** Bennett Conrad Huxley Lawrence Macaulay Wells Wodehouse Sheila Kaye-Smith (1887–1956) **Dr:** Coward	*The Collected Poems of Thomas Hardy* [new edtn] *Birds, Beasts and Flowers* *Poems* [pub. posthm.] *Riceyman Steps* *The Rover* *Antic Hay* *Kangaroo* *Told by an Idiot* *Men Like Gods* [sci. fi.] *Leave It To Psmith* *The End of the House of Alard* [popular novel] *The Young Idea*

INTER-WAR/MODERNIST

	declares independence of Transjordan – British mandate for Palestine in force; Turkish Republic estab.d – end of Ottoman Empire – Mustafa Kemal Atatürk, 1st President – Ankara becomes capital; [-1927] Canberra built as Federal Capital of Australia; S. Rhodesia granted internal self-gvnmt; disastrous earthquakes in Japan	[musical evocation of locomotive]; King Oliver's Creole Jazz Band [incls Louis Armstrong] records 'High Society', 'Dippermouth Blues'; 'Room Rent Blues'; [-1924] Clarence Williams Blue Five [incls Sidney Bechet] & Jelly Roll Morton's Orchestra make jazz records. **Art:** Le Corbusier, *Vers une architecture nouvelle* [theory]; Kirchner, 'The Amselfluh'; [-1936] Wyndham Lewis, 'Portrait of Edith Sitwell' [Tate]; [-1926] Spencer, 'Resurrection' [Tate]; Gabo, 'Column'; A. John, 'Madame Suggia' [Tate]; Klee, 'Landscape with Yellow Birds'. **Film:** Chaplin, 'A Woman of Paris'; Keaton, 'The Balloonatic'; Fred Newmeyer & Sam Taylor, 'Safety Last' [Harold Lloyd; early 'comedy of thrills']	Maugham Shaw Sean O'Casey (1884–1964) **Theory/Crit:** Eliot André Maurois **Lit. 'Events':**	*Our Betters* [1st pf.d NY, 1917] *St. Joan* [in NY; London, 1924] *The Shadow of a Gunman* [Abbey Theatre, Dublin] 'The Function of Criticism' *Ariel* [Fr. biog. of Shelley] W.B. Yeats, Nobel Prize for Literature
1924	[Jan.] Baldwin's gvnmt defeated – 1st [minority] Lab. gvnmt under Ramsay MacDonald [1st British PM to attend Assembly of League of Nations] – [Oct/Nov.] 'Zinoviev Letter' [allegedly from a Soviet leader to British Communist Party] coincides with Gen. Elec. campaign – detrimental to Labour – Cons. returned under Baldwin [413; Lab. 151, Lib. 40]; US 'Dawes Plan' for Ger. reparations in force – recovery duties reduced to 5% – evacuation of Ruhr agreed; non-Fascist lt. trade unions dissolved – opposition leaves parliament; [c.] USA limits immigration by national quota scheme; Britain recognises Soviet Union – Soviet constitution created – Lenin dies [Petrograd renamed Leningrad] – Joseph Stalin takes power & begins reorganisation of Soviets' resources ['5-Yr Plans'; v.1928] – Outer Mongolia joins USSR; N. Rhodesia becomes Crown Colony; Mallory & Irving lost near peak of Mount Everest	George V opens British Empire Exhibition, Wembley; photos 1st transmitted by wireless telegraph across Atlantic. **Int. Lit.:** O'Neill, *Desire Under the Elms* [play]; Frost, *New Hampshire, a poem*; T. Mann, *The Magic Mountain* [Ger. novel]. **Music:** Puccini, 'Turandot' [opera]; Holst, 'At the Boar's Head' [comic opera]; George Gershwin [comp] 'Lady Be Good' [US musical] & 'Rhapsody in Blue' [jazz orchestral work]. **Art:** André Breton, *Manifeste de Surréalisme* & (ed.) *La Révolution surréaliste*; Picasso, 'Still Life with Mandolin' & 'Red Tablecloth'; [-1926] Delaunay, 'Sprinters' [ser.]; Kandinsky, 'Shrill-Peaceful Rose Color'; Ernst, 'Two Children Threatened by a Nightingale'; Matthew Smith, 'Model Turning' [Tate]; [-1925] Joan Miró [pnt] 'Harlequin's Carnival' & 'Ploughed Land'. **Film:** Keaton, 'The Navigator'; Cecil B. De Mille, 'The Ten Commandments' [v.1956]. **Theory/Crit:** T.E. Hulme, *Speculations* [posthm.; ed., Herbert Read]; I.A. Richards, *Principles of Literary Criticism*; Woolf, 'Mr Bennett and Mrs Brown' [essay]. **Lit. 'Events':** Joseph Conrad dies; [-1931] James Woodforde, *Diary of a Country Parson, 1758–1802* [1st pub.d in 5 vols]	**P:** A.A. Milne (1882–1956) **Pr/F:** Firbank F.M. Ford Forster Galsworthy Macaulay Mansfield Wodehouse Margaret Kennedy (1896–1967) Mary Webb (1881–1927) P.C. Wren (1885–1941) **Dr:** Coward O'Casey	*When We Were Very Young* ['Christopher Robin' poems; *Now We Are Six*, 1927] *Sorrow in Sunlight* [aka *Prancing Nigger*] *Some Do Not* [1st novel in 'Tietjens' tetralogy, *Parade's End* (–1928)] *A Passage to India* *The White Monkey* [*The Silver Spoon*, 1926; *Swan Song*, 1928; novel trilogy pub.d as *A Modern Comedy*, 1929] *Orphan Island* *Something Childish, and Other Stories* [pub. posthm.] *The Inimitable Jeeves* *The Constant Nymph* [popular novel] *Precious Bane* [rural novel] *Beau Geste* [popular novel] *The Vortex* *Juno and the Paycock* [Dublin]
1925	Britain returns to Gold Standard; further legislation to protect British trade from foreign competition; Pensions Act: provides for Old Age, Widows, Orphans; Samuel Commission to examine coal industry – gvnmt paying c.£220m. in subsidies; BST made permanent [v.1916]; BBC broadcasts weekly to mainland Europe; Plaid Cymru [the Party of Wales] fnd.d; borders of Irish Republic & N. Ireland agreed; Locarno Pact (Treaties): European Powers guarantee borders of France, Germany & Belgium, agree not to attack each other & part of Rhineland to be demilitarised [v.1936]; [-1934] Hinderburg, President of Germany – Nazi party reconstituted;	Walter Chrysler fnds car corporation; *The New Yorker* fnd.d. **Int. Lit.:** Dreiser, *An American Tragedy*; Fitzgerald, *The Great Gatsby*; Dos Passos, *Manhattan Transfer*, Zora Neale Thurston's story 'Spunk' pub.d in Alain Locke (ed.), *The New Negro* [e.g. of 'Harlem Renaissance'; v.1919]; Anita Loos, *Gentlemen Prefer Blondes* [US novel]; Gide, *The Counterfeiters* [Eng. trans, 1931]; Kafka, *The Trial* [posthm.; Eng. trans, 1937]; Lion Feuchtwanger, *Jud Süss* [Ger. historical novel of Jewry]. **Music:** Alban Berg [comp] 'Wozzeck' [Aust. opera pf.d; wrtn, 1917–22]; Dmitri Shostakovitch [comp] '1st Symphony' [pf.d, 1926]; [-1927] Louis Armstrong's	**P:** Eliot **Pr/F:** Gerhardie Huxley Wodehouse Woolf Yeats Ivy Compton-Burnett (1892–1969) Warwick Deeping (1877–1950) T.F. Powys (1875–1953)	*The Hollow Men* *The Polyglots* *Those Barren Leaves* *Carry On Jeeves* *Mrs. Dalloway* *A Vision* [mystical prose] *Pastors and Masters* [novel] *Sorrell and Son* [popular novel] *Mr Tasker's Gods* [novel]

PERIOD	YEAR	INTERNATIONAL AND POLITICAL CONTEXTS	SOCIAL AND CULTURAL CONTEXTS	AUTHORS	INDICATIVE TITLES
		Mussolini begins to estab Fascist state in Italy; Cyprus becomes Crown Colony; Reza Khan, Shah of Persia	'Hot Five' record 'Cornet Chop Suey', 'Ory's Creole Trombone', 'Muskrat Ramble, 'Heebies Jeebies'; [–1927] Bessie Smith records 'Baby Doll', 'Cake-Walking Babies', 'J.C. Holmes Blues', 'St Louis Blues' [last 2 accompanied by Armstrong]. **Art:** 1st 'Surrealist' exhib.n, Paris; Picasso, 'The Three Dancers' [Tate]; [–1926] Matisse, 'Decorative Figure on an Ornamental Background'; Epstein [sculpt.] 'Rima' [Hyde Park]; Kokoshka, 'Amsterdam'; Miró, 'The Birth of the World'; Vassily Kandinsky [pnt] 'Swinging' [Tate]; 'Yves Tanguy [pnt] 'Extinction of Useless Lights'. **Film:** Chaplin, 'The Gold Rush'; Sergei Eisenstein [USSR], 'The Battleship Potemkin'; Newmeyer & Taylor, 'The Freshman' [Lloyd]	**Dr:** Coward Ben Travers (1886–1980) **Theory/Crit:** Middleton Murry Woolf **Lit. 'Events':**	*Hay Fever & Fallen Angels* *A Cuckoo in the Nest* ['Aldwych Farce'] *Keats and Shakespeare* *The Common Reader* [incls 'Modern Fiction'] G.B. Shaw, Nobel Prize for Literature
	1926	Miners' strike – [3–12 May] General Strike in Britain; Coal Mines Act: legalises 8-hr day; adoption of children legalised in England; Hadow Report on 'The Education of the Adolescent' [recommends secondary-modern schools; 1 of 6 influential education reports to 1934]; Electricity (Supply) Act estabs Central Electricity Board [–1933, sets up Grid system]; Council for the Preservation of Rural England fnd.d; [–1930] Simon Commission to investigate situation following 1919 Government of India Act; Germany admitted to League of Nations; Anglo-Egyptian Treaty: British troops withdraw to Suez Canal Zone; [–1928] Chiang Kai-shek leads army to unify republican China; Hirohito, Emperor of Japan	John Logie Baird 1st demonstrates a TV image; Reading University fnd.d; Fowler's *Dictionary of Modern English Usage* pub.d; Tawney, *Religion and the Rise of Capitalism* [economic history]. **Int. Lit.:** Ernest Hemingway, *The Sun Also Rises* [US novel; *Fiesta* in UK]; William Faulkner, *Soldier's Pay* [US novel]; Edna Ferber, *Show Boat* [US novel; Oscar Hammerstein musical, 1927]; Gide, *If It Die ...* [autobiog; Eng. trans, 1935]; Colette, *Le Fin de Chérie*; Kafka, *The Castle* [posthm.; Eng. trans, 1930]; Henri de Montherlant, *The Bullfighters* [Fr. novel; Eng. trans, 1927]; Georges Bernanos, *Sous le soleil de Satan* [Fr. novel]. **Music:** Constant Lambert [comp] 'Romeo and Juliet' [pf.d; ballet for Diaghilev]; [–1928] Jelly Roll Morton's 'Red Hot Peppers' record 'Black Bottom Stomp', 'The Chant', 'Doctor Jazz'. **Art:** [–1927] Picasso, 'Seated Woman'; Ernst, 'Histoire Naturelle' [portfolio of 'frottages' (pencil rubbings)]; René Magritte [pnt] 'The Menaced Assassin' & 'Rough Crossing'; L.S. Lowry [pnt] 'An Accident' [MAG]. **Film:** Niblo, 'Ben Hur' [Novarro]; Fritz Lang [Austr.], 'Metropolis'. **Lit. 'Events':** 1st Shakespeare Memorial Theatre burnt down [v.1879 & 1932]	**P:** Eliot Sassoon 'Hugh MacDiarmid' (Christopher Murray Grieve; 1892–1978) Edwin Muir (1887–1959) **Pr/F:** Firbank Christie Lawrence Milne Wells 'Henry Green' (Henry Vincent Yorke; 1905–73) T.E. Lawrence (1888–1935) **Dr:** O'Casey Maugham Travers	[c.] *Sweeney Agonistes* [unfinished verse play] *Satirical Poems* *A Drunk Man Looks at the Thistle* [long poem] *Chorus of the Newly Dead* *Concerning the Eccentricities of Cardinal Pirelli* *The Murder of Roger Ackroyd* *The Plumed Serpent* *Winnie-the-Pooh* *The World of William Clissold* *Blindness* [novel] *The Seven Pillars of Wisdom* ['Lawrence of Arabia's' memoirs; private edtn; public edtn, 1935] *The Plough and the Stars* *The Constant Wife* [in NY; London, 1927] *Rookery Nook* ['Aldwych Farce']
	1927	Cons. gvnmt passes Trade Disputes & Trade Unions Act outlawing general & sympathy strikes [repealed, 1945]; British Broadcasting Corporation (BBC) incorporated under Royal Charter [v.1922]; De Valera's Fianna Fail republican opposition party [fnd.d, 1926] enters Dáil in Ireland; [–1929] Britain breaks off diplomatic relations with USSR; Menin Gate war memorial, Belgium, unveiled; [–1935] French build Maginot Line [fortifications on eastern border with Germany]; 'Black Friday': Ger. economic system collapses; socialist riots in Vienna	[–1928] Baird demonstrates colour TV; Eddington, *Stars and Atoms* [popular science]; Julien Benda, *La Trahison des Clercs* [Fr. critique of political intellectuals]. **Int. Lit.:** S. Lewis, *Elmer Gantry* [novel]; Sinclair, *Oil!* [socialist novel]; Hemingway, *Men Without Women* [stories]; Thornton Wilder, *The Bridge of San Luis Rey* [US novel]; Mazo de la Roche, *Jalna* [Canadian popular novel; 1st in 'Whiteoak' family saga]; Kafka, *America* [Eng. trans, 1938]; Federico García Lorca, *Canciones* [Sp. gypsy songs]; Arnold Zweig, *Der Streit dem Sergeanten*	**P:** Eliot Victoria ('Vita') Sackville-West (1892–1962) **Pr/F:** W. Lewis Lawrence Mansfield T.F. Powys Woolf	'Journey of the Magi' [incl.d in *Ariel*; also 'A Song for Simeon', 1928, 'Animula', 1929, 'Mariana', 1930] *The Land* [long poem] *Time and Western Man* [phil.] *Mornings in Mexico* [travel writing] *Journal* [pub. posthm.] *Mr Weston's Good Wine* *To the Lighthouse*

INTER-WAR/MODERNIST

	History	Science/Music/Art/Film	Authors	Works
	– Palace of Justice burnt down; World Economic Conference in Geneva; Naval Disarmament Conference in Geneva; Sacco & Vanzetti executed in Washington; Sacco & Vanzetti Conference in Washington in USA despite conflicting evidence [v.1920]; Leon Trotsky ousted from Politburo in Stalin's struggle for power [exiled to Central Asia, 1928 – expelled from USSR, 1929]; Chiang Kai-shek suppresses Communist influence in Kuomintang – overthrows rival Nationalist gvnmt & estabs gvnmt at Nanking [new capital of China]; Charles Lindbergh, 1st solo transatlantic flight [NY-Paris, 33½ hrs]	**Music:** Holst, 'Egdon Heath' [orchestral work]; Vaughan Williams, 'Riders to the Sea' [opera]; Dmitri Shostakovitch [comp] 'Antigone' Symphony'; Arthur Honnegger [comp] 'Antigone' [opera; libretto by Jean Cocteau]; William Walton [comp] 'Sinfonia Concertante'; Louis Armstrong's 'Hot Seven' record 'Potato Head Blues', 'Weary Blues', 'Melancholy Blues'; Duke Ellington's Orchestra record 'Birmingham Breakdown', 'East St Louis Toodle-oo'. **Art:** Matisse, 'Woman wirth a Veil'; Sickert, 'Winston Churchill' [NPG]; Ernst, 'Vision Inspired by the Nocturnal Aspect of Porte St-Denis'; Raoul Dufy [pnt] 'Bay of Angels at Nice'. **Film:** [c.] 1st sound newsreel film; Keaton, 'The General'; Gance, 'Napoleon'; Alan Crosland, 'The Jazz Singer' [Al Jolson; 1st 'talking picture']; Joseph von Sternberg, 'Underworld'. **Lit. 'Events':** Arts Theatre Club opens	Elizabeth Bowen (1899–1973) Rosamond Lehmann (1901–90) 'Jean Rhys' (Gwen Williams, 1894–1979) Henry Williamson (1895–1977) **Dr:** Travers **Theory/Crit:** Forster Granville-Barker Robert Graves & Laura Riding	The Hotel [novel] Dusty Answer [novel] The Left Bank and Other Stories Tarka the Otter [nature novel] Thark ['Aldwych Farce'] Aspects of the Novel [–1945] Prefaces to Shakespeare [4 vols] A Survey of Modernist Poetry
1928	Women's Suffrage Bill [5th Reform Act]: vote given to all women over 21 [as for men already]; Companies Act: all Cos must keep proper accounts; National Party of Scotland fnd.d [v.1932 & 1934]; Ger. reparations problems continue unresolved; Kellogg-Briand Pact outlawing war signed in Paris [in force, 1929; became legal basis for Nuremberg trials, 1945–6]; Britain recognises Transjordan independence; Herbert Hoover, US President; [c.] '5-Yr Plan' in USSR; Chiang Kai-shek elected President of China; Amelia Earhart, 1st woman to fly the Atlantic	Alexander Fleming discovers penicillin; [c.] BBC transmits 1st [still] TV pictures; OED pub.d [12 vols – 70 yrs after 1st proposed]. **Int. Lit.:** Leslie Charteris, Meet the Tiger [1st of 'The Saint' detective novels]; Brecht, The Threepenny Opera [Ger. play, music by Kurt Weill]; Lorca, Romancero Gitano [Sp. poems; 2nd vol. 1935]; André Malraux, Les Conquérants [Fr. novel]. **Music:** Ravel, 'Boléro' [orchestral work]; Shostakovitch, 'The Nose' [satirical opera]; Stravinsky, 'Capriccio'; Gershwin, 'An American in Paris' [jazz tone-poem]; Duke Ellington, 'Creole Love Call', 'Black and Tan Fantasy', 'The Mooche'. **Art:** Breton, Surrealism and Painting; Picasso, 'Painter and Model' & 'Minotaur'; Derain, 'Still Life: Dead Game'; Magritte, 'Threatening Weather' [Penrose Coll.]; [c.] Man Ray makes Surrealist films & 'Rayographs' [photographic paintings]. **Film:** Keaton, 'Steamboat Bill Jnr'; Eisenstein, 'October'; Lang, 'The Woman on the Moon'; Luis Buñuel & Salvador Dali [Sp.], 'Le Chien Andalou'; Walt Disney, 'Plane Crazy' & 'Steamboat Willie' [1st Mickey Mouse cartoon with sound]. **Lit. 'Events':** Thomas Hardy dies	**P:** Hardy Lawrence Yeats **Pr/F:** Eliot Huxley Joyce Lawrence W. Lewis Milne Rhys Sassoon Shaw Woolf Edmund Blunden (1896–1974) Radclyffe Hall (1883–1943) Christopher Isherwood (1904–86) Edward Upward (b.1903) Evelyn Waugh (1903–66) **Dr:** O'Casey R.C. Sherriff (1896–1975)	Winter Words [posthm.] Collected Poems The Tower For Lancelot Andrewes [essays] Point Counter Point Anna Livia Plurabelle [chapter of Finnegan's Wake; v.1939] Lady Chatterley's Lover [private pub, Florence; v.1960] & The Woman Who Rode Away [stories] The Childermass [1st novel of trilogy; v.1955] The House at Pooh Corner Postures [aka Quartet; novel] Memoirs of a Fox-Hunting Man [1st Pt of fictional autobiog; v.1930* & 1936*] The Intelligent Woman's Guide to Socialism and Capitalism Orlando Undertones of War [memoirs & poems] The Well of Loneliness [banned lesbian novel] All the Conspirators [novel] 'The Railway Accident' [story; incl.d in Upward 1969] Decline and Fall [novel] The Siver Tassie Journey's End [WWI play; film, 1931]

PERIOD	YEAR	INTERNATIONAL AND POLITICAL CONTEXTS	SOCIAL AND CULTURAL CONTEXTS	AUTHORS	INDICATIVE TITLES
	1929	Baldwin gvnmt resigns – Gen. Elec.: 2nd minority Lab. gvnmt [287; Cons. 261, Lib. 59, others, 8] – Ramsay MacDonald, PM – 13 women MPs elected; [–1931] Margaret Bondfield, Minister of Labour – 1st British woman cabinet minister; Local Government Act: local authorities take over responsibility for social welfare from Poor Law Guardians in England; Hunger March of Glasgow unemployed to Trafalgar Square; new Tilbury Dock opens; [–1930] Young Plan for final settlement of Ger. reparations – Hague conference agrees Allied evacuation of Rhineland; NY Stock Market crash on Wall Street ('Black Tuesday') ushers in worldwide 'Great Depression' of 1930s; Nazi victory in Bavarian elections; all-Fascist parliament elected in Italy [99.4% vote for]; Eastern Pact: USSR, Estonia, Latvia, Poland, Romania, Turkey, Persia, Lithuania; [–1930] destruction of Russ. Kulak class [land-owning peasants] by Stalin; India gains Dominion status; unrest between Jews & Arabs in Palestine – anti-British riots – repressed [concessions made]; [c.] term 'apartheid' 1st used in SA to describe racial policy which separates the lives & development of whites & blacks; Airship 'Graf Zeppelin' flies round the world in 21½ days	BBC begins experimental TV programmes; The Listener 1st pub.d; Sir James Jeans, The Universe Around Us [popular astronomy]; US astronomer, Edwin Hubble, confirms that the universe is expanding. Int. Lit.: Dickinson, Further Poems [posthm.]; S. Lewis, Dodsworth; Hemingway, A Farewell to Arms; Faulkner, Sartoris & The Sound and the Fury; Rice, Street Scene [play]; Paul Claudel, Le Soulier de Satin [Fr. play]; Jean Cocteau, Les Enfants terribles [Fr. novel]; Erich Maria Remarque, All Quiet on the Western Front [Ger. war novel]; Axel Munthe, The Story of San Michele [popular Swed. autobiog.]. Music: Lambert, 'Rio Grande' [jazz idiom setting of Sacheverell Sitwell's libretto]; Ellington, 'Saturday Night Function'. Art: Museum of Modern Art, NY, opens; Picasso, 'Large Nude in Red Armchair'; Epstein, 'Night and Day' [façade for London Transport Building]; [–1930] Kokoshka, 'Jerusalem'; Henry Moore [sculpt.] 'Reclining Figure' [Leeds AG]. Film: Disney, 'Skeleton Dance' [1st of 'Silly Symphonies']; [>] Laurel & Hardy make their comedies [incls 'Two Tars']; Jacques Feyder [Belg.], 'The Kiss' [G. Garbo]; John Grierson [UK], 'Drifters' [influential social documentary] Lit. 'Events': the Book Society fnd.d; British Actors Equity fnd.d	**P:** Bridges Louis MacNeice (1907–63) **Pr/F:** Bowen Compton-Burnett Graves Green Richard Aldington (1892–1962) Richard Hughes (1900–76) Eric Linklater (1899–1974) John Cowper Powys (1872–1963) J.B. Priestley (1894–1984) **Dr:** Coward Shaw **Theory/Crit:** Richards Woolf	The Testament of Beauty [long poem] Blind Fireworks The Last September Brothers and Sisters Goodbye to All That [autobiog.] Living Death of a Hero [war novel] A High Wind in Jamaica [novel] Poet's Pub [novel] Wolf Solent [novel] The Good Companions [novel] Bitter Sweet The Apple Cart Practical Criticism A Room of One's Own
	1930	[>] World economic depression. Coal Mines Act estabs 7½-hr working day; Greenwood's Housing Act to promote slum clearance; London 5-Power Naval Disarmament Treaty; [c.] Aristide Briand, Fr. socialist, advocates United States of Europe; 107 Nazis elected to Reichstag – 2nd largest party in Germany; Mahatma Gandhi begins civil disobedience campaign in India – leads 200-mile march to sea to collect salt in symbolic defiance of gvnmt monopoly – arrested [released, 1931]; Simon Report on India pub.d – 1st London Round Table Conference on Indian self-gvnmt; Airship R101 destroyed on 1st flight to India – Britain ceases production; independence of Iraq recognised; Haile Selassie, Emperor of Ethiopia; Amy Johnson, 1st woman to fly solo from England to Australia; Chrysler Building, NY, completed [1046 ft high]	Daily Worker 1st pub.d; News Chronicle 1st pub.d; BBC broadcasts 1st TV programme synchronising sight & sound; [c.] Sir Frank Whittle experiments with gas turbines for jets; Youth Hostels Association (YHA) fnd.d; Freud, Civilisation and Its Discontents; Keynes, A Treatise on Money [economic theory]; Jeans, The Mysterious Universe. Int. Lit.: Faulkner, As I Lay Dying; José Ortega y Gasset, Revolt of the Masses [Sp. phil.]. Music: BBC Symphony Orchestra fnd.d – Adrian Boult, director; Stravinsky, 'Symphony of Psalms' [choral work]; Paul Hindemith [comp] 'Konzertmusik' [Ger. orchestral work]; William Grant Still [comp] 'Afro-American Symphony'; Duke Ellington opens at the Cotton Club, Harlem – records 'Mood Indigo'. Art: Courtauld Institute of Fine Art, London, fnd.d; Léger, 'Gioconda with Keys'; George Grosz [pnt] 'Couple' [Tate]; Piet Mondrian [pnt] 'Red, Blue and Yellow Composition' ['Neoplasticism']; [–1931] Alberto Giacometti, 'Suspended Ball' ['object-sculpture']; Edward Hopper [USA; pnt] 'Early Sunday Morning'; Grant Wood [USA; pnt] 'American Gothic'; Christopher Wood [pnt] 'Boat in the Harbour, Brittany' [Tate]. Film: Laurel & Hardy, 'Hog	**P:** Eliot Hardy W.[ystan] H.[ugh] Auden (1907–73) **Pr/F:** Christie R. Lehmann Wyndham Lewis Maugham Sackville-West Sassoon Walpole Waugh **Dr:** Coward Rudolph Besier (1878–1942) 'James Bridie' (O.H. Mavor, 1888–1951) Emlyn Williams (1905–87) **Theory/Crit:** William Empson **Lit. 'Events':**	Ash Wednesday Collected Poems [pub. posthm.] Poems Murder at the Vicarage ['Miss Marple'] A Note in Music The Apes of God Cakes and Ale The Edwardians Memoirs of an Infantry Officer [*] Rogue Herries [1st in 4-vol. saga 'The Herries Chronicle' (–1933)] Vile Bodies Private Lives The Barretts of Wimpole Street Tobias and the Angel & The Anatomist A Murder has been Arranged Seven Types of Ambiguity D.H. Lawrence dies; John Masefield, Poet

Christie' [Garbo]; Josef von Sternberg, 'The Blue Angel' & 'Morocco' [both M. Dietrich]; Alexander Dovzhenko [USSR], 'Earth'; Lewis Milestone, 'All Quiet on the Western Front'; Mervyn LeRoy, 'Little Caesar' [Edw. G. Robinson]; 'Animal Crackers' [Marx Bros]

1931

May Committee reports on financial state of Britain – heavy foreign withdrawals on Bank of England – financial crisis – Lab. gvnmt resigns – National gvnmt formed [Cons.-dominated, but MacDonald, PM] – Gold Standard abandoned – [Oct.] wins Gen. Elec. [558 to 56 opposition] – National Economy Act: salaries cut by 19% – unemployment reaches 2.5 m – protective duties levied on some imports; Act sets up Marketing Boards; Oswald Mosley leaves Lab. to fnd 'New Party' [v.1932]; world slump follows collapse of Credit Anstadt bank, Vienna & other Austr. & Ger. banks; revolution in Spain – Republic declared; Gandhi attends 2nd Round Table Conference on India – insists on all-India gvnmt – Moslems opposed – [>] in India, Gandhi renews civil disobedience campaign [incls 'fasts to death'] – New Delhi, new capital of India, fnd.d [designed by Sir Edwin Lutyens]; Statute of Westminster: British Dominions defined as sovereign states under Crown ['Commonwealth' gains currency]; [–1932] unrest amongst Russ. peasants – serious grain shortages; Japan invades Manchuria; Empire State Building, NY, completed [1250 ft high]

National Trust for Scotland fnd.d; 1st London trolley-bus runs; 1st outside TV broadcast – finish of Derby; zoo open at Whipsnade. **Int. Lit.:** Faulkner, *Sanctuary*; O'Neill, *Mourning Becomes Electra*; Pearl Buck, *The Good Earth* [US popular novel about China]; Robert Sherwood, *Reunion in Vienna* [US play]; Antoine de Saint-Exupéry, *Night Flight* [Fr. novel of flying; Eng. trans, 1932]; Georges Simenon pubs 1st 'Maigret' detective novels. **Music:** rebuilt Sadlers Wells Theatre opens; Walton, 'Belshazzar's Feast' [cantata; libretto, Osbert Sitwell]; Duke Ellington, 'Rockin' in Rhythm' & 'Limehouse Blues'. **Art:** Picasso, 'Large Still Life on a Pedestal Table & [sculpt.] 'Reclining Bather'; Epstein, 'Genesis' [marble; Granada TV]; G. Wood, 'Midnight Ride of Paul Revere'; Salvador Dali [pnt] 'The Persistence of Memory'; [–1932] Ben Shahn [USA; pnt] 'Passion of Sacco and Vanzetti' [satirical ser.; v.1920, 1927]. **Film:** Chaplin, 'City Lights'; Laurel & Hardy, 'Laughing Gravy'; 'Monkey Business' [Marx Bros]; Tod Browning, 'Dracula'; James Whale [UK], 'Frankenstein' [B. Karloff]; William Wellman, 'Public Enemy' [J. Cagney]

P: MacDiarmid — *First Hymn to Lenin and Other Poems*
Pr/F: Compton-Burnett — *Men and Wives*
Lawrence — *Apocalypse* [posthm.]
Rhys — *After Leaving Mr. Mackenzie*
Wodehouse — *The Jeeves Omnibus*
Woolf — *The Waves* & 'Preface' to *Life As We Have Known It* by Co-operative Working Women
A.J. Cronin (1896–1981) — *Hatter's Castle* [autobiog. novel]
James Hanley (1901–85) — *Boy* & *The Last Voyage* [novels]
Anthony Powell (1905–99) — *Afternoon Men* [novel]
Dr: Coward — *Cavalcade*
Priestley — *The Good Companions* [with Edward Knoblock] & *Dangerous Corner* [pub.d 1932]
Dodie Smith (1896–1990) — *Autumn Crocus*
Theory/Crit: Edmund Wilson — *Axel's Castle*

1932

Neville Chamberlain's Import Duties Act intros full protection – free trade abandoned – anti-protectionist Libs & Lab. peer, Philip Snowden, resign from National gvnmt – Ottawa conference estabs 'Imperial Preference' in trade – Wheat Act to protect market for home-producers; Great Hunger March of unemployed to London; Mosley renames New Party 'British Union of Fascists' [v.1931]; Act reforms juvenile court procedure & intros Approved Schools; Scottish Party fnd.d [v.1934]; De Valera & Fianna Fáil come to power in Irish Free State – sever most remaining constitutional ties with Britain – suspend repayment of land annuities from Ir. farmers to UK gvnmt – sets off 'Economic War' [–1938]; Lausanne Conference settles reparations & war debts [Germany to pay 3 milliard marks]; World Disarmament Conference opens at Geneva; Nazis become the largest party in Ger. Reichstag; Franklin D. Roosevelt, US President; Russo-Polish non-aggression pact [extended for 10 yrs, 1934]; Turkey admitted to L of Ns; Japan attacks China – occupies Shanghai – estabs puppet state of

Int. Lit.: Faulkner, *Light in August*; Hemingway, *Death in the Afternoon* [on bullfighting]; Erskine Caldwell, *Tobacco Road* [US novel & (1933) popular play]; Damon Ruyon, *Guys and Dolls* [US stories]; François Mauriac, *Le Noeud de Vipères* [Fr. novel]; [–1946] Romains, *Les Hommes de bonne volonté* [27-vol. Fr. novel cycle]. **Music:** Sir Thomas Beecham fnds London Philharmonic Orchestra; Arnold Schoenberg [comp] 'Moses and Aaron' [Austr. opera]; Benjamin Britten [comp] 'A Boy Was Born' [choral work]. **Art:** 'Socialist Realism' imposed on art in USSR; Picasso, 'The Dream'; [–1934] Ray, 'Observation Time – The Lovers'; W. Lewis, 'Rebecca West' [pencil drawing; NPG]; Hopper, 'Room in New York'; Spencer, 'The May Tree'; P. Nash illustr. Thomas Browne's *Urne Burial* & *The Garden of Cyrus* [v.1658]; [–1933] Giacometti, 'Palace at Four o'Clock in the Morning'. **Film:** 1st Venice Film Festival; Laurel & Hardy, 'The Music Box'; 'Horse Feathers' [Marx Bros]; Browning, 'Freaks'; von Sternberg, 'Shanghai Express' [Dietrich]; Whale, 'The Old Dark House' [Karloff]; Pandro Berman, 'Morning

P: Lawrence — *Last Poems* [posthm.]
MacDiarmid — *Scots Unbound and Other Poems*
Pr/F: Huxley — *Brave New World*
Isherwood — *The Memorial*
R. Lehmann — *Invitation to the Waltz* [novel]
Powell — *Venusberg*
J.C. Powys — *A Glastonbury Romance*
Shaw — *The Black Girl in Search of God*
Waugh — *Black Mischief*
'Lewis Grassic Gibbon' (James Leslie Mitchell; 1901–35) — *Sunset Song* [*Cloud Howe*, 1933 & *Grey Granite*, 1934; novel trilogy pub.d posthm. as *A Scot's Quair*, 1946]
Graham Greene (1904–91) — *Stamboul Train* [novel]
Charles Morgan (1894–1958) — *The Fountain* [novel]
Louis Golding (1895–1958) — *Magnolia Street* [novel]
Dr: Auden — *The Orators: an English Study*
Coward — *Words and Music* [revue; incls song 'Mad Dogs and Englishmen']

PERIOD	YEAR	INTERNATIONAL AND POLITICAL CONTEXTS	SOCIAL AND CULTURAL CONTEXTS	AUTHORS	INDICATIVE TITLES
		Manchukuo; Sydney Harbour Bridge opens; Amy Johnson flies solo to S. Africa & back	Glory' [K. Hepburn]; Frank Borsage, 'A Farewell to Arms' [G. Cooper]; Edmund Goulding [UK], 'Grand Hotel' [Garbo, Novarro]; George Fitzmaurice, 'Mata Hari' [Garbo, Novarro]; Howard Hawks, 'Scarface'. **Lit. 'Events'**: John Galsworthy, Nobel Prize for Literature; New Shakespeare Memorial Theatre, Stratford, opens; Michael Roberts (ed.) New Signatures [anthol.]	**Theory/Crit:** Antonin Artaud Eliot F.R. Leavis Q.D. Leavis Woolf	Manifesto of Theatre of Cruelty Selected Essays New Bearings in English Poetry & [–1953] edits Scrutiny [journal] Fiction and the Reading Public The Common Reader [2nd ser.]
	1933	Oxford Union debate 'That this House will in no circumstances fight for King and Country' passed by 275 votes to 153 – causes national outrage; Special Areas Act provides limited assistance to regions for slum clearance; London Passenger Transport Board amalgamates bus, tram & tube provision; 2nd Agricultural Marketing Act limits imports to control home production & keep prices up; Hitler appointed Chancellor of Germany – engineers Reichstag fire & accuses Communists – calls Gen. Elec. – non-Nazi parties terrorised & suppressed – arrogates absolute power to himself – 1st concentration camps set up – Germany leaves Disarmament Conference & L of Ns; Sp. right wing gains control of gvnmt – 'Falange' (Fascist Party) fnd.d; financial crisis in USA – Roosevelt announces 'New Deal' policies to defeat the US 'Great Depression' – 'Prohibition' repealed [v.1920]; USSR & USA estab. diplomatic relations for 1st time since Revolution of 1917; [–1932] 2nd '5-Yr Plan' in USSR; Japan withdraws from L of Ns	England's controversial 1932–3 'Body-line' cricket tour of Australia [Harold Larwood's fast bowling]; 1st 'supplement' to OED pub.d; Eddington, The Expanding Universe [popular astronomy]. **Int. Lit.:** Caldwell, God's Little Acre [novel]; Stein, Autobiography of Alice B. Toklas [auto]biog.]; Nathaniel West, Miss Lonelyhearts [US novel]; James Thurber, My Life and Hard Times [US autobio. humour]; Malraux, La Condition humaine [Fr. novel of revolutionary China; trans as Storm in Shanghai, 1934 & as Man's Estate, 1948]; [–1944] Duhamel, Chronique des Pasquier [Fr. family saga]; Ignazio Silone, Fontamara [It. novel of peasant life]; Federico Garcia Lorca, Blood Wedding [Sp. drama]. **Art:** Klee, 'Woman's Mask'; Ray, 'Portrait of Pablo Picasso'; W. Lewis, 'Red Scene' [Tate]; Spencer completes 'peace in war' murals at Burghclere Memorial Chapel, near Newbury, with 'Resurrection of the Soldiers' [ser. begun, 1923]; Ben Nicholson [pnt] 'Ben Nicholson and Barbara Hepworth' [NPG]. **Film:** British Film Institute (BFI) fnd.d; Disney, 'The Three Little Pigs' [in colour]; 'Duck Soup' [Marx Bros]; 'Sons of the Desert' [Laurel & Hardy]; Whale, 'The Invisible Man'; Merian C. Cooper & Ernest B. Schoedsack, 'King Kong'; Alexander Korda [UK], 'The Private Life of Henry VIII' [C. Laughton]; Reuben Mamoulian [USSR], 'Queen Christina' [Garbo]; Lloyd Bacon, 'Footlight Parade' & '42nd Street' [choreography, Busby Berkeley]; Wesley Ruggles, 'I'm No Angel' [M. West]; Lowell Sherman , 'She Done Him Wrong' [M. West, C. Grant]	**P:** Auden Yeats Stephen Spender (1909–95) **Pr/F:** Christie Powell Wells Vera Brittain (1893–1970) Stella Gibbons (1902–89) Walter Greenwood (1903–74) James Hilton (1900–54) 'George Orwell' (Eric Blair, 1903–50) Dorothy L. Sayers (1893–1957) **Theory/Crit:** Eliot Leavis & Denys Thompson Mario Praz **Lit. 'Events':**	The Dance of Death [verse play] The Winding Stair and Other Poems Poems Lord Edgware Dies From a View to a Death The Shape of Things to Come [plea to confront fascism; film, v.1936] Testament of Youth [memoirs] Cold Comfort Farm [parodic novel] Love on the Dole [working-class novel; dramatised (with R. Gow), 1935] Lost Horizon [novel] Down and Out in Paris and London [sociological memoirs] Murder Must Advertise ['Lord Peter Wimsey' detective novel] The Use of Poetry and the Use of Criticism [Harvard lectures, 1932–3] Culture and Environment The Romantic Agony Roberts (ed.) New Country [anthol.]; Open Air Theatre, Regents Park, fnd.d
	1934	Incitement to Disaffection Act: reverses Wilkes case decision [v.1763–6] that general powers of search are illegal; British Iron & Steel Federation formed to reorganise industry for efficiency; Unemployment Assistance Board intros means testing for poor relief – special commissioners appointed for depressed areas; Scottish National Party (SNP) fnd.d [unites parties of 1928 & 1932]; gvnmt subsidy to build SS 'Queen Mary' [launched 1936] & 'Queen	The British Council fnd.d [Royal Charter, 1940]; James Chadwick confirms the existence of the neutron; A.J.A. Symons, The Quest for Corvo [biog.]; [–1954] Arnold J. Toynbee, Study of History [10 vols]. **Int. Lit.:** John O'Hara, Appointment in Samara [US novel]; Lillian Hellman, The Children's Hour [US play]; Cocteau, La Machine infernale [play]. **Music:** Glyndebourne Festival Theatre [for opera] opens; [–1935] Gershwin, 'Porgy and Bess' [jazz opera];	**P:** MacDiarmid Dylan Thomas (1914–53) **Pr/F:** Christie Graves Greene Hilton Orwell	Stony Limits and Other Poems 18 Poems Murder on the Orient Express I, Claudius & Claudius the God [historical novels] It's a Battlefield Goodbye Mr Chips [film, v.1939] Burmese Days

INTER-WAR

Year	World Events	Science · Music · Art · Film	Authors	Works
	Elizabeth' [launched 1938]; France, with Britain & Italy, oppose Ger. rearmament; [June] Munich putsch: Hitler purges Nazi party of opposition – 100s murdered by SS ('Night of the Long Knives') – Pres. Hindenburg dies – Hitler becomes 'Reichsführer' (Chancellor) after plebiscite; Allied troops finally leave Rhineland; Ger.-Polish 10-yr non-aggression pact; USSR admitted to L of Ns; assassination of Leningrad Bolshevik, Kirov, ushers in Stalin's purges [v.1936]	Hindemith, 'Mathis der Maler' [Ger. symphony; opera later banned by Nazis]; Shostakovich, 'A Lady Macbeth of Mzensk' [Russ. opera – attacked for 'decadence' & withdrawn, 1936]; [>] Benny Goodman's ['Swing'] Orchestra estab.d. **Art:** Picasso, 'Woman Writing' & 'Bullfight'; [–1935] Epstein, 'Ecce Homo'; Dali, 'Mae West'; Dufy, 'Cowes Regatta'; Klee, 'Flowering'. **Film:** von Sternberg, 'The Scarlet Empress' [Dietrich]; Berman, 'The Little Minister' [K. Hepburn]; Korda, 'The Scarlet Pimpernel' [L. Howard]; Frank Capra, 'It Happened One Night' [C. Gable, C. Colbert]; George Cukor, 'David Copperfield' [W.C. Fields]; Alfred Hitchcock [UK], 'The Man Who Knew Too Much'; Leni Riefenstahl [Ger.], 'Triumph of the Will' [documentary of Nazi Nuremberg rally]	J.C. Powys Priestley Rhys Sayers Waugh Samuel Beckett (1906–89) **Dr:** Eliot **Theory/crit:** Cecil Day Lewis Eliot **Lit. 'Events':**	*Weymouth Sands* *English Journey* [account of 'condition of England' in 1930s] *The Nine Tailors* *Voyage in the Dark* [novel] *A Handful of Dust* *More Pricks than Kicks* [stories] *The Rock* [verse drama] *A Hope for Poetry* *After Strange Gods* Ban on Joyce's *Ulysses* lifted in USA – pub.d in UK, 1936; *Left Review* pub.d
1935	George V's Silver Jubilee; Macdonald resigns – National gvnmt wins Gen. Elec.: Baldwin (Cons.), PM; Government of India Act moves some way towards self-gvnmt, but Britain retains substantial power; Hore-Belisha intros beacons for pedestrian crossings & 30 mph limit in built-up areas; Italy invades Abyssinia – Hoare-Laval Pact: Anglo-Fr. deal with Italy – Foreign Sec. Hoare resigns – replaced by Anthony Eden – L of Ns imposes economic sanctions on Italy while rejecting Abyssinian appeals for help; Stresa Conference: Britain & France condemn unilateral repudiation of treaties as endangering European peace; Ger. Nuremberg Laws make Swastika official flag of Reich & deprive Jews of citizen's rights – plebiscite in Saar returns it to Ger. rule – Hitler repudiates Treaty of Versailles' military clauses – creates air force & restores full conscription in Germany; Fr.-Soviet & Czecho-Soviet pacts of mutual assistance; US 'New Deal': Labour Relations Act [right to organise freely without employers' coercion] & Social Security Act; Persia renamed Iran	London 'Green Belt' scheme intro.d; 1st British National Park in Snowdonia; Watson-Watt 1st demonstrates radar; Campbell: 1st land-speed record over 300 mph in racing-car 'Bluebird'; Sidney & Beatrice Webb, *Soviet Communism: A New Civilisation*. **Int. Lit.:** O'Hara, *Butterfield 8* [novel]; Thurber, *The Middle-Aged Man on the Flying Trapeze* [US humour]; Sherwood, *The Petrified Forest* [play]; John Steinbeck, *Tortilla Flat* [US novel]; Clifford Odets, *Waiting for Lefty* [US social protest play]; [–1939] Montherlant, *Les Jeunes Filles* [4-vol. novel]; Lorca, *Romancero Gitano* [Sp. songs & poems]. **Music:** R. Strauss, 'Die schweigsame Frau' [Ger. opera, with Stefan Zweig]; Ivor Novello [comp] 'Glamorous Night' [1st of his Drury Lane musicals; British Council]; Pierre Bonnard [pnt] 'Nude in a Bathtub'. **Film:** von Sternberg, 'The Devil Is a Woman' [Dietrich]; Whale, 'The Bride of Frankenstein' [Karloff]; Clarence Brown, 'Anna Karenina' [Garbo]; Frank Lloyd, 'Mutiny on the Bounty' [Laughton, C. Gable]; Hitchcock, 'The Thirty-Nine Steps' [R. Donat]; Mark Sandrich, 'Top Hat' [F. Astaire, G. Rogers]; Sam Wood, 'A Night at the Opera' [Marx Bros]	**P:** Eliot MacDiarmid MacNeice C.[ecil] Day Lewis (1904–72) **Pr/F:** Bowen Compton-Burnett Cronin Greene Hanley Isherwood Orwell C.S. Forester (1899–1966) Walter Brierley (1900–72) Cyril Connolly (1903–74) **Dr:** Auden & Isherwood Eliot E. Williams **Theory/Crit:** Empson **Lit. 'Events':**	'Burnt Norton' [& 'East Coker', 1940; 'The Dry Salvages', 1941; 'Little Gidding', 1942 – pub.d as *Four Quartets*, 1943] *Second Hymn to Lenin and Other Poems* *Poems* *Collected Poems, 1929–33* *The House in Paris* *A House and its Head* *The Stars Look Down* [popular novel] *England Made Me* *The Furys* *Mr Norris Changes Trains* *A Clergyman's Daughter* *The African Queen* [novel] *Means Test Man* [working-class novel] *The Rock Pool* [novel] *The Dog Beneath the Skin* *Murder in the Cathedral* *Night Must Fall* *Some Versions of Pastoral* Allen Lane fnds Penguin Books – [–1936] 1st 10 paperbacks pub.d

Period	Year	International and Political Contexts	Social and Cultural Contexts	Authors	Indicative Titles
	1936	George V dies – King Edward VIII accedes – constitutional crisis over proposed m. to Mrs Simpson [US divorcee] – Edward abdicates [becomes Duke of Windsor] – King George VI accedes; 'Jarrow March' of unemployed to London; 'Battle of Cable St.' in E. End of London between Mosley's 'blackshirts' [fascists] & opponents – Public Order Act intro.d banning political uniforms & paramilitary organisations; Churchill demands British rearmament – navy & air force improved; naval pact with France & USA; Dáil passes Executive Authority (External Relations) Act – limits role of Crown to diplomatic formalities in Irish Free State; Rome-Berlin Axis proclaimed by Mussolini [estab.d 1937]; Popular Front Coalition gvnmt in Spain – Falangists led by Gen. Franco rebel – set up 'Junta de Defesa Nacional' at Burgos: [–1939] Spanish Civil War – Republican gvnmt moves from Madrid to Valencia – European Powers agree to non-intervention – Germany & Italy recognise Franco as 'Chief of the Spanish State'; Italy captures Addis Ababa – It. king proclaimed Emperor of Ethiopia [occupied until 1941] – L of Ns lifts sanctions against Italy; Germany abrogates Locarno Pact [v.1925] – Nazis' 99% victory in elections – Hitler addresses Youth Rallies in Nuremberg on 'great national future' & 'lebensraum' [more 'living room'] – reoccupies demilitarised Rhineland without Allied protest – [>] construction of 'Siegfried Line' [western defence system] – 2yrs compulsory military service intro.d; [c.–1937] Moscow show trials & executions of former Bolshevik leaders & army chiefs for 'treason'; Emperor Hirohito forms cabinet of militarists in Japan	12m. UK citizens now take a summer holiday; BBC TV broadcasts 1st made from Alexandra Palace [discontinued, 1939–46]; XIth Olympics in new Berlin Stadium under Hitler; Rev. Dick Sheppard fnds Peace Pledge Union [pacifist movement]; [–1937] Billy Butlin opens 1st holiday camp at Skegness; *Life* magazine fnd.d in USA; Keynes, *General Theory of Employment, Interest, and Money* [economic theory]; A.J. Ayer, *Language, Truth and Logic* [anti-metaphysical phil.]. **Int. Lit.:** Faulkner, *Absalom, Absalom!*; Dos Passos, *USA* [novel trilogy: *42nd Parallel*, 1930; *1919*, 1932; *The Big Money*, 1936]; Sherwood, *Idiot's Delight* [play]; Djuna Barnes, *Nightwood* [US novel]; Margaret Mitchell, *Gone with the Wind* [US b-s. novel]; Bernanos, *Le Journal d'un curé de campagne* [novel]; Lorca, *The House of Bernarda Alba* [play]. **Music:** Prokoviev, 'Peter and the Wolf' [musical tale]; Novello, *Careless Rapture* [musical]. **Art:** Surrealist Exhibition in London; Lloyd Wright builds 'Falling Water' house, Bear Run, Pennsylvania; W. Lewis, 'Surrender of Barcelona' [Tate]. **Film:** Chaplin, 'Modern Times'; Korda, 'Things to Come' & 'The Man Who Could Work Miracles' [adaptns of H.G. Wells]; Capra, 'Mr Deeds Goes to Town' [Cooper]; Lang, 'Fury'; John Ford, 'The Plough and the Stars'; Basil Wright & Harry Watt [UK], 'Night Mail' [documentary; words by Auden; score by Britten]. **Lit. 'Events':** Rudyard Kipling dies; Victor Gollancz fnds Left Book Club; [–1941] John Lehmann pubs *New Writing* anthol.s	**P:** Auden D. Thomas Yeats (ed.) P.[atrick] J. Kavanagh (1905–67) **Pr/F:** Forster Huxley T.E. Lawrence R. Lehmann Orwell Sassoon Eric Ambler (1909–98) Daphne Du Maurier (1907–89) Winifred Holtby (1898–1935) Stevie Smith (1902–71) **Dr:** Auden & Isherwood Terence Rattigan (1911–77) **Theory/Crit:** Leavis C.S. Lewis	*Look, Stranger!* *Twenty-five Poems* *The Oxford Book of Modern Verse, 1892–1935* *Ploughman and Other Poems* *Abinger Harvest* [essays] *Eyeless in Gaza* *The Mint* [pub.d in USA; account of life as 'Aircraftman Ross'] *The Weather in the Streets* [sequel to 1932 novel] *Keep the Aspidistra Flying* *Sherston's Progress* [trilogy *; pub.d as *The Complete Memoirs of George Sherston*, 1937] *The Dark Frontier* [thriller] *Jamaica Inn* [novel] *South Riding, an English landscape* [novel] *Novel on Yellow Paper* [novel] *The Ascent of F6* [wrtn; pf.d, 1937, with music by Benjamin Britten] *French Without Tears* *Revaluation* *The Allegory of Love*
	1937	Coronation of George VI – last parade of British Empire; Duke of Windsor m. Mrs Simpson; Baldwin resigns – Neville Chamberlain (Cons). PM of National gvnmt; gvnmt announces rearmament policy; Air Raid Precautions (ARP) intro.d; [–1940] Hore-Belisha's army reforms; Matrimonial Causes Act legalises divorce for women on grounds of desertion [after 3 yrs], rape, insanity, cruelty & sodomy; De Valera intros new constitution for Irish Republic [now Eire] – independent but still in Commonwealth – removes MPs' oath of allegiance to Crown [under Anglo-Irish Treaty, 1921] – De Valera serves as Taoiseach [name changed from PM] to 1948 [re-elected, 1951–54, 1957–9]; internal civil war between Sp. republicans – capital	National Maritime Museum (NMM), Greenwich, opens; the *Daily Telegraph* absorbs the *Morning Post*; Nuffield College, Oxford, fnd.d; National Eisteddfod in Wales makes Welsh its official language; [–1938] nylon invented in USA – commercial production, 1939; [–1948] Joe Louis holds world heavyweight boxing title. **Int. Lit.:** Steinbeck, *Of Mice and Men*; Odets, *Golden Boy* [play]; Stevens, *The Man with the Blue Guitar* [poems]; Zora Neale Hurston, *Their Eyes Were Watching God* [US novel]; Malraux, *Days of Hope* [Fr. novel of Sp. Civil War; Eng. trans, 1938]; Giraudoux, *Électre* [Fr. play]; Nikolai Ostrovsky, *The Making of a Hero* [Russ. novel of communist revolution]. **Music:** Shostakovich, '5th Symphony';	**P:** Auden & MacNeice Stevie Smith John Betjeman (1906–84) David Jones (1895–1974) Rex Warner (1905–86) **Pr/F:** Christie Forester W. Lewis Orwell	*Letters from Iceland* [poems, letters & photographs] *A Good Time Was Had by All* *Continual Dew* [incls 'Death in Leamington' (1930) & 'Slough'] *In Parenthesis* [long poem of WWI] *Poems* *Death on the Nile* *The Happy Return* [1st 'Capt. Hornblower' novel] *The Revenge for Love* *The Road to Wigan Pier* [social & political memoir]

moved from Valencia to Barcelona – Germany & Italy withdraw from non-intervention agreement & actively support Franco – Basque town of Guernica bombed by Ger. planes; Indian Constitution in force – Burma & Aden [as Crown Colony] separated from India; Royal Commission on Palestine recommends end of mandate & creation of Jewish & Arab states; Roosevelt signs US Neutrality Act; [–1945] Sino-Jap. war resumes – Japanese seize Peking, Shanghai & Nanking – Chinese gvnmt of Chiang Kai-shek allies with Communist leaders Mao Tse-tung & Chou-en-lai to resist; Trotsky fnds '4th International' in opposition to the Soviet 'Comintern' [v.1919]; Golden Gate Bridge, San Francisco, completed

Bliss, 'Checkmate' [ballet]. **Art:** Picasso, 'Guernica' [v. preceding column; painting returned to Spain on restoration of democracy in 1981] & 'Weeping Woman' [ser.]; Brancusi, 'Endless Column' [steel sculpt.]; Dali, 'Metamorphosis of Narcissus' [Tate]; Tanguy, 'Days of Slowness'; Spencer, 'Cookham Moor' [MAG]; [–1940] David Smith [USA; sculpt.] 'Medals for Dishonour' [ser.]. **Film:** Laurel & Hardy, 'Way Out West'; Lang, 'You Only Live Once'; Disney, 'Snow White and the Seven Dwarfs' [1st full-length colour cartoon]; Korda, 'Elephant Boy'; Ford, 'Hurricane'; Wood, 'A Day at the Races' [Marx Bros]; Jean Renoir [Fr.], 'La Grande Illusion'; George Stevens, 'Swing Time' [Astaire, Rogers]
Lit. 'Events': The Readers' Union fnd.d; Left Book Club pubs Arthur Koestler, Spanish Testament & Spender, Forward From Liberalism; Laurence Olivier joins Old Vic – plays Hamlet, Coriolanus, Macbeth, Henry V

Sayers — The Busman's Honeymoon
Warner — The Wild Goose Chase [political fable]
Woolf — The Years
Lewis Jones (1897–1939) — Cwmardy [working-class novel]

J.R.R Tolkien (1892–1973) — The Hobbit [fantasy novel]

Dr: Sayers — The Zeal of Thy House [religious play]
Priestley — Time and the Conways & I Have Been Here Before

Theory/Crit:
Christopher Caudwell — Illusion and Reality

C. Day Lewis (ed.) — The Mind in Chains [incls Upward's 'Sketch for a Marxist Interpretation of Literature']
Ralph Fox — The Novel and the People
L.C. Knights — Drama and Society in the Age of Jonson
Alick West — Crisis and Criticism

1938

Eden resigns over Chamberlain's 'appeasing' policy towards Mussolini [pact recognises It. conquest of Abyssinia]; 50% of British families estimated below poverty line; Spens Report on 2ndry education proposes raising school leaving-age to 15 & widening provision [paves way for post-war legislation]; Women's Voluntary Service (WVS) fnd.d; Hitler meets Mussolini in Rome – assumes command of Ger. army – Ger. troops enter Austria – declared part of Ger. Reich ['Anschluss'] – British gvnmt persuaded to make concessions to Nazis as part of 'appeasement policy' – Chamberlain meets Hitler – [Sept.] 'Munich Crisis': Ger. troops occupy Sudetenland [Ger. part of Czechoslovakia] – British fleet mobilised & civilian gas-masks issued in Britain – 'Munich Agreement': Allies accept Nazi seizure of Sudeten; violent pogroms in Germany – anti-Jewish legislation in Italy; Franco's forces divide republican Spain – final offensive into Catalonia; Japan captures Canton & Hankow – Chiang Kai-shek retreats – tension between Chin. Nationalists & Communists – L of Ns declares Japan aggressor & invites support for China – Germany recognises Jap. Manchuria

Parliamentary committee recommends a week's holiday with pay as national standard; 'Xerography' [photocopying] invented; 1st 'Biro' ball-point pen made; fluorescent lighting intro.d in Britain; Otto Hahn splits uranium atom & discvs nuclear fission; British illustrated weekly, Picture Post, 1st pub.d; Jung, Psychology and Religion. **Int. Lit.:** Hemingway, The First Forty-Nine [stories]; E. E. Cummings, Collected Poems; Wilder, Our Town [play]; Jean-Paul Sartre, La Nausée [Fr. novel] & Le Mur [stories]; Jean Anouilh, Thieves' Carnival [Fr. play; Eng. trans, 1952]; Karen Blixen, Out of Africa [Dan. novel; film, 1985]. **Music:** Copland, 'Billy the Kid' [ballet]; Lambert, 'Horoscope' [ballet]. **Art:** International Exhibition of Surrealism, Paris; Dufy, 'The Regatta'; Klee, 'Flowering Harbour'; [c.] A. John, 'Dylan Thomas' [NMW]; W. Lewis, 'T.S. Eliot'; Barbara Hepworth [sculpt.] 'Forms in Echelon' [Tate]. **Film:** Eisenstein, 'Alexander Nevski' [score by Prokofiev]; Hitchcock, 'The Lady Vanishes' [M. Redgrave]; Hawks, 'Bringing Up Baby' [K. Hepburn; Grant]; Riefenstahl, 'Olympiad' [documentary of 1936 Games]; Gabriel Pascal & Anthony Asquith [UK], 'Pygmalion' [Howard]
Lit. 'Events': Orson Welles's radio production of H.G. Wells's War of the Worlds causes panic in USA

P: Auden — Selected Poems & (ed.) The Oxford Book of Light Verse
Day Lewis — Overtures to Death
Stevie Smith — Tender Only to One
Yeats — New Poems
Pr/F: Ambler — Epitaph for a Spy [thriller]
Beckett — Murphy [novel]
Bowen — The Death of the Heart
Du Maurier — Rebecca
Greene — Brighton Rock [1st 'Catholic' novel]
Hanley — The Hollow Sea
R. Hughes — In Hazard: A Sea Story
Isherwood — Lions and Shadows [autobiog.]
Orwell — Homage to Catalonia [memoirs of Sp. Civil War]

Stevie Smith — Over the Frontier
Upward — Journey to the Border [novella; incl.d in Upward 1969]

Warner — The Professor [political fable]
Waugh — Scoop
Dr: Auden & Isherwood — On the Frontier [pf.d; music by Britten]

Priestley — When We Are Married [farce]
Dodie Smith — Dear Octopus
Spender — Trial of a Judge [verse play]
E. Williams — The Corn Is Green
Theory/Crit:
Artaud — Le Théâtre et son double [trans 1957]
Caudwell — Studies in a Dying Culture
Cyril Connolly — Enemies of Promise
Louis NacNeice — Modern Poetry, a personal essay
Woolf — Three Guineas

PERIOD	YEAR	INTERNATIONAL AND POLITICAL CONTEXTS	SOCIAL AND CULTURAL CONTEXTS	AUTHORS	INDICATIVE TITLES
WORLD WAR II	1939	Franco's troops capture Barcelona – Madrid surrenders – Nationalists victorious – Sp. Civil War ends – Britain recognises Franco – Spain leaves L of Ns; [Mar.] British gvnmt issues guarantee to Poland, Greece & Romania against foreign aggression – Hitler invades & occupies Czechoslovakia [–1945]; Roosevelt's 'peace plea' to Hitler rejected – Mussolini invades & annexes Albania – Hitler denounces Polish non-aggression pact; [Aug.] Russo-German non-aggression pact – Ger. ultimatum to Poland – [Sept.] Germany & then USSR invade Poland – partitioned – USSR invades Finland – Britain, Australia, NZ & France declare war on Germany – **World War II begins:** British-Ger. naval engagements ensue; [Oct/Nov] USSR attacks Finland [expelled from L of Ns]; British Parliament passes Emergency Powers (Defence) Act – National Identity Cards issued [–1952] – National Service (Conscription) for men intro.d in Britain [for women, 1941; phased out, 1959–60] – wartime Ministries of Supply [–1959] & Information [–1946] estab.d – early-warning radar stations set up around British coast – barrage balloons used in defence against air attack – White Paper on Civil Defence; Eire neutral throughout WWII, but IRA outlawed; British Overseas Airways Corporation (BOAC) fnd.d	Entertainments National Service Association (ENSA) estab.d [provided entertainment for Allied troops/war workers on all fronts worldwide]; Sutton Hoo burial ship excavated in Suffolk; Sikorsky makes 1st functional helicopter in USA. **Int. Lit.:** Steinbeck, *The Grapes of Wrath*; West, *The Day of the Locust* [novel]; Raymond Chandler, *The Big Sleep* [US detective novel]; Saint-Exupéry, *Terre des Hommes* [novel]; T. Mann, *Lotte in Weimar* [novel]; Aleksei Arbuzov, *Tanya* [Russ. play]. **Music:** Novello, 'The Dancing Years' [musical]; 'We'll Hang Out the Washing on the Siegfried Line' [popular wartime song]; Irving Berlin [comp] 'God Bless America'. **Art:** Picasso, 'Cat and Bird'; Epstein, 'Adam' [Harewood House]; H. Moore, 'Reclining Figure', Matisse, 'Music'; Dali, 'Bacchanalia'; Kandinsky, 'Composition X'; Klee, 'Drunkenness'; Mondrian, 'Composition'; W. Lewis, 'Ezra Pound' [Tate]; P. Nash, 'Monster Field'; Shahn, 'Handball'; Ben Nicholson [pnt] 'White Relief'. **Film:** Korda, 'The Four Feathers'; Capra, 'Mr Smith Goes to Washington' [J. Stewart]; Ford, 'Stagecoach' [J. Wayne]; Renoir, 'La Règle du jeu'; Wood, 'Goodbye Mr Chips' [Donat, G. Garson]; Asquith, 'French Without Tears' [adptn of Rattigan]; Victor Fleming [producer, David Selznick], 'Gone With The Wind' [Gable, Howard, V. Leigh] & 'The Wizard of Oz' [J. Garland]; William Wyler, 'Wuthering Heights' [Olivier, M. Oberon]; Carol Reed [UK], 'The Stars Look Down' [M. Redgrave]; 'The Road to Singapore' [B. Crosby, B. Hope, D. Lamour; 1st of 6 'Road' movies]	**P:** Eliot MacNeice Spender Yeats **Pr/F:** Ambler Green Isherwood Isherwood & Auden L. Jones Joyce Orwell Powell Rhys Joyce Cary (1888–1957) B.L. Coombes (1893–1974) Richard Llewellyn (1907–83) 'Flann O'Brien' (Brian O'Nolan; 1911–66) **Dr:** Eliot Sayers **Theory/Crit:** Cleanth Brooks **Lit. 'Events':**	*Old Possum's Book of Practical Cats* *Autumn Journal* *The Still Centre* *Last Poems* [pub. posthm.] *The Mask of Dimitrios* [thriller] *Party Going* *Goodbye to Berlin* *Journey to a War* [account of visit to China] *We Live* [sequel to *Cwmardy*] *Finnegans Wake* *Coming Up for Air* *What's Become of Waring?* *Good Morning, Midnight* *Mister Johnson* [novel] *These Poor Hands* [working-class autobiog.] *How Green Was My Valley* [novel] *At Swim-Two-Birds* [novel] *The Family Reunion* *The Devil to Pay* *Modern Poetry and the Tradition* W.B. Yeats dies; Auden & Isherwood emigrate to NY; [–1950] Cyril Connolly fnds & edits *Horizon* magazine; Gielgud directs *The Importance of Being Earnest* with Edith Evans as Lady Bracknell

 1940–1959

World War II and the Post-War Period

INTRODUCTION

The present chapter deals with the two decades of the 1940s and 1950s – a period obviously dominated by the **Second World War*** and its aftermath, but with a strong sense through the 1950s, especially amongst the younger generation, that **Post-War*** exhaustion should give way to excitement, provocation, non-conformity and rebellion. [Suggested timeline narratives for the whole period are appended after the gloss on **(The) Post-War (Period)***.]

Chapter contents

7.1 THE SECOND WORLD WAR / WORLD WAR II (WWII)

The war between the the Allied Powers (initially France and Great Britain, later joined by the USA and the USSR) and the Axis Powers (Italy and Germany, later joined by Japan) from 1939 to 1945.

The historical process which led to the outbreak of war (France and Britain declared war on Germany on 3 September 1939) is covered by the gloss on the **Inter-War Period*** in Chapter 6. But in brief, it was determined by German resentment over the draconian terms of the Treaty of Versailles (1919) at the end of **World War I*** [Chapter 6]; the world economic crisis of 1929–30; the rise to power of a Fascist state in Italy under Mussolini throughout the 1920s and 1930s; the rise to power of the Nazi regime in Germany under Hitler from the early 1930s; the failure of the League of Nations (especially France and Britain) actively to police the peace; the illegal but unopposed rearmament of Germany and the remilitarisation of the Rhineland (1936); German, Italian and Japanese expansionist foreign policy in the late 1930s; the Spanish Civil War in which Germany and Italy supported Franco's Nationalists, and which became a proving ground for the new techniques of modern warfare; the unpreparedness of France and Britain for war; and their consequent policy of 'appeasement' in the face of German and Italian aggression. However, in 1939, with the Italian invasion of Albania, the German occupation of the whole of Czechoslovakia and the 'blitzkrieg' ('lightning war') invasion of Poland, the Allies declared war.

Following a non-aggression pact between the Soviet Union and Germany (August 1939), Poland was partitioned and the Soviets occupied Finland. Relying on the Maginot Line of defences [see Chapter 6, Inter-War* 'narratives' under Germany], the Allies remained immobile through the winter and early spring of 1939–40 (the period of the so-called 'Phoney War'), but in April–June 1940, Germany overran Denmark, Norway, the Netherlands, Belgium, and Luxembourg. In May, German forces turned the Maginot Line in Belgium, advanced rapidly through north-east France, and trapped the Allied troops on the coast at Dunkirk (who were then evacuated to Britain against the odds by a flotilla of miscellaneous craft). The French Army failed to withstand the German offensive and Paris fell in June 1940; the French signed an armistice the same month, allowing the German occupation of northern France, while the collaborationist Vichy government under General Pétain was set up in the south. General De Gaulle escaped to Britain where he instituted the 'Free French' movement. Winston Churchill became Prime Minister of the National Government in Britain in 1940, a year which saw the the 'blitz'[krieg] bombing of British cities and the 'Battle of Britain' in the air [August 1940–May 1941] to protect against it, but Britain escaped invasion. Japan joined the Axis Powers in 1940.

In 1940, Italy declared war on the Allies, involving Britain in the North Africa and Middle East campaigns; Bulgaria and Romania joined the Axis Powers; Greece repelled invasion by Italy then fell to a German/Bulgarian attack, which also crushed Yugoslavia and conquered Crete; Germany invaded the USSR, besieged Leningrad and reached Moscow by the winter of 1941, where Hitler's troops halted; British shipping was subjected to a German submarine campaign in an attempt to destroy the Atlantic supply routes; the United States remained neutral, whilst offering 'lend-lease' aid to Britain and the Soviet Union (supplying weapons and equipment in exchange for the right to use certain Allied bases), and Churchill and Roosevelt signed the 'Atlantic Charter' (outlining 'peace aims') in August 1941. But after taking Hong Kong, Japan made a surprise attack on the US fleet at Pearl Harbour (December 1941) which brought the United States into the war on the Allied side. The Philippines, Malaya, Singapore, Burma, Indonesia and many Pacific islands rapidly fell to the Japanese, until Allied victories in 1943–4 began to liberate them.

The tide of the war began to turn in the Allies' favour in 1942–3: following victory at the battle of El Alamein (1942), Allied forces drove the Axis Powers out of North Africa by May 1943; the invasion of Sicily and the advance up the Italian mainland forced Italy to surrender (September 1943; although German troops continued to fight there), Mussolini was deposed, peace made with the Allies, and Italy declared war on Germany; having routed the German Army after its massive offensive at Stalingrad (September 1942–February 1943), Soviet forces launched a counter-offensive which pushed all German forces out of the Soviet Union by August 1944.

Intensive 'round the clock' Allied bombing of Germany went on from 1942 to 1945, while knowledge of Hitler's 'Final Solution' to exterminate the Jews began to emerge.

On 6 June 1944 ('D-Day'), the Allied landings in Normandy began the process of driving the Gernman army out of France, liberating Paris in August 1944 and then Brussels, and crossing the Rhine in March 1945; the ongoing Soviet offensive forced Romania, Bulgaria and Finland to surrender, and by the spring of 1945, the USSR had overrun Eastern Germany; the Western and Eastern Allies met up in Saxony in April, and the Russians took Berlin on 2 May 1945 (Hitler committed suicide); an unconditional surrender was signed by a newly formed German government on 7 May 1945. Meanwhile, the Japanese were gradually being driven by Allied forces from Burma and other South-East Asian and Pacific territories; China regained most of the territory lost to Japan, and also annexed Formosa; the Soviet Union invaded Manchuria; and on 6 and 9 August 1945, the USA dropped an atomic bomb first on Hiroshima and then on Nagasaki; on 14 August, Japan surrendered and the Second World War ended. Peace treaties between the Allies and the Axis countries were signed gradually over the next 11 years.

The war cost upwards of 36 million lives worldwide (including six million Jews in the Holocaust, Hitler's 'ultimate solution' for their extermination); the destructive capacity of the world's super-powers had been immeasurably increased, especially by the invention of nuclear weapons; the balance of world power was now shared by America and the USSR (who dominated the whole of Eastern Europe); Germany (including Berlin) was divided into East and West, and occupied respectively by the Soviet Union and the Western Powers.

7.2 (THE) POST-WAR (PERIOD)

Although the term 'post-war' can be used to describe the period after any war, its contemporary currency is principally reserved for that following World War II* (this is confirmed by the fact that the years after World War I* [see Chapter 6] are normally referred to as 'the post-WWI period'). But while 'post-war' can, of course, define the entire subsequent period up to the present, it is most commonly used to define the second half of the 1940s and the 1950s.

Key Timeline Narratives 1940–1959

⤴ **The UK in Wartime**   In response to war, measures affecting civilian life were extensive: the Emergency Powers (Defence) Act of 1939 required National Identity Cards to be carried by all (until 1952), National Service (Conscription) was introduced for men the same year and for women in 1941 [phased out, 1959–63]; Ministries of Supply (–1959) and Information (–1946) were set up; Civil Defence, the Home Guard and auxiliary fire services were established; Purchase Tax (now VAT) was introduced in 1940, as was rationing (with a 'points' system) for food (the 'national loaf' appeared in 1942), clothing, petrol and other commodities (it was only gradually phased out from 1949–54), and income tax rose sharply (1941).

The war years also saw the beginnings of what would become in the post-war period the Welfare State (the Beveridge Report, 1942; the Norwood Report on secondary education, 1943; the Butler Education Act introducing secondary education for all, a White Paper proposing the National Health

Service (NHS), and the establishing of a Ministry of National Insurance, all 1944). [See below for more on the Welfare State.]

⮑ ***The Post-War International Context***   [Because of the complexity and eventfulness of this period, and to avoid simply repeating the information in the timeline tables, only a series of pointers will be given here.] Churchill's 'Iron Curtain' speech (1946) predicted the 'Cold War' between the Western and Eastern blocs (see, e.g., 1948–9) which dominated international relations throughout the period and fuelled the nuclear arms race [see, e.g., 1946, 1951, 1952, 1953, 1955, 1956, 1957]; the United Nations Organisation (UNO; later the UN) replaced the League of Nations (1945–6), and the North Atlantic Treaty Organisation (NATO) was founded (1949); the origins of the Common market are clearly apparent in the early 1950s and the Treaty of Rome (1957) established the European Economic Community (EEC).

East Germany became the German Democratic Republic (GDR) and West Germany the German Federal Republic in 1949 (occupation of the latter by the Western Powers ended and sovereignty was granted in 1952); in 1948–49, Ireland was fully inaugurated as the independent Republic of Ireland (Eire) and left the Commonwealth; India gained independence in 1947, and was partitioned as two states: India (Hindu) and Pakistan (Moslem; West Pakistan and East Pakistan were separated by India), with the partitioned state of Kashmir resulting in conflict between the two countries ever since. Independence stuggles flared up throughout the period: in Indo-China (e.g. French troops besieged in Dien Bien Phu, 1953–4), Egypt (e.g. the Suez Canal crisis, 1956), Kenya (the 'Mau Mau' guerrilla war against Britain, 1952–9), Cyprus (the EOKA guerrilla war against Britain, mid-1950s), and French North Africa (especially Algeria, mid-1950s). The Chinese Communists under Mao Tse-tung defeated the Nationalists and set up the People's Republic of China (1948–9), the Nationalists under Chiang Kai-shek set up a rival government on the islands of Formosa and Quemoy supported by the USA and a cause of severe tension [see, e.g., 1954–5], and Tibet suffered Chinese oppression throughout the 1950s; the Korean War (1950–3) between Communist North Korea and Nationalist South Korea drew in the Chinese Republic and the USA and UK; Zionist Jews occupied much of Palestine and declared the independent state of Israel (1948–9). In the USSR, 'de-Stalinisation' began under President Krushchev (1956), but the same year the Soviet Union invaded Hungary and crushed its pro-democrcay movement; in the USA, the communist witch-hunts of Senator McCarthy dominated the early 1950s, while the Supreme Court ruled that racial segregation in schools was unconstitutional (1954), leading to the Civil Rights Act of 1957 and race riots over integration in Little Rock, Arkansas, the same year, and in 1959, Alaska and Hawaii became the 49th, 50th and final States respectively; in Cuba (1957–9), Fidel Castro fought a guerrilla war against the dictator, President Batista, and overthrew his regime; in 1959, civil broke out in the ex-Belgian Congo [see next chapter for details].

⮑ ***UK Politics***   In 1945, the first majority Labour Government came to power [see **(The) Labour (Party)*** in Chapter 6 for more detail], and began the process of nationalising the UK's industries and building the Welfare State [see below]. Plural voting was abolished in 1948, and the Parliament Act of 1949 reduced the power of the Lords to delay legislation. In the General Election of 1950, Labour were re-elected but without an overall majority, and were split over NHS charges in 1951, thus allowing the Conservatives into power with a small majority under Churchill. In 1955, Churchill resigned, and the Conservatives, now under Anthony Eden, were returned with an increased majority; Eden resigned in 1957 (following the Suez debacle), and Harold Macmillan became Prime Minister; in 1959, he made his 'You've Never Had It So Good' speech, pointing to the increasing affluence of the nation during the

1950s, and won the third successive Conservative General Election victory. In 1958, the Liberals won a bye-election at Torrington, thus heralding the start of a gradual return from the political wilderness.

➲ **The Welfare State, Social Issues and Education in the UK**   The beginnings of the Welfare State during WWII have been noted in The UK in Wartime above, but it was the Labour Government of 1945–51 which introduced all the major legislation that brought about social and industrial reform. The Trades Disputes Act of 1927 (following the General Strike; see Chapter 6) was repealed in 1946, and the same year saw the nationalisation of the Bank of England and of civil aviation, and the passing of the National Insurance, National Health and New Towns Acts (National Insurance was Beveridge's main recommendation for state-supported security 'from the cradle to the grave', covering ill-heath, unemployment, retirement and family support; the NHS was fully inaugurated in 1948; Stevenage was designated as the first 'new town' in November 1946, and seven more sites to meet overspill from London were identified over the next three years).

From 1947 to 1950, coal, electricity, the railways, gas and steel were nationalised; a Town and Country Planning Act was passed, as were Acts covering subsidies for agricuture, provision by local authorities for children without proper homes, and Legal Aid and Advice; equal pay for women was introduced in the Civil Service in 1954; London was declared a 'smokeless zone' in 1955 following serious 'smog' during 1952–53 from which several thousand people died, and a Clean Air Act was passed in 1956; a Mental Health Act in 1959 instituted a regulatory framework for the treatment of mental disorders. The British Nationality Act of 1948 guaranteed freedom of entry to the UK from the Commonwealth and colonies, and in the course of the 1950s immigration from New Commonwealth countries (especially the Caribbean, India and Pakistan) expanded rapidly; race riots occurred in Nottingham and Notting Hill, London, in 1958. The Homicide Act was passed in 1957 abolishing the death penalty (with exclusions), the Wolfenden Commission reported in the same year on prostitution and homosexuality, making liberalising recommendations (which the Commons rejected in 1960), and the Street Offences Act of 1959 took prostitutes off the streets; in 1958, the Campaign for Nuclear Disarmament was founded and the first march took place to the Atomic Weapons Research Establishment at Aldermaston (set up, 1954–6).

The school leaving age was raised to 15 (1947), the General Certificate of Education (GCE) was introduced in 1951, the first LCC comprehensive school was opened at Kidbrooke, SE London (1954), and between 1948 and 1957, the civic universities of Nottingham, Southampton, Hull, Exeter and Leicester received their charters.

➲ **Science and Technology**   In science and medicine, c.1952 inoculation against polio was introduced (the 'Salk' vaccine was produced in 1955) and the first contraceptive pill made; in 1953, Crick and Wilson cracked the DNA code; in 1955, insulin was identified, and by about this time a sharp decline in deaths from tuberculosis in the UK had become apparent; interferon was discovered in 1957. A major technological narrative of this period is the rapid development of the nuclear industry (both of weapons [see The Post-War International Context above] and of nuclear power [see, e.g., 1954, 1955, 1956, 1957]); in 1941, the first British jet aircraft, the 'Gloster', powered by Sir Frank Whittle's engine, was test flown, the sound barrier was broken by a jet plane in 1952, and in 1956, the De Haviland 'Comet', the first passenger jet airliner, was brought into service; London Airport (now Heathrow) opened in 1946, with new terminals added in 1955, and Gatwick opened in 1958; Jodrell Bank radio telescope was begun in 1952 and went into operation in 1958; underground explorations for natural gas commenced around 1953; the first section of the M1, the UK's first motorway, opened in 1959; and in 1957, the USSR launched the first two of its 'Sputnik' space craft, and the 'space-race' began [see also 1958–9].

➲ **The Cultural Context**   During the early years of the war, the Entertainments National Service Association (ENSA, 1939; to provide all types of entertainment for war workers worldwide) and the Council for the Encouragement of Music and the Arts (CEMA, 1940) were founded. The latter became the Arts Council of Great Britain in 1942, and was granted its Royal Charter in 1946, the same year that the first Edinburgh Festival took place.

Sir Thomas Beecham founded the Royal Philharmonic Orchestra in 1947, the Aldeburgh Festival was established in 1948, as was the Institute of Contemporary Arts (ICA) in London. The Festival of Britain opened in 1951, with pavilions designed by Sir Basil Spence (who also produced the winning design for the new Coventry Cathedral the same year), as did the Royal Festival Hall (1951 also saw the first 'Archers' BBC radio programme broadcast); and the Royal Ballet was founded in 1957. The scheme for the Barbican redevelopment in London was launched in 1954, and in 1956, the Design Centre opened at the Haymarket.

In the arts, this was the period of the 'revolt into style' of the emerging post-war youth culture: of 'bebop' and 'cool' jazz (Charlie Parker, Dizzy Gillespie, Thelonious Monk, Miles Davis); of 'rock and roll' (Bill Haley, Fats Domino, Little Richard, Elvis Presley); of Teddy Boys, Beatniks and so-called Angry Young Men (Jack Kerouac, Allen Ginsberg, Lawrence Ferlinghetti; John Osborne, Kingsley Amis, Colin Wilson, John Wain); and of the first signs of 'Pop Art' in the visual arts (Eduardo Paolozzi, Jasper Johns, Peter Blake, Richard Hamilton, Jim Dine).

But two of the most striking British cultural narratives brought into bold relief by the timeline tables are the development of TV and of the theatre:

• **Television**   In 1946, the BBC resumed TV broadcasts to c.15,000 set owners in the UK; in 1948, the XIV Olympics in London were transmitted to c.120,000 homes; the coronation of Queen Elizabeth II in 1953 was shown on television and watched by millions, while in the USA, experiments with colour TV were underway. The Eurovision TV network was established in 1954, and the Television Act of the same year set up the Independent Television Authority (ITA; becomes ITV); Independent (commercial) TV commenced the following year, when there were by now c.4.5 million UK set owners; BBC TV first broadcast the 'Tonight' news programme and programmes for schools in 1957, followed by 'Panorama' in 1958.

• **Theatre**   In 1941, the Old Vic Theatre was bombed (rebuilt 1950), and until 1944, the company toured the country for CEMA [see above]; in 1943, the Bristol Old Vic was refounded and became the first UK theatre to receive state aid, and (1943–4) the Citizens' Theatre, Glasgow, was established; 1945–6 saw the setting-up of the new Old Vic Drama School, the temporary founding of the Young Vic Theatre [see 1970 in Chapter 8], and the founding of Joan Littlewood's Theatre Workshop (in 1953, it leased the Theatre Royal. Stratford, East London, and opened there in 1954); in 1949, the National Theatre Act was passed, and the NT's foundation stone was laid in 1951 (it opened finally in 1976). In 1955, Peter Brook directed Laurence Olivier in the RSC's revival of Shakespeare's *Titus Andronicus* and Paul Scofield in *Hamlet*, a production taken to Moscow (the first since 1917); 1956 saw John Osborne's *Look Back in Anger* at the Royal Court Theatre, London (amongst a programme of controversial new plays produced there by the English Stage Company under George Devine); in 1958–9, the Belgrade Theatre, Coventry, the Nottingham Playhouse and the Mermaid Theatre at Blackfriars, London, opened.

Timelines: 1940–1959

PERIOD	YEAR	INTERNATIONAL AND POLITICAL CONTEXTS	SOCIAL AND CULTURAL CONTEXTS	AUTHORS	INDICATIVE TITLES
WORLD WAR II	1940	George VI institutes George Cross & George Medal; Chamberlain Ministry resigns – [–1945] wartime Coalition gvnmt – Churchill (Cons.), PM; Purchase Tax & [–1954] food rationing intro.d; Germany invades Norway, Denmark, Low Countries – Holland & Belgium fall – British evacuate Dunkirk – [–1944] Ger. occupation of Channel Islands – Paris falls – Fr. gvnmt under Petain capitulates – 'collaborationist' gvnmt of unoccupied France based at Vichy – breaks off relations with Britain – 'Battle of Britain' to resist Ger. air attacks & 'blitz[krieg]' [bombing of British cities, incls destruction of Coventry Cathedral; v.1951] – 'Home Guard' formed & 'Fire Watching' made compulsory – Italy declares war on France & Britain – invades Greece – Japan joins Axis Powers; Pres. Roosevelt elected for 3rd term; Latvia, Estonia & Lithuania incorporated in USSR; Trotsky assassinated in Mexico City	Council for the Encouragement of Music & the Arts (CEMA) fnd.d [to take plays & concerts to evacuation areas – became the Arts Council of GB, 1942; v.1946]; Lascaux prehistoric cave-paintings discv.d in France; US scientists isolate plutonium. **Int. Lit.:** Hemingway, *For Whom the Bell Tolls*; O'Hara, *Pal Joey* [novel]; Chandler, *Farewell, My Lovely* [detective novel]; Richard Wright, *Native Son* [US novel]; Sherwood, *There Shall Be No Night* [play]; Mikhail Sholokhov, *And Quiet Flows the Don* [Russ. novel, 4 vols; Eng. trans]. **Music:** Stravinsky, 'Symphony in C major'. **Art:** UK War Artists scheme initiated; Matisse, 'Rumanian Blouse'; Kandinsky, 'Freshness'; Klee, 'Death and Fire'; Shahn, 'Willis Avenue Bridge'; [–1941] Henry Moore, 'Shelter Drawings' [London Underground during blitz]. **Film:** Chaplin, 'The Great Dictator' [satire on Hitler]; Disney, 'Pinocchio' & 'Fantasia'; Ford, 'The Grapes of Wrath' [H. Fonda]; Hitchcock, 'Rebecca' [Olivier]; Cukor, 'The Philadelphia Story' [K. Hepburn, C. Grant]; Thorold Dickinson [UK], 'Gaslight'	**P:** Auden Betjeman Day Lewis MacNeice **Pr/F:** Brittain Christie Greene F. O'Brien Orwell D. Thomas Arthur Koestler (1905–83) Michael Sadleir (1888–1957) C.P. Snow (1905–80) **Dr:** O'Casey	*Another Time* *Old Lights for New Chancels* *Poems in Wartime* *Poems 1925–1940* *Testament of Friendship* [memoirs] *Ten Little Niggers* *The Power and the Glory* *The Third Policeman* [wrtn; pub. posthm., 1967] *Inside the Whale* [essays] *Portrait of the Artist as a Young Dog* [autobiog.] *Darkness at Noon* [novel] *Fanny by Gaslight* [novel] *Strangers and Brothers* [1st novel in eponymous 11-vol. sequence (–1970): egs, v.1951, 1954, 1964] *The Star Turns Red*
	1941	Pres. Roosevelt announces 'Lend-Lease' scheme of aid: military bases leased to USA in return for supplies of materials and equipment to UK & USSR; British Air Training Corps (ATC) estab.d; Civil Defence & [–1948] National Fire Service estab.d; income tax at 50%; rationing 'points' system intro.d; heavy bombing raids on London – House of Commons destroyed; Bulgaria & Roumania join Axis Powers – Germany invades Greece [occupied to 1944] & Yugoslavia – battle for Crete – Rudolph Hess, Hitler's deputy, flies to Scotland to plead an Anglo-Ger. negotiated peace – Germany invades Russia – attacks Moscow – siege of Leningrad begins – Soviet-Jap. neutrality pact – Japan takes Hong Kong – bombs US fleet at Pearl Harbour, Hawaii – USA & Britain declare war on Japan – Axis Powers declare war on USA – Churchill & Roosevelt sign 'Atlantic Charter' [peace aims] – Gen. de Gaulle leads 'Free French' Resistance from London [begun 1940]	'Gloster', 1st British jet aircraft, flies. **Int. Lit.:** Fitzgerald, *The Last Tycoon* [posthm.]; Brecht writes *Mutter Courage und ihre Kinder* [pf.d, 1947> by his Berliner Ensemble, E. Germany]; [c.] Aragon, *La Grève-Coeur* [Fr. war poetry – against Vichy gvnmt]; Franz Werfel, *Das Lied von Bernadette* [Ger. novel]; [–1942] Ilya Ehrenburg, *The Fall of Paris* [Russ. war novel]. **Music:** [–1942] Shostakovitch, '7th (Leningrad) Symphony' [composed during siege]; I. Berlin, 'White Christmas' [song]; Michael Tippett [comp] 'A Child of Our Time' [oratorio]; [c.] 'bebop' music & dance become popular. **Art:** Matisse, 'Still Life with a Magnolia'; Brancusi, 'Cock' [sculpt.]; Hopper, 'Nighthawks'; P. Nash [as War Artist], 'Totes Meer' [Tate]; Spencer [as War Artist], 'Shipbuilding on the Clyde' [ser. to 1947; IWM]; [–1942] John Piper [pnt] 'Windsor Castle' [w/c ser.]. **Film:** Disney, 'Dumbo'; Reed, 'Kipps' [M. Redgrave; adaptn of H.G. Wells]; Ford, 'How Green Was My Valley'; Orson Welles, 'Citizen Kane'; John Huston, 'The Maltese Falcon' [Bogart]; Michael Powell [UK], '49th Parallel' [Olivier]; Humphrey Jennings [UK], 'Merchant Seamen' & 'Listen to Britain' [documentaries]	**P:** Auden Vernon Watkins (1906–67) **Pr/F:** Cary Christie Compton-Burnett P. Hamilton F. O'Brien Warner Woolf **Theory/Crit:** **Dr:** Coward John Crowe Ransom E. Wilson **Lit. 'Events':**	*New Year Letter* *The Ballad of Mari Lwyd* *A House of Children & Herself Surprised* [1st novel in trilogy*] *And Then There Were Nine* *Parents and Children* *Hangover Square* *An Béal Bocht* [Gaelic novel; Eng. trans as *The Poor Mouth*, 1973] *The Aerodrome* *Between the Acts* [pub. posthm.] *Blithe Spirit* *The New Criticism* *The Wound and the Bow* Virginia Woolf & James Joyce die; Old Vic bombed – company moves to Burnley & [–1944] tours for CEMA [v.1940]

1942

History: 'Beveridge Report' [on Social Insurance and Allied Services] lays foundation of post-war 'Welfare State'; wartime 'National Loaf' intro.d in Britain [standard size]; Gen. Eisenhower, C. in C. of US forces in Europe – RAF intensifies bombing raids on Germany – Germans occupy Vichy France – Fr. fleet scuttled by sabotage at Toulon – Spain & Portugal form Iberian Bloc – Rommel ('Desert Fox') takes Tobruk in N. Africa campaign ['Bailey Bridge' 1st used in this] – reaches El Alamein – British victory under Gen. Montgomery – Germans retreat W. from Egypt – allied landings in N. Africa – Germans capture Sebastopol – siege of Stalingrad begins – Japan invades & occupies Burma, Philippines, Singapore; build-up of US air force in Free China – bombs Tokyo; George Cross [v.1940] awarded to Malta for heroism in withstanding Ger. & It. bombardment; [>] Hitler's 'Final Solution' of exterminating the Jews underway

Culture: Birth of the author'; Assembly Rooms, Bath, bombed [reopened, 1963]; Roman treasure hoard discv.d at Mildenhall, Suffolk; J.S. Huxley, *Evolution: the Modern Synthesis* [scientific humanism]. **Int. Lit.:** Faulkner, *Go Down, Moses* [stories]; Chandler, *The High Window*; Wright, 'The Man who Lived Underground' [story]; Sartre, *Les Mouches* [play]; Anouilh, *Eurydice* [Fr. play; trans as *Point of Departure*, 1950]; Albert Camus, *The Outsider* [Eng. trans, 1946] & *The Myth of Sisyphus* [existential essays]; Paul Eluard, *Poésie et vérité* [poems]. **Music:** R. Strauss, 'Capriccio' [final opera]; Britten, 'Sinfonia da Requiem'. **Art:** Picasso, 'Nude with a Musician (Aubade)'; Miró, 'Women and Birds in Front of the Sun'; Mondrian, 'New York City' & [–1943] 'New York Boogie-Woogie'; Tanguy, '"Divisibilité Indéfinie"'; Lowry, 'River Scene'; Piper [as War Artist], 'Somerset Place, Bath' [Tate]; [–1950] Diego Rivera [pnt] murals for National Palace, Mexico City. **Film:** Disney, 'Bambi'; Wyler, 'Mrs Miniver' [Garson]; Welles, 'The Magnificent Ambersons'; Michael Curtiz, 'Casablanca' [Bogart, Ingrid Bergman]; David Lean [UK; with Noel Coward], 'In Which We Serve' [J. Mills]; Luchino Visconti [It.], 'Ossesione'

Authors / Works:
- **P:** Kavanagh — *Hunger* [long poem]
- Sidney Keyes (1922–43) — *The Iron Laurel*
- Alun Lewis (1915–44) — *Raiders' Dawn & The Last Inspection* [stories]
- **Pr/F:** Cary — *To be a Pilgrim* [*]
- C.S. Lewis (1898–1963) — *The Screwtape Letters* [religious essays]
- Waugh — *Put Out More Flags*
- **Dr:** Coward — *Present Laughter*
- Peter Ustinov (b.1921) — *House of Regrets*
- **Theory/Crit:** Woolf — *The Death of the Moth* [pub. posthm.]

1943

History: Ministry of Town & Country Planning estab.d; Norwood Report on 2ndry education: proposes grammar, modern & technical schools [influnces 1944 Education Act]; House Commons hears of Hitler's plan to exterminate the Jews; Nazi destruction of Warsaw Ghetto – [–1944] c.2–4m. people killed at Auschwitz extermination camp; Casablanca Conference: Churchill & Roosevelt agree 'unconditional surrender' terms for Germany – de Gaulle fnds National Liberation Front in Algiers – Allied 'round the clock' bombing of Germany – Allied victories in Tripoli & Tunisia – conquest of N. Africa – Allies invade Sicily & Italian mainland – Mussolini resigns – imprisoned, & then rescued by Ger. paratroopers – Italy surrenders & joins Allies against Germany – Fascist Party dissolved – continued Ger. resistance in Italy – Ger. army defeated & surrenders at Stalingrad – USSR launches successful offensive westwards – US & Austrl. victories over Japanese in SE Asia

Culture: Nuffield Foundation estab.d; J.S. Huxley, *Evolutionary Ethics*. **Int. Lit.:** Chandler, *The Lady in the Lake*; Brecht writes *The Life of Galileo* & *The Good Woman of Setzuan* [pf.d 1947> by Berliner Ensemble]. **Music:** Poulenc, 'La Figure humaine' [cantata]; Richard Rodgers & Oscar Hammerstein II [comp] 'Oklahoma!' & 'Carmen Jones'. **Art:** Matisse, 'Icarus' [paper cut-out]; Picasso, 'Woman in Green' & [sculpt.] 'Bull's Head' [bicycle seat & handlebars]; [–1944] Moore, 'Madonna and Child' [St Matthew's Church, Northampton]; Piper, 'Gordale Scar'; Victor Pasmore [pnt] 'Quiet River: the Thames at Chiswick' [Tate]; [–1946] Willem de Kooning [pnt] 'Pancho Villa Dead and Alive' ['Abstract Expressionism']. **Film:** Wood, 'For Whom the Bell Tolls' [Cooper, Bergman]; Lean, 'This Happy Breed' [Mills, S. Holloway]; Jennings, 'Fires Were Started' & 'The Silent Village' [documentaries]; Paul Rotha [UK], 'World of Plenty' [documentary]; 'Stalingrad' [USSR documentary]; Robert Stevenson [UK], 'Jane Eyre' [Welles]

Authors / Works:
- **P:** W.H. Davies — *Collected Poems* [posthm.]
- Eliot — *Four Quartets* [v.1935]
- Keyes — *The Cruel Solstice* [posthm.]
- D. Thomas — *New Poems*
- Keith Douglas (1920–44) — *Selected Poems*
- David Gascoyne (b.1916) — *Poems 1937–1942*
- **Pr/F:** Green — *Caught*
- Greene — *The Ministry of Fear*
- **Dr:** Coward — *This Happy Breed*
- Sayers — *The Man Born to be King* [series of radio plays]
- **Theory/Crit:** Leavis — *Education and the University* [incls 'A Sketch for an "English School"' & 'Mass Civilisation and Minority Culture']
- Richards — *How To Read A Page*
- E.M.W. Tillyard — *The Elizabethan World Picture*
- **Lit. 'Events':** Bristol Old Vic refnd.d – 1st theatre to receive state aid; [–1944] Citizens' Theatre, Glasgow, fnd.d; [–1945] Orwell literary editor of *The London Tribune*

1944

History: R.A. Butler's Education Act: intros 2ndry schooling for all children & '11+' selection exam; White Paper proposes National Health Service (NHS); strategic bombing of Germany increases – Ger. V1 & V2 rocket-propelled bombs ('Doodlebugs') attack

Culture: Britain's largest battleship, HMS 'Vanguard', launched. **Int. Lit.:** Saul Bellow, *Dangling Man* [US novel]; Anouilh, *Antigone* [pf.d in Ger.-occupied Paris]; Sartre, *Huis Clos* [play]; Camus, *Le Malentendu* [play]. **Music:** Bliss, 'Miracle in the

Authors / Works:
- **Pr/F:** Beckett — *Watt*
- Cary — *The Horse's Mouth* [novel*; film, 1959]
- R. Lehmann — *The Ballad and the Source*
- H.E. Bates (1905–74) — *Fair Stood the Wind for France* [novel]

Period	Year	International and Political Contexts	Social and Cultural Contexts	Authors	Indicative Titles
		Britain – Hitler survives bomb plot – purges army of all suspects – [6 June] 'D-Day': Allied landings in Normandy – Ger. retreat – Allied landings in S. France – Paris & Brussels liberated – France regains Lorraine – airborne landings fail at Battle of Arnhem – Belgium freed of Ger. troops – Ger. counter-attack in Ardennes [defeated, 1945] – Allied landings at Anzio – Monte Cassino bombarded – Rome surrenders – Allied landings in Greece – Leningrad relieved – USSR advances in Ukraine – invades Romania, Bulgaria & Hungary – captures Bucharest, Belgrade & Budapest – SE Asia liberated by US, Austrl. & British troops – Allies agree occupation zones for Germany & Berlin; Bretton Woods agreement on post-war economic reconstruction [proposes International Monetary Fund (IMF)]; Iceland declares itself independent of Denmark; Ho Chi Minh declares Vietnam independent of France	Gorbals' [ballet]; Aaron Copland [comp] *Appalachian Spring* [US orchestral work]. **Art:** Picasso, 'Enamelled Saucepan'; Chagall, 'Around Her'; Kandinsky, 'Tempered Élan'; [–1949] Léger, 'Leisure'; [–1945] Francis Bacon [pnt] 'Three Figures at the Base of a Crucifixion'; Graham Sutherland [pnt] 'Christ on the Cross' [St Matthew's Church, Northampton]. **Film:** [–1946] Eisenstein, 'Ivan the Terrible' & 'The Boyars' Plot'; Hawks, To Have and Have Not' [Bogart, L. Bacall]; Lean, 'Blythe Spirit'; Billy Wilder, 'Double Indemnity' [Robinson, F. MacMurray]; Laurence Olivier [UK], 'Henry V' [music by William Walton]; Alf Sjöberg [Swed.], 'Frenzy' [M. Zetterling; script, Ingmar Bergman]	L.P. Hartley (1895–1972) **Theory/Crit:** W.H. Auden Tillyard	*The Shrimp and the Anemone* [1st novel in trilogy*] *The Sea and the Mirror* *Shakespeare's History Plays*
1945		Churchill's Coalition gvnmt falls – Gen. Elec.: [–1951] 1st majority Lab. gvnmt – Clement Attlee, PM – SNP win Motherwell [1st parliamentary seat]; Welfare State & nationalisation legislation begins; Yalta Conference between Churchill, Stalin & Roosevelt – latter dies – Harry Truman, US President – Allies cross Rhine & overrun Germany from W. – USSR overruns Hungary, Poland, Austria & Germany from E. – takes Warsaw & Berlin – Soviet & US forces meet in Saxony – Hitler commits suicide – 'VE Day' [8 May: 'Victory in Europe'] – Italy liberated & Mussolini executed – Russia invades Manchuria – [6 & 9 Aug.] USA drops atom bombs on Hiroshima & Nagasaki – Japan capitulates – 'VJ Day' [2 Sept: 'Victory in Japan'] – [–1952] Allied occupation of Japan – **WWII ends;** Potsdam Conference: Allies to settle problems of post-war Europe – deeply divided; USA ends 'Lend-Lease' agreement; newsreels of Nazi death camps shown; [–1946] Nuremberg War Crimes Tribunal; San Francisco Conference fnds United Nations Organisation (UNO); Chinese Nationalists take Formosa from Japan – receive Soviet support; US & Soviet troops occupy former Jap.-held Korea; Arab League fnd.d in Cairo; Communist gvnmt estab.d in Vietnam	Family Allowance system intro.d in Britain; Harwell Atomic Research Centre estab.d [1st reactor built, 1947]; polythene perfected; BBC radio intros 'Light Programme'. **Int. Lit.:** Dickinson, *Bolts of Melody* [poems; posthm.]; Wright, *Black Boy* [autobiog. novel]; Tennessee Williams, *The Glass Menagerie* [US play, pf.d]; Elizabeth Smart, *By Grand Central Station I Sat Down and Wept* [US fiction]; [–1949] Sartre, *Roads to Freedom* [novel trilogy]; Camus, *Caligula* [play]. **Music:** Shostakovich, '9th Symphony'; Prokofiev, 'Cinderella' [ballet]; Britten, 'Peter Grimes' [opera]; Rodgers & Hammerstein, 'Carousel'; Novello, 'Perchance to Dream' [musical]. **Art:** [–1949] Moore, 'Family Group' [bronze; for Stevenage New Town]. **Film:** Renoir, 'The Southerner'; Asquith, 'The Way to the Stars' [M. Redgrave]; Jennings, 'A Diary for Timothy' [documentary; wrtn by E.M. Forster]; Lean, 'Brief Encounter' [Holloway, T. Howard, C. Johnson]; Hitchcock, 'Spellbound' [Bergman, G. Peck]; Wilder, 'The Lost Weekend'	**P:** Auden Betjeman Keyes A. Lewis Philip Larkin (1922–85) **Pr/F:** Green Orwell Waugh Nancy Mitford (1904–73) Osbert Sitwell (1892–1969) Flora Thompson (1876–1947) **Dr:** Priestley **Lit. 'Events':**	*For the Time Being & The Collected Poetry* *New Bats in Old Belfries* [incls 'A Subaltern's Love-song'] *Collected Poems* [posthm.] *Ha! Ha! Among the Trumpets* [posthm.] *The North Ship* *Loving* *Animal Farm* *Brideshead Revisited* *The Pursuit of Love* [novel] *Left Hand: Right Hand* [1st in 5-vol. autobiog. (–1950)] *Lark Rise to Candleford* [begun 1939; autobiog. trilogy] *An Inspector Calls* [pub. 1947] [–1946] new Old Vic Drama School & Young Vic Theatre set up [disbanded, 1951; reopened, 1970]; Joan Littlewood's Theatre Workshop fnd.d [v.1953]
1946		1927 Trades Disputes Act repealed; Bank of England & civil aviation nationalised; [–1948] National Insurance Acts implement Beveridge's	BBC resumes TV broadcasts [c.15,000 set owners in UK] – intros 3rd Programme [radio]; Arts Council of GB receives Royal Charter; Bertrand Russell, *History*	**P:** D. Thomas Henry Reed (1914–86)	*Deaths and Entrances* *A Map of Verona* [incls 'Naming of Parts']

of Western Philosophy; Benjamin Spock, *The Common Sense Book of Baby and Child Care* [30+ m. copies sold]. **Int. Lit.:** Sartre, *L'Existentialisme est un Humanisme* [phil. doctrines]; O'Neill, *The Iceman Cometh* [wrtn, 1939; pf.d, NY]; John Hersey, *Hiroshima* [1st account of A-bomb explosion]; Robert Lowell, *Lord Weary's Castle* [US poems]; Cocteau, *The Eagle Has Two Heads* [pf.d, London]; Jacques Prévert, *Paroles* [Fr. 'song-poems']. **Music:** Sir Thomas Beecham fnds Royal Philharmonic Orchestra; Hindemith, 'For Those We Love' [requiem; from Whitman's poem, 'When Lilacs Last in the Door-yard Bloom']; I. Berlin, 'Annie Get Your Gun' [musical]. **Art:** Picasso, 'Ulysses and the Sirens'; Léger, 'Farewell New York'; Hopper, 'Approaching a City'; Sutherland, 'Head of Thorns'; Sidney Nolan [Austrl; pnt] 'Ned Kelly' [1st of ser.]. **Film:** Cannes Film Festival fnd.d; Hitchcock, 'Notorious' [Ingrid Bergman]; Hawks, 'The Big Sleep' [Bogart, Bacall]; Wyler & Sam Goldwyn, 'The Best Years of Our Lives'; Ford, 'My Darling Clementine' [H. Fonda]; Watt, 'The Overlanders'; Lean, 'Great Expectations' [Mills, A. Guinness]; Jean Cocteau [Fr, with René Clément], 'La Belle et la Bête'

R.S. Thomas (1913–2000)
Pr/F: Douglas Green
Hartley
Isherwood
Larkin
Orwell
Mervyn Peake (1911–68)
Dr: Coward
O'Casey
Rattigan
Michéal MacLiammóir (1899–1978)
Christopher Fry (b.1907)
Lit. 'Events':

The Stones of the Field
Alamein to Zem Zem [posthm. war diary]
Back
The Sixth Heaven [*]
Prater Violet
Jill [novel]
'Politics and the English Language' [essay]
Titus Groan [1st novel in trilogy*, v.1950 & '59]
Peace in Our Time [pub. 1947]
Red Roses for Me
The Winslow Boy
Ill Met By Moonlight
A Phoenix Too Frequent
H.G. Wells dies; 1st Edinburgh Festival; Auden takes US citizenship; Peter Brook directs *Love's Labour's Lost*, Stratford Memorial Theatre

recommendations of state-supported security 'from the cradle to the grave'; National Health Act; New Towns Act [designates Stevenage as 1st to be built – Hatfield, Harlow, Crawley, Bracknell, Hemel Hempstead, Basildon, Welwyn Garden City designated over next 3 yrs]; London Airport [now Heathrow] opens; Churchill's 'Iron Curtain' speech in USA [between West & Eastern bloc] signals start of 'Cold War' [–1990]; [–1958] 4th Republic in France; republics declared in Italy, Albania, Bulgaria, Hungary, Philippines; UNO supersedes L of Ns – Security Council estabs right of veto – 1st meeting of General Assembly, London – UNESCO [UN Educational, Scientific & Cultural Organisation] also estab.d; Transjordan becomes independent kingdom of Jordan; [–1950] 4th Five-Yr Plan in USSR; Nanking re-estab.d as capital of China – Nationalists & Communists fail to agree new constitution; [–1954] Vietminh forces begin civil war in Indo-China; US Navy 1st tests atom bombs on Bikini Atoll

1947

Co-op opens 1st British self-service supermarket in Southsea; point-contact transistor invented & [c.] the bikini 1st worn; Christian Dior opens fashion house in Paris with his 'New Look'; Dead Sea Scrolls discv.d. **Int. Lit.:** *The Diary of Anne Frank* pub.d [Eng. trans, 1952]; T. Williams, *A Streetcar Named Desire* [film, 1951]; Arthur Miller, *All My Sons* [US play]; Camus, *The Plague* [Eng. trans, 1948]; Anouilh, *L'Invitation au château* [pf.d; v. Fry, 1950]; Jean Genet, *The Maids* [Fr. play; Eng. trans, 1953]; Moravia, *The Woman of Rome*; Primo Levi, *If This is a Man* [account of life in Auschwitz]. **Music:** Prokofiev, 'War and Peace' [opera]; Schoenberg, 'A Survivor from Warsaw [cantata]; [–1951] Charlie Parker Quintet [incls Miles Davis on trumpet] record modern jazz classics. **Art:** [–c.1960] Le Corbusier builds 'Unités d'Habitation' [large-scale Fr. housing blocks]; Matisse, 'Red Interior: Still Life on a Blue Table'; 'Negro Boxer' [paper cut-out] & [–1951] decorates chapel at Vence, France; Chagall, 'Bouquet of Flying Lovers' [Tate]; [>] Motherwell, 'Elegies to the Spanish Republic' [ser.]; Jackson Pollock [pnt] 'Shooting Star' & 'Cathedral' [US 'Action Painting'/'Abstract Expressionism']; Alberto Giacometti [sculpt.] 'Pointing Man' [Tate]. **Film:** Lean, 'Oliver Twist' [Guinness]; René Clair [Fr.], 'Le Silence est d'Or' [M. Chevalier]; Boulting Bros [UK], 'Brighton Rock' [R. Attenborough]; Jacques Tati [Fr., 'Jour de fête'

Pr/F: Compton-Burnett
Compton-Mackenzie
P. Hamilton
Hartley
Larkin
Pamela Hansford Johnson (1912–81)
Malcolm Lowry (1909–57)
Dr: MacNeice
Theory/Crit: Brooks
Lit. 'Events':

Manservant and Maidservant
Whisky Galore
The Slaves of Solitude
Eustace and Hilda [*]
A Girl in Winter [novel]
An Avenue of Stone [novel; sequel, *A Summer to Decide*, 1948]
Under the Volcano [novel]
The Dark Tower [verse plays for radio: pub.d]
The Well-Wrought Urn
[–1976] Harold Hobson, *Sunday Times* drama critic; [>] Bertolt Brecht forms Berliner Ensemble

Severest winter in Britain for 53 yrs; [1 Jan.] coal industry nationalised; Agriculture Act provides state subsidies; Town & Country Planning Act: county councils given powers of compulsory purchase & property owners require planning permission for alterations; school leaving-age raised to 15 [v.1938]; General Agreement on Tariffs & Trade (GATT) estab.d; US Marshall 'Recovery Plan' for aid in rebuilding post-war Europe; Four Powers wrangle over reconstruction of Germany; peace treaties with Hungary, Bulgaria, Romania, Finland & Italy [Allied troops leave]; Communist gvnmt in Poland; British announce withdrawal from Palestine [–1948]; India Independence Act: India partitioned as 2 Dominions: India [Hindu] & Pakistan [Moslem; E. & W. Pakistan are on either side of India] – Punjab split between them – dispute over Kashmir – ceded to India; [–1948] free emigration passage to Australia for British ex-service personnel; Chinese Nationalist troops capture Communist capital, Yenan

PERIOD	YEAR	INTERNATIONAL AND POLITICAL CONTEXTS	SOCIAL AND CULTURAL CONTEXTS	AUTHORS	INDICATIVE TITLES
POST-WAR	1948	NHS inaugurated; electricity industry, road transport & railways nationalised [British Road Services (BRS) & British Rail (BR) set up]; Children Act: Local Authorities responsible for those without proper homes; British Nationality Act guarantees freedom of entry to UK from Commonwealth & colonies; in Eire, John Costello, PM in Fine Gael-led coalition gvnmt: passes Republic of Ireland Act – Eire becomes a fully independent Republic [on Easter Monday, 1949] – leaves Commonwealth – UK gvnmt announces no change in constitutional status of N. Ireland without full agreement [entrenches Unionism]; UNO adopts Declaration of Human Rights & estabs World Health Organisation (WHO); Organisation of European Economic Co-operation (OEEC) estab.d; 'Cold War' intensifies: [–1949] USSR blockades W. Berlin – USA & Britain airlift in supplies; People's Republics estab.d in Czechoslovakia & Romania; Gandhi assassinated in India; SA gvnmt officially adopts 'apartheid'; Federation of Malaya estab.d; much of Palestine taken over by Zionist Jews – declare independent state of Israel – Arab League invades Palestine – 1st Arab-Israeli War; Communist troops invade China from Manchuria – set up People's Republic of N. China; N. Korea becomes a Communist republic – S. Korea Republic under US influence	Fresh meat ration in Britain reduced to 6d. p.w; XIV Olympics, London, televised – 120,000 TV owners in UK; Nottingham University receives Charter; [–1954] Churchill, *The Second World War* [6 vols]; Alfred C. Kinsey, *Sexual Behaviour in the Human Male* ['Kinsey Report']. **Int. Lit.:** Norman Mailer, *The Naked and the Dead* [US novel of WWII]; Irwin Shaw, *The Young Lions* [US novel]; Alan Paton, *Cry, the Beloved Country* [SA novel; film, 1952]; Mann, *Doktor Faustus* [novel]; Sartre, *Crime Passionel* [play]; Brecht, *The Caucasian Chalk Circle* [pf.d in English, NY; wrtn, 1944–5]. **Music:** Aldeburgh [arts] Festival estab.d ; [–1949] Vaughan Williams, 'The Pilgrim's Progress' [opera]; [>] Miles Davis & Gil Evans initiate 'Cool Jazz'. **Art:** Institute of Contemporary Arts (ICA), London, fnd.d; Le Corbusier, *Le Modulor* [archit. theory]; Motherwell, 'The Crossing'; Pollock, 'Composition Number I' & 'Summertime'. **Film:** Huston, 'The Treasure of Sierra Madre' [Bogart]; Hawks, 'Red River' [Wayne, M. Clift]; Asquith, 'The Winslow Boy' [adptn of Rattigan]; Welles, 'Macbeth'; Cocteau, 'Les Parents Terribles'; Wilder, 'A Foreign Affair'; Ford, 'Fort Apache' [Wayne, Fonda]; Hitchcock, 'Rope'; Powell, 'The Red Shoes' [ballet]; Olivier, 'Hamlet' [music by Walton]; Visconti, 'La Terra Trema'; Jules Dassin, 'The Naked City'; Charles Frend [UK], 'Scott of the Antarctic [Mills]; Vittorio De Sica [It.], 'Bicycle Thieves'	**P:** Auden **Pr/F:** Green Greene Kavanagh Waugh **Dr:** Fry Rattigan **Theory/Crit:** Eliot Robert Graves Leavis Jean-Paul Sartre **Lit. 'Events':**	*The Age of Anxiety* [dramatic poem] *Concluding* *The Heart of the Matter* *Tarry Flynn* [autobiog. novel] *The Loved One* *Thor, With Angels & The Lady's Not For Burning* *The Browning Version* [film, 1951] *Notes Towards the Definition of Culture* *The White Goddess* *The Great Tradition* *What is Literature?* [in French; Eng. trans 1950] T.S. Eliot, Nobel Prize for Literature
	1949	Clothes rationing ends; gas industry nationalised; Legal Aid & Advice Act; Parliament Act reduces power of Lords to delay legislation; Countryside Act estabs Areas of Outstanding Natural Beauty & National Parks Commission [v.1951–2]; devaluation of sterling [£ = $2.80]; North Atlantic Treaty Organisation (NATO) fnd.d; Council of Europe fnd.d; Federal gvnmt in W. Germany [Adenauer, 1st Chancellor] – German Democratic Republic (GDR) in Soviet-controlled East; Communist gvnmt in Hungary, 1st Soviet atomic explosions; Newfoundland becomes 10th Canadian province; Arab-Israeli armistice – partition of Jerusalem; Indo-Pakistan conflict over Kashmir; Indonesia declares independence from Holland; France gives Laos, Cambodia & Vietnam partial independence; Siam becomes Thailand; Mao Tse-tung & Communists defeat Nationalists & declare People's Republic of China	**Int. Lit.:** Frost, *Complete Poems*; Miller, *Death of a Salesman*; Genet, *Our Lady of the Flowers* [novel; Eng. trans, 1964]; Brecht, *Mother Courage* 1st pf.d. **Music:** Britten 'Let's Make an Opera!' [incls 'The Little Sweep']; Bliss, 'The Olympians' [opera]; Vaughan Williams, 'An Oxford Elegy' [setting to Arnold's poem, 'The Scholar Gypsy']; Novello, *King's Rhapsody*; Rodgers & Hammerstein, 'South Pacific'. **Art:** Picasso, 'Portrait of Françoise'; Epstein, 'Lazarus'; Miró, 'Women and Birds in the Moonlight' [Tate]; Sutherland, 'W.S. Maugham' [Tate]; Pollock, 'Number 8'; Mark Rothko [USA; pnt] 'Number 24' [abstract colour]; Patrick Heron [pnt] 'T.S. Eliot' [NPG]. **Film:** Reed, 'The Third Man' [Howard, Welles as Harry Lime; wrtn by Graham Greene]; Cocteau, 'Les Enfants Terribles'; Robert Rossen, 'All the King's Men' [B. Crawford]; Stanley Donen & Gene Kelly, 'On the Town' [musical]; Robert Hamer [UK], 'Kind Hearts and Coronets' [Guinness]; Alexander Mackendrick [UK], 'Whisky Galore' [adptn of Compton-Mackenzie]	**P:** MacNeice **Pr/F:** Bates Bowen Cary Greene Mitford Orwell Elizabeth Taylor (1912–75) Angus Wilson (1913–91) **Dr:** Eliot O'Casey **Theory/Crit:** Simone de Beauvoir René Wellek & Austin Warren **Lit. 'Events':**	*Collected Poems* *The Jacaranda Tree* *The Heat of the Day* *A Fearful Joy* *The Third Man* [film script; novel, 1950] *Love in a Cold Climate* *Nineteen Eighty-Four* *A Wreath of Roses* [novel] *The Wrong Set* [stories] *The Cocktail Party* *Cock-a-Doodle Dandy* *The Second Sex* [Eng. trans 1952] *Theory of Literature* National Theatre Act [v.1951]
	1950	Petrol rationing ends; Gen. Elec.: Lab. re-elected without overall majority – Attlee, PM; Scots Nationalists steal Stone of Scone from Coronation	**Int. Lit.:** Hemingway, *Across the River and into the Trees* [novel]; [–1951] T. Williams, *The Rose Tattoo* [of. Roy Bradbury, *The Martian Chronicles* [US sci.	**P:** Auden **Pr/F:** Beckett	*Collected Shorter Poems, 1930–1944* *Molloy* [in French; own trans, 1955; 1st novel in trilogy; publ.d in English, 1950]

throne, Westminster Abbey [recovered by 1952; v.1996]; [> 1950s] Peter Rachman collects inflated rents from prostitutes & W. Indians ['Rachmanism']; HMS 'Ark Royal' [aircraft carrier] launched; Klaus Fuchs convicted of disclosing atomic secrets to USSR; 'Schuman Plan' to pool W. Europe's coal & steel resources; Poland–GDR treaty estabs permanent border; N. Korea invades S. Korea – [–1953] Korean War: USA & UK support S. Korea, China supports N. Korea; Anglo-Egypt dispute over future of Sudan & Suez Canal Zone begins [v.1956]; Joseph McCarthy begins accusations of 'Un-American [anti-communist] Activities'; India declared an independent republic [within Commonwealth]; Chinese forces invade Tibet

fi, stories]; Ionesco, The Bald Prima Donna [play]. **Music:** [c.] Samba [dance] becomes popular; I. Berlin, 'Call Me Madam' [musical]; 'Guys and Dolls' [US musical]; Gian-Carlo Menotti [comp] 'The Consul' [US opera]; Peter Fricker [comp] 'Symphony No. 1'. **Art:** [–1955] Le Corbusier builds church of Notre-Dame-du-Haut, Ronchamp, France; [–1952] Epstein, 'Madonna and Child' [Convent, Cavendish Square, London]; Hepworth, 'Turning Forms' [Hertfordshire CC] & 'Contrapuntal Forms' [Harlow New Town; exhib.d Festival of Britain, 1951]; [–1952] de Kooning, 'Woman I'; Nicholson, 'Winter, November, 1950'; Pollock, 'Number 1, 1950 (Lavender Mist)' & 'Number 29' [black canvas]; [–1951] Giacometti, 'Falling Man'; Eduardo Paolozzi, 'Real Gold' [collage; early UK 'Pop Art'; Tate]. **Film:** Disney, 'Treasure Island'; Wilder, 'Sunset Boulevard' [Keaton, G. Swanson]; Huston, 'The Asphalt Jungle' [M. Monroe]; Cocteau, 'Orphée'; Henry King, 'The Gunfighter' [Peck]; Joseph Mankievitch, 'All About Eve' [Monroe, B. Davis]; Akira Kurosawa [Jap.], 'Rashomon'; Ingmar Bergman [Swed.], 'Summer Interlude'

Christie — A Murder Is Announced
Green — Nothing
Hartley — The Boat
Orwell — Shooting an Elephant [essays]
Peake — Gormenghast [*]
Wilson — Such Darling Dodos [stories]
William Cooper (1910–2002) — Scenes from Provincial Life [novel]
Doris Lessing (b.1919) — The Grass Is Singing [novel]
Dr: Fry — Venus Observed & Ring Round the Moon [trans of Anouilh – v.1947]

Theory/Crit:
Maurice Bowra — The Romantic Imagination
Lionel Trilling — The Liberal Imagination
Woolf — The Captain's Death Bed [posthm.]
Lit. 'Events': G.B Shaw & George Orwell die; Bertrand Russell, Nobel Prize for Literature; Old Vic rebuilt; Michael Redgrave plays Hamlet at Elsinore

1951

British Steel industry nationalised; budget intros NHS charges – Lab. split – Aneurin Bevan & Harold Wilson resign; Gen. Elect.: [–1955] small Cons. overall majority – Churchill, PM; balance of payments crisis in UK; London Foreign Exchange Market reopens for 1st time since 1939; 1st census in UK since 1931; [–1952] 1st National Parks designated [incls Lake & Peak Districts, Snowdonia, Dartmoor, N. Yorks Moors, Pembrokeshire Coast – others follow during 1950s]; General Certificate of Education (GCE) intro.d; Guy Burgess & Donald Maclean [UK diplomats & Soviet spies] defect to USSR [v.1963]; W. Germany joins Council of Europe; European Coal & Steel Community Treaty signed [UK becomes associate, 1954]; Egypt abrogates treaty with UK – British troops occupy Suez Canal Zone; Iranian gvnmt nationalises oil industry; 49 nations sign peace treaty with Japan [USSR, 1956]; India & Pakistan dispute future of Kashmir; USSR explodes A-bomb; Tibet under Chinese suzerainty

Festival of Britain – pavilions designed by Basil Spence [also wins design for new Coventry Cathedral; [–1953] Francis Crick & James Watson construct 'double-helix' model of DNA [v.1961]; 1st 'Miss World' contest; 'The Archers' radio programme begins; [c.] 1st electronic business computers in UK & USA. **Int. Lit.:** Mailer, Barbary Shore [novel]; [c.] J.D. Salinger, The Catcher in the Rye [US novel]; James Jones, From Here to Eternity [US war novel; film, 1953]; Herman Wouk, The 'Caine' Mutiny [US war novel; film, 1954]. **Music:** Royal Festival Hall opens; Auden [with C. Kallman], libretto for Stravinsky's opera 'The Rake's Progress'; E.M. Forster, libretto for Britten's opera, 'Billy Budd'; Rodgers & Hammerstein, 'The King and I'. **Art:** Dali, 'Christ of St John of the Cross' [Glasgow AG]; Hepworth, 'Vertical Forms' [Hatfield]; Sutherland, 'The Origins of the Earth' [panel for Festival of Britain]; Paolozzi, 'You can't beat the Real Thing' [V&A]; [–1952] Reg Butler [sculpt.] 'Unknown Political Prisoner' [Berkhamstead; v.1953]; David Smith, 'Hudson River Landscape' [US sculpt.]. **Film:** Huston, 'The African Queen' [K. Hepburn, Bogart]; Stevens, 'A Place in the Sun' [Clift, E. Taylor]; Reed, 'An Outcast of the Islands' [adptn of Conrad]; Vincente Minnelli, 'An American in Paris' [Kelly, L. Caron]; Elia Kazan, 'A Streetcar Named Desire' [Leigh, M. Brando]; Charles Crichton [UK], 'The Lavender Hill Mob' [Guinness, Holloway]

P: Douglas — Collected Poems [posthm.]
Pr/F: Beckett — Malone Meurt* [own trans as Malone Dies, 1956]
Forster — Two Cheers for Democracy [essays]
Greene — The End of the Affair
P. Hamilton — The West Pier [1st of 'Mr Gorse' novels*]
Powell — A Question of Upbringing [1st novel in 12-vol. sequence, A Dance to the Music of Time (–1975)]
Snow — The Masters [v.1940]
Spender — World Within World [autobiog.]
Williamson [v.1927] — The Dark Lantern [1st novel in 14-vol. sequence, A Chronicle of Ancient Sunlight]
Nicholas Monsarrat (1910–79) — The Cruel Sea [Charles Frend film, 1952]

Dr: Ustinov — A Sleep of Prisoners
John Whiting (1917–63) — The Love of Four Colonels / Saints Day & Penny for a Song

Theory/Crit:
Empson — The Structure of Complex Words
Arnold Kettle — An Introduction to the English Novel [vol. 1; vol. 2. 1953]
Lit. 'Events': National Theatre foundation stone laid [opens 1976]; Neville Coghill, The Canterbury Tales [modern trans]; the 'Arden Shakespeare' 1st pub.d; The Oxford Companion to the Theatre 1st pub.d

PERIOD	YEAR	INTERNATIONAL AND POLITICAL CONTEXTS	SOCIAL AND CULTURAL CONTEXTS	AUTHORS	INDICATIVE TITLES
	1952	George VI dies, Queen Elizabeth II accedes; war-time 'Utility' goods system & identity cards abolished [v.1939]; [~1953] 'smog' a problem in London [c.4000 die from it]; Christopher Craig & Derek Bentley convicted for murdering a policeman – Bentley hanged; 1st British A-bomb exploded off Australian coast; Bonn Conventions end occupation of German Federal Republic by W. Powers [v.1955] – joins European Coal & Steel Community as one of 6 participating states [beginning of Common Market]; Gen. Eisenhower, US President; [c.] 1st Hydrogen bomb exploded by USA – USS 'Nautilus', 1st nuclear submarine, begun; military coup in Egypt – King Farouk abdicates; Dr Nkrumah 1st PM of Gold Coast (Ghana); Mau Mau guerrillas active in Kenya – state of emergency declared – [~1958] leader Jomo Kenyatta sentenced to hard labour	[c.] contraceptive pill 1st produced; [c.] inoculation against polio 1st intro.d; myxomatosis 1st used in Britain to destroy rabbits [causes epidemic by 1953]; De Havilland 'Comet', 1st passenger jet airliner; 1st jet breaks the sound barrier; Jodrell Bank radio telescope begun; Southampton University fnd.d; [>] ancient city of Jericho excavated. **Int. Lit.:** Hemingway, *The Old Man and the Sea*; Kurt Vonnegut, *Player Piano* [US novel]; Anouilh, *The Waltz of the Toreadors* [pf.d]. **Music:** Vaughan Williams, 'Antarctica (7th) Symphony'; Tippett, 'The Midsummer Marriage' [opera; begun 1946]. **Art:** Matisse, 'Venus' & 'Flowing Hair' [pnt.d cut-outs]; Moore, decorative frieze for Time-Life Building, London & [~1953] 'King and Queen' [Tate]; [>] Jean Tinguely constructs his 1st 'Métamécaniques' [animated metal robotics]. **Film:** Chaplin, 'Limelight' [C. Bloom]; Disney, 'Robin Hood'; Donen & Kelly, 'Singin' in the Rain'; Kazan, 'Viva, Zapata!' [Brando, A. Quinn]; Welles, 'Othello'; Clair, 'Les Belles-de-Nuit' [G. Lollobrigida]; Fred Zinnemann, 'High Noon' [Cooper, Grace Kelly]; Cecil B. De Mille [US], 'The Greatest Show on Earth'	**P:** Auden D. Jones Muir D. Thomas **Pr/F:** Beckett Green Lessing Waugh Wilson Barbara Pym (1913–80) **Dr:** Rattigan Christie **Theory/Crit:** Frantz Fanon Leavis **Lit. 'Events':**	*Nones* *The Anathemata* *Collected Poems, 1921–1951* *Collected Poems, 1934–52* *L'Innommable** [in French; own trans. as *The Unnameable*, 1959] & *En Attendant Godot* [wrtn; pf.d Paris, 1953 & v.1955] *Doting* *Martha Quest* [1st novel in 5-vol. sequence, *Children of Violence** (–1969)] *Men at Arms* [1st novel in *The Sword of Honour* trilogy* (–1961)] *Hemlock and After* [novel] *Excellent Women* [novel] *The Deep Blue Sea* *The Mousetrap* [still running!] *Black Skin, White Masks* [trans, 1986] *The Common Pursuit* Universal Copyright Convention signed in Geneva
	1953	[June] Coronation of Elizabeth II – watched by millions on TV; sweets & sugar rationing end; N. Sea floods coast of Britain & Holland; [>] Gas Council begins to explore for underground natural gas; Korean War ends; Egypt becomes a republic – Anglo-Egypt agreement on self-gvnmt for Sudan; [~1961] Dag Hammarskjöld, Sec.-General of UN; Stalin dies – Malenkov succeeds; Marshall Tito, President of Yugoslavia; Cardinal Wyszynski imprisoned in Poland for indicting Communist authorities' attacks on RC Church; McCarthy heads US 'investigations' committee – communist witchunts intensify; in Indo-China, Fr. troops occupy Dien Bien Phu & Viet Minh forces invade Laos; British atomic weapon tested at Woomera, Australia; USSR explodes H-bomb; Hillary & Tensing reach peak of Mt Everest	Colour TV experiments in USA; Wittgenstein, *Philosophical Investigations* [posthm.]. **Int. Lit.:** Faulkner, *Requiem for a Nun*; Miller, *The Crucible* [pf.d]; T. Williams, *Camino Real* [pf.d]; Bellow, *The Adventures of Augie Marsh*; Chandler, *The Long Goodbye*; Bradbury, *Fahrenheit 451* [novel]; Salinger, *For Esmé – With Love and Squalor* [stories]; James Baldwin, *Go Tell it on the Mountain* [US novel]; Anouilh, *The Lark* [pf.d]; Max Frisch, *The Fire Raisers* [Swiss play]. **Music:** Walton, 'Orb and Sceptre' & 'Te Deum' [for Coronation]; Shostakovich, '10th Symphony'; Britten, 'Spring Symphony' & 'Gloriana' [for Coronation]; 'Paint Your Wagon' [US musical]; [~1954] Bill Haley & the Comets record 'Rock Around the Clock' & 'Shake, Rattle and Roll'. **Art:** 'Unknown Political Prisoner' International Sculpture Competition at Tate: Butler, 1st prize [v.1951], Hepworth 2nd prize; Pollock, 'Deep' & 'Ocean Greyness'; Bacon, 'Study After Velázquez's Portrait of Pope Innocent X'; Lynn Chadwick [sculpt.] 'Idiomorphic Figure'. **Film:** Disney, 'Peter Pan'; Tati, 'Monsieur Hulot's Holiday'; Zinnemann, 'From Here to Eternity' [Clift]; Benedek, 'The Wild One' [Brando]; Hawks, 'Gentlemen Prefer Blondes' [Monroe]; Mankiewicz, 'Julius Caesar' [Brando, J. Mason]; Wyler, 'Roman Holiday' [Peck,	**Pr/F:** Hamilton Hartley Lehmann Lessing Monsarrat Peake Woolf Brigid Brophy (b.1929) Ian Fleming (1908–64) John Wain (1925–94) **Dr:** Eliot Greene Morgan Rattigan **Theory/Crit:** Erich Auerbach **Lit. 'Events':**	*Mr Stimpson and Mr Gorse* [*] *The Go-Between* [Joseph Losey film, 1971; script by Harold Pinter] *The Echoing Grove* *Five* [5 short novels] *The Story of Esther Costello* *Mr Pye* *A Writer's Diary* [posthm.] *Hackenfeller's Ape* [novel] *Casino Royale* [1st 'James Bond' novel; film, 1967] *Hurry on Down* [novel] *The Confidential Clerk* *The Living Room* *The Burning Glass* *The Sleeping Prince* *Mimesis* [Eng. trans] Dylan Thomas dies; Winston Churchill, Nobel Prize for Literature; Theatre Workshop leases Theatre Royal, Stratford E., London [opens 1954]

1954

Total eclipse of the sun; food rationing ends in UK; UK Atomic Energy Authority Act: to promote industrial use; Landlord & Tenant Act: security of tenure for tenants; Civil Service intros equal pay for women; [>] immigration from Caribbean to Britain increases; IRA attack Omagh Barracks, N. Ireland – Flags & Emblems Act gives special protection to Unionist flag; Berlin Conference: UK, USA, France & USSR – Soviets reject proposal to reunify Germany; [-1955] W. European Union fnd.d; British troops evacuate Suez Canal Zone – Col. Nasser takes power in Egypt; Algerian nationalism erupts – Fr. troops sent to suppress revolt – [-1962] Algerian War; disturbances in Cyprus & Greece over 'Enosis' [unity with Greece]; US Senate censures McCarthy's methods; US Supreme Court declares racial segregation in schools unconstitutional; Communist Party banned in USA; Communist Vietnamese capture Dien Bien Phu – armistice in Indo-China signed at Geneva Conference – divided into N. & S. Vietnam at 17th Parallel – Ho Chi Minh, head of gvnmt in N. Vietnam

Television Act: Independent TV Authority (ITA) set up; Eurovision TV network estab.d; Hull University fnd.d; 1st LCC comprehensive school opens at Kidbrooke, SE London; [>] Barbican scheme of redevelopment in London; Roger Bannister runs 1st under 4-min. mile; Roman Temple of Mithras discv.d in London. **Int. Lit.**: Patrick White, *The Tree of Man* [Austrl. novel]; Moravia, *Roman Tales* [It. stories]; Françoise Sagan, *Bonjour Tristesse* [Fr. novel; film, 1958]. **Music**: Britten, 'The Turn of the Screw' [chamber opera']; Stravinsky, 'In Memoriam Dylan Thomas'; Menotti, 'The Saint of Bleecker Street' [US opera; pf.d]; 'Salad Days' [musical]; electronic 'Musique Concrète' in UK. **Art**: Picasso, 'Jacqueline' & 'Silvette David'; Léger, 'Two Women with Flowers' [Tate]; Tanguy; 'Multiplication of Arcs'; Mark Rothko [pnt] 'Ochre on Red on Red'; Jasper Johns [pnt] 'Flag above White' [US 'Pop Art']. **Film**: Cukor, 'A Star Is Born' [Garland, Mason; songs by Gershwin Brothers], Kazan, 'On the Waterfront' [Brando; R. Steiger]; Hitchcock, 'Rear Window' [Stewart] & 'Dial M for Murder' [both Grace Kelly]; Olivier, 'Richard III' [Bloom, R. Richardson; music by Walton], Kurosawa, 'Seven Samurai' [v.1960]; John Sturges, 'Bad Day at Black Rock' [S. Tracy]; Ralph Thomas [UK], 'Doctor in the House' [1st in series; More, D. Bogarde]; Federico Fellini [It.], 'La Strada' [Quinn]; John Hala & Joy Batchelor [UK], 'Animal Farm' [full-length cartoon adptn of Orwell]; Andrzej Wajda [Pol.], 'A Generation'; Linsay Anderson [UK], 'O Dreamland' & 'Thursday's Children' [documentaries]

P: Watkins — *Death Bell*
Thom Gunn (b.1929) — *Fighting Terms*
Pr/F: Huxley — *The Doors of Perception* [essays on mysticism & drugs]
Isherwood — *The World in the Evening*
Lessing — *A Proper Marriage* [*]
Wyndham Lewis — *Self-Condemned*
Snow — *The New Men* [v. 1940]
Tolkien — [-1955] *The Lord of the Rings* [3 vols]
Kingsley Amis (1922–95) — *Lucky Jim* [novel; Boulting Bros film, 1957]
William Golding (1911–93) — *Lord of the Flies* [novel; Peter Brook film, 1962]
George Lamming (b.1927, Barbados) — *The Emigrants* [novel]
Iris Murdoch (1919–99) — *Under the Net* [novel]
Dr: Fry — *The Dark is Light Enough*
Rattigan — *Separate Tables* [pub. 1955]
D. Thomas — *Under Milk Wood* [posthm.; radio play. 1st broadcast]
Whiting — *Marching Song*
Theory/Crit:
Kathleen Tillotson — *Novels of the Eighteen-Forties*
W.K. Wimsatt — *The Verbal Icon* [incls (with Monroe C. Beardsley) 'The Intentional Fallacy' (1946) & 'The Affective Fallacy' (1949)]

Lit. 'Events': [-1958 & 1960-3] Kenneth Tynan, drama critic on *The Observer*, [>] 'Beat(nik)' counter-culture develops

1955

Churchill resigns – Anthony Eden (Cons.), PM – Gen. Elec.: Cons. majority, 60; Attlee retires – Hugh Gaitskell, Lab. leader; 'credit squeeze' to control inflation; City of London becomes a 'smokeless zone'; decision to make H-bomb & construct 12 nuclear power stations in UK; Geneva Congress [of 72 states] on peaceful uses of atomic energy; British dispute with Chile & Argentina over Falkland Islands; Ger. Federal Republic (W. Germany) becomes a sovereign state – joins NATO; outbreak of violence in Cyprus [EOKA guerrillas] – State of Emergency declared; USSR signs Warsaw Treaty [unified E. European defence command]; Khrushchev & Bulganin lead USSR; S. Vietnam becomes a republic

[-1956] Independent [commercial] TV commences – ITV News begins – 4.5 m. UK TV sets; anti-polio 'Salk vaccine' produced; insulin identified; [c.] steep decline in deaths from tuberculosis in UK; Exeter University fnd.d. **Int. Lit.**: Miller, *A View from the Bridge* [pf.d]; T. Williams, *Cat on a Hot Tin Roof* [pf.d; film, 1958]; Vladimir Nabokov, *Lolita* [US novel]; J.P. Donleavy, *The Ginger Man* [US novel]; Alain Robbe-Grillet, *The Voyeur* [Fr. 'nouveau roman'; Eng. trans, 1958]. **Music**: Pierre Boulez [comp] 'Le Marteau sans maître' [Fr. orchestral work]. **Art**: Le Corbusier, *Le Modulor 2* [archit. theory]; Picasso, 'Women of Algiers, after Delacroix [Canvas O] [v.1834]; Dali, 'Last Supper'; Johns, 'Three Flags'; Tinguely 'constructs 'painting machines'; Chadwick, 'Seasons' [Arts Council]

P: Auden — *The Shield of Achilles*
Larkin — *The Less Deceived*
R.S. Thomas — *Song at the Year's Turning*
William Empson (1906–84) — *Collected Poems*
Laurie Lee (1914–97) — *My Many-Coated Man*
Norman MacCaig (1910–96) — *Riding Lights*
Pr/F: Amis — *That Uncertain Feeling*
Compton-Burnett — *Mother and Son*
Golding — *The Inheritors*
Graves — *Greek Myths* [prose versions]
Greene — *The Quiet American*
Hamilton — *Unknown Assailant* [*]
Hartley — *A Perfect Woman*

PERIOD	YEAR	INTERNATIONAL AND POLITICAL CONTEXTS	SOCIAL AND CULTURAL CONTEXTS	AUTHORS	INDICATIVE TITLES
			[–1957] Peter Blake [pnt] 'On the Balcony' [UK 'Pop Art'; Tate]; Sam Francis [pnt] 'Red and Yellow' [US 'Action' painting. **Film:** Disney, 'The Lady and the Tramp'; Kazan, 'East of Eden' [J. Dean]; Goldwyn, 'Guys and Dolls' [Brando; musical]; Wilder, 'The Seven Year Itch' [Monroe]; Mackendrick, 'The Ladykillers' [Guinness, P. Sellers]; Nicholas Ray, 'Rebel Without a Cause' [Dean]; Michael Anderson [UK], 'The Dam Busters' [M. Redgrave, R. Shaw]; Richard Brooks, 'The Blackboard Jungle' [S. Poitier]; Satyajit Ray [India], 'Pather Panchali' & [–1958] 'The World of Apu' [trilogy]; Karel Reitz & Tony Richardson [UK], 'Momma Don't Allow' [documentary] **Lit. 'Events':** Peter Brook directs Paul Scofield in Hamlet [1st theatre production taken to Moscow since 1917]	Laurie Lee W. Lewis D. Thomas Waugh Ruth Prawer Jhabvala (b.1927) Brian Moore (1921–99, Ulster) **Dr:** Beckett Enid Bagnold (1889–1981) **Theory/Crit:** Theodor Adorno Leavis Ezra Pound E.P. Thompson Trilling	A Rose for Winter [travel] Monstre Gai & Malign Fiesta [trilogy completed; v.1928.] Adventures in the Skin Trade [unfinished novel; posthm.] Officers and Gentlemen [*] To Whom She Will Marry [novel] Judith Hearne [novel; reprinted as The Lonely Passion of Judith Hearne, 1959] Waiting for Godot [London; own trans; v.1952] The Chalk Garden [NY; London, 1956] Prisms D.H. Lawrence: Novelist Literary Essays [ed. & intro., T.S. Eliot] William Morris: Romantic to Revolutionary The Opposing Self
POST-WAR	**1956**	White Paper on Technical Education in HE sector – Colleges of Advanced Technology (CATs) set up; Clean Air Act passed; Small Lotteries & Gaming Act legalises bingo & betting; petrol rationing reintro.d; Road Traffic Act intros vehicle testing & parking meters; Premium Bonds 1st intro.d; 1st large-scale nuclear power station opens at Calder Hall – 1st transatlantic telephone service links UK & N. America; [–1962] IRA campaign against British occupation in N. Ireland – Sinn Fein outlawed; Nasser nationalises Suez Canal – Israel attacks Egypt – UK & France send in troops – USA & UN condemn action & call for cease-fire – Eden withdraws – balance of payments crisis [UK humiliation signals end of status as independent world power]; guerrilla activity conts in Cyprus – [–1959] Archbishop Makarios deported for collusion; France recognises independence of Tunisia & Morocco; US Pres. Eisenhower re-elected; Khrushchev denounces Stalin – 'de-Stalinisation' policies in E. Bloc – Hungary seeks greater democracy & renounces Warsaw Treaty – USSR invades & crushes rebellion – ignores UN – proclaims martial law; Japan joins UN	Nancy Mitford (ed.), Noblesse Oblige [originates 'U/Non-U' classification]; [–1958] Churchill, History of the English-Speaking Peoples [4 vols]. **Int. Lit.:** O'Neill, Long Day's Journey into Night [pf.d Stockholm; wrtn, 1941]; Sagan, A Certain Smile [film, 1958]; Friedrich Dürrenmatt, The Visit [Swiss play]. **Music:** 'My Fair Lady' [musical of Shaw's Pygmalion; film, v.1964]; Elvis Presley, 'Heartbreak Hotel'; 'Hound Dog' & 'Love Me Tender'. **Art:** [–1959] Lloyd Wright builds Solomon R. Guggenheim Museum, NY; [–1964] Jørn Utzon's Sydney Opera House built; Design Centre opens in The Haymarket; Moore, 'Seated Figure against Curved Wall'; Hepworth, 'Stringed Figure (Curlew), Version II' [Tate]; [–1960] Vasarely, 'Ondho' ['Kineticist' painting]; Hopper, 'Sunlight on Brownstones'; Richard Hamilton, 'Just what it is that makes today's homes so different, so appealing' [collage; UK 'Pop Art']. **Film:** Huston, 'Moby Dick' [Peck]; Stevens, 'Giant' [E. Taylor, Dean – later killed in car crash]; Kelly, 'Invitation to the Dance'. M. Anderson & Mike Todd, 'Around the World in Eighty Days'; De Mille, 'The Ten Commandments' [Brynner, C. Heston; remake of 1924 epic]; Otto Peminger, 'The Man with the Golden Arm' [Sinatra]; Charles Walters, 'High Society' [B. Crosby, Grace Kelly]; Jack Lee [UK], 'A Town Like Alice'; Lewis Gilbert [UK], 'Reach for the Sky' [More]; Walter Lang [US], 'The King and I' [Kerr, Brynner]; Anatole Litvak, 'Anastasia' [Bergman, Brynner]; King Vidor, 'War	**P:** Kathleen Raine (1908–2003) **Pr/F:** Golding Lessing Macaulay West Wilson Dodie Smith Anthony Burgess (1917–93) Gerald Durrell (1925–95) Hammond Innes (1913–98) Sam Selvon (1923–94; Trinidad) **Dr:** Ustinov Brendan Behan (1923–66; Ireland) John Osborne (1929–94) N.F. Simpson (b.1919) **Theory/Crit:** Leavis Trilling Colin Wilson **Lit. 'Events':**	Collected Poems Pincher Martin Retreat to Innocence The Towers of Trebizond The Fountain Overflows Anglo-Saxon Attitudes The Hundred and One Dalmatians [Disney film, 1961] Time for A Tiger [novel; 1st in 'Malayan Trilogy' (–1959)] My Family asnd Other Animals [memoirs] The Mary Deare [novel] The Lonely Londoners [novel] Romanoff and Juliet The Quare Fellow [London; Dublin, 1954; film, 1962] Look Back in Anger [Tony Richardson film, 1959] A Resounding Tinkle D.H. Lawrence: Novelist A Gathering of Fugitives The Outsider Copyright Act [made necessary by development of radio, TV, films & records];

and Peace' [Fonda, A. Hepburn]; Bergman, 'The Seventh Seal' [M. von Sydow]; Roger Vadim [Fr.], 'And God Created Woman' [B. Bardot]; Elvis Presley, 'Love Me Tender'; Joshua Logan, 'Bus Stop' [Monroe]

covers reproduction of any original literary work in any form in public; [–1961] Auden, Professor of Poetry, Oxford; Robert Conquest (ed.), *New Lines* anthology – launches 'The Movement' poets [incls Larkin, Amis, Wain, Thom Gunn, D.J. Enright, Donald Davie, Elizabeth Jennings]; Berliner Ensemble visits London [after Brecht's death]; English Stage Co. opens at Royal Court Theatre [prog. incls *Look Back in Anger*]

P: Gunn — *The Sense of Movement*
Stevie Smith — *Not Waving but Drowning*
Ted Hughes (1930–98) — *The Hawk in the Rain*
Dom Moraes (b.1938; India) — *A Beginning*

Pr/F: Compton-Burnett — *A Father and his Fate*
Fleming — *From Russia with Love* [film, 1963]
Hartley — *The Hireling*
Murdoch — *The Sandcastle*
Selvon — *Ways of Sunlight* [stories]
Wilson — *A Bit off the Map* [stories]
John Braine (1922–86) — *Room at the Top* [novel; Jack Clayton film, 1958]
Lawrence Durrell (1912–90) — *Justine* [1st novel in *Alexandria Quartet* (–1960)]
Colin MacInnes (1914–76) — *City of Spades* [novel]
V.S. Naipaul (b.1932; Trinidad) — *The Mystic Masseur* [novel]
Muriel Spark (b.1918; Scotland) — *The Comforters* [novel]

Dr: Beckett — *Fin de partie* [own trans as *Endgame*, 1958]
Greene — *The Potting Shed* [NY]
Osborne — *The Entertainer* [Tony Richardson film, 1960] & [with A. Creighton] *Epitaph for George Dillon*
Harold Pinter (b.1930) — *The Room & The Dumb Waiter* [wrtn; pf.d as double bill, 1960]

Theory/Crit:
Richard Altick — *The English Common Reader*
Northrop Frye — *Anatomy of Criticism*
Noam Chomsky — *Syntactic Structures*
Richard Hoggart — *The Uses of Literacy*
Walter Houghton — *The Victorian Frame of Mind*
Irving Howe — *Politics and the Novel*
Ian Watt — *The Rise of the Novel*
Wimsatt & Brooks — *Literary Criticism: A Short History* [4 vols]
Ivor Winters — *The Function of Criticism*

1957

Eden resigns – Harold Macmillan (Cons.), PM; Homicide Act abolishes death penalty [excluding murder of police officers]; Wolfenden Report on homosexuality & prostitution recommends liberalising proposals – rejected by Commons, 1960; fire at Windscale nuclear reactor causes radioactive fall-out; British armed forces reduced & rationalised; internment of IRA activists intro.d in Ulster & Eire; 1st British H-bomb exploded at Christmas Island; Treaty of Rome estabs the European Economic Community (EEC or 'Common Market') amongst 6 states [France, Italy, W. Germany, Belgium, Holland, Luxembourg] – Britain stays out; [–1966] Willy Brandt, mayor of W. Berlin; Suez Canal reopens – British & Fr. firms taken over by Egypt; Civil Rights Act in USA – race riots in Little Rock, Arkansas, over integration of Afro-Americans in high schools; guerrilla activity led by Fidel Castro against Cuban dictator, Pres. Batista; independence for Ghana & Federation of Malaya [Malaysia]; USSR launches 'Sputniks I & II', 1st space-craft; Fuchs & Hilary lead S. Pole expedition

UK epidemic of Asian flu; BBC 1st broadcasts 'Tonight' & schools progs; interferon [body's anti-virus substance] disc.d; Leicester University fnd.d; C. Northcote Consumers' Association fnd.d; C. Northcote Parkinson, *Parkinson's Law: the Pursuit of Progress* ['work expands to fill the time available']. **Int. Lit.:** T. Williams, *Orpheus Descending* [play]; Ray Lawler, *Summer of the Seventeenth Doll* [Austrl. play; pf.d London]; Jack Kerouac, *On the Road* [US 'Beat' novel]; John Cheever, *The Wapshot Chronicle* [US novel]; White, *Voss* [Austrl. novel]; Genet, *The Balcony* [pf.d London]; Robbe-Grillet, *Jealousy* [Eng. trans, 1959]; Moravia, *Two Women* [It. novel]; Boris Pasternak, *Dr Zhivago* [Russ. novel; trans, 1958]. **Music:** Royal Ballet formed; Auden [with Kallman] trans libretto to Mozart's 'The Magic Flute'; Leonard Bernstein [comp] 'West Side Story' [score for Sondheim musical]; 'My Fair Lady' [musical of Shaw's *Pygmalion*]; Presley, 'Jailhouse Rock'. **Art:** Picasso, 'Las Meninas'; Interior Compositon' [v. 1656–7, Velásquez] & 'La Baignade' [mural, UNESCO, Paris]; [–1959] Miró, 'Wall of the Moon' & 'Wall of the Sun' [ceramic murals, UNESCO]; [–1958] Epstein, 'Christ in Majesty' [Llandaff Cathedral]; Moore, 'Reclining Figure' [UNESCO]; Blake, 'Children Reading Comics' [RCA]; Hamilton, 'Hommage à Chrysler Corp'; Rothko, 'White and Greens on Blue'. **Film:** Sturges, 'Gunfight at the OK Corral' [K. Douglas]; Lean & Sam Spiegel, 'Bridge on the River Kwai' [Guinness; score by Malcolm Arnold]; Bergman, 'Wild Strawberries' [V. Sjöström, von Sydow]; Olivier, 'The Prince and the Showgirl' [Monroe]; Presley, 'Loving You'; Kurosawa, 'Throne of Blood' [adptn of *Macbeth*]; Wajda, 'Kanal'; Stanley Kubrick, 'Paths of Glory' [Douglas]; Mankiewicz, 'The Quiet American' [M. Redgrave; adptn of Greene]; Sidney Lumet, 'Twelve Angry Men' [H. Fonda]; Mikhail Kalatozov [USSR], 'The Cranes Are Flying'; Anderson, 'Every Day Except Christmas' [documentary]

PERIOD	YEAR	INTERNATIONAL AND POLITICAL CONTEXTS	SOCIAL AND CULTURAL CONTEXTS	AUTHORS	INDICATIVE TITLES
	1958	Elizabeth II's son, Charles, made Prince of Wales [v.1969]; race riots in Notting Hill & Nottingham; Life Peerages created; Libs win Torrington by-election [start of gradual political recovery]; Gatwick airport opens as alternative to Heathrow; Jodrell Bank radio telescope begins to operate; Campaign for Nuclear Disarmament (CND) fnd.d – 1st Aldermaston march; [–1969] Gen. de Gaulle, President of 5th Republic in France – Fr. troops leave Morocco & Tunisia; USSR demands that Berlin be a 'Free City' – NATO rejects; [–1969] Ayub Khan, President of Pakistan; W. Indies Federation fnd.d; military coup in Iraq – royal family murdered – becomes a republic; conflict between Greek & Turkish Cypriot communities; Yemen attacks Aden border – state of emergency declared; Hendrik Verwoerd, SA Premier – strong proponent of apartheid & for SA to become a republic [v.1961]; USA & USSR launch several space exploration rockets	BBC 1st broadcasts 'Panorama'; Munich air disaster – among 23 killed, 8 Man. Utd football players ['Busby's Babes']; electronic computers widely in use; reports of 'Yeti' ('Abominable Snowman') in high Himalayas; J.K. Galbraith, *The Affluent Society* [US economic theory]. **Int. Lit.:** Brecht, *The Resistible Rise of Arturo Ui* [pf.d posthm.]; Truman Capote, *Breakfast at Tiffany's* [US novel; film, 1961]; Leon Uris, *Exodus* [US novel; Otto Preminger film, 1960]; Chinua Achebe, *Things Fall Apart* [Nigerian novel]; Laurens Van Der Post, *The Lost World of the Kalahari* [SA travel writing]; Giuseppe di Lampedusa, *The Leopard* [It. novel; trans. 1960; Visconti film, 1963]. **Music:** Presley conscripted into US army; Britten, 'Noye's Fludde' [miracle play set to music]; Rodgers & Hammerstein, 'The Flower Drum Song'. **Art:** 'The New American Painting' exhib.n tours Europe; Francis, 'Blue on a Point'; Paolozzi [sculpt.] 'Japanese War God'; [–1960] Yves Klein, 'Anthropometries' [imprints on paper of nude models coated with blue paint]. **Film:** Hitchcock, 'Vertigo' [Stewart, K. Novak]; Tati, 'Mon Oncle'; Wyler, 'The Big Country' [Peck, Heston]; Gilbert, 'Carve Her Name with Pride' [P. Scofield]; Bergman, 'The Face'; Brooks, 'Cat on a Hot Tin Roof' [E. Taylor, P. Newman]; Wajda, 'Ashes and Diamonds'; Presley, 'King Creole'; Reitz, 'We Are the Lambeth Boys' [documentary]; Mark Robson, 'The Inn of the Sixth Happiness' [Ingrid Bergman]; Edward Dmytryk, 'The Young Lions' [Brando, Clift, M. Schell]; John Cassavetes, 'Shadows' [improvisation by actors]; [>] 'Carry On Sergeant', 1st in ser. of 'Carry On' movies **Lit. 'Events':** Belgrade Theatre, Coventry, opens	**P:** Betjeman **Pr/F:** Amis Bates Fleming Jhabvala Lessing Murdoch Pym Wain Wilson Sean O'Faolain (1900–91) Alan Sillitoe (b.1928) **Dr:** Behan Eliot Rattigan Pinter John Arden (b.1930) Shelagh Delaney (b.1939) Willis Hall (b.1929) Ann Jellicoe (b.1927) John Mortimer (b.1923) Peter Shaffer (b.1926) Arnold Wesker (b.1932) **Theory/Crit:** Kenneth Allsop Praz Tillyard Raymond Williams	*Collected Poems* [b-s; enlarged edtn, 1962] *I Like It Here* *The Darling Buds of May* *Dr No* [Terence Young, 1st 'Bond' film, 1962] *Esmond in India* *A Ripple from the Storm* [*] *The Bell* *A Glass of Blessings* *The Contenders* *The Middle Age of Mrs Eliot* *Stories of Sean O'Faolain* [coll. edtn] *Saturday Night and Sunday Morning* [novel; Karel Reitz film, 1960] *The Hostage* *The Elder Statesman* *Variations on a Theme* *The Birthday Party* [film, 1969] *Live Like Pigs* *A Taste of Honey* [Tony Richardson film, 1961] *The Long and the Short and the Tall* [film, 1961] *The Sport of My Mad Mother* *The Dock Brief & What Shall We Tell Caroline?* [as double bill] *Five Finger Exercise* *Chicken Soup with Barley* [1st play of trilogy*] *The Angry Decade* *The Flaming Heart* *The Epic Strain in the English Novel* *Culture and Society*
	1959	Driest British summer for 200 yrs; Macmillan coins 'You've never had it so good' slogan & wins 3rd successive Cons. Gen. Elec. victory; NCB to close 250 pits by 1965; Street Offences Act takes prostitutes off streets; Obscene Publications Act [used to prosecute Penguin Books for publishing *Lady Chatterley's Lover*, v.1960]; Crowther Report recommends raising school leaving age to 16 & better educational provision for '15 to 18' age-group; Seán Lemass succeeds De Valera as Taoiseach – signals start of modern Ireland; European Free Trade Association (EFTA) estab.d by 'Outer 7' [UK, Austria, Denmark, Norway, Portugal,	*The Manchester Guardian* renamed *The Guardian*; [–1961] 'New University' of Sussex fnd.d at Brighton; 1st section of the M1, UK's 1st motorway, opens. **Int. Lit.:** Lowell, *Life Studies* [poems]; Bellow, *Henderson the Rain King*; Mailer, *Advertisements for Myself* [essays]; William Burroughs, *Naked Lunch* [US novel]; T. Williams, *Sweet Bird of Youth*; Edward Albee, *The Zoo Story* [US play; pf.d Berlin]; Genet, *The Blacks* [pf.d; Eng. trans, 1961]; Anouilh, *Becket* [pf.d]; Ionesco, *Rhinoceros* [pub.d; pf.d, 1960]; Günter Grass, *The Tin Drum* [Ger. novel; Eng. trans, 1962; film, 1979]. **Music:** Rodgers & Hammerstein, 'The Sound of Music'; Lionel Bart [comp] 'Fings Ain't	**P:** Geoffrey Hill (b.1932) **Pr/F:** Fleming Golding Huxley Lee MacInnes Naipaul Peake Sillitoe Spark Wain	*For the Unfallen: Poems 1952–1958* *Goldfinger* [Guy Hamilton film, 1964] *Free Fall* 'Brave New World Revisited' [essay] *Cider with Rosie* [autobiog.] *Absolute Beginners* *Miguel Street* *Titus Alone* [*] *The Loneliness of the Long Distance Runner* [stories; Tony Richardson film, 1963] *Memento Mori* *A Travelling Woman*

Sweden & Switzerland]; agreement between all sides in Cyprus [v.1960]; self-gvnmt for Jamaica; Pope John XXIII calls 2nd Vatican Council [1st, 1870] seeking church unity [opens, 1962]; UN condemns Apartheid; Alaska becomes 49th US State, Hawaii 50th & last; Castro seizes power in Cuba – Batista flees; civil war begins in Belgian Congo; uprising in Tibet against Chinese – suppressed – Dalai Lama flees to India; space & moon probes by USA & USSR – training of astronauts begins

Wot They Used T'be' [Theatre Workshop musical; film, 1960]. **Art:** Frank Lloyd Wright builds Guggenheim Museum of Art, NY; Epstein, 'Monument to the Dead of the Working Class'; Moore, 'Animal Farm' [Zoological Soc.] & 'Two-Piece Reclining Figure No. I'; Blake, 'Kim Novak Wall'; [–1960], Jim Dine, 'Car Crash' [pnt & collage; US 'Pop Art']; [–1950] Alexander Calder [USA] constructs 'Red Polygons (Red Flock)' [mobile]. **Film:** Disney, 'Sleeping Beauty'; Preminger, 'Anatomy of a Murder' [G. C. Scott, L. Remick]; Wilder, 'Some Like It Hot' [Monroe, T. Curtis, J. Lemmon]; Goldwyn, 'Porgy and Bess' [Poitier; songs by Gershwin Bros]; Wyler, 'Ben Hur' [Heston, Novarro (v.1926)]; Powell, 'Peeping Tom'; Makiewicz, 'Suddenly Last Summer' [Clift]; Kramer, 'On the Beach' [Astaire, Peck]; Bergman, 'The Virgin Spring'; Reed, 'Our Man in Havana' [adptn of Greene; Guinness, N. Coward]; Boulting Bros, 'I'm All Right Jack' [Sellers, M. Rutherford]; Michelangelo Antonioni [It.], 'L'Avventura' [M. Vitti; 1st in trilogy – v.1960,1962]; Fellini, 'La Dolce Vita' [M. Mastroianni, A. Aimée, A. Ekberg]; François Truffaut [Fr.], 'Les Quatre Cents Coups'; Jean-Luc Godard [Fr.], 'A Bout de souffle' ('Breathless') [J-P Belmondo, J. Seberg]; Alain Resnais [Fr.], 'Hiroshima, Mon Amour' [co-wrtn with Marguerite Duras]; Ronald Neame [UK], 'The Horse's Mouth' [Guinness; adptn of Cary]; Bryan Forbes & Richard Attenborough [UK], 'The Angry Silence'

Malcolm Bradbury (1932–2000)

Andrew Sinclair (b.1936)

Keith Waterhouse (b.1929)

Dr: Arden

Beckett

Greene

Osborne

Simpson

Wesker

Theory/Crit:

Ferdinand de Saussure

Lit. 'Events':

Eating People is Wrong [novel]

The Breaking of Bumbo & My Friend Judas [novels]

Billy Liar [novel; John Schlesinger film, 1963]

Serjeant Musgrave's Dance

Krapp's Last Tape [in French; pf.d with *Endgame*, 1958; Eng. broadcast, 1960]

The Complaisant Lover

The World of Paul Slickey [musical]

A Slight Ache & The Dwarfs [on radio; on stage, 1961, 1964]

One Way Pendulum

Roots [*] & *The Kitchen*

Course in General Linguistics [Eng. trans; 1st pub, 1915]

Nottingham Playhouse & Mermaid Theatre, London, open; C.P. Snow's Rede Lecture, 'Two Cultures [Arts v. Sciences] and the Scientific Revolution' [Leavis reacts with *Two Cultures?*, 1962]

1960–1979

The Nineteen-Sixties and Seventies

INTRODUCTION

Unlike the 1960s, which is still known by its familiar soubriquet, 'The Swinging Sixties', the 1970s has no commonly used nickname – although 'The Sour/Discordant Seventies' might describe the decade fairly accurately. The terms **Contemporary*** and **Postmodernist***, which sometimes include the years 1960–79, are reserved for Chapter 9, and the reasons for such a location given there. Here, although there are clearly major continuities between them, the narratives discernible in the timeline tables are outlined separately below for each of the two decades both for clarity and because each seems to have – not unlike the 1920s and 1930s – a distinctive character: one evincing euphoria and hopefulness, the other disenchantment and frustration.

Chapter contents

8.1 NINETEEN-SIXTIES

Key Timeline Narratives 1960–1969

➲ *The International Context*

- ***British Colonies in Africa and Elsewhere***   Ushered in by Harold Macmillan's 'Wind of Change' speech at Cape Town in 1960, the period, and especially the earlier part of it (although the process continues into the 1970s), saw independence achieved by the majority of Britain's African colonies, as well as by those in the Caribbean and elsewhere (many registering this by changing their name), while despite the resistence of the white settlers in Algeria, the country became independent from France in 1962. By 1967 (when the UK also withdrew its troops from Aden [The People's Republic of Yemen, 1968]), a White Paper proposing a drastic reduction by the mid-1970s in British military commitments 'East of Suez' was a *de facto* recognition of the UK's declining status as a world power. However, independence also led to acute tensions in many of the new states, the most serious in the 1960s being in the Congo (1961–2), Cyprus (1964) and Nigeria (1968–70, when secessionist Biafra surrenders).

    A rather different issue in Africa, however, and one that bedevilled the Labour Governments of 1964 and 1966 under Harold Wilson, was that of Southern Rhodesia which, under its Prime Minister, Ian Smith, made a Unilateral Declaration of Independence (UDI) in 1965 to ensure the continuation of white rule there, and became an illegal regime subject to UN sanctions (it was not until 1979–80 that majority rule was declared and Rhodesia became the independent state of Zimbabwe).

    As witnessed by the Sharpeville massacre of 1960 (police shot black Africans on a peaceful march), the apartheid regime in South Africa became increasingly repressive and isolated from the international community (it withdrew from the Commonwealth as a republic in 1961). The first Bantustan (a theoretically 'independent' homeland for black Africans) was set up in 1963 [but see 1976 for Transkei], Nelson Mandela was tried, convicted and given life imprisonment in 1964 for political offences (released 1990), and in 1968–9, the government refused to admit the MCC touring team for including the South African-born coloured cricketer, Basil D'Olivera [see also 1970, when a mass campaign results in the cancellation of a South African cricket tour to the UK, and South Africa is expelled from the Olympic Committee and banned from the Davis Cup].

- ***The USA and USSR***   As John F. Kennedy became US President in 1960, relations between the two super-powers were severely strained, especially over Cuba where Fidel Castro had expropriated US firms and aligned the island with the Soviet bloc. Following the USA's failed 'Bay of Pigs' invasion of Cuba in 1961, the stand-off between the USA and the USSR intensified in 1962 over the building of a Soviet missile base there and nuclear war was only narrowly averted. Thereafter, relations eased a little (e.g. a 'hot line' was established in 1963 between the presidents of the two states to preclude such potentially disastrous events occurring [Kennedy was assassinated the same year]), although a series of spying revelations throughout the 1960s [see, for example, 1960, 1961, 1962, 1963, 1965] and the Soviet-led invasion of Czechoslovakia during the 'Prague Spring' of 1968 did little to thaw the continuing 'Cold War' climate.

    While 'de-Stalinisation' nevertheless continued in the USSR under President Brezhnev, the USA was wrestling with both the Vietnam War [see below], and the black Civil Rights movement (at its height between c.1961 and 1968 – the year President Lyndon Johnson's Civil Rights Bill was finally passed, Martin Luther King and Robert Kennedy were assassinated, and Richard Nixon was elected President).

- **Vietnam War**   The single most dominant international event of the whole period (ends 1973–4), its origins began in the late 1950s when North Vietnamese guerrillas (Viet Cong) started infiltrating South Vietnam. In 1962, the USA established a military command in the South, and in 1964 when N. Vietnam and S. Vietnam went to war, the 'Gulf of Tonkin' episode (N. Vietnamese bombed US warships) led to retaliatory bombing of the North and the *de facto* involvement of the USA. By 1965, the USA had substantially increased its offensive capability, and US anti-war demonstrations began. The Viet Cong 'Tet Offensive' (1968) threatened Saigon, the same year as US troops massacred civilians at My Lai. The war seriously divided US public opinion, and caused huge demonstrations at home and abroad [see, for example, 1967, 1968, 1969]. [For the continuation of the war, see Asia in the 1970s below.]
- **Other Conflicts**   In China, the 'Cultural Revolution' began in 1966 with the purging by Red Guards of 'revisionists'; tension between China and India was high (see 1962), and between India and Pakistan, who were at war over Kashmir from 1965 to 1966. In 1967, the radical guerrilla, Che Guevara, was killed in Bolivia, and the Arab-Israeli 'Six-Day War' broke out, with Egypt, Syria and Jordan defeated, the beginning of the Israeli occupation of the Gaza Strip (coastal region of SW Palestine), Sinai, the West Bank (of the Jordan River), and the annexing of the Jordanian part of Jerusalem.
- **Europe**   Significant events include: the resistance of France to Britain joining the Common Market (1961, 1963, 1967), and France's withdrawal from NATO (1966); East Germany (GDR) sealing the border of West and East Berlin by building the Berlin Wall (1961); the military coup in Greece (1967) and Greece's withdrawal from the Council of Europe (1969); the unrest across Europe (especially in Paris) of students and workers in May 1968 (similar unrest occurred in the USA).

➲ **UK Politics**   The Liberals continued their political revival by winning the Orpington by-election in 1962; in 1963, Alec Douglas-Home became Prime Minister on Macmillan's resignation (following the 'Profumo Affair' involving John Profumo, Minister of War, the call-girls Christine Keeler and Mandy Rice-Davies, and a Soviet diplomat); and Harold Wilson, became Labour Party leader on Gaitskell's death, then winning the General Election of 1964 with a small majority. Edward Heath became Conservative Party leader in opposition in 1965, and in 1966 the Wilson Labour Government was again returned, this time with an increased majority.

Significantly, in the same year, Plaid Cymru (the Party of Wales; *v.*1925) won its first parliamentary seat at Carmarthen, thus heralding a revival of Welsh nationalism (endorsed by the Welsh Language Act of 1967, which gave Welsh equal legal validity with English), and in 1967, the Scottish National Party (SNP; *v.*1934) won the Hamilton by-election. In 1967, too, the first 'Ombudsman' (Parliamentary Commissioner for Administration: to investigate complaints about government departments) was appointed, and the Representation of the People Act of 1969 lowered the voting age to 18. Prince Charles was formally invested that year by the Queen at Caernarvon Castle as Prince of Wales, a title he had held since 1958. One of the most significant political developments of the period, however – which also fundamentally transformed social and cultural life in the following decades – was the emergence of a new Women's Movement mobilised by radical feminist theory and action (this was not, of course, a specifically British phenomenon).

➲ **UK Industrial and Social Relations**   Despite the setting-up in 1962 of the National Economic Development Council ('Neddy') to orchestrate economic planning, the abolition of Resale Price Maintenance (RPM) by the Tories in 1964 to promote more competition, and the establishing of a

Prices and Incomes Board by Labour in 1965, the UK economy throughout the 1960s was fragile: a sterling crisis in July 1966 brought about deflation and a wage-freeze; as a result, the trade gap widened, and in 1967, the pound was devalued by 14.3 per cent. Such problems did not ease industrial relations: in 1966, immediately following the Labour election victory, there was a seamen's strike, and in 1969, the Wilson Government published a White Paper, 'In Place of Strife', proposing trade union reform (including governmental powers to demand strike ballots and 'cooling-off' periods in industrial; disputes) and published an Industrial Relations Bill. This provoked a mass strike on May Day and was withdrawn, thus heralding the difficulties successive governments in the 1970s would have with the trades unions.

Nevertheless, the Labour Governments from 1964–70 introduced much social reform legislation which helped to make the UK a more liberal society: this covered consumer protection, rating and valuation (both 1962) and monopolies and mergers (1965); the abolition of the death penalty (1965); the legalisation of abortion and of homosexual acts between consenting adults, the introduction of breathalysers for road safety (all 1967); clean air, trades descriptions (both 1968); and divorce (1969). The Greater London Council (GLC) was established in 1965, and the 'Save As You Earn' (SAYE) scheme in 1969.

Less popular was the Beeching Report of 1963 on the streamlining of the British railway system, which led to extensive reductions in services provided.

- **Immigration**   From the New Commonwealth countries, this was at its height in the early 1960s, and restrictions were introduced by the Commonwealth Immigrants Acts of 1962 and 1968 (when there was an influx of expelled Kenyan Asians into Britain and the Tory right-winger, Enoch Powell, made his 'rivers of blood' speech against immigration). On the other hand, the Race Relations Act of 1965 legislated against discrimination and set up the Race Relations Board to deal with complaints, while that of 1968 extended anti-discrimination to housing and employment, allowed the Race Relations Board to inititiate proceedings, and established the Council of Community Relations (1969; v.1976 also) to improve race relations.

- **Education**   Major initiatives included: the Newsome Report on secondary education in the UK (1963) which proposed raising the school leaving-age to 16 (achieved in 1972); the requirement in 1965 of Local Education Authorities to submit plans for a comprehensive school system in their area; the Robbins Report of 1963 on the expansion of higher education in the UK, and the founding throughout the first half of the 1960s of the 'New Universities' (e.g. Sussex, Essex, Warwick, Coleraine, Heriot-Watt, Kent, Strathclyde); the founding of the Council for National Academic Awards (CNAA) and degree-awarding Polytechnics [see 1964–6; and also 1992 when the Polys became universities]; and the founding of the Open University using radio and TV for distance learning in 1969.

- **Northern Ireland**   The 'Troubles' of the next 30 years began with civil rights demonstrations in Londonderry in 1968, the escalation of violence involving both Catholics and Protestants and the deployment of British troops to restore order in 1969 [see 1970s below for further details].

⊃ **Science and Technology**   In science, the connection between smoking and disease was established; the measles vaccine developed (1963); in 1967, Dr Christian Barnard performed the first live heart-transplant operation in South Africa, and in 1968, the UK's first heart-transplant patient survived for 46 days; in 1969, the first human embryo was fertilised in a test-tube in Cambridge [see also 1974]. In 1962, however, the Thalidomide drug disaster amongst pregnant women (causing severe birth deformities) indicated that medical intervention could have a downside.

Despite international attempts to limit the proliferation of nuclear weapons [see 1962–3, 1968], the testing and possession of them continued: the UK obtained its first 'Polaris' missiles between 1960 and 1966; France exploded a bomb in 1960 and an H-bomb in 1968; and China three bombs (1963–6) and an H-bomb (1967). Peaceful technological developments included: the first successful laser (1960); the launching of 'Telstar', the US telecommunications satellite (1962); the agreement between France and Britain in 1962 to build 'Concorde', the first supersonic airliner, and its first public flight in 1969; the first 'Hovercraft' service (1966); UK colour TV on BBC2 (1967) and on BBC1 and ITV (1969).

But perhaps the two most significant technological narratives of the 1960s were the exploration for and first landing of North Sea oil and natural gas by the UK [see 1964, 1965, 1967]; and the rapid development of space exploration: the USSR's Sputnik V in 1960 which orbited the earth with two dogs on board; the first men in space (Yuri Gargarin [USSR] and then Alan Shephard [USA]) in 1961; the US 'Ranger' spacecraft hitting the Moon (1962); the first woman in space (USSR, 1963); the transmission of photographs by US 'Ranger' (Moon) and 'Mariner' (Mars) in 1964; the first space walk by a Soviet astronaut (1965) and then one by US Buzz Aldrin (1966, the same year as US 'Surveyor' landed on the Moon and sent back photographs of its surface); the landing of 'Venus IV' on Venus (USSR, 1967); the journey to the Moon and back, having done ten orbits of it, by US spacecraft 'Apollo 8' containing three astronauts (1968); and finally in 1969, the televised landing on the Moon of US 'Apollo 11' astronauts, Neil Armstrong and Buzz Aldrin, who brought rock samples back to earth.

➲ Social and Cultural 'Signs of the Times'

- **Disasters**   The Aberfan coal-tip slip in 1966 which engulfed a school wiping out 116 Welsh children and 28 adults; the wrecking of the 'Torrey Canyon' oil tanker off Land's End in 1967 causing extensive pollution (environmenal consciousness grows during the Sixties [Rachel Carson's *The Silent Spring* on the dangers of modern pesticides was published in 1963, and the UN report, *Problems of the Human Environment*, stressed the urgent need for conservation in 1969; see 1970s below for the rapid development of this issue]).
- **Crimes and Trials**   The obscenity trial at the Old Bailey in 1960 of Penguin Books for publishing D.H. Lawrence's novel, *Lady Chatterley's Lover* (their victory was a mile-stone in loosening censorship and is sometimes seen as ushering in the 'permissiveness' of the 1960s); the Great Train Robbery of 1963, and the ensuing trial of the robbers; the trial in 1966 of the Moors Murderers, Ian Brady and Myra Hindley; the trial of the London gangsters, Ronnie and Reggie Kray, for murder in 1969.
- **Sport**   The victory of Cassius Clay over Sonny Liston in 1964 to become world heavyweight boxing champion (he then joined the 'Black Muslim' movement and changed his name to Muhammad Ali); the victory of the English football team over Germany in the World Cup in 1966.
- **The Swinging Sixties**   *Time* magazine identified London as a 'swinging city' in 1966, and in 1967, articles appeared in the *Guardian* newspaper by Margaret Drabble and Mary Quant on 'the permissive society' and 'the sexual revolution' (Quant's own fashion design was itself a hallmark of 1960s' style).
- **Art**   The predominance of 'Pop Art', especially in the USA and UK, throughout the decade.
- **Popular Music**   The release of the Beatles' first LP, 'Please Please Me', in 1963, of the Rolling Stones' first single, 'Come On', the same year, and the two groups' huge success during the rest of the decade; broadcasting from 'pirate' radio stations on ships outside British waters (see 1964); the release in 1966 of 'The Jimi Hendrix Experience's' first single, 'Hey Joe', and first album, 'Are

You Experienced?'; The Who at the Monterey Pop Festival in 1967; the Woodstock and Isle of Wight rock festivals in 1969, and John Lennon and Yoko Ono's 'bed-in' protest that year against the Vietnam War; the proliferation of 'pop' musicals throughout the period (including 'Oliver!' [1960], 'Oh, What a Lovely War' [1963], 'Joseph and the Amazing Technicolor Dreamcoat' and 'Hair' [both 1968], 'Oh! Calcutta!' [1969]).

- **Theatre**   The UK theatre continued to develop dynamically, with the RSC making the Aldwych Theatre its London base under Peter Hall (1960); the setting-up of the National Theatre Board and National Theatre Company under Laurence Olivier (housed at the Old Vic until the NT itself was built [see 1976]), and the opening of the Chichester Festival Theatre, also under Olivier (both 1962); the opening of the Travers Theatre, Edinburgh (1963), the Octagon Theatre, Bolton (1967), the Open Space Theatre, London (1968) and the Theatre Upstairs at the Royal Court, London (1969); the planning of the Barbican Theatre as the future home of the RSC (1965); and the abolition of censorship by the Lord Chamberlain in the Theatres Act of 1968.

- **Satire**   The new sense of liberation in the 1960s saw a boom in satire: the review 'Beyond the Fringe' (Peter Cook, Dudley Moore, Jonathan Miller, Alan Bennett) opened at the Edinburgh Festival in 1960 and then moved to the Establishment Club, London; 'That Was The Week That Was' ('TW3') was first broadcast on TV in 1962, and *Private Eye* magazine was launched the same year.

- **Theory and Criticism**   It is from the mid- to late 1960s that the so-called 'Moment of Theory' is usually dated (including Marxism, Feminism and Structuralism). The exponential growth of work in this area can be followed through the **Theory/Crit.** sections of the timeline tables for this and subsequent decades. Dates of translation indicate how relatively late European theory entered the British cultural arena.

8.2 NINETEEN-SEVENTIES

Key Timeline Narratives 1970–1979

⊃ *The International Context*

- **Africa**   Repression in apartheid *South Africa* continued with the massacre of demonstrators at Soweto in 1976 and the death in custody of the black civil rights leader, Steve Biko – the same year that the UN banned arms sales to South Africa. Prime Minister Ian Smith declared *Rhodesia* a republic in 1970, but by 1976 the process of transition to (black) majority rule was underway, the end of white rule was agreed in 1978, and in 1979, conflict and illegal UDI ended [see 1960s: British Colonies in Africa], UN sanctions were lifted, and Bishop Muzorewa became the first black President of Zimbabwe (for 6 months, until elections; see 1980).

  In *Uganda*, an army coup in 1971 put Idi Amin in power whose ruthless military dictatorship saw the expulsion of all Ugandan Asians with British passports (some 25,000 entered the UK) and the killing of hundreds of thousands of 'opponents' to the regime [see 1974]; but in 1978–9, Tanzania sent in troops and Amin was deposed (1979). Following the overthrow of the fascist dictatorhip in Portugal in 1974 [see below, Europe], *Mozambique* and *Angola* became independent, but long-running civil wars immediately ensued.

- **Asia**   The war in *Vietnam* ground on with the US-led invasion of Cambodia (Kampuchea; 1970) and Laos (1971), mounting US casualties, huge anti-war demonstrations at home (e.g. Washington, 1971), and continuing military successes by the Viet Cong – resulting in a ceasefire in 1973 and the USA withdrawing its troops. However, the war in Indo-China was not over, with pro-

Chinese communist Khmer Rouge guerrillas led by Pol Pot fighting government troops in *Cambodia* (1974) and taking the capital Phnom Pen in 1975 (between two and three million people died in the regime's brutal 'killing fields' policy); but further Viet Cong victories in Cambodia and against South Vietnam led to the fall of Saigon and the end of the Vietnam War in 1975, the reunification of Vietnam in 1976 with Hanoi as its capital, the Vietnamese invasion and occupation of Cambodia in 1978, and the overthrow of Pol Pot's Khmer Rouge regime in 1979.

Conflict broke out on the Indian sub-continent in 1971 when *India* and *Pakistan* went to war, Pakistan was defeated and East Pakistan [see 1947] declared itself the independent state of *Bangladesh* (which joined the Commonwealth in 1972, as Pakistan left it). Zulfikar Bhutto became President of Pakistan in 1971, and did much to rebuild and reform the country, but he was ousted by a military coup led by General Zia Ul-Haq in 1977, sentenced to death in 1978, and finally executed in 1979 (after worldwide protest). Zia then introduced a policy of Islamisation in Pakistan.

• **The Americas**   In the earlier part of the decade, the *United States* was still traumatised by the Vietnam War [see above] and domestic opposition to it (six student demonstrators were killed by the National Guard at Kent and Jackson State Universities in 1970), and then from 1972 by the 'Watergate' scandal in Washington in which President Nixon's senior aides were implicated, Nixon himself was subpoenad for refusing to hand over secret tape-recordings (1973), and resigned under threat of impeachment in 1974.

In South America, *Chile* elected Salvator Allende its (Marxist) President in 1970, who instituted liberalising policies, but was overthrown and killed in a military coup led by General Augusto Pinochet in 1973; Pinochet became President of a brutally repressive regime until the late-1980s. In 1978, the Sandinista guerrillas fermented conflict in *Nicaragua*, overthrew the US supported Somoza dictatorship, and formed a government in 1979.

• **The Middle East and Iran**   In 1970, there was a civil war in Jordan between government troops and guerrillas of the Popular Front for the Liberation of Palestine (PLO); in 1972, 11 Israeli athletes were murdered at the Munich Olympics and 26 people died in an attack at Tel Aviv airport; the Arab-Israeli Yom Kippur War broke out in 1973 when *Egypt* and *Syria* invaded *Israel*, a counter-attack by Israel led to a ceasefire after three weeks, and UN peace-keeping forces were deployed, but the subsequent hike in oil prices and reduced production by the Arab states (–1974) caused a major energy crisis, especially in the West. In 1974, Israel withdrew from the Suez Canal (which reopened after 8 years in 1975) and signed a truce with Syria, but began bombing Palestinian refugee camps in the *Lebanon*, the same year that the UN recognised the Palestine Liberation Organisation (PLO). A civil war between Christian and Muslim militias commenced in Lebanon in 1975 (ceasefire 1976). Israeli and Egyptian leaders visted each others' countries in 1977 on a peace mission, and in 1978, the US President, Jimmy Carter, brokered the Camp David peace accord between Israel and Egypt. However, continuing PLO guerrilla activity on the one hand (see 1978 and 'Terrorism' below), and on the other, Israel's establishing of Jewish settlements on the West Bank (1977; v.1967) and bombing of Palestinian camps in South Lebanon (1978) ensured that tension in the Middle East remained high.

In *Iran*, despite social reform and the nationalisation of the Western-owned oil industry (1973), the Shah's regime came into increasing conflict with Islamic fundamentalists, culminating in violent demonstrations against it, martial law imposed, an oil strike which cut off all exports (1978), and in 1979, a revolution which deposed and exiled the Shah and established the Ayatollah Khomeini as ruler of an Islamic republic. The Shah's exile in the USA caused the seizing of hostages in the US Embassy in Teheran, a crisis which lasted until 1981. Once again, the price of oil increased.

- **Europe and the USSR**   In 1970, West Germany signed a peace treaty with the USSR and with Poland (recognising national boundaries), and throughout the period there was a move towards greater European unity, with the Helsinki Agreement of 1975 underwriting security, co-operation and human rights, the first direct elections to the European Parliament in 1979 and the institution of the European Monetary System (EMS) the same year (although Mrs Thatcher demanded reduced contributions by the UK to the EEC). However, between 1972 and 1973, the UK and Iceland were involved in the so-called 'Cod War' over fishing limits.

  The 1970s also saw a number of liberalising initiatives in European states: Wladyslaw Gomulka attempted to put Poland on the road to more freedom and independence, but riots in Gdansk and other Baltic ports over price increases forced him to resign (1970–1); in 1974, a military coup in Portugal overthrew the country's fascist regime, and free elections were held in 1975 with a socialist majority returned; in Greece, military rule by the 'Colonels' Junta' also ended in 1974, free elections were held and the monarchy deposed (Greece joined the EEC in 1979); General Franco died in 1975, and the Spanish monarchy was restored under King Juan Carlos I, who oversaw the gradual restoration of democracy in Spain; and in 1977, dissident Czech intellectuals published 'Charter 77' demanding civil rights. Such pressures towards democratisation and liberalisation in East European states reached their climax in the late-1980s, but the Seventies ended ominously with the USSR's ill-fated invasion of Afghanistan (1979).

- **'Terrorism'**   [Scare-quotes are used here to signal how equivocal the term is, most particularly because what is terrorism to one is legitimate political action to another.] The 1970s saw a rapid escalation in the use of violent strategies to achieve political goals: hijacking (especially of airliners), kidnapping, hostage-taking, assassination, bombings and shootings. Instances include: in 1970, the beginning of the Baader-Meinhof 'Red Army Faction' terror campaign against the 'materialist order' in West Germany, and the hijacking of three planes to Jordan by the PLO, the crew and passengers held hostage and then released, and the planes blown up; the bombing in 1971 of a UK government minister's house by the 'Angry Brigade' in protest at the Industrial Relations Act [see below]; the killing of 11 Israeli athletes by pro-Palestinian guerrillas at the Munich Olympic Games in 1972, and the attack on Tel Aviv airport in which 26 people died the same year; 70 hostages taken by Palestinian guerrillas at an OPEC meeting in Vienna (1975); the hijacking of an airliner by PLO guerrillas and the rescue of hostages by Israeli forces at Entebbe airport, Uganda; the hijacking of a Lufthansa airliner by the Red Army Faction to try and secure the release of Andreas Baader at Mogadishu, Somalia, in 1977 (87 hostages were freed after five days; Baader committed suicide); the 'Red Brigades' in Italy kidnapped and killed Aldo Mori, a former Prime Minister (1978); Muslim extremists seized the Grand Mosque at Mecca, Saudi Arabia. [IRA activity in the UK is outlined under *Ireland* below.]

- **Nuclear and Environmental Issues**   As noted at the end of the section on the 1960s, concerns about nuclear proliferation, the environment and conservation were becoming an international issue; the 1970s saw attempts at regulation rapidly increase. While France might resume nuclear tests in the Pacific, there was international outcry against it (1973), and more generally there were attempts to attain international agreements to limit nuclear capacity: for example, in 1971, 40 nations signed a treaty banning nuclear weapons on the seabed, and the first Strategic Arms Limitation Talks (SALT) began to try and reduce anti-ballistic missiles (treaty signed by USA and USSR, 1972), while a major nuclear accident at Three Mile Island in the USA (1979) concentrated minds about the dangers of domestic use.

  To stress the urgent need to preserve natural resources, 1970 was nominated European

Conservation Year; there was the first UN World Conference on the Human Environment in Stockholm in 1972, with the UN adopting a Declaration on it the following year; by 1974, serious anxiety was being expressed about the danger to the ozone layer from CFCs ('greenhouse gases'); and oil spills of the kind listed under Signs of the Times: Disasters, below, in the late-1970s underlined the dangers of pollution. In 1979, bans on whale fishing were introduced to protect endangered species.

• *Science and Technology*   In the earlier part of the 1970s, space exploration continued, as did that for oil in the North Sea (the first oil landed in the UK, 1975); the first Boeing 747 'Jumbo Jet' was launched in 1970, while cut-price shuttle flights between London and New York became available in 1977; the world's first 'test-tube baby' was officially born in 1974 (see also 1969); the first UK baby was born after *in vitro* fertilisation in 1978; and a campaign by the World Health Organisation (WHO) to eradicate smallpox begins to succeed (1976; its complete eradication was announced by WHO in 1980). But perhaps the most significant narrative, in its relative infancy, was the appearance as the decade progressed of microprocessors, portable and home computers, floppy disks, home video recorders, digital watches, computer games, and Sony Walkman cassette players.

⮑ *UK Politics and the Economy*   [This gloss should be read in conjunction with the following one, as the issues here were closely inter-related.] Following Labour's failure to institute its policy of 'In Place of Strife' for industrial relations (1969), the Conservatives came to power in the General Election of 1970 with Edward Heath as Prime Minister. A period of extreme tension ensued between the Government and the trades unions, exacerbated by a weak economy [see 1972] further battered by a huge rise in the price of oil (1973–4) following the Arab–Israeli Yom Kippur War and the nationalisation of the foreign oil industry in Iran [see Africa, above, Middle East and Iran]. A 'State of Emergency' was declared in 1973.

The General Election of 1974 restored Wilson's Labour Party to (minority) government, which inherited industrial turmoil and an economy suffering from severe inflation (c.25% by 1975, when the Government had to seek a loan of £1 billion from the International Monetary Fund [IMF]). The 'Social Contract' between the TUC and the Government to restrain pay rises was instituted in 1974, but economic and social problems intensified; Wilson resigned in 1976, and James Callaghan became Prime Minister; the pound fell below two to the dollar the same year, inflation remained high, a further huge loan was sought from the IMF; and cuts in public-sector spending resulted in more strikes. The Liberal leader, Jeremy Thorpe, was forced to resign over the Norman Scott affair (he was accused and acquitted of conspiracy to murder in 1979), and David Steel replaced him. Labour was kept in power by a pact with the Liberals ('Lib-Lab Pact') in 1977, but the collapse of the 'Social Contract' the same year, and of the 'Lib-Lab Pact' in 1978 left Labour seriously exposed. The 'Winter of Discontent' (1978–9) began, devolution referenda in Wales and Scotland failed to reach the required 40 per cent of the electorate (March 1979; see below), the SNP tabled a successful vote of 'no confidence' in the Government at the end of March, and in the subsequent General Election, the Conservative victory brought Margaret Thacher to power (–1990) and a series of Conservative Governments until 1997.

In the General Election of 1970, Plaid Cymru won 175,000 votes and the SNP 11 per cent of the vote, the first time a fourth party in the UK had taken such a significant share. In 1974, Plaid Cymru took three seats from Labour, and the SNP won 11 seats and 30 per cent of the Scottish vote. Pressure for devolution mounted, and the minority Callaghan Government in 1976 intoduced a Scotland and Wales Bill which proposed separate assemblies for both countries to manage social services and local government but with no powers of taxation and Westminster retaining the veto. The Bill failed in 1977; separate Bills for each country were introduced later the same year (including provision for referenda), and passed in 1978. The referenda were held in March 1979, with a large defeat for devolution in Wales, considerable support for it in Scotland but not enough to secure its passage, and the subsequent vote of 'no confidence' by the SNP which brought down the Labour Government [see above].

In 1970, the UK reopened negotiations to join the EEC, the Commons voted in favour in 1971, and in 1973, together with Eire and Denmark, Britain became a full member (having agreed to the controversial Common Agricultural Policy [CAP]). In a referendum of 1975, 67 per cent of those who voted were in favour of continued membership, although after 1979, relations between the Thatcher Government and the EEC were often severely strained [see Chapter 9].

⊃ **UK Industrial Relations**   As is clearly apparent from UK Politics, set out above, a major narrative in the 1970s was the conflict between the government and the trades unions. The Heath Government in 1970 inherited a situation in which strikes were causing nationwide power cuts, but its Industrial Relations Act of 1971 soured the situation further by establishing an Industrial Relations Court with extensive powers to delimit strike action. Despite turning out to be ineffectual, the legislation engendered deep hostility, with the first national miners' strike since 1926 following in 1972–3 which caused widespread power cuts, and a State of Emergency was declared. The strike ended with a 32 per cent pay rise recommended for the miners, but the same year saw the gaoling of the 'Pentonville Five' (dockers) for defying the Industrial Relations Act and their being released after union agitation.

Pay and price freezes continued in 1973, 2 million workers struck on May Day, the miners' began an overtime ban which again led the Government to declare a State of Emergency and to introduce a 'Three-Day Week' in industry. When it came to power in 1974, the Wilson Government repealed the Industrial Relations Act and announced a 'Social Contract' with the TUC. The Employment Protection Act of 1975 set up the Advisory, Conciliation and Arbitration Service (ACAS); however, the same year, wage increases spiralled, inflation hit 25 per cent, 1.5 million were unemployed, there were many bankruptcies, and the UK economy was effectively broke. A voluntary agreement with the TUC on wage-restraint the same year held good for the next two years, and helped to bring inflation down, but the Callaghan Government was forced by the IMF in 1976 [see above] to introduce swingeing cuts in public spending which were deeply unpopular and caused further industrial strife.

With the collapse of the 'Social Contract' in 1977, free collective bargaining resumed, a Prices Commission was founded to freeze prices, there was a firemem's strike and mass pickets in confrontation with the police at the Grunwick dispute in East London. The government's attempts to limit pay rises again foundered in 1978 and the 'Winter of Discontent' was ushered in, with 1.5 million public-sector workers on 24-hour strikes against wage-restraint.

A further feature of the industrial scene during the 1970s was extensive government intervention: the Industry Act of 1975 set up the National Enterprise Board; the British National Oil Corporation (BNOC) was established the same year; and British Aerospace and British Shipbuilders were set up in 1977 to run the nationalised aviation and ship-building industries respectively. Government also saw its role as shoring up 'lame duck' companies: in 1970–1, facing bankrupcy, Rolls Royce was nationalised; also in 1971, the government rescued Upper Clyde Shipbuilders, after initially refusing assistance and a union 'work-in' in protest against the company's liquidation; in 1975, the British

Leyland Motor Corporation (BLMC) lost £76 million, the government pumped in huge amounts of public money to head off bankrupcy (again in 1977), and the company was reorganised as British Leyland (its subsequent history was to be one of falling market share, disaggregation and finally of being sold off altogether).

⊃ **UK Social Issues**   In 1971, the UK adopted decimal currency, and VAT (at 8 per cent, with exemptions) replaced Purchase Tax in 1973. Queen Elizabeth's Silver Jubilee took place in 1977. The Equal Pay Act of 1970 sought to eradicate discrimination between the sexes in employment (whilst still excluding thousands of part-time women workers), and the Sex Discrimination Act of 1976 consolidated this; the Divorce Law Reform Act (1971) acknowledged that the principal ground for divorce in the UK was now the breakdown of marriage; and free family planning became available on the NHS in 1974.

In 1971, the Immigration Act further restricted the rights of Commonwealth subjects to settle in the UK; conversely, the Race Relations Act of 1976 established the Commission for Racial Equality and reinforced legislation against incitement to racial hatred; nevertheless, there were riots at the Notting Hill Carnival in 1976 and violent clashes between anti-Fascists and the National Front throughout the late-1970s. The Local Government Act (1972; in force, 1974) created new counties (e.g. Avon, Humberside, Cleveland) and merged others (e.g. Hereford and Worcester).

As Education Minister, Mrs Thatcher ended free milk in schools in 1971, although the school leaving age was raised from 15 to 16 the following year; the subsequent Labour Government pressed ahead with its policy of making comprehensive education the norm (1975–6); the first Open University broadcast was made in 1971; and in 1972, men's Cambridge colleges admitted their first women students, and five Oxford colleges announced that they would do the same.

⊃ **Northern Ireland**   The 'Troubles' in Ulster and elsewhere in the UK intensified during the 1970s. 1970–1 saw the formation of the Social Democratic and Labour Party (SDLP; John Hume became leader in 1979), the Rev. Ian Paisley's Democratic Unionist Party, the Ulster Defence Regiment (UDR) and the Ulster Defence Association (UDA), but also such terrorist groups as the Provisional IRA, the Ulster Volunteer Force (UVF) and the Ulster Freedom Fighters (UFF), initiating a wave of shootings, bombings and rioting.

The first major offensive by the Provisionals was in 1971; the Special Powers Act of the same year introduced internment without trial in Northern Ireland; and the Long Kesh camp was established. In January 1972, 13 civil rights marchers were shot dead by paratroopers in the 'Bloody Sunday' massacre in Londonderry; 22 bombs in one day in Belfast caused the army to launch 'Operation Motorman' to reopen 'no-go' areas in Londonderry and Belfast; the number of British troops in Ulster had risen from 6000 in 1969 to 20,000 in 1972 (with mounting casualties); and the British Government was forced to suspend the Stormont Assembly and impose direct rule from London.

In 1973, the bombing campaign spread to the UK mainland, with bombs at the Old Bailey and elsewhere, a campaign which continued throughout the 1970s (see, e.g., Guildford, Woolwich and Birmingham [1974]; 'Balcombe Street Siege' [1975]; 1976). In 1973–4, the Sunningdale Agreement and the establishing of a non-sectarian power-sharing Executive in place of the Stormont Government was intended to resolve the political difficulties, but rejection by the Ulster Unionist Council and the Protestant workers' strike in 1974 caused direct rule to be reintroduced. The Special Armed Services (SAS) were sent to Ulster in 1975, the same year that the Irish National Liberation Army (INLA) was formed; in 1976, the Women's Peace Movement in Northern Ireland was founded (awarded the Nobel Peace Prize, 1977); 'dirty protests' by IRA prisoners in the H-Blocks began in

1978; and in 1979, the IRA killed 18 soldiers at Warrenpoint and assassinated Lord Mountbatten, while the INLA killed Airey Neave, MP, with a car-bomb at the House of Commons.

➲ Social and Cultural 'Signs of the Times'

- **Disasters** A cyclone and tidal wave engulfed East Pakistan in 1970 causing huge damage and loss of life, and in 1974, as Bangladesh [see above, Asia], monsoon floods covered half the country leaving 10 million homeless; in 1971, the crush barriers collapsed at the Ibrox football stadium, Glasgow, killing 66 fans; from 1973, continuing drought caused severe famine in Ethiopia and the Horn of Africa more generally; an explosion at Flixborough chemical works, UK, killed 29 people; 41 people were killed in the Moorgate underground crash in London in 1975, and c. 580 passengers died when two Jumbo jets collided on the ground at Tenerife airport in 1977; Dutch Elm disease destroyed 6.5 million trees in the UK in 1975; in 1977, the North Sea was badly polluted after an oil rig accident in the Ekofisk field, as were the Brittany coast in 1978 by the wrecked oil tanker 'Amoco Castle' and the Gulf of Mexico by a huge oil spill in 1979, the same year that witnessed a major nuclear accident at Three Mile Island, USA.
- **Buildings and Exhibitions** 1972 saw the 'Treasures of Tut'ankhamun' exhibition at the British Museum; in 1973, the new London Bridge, Sydney Opera House and the World Trade Centre, New York, all opened; the first McDonald's restaurant opened in London in 1974; the Museum of London and the National Exhibition Centre, Birmingham, opened in 1976; Richard Rogers' Pompidou Centre opened in Paris in 1977; in 1978, Norman Foster designed the Salisbury Centre at the University of East Anglia and Warwick Castle was sold to Mme Tussauds; in 1979, plans to redevelop London's docklands were announced and the National Heritage Fund established.
- **Sport** 1972 saw Bobb Fischer beat the title-holder, Boris Spassky, in the world chess championship; in boxing, Muhammad Ali defeated both Joe Frazier and then George Foreman in 1974 to retain the world heavyweight title, which he also won for the third time in 1978; in 1977, Virginia Wade finally took the Ladies Singles title at Wimbledon, and 'Red Rum' won the Grand National for the third time.
- **Theatre** The second Young Vic Theatre opened in 1970, and the Crucible Theatre, Sheffield, was built in 1971, the same year that Trevor Nunn succeeded Peter Hall as director of the RSC (Hall took over from Laurence Olivier as director of the National Theatre Company in 1972); the English National Opera was established at the London Colliseum in 1974; the Royal Exchange Theatre, Manchester, opened in 1976, as, finally, did the National Theatre, London (some 25 years after its foundation stone was laid).
- **Popular Music** In 1970, Jimi Hendrix died in London, the Beatles released the LP 'Let It Be' and then began to split up; the Rolling Stones continued to produce successful albums [see, e.g., 1971, 1972, 1978], as did Bob Marley (e.g. 1972, 1976); The Who produced 'Tommy' (rock opera, 1972); in 1976–7, 'Punk' counter-culture arrived with The Clash, The Buzzcocks and The Sex Pistols (with the latter giving their infamous 'obscene' TV interview); musicals of the period include: 'Jesus Christ Superstar' (1971), 'Godspell' (1971), 'A Little Night Music' and 'The Rocky Horror Show' (both 1973), 'Jeeves' (1975), 'Pacific Overtures' (1976), 'Annie' (1977), 'Evita' (1978), and 'Sweeney Todd' (1979).
- **Visual Arts** The decade saw the development of 'Installation Art' [see, e.g., 1975, 1976, 1979].
- **Theory/Criticism** The column entries in the timeline tables indicate the rapid consolidation of Feminism, Marxism, Poststructuralism, Reader-Response theory, neo-Freudianism, and early essays in Deconstruction, Postmodernism and Postcolonialism.

Timelines: 1960–1979

PERIOD	YEAR	INTERNATIONAL AND POLITICAL CONTEXTS	SOCIAL AND CULTURAL CONTEXTS	AUTHORS	INDICATIVE TITLES
NINETEEN-SIXTIES	1960	[>] Betting and Gaming Act leads to huge bingo craze; [~1961] UK 1/4d. [farthing] ceases to be legal tender; US 'Polaris' missiles to be based at Holy Loch, Scotland; Macmillan's 'wind of change' speech at Cape Town signals onset of African independence – [>] many states [incl. Nigeria, Somalia & Belgian Congo] become independent – civil war in Congo as Katanga province secedes – UN intervenes; Cyprus becomes an independent republic – Archbishop Makarios, President; John F. Kennedy, US President; US firms in Cuba expropriated – Castro aligns with Soviet bloc – USA ends aid; US 'spy plane' shot down over USSR – pilot imprisoned; Leon Brezhnev, President of USSR; massacre of black S. Africans on Pan-African demonstration shot by police in Sharpeville; [~1961] Adolph Eichmann, Gestapo leader, captured by Israelis in Argentina – tried & executed in Israel; 'Sputnik V' with 2 dogs on board successfully orbits Earth; France explodes 1st nuclear bomb in Sahara; Brasilia [begun 1957] becomes new capital of Brazil	10.5m. TV sets in UK; [Dec.] TV 'soap' 'Coronation Street' begins – [~1969] Jack Rosenthal writes c.150 episodes; BBC White City TV Centre opens; 1st successful laser developed; 1st communications satellite launched; New Left Review begins; Ayer, Logical Positivism [phil.]. Int. Lit.: Lillian Hellman, Toys in the Attic [US play]; John Barth, The Sot-Weed Factor [US novel]; John Updike, Rabbit, Run [US novel; 1st in trilogy* – v.1971, 1981]; Wilson Harris, The Palace of the Peacock [Caribbean novel]. Music: Britten, 'A Midsummer Night's Dream' [opera]; Walton, '2nd Symphony'; Bliss, 'Tobias and the Angel' [opera; stage, 1961]; Bart, 'Oliver' & 'Lock Up Your Daughters' [musicals]; Presley, 'It's Now or Never'. Art: [c.] 'Optical' Art develops in USA & Europe; Pasmore, 'Yellow Abstract' [Tate]; Giacometti, 'Walking Man'; de Kooning, 'Door to the River'; [c.] David Smith develops 'Zig' & 'Cubi' sculptural forms in USA; Johns, 'Painted Bronze (Ale Cans)'; Dine, 'Shoes Walking on My Brain' [pnt & objects]; Robert Rauschenberg [pnt] 'Pilgrim'; Andy Warhol [pnt] 'Saturday's Popeye'. Film: Sturges, 'The Magnificent Seven' [Brynner; remake of 'Seven Samurai' – v.1954]; Hitchcock, 'Psycho' [A. Perkins]; Huston, 'The Misfits' [C. Gable, Monroe; wrtn by Arthur Miller]; Kramer, 'Inherit the Wind' [Tracy]; Kubrick, 'Spartacus' [Douglas, P. Ustinov]; Wayne, 'The Alamo'; Asquith, 'The Millionairess' [Sellers, Loren]; Neame, 'Tunes of Glory' [J. Mills, Guinness]; Antonioni, 'La Notte' [Mastroianni, J. Moreau]; Visconti, 'Rocco and His Brothers' [C. Cardinale]; Wilder, 'The Apartment' [Lemmon, S. MacLaine]; Daniel Mann, 'Butterfield 8' [E. Taylor]; Louis Malle [Fr.], 'Zazie dans le Métro'; Joseph Losey [UK], 'The Criminal' [S. Baker]; John Schlesinger [UK], 'Terminus' [documentary]. Lit. 'Events': Unexpurgated text of Lady Chatterley's Lover pub.d by Penguin Books after Old Bailey obscenity trial; Peter Hall, director of new Royal Shakespeare Co. makes Aldwych Theatre RSC's London base; Franco Zeffirelli's Romeo and Juliet at Old Vic; satirical revue, 'Beyond the Fringe', at Edinburgh Festival	**P:** Auden Betjeman T. Hughes Edward Lucie-Smith (b.1933) Sylvia Plath 1932–63; b. USA) **Pr/F:** Amis Jhabvala MacInnes Moore Moraes Spark Lynn Reid Banks (b.1929) Stan Barstow (b.1928) David Lodge (b.1935) Olivia Manning (1908–80) Edna O'Brien (b.1932) David Storey (b.1933) Raymond Williams (1921–88) **Dr:** Arden Delaney Mortimer Pinter Rattigan Wesker Robert Bolt (1924–95) **Theory/Crit:** Leslie Fiedler Aldous Huxley George Steiner Trotsky	Homage to Clio Summoned by Bells [verse autobiog.] Lupercal A Tropical Childhood and Other Poems A Winter Ship [pub. anon.] & The Colossus and Other Poems Take a Girl Like You The Householder Mr Love and Justice The Luck of Ginger Coffey Gone Away [travel] The Ballad of Peckham Rye & The Bachelors The L-Shaped Room [novel; Bryan Forbes film, 1962] A Kind of Loving [novel; John Schlesinger film, 1962] The Picturegoers [novel] [–1965] The Balkan Trilogy [war novels; v.1977] The Country Girls [1st novel in trilogy*] This Sporting Life [novel; Lindsay Anderson film, 1963] Border Country [novel] The Happy Haven The Lion in Love The Wrong Side of the Park The Caretaker [Clive Donner film, 1963] Ross [about T.E. Lawrence] I'm Talking About Jerusalem [*] A Man for All Seasons [Fred Zinnemann film, 1967] Love and Death in the American Novel Collected Essays Tolstoy or Dostoevsky Literature and Revolution [Eng. trans; 1st pub. 1924]
	1961	UK Census: population, 52.5m.; betting shops open in UK; mass arrests of anti-nuclear demonstrators in Trafalgar Square; [c.] Caribbean &	Crick et al determine the structure of DNA & thus break the genetic code [v.1951]; New Testament of New English Bible pub.d [OT, 1970]; world's largest	**P:** Gunn MacNeice John Fuller (b.1937)	My Sad Captains Eighty-Five Poems & Solstices Fairground Music

1960

Asian immigration at its height [esp.ly to 'beat the ban' intro.d by the Commonwealth Immigrants Act of 1962]; Lonsdale, Blake & Krogers spy trials in UK; UK applies to join Common Market, as does Eire; GDR seals border of W. & E. Berlin – Berlin Wall built; Iraq claims Kuwait – British troops deployed; white settlers (OAS) in Algeria fight against independence from France; Congo: UN troops fight Katanga – secession ends; unsuccessful 'Bay of Pigs' invasion of Cuba by USA; US 'freedom riders' from Montgomery, Alabama, travel by bus to Jackson, Mississippi; [–1962] SA becomes a republic & leaves Commonwealth; 'de-Stalinisation' process in USSR – body removed from Lenin Mausoleum – cities renamed; independence for Tanganyika & Sierra Leone; [–1962] Indian troops annex Goa [from Portugal]; UN Sec.-General, Dag Hammarskjöld, killed in air crash; USSR's Yuri Gargarin 1st man in space – Alan Shepard, 1st US astronaut in space

& fastest computer 'Atlas' in use at Harwell atomic research station; *Webster's New* [3rd] *International Dictionary* pub.d. **Int. Lit.:** Salinger, *Franny and Zooey* [2 stories; wrtn, 1955, 1957]; T. Williams, *The Night of the Iguana*; Joseph Heller, *Catch-22* [US war novel; Mike Nichols film, 1970]; Grass, *Cat and Mouse* [Eng. trans, 1963]; Frisch, *Andorra* [play]; Genet, *The Screens* [pf.d]; Van Der Post, *The Heart of the Hunter*. **Art:** Goya's 'Duke of Wellington' stolen from NG [recovered, 1965]; Picasso [sculpt.] 'Woman with a Tray and a Bowl'; [–1962] William Roberts, 'The Vorticists at the Restaurant de la Tour Eiffel: Spring 1915' [Tate]; [–1962] Moore, 'Three-Piece Reclining Figure No. I'; Tinguely, 'Study for the End of the World' [1st in ser. of self-destroying monster sculptures]; Klein, 'Fire Paintings'; Vasarely, 'Orion' ['Op Art']; David Hockney [pnt] 'I'm in the Mood for Love' [RCA]; Roy Lichtenstein [pnt] 'Popeye' & 'Washing Machine'; Claes Oldenburg, 'Plate of Meat' [wire, plaster, etc]; Tom Wesselmann [pnt] 'Great American Nude # 1'. **Film:** TV causes cinema audiences to decline by 33% since 1948 – over 1500 cinemas closed; Bergman, 'Through a Glass Darkly'; De Sica & Carlo Ponti, 'Two Women' [Belmondo, Loren]; Mann, 'El Cid' [Heston, Loren]; Forbes, 'Whistle Down the Wind' [H. Mills]; Resnais, 'Last Year at Marienbad' [co-wrtn with Alain Robbe-Grillet]; Truffaut, 'Jules et Jim' [Moreau]; Malle, 'Vie Privée' [Bardot]; Clayton, 'The Innocents' [adptn of Henry James, 'The Turn of the Screw']; Rossen, 'The Hustler' [Scott, Newman]; Brando, 'One-Eyed Jacks'; J. Lee Thompson [UK], 'The Guns of Navarone' [Peck, R. Hughes]; Luis Buñuel [Sp.], 'Viridiana'; Blake Edwards, 'Breakfast at Tiffany's' [A. Hepburn]; Sam Peckinpah, 'Guns in the Afternoon' [J. McCrea]; Robert Wise, 'West Side Story' [G. Chakiris, N. Wood].

Pr/F: Cooper	*Scenes from Married Life*
Fleming	*Thunderball* [film, 1965]
Greene	*A Burnt-out Case*
R. Hughes	*A Fox in the Attic* [1st novel in unfinished series, 'The Human Predicament'; v.1973]
Murdoch	*A Severed Head* [adapted as play, with J.B. Priestley, 1963]
Naipaul	*A House for Mr Biswas*
Spark	*The Prime of Miss Jean Brodie* [Ronald Neame film, 1969]
Waugh	*Unconditional Surrender* [*]
Wilson	*The Old Men at the Zoo* [TV adptn, 1983]
Dr: Beckett	*Happy Days* [in NY]
Jellicoe	*The Knack* [Richard Lester film, 1965]
Osborne	*Luther*
Pinter	*The Collection* [on TV]
Whiting	*The Devils* [Ken Russell film, 1971]
Henry Livings (b.1929)	*Stop It, Whoever You Are* & *Big Soft Nellie*
Theory/Crit:	
Empson	*Milton's God*
Martin Esslin	*The Theatre of the Absurd*
Fanon	*The Wretched of the Earth* [Eng. trans]
Orwell	*Collected Essays* [posthm.]
Steiner	*The Death of Tragedy*
R. Williams	*The Long Revolution*
Lit. 'Events':	'The Age of Kings' on TV [Shakespeare's history plays]

1962

Libs win Orpington by-election [continues party revival]; Lords reform: successor to a peerage can renounce it for life [Anthony Wedgwood Benn does this in 1963 after passing of Peerage Act]; National Economic Development Council ('Neddy') estab.d to plan national economy; Welsh Language Society fnd.d to promote language – from 1963, English names painted out on road signs; IRA calls off campaign in Ulster; schemes initiated to put fluoride in water; Thalidomide drug disaster amongst pregnant women [produces severe abnormalities in babies]; Commonwealth Immigrants Act [intros restrictions on right of entry; & 1968]; Co-ordinating Committee Against Racial Discrimination (CCARD) & Conference of Afro-Asian-Caribbean Organizations (CAACO) fnd.d in

1st issue of *Private Eye*, satirical magazine, pub.d; TV satire prog. 'That Was The Week That Was' ('TW3'), 1st broadcast; US 'Telstar' communications satellite launched; Anthony Sampson, *Anatomy of Britain*. **Int. Lit.:** Nabakov, *Pale Fire* [novel]; Albee, *Who's Afraid of Virginia Woolf?* [pf.d; Mike Nichols film, 1966 – with Burton & Taylor]; James Clavell, *King Rat* [US novel]; Durrenmatt, *The Physicists* [pf.d]; Solzhenitsyn, *One Day in the Life of Ivan Denisovitch* [novel; Casper Wrede film, 1971]; Yevegeny Yevtushenko, *Babi Yar* [poem]. **Music:** Stravinsky, 'The Flood' [opera]; Britten, 'War Requiem' [pf.d in Coventry Cathedral]; Tippett, 'King Priam' [opera]; Bart, 'Blitz!' [musical]; The Beatles release 'Love Me Do', 'She Loves Me', 'Let Me Hold Your Hand'; Bob Dylan, 'Blowin' in the Wind'. **Art:** for new Coventry

P: Stevie Smith	*Selected Poems*
Watkins	*Affinities*
Roy Fuller (1912–91)	*Collected Poems, 1936–1961*
Pr/F: Braine	*Life at the Top*
Burgess	*A Clockwork Orange* [Stanley Kubrick film, 1971]
Huxley	*Island*
Isherwood	*Down There on a Visit*
Lessing	*The Golden Notebook* [new edtn with 'Preface', 1972]
Lodge	*Ginger, You're Barmy*
Murdoch	*An Unofficial Rose*
O'Brien	*The Lonely Girl* [*; as *The Girl with Green Eyes*, 1964]

PERIOD	YEAR	INTERNATIONAL AND POLITICAL CONTEXTS	SOCIAL AND CULTURAL CONTEXTS	AUTHORS	INDICATIVE TITLES
NINETEEN-SIXTIES		UK; William Vassall, Admiralty clerk, imprisoned for spying for USSR; UK & France sign agreement to build 'Concorde' [1st supersonic airliner; v.1969]; Geneva Conference estabs coalition gvnmt in Laos & guarantees its neutrality; [–1965] Vatican Council meets; Cuban crisis over Soviet missile base – USA blockades Cuba – Soviet ships deployed – base finally dismantled – possibility of nuclear war averted; USA estabs a military command in S. Vietnam [v.1964]; China attacks Indian border at NE Frontier; independence for Algeria from France; independence for Uganda, Jamaica, Trinidad & Tobago, Rwanda, W. Samoa, Tanganyika, under Julius Nyerere, becomes a republic; trial of Nelson Mandela begins in Johannesburg sentenced to life imprisonment [v.1990]; US 'Ranger' spacecraft hits the Moon	Cathedral: Sutherland, 'Christ in Majesty' tapestry; Epstein, 'St Michael' sculpture; Piper, stained-glass; NG buys da Vinci cartoon for 'Virgin and Child'; Chadwick; 'Pyramids'; Sutherland, 'Baron [Kenneth] Clark' [NPG]; Rothko, 'Number 2'; Dine, 'Tennis Shoe'; Johns, 'Double Flag'; Oldenburg, 'Green Ladies Shoes' [wire, etc] & 'Hamburger' set. [plaster]; Lichtenstein, 'Blam' & 'Masterpiece'; Rauschenberg, 'Dylaby'; Warhol, 'Big Campbell's Soup Can (19¢)' & 'Marilyn Monroe Diptych' [Tate]; Klein, 'Portrait Relief of Arman' [cast from living model]; Paolozzi, 'Four Towers' [aluminium & pnt; SNG]; Blake, 'Toy Shop' [mixed media; Tate]; R.B. Kital [pnt] 'Good News for Incunabulists'. **Film:** Marilyn Monroe dies; Bergman, 'Winter Light'; Welles, 'The Trial' [Perkins, Cardinale]; Ford, Henry Hathaway & George Marshall, 'How the West was Won' [Cinerama; Peck]; Lean & Spiegel, 'Lawrence of Arabia [wrtn by Robert Bolt; Guinness, P. O'Toole, O. Sharif]; Godard, 'Vivre sa vie' [A. Karina]; Robert Mulligan, 'To Kill a Mockingbird' [Peck]; Antonioni, 'L'Eclisse'; Kubrick, 'Lolita' [Mason]; John Frankenheimer, 'Birdman of Alcatraz' & 'The Manchurian Candidate'; Roman Polanski [Pol.], 'Knife in the Water'; Peter Ustinov [UK], 'Billy Budd' [T. Stamp, R. Ryan]; Basil Deardon [UK], 'Victim' [Bogarde]; [>] Ken Loach makes 'Z Cars' for TV. **Lit. 'Events':** National Theatre Board set up to run NT Co. directed by Olivier & housed at Old Vic until NT was built [v.1976]; Chichester Festival Theatre (Olivier, director) opens with Redgrave in Uncle Vanya; A. Alvarez (ed.). The New Poetry [intros new US poetry into UK]	Upward Wain Wilson Len Deighton (b.1929) 'John Le Carré' (David Cornwell, b.1931) Penelope Mortimer (1918–99) **Dr:** Livings Shaffer Wesker Edward Bond (b.1935) David Mercer (1928–80) David Rudkin (b.1936) James Saunders (b.1925) **Theory/Crit:** Auden Georg Lukács Marshall McLuhan	In the Thirties [1st novel in trilogy, The Spiral Ascent *] Strike the Father Dead Late Call The Ipcress File [thriller; Sidney J. Furie film; 1965] A Murder of Quality [novel] The Pumpkin Eater [novel; Jack Clayton film, 1963; script by Pinter] Nil Carborundum The Private Ear & The Public Eye [double bill] Chips With Everything The Pope's Wedding A Climate of Fear & A Suitable Case for Treatment Afore Night Come Next Time I'll Sing to You The Dyer's Hand The Historical Novel [Eng. trans; (1937)] The Gutenberg Galaxy
	1963	Macmillan resigns – Alec Douglas-Home (Cons.), PM; Gaitskell dies – Harold Wilson, Lab. leader: speech on harnessing 'the white heat of the technological revolution'; UK to purchase 'Polaris' missiles from USA; Newsome Report ['Half Our Future'] on 2ndry education in UK proposes raising school leaving-age to 16 [achieved, 1972]; Robbins Report on expansion of UK higher education system: HE to be available to all qualified candidates – calls for 197,000 university places by 1967/8; Beeching Report on reshaping UK rail system – leads to drastic reductions in service; 'Profumo affair': John Profumo, Minister for War, resigns over sex scandal – alleged security lapse involving Soviet diplomat, Stephen Ward, Christine Keeler & Mandy Rice-Davies; Great Train Robbery	The Sun newspaper 1st pub.d; measles vaccine developed; John Robinson, Bishop of Woolwich, pubs controversial book, Honest to God; York University fnd.d; [c.] Polaroid colour prints 1st produced; E.P. Thompson, The Making of the English Working Class [history]; Rachel Carson, The Silent Spring [on dangers of modern pesticides]. **Int. Lit.:** Updike, The Centaur; Vonnegut, Cat's Cradle; Thomas Pynchon, V [US novel]; Mary McCarthy, The Group [US novel]; Sidney Lumet film, 1965]; Grass, Dog Years [Eng. trans, 1965]; Ionesco, Exit the King [pf.d, London]; Rolf Hochhuth, The Representative [Ger. play attacking Pope Pius XII]. **Music:** Ashton, 'Marguérite and Armand' [ballet, with Nureyev & Fonteyn]; Joan Littlewood directs Theatre Workshop's musical Oh, What a Lovely War [film,	**P:** Eliot MacNeice **Pr/F:** Amis Burgess Le Carré Murdoch Naipaul Plath Sillitoe Spark Storey Margaret Drabble (b.1939) Nell Dunn (b.1936)	Collected Poems, 1909–1962 The Burning Perch One Fat Englishman Inside Mr Enderby [1st novel in trilogy (–1974)] & Honey for the Bears The Spy Who Came in from the Cold [Martin Ritt film, 1965] The Unicorn Mr Stone and the Knight's Companion The Bell Jar [novel] The Ragman's Daughter [stories] The Girls of Slender Means Radcliffe A Summer Bird-Cage [novel] Up the Junction [stories]

The Collector [novel; William Wyler film, 1965] — John Fowles (b.1926)
Travelling People [novel] — B.S. Johnson (1933–73)
The Workhouse Donkey — Dr: Arden
Comédie [own trans as *Play*, London, 1964] — Beckett
Kelly's Eye — Livings
The Lover — Pinter
Man and Boy — Rattigan
Photo-Finish — Ustinov
The Rhetoric of Fiction — Theory/Crit: Wayne C. Booth
The Feminine Mystique — Betty Friedan
Structural Anthropology [(1958); Eng. trans] — Claude Lévi-Strauss
The Meaning of Contemporary Realism [(1950); Eng. trans] — Lukács
Concepts of Criticism — Wellek

of £2.5m. – trial of Ronnie Biggs, Bruce Reynolds et al; Kim Philby identified as 'Third Man' in Burgess & Maclean spying ring [v.1951] – flees to Moscow; De Gaulle vetoes UK entry to EEC; USA, USSR & UK sign Nuclear Test Ban Treaty; Martin Luther King leads campaign for black civil rights in Birmingham, Alabama – rioting – Pres. Kennedy takes Civil Rights Bill to US Congress – Kennedy & black leader, Medgar Evers, assassinated – Lyndon Johnson, President; 1st Bantustan ['independent' enclave for SA blacks] set up in Transkei; Organisation of African Unity (OAU) fnd.d; independence for Kenya [republic, 1964]; USSR puts 1st woman in space

1969]; Beatles' 1st LP, 'Please Please Me'; Dylan, 'The Freewheelin' Bob Dylan' [album]; Rolling Stones release 1st single, 'Come On'. **Art:** [–1965] Moore, 'Reclining Figure, Lincoln Center Sculpture' [NY]; Bacon, 'Man and Child' [Marlborough AG]; Lichtenstein, 'The Drowning Girl', 'I Know … Brad' & 'Whaam!'; Warhol, 'Early Colored Liz' [silkscreen] & 'White Car Crash 19 times'; Blake, 'Bo Diddley'; Hockney, 'Domestic Scene, Broadchalk, Wilts'; Patrick Caulfield [pnt] 'Engagement Ring'; Joe Tilson, 'Nine Elements' [mixed media; SNG]; Lewis Morley, 'Christine Keeler' [photo; NPG; v.'Profumo affair']. **Film:** Hitchcock, 'The Birds'; Bergman, 'The Silence'; Fellini, '8½' [Mastroianni]; Mankiewicz, 'Cleopatra' [E. Taylor]; Mann, 'The Fall of the Roman Empire'; Richardson, 'Tom Jones' [script by Osborne; Finney, L. Redgrave, D. Warner, S. York]; Losey, 'The Servant' [Bogarde, S. Miles; Pinter's adptn of Robert Maugham novel]; Resnais, 'Muriel'; Malle, 'Le Feu Follet'; Martin Ritt, 'Hud'; Andy Warhol, 'Sleep' [3-hr silent 'movie' of man sleeping]; Stanley Baker [UK], 'Zulu' [M. Caine]. **Lit. 'Events':** attempt to republish John Cleland's novel, *Fanny Hill* [v.1748], prosecuted under Obscene Publications Act; Travers Theatre, Edinburgh, opens

---

1964

Collected Poems — P: Kavanagh
The Whitsun Weddings — Larkin
Confessions and Histories — Lucie-Smith
Earthworks — Tony Harrison (b.1937)
You Only Live Twice ['Bond'; film, 1967] — Pr/F: Fleming
The Snow Ball — Brophy
Nothing Like the Sun — Burgess
The Garrick Year — Drabble
The Spire — Golding
A Single Man — Isherwood
Albert Angelo — Johnson
African Stories [coll.] — Lessing
Girls in Their Married Bliss [*] — O'Brien
The Housing Lark — Selvon
The Corridors of Power [v.1940] — Snow
Late Call — Wilson
The Terminal Beach [stories] — J.G. Ballard (b.1930)
How It Is — Dr: Beckett
Eh? — Livings
Inadmissible Evidence — Osborne
A Scent of Flowers — Saunders
The Royal Hunt of the Sun [Irving Lerner film, 1969] — Shaffer
Entertaining Mr Sloane [Douglas Hickox film, 1969] — Joe Orton (1933–67)

Cons. gvnmt abolishes Resale Price Maintenance (RPM) to promote competition [supermarkets can now undercut small shopkeepers]; Gen. Elec.: small Lab. majority – Wilson, PM; Ministry of Technology formed – Department of Education has 1st Council for National Academic Awards (CNAA) fnd.d [to validate degrees in non-university-sector colleges; v.1966]; gvnmt licences granted to drill for oil & gas in N. Sea; 'Mods' & 'Rockers' riot at UK holiday resorts; contraceptive pills banned for UK RCs; Greeks & Turks fight in Cyprus – Makarios calls in UK & UN peace-keepers; Martin Luther King awarded Nobel Peace Prize; US Pres. Johnson signs Civil Rights Bill – re-elected with large majority; S. & N. Vietnamese troops at war – 'Gulf of Tonkin' incident: Vietcong attack US warships – retaliatory bombing of N. Vietnam begins; Khruschev resigns – Brezhnev & Kosygin now Soviet leaders; [–1966] China explodes 3 nuclear bombs; Ian Smith becomes PM of S. Rhodesia (later Zimbabwe; v.1965–6); independent republics in Malta, Nyasaland (Malawi), N. Rhodesia (Zambia), Tanganyika & Zanzibar (united as Tanzania); US 'Ranger' [Moon] & 'Mariner' [Mars] spacecraft send back photographs

The *Daily Herald* [ex-Labour newspaper] closes; 1st *Observer* colour supplement; BBC TV launches BBC2; 'New Universities' of Essex, E. Anglia, Kent, Lancaster, fnd.d; Forth Road Bridge opens; Cassius Clay beats Sonny Liston for world heavyweight boxing title – joins 'Black Muslim' sect & changes name to Muhammad Ali; [>] 'Hippy' counter-culture develops. **Int. Lit.:** Cheever, *The Wapshot Scandal* [novel]; Hemingway, *A Moveable Feast* [autobiog. sketches; posthm.]; Lowell, *For the Union Dead* [poems]; Bellow, *Herzog*; A. Miller, *After the Fall* [pub.d] & *Incident at Vichy* [pf.d]; Gore Vidal, *Julian* [US novel]. **Music:** [c.] 'pirate' station, 'Radio Caroline', broadcasts from ship outside British waters; Stravinsky, 'Elegy for J.F.K'; Beatles, 'Beatles For Sale' [album] – 1962 singles released in USA to hysteria – global 'Beatlemania' – Richard Lester film, 'A Hard Day's Night'; Rolling Stones tour USA; Dylan, 'The Times They Are A-Changin' & 'It Ain't Me, Babe'. **Art:** Oldenburg, 'Giant Soft Toothpaste' [mixed media]; Warhol, 'Boxes' [assembly]; Hamilton, 'Epiphany (Slip It To Me)'; George Segal [USA], 'Woman Standing in a Bath Tub' [mixed media]. **Film:** UK film audiences 50% less than in 1957; Disney, 'Mary Poppins' [J. Andrews]; Cukor, 'My Fair Lady' [A. Hepburn, Holloway, R. Harrison]; Hitchcock, 'Marnie'; Kubrick, 'Dr Strangelove' [Scott, Sellers]; Godard, 'Une Femme Mariée' [Karina];

PERIOD	YEAR	INTERNATIONAL AND POLITICAL CONTEXTS	SOCIAL AND CULTURAL CONTEXTS	AUTHORS	INDICATIVE TITLES
			Antonioni, 'The Red Desert' [Vitti; R. Harris]; Losey, 'King and Country' [Bogarde]; Forbes, 'Séance on a Wet Afternoon' [Attenborough]; Warhol, 'Blow Job'; Pier Paolo Pasolino [It.], 'The Gospel According to St Matthew'; Peter Glenville [UK], 'Becket' [Burton, O'Toole]; Michael Cacoyannis [Grk], 'Zorba the Greek' [Quinn]; [–1967] Segei Bondarchuk [USSR], 'War and Peace' [4 pts]; Grigori Kozintsev [USSR], 'Hamlet'; Hiroshi Teshigahara [Jap.], 'Woman of the Dunes'; Tony Essex [UK], 'The Great War' [ser. of TV films based on archive material]; Peter Watkins, 'Culloden' [TV documentary]	Brian Friel (b.1929; Ulster) **Theory/Crit:** Chomsky Jan Kott Herbert Marcuse McLuhan John Willett **Lit. 'Events':**	*Philadelphia! Here I Come!* *Current Issues in Linguistic Theory* *Shakespeare Our Contemporary* *One-Dimensional Man* *Understanding Media* *Brecht on Theatre* [ed. & trans] Peter Brook directs Peter Weiss's *Marat/Sade* [Aldwych]
	1965	Churchill dies – Edward Heath replaces Alec Douglas-Home as Cons. opposition leader; Labour sets up Prices & Incomes Board; Murder (Abolition of Death Penalty) Act; Race Relations Act makes discrimination illegal – Race Relations Board set up [v.1968] – Campaign Against Racial Discrimination (CARD) estab.d; Greater London Council (GLC) estab.d; LEAs required to submit plans for comprehensive schools; gvnmt announces CATs [v.1956] to be awarded university status [v.1966/7]; 1st woman High Court judge in England; [>] BP explores for oil under N. Sea; 70 mph speed limit intro.d on UK roads; Gerald Brooke, UK lecturer imprisoned in Moscow for subversion [exchanged for Krogers, 1969]; Spain renews claims on Gibraltar; NLF guerrillas active in Aden – UK assumes direct rule; Unilateral Declaration of Independence (UDI) by PM Smith of Rhodesia – regime declared illegal – UN votes mandatory sanctions; black activist, Malcolm X, assassinated in USA – race riots in Watts, Los Angeles – many dead & injured – extensive damage to property – Ku Klux Klan murder Civil Rights worker; civil war in Dominican Republic – US troops sent in; army takes over gvnmt in S. Vietnam – USA substantially increases combat troops for offensive action; anti-Vietnam war protestors besiege Pentagon; India & Pakistan at war over Kashmir; independence for Gambia; Soviet astronaut makes 1st 'space walk'	BBC's '24 Hours' news prog. 1st broadcast; Ulster (Coleraine) & Warwick Universities fnd.d; Post Office Tower, London, opens; 1st Commonwealth Festival of the Arts in UK. **Int. Lit.:** Mailer, *An American Dream*; Updike, *Of the Farm*; Vonnegut, *God Bless You, Mr. Rosewater*; Albee, *Tiny Alice* [pub.d]; Jerzy Kosinski, *The Painted Bird* [Holocaust novel]; Derek Walcott, *The Castaway and Other Poems* [Trinidadian poems]. **Music:** Sir Harrison Birtwhistle [comp] 'Tragoedia' & 'Ring a Dumb Carrillon'; Sir Kenneth MacMillan [choreograph] 'Romeo and Juliet' [ballet]; Beatles receive the MBE; Rolling Stones, 'The Last Time'; Dylan, 'Mr Tambourine Man', 'It's All Over Now, Baby Blue' & 'Like a Rolling Stone'. **Art:** Lichtenstein, 'White Brushstroke # 1'; Hockney, 'Rocky Mountains and Tired Indians' [SNG]; Tilson, 'P.C from N.Y.' [screenprint]; Mel Ramos [pnt] 'Miss Cushion Air (Miss Firestone)'. **Film:** Godard, 'Alphaville'; Malle, 'Viva Maria' [Bardot, Moreau]; Fellini, 'Juliet of the Spirits' [G. Masina]; Wise, 'The Sound of Music' [Andrews]; Lean, 'Dr Zhivago' [wrtn by Robert Bolt; Sharif, Christie]; Lester, 'Help!' [Beatles]; Schlesinger, 'Darling' [Christie]; Polanski, 'Repulsion' [C. Deneuve]; Watkins, 'The War Game' [controversial documentary rejected by BBC TV]; James Ivory [US], 'Shakespeare Wallah' [script by Jhabvala]; Ken Russell, 'Debussy' [TV documentary]; 'A Passage to India' [TV film]. **Lit. 'Events':** T.S. Eliot dies; Barbican Theatre planned as future home for RSC	**P:** Auden Gascoyne MacCaig Plath George Barker (1913–91) **Pr/F:** Bradbury Deighton Drabble Fleming Le Carré Lessing Lodge Moore Murdoch O'Brien Sillitoe Spark **Dr:** Arden Bond Mercer Osborne Pinter Shaffer Frank Marcus (b.1928) Dennis Potter (1935–94) **Theory/Crit:** Mikhail Bakhtin Victor Shklovsky	*About the House* *Collected Poems* *Measures* *Ariel* [posthm.] *Collected Poems, 1930–1965* *Stepping Westward* *Funeral in Berlin* *The Millstone* [film, 1969 – as 'A Touch of Love'] *The Man with the Golden Gun* [posthm.] *The Looking-Glass War* *Landlocked* [*] *The British Museum is Falling Down* *The Emperor of Ice-Cream* *The Red and the Green* *August is a Wicked Month* *The Death of William Posters* *The Mandelbaum Gate* *Armstrong's Last Goodnight & Left-Handed Liberty* *Saved* *The Governor's Lady & Ride a Cock Horse* *A Patriot for Me* [refused a licence – pf.d privately] *Tea Party* [on TV] & *The Homecoming* *Black Comedy* *The Killing of Sister George* [film, 1969] *Vote, Vote, Vote for Nigel Barton & Stand Up for Nigel Barton* [on TV] *Rabelais and His World* [Eng. trans] 'Art as Technique' [(1917); Eng. trans]
	1966	Gen. Elec.: Lab. re-elected with increased majority: Wilson, PM; Plaid Cymru wins Carmarthen by-election; sterling crisis in UK – wage freezes intro.d;	*The Times*' front page carries news for 1st time; opening of Parliament 1st televised; Centre Point, London, built; Tay & Severn road bridges	**P:** MacNeice Moraes Stevie Smith	*Collected Poems* [posthm.] *Poems, 1955–1965* *The Frog Prince*

Year	History / Society	Culture (Lit., Music, Art, Film)	Authors	Works
	prototype Dounreay nuclear power station begun; UK's 1st Polaris submarine, 'HMS Resolution', launched; CATs become Universities [e.g. Bath, Bradford, Brunel, City, Heriot-Watt, Surrey, UWIST, Loughborough, Strathclyde] – Anthony Crosland, Education Minister, announces that 27 [later 30] technical colleges will be redesignated Polytechnics & award CNAA-validated degrees [v.1964]; PMs Wilson & Smith meet on HMS 'Tiger' to negotiate on UDI for Rhodesia – UK proposals rejected – UN sanctions imposed; coal-tip slide in Aberfan, Wales, kills 116 local schoolchildren & 28 adults; 'Moors Murderers', Ian Brady & Myra Hindley, receive life sentences; European 'Six' adopt Common Farm Policy; France withdraws from NATO; race riots in Chicago, Cleveland & Brooklyn; Verwoerd, S. African PM, assassinated – B.J. Vorster, PM; Tashkent declaration to end Indo-Pakistani war; Indira Gandhi, Indian PM; independence for Barbados, Basutoland (Lesotho), Bechuanaland (Botswana), British Guiana (Guyana); 'Cultural Revolution' begins in China – 'Red Guards' purge 'Revisionists'; 'Buzz' Aldrin makes spacewalk from US 'Gemini 12' – US 'Surveyor 1' lands on Moon & transmits photos of surface	completed; Hovercraft service begins; England beat Germany in the World Cup at Wembley; Time magazine identifies London as a 'swinging' city. **Int. Lit.:** Barth, *Giles Goat-boy*; Capote, *In Cold Blood* [US 'faction']; Pynchon, *The Crying of Lot 49*; Jacqueline Susann, *Valley of the Dolls* [US b-s. novel; film, 1967]; White, *The Solid Mandala*; Christina Stead, *Cotters' England* [Austrl. novel]; Yevtushenko, *Poems* [Eng. trans]. **Music:** Rolling Stones, Mick Jagger & Keith Richard, on drugs charges; Malcolm Williamson [comp] 'The Violins of St Jacques' [opera]; Beatles, [LP] 'Revolver'; The Who, 'My Generation'; Jimi Hendrix forms band 'Jimi Hendrix Experience' in UK – 1st single, 'Hey Joe', instant success. **Art:** Caribbean Artists Movement (CAM) fnd.d in London [1st public meetings, 1967]; floods damage art treasures in Florence; Pasmore, 'Construction Relief' [Marlborough Gall.]; Oldenburg, 'Soft Medecine Cabinet' [mixed media]; [–1967] Allen Jones [pnt] 'Perfect Match'. **Film:** Antonioni, 'Blow-up' [S. Miles, D. Hemmings, V. Redgrave]; Bergman, 'Persona' [L. Ullmann, B. Andersson]; Houston, 'The Bible' [R. Harris]; Welles, 'Chimes at Midnight' [Welles's Falstaff]; Losey, 'Modesty Blaise' [Bogarde, Vitti]; Gilbert, 'Alfie' [Caine, S. Winters, V. Merchant]; Reitz, 'Morgan – a Suitable Case for Treatment' [Warner, V. Redgrave]; Warhol, 'The Chelsea Girls'; Polanski, 'Cul-de-Sac'; Truffaut, 'Fahrenheit 451' [adptn of Ray Bradbury sci-fi novel]; Gillo Pontecorvo [It.], 'The Battle of Algiers'; Stuart Burge [UK], 'Othello' [Olivier]; Tony Garnett & Ken Loach, 'Cathy Come Home' [BBC TV docu-drama on homelessness in UK]. **Lit. 'Events':** Jonathan Miller's TV version of *Alice in Wonderland*	R.S. Thomas Basil Bunting (1900–85) Seamus Heaney (b.1939; Ulster) **Pr/F:** Fowles Greene Isherwood Johnson Murdoch Rhys R. West Woolf David Caute (b.1936) Paul Scott (1920–78) **Dr:** Orton Mercer Potter Tom Stoppard (b.1937) **Theory/Crit:** Kenneth Burke Frank Kermode John Searle Susan Sontag Lévi-Strauss Trilling R. Williams	*Pietà* *Briggflatts* *Death of a Naturalist* *The Magus* [rev.d version, 1977] *The Comedians* *Exhumations* [misc. writings] *Trawl* *The Time of the Angels* *Wide Sargasso Sea* *The Birds Fall Down* *Collected Essays* [posthm.] *The Decline of the West: a novel* *The Jewel in the Crown* [1st novel in 'The Raj Quartet' (–1975); TV adptn, 1984] *Loot* *Belcher's Luck* *Where the Buffalo Roam* [on TV] *Rosencrantz and Guildenstern Are Dead* [Edinburgh; Old Vic, 1967] *Language as Symbolic Action* *The Sense of an Ending* *Speech Acts* *Against Interpretation* *The Savage Mind* *Beyond Culture* *Modern Tragedy*
1967	1st Parliamentary 'Ombudsman' appointed; trade gap widens – devaluation of pound by 14.3%; Welsh Language Act gives Welsh equal legal validity with English; SNP wins Hamilton by-election; UK neo-fascist groups fnd National Front; Abortion Act permits termination of pregnancy; Sexual Offences Act permits homosexual acts between consenting adults; Decimal Currency Act announces UK decimalisation [v.1971]; Road Safety Act allows police to breathalyse drivers; foot & mouth disease in UK – 422,000 animals culled; 1st N. Sea natural gas landed in UK; Defence White Paper proposes severe cuts & withdrawal from East of Suez commitments by mid-1970s; Plowden Report on *Children and Their Primary Schools*; gvmnt applies for EEC membership – De Gaulle blocks it for 2nd time; anti-Vietnam War demonstrations in London; Northern Ireland Civil	UK colour TV begins on BBC2; BBC radio progs change to Radio 1, 2, 3, 4 – local radio stations begin; articles in the *Guardian* by Margaret Drabble & Mary Quant on 'the permissive society' & the sexual revolution'; Francis Chichester's solo voyage round world in 'Gypsy Moth IV'; Donald Campbell killed in 'Bluebird' trying to break own water speed record; Stirling & Salford Universities fnd.d; [–1968] George Best of Man. Utd at height of football career; Dr Christian Barnard performs 1st heart transplant in S. Africa; Desmond Morris, *The Naked Ape* [human zoology]. **Int. Lit.:** Lowell, *Near the Ocean* [poems]; Mailer, *Why Are We in Vietnam?*; Alison Lurie, *Imaginary Friends* [US novel]; William Styron, *The Confessions of Nat Turner* [US novel]; Hochhuth, *Soldiers* [Ger. play attacking W. Churchill; banned in London; v.1968]; Gabriel Garcia Marquez, *One Hundred Years of Solitude* [Columbian novel;	**P:** Fuller Hughes Watkins Elizabeth Jennings (1926–2001) Roger McGough (b.1937) Brian Patten (b. 1946) **Pr/F:** Ballard Drabble Dunn Golding Isherwood Naipaul Wilson Angela Carter (1940–92)	*The Tree that Walked* *Wodwo* [poetry & prose] *Selected Poems 1930–1960* *Collected Poems* [& 1987] *Frinck, a Life in the Day of* & (et al eds), *The Mersey Sound* [anthol.] *Little Johnny's Confession* *The Disaster Area* [stories] *Jerusalem the Golden* *Poor Cow* *The Pyramid* *A Meeting by the River* *The Mimic Men* *No Laughing Matter* *The Magic Toyshop* [novel; film, 1987]

Period	Year	International and Political Contexts	Social and Cultural Contexts	Authors	Indicative Titles
		Rights Association (NICRA) fnd.d; 'Torrey Canyon' oil tanker aground off Land's End; military coup in Greece – George Papadopoulos leads gvnmt; Arab-Israeli 'Six-Day War' – Egypt, Jordan & Syria defeated – Israel occupies Gaza Strip, Sinai & West Bank; race riots in Detroit & Newark, N.J.; British withdrawal from Aden – People's Republic of S. Yemen proclaimed [1968]; guerrilla, Che Guevara, killed in Bolivia; state of Biafra secedes from Nigeria in civil war [defeated, 1970]; Soviet spacecraft 'Venus IV' lands on Venus; [c.] China explodes H-bomb	trans, 1970]; Arbuzov, *The Promise* & *It Happened at Irkutsk* [Russ. plays pf.d in UK]. **Music:** Q. Elizabeth Hall, London, opens on South Bank; Beatles, [LP] 'Sgt. Pepper's Lonely Hearts Club Band' [cover by Peter Blake] & 'The Magical Mystery Tour' [film]; Hendrix Experience's 1st album, 'Are You Experienced?'; The Who at Monterey Pop Festival. **Art:** Royal College of Art receives Charter; Warhol, 'Marilyn Monroe (Marilyn)' [10 screen-prints]; Hockney, 'A Bigger Splash' [Tate]. **Film:** Disney, 'The Jungle Book'; Buñuel, 'Belle de jour' [Deneuve]; Godard, 'Weekend'; Kramer, 'Guess Who's Coming to Dinner?' [K. Hepburn, Tracey, Poitier]; Lester, 'How I Won the War' [R. Kinnear, M. Crawford]; Losey, 'Accident' [Baker, Bogarde; adptn by Pinter]; Brook, 'Marat/Sade' [G. Jackson]; Schlesinger, 'Far From the Madding Crowd' [adptn of Hardy; Christie, Bates, Stamp, P. Finch]; Truffaut, 'The Bride Wore Black'; Mike Nichols, 'The Graduate' [Bancroft, D. Hoffman]; Arthur Penn , 'Bonnie and Clyde' [W. Beatty, F. Dunaway]; Joshua Loghan, 'Camelot'; Robert Aldrich, 'The Dirty Dozen' [L. Marvin]; George Roy Hill, 'Thoroughly Modern Millie' [Andrews, M. Tyler Moore]; Ken Loach [UK], 'Poor Cow' [C. White]; Vilgot Sjöman [Swed.], 'I am Curious – Yellow'; Joseph Strick [UK], 'Ulysses' [adptn of Joyce; UK film censors refuse certificate]; Franco Zeffirelli [It.], 'The Taming of the Shrew' [E. Taylor, Burton]	Michael Frayn (b.1933) William McIlvanney (b.1936; Scotland) William Trevor (b.1928; Ireland) Fay Weldon (b.1933) **Dr:** Orton Pinter Alan Ayckbourn (b.1939) Peter Nichols (b.1927) Charles Wood (b.1932) **Theory/Crit:** Roland Barthes McLuhan (with Quentin Fiore) Steiner Lit. **'Events':**	*Towards the End of the Morning* [novel] *Remedy is None* [novel] *The Day We Got Drunk on Cake* [stories] *The Fat Woman's Joke* [novel] *The Erpingham Camp* [TV play, 1966] & *The Ruffian on the Stair* [radio play, 1963; pf.d as double bill, 'Crimes of Passion'] *The Basement* *Relatively Speaking* *A Day in the Death of Joe Egg* *Dingo* *Writing Degree Zero* [Eng. trans; (1953)] & *Elements of Semiology* [Eng. trans; (1964)] *The Medium is the Massage* *Language and Silence* Publishers' Association fnd.d; 26-Pt serial of *The Forsyte Saga* on TV; Octagon Theatre, Bolton, built
NINETEEN-SIXTIES	**1968**	Clean Air Act makes cities 'smokeless zones'; Countryside Commission estab.d: conservation areas & scheduled ancient monuments intro.d; Second Race Relations Act extends anti-discrimination legislation & replaces Race Relations Board [v.1965] with Community Relations Commission; Trade Descriptions Act; Gaming Board estab.d to regulate gambling, betting, bingo, etc; mass anti-Vietnam war demonstration in Grosvenor Square, London; influx of expelled Kenyan Asians into UK – 2nd Commonwealth Immigration Bill intros further restrictions & denies Kenyan passport-holders automatic entry [as promised at independence, 1963]; Enoch Powell delivers 'rivers of blood' [anti-immigration] speech; Civil Rights demonstrations in Londonderry – violence escalates – N. Ireland 'Troubles' begin – IRA revitalised – Bernadette Devlin fnds People's Democracy Movement; [–1969] Welsh nationalists explode bombs in Wales; Nuclear Non-Proliferation Treaty signed by 61 countries; France explodes H-bomb;	1st & 2nd class postage intro.d; 15.1m. TV sets in UK; end of steam trains in UK; UK's 1st heart transplant patient survives 46 days; London Bridge sold to US oil co. – re-erected over Colorado River. **Int. Lit.:** Mailer, *Armies of the Night* [re. anti-Vietnam march on Pentagon, 1967]; Miller, *The Price* [pf.d]; Updike, *Couples*; Gore Vidal, *Myra Breckinridge* [US novel; Michael Sarne film, 1970]; Tom Wolfe, *The Electric Kool-Aid Acid Test* [account of Ken Kesey & the 'Merry Pranksters']; Solzhenitsyn, *Cancer Ward* [Eng. trans, Pt I, Pt II, 1969] & *The First Circle* [Eng. trans]; Arbuzov, *Confession at Night* [Russ. play pf.d in UK]. **Music:** Rolling Stones, 'Jumpin' Jack Flash' & 'Beggar's Banquet' [album]; Hendrix, 'Axis: Bold As Love' & 'Electric Ladyland' [albums]; R.R. Bennett [comp] 'A Penny for a Song' [opera]; Tim Rice & Andrew Lloyd Webber, 'Joseph and the Amazing Technicolor Dreamcoat' [pop oratorio'; pf.d, Edinburgh, 1972]; musicals, 'Cabaret' & 'Hair' 1st pf.d. **Film:** Anderson, 'If...' [M. McDowell, C. Noonan];	**P:** G. Hill Lucie-Smith **Pr/F:** Amis Hughes Le Carré Moore Murdoch Orwell Rhys P.H. Newby (b.1918) **Dr:** Ayckbourn Bond Osborne Pinter Potter Stoppard	*King Log* *Towards Silence* *I Want It Now* *The Iron Man* [children's stories] *A Small Town in Germany* *I Am Mary Dunne* *The Nice and the Good* *Collected Essays, Journalism and Letters* [posthm.] *Tigers Are Better Looking* [stories] *Something to Answer For* [novel; 1st Booker Prize winner, 1969] *How the Other Half Loves* *Early Morning & Narrow Road to the Deep North* *The Hotel in Amsterdam* *Landscape* [radio play; pub.d 1969 with Silence] *A Beast With Two Backs* [on TV] *The Real Inspector Hound*

1968

[May] student & workers uprisings in Paris – student unrest across Europe & USA; Martin Luther King & Robert Kennedy assassinated in USA – US Civil Rights Bill passed; Richard Nixon, US President; 'Prague Spring' [liberal reforms] – Warsaw Pact led by USSR invades Czechoslovakia – [–1970] liberal leaders expulsed; Viet Cong 'Tet Offensive' threatens Saigon; My Lai massacre by US troops in Vietnam – trial of Lieutenant William Calley, 1969–71; independence for Mauritius; [–1969] S. Africa refuses MCC touring team which includes Basil D'Olivera [S. African-born coloured cricketer]; US spacecraft 'Apollo 8' containing 3 astronauts travels to Moon, does 10 orbits & returns safely

Bergman, 'The Shame'; Kubrick, '2001: A Space Odyssey'; Polanski, 'Rosemary's Baby' [Cassavetes, M. Farrow]; Reed, 'Oliver!' [O. Reed]; Reisz, 'Isadora'; Resnais, 'Je t'aime, Je t'aime'; Richardson, 'The Charge of the Light Brigade' [V. Redgrave, Hemmings]; Warhol [with Paul Morrissey], 'Flesh' [J. Dallesandro]; Wise, 'Star!' [Andrews]; Wyler, 'Funny Girl' [B. Streisand]; Zeffirelli, 'Romeo and Juliet' [M. York, N. Parry, J. McEnery]; Mel Brooks, 'The Producers'; George Dunning [UK], 'Yellow Submarine' [cartoon sponsored by Beatles]; Albert Finney [UK], 'Charlie Bubbles' [Finney, B. Whitelaw]; Jack Gold [UK], 'The Bofors Gun'; Ken Hughes [UK], 'Chitty Chitty Bang Bang' [D. Van Dyke et al]. **Lit. 'Events':** C. Day Lewis, Poet Laureate; [–1973] Roy Fuller, Professor of Poetry, Oxford; Theatres Act abolishes censorship by Lord Chamberlain [Hochhuth's Soldiers – v.1967 – can now be performed in London]; Charles Marowitz's Open Space Theatre, London, opens

Author	Work
Alan Bennett (b.1934)	Forty Years on
Peter Barnes (b.1931)	The Ruling Class
Christopher Hampton (b.1946)	Total Eclipse
John Wells (b.1936)	Mrs Wilson's Diary
Theory/Crit:	
Auden	Secondary Worlds
Walter Benjamin	Illuminations [Eng. trans (1955); incls 'The Work of Art in the Age of Mechanical Reproduction' (1936)]
Mary Ellman	Thinking About Women
Vladimir Propp	Morphology of the Folktale [Eng. trans (1958)]

1969

Formal investiture of Charles, Prince of Wales, by Queen at Caernarvon Castle [v.1956]; Divorce Reform Act improves conditions for women; Representation of the People Act lowers voting age to 18 [becomes age of majority]; White Paper, 'In Place of Strife', proposes trade union reforms – gvnmt pubs Industrial Relations Bill – 100,000 workers strike on May Day opposing it – withdrawn; Save As You Earn (SAYE) scheme intro.d; Kray twins sentenced for murder; sectarian disturbances in N. Ireland – 6 killed in Belfast riots – Protestants besiege Bogside in Londonderry – British troops sent in to restore order – Bernadette Devlin elected MP; De Gaulle loses referendum & resigns – Georges Pompidou, President of France; Willy Brandt, Chancellor of W. Germany; Spain closes border with Gibraltar [v.1985]; Mrs Golda Meir, PM of Israel; Canada becomes officially bilingual [English & French]; nationwide demonstrations in USA against continuing Vietnam War; Tom Mboya, Kenyan politician, assassinated; US 'Apollo 11' astronauts, Neil Armstrong & Buzz Aldrin, 1st human beings to set foot on Moon – TV pictures of landing transmitted to Earth – rock samples brought back; [>] hi-jacking of airliners becomes international problem; UN report, Problems of the Human Environment, stresses urgent need for conservation

Ecologist magazine fnd.d; colour on BBC1 & ITV; human egg fertilized in test tube at Cambridge ('Test-tube Baby'); 1st UK decimal coin (50p. piece) circulates – old ½d. withdrawn; 1st public flight of 'Concorde'; Open University fnd.d [part-time courses using radio & TV]. **Int. Lit.:** Vonnegut, Slaughterhouse – 5; Maya Angelou, I Know Why the Caged Bird Sings [1st in 4-vol. US autobiog.]; Philip Roth, Portnoy's Complaint [US novel]; Margaret Atwood, The Edible Woman [Canadian novel]. **Music:** 500,000 attend rock festival at Woodstock, NY; 150,000 attend Bob Dylan pop concert on Isle of Wight – releases 'Lay, Lady, Lay'; John Lennon & Yoko Ono stage 'bed-in' protest against Vietnam war; K. Tynan's review 'Oh! Calcutta!' pf.d in NY [London, 1970]; Beatles, 'Abbey Road' [album]; Rolling Stones, 'Honkey Tonk Woman' & 'Let It Bleed' [album]; The Who, 'Tommy' [rock opera]; Tippett, 'The Knot Garden' [opera pf.d]; Richard Bennett, 'Jazz Pastoral' & 'Victory' [opera]. **Art:** Carl Andre's 'bricks' sculpture exhibited at Tate; Lichtenstein, 'Rouen Cathedral II (seen at 3 different times of day)'; Segal, 'Artist in His Loft' [mixed media]; Tilson, 'Snow White and the Black Dwarf' [screenprint & oil]; A. Jones, 'Table' [fibreglass kneeling woman supporting glass top]. **Film:** Antonioni, 'Zabriskie Point'; Fellini, 'Fellini-Satyricon'; Hamilton, 'Battle of Britain' [Olivier, More, York; music by Walton]; Hill, 'Butch Cassidy and the Sundance Kid' [R. Redford, P. Newman]; Lester, 'The Bed Sitting-Room' [Tushingham, Richardson]; Garnett & Loach, 'Kes'; Peckinpah, 'The Wild Bunch'; Schlesinger, 'Midnight Cowboy [Hoffman,

Author	Work
P: Auden	City Without Walls
Heaney	Door into the Dark
Douglas Dunn (b.1942; Scotland)	Terry Street
Michael Longley (b.1939; Ulster)	No Continuing City
Pr/F: Amis	The Green Man
Brophy	In Transit
Carter	Heroes and Villains [novel]
Drabble	The Waterfall
Fowles	The French Lieutenant's Woman [Karel Reisz film, 1981; script by Pinter]
Johnson	The Unfortunates
Lee	As I Walked Out One Summer Morning [autobiog.]
Lessing	The Four-Gated City [*]
Murdoch	Bruno's Dream
Upward	The Railway Accident and Other Stories [v.1928, 1933] & The Rotten Elements [*]
Dr: Livings	Honour and Offer
Nichols	The National Health
Orton	What the Butler Saw [posthm.]
Osborne	West of Suez
Pinter	Night & Silence
Potter	Son of Man [on TV]
Storey	In Celebration
Wood	H: Monologues at Front of Burning Cities
Howard Brenton (b.1942)	Magnificence
Theory/Crit:	
Louis Althusser	For Marx [Eng. trans.]
Perry Anderson	'Components of the National Culture'

PERIOD	YEAR	INTERNATIONAL AND POLITICAL CONTEXTS	SOCIAL AND CULTURAL CONTEXTS	AUTHORS	INDICATIVE TITLES
			J. Voight]; Richard Attenborough [UK], 'Oh! What a Lovely War' [J. Mills, M. Smith]; Dennis Hopper & Peter Fonda, 'Easy Rider' [& J. Nicholson]; Gene Kelly, 'Hello Dolly' [Streisand]; Ken Russell, 'Women in Love' [Jackson, Reed; adptn of D.H. Lawrence]; Franklin J. Schaffner, 'Patton – Lust for Glory' [Scott]. **Lit. 'Events'**: Samuel Beckett, Nobel Prize for Literature; Booker Prize for fiction begins [v. Newby, 1968]; Theatre Upstairs opens at Royal Court; Michael Horowitz (ed.), *Children of Albion: Poetry of the Underground in Britain* [anthol.]	Benjamin Leavis	*Charles Baudelaire: A Lyric Poet in the Age of High Capitalism* [Eng. trans] *English Literature in Our Time and the University*
1970		Equal Pay Act prevents discrimination between men & women; strikes cause nationwide electric power cuts – emergency powers declared; gvnmt requires local authorities to set up social services apparatus; Gen. Elec.: Cons. victory – Edward Heath, PM – Plaid Cymru & SNP make significant gains; [–1971] Rolls Royce Co. in financial crisis – rescued by gvnmt aid; marches banned in N. Ireland – Provisional IRA formed – Ulster Defence Regiment (UDR) formed in Belfast – Social Democratic & Labour Party (SDLP) fnd.d; UK reopens negotiations to join EEC; W. German peace treaty with USSR & with Poland [recognises national boundaries]; Baader-Meinhof 'Red Army Faction' begin terrorist campaign in W. Germany; Smith decares Rhodesia a republic; USA invades Cambodia; 6 US student demonstrators killed by National Guard at Kent State & Jackson State Universities; Salvador Allende [Marxist] narrowly elected president of Chile; civil war in Jordan between gvnmt troops & Popular Front for the Liberation of Palestine (PLO) guerrillas – PLO hijacks 3 aircraft to Jordan in Europe – planes blown up – crew & passengers held hostage then released; independence for Fiji, Tonga & W. Samoa; US spacecraft 'Apollo 13' explodes on way to Moon – crew escape in lunar module; cyclone & tidal wave strikes E. Pakistan – huge damage & death-toll; European Conservation Year: urgent need to preserve natural resources	Mass campaign against S. African cricket tour to UK – cancelled – SA expelled from Olympic Committee; Boeing 747 'Jumbo Jet' intro.d. **Int. Lit.**: Lowell, *Notebook* [poems]; Bellow, *Mr Sammler's Planet*; Updike, *Bech: A Book*; Lurie, *Real People*; Toni Morrison, *The Bluest Eye* [US novel]; White, *The Vivisector*; Henri Charrière, *Papillon* [Fr. novel of penal colony]. **Music:** Shostakovitch, '14th Symphony'; Lloyd Webber & Rice, *Jesus Christ Superstar* ['rock opera'; staged 1971; film, 1973]; Jimi Hendrix dies in London; Beatles, 'Let It Be' [album] – group splits up [officially, 1971]; Rolling Stones, 'Sticky Fingers' [album]. **Film:** British Board of Film Censors intros gradings 'U & A' [all ages], 'AA' [14+], 'X' [18+]; Bondarchuk, 'Waterloo' [Steiger, C. Plummer, V. McKenna et al]; Hughes, 'Cromwell' [Guinness, R. Harris, D. Tutin et al]; Lean, 'Ryan's Daughter' [wrtn by Robert Bolt; J. Mills, S. Miles et al]; Logan, 'Paint Your Wagon' [Marvin, Eastwood, Seberg]; Penn, 'Little Big Man' [Hoffman, Dunaway]; Richardson, 'Ned Kelly' [M. Jagger]; Warhol [with Morrissey], 'Trash'; Robert Altman, 'M*A*S*H' [D. Sutherland, R. Duvall, E. Gould]; Arthur Hiller, 'Love Story' [A. MacGraw, R. O'Neal; adptn of Erich Segal novel]; Michael Wadleigh, 'Woodstock' [documentary]	**P:** Harrison Hughes **Pr/F:** Forster Hansford Johnson Murdoch O'Brien Spark Susan Hill (b.1942) **Dr:** Beckett Bolt Hampton Mercer Shaffer Storey David Hare (b.1947) Howard Barker (b.1946) **Theory/Crit:** Shulamith Firestone Germaine Greer F.R. & Q.D. Leavis J. Hillis Miller Kate Millett **Lit. 'Events':**	*The Loiners* *Crow: From the Life and Songs of the Crow* [rev.d edtn, 1972] *Maurice* [posthm.] *The Honour's Board* *A Fairly Honourable Defeat* *A Pagan Place* *The Driver's Seat* *I'm the King of the Castle* [novel] *Breath* *Vivat! Vivat! Regina!* *The Philanthropist* *After Haggerty & Flint* *The Battle of Shrivings* *The Contractor & Home* *Slag* *Cheek* *The Dialectic of Sex* *The Female Eunuch* *Dickens the Novelist* *Thomas Hardy: Distance and Desire* *Sexual Politics* 2nd Young Vic Theatre opens [v. 1945]; Brook's *A Midsummer Night's Dream* at Aldwych
1971		Nationwide demonstrations & strikes [incl. 1st postal strike] against Industrial Relations Act – 'Angry Brigade' bomb gvnmt minister's home in protest; union's 'work-in' at Upper Clyde Shipbuilders in protest at Co.'s liquidation – gvnmt steps in with rescue package; Immigration Act further restricts right of Commonwealth citizens to settle in UK; Commons vote in favour of joining EEC; Mrs Thatcher [as Education Minister] ends free	Decimal currency adopted in UK; 1st Open University broadcast; Greenpeace fnd.d; [–1972] microprocessors in computers invented – 1st pocket calculator in UK costs £79.95; crush barriers at Ibrox football stadium, Glasgow, collapse – 66 killed; Disney World, Florida, opens. **Int. Lit.:** Kosinski, *Being There*; Updike, *Rabbit Redux* [*]; Wouk, *The Winds of War*; Solzhenitsyn, *August 1914* [Eng. trans, 1972]. **Music:** Bernstein, 'Mass for the Late	**P:** G. Hill Hughes Patten Plath George MacBeth (1932–92; Scotland) **Pr/F:** Amis Burgess	*Mercian Hymns* [30 prose poems] *Selected Poems, 1957–1967* *Walking Out: The Early Poems of Brian Patten* *Crossing the Water & Winter Trees* [posthm.] *Collected Poems 1958–1970* *Girl, 20* *MF*

milk in schools; Special Powers Act reintros internment without trial in N. Ireland – Long Kesh camp estab.d – wave of riots, shootings & bombings – UVF bomb kills 15 in a Belfast bar – Ulster Defence Association (UDA) fnd.d – Ian Paisley's Democratic Unionist Party fnd.d; China admitted to UN – Taiwan vacates seat; U Thant resigns – Kurt Waldheim, UN Sec.-General; 40 nations sign treaty banning nuclear weapons on seabed; Strategic Arms Limitation Talks agree to limit anti-ballistic missiles; Congo renamed Zaire; army coup places Idi Amin in power in Uganda; war between India & Pakistan – Pakistan defeated – E. Pakistan declares itself independent state of Bangladesh; Zulfikar Bhutto, President of Pakistan; US troops enter Laos [US losses in Vietnam now c.45,000]; 200,000 people demonstrate against Vietnam war in Washington; independence for Bahrain; 'Apollo 14' & '15' land on Moon – 1st moon drive; US & USSR launch space probes towards Mars

President Kennedy'; The Who, 'Who's Next' [album]; 'Godspell' [US musical] opens in London. **Film:** Kozintsev, 'King Lear'; Kubrick, 'A Clockwork Orange' [v. Burgess, 1962]; Garnett & Loach, 'Family Life'; Losey, 'The Go-Between' [v. Hartley, 1953]; Nichols, 'Carnal Knowledge' [J. Nicholson et al]; Peckinpah, 'Straw Dogs' [D. Warner]; Polanski, 'Macbeth'; Schlesinger, 'Sunday, Bloody Sunday' [Jackson, Finch]; Visconti, 'Death in Venice' [Bogarde; adptn of Thomas Mann]; Warhol, 'Sex'; William Friedkin, 'The French Connection' [G. Hackman]; Lionel Jeffries [UK], 'The Railway Children'; Norman Jewison, 'Fiddler on the Roof' [Topol]; Alan J. Pakula, 'Klute' [J. Fonda. **Lit. Events':** Trevor Nunn succeeds Hall as RSC director; Crucible Theatre, Sheffield, built; NY Co. 'Living Theatre' at the Roundhouse. **Theory/Crit:** Althusser, *Lenin and Philosophy and Other Essays* [Eng. trans; incls 'Ideology and Ideological State Apparatuses']; Paul de Man, *Blindness and Insight*; Antonio Gramsci, *Selections from the Prison Notebooks* [Eng. trans]; Roman Jakobson/M. Halle, *Fundamentals of Language* [2nd edtn]; Fredric Jameson, *Marxism and Form*; Kermode, *Modern Essays & Extraterritorial*; Steiner, *In Bluebeard's Castle*

Author	Work
Carter	*Love*
Caute	*The Occupation: a novel*
Greene	*A Sort of Life* [autobiog.]
S. Hill	*Strange Meeting*
Johnson	*House Mother Normal*
Le Carré	*The Naïve and Sentimental Lover*
Lessing	*Briefing for a Descent into Hell*
Murdoch	*An Accidental Man*
Naipaul	*In a Free State* [Booker]
Weldon	*Down Among the Women*
Frederick Forsyth (b.1938)	*The Day of the Jackal* [novel; film, 1973]
Tom Sharpe (b.1928)	*Riotous Assembly* [novel]
Dr: Bennett	*Getting On*
Bond	*Lear*
Osborne	*West of Suez*
Nichols	*Forget-Me-Not-Lane*
Pinter	*Old Times*
Storey	*Traitor, Paper Roses & Casanova* [on TV]
	The Changing Room
Simon Gray (b.1936)	*Butley*

1972 Over 1m. unemployed; miners' 6-week strike ends with recommended 32% pay rise – widespread power cuts – State of Emergency declared; UK economic crisis – White Paper, 'A Programme for Inflation', proposes 90-day freeze on increases in pay & prices; 5 dockers ('Pentonville Five') gaoled for defying Industrial Relations Act – released after union agitation; 'Angry Brigade' members sentenced to 10 years; [Jan.] 13 civil rights marchers in Londonderry shot dead by paratroopers in 'Bloody Sunday' massacre – 22 IRA bombs in 1 day in Belfast results in army 'Operation Motorman' against 'no-go' areas – 100th soldier killed – direct rule from London imposed – IRA bomb kills 7 in Officer's Mess, Aldershot; [–1973] 'Cod War' between UK & Iceland over fishing limits; Baader-Meinhof, Ger. terrorist group, leaders arrested; Pres. Nixon re-elected in USA – 'Watergate' break-in at Washington – former White House aides indicted; US Senate passes Equal Rights amendment; Strategic Arms Limitation Treaty (SALT) signed by USA & USSR; 11 Israeli athletes killed by pro-Palestinian guerrillas at Munich Olympics – 25 killed by Jap. Red Army terrorists in Tel Aviv airport; Pakistan leaves Commonwealth – Bangladesh joins; Ceylon becomes republic of Sri Lanka; Amin orders

UK school leaving-age raised from 15 to 16; 1st UK hypermarket opens; Cambridge colleges admit women students [Oxford colleges later follow suit]; Bobby Fischer beats title-holder Boris Spassky in world chess championship, Reykjavik. **Int. Lit.:** A. Miller, *The Creation of the World and Other Business* [play]; Atwood, *Surfacing*; van der Post, *A Story Like the Wind* [life in SA]; Eudora Welty, *The Optimist's Daughter* [US novel]; Thomas Keneally, *The Chant of Jimmy Blacksmith* [Austrl. novel]. **Music:** Shostakovitch, '15th [Last] Symphony'; Harrison Birtwhistle [comp] 'The Triumph of Time' [orchestral work]; Bob Marley, 'Catch a Fire' [album]; Rolling Stones, 'Exile on Main Street' [album]. **Art:** 'Treasures of Tut'ankhamun' exhibition at BM; A. Jones [pnt] 'Bare Me'. **Film:** Buñuel, 'The Discreet Charm of the Bourgeoisie'; Fellini 'Roma'; Hitchcock, 'Frenzy' [all-star cast]; Mankiewicz, 'Sleuth' [Olivier, Caine; adptn of Anthony Shaffer play]; Bernardo Bertolucci [It.], 'Last Tango in Paris' [Brando, M. Schneider]; Francis Ford Coppola, 'The Godfather' [Pt I; Pacino, Brando, D. Keaton; Pt II, 1974; Pt III, 1990]. **Theory/Crit:** Barthes, *Mythologies* [(1957); Eng. trans] & *Critical Essays* [(1964); Eng. trans]; John Berger, *Ways of Seeing*; Aimé Césaire, *Discourse on Colonialism*; Gilles Deleuze & Félix Guattari, *Anti-Oedipus*; Michel

Author	Work
P: Dunn	*The Happier Life*
Fuller	*Cannibals and Missionaries*
Heaney	*Wintering Out*
K. Raine	*The Lost Country*
Donald Davie (1922–95)	*Collected Poems, 1950–1970*
Pr/F: Carter	*The Infernal Desire Machine of Doctor Hoffman*
Drabble	*The Needle's Eye*
Forsyth	*The Odessa File*
S. Hill	*The Bird of Night*
Moore	*Catholics*
Sharpe	*Indecent Exposure*
Storey	*Pasmore*
Trevor	*The Ballroom of Romance* [stories]
Richard Adams (b.1920)	*Watership Down* [novel]
John Berger (b.1926)	*G* [novel; Booker]
James Herriot (b.1916)	*All Creatures Great and Small* [novel]
Dr: Ayckbourn	*Time and Time Again & Absurd Person Singular*
Beckett	*Not I*
Hare	*The Great Exhibition*
Potter	*Follow the Yellow Brick Road* [on TV]
Stoppard	*Jumpers*

PERIOD	YEAR	INTERNATIONAL AND POLITICAL CONTEXTS	SOCIAL AND CULTURAL CONTEXTS	AUTHORS	INDICATIVE TITLES
		expulsion of all Ugandan Asians with British passports – UK to admit 25,000; 1st UN World Conference on Human Environment, Stockholm	Foucault, *The Archeology of Knowledge* [(1969); Eng. trans]; Jameson, *The Prison-House of Language*; Lukács, *Studies in European Realism* [(1957); Eng. trans]; Trilling, *Sincerity and Authenticity*	Wesker Caryl Churchill (b.1938) Lit. 'Events':	*The Old Ones* *Owners* John Betjeman, Poet Laureate; feminist magazine, *Spare Rib*, fnd.d; Peter Hall succeeds Olivier as National Theatre Co. director
1973		Pay & price freeze conts – 2m. workers strike on May Day – State of Emergency declared – miners begin overtime ban – [–1974] 3-Day Week intro.d; VAT (8%) intro.d; UK, Eire & Denmark join EEC; Ulster poll shows large majority wish to remain part of UK – N. Ireland Bill intros anti-terrorism measures [incls trial without jury] – Stormont gvnmt abolished – Sunningdale Agreement leads to power-sharing N. Ireland Assembly – IRA bomb at Old Bailey; compensation for Thalidomide victims finally settled [v.1962]; French resume nuclear tests in Pacific – international outcry; US/Viet Cong ceasefire in Vietnam – USA withdraws troops [conflict in Indo-China conts, v.1975]; Yom Kippur War: Egypt & Syria invade Israel – counter-attack – ceasefire after 3 weeks – UN peace-keeping force deployed – [–1974] Arab oil states increase prices by up to 100% & cut production – major energy crisis for West; Shah nationalises foreign oil industry in Iran; Watergate: Nixon aides resign – Nixon subpoenad for refusing to hand over secret tape-recordings – Pulitzer Prize awarded to *Washington Post* for its role in the Watergate affair; Pres. Allende of Chile overthrown & killed in military coup by Gen. Pinochet; independence for Bahamas; [>] drought causes famine in Ethiopia & Horn of Africa; severe flooding in Indian sub-continent & Mississippi, USA; UN adopts Declaration on the Human Environment	Princess Anne's wedding on TV – 500m. viewers worldwide; new London Bridge, Sydney Opera House & World Trade Centre, NY, open; LBC & Capital Radio, 1st legal UK commercial radio stations, begin broadcasting. **Int. Lit.:** Lowell, *The Dolphin* [poems]; Kosinski, *The Devil Tree* [rev.d edtn, 1982]; Vonnegut, *Breakfast of Champions*; Pynchon, *Gravity's Rainbow*; Mailer, *Marilyn* [pictorial life of Monroe]; Morrison, *Sula* ; Erica Jong, *Fear of Flying* [US novel]; Alice Walker, *In Love and Trouble* [US stories]; White, *The Eye of the Storm* [Nobel Prize for Literature]; [–1975] Solzhenitsyn, *The Gulag Archipelago* [3 vols; pub.d in West; on Stalinist terror]. **Music:** 'The Rocky Horror Show' [musical] opens in London; Britten, 'Death in Venice' [opera]; Stephen Sondheim [comp] 'A Little Night Music' [musical]; MacMillan, 'The Seven Deadly Sins' [ballet]. **Art:** Picasso dies; Warhol, 'Mao' [silkscreen series; Saatchi Coll.]. **Film:** Altman, 'The Long Goodbye' [Gould; adptn of Raymond Chandler]; Hamilton, 'Live and Let Die' [R. Moore as 'Bond', J. Seymour]; George Lucas, 'American Graffiti' [R. Dreyfuss]; William Friedkin, 'The Exorcist' [von Sydow]; George Roy Hill, 'The Sting' [Redford, Newman, R. Shaw]; Terrence Malick, 'Badlands' [M. Sheen, S. Spacek]; Sydney Pollack, 'The Way We Were' [Redford, Streisand]. **Theory/Crit:** Adorno & Max Horkheimer, *The Dialectic of Enlightenment* [1944]; Eng. trans]; Auden, *Forewords and Afterwords*; Bakhtin, *Problems of Dostoevsky's Poetics* [c.1929]; Eng. trans]; Benjamin, *Understanding Brecht* [(1966); Eng. trans; incls 'The Author as Producer' (1934)]; Harold Bloom, *The Anxiety of Influence*; Jacques Derrida, '*Différance*' [(1966); Eng. trans]; Clifford Geertz, *The Interpretation of Cultures*; Roman Ingarden, *The Literary Work of Art* [(1931); Eng. trans]; Jill Johnson, *Lesbian Nation*; Adrienne Rich, *On Lies, Secrets and Silence* [expanded edtn, 1979]; V.N. Volosinov, *Marxism and the Philosophy of Language* [(1929); Eng. trans]	**P:** Longley McGough R.S. Thomas Paul Muldoon (b.1951, Ulster) **Pr/F:** Ballard Greene R. Hughes B.S. Johnson Lessing Murdoch Wilson Martin Amis (b.1949) John Banville (b.1945; Ireland) Beryl Bainbridge (b.1934) J.G. Farrell (1935–79) **Dr:** Ayckbourn Bennett Bond Brenton & Hare Friel Hampton Shaffer Storey Trevor Griffiths (b.1935) Lit. 'Events':	*An Exploded View* *Gig* *Selected Poems, 1946–1968* *New Weather* *Vermilion Sands* [stories] *The Honorary Consul* *The Wooden Shepherdess* [2nd & last novel in unfinished ser.; v.1961] *Christie Mairy's Own Double-Entry & Aren't You Rather Young To Be Writing Your Memoirs?* [stories] & *Everyone Knows Somebody Who's Dead* [stories] *The Summer Before the Dark* *The Black Prince* *As If By Magic* *The Rachel Papers* [novel] *Birchwood* [novel] *The Dressmaker* [novel] *The Siege of Krishnapur* [novel; Booker] [–1974] *The Norman Conquests* [trilogy; pub.d 1975] *Habeas Corpus* *The Sea & Bingo: Scenes of money and death* *Brassneck* *The Freedom of the City* *Savages* *Equus* *Cromwell & The Farm* *The Party* W.H. Auden & Noel Coward die; Larkin edits *The Oxford Book of Twentieth-Century English Verse*

1974

Miners' overtime ban conts – train drivers strike; [Feb] Gen. Elec.: Lab. form minority gvnmt – Wilson, PM; State of Emergency, strikes & 3-day week end – Pay Board & statutory wage controls scrapped – 'Social Contract' between gvnmt & TUC to restrain pay rises – Trade Union & Labour Relations Act replaces 1971 Act; [Oct] Gen. Elec.: Lab. gains small overall majority; Ulster Unionist Council rejects Sunningdale Agreement – Protestant workers' strike leads to state of emergency – power-sharing Assembly prorogued – direct rule from Westminster reinstated; IRA bombing campaign incls Guildford, Woolwich & 20+ people killed in Birmingham pub – Prevention of Terrorism Act proscribes IRA & gives police sweeping powers; fascist regime overthrown by military coup in Portugal; military rule ['Colonels' Junta'] in Greece ends – free elections held – monarchy deposed; in USA, Nixon resigns over Watergate cover-up under threat of impeachment – Gerald Ford, President; world shortage of oil conts; Israel withdraws from Suez Canal – truce with Syria – bombs Palestinian refugee camps in Lebanon – UN recognises PLO; c.250,000 deaths in Uganda since Amin came to power; Haile Selassie deposed in Ethiopia; Khmer Rouge fight gvnmt troops in Cambodia; monsoon floods in Bangladesh cover 50% of country – 10m. homeless; [>] increasing anxiety over danger to ozone layer from 'greenhouse gases' (CFCs)

BBC's Ceefax Teletext 1st broadcast; gvnmt intros admission charges for national galleries & museums; free family planning available on NHS; major oil fields discv.d in N. Sea – 3 more drilling platforms authorised; world's 1st 'test-tube baby' officially born; 1st 'McDonald's' opens in London; Lord Lucan 'missing' after nanny's murder; USSR expels Solzhenitsyn; [Jan.] Muhammad Ali defeats Joe Frazier & [Oct.] regains world boxing title by beating George Foreman; Carl Bernstein & Bob Woodward, *All the President's Men* [*Washington Post* 'Watergate' journalists; Alan Pakula film, 1976]. **Int. Lit.:** Heller, *Something Happened*; Lurie, *The War Between the Tates*; Keneally, *Blood Red, Sister Rose*; J.M. Coetzee, *Dusklands* [SA novel]; Athol Fugard, *Sizwe Banzi is Dead* [SA play]; Peter Carey, *The Fat Man in History* [Austrl. stories]. **Music:** English National Opera estab.d at London Coliseum; [–1982] Birtwhistle, 'The Masque of Orpheus' [opera]; Thea Musgrave [comp] 'The Voice of Ariadne' [opera]. **Film:** Clayton, 'The Great Gatsby' [Redford, Farrow; adptn of Scott Fitzgerald]; Coppola, 'The Godfather II'; Lumet, 'Murder on the Orient Express' [all-star cast; adptn of Agatha Christie]; Polanski, 'Chinatown' [Huston, Nicholson, Dunaway]; Brooks, 'Blazing Saddles' & 'Young Frankenstein' [both G. Wilder]; John Guillermin, 'The Towering Inferno' [all-star cast]; Tobe Hooper, 'The Texas Chainsaw Massacre'. **Theory/Crit:** Wolfgang Iser, *The Implied Reader*; Julia Kristeva, *About Chinese Women* [Eng. trans]

P: Auden — *Last Poems* [posthm.]
Dunn — *Love or Nothing*
Larkin — *High Windows*
Lucie-Smith — *The Well-Wishers*
Anne Stevenson (b.1933) — *Correspondences*

Pr/F: Bainbridge — *The Bottle Factory Outing*
Carter — *Fireworks* [stories]
Forsyth — *The Dogs of War*
Fowles — *The Ebony Tower* [stories]
S. Hill — *In the Springtime of the Year*
Le Carré — *Tinker, Tailor, Soldier, Spy* [TV ser., 1979]
Lessing — *The Memoirs of a Survivor* [film, 1981]
Murdoch — *The Sacred and Profane Love Machine*
Sharpe — *Porterhouse Blue*
Spark — *The Abbess of Crewe*
Buchi Emecheta (b.1944, Nigeria) — *Second-Class Citizen* [novel]

Dr: Ayckbourn — *Absent Friends & Confusions*
Brenton — *The Churchill Play*
Hare — *Knuckle*
Nichols — *Chez Nous*
Potter — *Joe's Ark* [on TV]
Stoppard — *Travesties*
Storey — *Life Class*
Willy Russell (b.1947) — *John, Paul, George, Ringo ... and Bert*

1975

Inflation around 25% – c.1.5m. unemployed – Wilson imposes £6 p.w. limit on wage-rises – many bankruptcies – gvnmt seeks £1b. loan from IMF; Industry Act sets up National Enterprise Board – British National Oil Corporation (BNOC) estab.d; British Leyland car company taken over by gvnmt; Employment Protection Act estabs workers' rights – sets up Advisory, Conciliation & Arbitration Service (ACAS); Sex Discrimination Act improves conditions of women employees; Mrs Thatcher elected Cons. Party leader; explosion at Flixborough chemical plant kills 29; referendum confirms UK's continuing EEC membership – 67% in favour; internment in N. Ireland suspended – SAS sent to Ulster – INLA formed – UVF made illegal – 'Birmingham Six' [alleged bombers] jailed for life [v.1991]; Helsinki Agreement: states sign pact on security, co-operation & human rights in Europe; Palestinian terrorists take 70 hostages at OPEC meeting in Vienna; Franco dies in Spain – monarchy restored; 1st free elections in Portugal for 50 yrs – socialist majority – independence for Mozambique & Angola [civil war begins]; conflict in USA over

International Women's Year; 1st N. Sea oil landed in UK; 41 killed in Moorgate tube train crash; 17.7m. UK TV sets; portable computers & floppy discs developed; 1st home video recorders intro.d; Dutch Elm disease kills 6.5m. trees in UK; Andrei Sakharov, Soviet human rights campaigner, wins Nobel Peace Prize. **Int. Lit.:** Bellow, *Humboldt's Gift*; Márquez, *The Autumn of the Patriarch* [Eng. trans, 1976]; Carlos Fuentes, *Terra Nostra* [Mex. novel]. **Music:** Sir Peter Maxwell Davies [comp] 'Symphony'; Lloyd Webber & Ayckbourn, 'Jeeves' [musical play]. **Art:** Nam June Paik, 'Video Fish' [video installation, Paris]. **Film:** Altman, 'Nashville'; Antonioni, 'The Passenger' [Nicholson, Schneider]; Forman, 'One Flew Over the Cuckoo's Nest' [Nicholson]; Kubrick, 'Barry Lyndon' [O'Neal, M. Berenson, P. Magee; adptn of Thackeray]; Spielberg, 'Jaws'; Terry Gilliam & Terry Jones [UK], 'Monty Python and the Holy Grail' [J. Cleese, M. Palin et al]; Jim Sharman, 'The Rocky Horror Picture Show'; Peter Weir [Austrl.], 'Picnic at Hanging Rock'; Loach & Garnett, 'Days of Hope' [on TV]. **Theory/Crit:** Barthes, *S/Z* (1970) [Eng. trans]; Jean Baudrillard, *The Mirror of Production* [(1973);

P: Fuller — *The Mountain in the Sea*
Graves — *Collected Poems, 1975*
Heaney — *North & Stations*
Stevie Smith — *Collected Poems* [posthm.]
Adrian Henri (b.1932) — *The Best of Henri: Selected Poems 1960–1970*

Pr/F: M. Amis (b.1948) — *Dead Babies*
Bradbury — *The History Man*
Jhabvala — *Heat and Dust* [Booker; film, 1982]
Lodge — *Changing Places*
McIlvanney — *Docherty*
Moore — *The Great Victorian Collection*
Murdoch — *A Word Child*
Naipaul — *Guerrillas*
Selvon — *Moses Ascending*
Trevor — *Angels at the Ritz* [stories]
Weldon — *Female Friends*
Maureen Duffy (b.1933) — *Capital: a fiction*
Ian McEwan (b.1948) — *First Loves, Last Rites* [stories]

Dr: Ayckbourn — *Bedroom Farce*
Barker — *Stripwell*

PERIOD	YEAR	INTERNATIONAL AND POLITICAL CONTEXTS	SOCIAL AND CULTURAL CONTEXTS	AUTHORS	INDICATIVE TITLES
		school 'bussing' to end racial segregation; Suez Canal reopens after 8 yrs; [−1978] civil war in Lebanon between Xtians & Muslims; Communist victories in Cambodia & Vietnam – Saigon retaken – Vietnam War ends, but Khmer Rouge take Phnom Pen, Cambodia [v. 1978–9]	Eng. trans]; Bloom, A Map of Misreading; Jonathan Culler, Structuralist Poetics; Foucault, Discipline and Punish [(1975)]; Eng. trans]; Lucien Goldmann, Towards a Sociology of the Novel [(1964); Eng. trans]; Ihab Hassan, The Postmodern Turn & Paracriticisms; Juliet Mitchell, Psychoanalysis and Feminism; Tzvetan Todorov, The Fantastic [(1970); Eng. trans]; Monique Wittig, The Lesbian Body [(1973); Eng. trans]	Bond Churchill Gray Griffiths Hare Pinter Potter Russell Pam Gems (b.1925) Stephen Poliakoff (b.1952)	The Fool: Scenes of bread and love Objections to Sex and Violence Otherwise Engaged Comedians Teeth 'n' Smiles No Man's Land Brimstone and Treacle [banned until 1987] Breezeblock Park [on stage], Break-In & Death of a Young Young Man [on TV] Dusa, Stas, Fish and Vi Hitting Town & City Sugar
	1976	Wilson resigns – James Callaghan (Lab.), PM; Jeremy Thorpe resigns as Lib. leader – David Steel elected; economic crisis in Britain – inflation at 17% – £ falls below $2 – £2.3b. loan obtained from IMF – strikes follow public-sector spending cuts; Race Relations Bill extends legislation against incitement to racial hatred & estabs Commission for Racial Equality; Bill to nationalise ship-building & aircraft industries [v.1977]; Callaghan launches 'Great Debate' on modernising UK education – Education Bill to make comprehensive education system compulsory; Bill to create separate assemblies for Scotland & Wales [fails 1977]; Notting Hill Carnival riots; N. Ireland Convention dissolved – [Feb.–June] IRA bombing campaign in England – 'Guildford Four' [alleged bombers] sentenced to life [v.1989] – New Women's Peace Movement formed in Ulster; Jimmy Carter, President of USA; PLO guerrillas hijack plane – Israeli troops rescue hostages at Entebbe airport, Uganda; S. Africa: massacre of demonstrators in Soweto – Transkei becomes 1st 'independent' black homeland; Rhodesia announces transition to black majority rule; China, Chairman Mao dies – leadership struggle ensues; Vietnam reunified – capital, Hanoi; US 'Viking II' lands on Mars – transmits 1st photos of surface; WHO's 2-yr campaign begins to eradicate smallpox [v.1980];	Worst drought in UK for 250 yrs; [c.] digital watches become cheaply available; [>] GLC abandons high-rise housing; Museum of London & National Exhibition Centre, Birmingham, open. **Int. Lit.:** Atwood, Lady Oracle; Vonnegut, Slapstick: Or Lonesome No More; Alex Haley, Roots [US history]; Lisa Alther, Kinflicks [US b-s. novel]. **Music:** Sondheim, 'Pacific Overtures' [musical]; Philip Glass [comp] 'Einstein on the Beach' [opera]; [−1978] Krzysztof Penderecki [comp] 'Paradise Lost' [opera]; Marley, 'Rastaman Vibration' [album]; [>] 'Punk' counter-culture arrives with The Clash, The Buzzcocks & The Sex Pistols release 'Anarchy in the UK' & give 'obscene' interview on Thames TV's 'Today' prog. **Art:** The Arts Britain Ignores pub.d – Minorities Arts Advisory Service (MAAS) formed. **Film:** Schlesinger, 'Marathon Man' [Olivier, Hoffman]; John G. Avildsen, 'Rocky' [S. Stallone]; Derek Jarman [UK], 'Sebastiane'; Alan Parker, 'Bugsy Malone' [J. Foster]; Frank Pierson, 'A Star Is Born' [Streisand, K. Kristofferson]; Martin Scorsese, 'Taxi Driver' [De Niro, Foster]; Garnett & Loach, 'The Price of Coal' [on TV]. **Theory/Crit:** Barthes, The Pleasure of the Text (1973); Eng. trans]; de Man, The Rhetoric of Romanticism; Chomsky, Reflections on Language; Derrida, Of Grammatology (1967); Eng. trans]; Terry Eagleton, Criticism and Ideology & Marxism and Literary Theory; Foucault, The History of Sexuality [vol. 1; Eng. trans]; Ellen Moers, Literary Women; A. Rich, Of Woman Born; V.N. Volosinov, Freudianism: A Marxist Critique (1926); Eng. trans]; R. Williams, Keywords	**P:** Gunn Hughes Longley **Pr/F:** Moore Murdoch Rhys Sharpe Storey Trevor Neil Jordan (b.1950) Emma Tennant (b.1943) **Dr:** Ayckbourn Bond Brenton Churchill Griffiths Hampton Russell Storey David Edgar (b.1948) **Lit. 'Events':**	Jack Straw's Castle Season Songs Man Lying on a Wall The Doctor's Wife Henry and Cato Sleep It Off, Lady [stories] Witt Saville [novel; Booker] The Children of Dynmouth Nights in Tunisia [stories] Hotel de Dream [novel] Just Between Ourselves The White Devil [adptn] & A-A-America [in 2 pts] Weapons of Happiness Light Shining in Buckinghamshire Bill Brand [on TV] Treats One for the Road [stage] & Our Day Out [on TV] Mother's Day Destiny National Theatre opens [25 yrs after foundation stone was laid]; Royal Exchange Theatre, Manchester, opens
	1977	Queen's silver jubilee; Roy Jenkins leaves gvnmt to be President of EEC Commission [& v.1981]; Lib-Lab pact keeps gvnmt in office – 'Social Contract' collapses [free collective bargaining resumes]; Prices Commission to freeze prices [up c.70% since	Virginia Wade wins Wimbledon; Red Rum wins Grand National for 3rd time; Gay News fined £1000 for blasphemy in UK; 1st cut-price shuttle flights London-NY; US Apple Co. produces 1st boom in sales of home computers; Galbraith, The Age of	**P:** Graves Hughes Muldoon Tom Paulin (b.1949, Ulster)	New Collected Poems Gaudette Mules A State of Justice

1974]; British Leyland threatens lock-out because of strikes – gvnmt threatens to withhold public money but capitulates; British Aerospace & British Shipbuilders fnd.d to run nationalised industries; mass pickets clash with police at Grunwick film-processing factory, E. London, in union-recognition dispute; firemen's strike – army provides fire-services; anti-Fascists clash with National Front in Lewisham, SE London & Birmingham; founders of Women's Peace Movement, N. Ireland, awarded Nobel Peace Prize; N. Sea badly polluted after oil rig accident in Ekofisk field; French is made the sole official language of Quebec; dissident Czech intellectuals publish 'Charter 77' demanding civil rights; USA & Panama sign defence & neutrality treaty [re. Canal] until 1999; Israel begins to estab. settlements on W. Bank [v.1967]; UN bans arms sales to SA – Steve Biko, black civil rights leader, dies in detention; military coup by Gen. Zia ousts Pres. Bhutto in Pakistan [sentenced to death, 1978]; after 5 days, 87 plane hijack hostages freed at Mogadishu, Somalia; Vietnamese 'boat-people' begin to seek their freedom; 2 jumbo jets collide on ground in Tenerife air disaster – 582 die

Uncertainty [hist/sociol]; Tom Nairn, The Break-Up of Britain [sociol.]. **Int. Lit.**: Lowell, Day by Day [poems]; Atwood, Dancing Girls [stories]; Coetzee, In the Heart of the Country; Jong, How to Save Your Own Life; Kosinski, Blind Date; Morrison, Song of Solomon; Grass, The Flounder [Eng. trans, 1978]; David Mamet, American Buffalo [US play]. **Music:** Maria Callas & Elvis Presley die; Sex Pistols release 'God Save the Queen' & 'Never Mind the Bollocks, Here's the Sex Pistols' [album – advance orders of 100,000 copies]; Tippett, 'The Ice Break' [opera]; 'Annie' [musical play]. **Art:** Richard Rogers's Pompidou Centre, Paris, opens. **Film:** Groucho Marx & Bing Crosby die; Altman, '3 Women' [Spacek, S. Duvall, J. Rule]; Attenborough, 'A Bridge Too Far' [all-star cast]; Lucas, 'Star Wars' [Guinness, C. Fisher et al]; Spielberg, 'Close Encounters of the Third Kind'; Woody Allen, 'Annie Hall' [D. Keaton]; John Badham, 'Saturday Night Fever' [J. Travolta]; David Lynch, 'Eraserhead'; Zeffirelli, 'Jesus of Nazareth' [on TV]. **Theory/Crit:** Barthes, Image-Music-Text [Eng. trans]; incls 'The Death of the Author']; Ernst Bloch et al, Aesthetics and Politics; Rosalind Coward & John Ellis, Language and Materialism; Foucault, 'Intellectuals and Power' [Eng. trans]; Jacques Lacan, Écrits [Eng. trans; (essays over many yrs] & The Four Fundamental Concepts of Psychoanalysis [(1973); Eng. trans]; Elaine Showalter, A Literature of Their Own; Barbara Smith, Toward a Black Feminist Criticism; Todorov, The Poetics of Prose [(1971); Eng. trans]; R. Williams, Marxism and Literature

Pr/F: Bainbridge	Injury Time
Carter	The Passion of New Eve
Drabble	The Ice Age
Fowles	Daniel Martin
Isherwood	Chrisopher and His Kind [autobiog.]
Le Carré	The Honourable Schoolboy
Manning	[–1980] The Levant Trilogy; with The Balkan Trilogy (v. 1960) forms Fortunes of War]
McIlvanney	Laidlaw
Pym	Quartet in Autumn
Scott	Staying On [sequel to Raj Quartet; Booker]
Tolkein	The Silmarillion [posthm.]
Upward	No Home but the Struggle [*]
Bruce Chatwin (1940–89)	In Patagonia [travel]
Dr: Ayckbourn	Ten Times Table
Bennett	The Old Country
Brenton	Epsom Downs
Churchill	Traps
Nichols	Privates on Parade
Stoppard	Professional Foul [for TV] & Every Good Boy Deserves Favour [with LSO conducted by André Previn]
Barrie Keefe (b.1945)	A Mad World, My Masters
Lit. 'Events':	Virago Press publishes its first book

1978

1st live broadcasts from the Commons; Lib-Lab pact ends, but Callaghan gvnmt carries on – proposes 5% limit for pay rises – TUC & Lab. Party Conference reject wage-restraint – Commons rejects sanctions against employers breaching 5% limit – Ford car workers get 17% wage increase after 9-wk strike – [–1979] 'Winter of Discontent' begins; gvnmt approve plans for nuclear reprocessing plant at Windscale, Cumbria; anti-Nazi carnival in London; IRA bomb kills 14 in Belfast – 'dirty protests' by H-block IRA prisoners in Ulster – UK criticised for interrogation techniques used in N. Ireland; wrecked oil tanker 'Amoco Cadiz' pollutes Brittany coast; 'Red Brigades' kidnap & kill Aldo Mori, former It. PM; Pope John Paul I [Polish] – 1st non-It. pope for 450 yrs; US Pres. Carter brokers Camp David peace agreement between Israel & Egypt; Arab guerrillas kill 37 Israelis in bus attack – Israel bombs PLO camps in S. Lebanon; violent demonstrations against Shah's rule in Iran – martial law imposed – oil strike cuts off all exports; end of white rule in Rhodesia agreed by late 1978;

UK's 1st statutory May Day holiday; 1st UK baby born after in vitro fertilisation; [–1979] publication of Times & Sunday Times suspended by strikes; Muhammad Ali wins world heavyweight boxing title for 3rd time. **Int. Lit.:** Updike, The Coup; Wouk, War and Remembrance; Mamet, The Water Engine [pf.d]; John Irving, The World According to Garp [US novel]; Paul Theroux, Picture Palace [US novel]; Georges Perec, Life a User's Manuel [Fr. fiction; Eng. trans, 1987]; Milan Kundera, The Book of Laughter and Forgetting [Czech novel; Eng. trans 1980]. **Music:** 'Rock Against Racism' festival in London; Rolling Stones, 'Some Girls' [album]; MacMillan, 'Mayerling' [ballet]. **Art:** 'State of British Art' conference at ICA; Norman Foster designs Sainsbury Centre at University of East Anglia. **Film:** Bergman, 'Autumn Sonata' [Ingrid Bergman]; Malle, 'Pretty Baby' [Sarandon, B. Shields]; Michael Cimino, 'The Deer Hunter' [De Niro, M. Streep]; Richard Donner, 'Superman' [Brando, Hackman, C. Reeve et al]; Blake Edwards [UK], 'Revenge of the Pink Panther'

P: Bunting	Collected Poems
Harrison	From 'The School of Eloquence' and other poems
Hill	Tenebrae
Hughes	Cave Birds
MacCaig	Old Maps and New: Selected Poems
MacDiarmid	Complete Poems 1920–1976
U.[rsula] A. Fanthorpe (b.1929)	Side Effects
Andrew Motion (b.1952)	The Pleasure Steamers
Craig Raine (b.1944)	The Onion, Memory
Charles Tomlinson (b.1927)	Selected Poems 1951–1974 & The Shaft
Pr/F: K. Amis	Jake's Thing
M. Amis	Success
Farrell	The Singapore Grip
Greene	The Human Factor
McEwan	In Between the Sheets [stories] & The Cement Garden [novel]
Mortimer	Rumpole of the Bailey [TV ser., 1979]

Period	Year	International and Political Contexts	Social and Cultural Contexts	Authors	Indicative Titles
		[-1979] Tanzania sends troops into Uganda – Gen. Amin deposed; civil rights dissidents jailed in Moscow; [-1979] Sandinistas ferment conflict in Nicaragua; mass suicide in Guyana of 913 members of US cult, the People's Temple; Vietnam invades Kampuchea (Cambodia); independence for Solomon Islands	[Sellers, H. Lom]; Randal Keiser, 'Grease' [Travolta, O. Newton-John]. **Theory/Crit:** Derrida, *Writing and Difference* [(1967); Eng. trans]; Judith Fetterley, *The Resisting Reader: A Feminist Approach to American Fiction*; Iser, *The Act of Reading*; Pierre Macherey, *A Theory of Literary Production* [(1966); Eng. trans]; Susie Orbach, *Fat is a Feminist Issue*; Michael Riffaterre, *Semiotics of Poetry*; Edward Said, *Orientalism*; E.P. Thompson, *The Poverty of Theory*; Hayden White, *Tropics of Discourse*	Murdoch Tennant Weldon A.[ntonia] S.[usan] Byatt (b.1936) Michèle Roberts (b.1949) **Dr:** Ayckbourn Barker Bond Gems Gray Hare Mercer Pinter Potter Russell Stoppard	*The Sea, The Sea* [Booker] *The Bad Sister* *Praxis* *The Virgin in the Garden* [novel] *A Piece of the Night* [novel] *Joking Apart* *The Hang of the Goal* *The Woman* *Piaf* *The Rear Column* *Plenty* [film, 1985] & *Licking Hitler* [TV film] *Cousin Vladimir* *Betrayal* *Pennies from Heaven* [on TV] *The Daughters of Albion* [on TV] *Night and Day*
	1979	1.5m. public service workers on 24-hour strikes against pay restraint [incls ambulance drivers, NHS ancillary staff & refuse collectors]; Callaghan gvnmt depends on SNP support – devolution referenda in Scotland & Wales fail – [Mar.] gvnmt defeated on 'no confidence' vote tabled by SNP – Gen. Elec.: Cons. victory: majority of 43 – Margaret Thatcher, 1st woman PM; Anthony Blunt, surveyor of the Queen's pictures, named as 'fourth man' in Burgess, Maclean & Philby Soviet spy network [v.1951, 1963]; IRA kill Lord Mountbatten – also 18 soldiers at Warrenpoint – INLA kill Airey Neave, Tory MP, with car bomb at Commons; 1st direct elections to European Parliament – European Monetary System (EMS) estab.d – Greece joins EEC; major nuclear accident at Three Mile Island plant in USA; Shah deposed & exiled in Iranian revolution – Ayatollah Khomeini, ruler of Islamic republic – [-1981] US embassy hostages seized in Teheran; Muslim extremists seize Grand Mosque at Mecca, Saudi Arabia; illegal UDI in Rhodesia ends – UN sanctions lifted – Bishop Muzorewa, 1st black PM of Zimbabwe; ex-Pres. Bhutto executed in Pakistan – Islamic laws intro.d; USSR invades Afghanistan; Vietnam occupies Cambodia – Khmer Rouge overthrown – Pol Pot regime accused of killing 3m. people; huge oil spillage in Gulf of Mexico; whaling by factory ships & all whaling in Indian Ocean banned to protect species	Mother Theresa awarded Nobel Peace Prize; National Heritage Fund estab.d; 1st mass-marketing of computer games; Sony Walkman cassette players 1st intro.d; storms strike Fastnet yacht race – 17 killed. **Int. Lit.:** Baldwin, *Just Above My Head*; Kosinski, *Passion Play* [novel]; Lurie, *Only Children*; Mailer, *The Executioner's Song* [re. convicted killer, Gary Gilmore]; Heller, *Good as Gold*; Roth, *The Ghost Writer* [1st novel in 'Zuckerman' trilogy]; Styron, *Sophie's Choice* [Alan Pakula film, 1982]; Vonnegut, *Jailbird*; Atwood, *Life Before Man*; White, *The Twyborn Affair*. **Music:** Sondheim, 'Sweeney Todd' [musical]. **Art:** Dani Karavan, 'Homage to Galileo Galilei' [laser installation, Florence]. **Film:** Allen, 'Manhattan' [Keaton, Streep]; Coppola, 'Apocalypse Now' [Brando, Duvall, Hopper, H. Ford, M. Sheen]; T. Jones, 'Monty Python's Life of Brian' [Cleese, Gilliam et al]; Polanski, 'Tess' [N. Kinski; adptn of Hardy]; Gillian Armstrong [Austrl.], 'My Brilliant Career'; Robert Benton, 'Kramer vs Kramer' [Hoffman, Streep]; George Miller [Austrl.], 'Mad Max' ['Mad Max 2', 1981]; Stuart Rosenberg, 'The Amityville Horror' [Steiger]; Robert Wise, 'Star Trek: The Motion Picture'. **Theory/Crit:** Althusser & Etienne Balibar, *Reading 'Capital'* [(1965); Eng. trans]; Tony Bennett, *Formalism and Marxism*; de Man, *Allegories of Reading*; Umberto Eco, *The Role of the Reader* & *A Theory of Semiotics*; Sandra Gilbert & Susan Gubar, *The Madwoman in the Attic*; Stuart Hall et al [eds], *Policing the Crisis*; Hartman (ed.), *Deconstruction and Criticism* [incls Bloom, de	**P:** Dunn Fuller Gunn Heaney Hughes Jennings Longley McGough Raine Denise Levertov (1923–97) Derek Mahon (b.1941, Ulster) **Pr/F:** Carter Golding Collins Lessing Naipaul Tennant Zoe Fairbairns (b.1948) D.M. Thomas (b.1935) **Dr:** Ayckbourn Bond Brenton Churchill Gray	*Barbarians* *Lies and Secrets* *Selected Poems, 1950–1975* *Field Work* *Moortown & Remains of Elmet* [with photographer, Fay Godwin] *Selected Poems & Moments of Grace* *The Echo Gate* *Holiday on Death Row* *A Martian Sends a Postcard Home* *Collected Earlier Poems 1940–1960* *Poems, 1962–1978* *The Bloody Chamber* [stories] & *The Sadeian Woman: An Exercise in Cultural History* *Darkness Visible* *The Bitch* *Shikasta* [1st in ser. of 5 vols of 'space fiction', *Canopus in Argos: Archives* (–1982)] *A Bend in the River* *Wild Nights* *Benefits* [novel] *The Flute-Player* [novel] *Sisterly Feelings* *The Worlds* [pub.d 1980] *Sore Throats* *Cloud Nine* *Close of Play*

Man, Derrida, J.H. Miller]; Mary Jacobus (ed.), *Women Writing and Writing About Women* [incls Showalter, 'Towards a Feminist Poetics']; Colin MacCabe, *James Joyce and the Revolution of the Word*; Marcuse, *The Aesthetic Dimension*; Elaine Marks, 'Lesbian Intertextuality'; Francis Mulhern, *The Moment of 'Scrutiny'*; R. Williams, *Politics and Letters*; Wittig & Sandi Zeig, *Lesbian Peoples*

Keefe

Potter

Russell
Shaffer

Sus
Blue Remembered Hills [on TV; on stage, posthm., 1996]
Lies [on TV]
Amadeus [Milos Forman film, 1984]

9 1980–1999

The Contemporary Period

INTRODUCTION

This final chapter once again deals with two decades: the 1980s and 1990s, bringing us up to the end of the second millennium. As before, in pursuit of clarity the timeline narratives are given separately for each decade. But the problem here, as we approach our own recent past, is the seemingly exponential growth of possible material to include, since time and historians have not yet had a chance to select out the salient grand narratives of our times. As Salman Rushdie tellingly put it in *Midnight's Children*: 'the further you get from the past, the more concrete and plausible it seems – but as you approach the present, it inevitably seems more and more incredible.' For the last 20 years of the 20th Century, the reader is invited to reshape the materials presented here to forge their own narrative of the 'incredible' present.

Chapter contents

9.1 CONTEMPORARY

A slippery adjective, whose meanings the dictionary gives as: 'living, occurring or originating at the same time; belonging to or occurring in the present; modern in style or design'.

The second sense is the principal one in our context here, but the third sense cited may cause some confusion by conflating the words 'contemporary' and 'modern' [see the comments on 'modern' in the gloss on **Modernism*** in Chapter 6], especially as a more specific use of 'contemporary' in relation to style and design is sometimes reserved for the house decoration and furniture of the 1950s. But the biggest problem with using 'contemporary' as a term in cultural periodisation when it means 'belonging to or occurring in the present' is: how far back does 'the present' extend? Usage varies here, and it is not uncommon even now to find that 'Contemporary Literature' courses in fact begin in the 1950s. While recognising that a definition of 'the present' which includes the last 20 years of the 20th Century is dubious if not comic, the term still has such general currency in cultural and literary history that it seems appropriate to continue to use it here for the period of the 1980s and 1990s (and rather less controversial than calling it 'The **Postmodern*** Period').

9.2 NINETEEN-EIGHTIES

Key Timeline Narratives 1980–1989

⮑ *The International Context*

- *Africa* In 1980, the parliamentary elections in the newly independent *Zimbabwe* resulted in victory for the ZANU Party which won 57 of the 63 seats (ZAPU took the rest), with Robert Mugabe as Prime Minister; in 1987, Mugabe persuaded parliament to combine the roles of head of state and head of government and became the country's first (and so far only) executive President; and the following year, ZANU and ZAPU merged to make Zimbabwe effectively a one-party state.

  A new constitution in *South Africa* in 1984 caused serious rioting in the black townships, followed by a state of emergency in 1985 when President Botha rejected the principle of 'one man, one vote' and 100,000 black squatters were to be moved into new townships (Britain refused to implement full economic sanctions against South Africa at a conference of Commonwealth Prime Ministers the same year); large-scale anti-apartheid unrest continued in 1986, with many detained and riots in Soweto, and again in 1989, when 23 people were killed near Cape Town [see the early 1990s, below, for constitutional reform in South Africa].

  Relations between Colonel Gadafy's *Libya* and the West reached breaking-point with the siege of the Libyan People's Bureau in St James's Square, London, and the shooting there of WPC

Fletcher; US planes bombed Libya in 1986, and the bombing of Flight 103 over Lockerbie, Scotland in 1988 [see 'Signs of the Times': Disasters, below] was widely held to have been instigated by Lybia.

- **Asia**   In *China*, despite the more liberal reinterpretation of Maoism which followed the trial and sentencing in 1980–1 of 'the Gang of Four' (including Mao Tse-tung's widow) which had held power since Mao's death in 1976, the decade ended with a massacre by the army of pro-democracy demonstrators during a huge rally in Tiananmen Square, Beijing, in 1989.

  In Assam, *India*, in 1983, 600 Muslim refugees were killed in a sectarian massacre; Hindu-Muslim riots in 1984 led to the occupation of the Golden Temple of Amritsar by Sikh militants and its storming by government troops, during which over 800 people died; the Prime Minister, Indira Gandhi, was then assassinated by her Sikh bodyguards in retaliation, causing a backlash in its turn by Hindus who massacred 3000 Sikhs; a bomb was suspected of destroying an Air India flight over the Atlantic in 1985, killing over 320 people.

  Martial law was lifted in Pakistan in 1985, and ex-President Bhutto's daughter, Benazir Bhutto, returned to her country in 1986 to lead the main opposition party. Following General Zia's death in a plane crash in 1988, she was elected Prime Minister and took Pakistan back into the Commonwealth in 1989.

  During the 1980s, Bangladesh was ravaged by cyclones, tidal waves and flooding [see 'Signs of the Times': Disasters, below]. Racial conflict between Sinhalese and Tamils seeking separation from *Sri Lanka* intensified in this period [see, e.g., 1983, 1987]. In 1984–5, the UK agreed to relinquish the sovereignty of *Hong Kong* to China by 1997.

- **The Americas**   In 1982, royal assent was given to the Canada Bill, and the new constitution contained therein finally freed *Canada* from any control by the UK Parliament. In 1980, the *USA* made a bungled attempt to free the hostages in the American Embassy in Tehran [see Chapter 8, 1979, and gloss on International Context], Jimmy Carter was defeated in the Presidential Elections and Ronald Reagan came to power; 1981 saw an assassination attempt on President Reagan, and the Iran hostages were finally freed after 444 days in captivity. Iin 1983, the USA invaded Grenada, and began to support the Contra rebels in *Nicaragua* against the Marxist Sandinista government [see Chapter 8, 1978–9], but on President Reagan's re-election in 1985, such aid was banned and a trade embargo instituted in its place; by 1986, the USA was embroiled in the 'Irangate' scandal in which profits from an exchange of arms for hostages with Iran were diverted to the Nicaraguan Contra rebels even though Congress had refused funding; President Noriega of Panama was indicted for drug-smuggling in 1988, and in 1989 US troops invaded Panama and ousted him.

  In April 1982, after years of claiming territorial rights, *Argentina*, under its military rulers, invaded the Falkland Islands and the Falklands War began: the UK dispatched a 'task force', HMS 'Sheffield' was sunk, as was the Argentine ship 'General Belgano', and fighting ended in June with the surrender of the Argentine forces at Port Stanley; civilian rule was re-established in Argentina in 1983, with members of the ex-military junta facing prosecution for their part in an earlier internal 'dirty war' in which so many civilians were 'disappeared'.

- **The Middle East, Iran and Iraq**   Conflict escalated in the region throughout the 1980s: in 1980, Israel declared all of Jerusalem its capital city; in 1981, President Sadat of Egypt was assassinated, Israel annexed the Golan Heights, bombed a nuclear reactor in Baghdad, and bombed Beirut which was the centre of intense fighting in Lebanon; in 1982, Sinai was returned to Egypt by the Israelis (it had been occupied since the war of 1967), but they also invaded Lebanon and besieged Beirut from which the PLO and Syrian forces began to withdraw, leaving the Christian militias to carry out massacres in the Palestinian refugee camps. In 1983–4, in Beirut, suicide lorry-bombs wrecked a US Marine base, the US Embassy and the barracks of French UN peace-keeping troops, killing hundreds and leading to the evacuation of the UN peace-keeping force; and Terry Waite, the Archbishop of Canterbury's envoy on a hostage-releasing mission, was kidnapped in Lebanon in 1987 (released in 1991 after 2,353 days in captivity). However, something of a breakthrough in Arab-Israeli relations came towards the end of the decade when Yasser Arafat, the PLO leader, recognised Israel's right to exist (1988).

By 1980, the tension between Iran and Iraq (under Saddam Hussein) was mounting, and in 1983 Iran launched a major offensive across the border; the bitter war dragged on through the mid-1980s until an Iraqi gas attack on the Iranians in 1988 which killed some 5000 people led to a cease-fire the same year.

• **The USSR and Europe**   The Soviet invasion of Afghanistan in 1979 drew international censure, with the USA, West Germany, China and Japan amongst other nations boycotting the Moscow Olympics in 1980 in protest (in retaliation, the USSR and 16 other states boycotted the Los Angeles games in 1984). After many set-backs against the mujahideen, Soviet troops withdrew in 1988–9, ten years after they had first invaded and with little to show for it. Despite the Soviet Union being called 'the evil empire' by US President Reagan in 1983 when he proposed the 'Star Wars' missile shield in space, the decade was otherwise characterised by the gradual liberalisation of the USSR, especially after Mikhail Gorbachev came to power in 1985 and introduced policies of 'glasnost' (openness) and 'perestroika' (reconstruction).

Throughout the early 1980s, signs of a movement in Eastern Europe towards greater democratic freedom were apparent in the Gdansk shipyard strikes in Poland which had led to the creation of the independent trade union federation, 'Solidarity'. Although martial law was imposed in 1981 and Solidarity banned (1982), the Pope's visit to Poland in 1983 when he supported the right to join free trade unions indicated that the old repressive order was under threat. In 1986, over 200 Polish political prisoners were released from confinement, as were a number of leading Soviet dissidents. Demonstrations for liberal reform occurred in Hungary in 1987, and by 1988, there was widespread unrest in the USSR's satellite states; contested elections were approved for the first time, and large-scale troop reductions were made throughout the Soviet bloc.

In 1989, Presidents Gorbachev and George Bush (who had become US President in 1988) met off Malta and declared the 'end of the Cold War'; there were revolutions in Poland, Hungary, Czechoslovakia, Bulgaria, Romania and East Germany, where the demolition of the Berlin Wall came to symbolise the end of the East European Communist past. A series of 'Summits' between Gorbachev and Ronald Reagan, who became US President in 1980 and was returned for a second term in 1985, were also instrumental in achieving a significant reduction in the super-powers' stockpile of nuclear arms [see 1985, 1986, 1987].

Spain became a member of NATO in 1982 , and opened the border with Gibraltar to pedestrians (it was fully opened in 1985); Spain and Portugal joined what was now the European Community (EC) in 1986, the year of the Single European Act (which Mrs Thatcher signed on behalf of the UK) and of agreement to build the Channel Tunnel (–1987). In 1986, the Swedish Prime Minister, Olaf Palme, was assassinated in Stockholm.

• **Nuclear and Environmental Issues**   Intensifying concern over global warming, environmental pollution and endangered species [see e.g. 1982, 1985 and 'Signs of the Times': Disasters, below] caused the growth of 'Green' [ecology] political parties in Europe and elsewhere from 1980 onwards; in 1984, the warmest weather on record (in 1981 and 1983) was blamed on the 'greenhouse effect'; in 1986, the first hole in the ozone layer was detected over Spitzbergen, while in 1987, its thinning was attributed to the industrial nations' proliferation of CFCs, the same year that a rise in sea-levels and the onset of ever more destructive hurricanes were predicted.

Related to these anxieties [see also Science, Technology and Health, below] was the anti-nuclear movement (most active in the first half of the 1980s): in 1980, the British Government agreed to buy US 'Trident' missiles and to have NATO 'Cruise' missiles based in the UK, causing 60,000 people to demonstrate against it and the Labour Party Conference to vote for unilateral nuclear disarmament (1980–1); in 1981, there were anti-nuclear demonstrations across Europe and the USA, including a 150,000-strong one in London against the siting of 'Cruise' missiles at Greenham Common, where the first Women's Peace Camp was set up and thousands of women demonstrated (1981–2; it was cleared by police and bailiffs in 1984).

Huge anti-nuclear-weapons demonstrations took place in West Germany, Italy, Austria, Sweden and Spain in 1983, the year that 'Cruise' missiles first arrived at Greenham Common and UK demonstrations culminated in a 250,000-strong rally in Hyde Park; in 1985, the Greenpeace protest ship 'Rainbow Warrior' was sabotaged off New Zealand by the French secret service; in 1986, a nuclear reactor at Chernobyl, USSR, exploded, causing many deaths and fall-out which contaminated the Soviet Union and parts of Europe for years afterwards. Some international political initiatives to limit nuclear weapons were also made in the period: the Strategic Arms Reduction Talks (START) opened in Geneva in 1982 (the treaty was finally signed in 1991), and the East–West thaw following Mikhail Gorbachev's coming to power in the Soviet Union in 1985 resulted in arms limitation 'Summits', as noted in the gloss on The USSR and Europe above.

• *Science, Technology and Health*   Space exploration slowed down because of the huge costs involved; nevertheless, the US space shuttle 'Discovery' made its first flight in 1984; 'Challenger' followed, but exploded in 1986, killing its crew of seven; and the US space-craft 'Voyager II' transmitted photographs of Neptune back to earth in 1989. Advances in information technology (IT) led to the wide availability of home computers, PCs and computer games [see 1981, 1982 (Sinclair's 'ZX Spectrum' PCs), 1983, 1984 (Apple Mac PCs with the first 'mouse'), 1985 (Amstrad word-processors)]; 'Vodaphone' introduced the first cellular radio network in the UK (1984) and the first mobile 'phones were in use by c.1986; from 1987, cassettes began to replace vinyl discs as the main form of recorded music, and by 1988 the first compact discs were being developed.

From c.1982 onwards, there were major advances in genetic science and engineering; 1983 saw the first UK heart and lung transplant (the first triple transplant of heart, lungs and liver was performed in Cambridge in 1986), and in 1984, the first UK 'test-tube' triplets were born. In 1983, the High Court in Britain upheld a doctor's right to prescribe the contraceptive pill to under-16 year olds without their parents' consent; during 1983–4, a UK government enquiry into the high incidence of cancer amongst those living near the Sellafield nuclear power station reported that childhood leukaemia there was ten times the national average; and the sale of meat from infected cattle began the BSE crisis in the UK in 1988.

However, the most devastating international health problem was the rapid development of the AIDS epidemic worldwide. The first reports of the disease appeared in 1981; by 1983, around 2000 people in the USA were affected and AIDS had spread to Europe; the AIDS virus was identified in

1984–5; 1985 saw the first UK baby to die of the disease, blood-donors began to be screened, and the World Health Organisation (WHO) declared an epidemic. By 1986, over 270 people had died of AIDS in the UK (one person a day by 1987), and the government launched a £20 million public awareness campaign; and by 1988, it was estimated that between five and ten million people worldwide were HIV positive.

UK Politics and the Economy   In its first budget in 1979, the new Tory Government under Mrs Thatcher introduced a series of policy initiatives which dominated the decade and effected radical changes in British political and social life: monetarism lay at the heart of these (the theory that the economy – and specifically inflation – can be regulated by controlling the supply of money in circulation), as did the rolling-back of the state through free market economics and deregulation (i.e. lifting government restrictions to stimulate competition); the resulting measures included: a cut of £4000 million in public spending, adversely affecting public-sector employment, a cut in income tax and a rise in VAT from 8 per cent to 15 per cent. A second budget in 1980 again cut public spending by a large amount, and plans to sell off nationalised industries became part of the agenda (part of British Petroleum was sold off in 1979 and its huge share sale was floated in 1987; state holdings in British Aerospace were sold in 1980 and in Britoil, 1982, 1985). One significant sign of new Tory policy was the Housing Act of 1980 which gave council house tenants the 'Right to Buy'. In 1981, the budget announced cuts in defence spending and in higher education.

Thatcherite economics in the early 1980s initially caused inflation to soar, the economy to go into recession and unemployment to rise to an unprecedented post-war figure of 3.3 million (1982–3), but the results in the longer term were deflationary, and by 1983 the economy was growing, inflation had fallen to the lowest level for 15 years, and unemployment, while still very high, was on the wane. Bolstered by the patriotoic fervour generated by the Falklands War in 1982 [see The International Context: The Americas, above], and by a budget earlier in 1983 which had lifted personal tax allowances above the rate of inflation and increased the size of mortgage loans available for tax relief, Mrs Thatcher called a General Election in which the Conservatives were returned with the biggest working majority of any government since 1945.

The defeat of the Miners' strike in 1984–5 [see UK Industrial Relations, below] was a decisive event in unleashing the implementation of the new Tory policies: a Local Government Act of 1986 abolished the GLC led by the Labour left-winger, Ken Livingstone (it was one of 50 such acts during Mrs Thatcher's terms of office which limited the powers of local government and increased centralisation); privatisation of state-owned companies proceeded rapidly during the second half of the decade (including Cable and Wireless, British Telecom, British Gas, British Airways, the British Airports Authority, the National Bus Company, British Steel and the water companies; the process continued into the **1990s*** – see below); in the 'Big Bang' of 1986, the London Stock Exchange was deregulated.

As a result of privatisation and legislation to restrict trade union activity [see, e.g. the Employment Acts of 1980, 1982, 1988–90 and UK Industrial Relations, below], strikes became less common in the later 1980s. Despite a 27 per cent devaluation of the pound in 1985, the economy boomed (partly through revenues from privatisation and from North Sea oil and gas), unemployment fell, and share and home ownership (helped by tax relief on mortgages) became central to Mrs Thatcher's vision of a new Britain (house prices in the south of England rose by 25 per cent in 1987). Despite the London Stock Market crash on 'Black Monday' 1987, when 20 per cent was wiped off share values, the budget of that year again cut income tax and introduced personal pension plans (which also received tax relief), following which – and on the back of the 'feel-good factor'– a General Election was called and a large overall majority was again at the disposal of the Tory Government.

With public spending the lowest for 20 years, the budget of 1988 further reduced income tax, but combined with the availability of plentiful credit, a consumer boom ensued, interest rates rose, as did inflation and imports: with a balance of payments deficit of £20 billion in 1989, the economy was in deep trouble. The introduction of the Poll Tax in place of rates in Scotland (1989) and the rest of the UK in 1990 was bitterly resented; despite having signed the Single European Act in 1986, Mrs Thatcher's attitude towards the EC was always wary, and this culminated in her row in 1989–90 with her Deputy PM, Geoffrey Howe, and her Chancellor, Nigel Lawson, over joining the ERM and the single currency. The Cabinet was in disarray; and the 'Iron Lady' had suddenly become vulnerable. She lost the Conservative Party leadership election in 1990.

Elsewhere in British politics, ideological change was also occurring. In 1980, James Callaghan retired as leader of the Labour Party, and Michael Foot, a veteran left-winger, won the leadership contest over Dennis Healey; a conference agenda was then introduced (led by Tony Benn) which pushed the party, and any future Labour Government, much further to the left: public ownership of the economy would be extended; protectionism would be introduced; the House of Lords would be abolished; Britain would leave the EEC; unilateral nuclear disarmament would become Labour policy; and re-selection processes would allow constituency parties to de-select sitting MPs as official candidates. A special conference early in 1981 voted for the Labour Party leader to be elected by an electoral college comprising representatives from MPs, the trade unions and constituency associations, rather than by MPs alone. This programme split the Labour Party and made it unelectable in the face of Thatcherite conservatism during the 1980s (for example, in the General Election of 1983, its manifesto contained a number of the key policies outlined above which failed to appeal either to traditional Labour voters or the undecided).

Outraged by the leftist tendency of the party, and by the electoral college in particular, three former cabinet ministers, David Owen, Shirley Williams and William Rodgers, left the party and joined another ex-minister, Roy Jenkins [see Chapter 8, 1977], to form the Social Democratic Party (SDP), which immediately made an alliance with the Liberals, and in so doing sought to 'break the mould' of British politics by creating a viable third party. In the General Election of 1983, the alliance won 23 seats and 25 per cent of the vote, but despite this success, it failed to 'break the mould' in the 1987 General Election, and in 1988, most of the SDP merged with the Liberals to become the Social Democratic and Liberal Party (SDLP; David Owen continued to lead the remaining SDP until it was finally wound up in 1990).

In 1983, Neil Kinnock replaced Foot as Labour Party leader, denounced the Trotskyite Militant Tendency within the party in a Conference speech in 1985 (members of it were later expelled), and the slow process to electoral recovery began (in 1987, Labour increased its share of the vote and number of parliamentary seats); a Labour review document in 1989, 'Meet the Challenge, Make the Change', discarded many left-wing policies (including price and import controls, high income tax, a wealth tax, unilateral nuclear disarmament, and rescinding restrictions on trades unions) and inclined towards a free market economy.

⮑   *UK Industrial Relations*   Given the so-called 'ungovernability' of the 1970s and the political situation in the 1980s as described above, it was inevitable that the Government's relations with the trades unions would be confrontational. In 1980, the first of a series of Employment Acts was introduced to curb what Mrs Thatcher saw as intolerable trade-union militancy, banning secondary picketing (i.e. disallowing pickets from elsewhere than the dispute itself), expanding exemptions from 'closed shops', and offering funds for secret ballots before strikes and for the election of officials (a second Employment Act in 1982 further legislated against 'closed shops'). Also in 1980, a three-month strike by British Steel workers ended in failure, the industry thereafter being restructured, and with over two million unemployed (the highest since 1935), there was a trade-union 'Day of Action' protesting at the Government's economic and industrial relations policies.

This was followed in 1981 by a 'People's March for Jobs' from Liverpool to London, the same year that it was announced 50 pits were to close in the UK with the loss of 30,000 mining jobs, unofficial stoppages forced the Government to reverse the decision, and Arthur Scargill became National President of the NUM. 1982 saw unsuccessful disputes on the railways and in the NHS; the National Graphical Association was fined and had its assets confiscated in 1983 for attempting to impose a 'closed shop' at a printing plant in Warrington, and a second 'Day of Action' failed to prevent the Government's banning of trade unions at GCHQ in Cheltenham in 1984. But it was the defeat of the Miners' Strike of 1984–5 which permanently weakened the British trade union movement: the miners were divided, the NCB held firm, the police were used in an offensive capacity, violent clashes were televised, the High Court ruled the strike illegal and sequestered the union's funds, and when the strike was finally called off in 1985, the pit closures were instituted and the miners remained divided.

Thereafter, the incremental programme of anti-union confrontation and legislation continued: a teachers' pay dispute in 1985 which disrupted schools led to the abolition of the Burnham negotiating committee in 1986 and the imposition of a pay settlement; in 1986–7, there were violent clashes between print-workers' pickets and police at Rupert Murdoch's new News International print works in Wapping, East London, over a 'single-union agreement' with electicians which broke the print unions' restrictive practices in terms of manning levels – again, fines and sequestration followed; troops were used to drive ambulances during the London ambulance workers' strike of 1989–90; and the 1988–90 Employment Acts, amongst other restrictions on trade union activity, gave union members the right to ignore a ballot on industrial action, banned strikes in support of 'closed shops', and required the unions themselves to disown unofficial action.

● **UK Social Issues and Education**   Apart from the social problems incident on the cuts in public spending, high unemployment and industrial conflict, the tensions in Thatcher's Britain in the 1980s revealed themselves in the riots – especially between black youths and the police – in Brixton and Southall, South London, Toxteth, Liverpool, Moss Side, Manchester, and elsewhere in the spring of 1981, and in Brixton again, Handsworth, Birmingham, and on the Broadwater Farm estate in Tottenham, North London, in 1985.

Despite Mrs Thatcher's reassurances about the NHS being safe in her hands, significant changes were made to it: in 1983, it was required to put its support services out to public tender; prescription charges rose to £2 in 1985 and charges were introduced for eye-tests and dental work in 1988; and a White Paper, 'Working for Patients', in 1989 outlined sweeping reforms for the NHS, including the creation of an 'internal market' and stressing the need for 'value for money' and 'cost effectiveness' (by 1989, the NHS was costing £26 billion per annum to run).

In education, significant developments were: the cut-backs in grants to universities and in student numbers in 1981 and beyond (in retaliation for which Oxford University refused Mrs Thatcher an honorary degree in 1985); the banning of corporal punishment in schools by the European Court in 1982; the first GCSE examinations in 1988; and Kenneth Baker's Education Act of the same year which introduced the national curriculum and devolved much responsibility for managing the education process to the schools themselves.

↪ **Northern Ireland**   An Anglo-Irish summit in Dublin in 1980 agreed on common interests, but the same year (and into 1981) IRA prisoners in the H-Blocks at the Maze prison began a series of hunger strikes which resulted in ten deaths, including that of Bobby Sands (May–October 1981, and recently elected as an MP for Tyrone), after which the strikes were called off. The IRA continued to plant devastating bombs in Ulster and mainland Britain throughout the 1980s, including one at the Grand Hotel, Brighton, during the Conservative Party conference of 1984, which was probably intended to kill Mrs Thatcher but caused the death of five others [see also 1982, 1983, 1987, 1989]. In 1983, the All Ireland Forum was founded between the Irish Government and the Northern Irish SDLP and Alliance Party, but was rejected by both Unionists and Mrs Thatcher; the same year Gerry Adams became President of Sinn Féin and MP for West Belfast, and there was a mass break-out of 134 IRA prisoners from the Maze prison.

The Anglo-Irish Agreement of 1985, which was intended to involve the Dublin Government in finding a solution to the Northern Ireland problem, outraged Unionists and all 15 of their MPs resigned in protest; 1987–8 saw the SAS actively involved in 'the Troubles' (controversially killing three IRA members in Gibraltar in 1988 – at their funeral, three mourners were killed by Loyalist paramilitaries, and at their subsequent funeral, two undercover British soldiers were killed); also in 1988, the right to silence was abolished in Norther Ireland courts and the Government banned radio and TV interviews with members of the IRA and other sectarian groups.

↪ **Social and Cultural 'Signs of the Times'**

• **Disasters**   Drought and famine in East Africa, especially in Somalia and Ethiopia where refugees from the war were worst affected, was one of the decade's most pressing problems [see, e.g., 1980, 1984–5 (when the UN estimated c.19 million Africans were starving) and 1987], equalled only perhaps by the recurrent monsoon floods, cyclones and tidal waves which devastated Bangladesh [see 1984, 1985, 1987, 1988]. Other natural disasters included: in 1985, an earthquake which destroyed much of Mexico City and a volcano eruption in Columbia which killed some 25,000 people; c.1700 people killed by gases escaping from a volcanic lake in the Cameroons (1986); serious drought in India and gales over southern England which caused extensive damage (1987); floods in China and on the Nile, drought in the US midwest and earthquakes in India and Armenia (1988); and an earthquake which wrecked parts of San Fransisco in 1989.

Man-made disasters (leaving aside Chernobyl; see Nuclear and Environmental Issues, above) included: the collapse in 1980 of a floating hostel for oil-rig workers in the North Sea, killing over 120 people; the destruction of a Korean passenger plane by a Soviet jet fighter over Siberia in which nearly 270 people died; an explosion at a chemical plant at Bhopal, India, causing extensive casualties; the death of 41 fans caused by UK football hooligans at the Juventus–Liverpool European Cup Final in the Heysel Stadium, Belgium, and a fire in Bradford City FC's grandstand which killed 52 spectators (both 1985); 400 pilgrims were killed when Iranian Muslims rioted on a pilgrimage to Mecca, the cross-Channel car ferry, 'Herald of Free Enterprse', sank off Zeebrugge, Belgium, with the loss of 192 lives, and a fire at King's Cross tube station, London, killed 30 people (all 1987). A bomb on Pan Am Boeing 747, Flight 103, over Lockerbie, Scotland, killed a total of over 280 people, an explosion on the North Sea oil rig, 'Piper Alpha', which claimed 166 lives, and the Clapham Junction rail crash in which 35 people died (all 1988). The Kegworth plane crash on the M1 motorway which killed 44 people, the Hillsborough stadium disaster where 94 Liverpool football fans were crushed to death, the sinking of the 'Marchioness' pleasure-boat on the Thames, London, when 51 party-goers drowned, and a huge oil spill from the damaged tanker 'Exxon Valdez' in Alaska (all 1989).

- **Crimes and Trials** In the UK in the 1980s these included: the conviction of Peter Sutcliffe (the 'Yorkshire Ripper') in 1981; the Brinks-Mat robbery when £25 million in gold bars was stolen, and the kidnapping of the Irish 1981 Derby winner, 'Shergar', with a ransom demand of £2 million (both 1983). The rampage of a gunman in Hungerford, Berkshire, in which 16 people were killed and 14 injured, the prosecution of Guinness company executives on charges of illegal share-dealing, the unsuccessful attempt by the Government to suppress MI5 officer Peter Wright's autobiography, *Spycatcher*, and the trial of Cynthia Payne for running a brothel (all 1987). In 1989, the convictions of the 'Guildford Four' pub bombers were overturned and they were freed after 14 years in gaol (as were those of the 'Birmingham Six' in 1991, after 16 years in prison; see Chapter 8, 1974).

- **Buildings and 'Openings'** In 1980, the Humber Bridge was completed (opened 1981), and Covent Garden, London, reopened as a shopping centre; the Nat West Tower opened in London in 1981; the Barbican Centre, London, opened in 1982 and the RSC moved in, the same year that approval was granted for the new British Library building in the Euston Road and the Thames Barrier at Woolwich was completed. In 1984, Prince Charles made his infamous criticism of contemporary architecture at the Royal Institute of British Architects (RIBA); in 1985–6, Richard Roger's Lloyd's Building in London was completed and opened, and the Swan Theatre, Stratford-upon-Avon, opened in 1986.

- **Sport** Björn Borg won the Wimbledon men's tennis singles for the fifth consecutive year in 1980; in 1981, the first woman cox participated in the Oxford and Cambridge boat race (the same year that the Church of England voted to ordain women deacons), and the first London Marathon was run; 1984 saw the ice-skaters, Torville and Deane, win the 'Grand Slam' of World, Olympic and European titles. After the Heysel stadium outrage of 1985 [see above, Disasters], British football clubs were banned from European competitions; and in 1986, 30 million people worldwide participated in Sportaid's 'Race Against Time' programme on behalf of refugees in Africa.

- **UK TV** A fourth TV channel (in both English and Welsh) was announced in 1980 (Channel Four was inaugurated in 1982), and a franchise granted for breakfast TV; 750 million people worldwide watched the Royal Wedding of Prince Charles and Princess Diana on TV in 1981; three new regional commercial TV services began in 1982, and in 1984, cable TV was introduced into the UK. The BBC launched full day-time TV in 1986 (by 1987, there was TV available 24 hours a day), and British Satellite Broadcasting (BSB) was awarded the first UK franchise for satellite TV. In 1988, the Broadcasting Standards Council was set up to curb sex and violence on TV; and in 1988–89, proceedings in the House of Commons were first televised.

- **Popular Music** In 1980, there was a two-month strike by musicians at the BBC in protest at plans to scrap several of its orchestras, and John Lennon was murdered in New York; Bob Marley died in 1981 aged 36; Michael Jackson's album 'Thriller' appeared in 1982 (by 1984, it had sold between 35 and 40 million copies). In 1984, Bob Geldoff established the charity 'Bandaid' and sales of a single, 'Do They Know It's Christmas', raised £8 million; Geldoff followed this in 1985 by organising two simultaneous ten-hour 'Live Aid' pop concerts (for Ethiopian relief) at Wembley, London, and the JFK Stadium, Philadelphia, with live TV transmission worldwide watched by 1.5 billion viewers, and which raised well over £50 million. 1989 saw the release of Madonna's 'Like a Prayer'.

Musicals of the decade included: 'Cats' (1981), 'Starlight Express', 'Sunday in the Park with George' (both 1984), 'Les Miserables' (1985), 'The Phantom of the Opera' and 'Chess' (both 1986).

If the demolition of the Berlin Wall in 1989 was one sign that the 1990s might be a rather different decade, so too, perhaps, was the declaration in the same year of a *fatwa* by religious leaders in Iran on the Anglo-Indian novelist Salman Rushdie and on Penguin Books for publishing *The Satanic Verses* (1988). While Rushdie went into hiding under threat of death, Muslims in Bradford burnt the offending novel.

9.3 NINETEEN-NINETIES

Key Timeline Narratives 1990–1999

➲ *The International Context*

- ***Africa*** The 1990s saw the end of apartheid in *South Africa*, with the lifting of a 30-year ban on the African National Congress (ANC), the freeing of Nelson Mandela [see 1990] and his historic meeting with President de Klerk (1990); in 1992, constitutional reforms gave legal equality to black South Africans, which were overwhelmingly supported by the white population. The South African Communist Party leader, Chris Hani, was assassinated in 1993, and there were violent battles in Johannesburg between ANC supporters and Zulus in 1994, but the same year, Nelson Mandela was inaugurated as President of the new South Africa, and in 1995, the royal visit by Queen Elizabeth was the first such since 1947.

   While the government of *Angola* signed a peace treaty with UNITA rebels in 1994, which ended the long-running civil war, the same year saw the onset of tribal massacres in *Rwanda* when 100,000 people were killed in two weeks. Hutus were then massacred by Tutsis in 1995, and in 1996 a Tutsi offensive drove millions of refugees into *Zaire*, where, in 1997, rebel troops were victorious over the government, President Mobuto was forced to resign, and Laurent Kabila became President of the renamed Democratic Republic of Congo. Tourists in *Egypt* were killed by Islamic extremists in 1996 and 1997; and in *Nigeria*, the government executed the dissident writer and environmental activist, Ken Saro-Wiwa, in 1995 despite international protest. In 1998, President Mugabe of *Zimbabwe* ordered the confiscation of white-owned farms; and in 1999, Colonel Gaddafi of *Libya* finally agreed to the trial in the Netherlands of two Libyans suspected of the 1988 bombing of Pan Am Flight 103 over Lockerbie, Scotland.

- ***Asia*** In *India*, Rajiv Gandhi, ex-Premier and Indira Gandhi's eldest son, was assassinated in 1991; ferocious Hindu-Muslim riots occcurred in 1992, and 300 people were killed by bombings in Bombay in 1993. Tension in the region was increased from 1998 by India and Pakistan competing in the testing of nuclear weapons; and by 1999, conflict was again mounting between India and Muslim guerrillas over Kashmir.

   The sovereignty of *Hong Kong* was handed over to *China* by the UK in 1997 [see 1984] after

156 years of British rule. In *Japan* in 1995, Sarin nerve gas was released in five trains on the Tokyo underground by a terrorist group, causing many casualties.

However, it was the escalation of the long-running conflict in Afghanistan which increasingly came to dominate the period (and beyond): radical Muslim mujahedeen attacked Kabul in 1992, and in 1995, Taliban fighters again besieged the capital, which fell to them in 1996, when a strict Islamic regime was introduced. 1997 saw a Taliban offensive to establish control over the remaining third of the country. In response to the bombings of its embassies in 1998 [see, below], the United States launched missile strikes on Afghanistan – thus presaging future events.

- *USA*   The United States was centrally involved in the Gulf War of 1990–1 and later confrontations with Iraq [see below]; US marines were sent into Somalia in 1992–3 to secure the capital, Mogadishu, from control by warlords such as General Aidid (the UN took over, only leaving in 1995), and in 1994, they managed a peaceful occupation of Haiti; US troops were also involved in attempts to bring peace to the conflict in Bosnia (e.g. 1996). US forces and embassies abroad were subjected to bomb attacks in the second half of the decade [see 1996 and 1998 – when US embassies in Nairobi, Kenya, and Dar-es-Salaam, Tanzania, were bombed killing over 250 people, the chief suspect being Osama bin Laden].

But much attention during the decade was focused on domestic matters: there were severe race riots in Los Angeles in 1992, the year Bill Clinton was elected President, but in 1994 he was handicapped in his role by elections which resulted in Republican majorities in both Houses of Congress. Despite being embroiled with his wife, Hillary Clinton, in the 'Whitewater' fraud case in 1996, he was re-elected President the same year, only to be involved in the 'Zippergate' scandal (his affair with Monica Lewinsky) in 1998. He was impeached the same year, but remained President, and was acquitted in 1999.

Other domestic events which shocked the USA in this period were the FBI siege of the Branch Davidian cult HQ at Waco, Texas, in which scores died in the ensuing inferno; the trial for the murder of his wife and her friend by O. J. Simpson, the ex-US-football star, followed by the controversial not-guilty verdict (1994–5); and the huge car-bomb which destroyed the federal building in Oklahoma City in 1995 in which 167 people died and for which a right-wing US citizen, Timothy McVeigh, was arrested and convicted.

- *Iraq and the Middle East*   In 1990, the UK impounded a 'supergun' bound for *Iraq*; in the same year, the Iraqi invasion of Kuwait under President Saddam Hussein was condemned by the super-powers who began sending troops to the Gulf, and in 1991, 'Operation Desert Storm' led by the USA and UK launched the Gulf War in which Iraq was defeated and had harsh sanctions imposed upon it (including the deployment of UN weapons inspectors seeking information about Iraq's armament programme); half a million Kurdish refugees fled Iraq. Tension mounted again in 1997 when Saddam Hussein expelled six US weapons inspectors working for the UN, and in 1998, after the inspectors had been refused full access to missile sites, the Western allies launched 'Desert Fox' air-strikes on Iraq.

Elsewhere in the Middle East, Western hostages held in Beirut were freed (Brian Keenan in 1990 after 1597 days in captivity; Terry Waite and Thomas Sutherland in 1991 after 2353 days; and John McCarthy the same year after five years and three months). However, the conflict between *Israel* and the *Palestinians* continued [see, e.g., 1990, 1993, 1994, 1996, 1997], but despite the violence and the assassination in 1995 of the Israeli Prime Minister, Yitzhac Rabin, some progress was made towards a peaceful solution: in 1993, the US President, Bill Clinton, brokered a peace accord between Israel and the PLO, which allowed limited Palestinian autonomy in the Gaza Strip and West Bank [see 1993]; the PLO leader, Yasser Arafat, returned to Palestine in 1994 after 27 years in exile, was victorious in elections to inaugurate the Palestinian Authority in 1996 and became its first President, the PLO then deleting the destruction of Israel from its charter (notwithstanding attacks by Hamas and Hezbullah guerrillas the same year, and Israeli retaliatory strikes into the West Bank and Beirut). In 1997, Israel began to withdraw from Hebron after 30 years' occupation, despite suicide-bomb attacks in Israeli cities.

- *USSR/Russia*   The decade began (1990–1) with social unrest in the Soviet republics; a hard-line Communist coup which ousted President Gorbachev but then collapsed; the rapid spread of 'perestroika' [see 1985]; the dissolution of the USSR into independent states (e.g. Russia, Ukraine, Georgia, etc.), the resignation of Gorbachev as President of the Soviet Union and the election of Boris Yeltsin as President of the Russian Republic (all 1991). Russia struggled throughout the 1990s to ward off political, social and economic chaos [see, e.g., 1992, 1993, 1998], and from 1994–6, the new state invaded the breakaway 'republic' of Chechnya and bombarded its capital, Grozny; a peace agreement was signed in 1996 and Russian troops withdrew; but separatist Muslim guerrillas continued to press for independence, and in 1999, Russia again attacked Chechnya.

  Otherwise, with the Cold War ended, international relations improved and attempts were again made to introduce arms control [but see France,1995–6, and India-Pakistan, 1998]: the START treaty was finally signed in 1991 [see 1982]; and the UK Prime Minister, John Major, and President Yeltsin of Russia agreed on weapons control in 1992. In 1996, the UN endorsed a Comprehensive Test Ban Treaty for nuclear weapons; Presidents Clinton and Yeltsin met at the Helsinki Summit in 1997, the same year that NATO and Russia signed the Founding Act on Mutual Relations, Co-operation and Security – thus formally ending 50 years of hostility in Europe. 1997 also saw the Oslo and Ottawa international treaties to install a total ban on landmines (the campaign for which had been one of Princess Diana's principal causes – including visits to Angola and Bosnia in 1997, the year of her death) – however, the United States, Russia and China refused to sign.

- *Europe*   West and East Germany were reunified in 1990, and the UK joined the ERM [see UK Politics, below]; in 1991, the Maastricht Treaty was signed by EC leaders with a commitment to introduce a single European currency in 1999, but while John Major [now Prime Minister – see UK Politics, below] declared that the UK should be 'at the very heart of Europe', he retained an opt-out clause from joining either the Euro or the 'Social Chapter' (increased welfare costs to employers would threaten UK industry; in fact, because of Conservative 'Eurosceptic' opposition, fuelled by a Danish referendum rejection of the Maastricht Treaty [1992], and a very small majority after the General Election of 1992, the UK Parliament only ratified Maastricht in 1993). Financial speculation and high German interest rates forced the UK ignominiously out of the ERM on 'Black Wednesday' 1992; the EC single market was inaugurated in 1993; and because of the BSE crisis, the EC banned the export of British beef worldwide in 1996 [later revoked, but a government cull of cattle over 30 months old was instituted]. In the same year, Labour announced its intention to hold a referendum before the UK joined the European single currency [see also 1997]. On 1 January 1999, the 'Euro' was launched in 11 countries [but not in the UK]; also in 1999, economic tension between the EC and the USA grew over the importation of Caribbean rather than South American bananas (US sanctions were imposed on EC luxury goods).

  In contrast to the process of European unification, the other main narrative in Europe in the 1990s was the breakdown into ferocious civil war of the 'old' Yugoslavia (involving Serbia, Croatia,

Bosnia, and ethnic Albanians); the Serbian siege of Serajevo [see 1992, 1994] and the 'ethnic cleansing' of Bosnian Muslims (1992); the Serbian attack on Zagreb and the overunning of the UN 'safe haven' of Srebrenica, the seizing of 350 UN peacekeepers at Gorazde, the bombing of Serbia by NATO, and a Bosnian peace accord signed in Paris, with NATO to police the peace (all 1995); the discovery of mass graves near Srebrenica, the opening of a Bosnian war crimes tribunal at the Hague, and huge pro-democracy demonstrations in Serbia against President Milosevic (all 1996); the Kosovo-Serb conflict of 1998–99, in which ethnic Albanians were 'cleansed' (massacred), NATO again launched airstrikes on Serbia, President Milosevic was indicted as a war criminal, and the Federal Republic of Yugoslavia (Serbia) withdrew from Kosovo, which became an international protectorate policed by 50,000 NATO peace-keeping troops.

➲ The Environment, Health, Science and Technology

- **The Environment**   Concerns about the Environment continued to grow during the 1990s: in 1990, the UK decided that in future all new cars should run on lead-free fuel; 1992 saw the worst drought in Britain since 1745, the same year that industrial nations sought to phase out the use of CFCs as the ozone layer depleted – a process confirmed for the Northern Hemisphere in 1995, the hottest year on record at that point and taken to be proof of global warming [but see also 1997 which beat that record, when it was calculated that spring was starting eight days earlier than in the past]. In 1995, the world population was estimated to have grown by 100 million to reach 5.7 billion.

- **Health and Science**   Issues to do with Health and Science in the decade included: the continuation of the UK BSE crisis [in 1990, the Agriculture Minister, John Gummer, was seen on TV advising his four-year-old daughter to eat beef-burgers in an attempt to stem public concern); the devastation worldwide caused by AIDS (Freddie Mercury of the pop group 'Queen' died of it in 1991, the ballet-dancer, Rudolf Nureyev, in 1993), with medical experts in 1997 claiming that 40 million people would be infected by the year 2000. In 1995, the Ebola virus killed over 150 people in Zaire, the breast cancer gene was discovered, scientists announced that it was now possible to transplant pigs' organs into human beings, and in the UK the first nationwide DNA database was established.

  In 1996, the WHO began to tackle the worldwide problem of obesity, an outbreak of food-poisoning from eating cooked meat killed 12 people in Scotland, and experts claimed there was no proof of the condition 'Gulf War Syndrome'. 'Dolly the Sheep' became the first live animal to be created from a cloned cell in 1997; and from 1998, the anti-impotence drug 'Viagra' came on the market and sold in large quantities; 1998 also saw the striking-off of two doctors at Bristol Royal Infirmary responsible for the deaths of 29 children after heart surgery; and in 1999, the WHO warned of the return of tuberculosis as a worldwide threat.

- **Technology**   In Technology, achievements in space included the docking of the US space shuttle 'Discovery' with the Russian space station 'Mir' in 1995, and the landing of the US space probe 'Pathfinder' on Mars in 1997. The French and British ends of the Channel Tunnel finally joined up in 1990 (Eurotunnel was opened to rail traffic a couple of years later, and the Eurostar terminal at Waterloo Station in 1995). Use of the Internet expanded exponentially during the 1990s; and in 1995, Microsoft launched 'Windows 95' (Bill Gates became the richest man in the world), but in 1997, a US judge ordered the company to sell internet software separately from 'Windows' in order to avoid a monopoly over access to the World Wide Web. In 1996, the Hubble space telescope revealed five time more galaxies in the universe than had been estimated hitherto; the approach of the year 2000 in 1999 intensified fears of a 'millennium bug' which would cause computers to crash worldwide.

○ *UK Politics and the Economy*   the British economy was in recession in 1990, with inflation higher than at any point since the Conservatives came to power in 1979, but despite Mrs Thatcher's misgivings, her government announced that the UK would join the ERM – although not the single European currency [for the UK's relations with the EC during the 1990s, see International Context: Europe, above]. The Cabinet was split over Europe; Mrs Thatcher's Deputy Prime Minister resigned and later joined the anti-Thatcher camp in the Tory leadership election [see below]. In the same year, the Community Charge [see also 1989 and **1980s*** UK Politics and Economy, above] was introduced into England and Wales, causing bitter resentment and an anti-Poll Tax riot in London (the Major Government scrapped it for a new Property Tax in 1991). This combination of factors led to a leadership contest in the Conservative Party, which Mrs Thatcher lost after the second ballot, and she fell from power in late November 1990, with John Major becoming party leader and Prime Minister in her stead, and in the same year, the rump of the SDP under David Owen [see 1988, and 1980s* UK Politics, above] was finally wound up.

Although widely expected to lose, the Major Government, having introduced a pre-election budget which halved road tax and doubled the value of Personal Equity Plans (PEPs), was returned to power in the General Election of 1992, thus securing a fourth successive Conservative victory, albeit with a very small majority which constrained Major's policies thereafter. Neil Kinnock resigned as leader of the Labour Party (which had nevertheless improved its performance in the General Election), and was replaced by John Smith. The same year, the Labour MP, Betty Boothroyd, became the first woman Speaker of the Commons in 600 years, while Paddy Ashdown, leader of the Lib-Dems, admitted an affair with his secretary five years before (he was to resign in 1999), and David Mellor, the Conservative Heritage Secretary, resigned over a sex scandal – the first in a number of instances of 'sleaze' in British politics throughout the 1990s [see 1993, 1994, 1995, 1997, 1998].

During 1992–3, the UK economy went even deeper into recession with over three million unemployed at one point [see also UK Social Issues, below]; there was an economic crisis on 'Black Wednesday' 1992 when Britain was forced out of the ERM and interest rates were raised for a short while to 15 per cent in an effort to protect the pound. In 1993, Major dismissed his Chancellor of the Exchequer, Norman Lamont, and the government was in disarray, a situation compounded by the Conservatives' terrible local election results (1993–5) and the collapse of their local power base. In 1994, John Major introduced his 'Back to Basics' campaign on behalf of 'family values', but 'sleaze' [see above] undermined it; in 1995, the embattled Prime Minister resigned from and then rewon the party leadership; in 1996, the Tories lost their Commons majority, and Major's government struggled on until the General Election of 1997.

John Smith died suddenly in 1994, and Tony Blair succeeded him as Labour Party leader, managing the following year to persuade party members to drop 'Clause Four' (the commitment to public ownership of the means of production) from the Labour constitution, where it had been enshrined since 1918 – thus effectively launching 'New Labour'. In the General Election of 1997, the unpopularity of the Tories and Blair's successful campaigning assured that Labour won a large majority (the Conservatives lost all their seats in Scotland and Wales), and Tony Blair became Prime Minister, with Gordon Brown as Chancellor of the Exchequer. They led a 'New Labour' Government which embraced a free market economy and had learned and inherited much from the Conservative Ministries of the last 18 years.

Referenda on devolution for Scotland and Wales were held in 1997 (nearly 75 per cent of the vote in Scotland was in favour, but only 50.3 per cent in Wales); and in 1999, the first elections to the Scottish and Welsh Assemblies left Labour as the largest party in each but without an overall majority in either. The Stone of Scone, stolen by King Edward I of England in 1296, was returned from Westminster to Scotland in 1996, 700 years later. In 1998, a referendum in London voted in favour of an elected mayor and assembly, and the independent ex-Labour candidate Ken Livingstone [see 1981, 1986] later won the election.

⮕ *UK Industrial and Social Issues and Education*   Conservative policies from the 1980s continued into the early 1990s [see above for the 'Poll Tax'], with the electricity industry privatised in 1990, the railways in 1993, and coal sold off in 1994; trade union reform was further engineered by the Employment Act of 1990 [see 1988–90, and 1980s* UK Industrial Relations, above] and the Trade Union Reform and Employments Rights Act of 1993, which decreed that pre-strike ballots should be by post and no strike action should begin until seven days after the result of the ballot was announced; 26 wage councils were abolished the same year so that the market would set wage levels.

In the early 1990s, the recession [see above] meant that around three million people were unemployed, and that the rise in individual debt fuelled by the credit boom of the 1980s [see 1980s* UK Politics, above] became a serious problem for large numbers of people, as did mortgage repayments for the newly enlarged property-owning class (by mid-1992, repossessions of houses through defaulting on mortgage repayments were running at an annual rate of 75,000 and around 300,000 mortgage-holders were six months or more in arrears with payments).

Racial tension persisted throughout the decade [see, e.g., 1995, 1999], but focusing centrally on the murder of the black teenager, Stephen Lawrence, in Eltham, SE London, in 1993, and the subsequent enquiries into the police handling of the investigation [see 1997, 1998]; the Macpherson Report of 1999 found that the London police force was institutionally racist.

Anxieties about the moral fabric of late millennial Britain were focused by other crimes in the decade: two-year-old James Bulger was murdered by two 11-year-old boys; Rosemary West went on trial for the Cromwell Street, Gloucester, murders in 1995, her husband, Fred, having hanged himself in his prison cell at the beginning of the year; in 1996, a gunman at a school in Dunblane, Scotland, shot dead 16 children and a teacher; a former Tory cabinet minister, Jonathan Aitken, lost his libel case against the *Guardian* newspaper over corruption allegations in 1997, and went on trial for perjury in 1998 (he was gaoled in 1999); and Jill Dando, the TV presenter, was gunned down on her own doorstep in 1999. 1998 saw the first large-scale pro-countryside demonstration in the UK.

Issues to do with sex and gender included: in addition to the first woman Speaker in the Commons [see UK Politics, above], the vote of the Church of England Synod in favour of the ordination of women (1992), and the ordination of the first women priests in 1994; the appointment of Stella Rimmington as the first woman head of MI5 (1993); and the lifting of the 200-year-old ban on women members by cricket's ruling body, the MCC, in 1998. (Mary Robinson became the first woman President of Eire in 1990, followed by Mary McAleese in 1997.) In 1994, Parliament lowered the age of consent for homosexuals from 21 to 18, and in 1997, it was effectively lowered again from 18 to 16.

In education, the first 'league tables' for the achievements of seven-year-olds were published in 1991; in 1992, the old Polytechnics [see 1964–6] were incorporated as another group of 'new' universities; and in 1997, legislation was introduced to abolish maintenance grants for HE students and to make them pay tuition fees.

Northern Ireland   The decade opened with more IRA bomb attacks in Ulster (1990, 1992, 1993) and in mainland Britain (including the murder of Conservtive MP, Ian Gow [1990], a mortar attack on the Cabinet Office at Downing Street [1991], and devastating bombs in the City of London and one in Warrington which killed two children [1992–3]). However, with the total number of victims of 'The Troubles' killed reaching 3000 in 1992, and following the 1993 bombs, the IRA called its first ceasefire the same year, and the Irish and British Prime Ministers signed the 'Downing Street Declaration' and the 'Joint Initiative' for peace in Northern Ireland, in which a shared sovereignty was agreed which would both protect the rights of Nationalists while not forcing Unionists into a united Ireland; Sinn Féin would be included in the talks if IRA violence ceased.

In 1994, the IRA announced a full ceasefire after 25 years of guerrilla warfare, and the loyalist paramilitaries followed suit. In 1995, the two governments published a joint framework document for the future of Northern Ireland, the broadcasting ban of 1988 was lifted, and the first face-to-face talks for a quarter of a century took place between British ministers and Sinn Féin leaders. All-party talks ran into difficulties early in 1996 over the decommissioning of IRA weapons, and the ceasefire was shattered by huge bombs first at Canary Wharf in London's Docklands and then in Manchester. After the General Election of 1997, a second IRA ceasefire was announced (partly under presssure from the USA), all-party talks resumed (Tony Blair was the first UK Prime Minister to meet Sinn Féin leaders), and culminated on 10 April 1998 with the 'Good Friday Agreement' which paved the way for the resumption of provincial self-government in Northern Ireland. An Executive and an Assembly were created (first meeting in July the same year), and North–South councils were set up to consider matters of common interest.

A referendum in May 1998 showed 71 per cent of people in Ulster in favour of the Agreement, but while Blair announced an enquiry into the 'Bloody Sunday' killings of 1972, the 'Real IRA', a splinter-group opposed to the Agreement, exploded a bomb in the town centre of Omagh which killed nearly 30 people. 1999 saw the full inauguration of devolved government to the province, but disagreements between Unionists and Sinn Féin about decommissioning and the Executive were already putting the 'Good Friday Agreement' at risk.

Social and Cultural 'Signs of the Times'

• **Disasters**   Natural disasters included: continuing famine in the Horn of Africa, with an estimated seven million people at risk in Sudan in 1991; further cyclones and widespread flooding in Bangladesh [see 1991, 1998]; severe flooding in the US Midwest (1993); major earthquakes in Los Angeles (1994), Kobe, Japan – in which over 4000 people perished (1995), and a devastating one in Columbia (1999).

Man-made disasters (excluding Bosnia, Kosovo and Rwanda – see above, International Contexts: Europe, and Africa) included: a huge oil slick in the Gulf as a consequence of the war and the fires raging in the Kuwaiti oil-fields as Iraqi troops withdrew (1991); Windsor Castle severely damaged by fire (1992); extensive oil damage in the Shetland Isles from the wrecked tanker 'Braer' (1993); the death of over 900 people when the car-ferry 'Estonia' sank in the Baltic

Sea (1994); a fire on a freight train in the Channel Tunnel (1996); the death of over 200 Muslim pilgrims in an encampment fire at Mecca, Saudi Arabia, and of Princess Diana in a car crash in Paris (1997); and a fire in the Mont Blanc Tunnel between France and Italy in which 40 people died (1999).

- **The Royals**   In 1992, Andrew Morton's controversial book, *Diana: Her True Story*, was published, and it was announced that Prince Charles and Pricess Diana were to separate; while the Queen agreed to pay income and capital gains tax from 1993. Princess Diana was interviewed on BBC TV's 'Panorama' programme about her marriage to Prince Charles in 1995, and the Queen called for a royal divorce; in 1996, the Prince and Princess agreed to divorce, as did the Duke and Duchess of York ('Fergie'). The Queen and Duke of Edinburgh made a less than successful visit to India in 1997, the same year that Princess Diana was killed in the Paris car crash; and in 1999, it was estimated that 200 million people worldwide watched the wedding of Prince Edward and Sophie Rhys-Jones (the Duke and Duchess of Wessex) on TV.

- **Sport**   Footballer, Paul Gascoigne ('Gazza'), wept on England's defeat by West Germany in the World Cup of 1990; US boxer, Mike Tyson, was sentenced to six years in gaol for rape; and in an England–West Indies test match, Brian Lara became the highest scoring batsman in test history. In 1997, the Grand National horse race was postponed because of the threat of IRA bombs; and in 1999, the UK Government prevented BSkyB's takeover bid for Manchester United FC, the same year that the club won the 'treble' (FA Cup, UK Premiership and European Champions Cup).

- **Popular Music**   1990 saw the Royal Opera House, Covent Garden, cancelling new productions because of a £4 million deficit (in 1998, it had to close for a year because of another financial crisis), and West End musicals were also in trouble, but the 'Three Tenors' concert for the World Cup in Rome was a great success. In 1991, Mozart's operas were widely performed in bicentennial celebrations, Princess Diana attended Pavrotti's free thirtieth-anniversary celebration concert in Hyde Park, Placido Domino sang in Windsor Great Park, and Bryan Adams's single '(Everything I Do) I Do It for You' had a record-breaking 16 weeks at Number One in the charts. In 1992, Madonna published her book of photographs, *Sex*; the musical 'Sunset Boulevard' opened in London in 1993; 350,000 people attended the twenty-fifth anniversary of the original Woodstock pop concert at Saugerties, New York State, in 1994; in 1997, Elton John's tribute to Princess Diana, 'Candle in the Wind', sold 31.8 million copies in a month to become the best-selling single ever; and in 1999, Sir Simon Rattle became conductor of the Berlin Symphony Orchestra.

- **Cultural Events**   In 1993–4, legislation was passed allowing shops to open on Sundays, and in 1994, the first draw in the UK National Lottery occurred (a record jackpot of £42 million was won in 1996). The comic *Viz* became a best-selling magazine in 1991, while *Punch* closed in 1992 after 150 years; Damien Hirst's art-work comprising a preserved shark in a tank was exhibited in 1991, and in 1993, the Whitney Biennial Exhibition in New York was seen as a Postmodernist* landmark in the visual arts. The replica Globe Theatre opened on London's South Bank in 1996; 10 million 'Tamagotchi' toys were sold in 1997; in 1998–9, some ten years after it was imposed, the *fatwa* on the novelist, Salman Rushdie, was lifted, and the UK and Iran could once again exchange ambassadors; but what more fitting moment and symbolic Postmodern* artefact with which to end this chronicle of 500 years of history and cultural production than the opening of the Millennium Dome at Greenwich, London, as the year 2000 ticked towards us.

9.4 POSTMODERNISM / POSTMODERNITY / POSTMODERN

As with their ostensibly relational term, Modernism* [see Chapter 6], the concepts under consideration here are exceedingly difficult to define with any degree of precision or agreement in respect of chronology, meaning or application. What follows, therefore, is a partial (in both senses of the word) working definition of the terms which attempts to distil the more generally accepted characteristics they imply, whilst recognising that the definition would undoubtedly be challenged by others in both scope and substance.

Although the terms have a longer lexical history, their prevalent usage occurs in the **Post-(WW II) Period*** [see Chapter 7; some critics nevertheless perceive 'postmodern' features in the cultural production of earlier periods]. Commentators also differ as to whether the whole period since 1945 should be considered 'postmodern' (some date its beginnings in the 1950s – especially in architecture; others from the cultural revolutions of the 1960s – for example, in 'Pop Art'; others from the economic and social problems of the 1970s; and others again as specifically characterising the 1980s and 1990s). The present definition will take it that Postmodernism is a post-war phenomenon, but one whose features are most clealy apparent in the last two decades of the 20th Century – as evidenced by the plethora of theoretical and critical books on the subject [see timeline tables: Theory/Crit.].

While often used interchangeably, it is helpful to distinguish between the three terms – if only simplistically. 'Postmodern' and 'Postmodernity' are best used to describe the social conditions and developments in post-war 'late-capitalist' economies and advanced media societies, reserving 'Postmodernism' for cognate movements in the general culture and in the arts (for, like Modernism, it is both international and inflected variously in different art forms). In this way the world of Reaganite and Thacherite economics, information and communications technology, the Gulf War, global warming, AIDS and genetic engineering may be termed 'Postmodern', while self-reflexivity, playfulness, parody, pastiche and bricolage in the arts can be described as 'Postmodernist'. The focus here will be on this last term.

What is the force of the 'Post' in 'Postmodernism', and what is Postmodernism's relationship to 'Modernism'? Once again commentators differ, most especially over whether the term seems to denote a later continuation of Modernism (merely describing developments which succeed and extend Modernism's main achievements), or a radical break with its dominant aesthetic and ideological features. Equally, depending on one's point of view, Postmodernism displays either an abhorrent commodification of culture and a cynical denial of tradition and value (as enshrined in canonic Modernist texts), or a welcome release from the stagnant orthodoxies of 'high culture' and a newly democratic resurgence of creative diversity. The definition offered below will be seen to comprise a composite but modified version of these two positions.

Postmodernist theories (in tandem with Poststructuralism; see Theory/Crit. in the timeline tables for examples of this cognate theoretical field) tend to posit the discursive nature of all experience, and the impossibility, therefore, of arriving at any absolute certainty or truth (hence, perhaps, the apposite indeterminacy of the concept itself). What Jean-François Lyotard, in *The Postmodern Condition* (see 1984: Lyotard [1979]), called the 'grand narratives' of social and intellectual progress initiated by the Enlightenment are discredited, since any grounding of such ideas in notions of 'history' or 'reality' is no longer possible in the comprehensively 'textualised' world of images and simulations which characterises the contemporary age. Equally, when Jean Baudrillard (see 1983: Baudrillard [1981]) proposes that the modern condition means the 'loss of the real' – that history and reality, in our hyper-real world of images and simulations, have been replaced by 'simulacra' (the dictionary definition of a simulacrum is 'a thing made to resemble some other thing, an inferior or deceptive likeness'; in other words, for Baudrillard, a deceptively 'real' representation of an always already unreal 'reality') – then knowing anything substantively becomes deeply problematical. To put it another way, in the world of conspicuous consumerism and advanced technologies driven by late 20th-Century monopoly capitalism, all meaning – political, religious, historical, social, cultural – is replaced by pastiche and style: a world of hollow and empty signifiers, a ceaseless procession of chimerical images. The fundamental political and cultural pessimism such thinking may imply none the less signals a 'condition' that does coincide with aspects of late-millennial life: Baudrillard may have been tastelessly *outré* in suggesting that the Gulf War of 1991 'Did Not Take Place', but his perception of it as a media event, a TV simulation, was not without point (see 1991: Baudrillard).

A Marxist critique of Postmodernism, but one which nevertheless seems to confirm its principal characteristics, is Fredric Jameson's *Postmodernism, or the Cultural Logic of Late Capitalism* (see 1991: Jameson; the title essay was first published in 1984). Jameson sees a fundamental connection between the 'electronic and nuclear-powered' technology of the multinational global economy and the 'depthless', fragmented, random and heterogeneous style of Postmodernist culture. Such a commodity culture, he claims, is no longer rebuffed or parodied (as it might be in Modernism), but directly incorporated into Postmodern art (as, for example, in Andy Warhol's paintings of Campbell's soup cans): it is, in effect, 'pastiche' (or 'blank parody'), the imitation of another style without any critical distance on the process of recycling, since the absolute extension of the commodity system obviates any recourse to discourses outside it which would allow for appraisal or critique: the parody, then, *becomes* the thing parodied.

The artist, so the argument runs, in the continuous present made available by computers and media technologies, can only resort to mimicry of other styles (often from the past: 'recycled images') without purpose, irony or satire, but merely as a form of 'nostalgia' which represents, not the 'real' past, but only our ideas and stereotypes of it (as promoted by the heritage industry, for example, or television's 'classic' historical dramas and adaptations). This tendency, therefore, also endows present reality and history with a glossy patina of its own simulated and fallacious past. The crucial distinction between Modernism* and Postmodernism seems to lie here: for where the former's formal experiments were intended to give a fuller and more truthful account of reality, and its artistic production to propagate aesthetic, moral and cultural values in the face of a modern alienating mass civilisation, the latter cannot recognise a 'real' reality to be accessed behind the factitious representations of it and can assume no stable premises in which to ground value. In other words, in a world dominated by the threat of annihilation by nuclear holocaust (in Martin Amis's view, the only experience of this we can conceivably have is the one we are currently living through – that is, waiting for it to happen), the End of History becomes the only 'reality' and one which negates any humanistic notions of progress, futurity or human agency. All that remains for us is a conspicuous display of Postmodern 'playfulness'.

However, despite such an apparently passive and pessimistic disposition, favourable arguments for Postmodernism are made in a number of ways, not least by acknowledging the knowing self-consciouness of much of its artistic production which the above account would seem to deny:

First, if indeed its depiction of the contemporary world is recognisable in terms of our experience of living in it, then Postmodernist representation of it may help us, by a paradoxical twist, to understand it better (hence becoming a new form of mimesis or 'realism'!): a pastiche of commodification, for example, may expose the ways in which that process works upon us.

Second, Postmodernism's characteristic postures offer a critique of essentialist and exclusive models of the human subject in their tendency to 'decentre' unitary and normative conceptions of sexual, ethnic, racial and cultural identity, thus having close affiliations with the politicised theoretical and artistic agendas of Feminism and Postcolonialism and of African-American, Women-of-Colour, Lesbian, Gay and Queer theory and writing.

Third, Postmodernism's self-ironic eclecticism, especially in its importation of tropes from popular cultural forms, has challenged the exclusiveness of Modernist and other high art movements, and has at once widened the range of imagery available to be drawn on and forged immediate and direct relations with the contemporary environment.

Fourth, and in connection, its celebration of the endless 'play' of signification in any discursive 'simulacrum' encourages a kind of anarchic freedom in the 'depthless' provisionality of the (re)cycling of signifiers.

In both these last two respects, Postmodernism, whilst also helping to define current manifestations of modernity, has also radically challenged the hegemony of high culture (so that 'Literature', for example, becomes merely one set of discursive texts in the 'technological' continuum of popular-cultural production and reproduction of all forms of art). To take just one example of this transgressive tendency (from the visual arts): the reproduction of cartoon-strip images in the 'Pop' paintings of Roy Lichtenstein are visually striking in themselves and – while not necessarily ironically exposing the 'crudity' and 'commercialism' of the source material, as Modernism might have done – they neverthelss simultaneously defamiliarise the cartoon form and celebrate its potential as a source of dynamic contemporary iconography.

British Postmodernist Fiction

In the international literary context, the impact of Postmodernism has been seen most extensively in fiction, where a roll-call of novelists would include: John Barth, Thomas Pynchon, Donald Barthelme, William Burroughs, Alain Robbe-Grillet, Marguerite Duras, Carlos Fuentes, Gunter Grass, Gabriel García Màrquez, Isabel Allende, Jorge Luis Borges, J. M. Coetzee and Toni Morrison. This is true, too, of contemporary British writing, although plays like Mark Ravenhill's *Fucking and Shopping* and Sarah Kane's *Blasted* in the 1990s, with their 'commodified' display of sex and violence, would be examples of Postmodernist drama.

Among the principal characteristics of British Postmodernist fiction are: the strategic exposure of the fallacy of 'realism'; an exuberant promotion of the non-representational, and the deployment of fictive modes like fantasy, gothic, fabulation and magic realism; self-reflexivity and self-referentiality about writing fiction ('metafiction'); a teasing disturbance of fictional conventions such as 'character' and 'plot', and a reluctance to release the 'meaning' of the text; a concern with the fictional writing/re-writing of history ('historiographic metafiction'; see 1989: Linda Hutcheon); the 're-vision' (re-casting in modern form) of canonic novels from the past; the celebration of sexual, racial and regional identity and diversity; immersion in the imagery and texture of contemporary urban existence; the notation, prior to the year 2000, of millennial angst and fear of apocalypse; and a self-conscious delight in style – in the artifice of writing itself, whether it be playful, provocative, introspective, heteroglossic, demotic, mannered, minimalist or pyrotechnical.

Timelines: 1980–2000

PERIOD	YEAR	INTERNATIONAL AND POLITICAL CONTEXTS	SOCIAL AND CULTURAL CONTEXTS	AUTHORS	INDICATIVE TITLES
	1980	Gvnmt intros radical monetarist & industrial relations policies: cut public spending & sell off nationalised industries – budget lowers personal taxes but almost doubles VAT – Employment Act imposes restrictions [e.g. no secondary picketing] on trades unions [v.1982, 1988–90] – inflation hits 21.8% – over 2m. unemployed [highest since 1935] – trade-union 'Day of Action' results; Housing Act gives tenants 'right to buy' their council houses; Callaghan retires – Michael Foot, Lab. leader; Iranian Embassy siege with hostages in London – SAS end it; NATO to base US 'Cruise' missiles in UK; 60,000-strong anti-nuclear demonstration in UK; internment abolished in N. Ireland – [–1981] 'H-Block' hunger strikes by IRA prisoners in Maze prison; ZANU party wins 57 of 63 seats in Rhodesian elections – Robert Mugabe, PM of independent Zimbabwe; Ronald Reagan, US President; USA, W. Germany, China & Japan boycott Moscow Olympics in protest at Soviet invasion of Afghanistan – Islamic conference demands withdrawal; Gdansk shipyard strikes in Poland lead to independent trade union federation, 'Solidarity'; c.1.3m. refugees from war in Ethiopia enter Somalia – 10m. face famine in E. Africa; WHO announces eradication of smallpox; UNESCO reports that ⅓ of world's population cannot read or write; [>] growth of 'Green' [ecology] Parties in Europe [v.1989]	6d. pieces no longer legal tender; over 120 killed in collapse of floating hostel for N. Sea oil-rig workers; UK breakfast TV franchise set up; Humber Bridge completed [opens 1981]; Covent Garden market re-opens as shopping centre; Björn Borg wins Wimbledon men's singles for 5th consecutive year. **Int. Lit.:** Coetzee, *Waiting for the Barbarians*; Marge Piercy, *Vida* [US novel]; Jane Smiley, *Barn Blind* [US novel]; Christopher Hope, *A Separate Development* [SA novel]. **Music:** 2-mth strike by BBC musicians over plan to scrap 5 orchestras; John Lennon murdered in USA; Glass, 'Satyagraha'; Marley, 'Uprising' [album]. **Film:** Comino, 'Heaven's Gate' [Kristofferson, J. Hurt]; Kubrick, 'The Shining' [Nicholson, Duvall]; Lynch, 'The Elephant Man' [Hopkins, Hurt, Bancroft, Gielgud]; Scorsese, 'Raging Bull' ['Star Wars' sequel]; John Landis, 'The Blues Brothers' [Aretha Franklin, Ray Charles, James Brown et al]; Alan Parker, 'Fame'. **Theory/Crit:** Michèle Barrett, *Women's Oppression Today: Problems in Marxist Feminist Analysis*; Catherine Belsey, *Critical Practice*; Pierre Bourdieu, *The Logic of Practice*; Stanley Fish, *Is There a Text in This Class?*; Foucault, *Power/Knowledge* [(1977); Eng. trans]; Gérard Genette, *Narrative Discourse*; Stephen Greenblatt, *Renaissance Self-Fashioning*; Geoffrey Hartman, *Criticism in the Wilderness*; Barbara Johnson, *The Critical Difference*; Annette Kolodny, 'Dancing Through the Minefield'; A. Rich, 'Compulsory Heterosexuality and Lesbian Existence'; Dale Spender, *Man Made Language*; R. Williams, *Problems in Materialism and Culture*	**P:** Heaney Muldoon Paulin Lynton Kwesi Johnson (b.1952; Jamaica) Medbh McGuckian (b.1950; Ulster) **Pr/F:** Bowen Burgess Chatwin Drabble Golding Greene Jordan Le Carré Lodge Murdoch Weldon Wilson Penelope Lively (b.1933) Adam Mars-Jones (b.1954) Bernard MacLaverty (b.1942; Ulster) Graham Swift (b.1949) **Dr:** Ayckbourn Brenton Frayn Friel Russell Storey **Lit. 'Events':**	*Selected Poems, 1865–1975* *Why Brownlee Left* *The Strange Museum* *Inglan Is a Bitch* *Single Ladies: Sixteen Poems & Portrait of Joanna* *Collected Stories* *Earthly Powers* *The Viceroy of Ouidah* [travel] *The Middle Ground* *Rites of Passage* [1st of trilogy*; Booker] *Dr Fischer of Vienna & Ways of Escape* [autobiog.] *The Past* [novel] *Smiley's People* [novel; TV ser., 1981] *How Far Can You Go?* *Nuns and Soldiers* *Puff Ball* *Setting the World on Fire* *Judgement Day* [novel] *Lantern Lecture* [stories] *Lamb* [novel] *The Sweet Shop Owner* [novel] *Season's Greetings* *The Romans in Britain* *Make and Break* *Translations* *Educating Rita* [film, 1983] *Early Days* RSC's *Nicholas Nickleby* pf.d [adaptn by David Edgar]
	1981	Unemployment reaches 2.5m. – Liverpool-London 'People's March for Jobs'; budget announces cuts in defence spending, grants to universities & number of student places; Lab. Party & TUC Conferences vote for unilateral nuclear disarmament [v.1989] – Lab. electoral college estab.d to select leader – 'Gang of Four' [ex-Ministers Roy Jenkins, Shirley Williams, David Owen & William Rodgers] leave Lab. & fnd Social	Royal Wedding of Charles & Diana [750m. watch it worldwide on TV]; C of E votes to ordain women as deacons; [–1982] Women's Peace Camp set up at Greenham Common US airforce base, Berkshire, where Cruise missiles are to be stockpiled – 150,000 demonstrate in London against their siting; 1st woman elected a fellow of All Souls College, Oxford – 1st woman cox in Oxford & Cambridge Boat Race; 1st London Marathon; cheap home computers	**P:** Dunn Harrison Motion Patten Plath C. Raine K. Raine Tomlinson	*St Kilda's Parliament* *Continuous, A Kumquat for John Keats & U.S. Martial* *Independence* *Love Poems* *Collected Poems* [ed. Ted Hughes] *A Free Translation* *Collected Poems* *The Flood*

CONTEMPORARY

Democratic Party (SDP) – form alliance with Libs [Jenkins becomes party leader, 1982]; London Docklands Development Corporation set up to regenerate E. London; 50 UK pits employing 30,000 miners to close – unofficial stoppages reverse gvnmt decision to remove subsidies – Arthur Scargill becomes National President of NUM; British Nationality Act restricts right to live in Britain to British citizens; serious rioting in Brixton, Southall, Toxteth & Moss Side – 13 black youths burnt to death in Deptford fire ('New Cross Massacre'); 'Yorkshire Ripper' (Peter Sutcliffe) sentenced to life; [May] Maze hunger-striker, Bobby Sands, recently elected Tyrone MP, dies – [Oct.] 10th prisoner dies – hunger strikes called off; anti-nuclear demonstrationa across Europe & in USA; François Mitterrand, President of France; 'Solidarity' strikes in Poland – martial law imposed – US economic sanctions; US Embassy hostages in Teheran freed after 444 days; Pres. Sadat of Egypt assassinated; Israel bombs nuclear reactor in Bahdad – annexes Golan Heights – bombs Beirut – intense fighting in Lebanon; [c.] 1st reports of AIDS widely available – IBM intros PC; [>] cable TV intro.d into UK. **Int. Lit.:** Morrison, *Tar Baby*; Updike, *Rabbit is Rich* [*]; Vidal, *Creation*; Carey, *Bliss* [novel]; Gillian Slovo, *The Betrayal* [SA novel] & *Ties of Blood*; Márquez, *Chronicle of a Death Foretold* [Eng. trans, 1982]. **Music:** Lloyd Webber, 'Cats' [musical of T.S. Eliot's 'Old Possum' poems]; Bob Marley dies aged 36; Rolling Stones, 'Tattoo You' [album]; MacMillan, 'Isadora' [ballet]. **Art:** 'New Spirit of Painting' exhibition, London; Warhol, 'Dollar Signs' [silkscreen]; Anish Kapoor, 'To Reflect an Intimate Part of the Red' [mixed media installation, London]. **Film:** Boorman, 'Excalibur' [H. Mirren, N. Terry, N. Williamson]; Spielberg, 'Raiders of the Lost Ark' [H. Ford, K. Allen; 1st in 'Indiana Jones' trilogy – sequels, 1984, 1989]; Weir, 'Gallipoli' [M. Gibson]; Bill Forsyth [UK], 'Gregory's Girl'; Hugh Hudson [UK], 'Chariots of Fire' [script by Colin Welland]; 'Brideshead Revisted' [TV adaptn of Waugh novel by John Mortimer]. **Theory/Crit:** Bakhtin, *The Dialogic Imagination: Four Essays* (1975); Eng. trans]; Hélène Cixous, 'The Laugh of the Medusa' & 'Sorties' ((1975); Eng. trans] in Elaine Marks & Isabelle de Courtivron (eds), *New French Feminisms*; Culler, *The Pursuit of Signs*; Derrida, *Dissemination & Positions* [(1972); Eng. trans]; Eagleton, *Walter Benjamin or Towards a Revolutionary Criticism*; Roger Fowler, *Literature as Social Discourse*; Hartman, *Saving the Text*; bell hooks, *Ain't I A Woman: Black Women and Feminism*; Jameson, *The Political Unconscious*; Cherríe Moraga & Gloria Anzaldúa, *This Bridge Called My Back: Writings by Radical Women of Color*; Williams, *Culture*; Wittig, 'One Is Not a Woman Born'; Robert Young (ed.), *Untying the Text: A Post-Structuralist Reader* [incls Foucault, 'The Order of Discourse' (1970)]

D.J. Enright (1920–2002) — *Collected Poems*

Pr/F: M. Amis — *Other People: a Mystery*
Banville — *Kepler*
McEwan — *The Comfort of Strangers* [novel]
Moore — *The Temptation of Eileen Hughes*
O'Faolain — *Collected Stories*
Osborne — *A Better Class of Person* [autobiog.]
Spark — *Loitering with Intent* [novel]
Swift — *Shuttlecock* [novel]
D.M. Thomas — *The White Hotel*
Julian Barnes (b.1946) — *Metroland* [novel]
William Boyd (b.1952) — *A Good Man in Africa* [novel]
Alasdair Gray (b.1934; Scotland) — *Lanark: A Life in Four Books* [novel]
Caryl Phillips (b.1958; St Kitts) — *Strange Fruit* [novel]
Jonathan Raban (b.1942) — *Old Glory* [travel]
Salman Rushdie (b.1947; India) — *Midnight's Children* [Booker]

Dr: Ayckbourn — *Making Tracks*
Bond — *Restoration*
N. Dunn — *Steaming*
Gray — *Quartermaine's Terms*
Nichols — *Passion Play*
Stoppard — *On the Razzle*
Wells — *Anyone for Denis?*

Lit. 'Events': Peter Hall's *The Oresteia* at National Theatre [adaptn by Tony Harrison]

1982

Pope visits UK [1st since 1531]; Falklands War: [Ap.] Argentina invades Falkland Islands – UK 'task force' dispatched – HMS 'Sheffield' sunk – UK sinks 'General Belgrano' – [June] Argentines surrender to UK troops at Port Stanley – fighting ends; 3.25m. unemployed in UK; 2nd Employment Act places tight restrictions on unions & 'closed shops' [v.1980, 1988–90]; Lab. Party to expel members of Militant Tendency; Britoil & Cable & Wireless privatised; BT telephone monopoly ended [v.1983]; Laker Airways ('Skytrain') & De Lorean car co. fail; IRA bombs in Hyde Park & Regent's Park, London, kill soldiers, & civilians in Ballykelly; [Dec.] 30,000 women demonstrate at Greenham Common; Strategic Arms Reduction Talks (START) open in Geneva [v.1991]; European Court bans corporal 3 regional commercial TV services & 4th BBC TV channel inaugurated [Channel 4 to use both English & Welsh & aim progs at multicultural minority audiences]; Sinclair produces the ZX Spectrum, biggest-selling UK-designed computer; [>] rapid developments in genetic engineering & computer games; 1st compact discs on sale; Barbican Centre & Thames Barrier, Woolwich, completed; Henry VIII's flagship 'Mary Rose' raised in Solent [sank, 1545]. **Int. Lit.:** Bellow, *The Dean's December*; Atwood, *Bodily Harm*; Keneally, *Schindler's Ark* [Booker Prize; Steven Spielberg film (as 'Schindler's List'), 1993]; Alice Walker, *You Can't Keep a Good Woman Down* [stories]. **Music:** Michael Jackson, 'Thriller' [album; by 1984, sells 35–40m. copies]. **Art:** National Black Art Convention held in UK – MAAS

P: Fanthorpe — *Standing To*
Fuller — *The Individual and His Times: Selected Poems*
Gunn — *The Passages of Joy*
Jennings — *Celebrations and Elegies*
MacBeth — *Poems from Oby*
McGough — *Waving at Trains*
McGuckian (b.1949) — *The Flower Master*
Mahon — *The Hunt by Night*
James Fenton (b.1949) — *The Memory of War: Poems 1968–1982* [& *Children in Exile*, 1983]
Adrian Mitchell (b.1932) — *For Beauty Douglas: Adrian Mitchell's Collected Poems 1953–1979*
Edwin Morgan (b.1920; Scotland) — *Poems of Thirty Years*

Pr/F: Barnes — *Before She Met Me*
Boyd — *An Ice-Cream War*

PERIOD	YEAR	INTERNATIONAL AND POLITICAL CONTEXTS	SOCIAL AND CULTURAL CONTEXTS	AUTHORS	INDICATIVE TITLES
		punishment in schools; Spain joins NATO – opens frontier with Gibraltar to pedestrians; Brezhnev dies – Andropov, Soviet President; food riots in Poland – 'Solidarity' banned; Canada Bill gains Royal Assent – new constitution finally frees it of UK Parliament; Israel returns Sinai to Egypt [occupied since 1967]; Israel invades Lebanon – Beirut besieged – PLO & Syrian forces begin withdrawal – Palestinians massacred by Lebanese Xian militia in refugee camps; [>] growing concern worldwide about all aspects of environmental pollution & endangered species	[v.1976] pubs 1st national register of black artists & cross-cultural arts magazine, *Artrage*; 'Zeitgeist' art exhibition, Berlin. **Film:** Attenborough, 'Gandhi' [B. Kingsley, J. Gielgud, T. Howard, J. Mills]; Bergman, 'Fanny and Alexander'; Coppola, 'One From The Heart' [Kinski]; Spielberg, 'E.T. The Extra-Terrestrial' & [with Tobe Hooper], 'Poltergeist'; Tony Garnett, 'Handgun' ("Deep in the Heart"); Ted Kotcheff, 'First Blood' [Stallone; 1st Rambo movie]; Alan J. Pakula, 'Sophie's Choice' [Streep, K. Kline; adptn of William Styron novel]; Sydney Pollack, 'Tootsie' [Hoffman, J. Lange]; Ridley Scott, 'Blade Runner' [H. Ford]; 'Barchester Chronicles' [TV adptn of Trollope]. **Theory/Crit:** Barthes, *A Barthes Reader* [ed. Susan Sontag]; Centre for Contemporary Cultural Studies, Birmingham University, *The Empire Strikes Back: Race and Racism in '70s Britain*; Culler, *On Deconstruction*; Derrida, *White Mythology* [Eng. trans]; Eagleton, *The Rape of Clarissa*; Shoshana Felman (ed.), *Literature and Psychoanalysis*; Genette, *Figures of Literary Discourse*; Hans Jauss, *Towards an Aesthetic of Reception*; Kristeva, *The Powers of Horror* [(1980); Eng. trans]; Hillis Miller, *Fiction and Repetition*; Christopher Norris, *Deconstruction*; Michael Ryan, *Marxism and Deconstruction*; Todorov, *Introduction to Poetics* [Eng. trans]; Sontag, *A Susan Sontag Reader* [ed., Elizabet Hardwick]; Alice Walker, *In Search of Our Mothers' Gardens: Womanist Prose*; Wittig, 'The Category of Sex'	Burgess Chatwin Fowles Greene Plath Weldon Peter Ackroyd (b.1949) Kazuo Ishiguro (b.1954; Japan) Timothy Mo (b.1950; Hong Kong) Marina Warner (b.1946) **Dr:** Ayckbourn Bennett Bond Churchill Frayn Hampton Hare Nichols Pinter Stoppard Lit. **'Events':**	*The End of the World News* *On the Black Hill* [novel] *Mantissa* *Monsignor Quixote* *The Journals of Sylvia Plath* [ed. Ted Hughes] *The President's Child* *The Great Fire of London* [novel] *A Pale View of Hills* [novel] *Sour Sweet* [novel] *The Skating Party* [fiction] *Way Upstream* [pub.d 1983] *Objects of Affection* [5 TV plays] *Summer* *Top Girls* *Noises Off* *Tales from Hollywood* *A Map of the World* *Poppy* [musical play] *Other Places* [3 short pieces] *The Real Thing* New British Library building in Euston Rd approved; RSC moves to Barbican – opens with Nichols's *Poppy* [v. above]
	1983	Pre-election budget increases tax allowances & mortgage loans eligible for interest relief; inflation [3.7%] lowest for 15 yrs – unemployment falls; Gen. Elec.: Lab. manifesto proposes nuclear disarmament & withdrawal from EEC [v.1989] – Cons re-elected with increased majority – Thatcher, PM – Libs & SDP gain 25% of vote & win 23 seats; Foot & Jenkins resign as party leaders – replaced by Neil Kinnock, Lab. & David Owen, SDP; High Court upholds doctors' right to prescribe 'the Pill' to under-16s without parents' consent; enquiry into high incidence of cancer around Sellafield nuclear power station; Gerry Adams, President of Sinn Féin & MP for W. Belfast – 134 IRA prisoners in mass break-out at the Maze – IRA car-bomb explodes outside Harrods, London, killing 5; 1st Cruise missiles arrive at Greenham Common – anti-nuclear demonstrations culminate in ¼m. rally in Hyde Park – huge anti-nuclear protests elsewhere in Europe; Pres. Reagan calls USSR the 'evil empire' &	1st UK heart & lung transplant; £1 coin 1st intro.d; £25m. gold bars stolen from Brinks-Mat in UK; Irish 1981 Derby winner, Shergar, kidnapped – £2m. ransom demand; seat-belts compulsory in UK – wheel-clamping intro.d in London; BBC TV's 'Breakfast Time' [1st UK early morning prog.]. **Int. Lit.:** Mamet, *Glengarry Glen Ross* [play]; Theroux, *The Kingdom by the Sea* [travel in UK]; Coetzee, *Life and Times of Michael K* [Booker Prize]; Walker, *The Color Purple* [novel; Steven Spielberg film, 1985]; William Kennedy, *Ironweed* [US novel]; Neil Simon, *Brighton Beach Memoirs* [US play; 1st in trilogy]. **Art:** MAAS Nicholas Gage, *Eleni* [US biog. history]. **Art:** MAAS – exclusively 'Black-Art' Gallery opens – Committee of Asian Artists (CAA) organises alternative 'Festival of India'; Duane Hanson [constr.] 'Bus Stop Lady' [mixed media lifesize figure]. **Film:** Allen, 'Zelig' [Farrow]; Coppola, 'Rumble Fish' [Hopper, M. Dillon, M. Rourke]; Gilliam & Jones, 'Monty Python's The	**P:** Davie Fuller G. Hill Hughes MacCaig Motion Muldoon Paulin R.S. Thomas Fleur Adcock (b.1934; NZ) John Agard (b.1949, Guyana) Grace Nichols (b.1950; Guyana) Peter Porter (b.1929; Australia) J.[eremy] H. Prynne (b.1936)	*Collected Poems, 1971–1983* *The Beautiful Inventions* *The Mystery of the Charity of Charles Péguy* *River* *A World of Difference* *Secret Narratives* *Quoof* *Liberty Tree* *Later Poems, A Selection* *Selected Poems* [further coll., 2000] *Limbo Dancer in Dark Glasses* *i is a long-memoried woman* [poem sequence; film, 1990] *Collected Poems* *Poems*

CONTEMPORARY

1983

proposes 'Star Wars' missile shield in space; USA supports Contra rebels against marxist Sandinista gvnmt in Nicaragua; suicide lorry-bombs in Beirut wreck US marine base [241 killed], US Embassy & Fr. barracks of UN 'peace-keeping' troops [58 killed]; Iran launches major offensive across Iraq border; racial violence between Sinhalese & Tamils in Sri Lanka; AIDS affects 2000 in USA – spreads to Europe

Meaning of Life' [Cleese et al]; Scorsese, 'The King of Comedy' [De Niro; J. Lewis]; Richard Marquand, 'Return of the Jedi' [3rd 'Star Wars' movie]; Lewis Gilbert [UK], 'Educating Rita' [Caine, J. Walters, M. Lipman; Willy Russell adptn of his play]; 'Peter Greenaway [UK], 'The Draughtsman's Contract' [J. Suzman]; John MacKenzie [UK], 'The Long Good Friday' [Hoskins, Mirren; script by Barrie Keefe]; Barbra Streisand, 'Yentl' [script by Jack Rosenthal]; Peter Yates [UK], 'The Dresser' [Finney, Coutenay, E. Fox,]; Loach, 'Questions of Leadership' [UK TV documentary series banned on political grounds]

Theory /Crit: Benedict Anderson, *Imagined Communities*; Baudrillard, *Simulacra and Simulations* [(1981); Eng. trans]; Eagleton, *Literary Theory: an Introduction*; Lisa Jardine, *Still Harping on Daughters: Women and Drama in the Age of Shakespeare*; Kermode, *The Art of Telling*; Jerome McGann, *A Critique of Modern Textual Criticism*; Norris, *The Deconstructive Turn*; Riffaterre, *Text Production*; Said, *The World, the Text and the Critic*; B. Smith (ed.), *Home Girls: A Black Feminist Anthology*; R. Williams, *Towards 2000*

Lit. 'Events': William Golding, Nobel Prize for Literature

Pr/F: Ackroyd — *The Last Testament of Oscar Wilde*
Bradbury — *Rates of Exchange*
Deighton — *Berlin Game* [1st in Game, Set and Match trilogy (–1986)]
Fairbairns — *Stand We At Last*
Fuller — *Flying to Nowhere* [novel]
S. Hill — *The Woman in Black* [also a play]
Jordan — *The Dream of a Beast* [novel]
Le Carré — *The Little Drummer Girl*
McIlvanney — *The Papers of Tony Veitch*
MacLaverty — *Cal* [Pat O'Connor film, 1984]
Roberts — *The Visitation*
Rushdie — *Shame*
Selvon — *Moses Migrating*
Swift — *Waterland*
Tennant — *Woman Beware Woman*
Trevor — *Fools of Fortune & The Stories of William Trevor*
Weldon — *The Life and Loves of a She-Devil*
Howard Jacobson (b.1942) — *Coming From Behind* [novel]
James Kelman (b.1946, Scotland) — *Not Not While the Giro, and Other Stories*
Dr: Barker — *Victory & Crimes in Hot Countries*
Bennett — *An Englishman Abroad* [on TV]
Brenton — *The Genius*
Churchill — *Fen*
Edgar — *Maydays*
Russell — *Blood Brothers*
Alan Bleasdale (b.1946) — *Boys from the Blackstuff* [5 TV plays]

1984

[–1985] miners' strike: violent clashes with strike-breaking miners at Notts & Derbys pits & riot police at Orgreave coke works, Yorks – High Court rules strike illegal, fines NUM & sequesters funds; 'Day of Action' fails to prevent banning of trade unions at GCHQ, Cheltenham; BT privatised & [–1985] National Bus Co; IRA bombs Grand Hotel, Brighton, at Cons. Party conference – 5 killed; Greenham Common women's peace camp cleared by bailiffs & police; WPC Fletcher shot & killed at Libyan People's Bureau, London; GLC declares 1984 'Anti-Racist Year', but racist attacks on Asians increase; gvnmt report says childhood leukaemia 10 times national average near Sellafield nuclear plant; UK agrees to relinquish sovereignty of Hong Kong to China in 1997; US troops killed by suicide bombers in Beirut –UN peace-keeping force evacuated; Hindu-Muslim riots in India – troops storm Golden Temple of Amritsar occupied by Sikh militants – over 800 die – Sikh bodyguards assassinate PM, Indira Gandhi – 3000 Sikhs massacred in Hindu backlash; chemical plant at Bhopal, India, explodes

£1 note & 1/2p coin phased out; 1st cellular radio network, Vodaphone, intro.d in UK; Apple Mac PCs [1st with 'mouse'] launched; UK's 1st test-tube triplets born; ice-skaters, Torvill & Dean, win 'Grand Slam' of World, Olympic & European titles. **Int. Lit.:** Heller, *God Knows*; Lurie, *Foreign Affairs*; Smiley, *Duplicate Keys* [thriller]; Updike, *The Witches of Eastwick*; Vidal, *Lincoln* [novel]; Hope, *Kruger's Alp*; Allende, *Of Love and Shadows*; Kundera, *The Unbearable Lightness of Being* [David Kaufman film, 1988]; Walker, *In Search of Our Mothers' Gardens* [essays]; Keri Hulme, *The Bone People* [NZ novel; Booker Prize, 1985]; Anita Desai, *Clear Light of Day & In Custody* [Indian novels]; Jamaica Kincaid, *At the Bottom of the River* [stories of Antigua]. **Music:** Glass, 'Akhnaten' [opera]; Lloyd Webber, 'Starlight Express' [musical]; Sondheim, 'Sunday in the Park with George' [musical]; Madonna, 'Like a Virgin'; Bob Geldof estabs 'Band Aid' charity rock group – releases single, 'Do They Know It's Christmas' – raises £8 million. **Art:** Turner Prize for art 1st awarded; Prince Charles criticises modern

P: Fanthorpe — *Voices Off*
Harrison — *Selected Poems*
Heaney — *Station Island*
Kavanagh — *Patrick Kavanagh: The Complete Poems* [posthm.]
Lucie-Smith — *Beasts with Bad Morals*
McGuckian — *Venus and the Rain* [rev.d edtn, 1994]
Mitchell — *On the Beach at Cambridge: New Poems*
Nichols — *The Fat Black Woman's Poems*
Raine — *Rich*
Tomlinson — *Notes from New York*
David Dabydeen (b.1955; Guyana) — *Slave Song*
C.H. Sisson (1914–2003) — *Collected Poems*
Pr/F: K. Amis — *Stanley and the Women*
M. Amis — *Money*
Ballard — *The Empire of the Sun* [Stephen Spielberg film, 1987]
Barnes — *Flaubert's Parrot*
Boyd — *Stars and Bars*
Carter — *Nights at the Circus* [novel]

PERIOD	YEAR	INTERNATIONAL AND POLITICAL CONTEXTS	SOCIAL AND CULTURAL CONTEXTS	AUTHORS	INDICATIVE TITLES
		– extensive casualties; [–1985] disastrous famine in Ethiopia – international aid operation begins; USSR & 16 other states boycott Los Angeles Olympics; 1st flight of US space shuttle 'Discovery'; 'greenhouse effect' blamed for 1981 & 1983 weather – warmest on record – monsoon floods in Bangladesh destroy 0.5m. homes; AIDS virus finally identified	architecture at RIBA. **Film:** Allen, 'Broadway Danny Rose' [Farrow]; Coppola, 'The Cotton Club' [Hoskins, R. Gere]; Huston, 'Under the Volcano' [Finney, J. Bisset; adptn of Malcolm Lowry novel]; Lean, 'A Passage to India' [Guinness, P. Ashcroft, N. Havers et al; adptn of E.M. Forster]; Martin Brest, 'Beverley Hills Cop' [E. Murphy]; James Cameron, 'The Terminator' [A. Schwarzenegger]; Wes Craven, 'A Nightmare on Elm Street'; Roland Joffe & David Puttnam [UK], 'The Killing Fields'; Neil Jordan [Ir/UK], 'The Company of Wolves' [co-adptn of Angela Carter's story]; Sergei Leone, 'Once Upon a Time in America' [De Niro, J. Woods]; Ivan Reitman, 'Ghostbusters' [S. Weaver]; Edgar Reitz [Ger.], 'Heimat' [for TV; 2nd film, 1992]; Wim Wenders, 'Paris, Texas' [Kinski] **Theory/Crit:** Adorno, *Aesthetic Theory* [(1970); Eng. trans]; Bourdieu, *Distinction: A Social Critique of the Judgement of Taste*; Louis Henry Gates Jr. (ed.), *Black Literature and Literary Theory* [incls Wole Soyinka 'The Critic and Society']; hooks, *Feminist Theory: From Margin to Center*; Jameson, 'Postmodernism, or The Cultural Logic of Late Capitalism' [v.1991]; Kristeva, *Revolution in Poetic Language* [1974]; Eng. trans] & *Desire in Language* [(1980); Eng. trans]; Audre Lorde, *Sister/Outsider*; Jean-François Lyotard, *The Postmodern Condition* [(1979); Eng. trans]; Mitchell, *Women: The Longest Revolution*; Toni Morrison, 'Rootedness: The Ancestor as Foundation'; R. Williams, *Writing in Society*	Forsyth Golding Gray Jacobson Kelman Lessing ('Jane Somers') Lodge McIlvanney Spark Linda Anderson (b.1949; Ulster) Iain Banks (b.1953; Scotland) Anita Brookner (b.1928) Jennifer Johnston (b.1930; Ireland) Agnes Owens (b.1926; Scotland) Sue Townsend (b.1946) **Dr:** Ayckbourn Barker Brenton Churchill Gems Gray Pinter Poliakoff Liz Lochhead (b.1947, Scotland) **Lit. 'Events':**	*The Fourth Protocol* *The Paper Men* *1982, Janine* *Peeping Tom* [novel] *The Busconductor Hines* [novel] *The Diaries of Jane Somers* [1st pub.d as 2 novels under pseudonym] *Small World: An Academic Romance* *These Words: Weddings and After* [essay & poetry] *The Only Problem* *To Stay Alive* [novel] *The Wasp Factory* [novel] *Hotel du Lac* [novel; Booker] *The Railway Station Man* [novel] *Gentlemen of the West* [novel] *The Secret Diary of Adrian Mole, Aged 13 3/4* [fiction] *It Could Be Any One of Us* & *Intimate Feelings* *The Power of the Dog* *The Genius* & *Bloody Poetry* *Softcops* *Camille* *The Common Pursuit* *One for the Road* *Breaking the Silence* *Dreaming Frankenstein and Collected Poems* [reissued 1994] & *Sweet Nothings* [on TV] Ted Hughes, Poet Laureate; 1st distribution of royalties to authors from Public Lending Rights
CONTEMPORARY	**1985**	£ = $1.07 – devalued by 27% in 1 yr; miners' strike ends without victory [> weakens UK trade union movement]; Kinnock's speech at Lab. Conference attacks 'Militant Tendency' [esp.ly in Liverpool]; rioting in Brixton, Handsworth, Birmingham [Cherry Groce shot by police] & Broadwater Farm, Tottenham [PC Blakelock murdered]; Anglo-Irish Agreement gives Eire consultative role in N. Ireland affairs – all 15 Ulster Unionist MPs resign in protest – gvnmt exerts pressure on BBC to drop its documentary on N. Ireland – 1st 1-day strike by	1st UK baby dies of AIDS – blood-donors screened; Oxford University refuses Mrs Thatcher honorary degree because of education cuts; UK football hooligans cause death of 41 fans at Juventus v. Liverpool European Cup final at Heysel stadium, Belgium – UK clubs banned from European competitions; fire during match in Bradford City FC's grandstand kills 52 spectators; Amstrad launch popular domestic word-processor; Randolf Quirk et al, *A Comprehensive Grammar of the English Language*. **Int. Lit.:** Roth, *Zuckerman Bound* [trilogy	**P:** Dunn Fuller Harrison G. Hill Longley Motion Tomlinson	*Elegies* *Selected Poems 1954–1982* *V.* [long poem; TV film, 1987, caused press furore], *The Fire-Gap*, *The Mysteries* [verse adptn of medieval plays; pf.d NT] & *Dramatic Verse 1973–1985* [coll. adptns for theatre] *Collected Poems* *Poems 1963–1983* *Dangerous Play: Poems 1974–1984* *Collected Poems*

1986

journalists in BBC's history; Spain fully opens border with Gibraltar; Arab terrorist attacks at Rome & Vienna airports – It. cruise ship hijacked; US Pres. Reagan begins 2nd term; USA bans aid to Contra rebels in Nicaragua – trade embargo against Sandinista gvnmt; 100,000 black squatters moved to new townships – riots & state of emergency in SA; Mikhail Gorbachev in power in USSR: [>] 'glasnost' (openness) & 'perestroika' (reconstruction) – Reagan/Gorbachev talks in Geneva agree 50% cut in nuclear weapons; Greenpeace protest ship, 'Rainbow Warrior', sabotaged & sunk by Fr. secret service in NZ; UN estimates c.19m. Africans face famine; increasing global concern over pollution & conservation; Air India flight blown up over Atlantic killing 329; cyclone & tidal wave kill 10,000 in Bangladesh – massive earthquake destroys large parts of Mexico City [c.7000 die] – volcano in Columbia kills 25,000; WHO declares AIDS an epidemic; [>] genetic science develops rapidly

(v.1979) & sequel, *The Prague Orgy* (1985); Vonnegut, *Galapagos*; Don DeLillo, *White Noise* [US novel]; Brett Easton Ellis, *Less Than Zero* [US novel]; Garrison Keillor, *Lake Wobegon Days* [US humour]; Keneally, *A Family Madness* [novel]; Carey, *Illywhacker*; Atwood, *The Handmaid's Tale* [film, 1990]; Kincaid, *Annie John* [novel]; Allende, *The House of the Spirits*; Fuentes, *The Old Gringo* [Eng. trans 1986]; R.K. Narayan, *Under the Banyan Tree* [Indian stories]; Ken Suro-Wiwa, *Sozaboy, a Novel in Rotten English* [Nigerian novel]. **Music:** 'Les Miserables' [musical] opens; Geldof organises 10-hr 'Live Aid' pop concerts [for Ethiopia] at Wembley & JFK Stadium, Philadelphia – worldwide live TV transmission – 1½ billion viewers – c.£40m. raised. **Art:** 'Neue Slowenische Kunst' exhibition, London; Warhol, 'Raphael 1 – $6.99' & 'Queen Elizabeth II' [silkscreen prints; NPG]; CRE report, 'The Arts of Ethnic Minorities', promotes diversity; 'Vision & Voice', UK black visual arts conference, Birmingham – 'Black Art/White Institutions' conference, London. **Film:** Gilliam, 'Brazil' [De Niro et al]; Huston, 'Prizzi's Honour' [Nicholson, K. Turner]; Kurosawa, 'Ran' [adptn of *King Lear*]; Weir, 'Witness' [H. Ford]; Hector Babenco [Brazil], 'Kiss of the Spider Woman'; Chris Bernard [UK], 'Letter to Brezhnev'; Lasse Hallström [Swed.], 'My Life as a Dog'; David Hare [UK], 'Wetherby' [V. Redgrave, Holm, J. Dench; wrtn by Hare]; Sydney Pollack, 'Out of Africa' [Redford, Streep; adptn of Karen Blixen (Isak Dinesen) memoirs, 1938]; Robert Zemeckis, 'Back to the Future'; ITV 'soap' 'Eastenders' begins. **Theory/Crit:** Jonathan Dollimore & Alan Sinfield (eds), *Political Shakespeare: New Essays in Cultural Materialism*; Gates (ed.), *'Race,' Writing and Difference* [incls essays by Bhaba, Derrida & Spivak]; Donna Harraway, 'A Manifesto for Cyborgs'; Alice Jardine, *Gynesis: Configurations of Women in Modernity*; Luce Irigaray, *Speculum of the Other Woman* [(1974); Eng. trans] & *This Sex Which Is Not One* [(1977); Eng. trans]; McGann, *The Beauty of Inflections*; Toril Moi, *Sexual/Textual Politics*; Eve Kosofsky Sedgwick, *Between Men: English Literature and Male Homosocial Desire*; Gayatri Chakravorty Spivak, 'Three Women's Texts and a Critique of Imperialism'; Jeffrey Weeks, *Sexuality and its Discontents*

Author	Work
Fred D'Aguiar (b.1960; roots in Guyana)	*Mama Dot*
Benjamin Zephaniah (b.1958; roots in Jamaica)	*The Dread Affair*
Pr/F: Ackroyd	*Hawksmoor*
Brookner	*Family and Friends*
Burgess	*Kingdom of the Wicked*
Byatt	*Still Life* [sequel to 1978 novel]
Carter	*Black Venus* [stories]
Dunn	*Secret Villages* [novel]
Fowles	*A Maggot*
Lessing	*The Good Terrorist*
McIlvanney	*The Big Man*
Moore	*Black Robe*
Mortimer	*Paradise Postponed* [novel; TV ser., 1986]
Murdoch	*The Good Apprentice*
Phillips	*The Final Passage*
Raban	*Foreign Land* [novel]
	Night Shift [novel]
Dermot Bolger (b.1959, Ireland)	*Crusoe's Daughter* [novel]
Jane Gardam (b.1928)	*The Killeen* [novel]
Mary Leland (b.1941; Ireland)	*The Unbelonging* [novel]
Joan Riley (b.1958; Jamaica)	*Oranges Are Not The Only Fruit* [novel]
Jeanette Winterson (b.1959)	
Dr: Ayckbourn	*The Castle & Woman in Mind*
Barker	*Downchild*
Bleasdale	*Are You Lonesome Tonight?* [musical about Presley]
Bond	*The War Plays* [trilogy; pub.d]
Brenton & Hare	*Pravda: A Fleet Street Comedy*
Edgar	*Entertaining Strangers*
Hanif Kureishi (b.1954)	*My Beautiful Laundrette* [screenplay for Stephen Frears film, 1985]
Frank McGuinness (b.1956; Ireland)	*Observe the Sons of Ulster Marching Towards the Somme*
David Pownall (b.1938)	*Master Class*
Lit. 'Events':	Philip Larkin dies
P: Adcock	*The Incident Book*
Fanthorpe	*A Watching Brief*
Hughes	*Flowers and Insects: some birds and a pair of spiders*
Levertov	*Selected Poems*
Longley	*Poems*

Halley's Comet reappears; UK gvnmt launches £20m. campaign against AIDS – 278 deaths to date; 1st triple transplant [heart, lungs, liver] pf.d in Cambridge; BBC launches full day-time TV; British Satellite Broadcasting (BSB) awarded 1st franchise for satellite TV; the *Independent* & *Today* newspapers

Hestletine & Brittan resign from Thatcher gvnmt over future US ownership of Westland Helicopters; Local Gvnmt Act abolishes GLC & metropolitan counties; Teachers' Pay & Conditions Act abolishes Burnham negotiating committee & imposes pay settlement; privatisation of British Gas [–1990],

PERIOD	YEAR	INTERNATIONAL AND POLITICAL CONTEXTS	SOCIAL AND CULTURAL CONTEXTS	AUTHORS	INDICATIVE TITLES
CONTEMPORARY		British Airways (BA) [–1988] & TSB; 'Big Bang': London Stock Exchange deregulated and computerised; [–1987] violent clashes between police & print-workers' pickets at Rupert Murdoch's News International plant in Wapping over 'single union agreement' with electricians to use new newspaper print technology; Nissan car co. opens new plant in Sunderland; agreement finally reached to build Channel Tunnel; Thatcher signs Single European Act: gives greater powers to European Parliament & abolishes key veto rights by a single state; Spain & Portugal join European Community (EC); leading Soviet dissidents released & 225 political prisoners in Poland; Swedish PM, Olaf Palme, assassinated; 'Irangate' scandal in USA: arms exchanged for hostages with Iran – profits diverted to Nicaraguan Contra rebels after Congress refuses funding; anti-apartheid unrest continues in SA – riots in Soweto; Benazir Bhutto [ex-Pres. Bhutto's daughter] returns to Pakistan from exile; US space shuttle, 'Challenger', explodes – 7 crew die; nuclear disaster at Chernobyl, USSR; gases from volcanic lake in Cameroons kill 1700; 1st hole in ozone layer detected over Spitzbergen; 30m. people worldwide in Sportaid's 'Race Against Time' for starving African refugees	launched; OED Supplement (OEDS) completed. Int. Lit.: Updike, Roger's Version; Coetzee, Foe; Walcott, Collected Poems 1948–1984. Music: Lloyd Webber, 'The Phantom of the Opera' & with Rice, 'Chess' [musicals]; Art: Arts Council report, 'The Arts & Ethnic Minorities: Action Plan'; 'Black Visual Arts Forum' at ICA; Richard Roger's Lloyd's building, London, opens; Tom Phillips [pnt] 'Iris Murdoch' [NPG]. Film: Allen, 'Hannah and Her Sisters' [Caine, Fisher, Farrow, B. Hershey]; Jarman, 'Caravaggio'; Lynch, 'Blue Velvet' [Hopper, I. Rossellini]; Alex Cox, 'Sid and Nancy' [based on life of 'punk' Sid Vicious]; Claude Berri [Fr.], 'Jean de Florette' [G. Depardieu, Y. Montand]; James Cameron, 'Aliens' [Weaver]; Peter Faiman [Austrl.], 'Crocodile Dundee' [P. Hogan]; Neil Jordan [UK], 'Mona Lisa' [Caine, Hoskins]; Spike Lee, 'She's Gotta Have It'; Ismail Merchant & James Ivory, 'A Room with a View' [M. Smith, Dench, D. Elliott, D. Day-Lewis, H. Bonham-Carter; adptn of Forster; script by Jhabvala]; Tony Scott, 'Top Gun' [T. Cruise, K. McGillis]; Oliver Stone, 'Platoon' [T. Berenger] & 'Salvador' [Woods, J. Belushi]; Andrei Tarkovsky [USSR], 'The Sacrifice'. Theory/Crit: de Man, The Resistance to Theory; Eagleton, Against the Grain: Essays; Eco, Travels in Hyperreality; Jacobus, Reading Woman; Cora Kaplan, Sea Changes: Culture and Feminism; Lyotard, 'Defining the Postmodern' [Eng. trans]; Moi (ed.), The Kristeva Reader [incls 'Women's Time' (1979)]; Ngugi wa Thiong'o, Decolonising the Mind: The Politics of Language in African Literature; A. Rich, Blood, Bread, and Poetry: Selected Prose; Said, 'Orientalism Reconsidered'; Showalter (ed.), The New Feminist Criticism; Wellek, A History of Modern Criticism 1750–1950 [6 vols]	Wendy Cope (b.1945) Pr/F: K. Amis Carter (ed.) Caute Ishiguro Le Carré Mo Nichols Phillips Powell Raban Trevor Weldon Jim Crace (b.1946) Ian Rankin (b.1960; Scotland) Dr: Bennett Bleasdale Gems Potter Lit. 'Events':	Making Cocoa for Kingsley Amis The Old Devils [Booker] Wayward Girls & Wicked Women [anthol. of stories] News from Nowhere An Artist of the Floating World A Perfect Spy An Insular Possession Whole of a Morning Sky [novel] A State of Independence The Fisher King Coasting [autobiog. travel] The News from Ireland [stories] The Shrapnel Academy Continent Knots and Crosses [detective thriller] Kafka's Dick & The Insurance Man [on TV] The Monocled Mutineer [on TV] The Danton Affair The Singing Detective [on TV] Swan Theatre, Stratford, opens
	1987	Pre-election budget lowers income tax, raises inheritance tax threshold & intros personal pension plans; Gen. Elec.: Cons re-elected for 3rd time – Thatcher, PM – large overall majority – Lab. improves on 1983 – Lib-SDP Alliance does less well; British Airports Authority (BAA) & Rolls Royce privatised – gvnmt floats Eurotunnel & BP share sale [world's biggest]; unemployment falls to 2.65m. [lowest for 5 yrs]; 'Black Monday' London stock exchange crash: 20%/£50.6b. wiped off shares – subsequent US Wall St crash larger than 1929; gunman kills 16 & wounds 14 in Hungerford, Berkshire; SAS kill 8 IRA members in Loughall – Enniskillen Remembrance Day bombing [11 killed] – bombing at British military base, W. Germany [31 injured]; 'Herald of Free Enterprise' cross-Channel car ferry sinks at Zebrugge, Belgium	[Oct.] gales over SE England cause extensive damage; fire at King's Cross tube station kills 30; 1 person a day in UK now dying of AIDS; house prices in S. England rise by 25%; 24-hr TV now available in UK; Peter Wright, Spycatcher [autobiog. of MI5 officer – gvnmt's unsuccessfull attempt to suppress it]; 'The New Man' concept is in the news. Int. Lit.: Morrison, Beloved; Wolfe, The Bonfire of the Vanities; Carrie Fisher, Postcards from the Edge [US novel]; Allende, Eva Luna. Music: [>] cassettes replace vinyl discs as main form of recorded music. Art: Third Text & Bazaar [ethnic minority arts magazines] 1st pub.d; sale of Van Gogh's 'Irises' [£30m.] & 'Sunflowers' [£24.7m.]; David Buckland [pnt] 'Harold Evans and Tina Brown' [NPG]. Film: Attenborough, 'Cry Freedom'; Bertolucci, 'The Last Emperor' [O'Toole]; Donner, 'Lethal Weapon'	P: G. Barker Heaney Motion Muldoon Ciaran Carson (b.1948, Ulster) Carol Ann Duffy (b.1955, Scotland) Kathleen Jamie (b.1962, Scotland) Sean O'Brien (b.1952) Peter Redgrove (b.1932) Pr/F: Ackroyd M. Amis Banks	Collected Poems The Haw Lantern Natural Causes The Irish for No Selling Manhattan The Way We Live The Frighteners The Moon Disposes: Poems 1954–1987 Chatterton Einstein's Monsters [stories & essay] Espedair Street

1987

[192 killed]; war criminals trials begin in Israel & France; democratisation continues in USSR – demonstrations in Hungary for liberal reform; Reagan & Gorbachev Washington summit: all land-based, intermediate-range weapons to be dismantled; Terry Waite, Archbishop of Canterbury's representative on hostage-release mission, kidnapped in Lebanon; Iranian Muslims riot on pilgrimage to Mecca – 400 killed; Robert Mugabe becomes President of Zimbabwe; serious drought in India & flooding in Bangladesh [24m. homeless]; UN warns of famine in Ethiopia, Mozambique & Angola; thinning of ozone layer attributed to industrial nations' proliferation of CFCs – rise in sea-levels & more destructive hurricanes predicted

[Gibson]; Huston, 'The Dead' [adptn of final story in Joyce's Dubliners]; Kubrick, 'Full Metal Jacket'; Spielberg, 'Empire of the Sun' [Havers, J. Malkovitch, M. Richardson; adptn of J.G. Ballard; script by Tom Stoppard]; Stone, 'Wall Street' [M. Sheen, C. Sheen, M. Douglas; Gabriel Axel [Den.], 'Babette's Feast'; John Boorman [UK], 'Hope and Glory' [Miles]; Barry Levinson, 'Good Morning, Vietnam' [R. Williams]; Adrian Lyne, 'Fatal Attraction' [Douglas, G. Close]; Leonard Nimoy, 'Three Men and a Baby'; Brian De Palma, 'The Untouchables' [Connery, De Niro, K. Cosner, A. Garcia]. **Theory/Crit:** Gloria Anzaldúa, Borderlands/La Frontera: The New Mestiza; Hazel Carby, Reconstructing Womanhood: The Emergence of the Afro-American Woman Novelist; Chomsky, On Power and Ideology; Gates, Figures in Black; E.D Hirsch, Cultural Literacy; Paul Gilroy, There Ain't No Black in the Union Jack; Johnson, A World of Difference; Teresa De Laurentis, Technologies of Gender; J.H. Miller, The Ethics of Reading; Toril Moi (ed.), French Feminist Thought; Foucault, The Foucault Reader [ed., Paul Rabinov; incls 'What is an Author?' (1969)]; Lynne Segal, Is the Future Female?; Spivak, In Other Worlds; H. White, The Content of the Form: Narrative Discourse and Historical Representation

Author	Work
Boyd	The New Confessions
Brookner	A Friend from England
Chatwin	The Songlines [travel/anthropology]
Drabble	The Radiant Way [1st in trilogy*]
Golding	Close Quarters [*]
Johnston	Fool's Sanctuary
Lively	Moon Tiger [Booker]
McEwan	The Child in Time
Murdoch	The Book and the Brotherhood
Naipaul	The Enigma of Arrival
Moore	The Colour of Blood
Owens	Like Birds in the Wilderness
Potter	The Hearts and Lives of Men
Weldon	Blackeyes [novel; TV adptn, 1988]
Winterson	The Passion
Melvyn Bragg (b.1939)	The Maid of Buttermere [novel]
Dr: Ayckbourn	Henceforward & A Small Family Business [pub.d]
Barker	The Possibilities
Bennett	Talking Heads [6 monodramas on TV]
Churchill	Serious Money
Edgar	That Summer [pub.d]
Kureshi	Sammy and Rosie Get Laid [screenplay for Stephen Frears film]
Lochhead	Mary Queen of Scots Got Her Head Chopped Off
Poliakoff	Coming in to Land
Shaffer	Lettice and Lovage
Timberlake Wertenbaker (b.1951; USA)	Our Country's Good [uses Farquhar's The Recruiting Officer – v.1706]
Lit. 'Events':	RSC's Les Liaisons dangereuses [adaptn by Christopher Hampton, 1986]

1988

Budget again reduces income tax [standard rate 25%, higher rate 40%] – public spending lowest for 20 yrs; NHS charges intro.d for eye-tests & dental work; Libs & SDP [v.1990] merge to form SDLP; [–1990] Emploment Acts impose further restrictions on trades unions [e.g. on ballots, 'closed shops', unofficial action]; national curriculum intro.d in schools – 1st GCSE exams; British Steel privatised; bomb on Pan Am Boeing 747, Flight 103, over Lockerbie, Scotland, kills 270 in total; right to silence abolished in N. Ireland courts – 3 IRA members killed by SAS in Gibraltar [gvnmt protests at Thames TV documentary 'Death on the Rock'] – 3 mourners killed at their funeral by Loyalists – 2 British soldiers killed at subsequent funeral – gvnmt bans radio & TV interviews with Ulster paramilitaries; Reagan leaves office – George Bush, US Pres; PLO leader Yasser Arafat recognises

Over 150 killed when N. Sea oil rig, 'Piper Alpha', explodes; rail crash at Clapham Junction kills 35; meat from infected cattle being sold in UK – BSE crisis begins; Broadcasting Standards Council set up to curb sex & violence on TV; 'Turin Shroud' a medieval fake [dated to 13th–14th Century]; [>] compact discs developed; Stephen Hawking, A Brief History of Time [b-s. science]. **Int. Lit.:** Vonnegut, Bluebeard; Mamet, Speed-the-Plow [play]; Atwood, Cat's Eye; Hope, White Boy Running [non-fict. about SA]; Carey, Oscar and Lucinda [Booker Prize; film, 1997]; Màrquez, Love in the Time of Cholera; Desai, Baumgartner's Bombay; Kincaid, A Small Place [Antiguan history]. **Art:** 'African & Asian Visual Artists' Archive' (AAVAA) & 'Autograph' [black photographers' association] launched; Wesselman, 'Big Blonde # 2'; 'Visions of Britain' on TV – Prince Charles attackes modern architecture & promotes

Author	Work
P: Dunn	Northlight
Larkin	Collected Poems [posthm.]
Jo Shapcott (b.1953)	Electroplating the Baby
Pr/F: Chatwin	Utz [novel]
Crace	The Gift of Stones
Lessing	The Fifth Child
Lodge	Nice Work
Mortimer	Summer's Lease
Rushdie	The Satanic Verses
Spark	A Far Cry from Kensington
Swift	Out of This World
Trevor	The Silence in the Garden
Warner	The Lost Father [novel]
Weldon	Leader of the Band
Roddy Doyle (b.1958; Ireland)	The Commitments [1st novel in 'BarrytownTrilogy' * (–1991); Alan Parker film, 1991]

PERIOD	YEAR	INTERNATIONAL AND POLITICAL CONTEXTS	SOCIAL AND CULTURAL CONTEXTS	AUTHORS	INDICATIVE TITLES
CONTEMPORARY		Israel's right to exist; Iraqi gas attack on Iranians kills 5000 – cease-fire agreed; Pres. Zia of Pakistan killed in mid-air explosion – Benazir Bhutto elected; USSR begins military withdrawal from Afghanistan – unrest in Soviet satellite states – contested elections approved – large troop reductions in E. Europe herald end of Cold War [v.1989]; Zimbabwe effectively becomes a one-party state [Pres. Mugabe's ZANU party]; terrible floods in Bangladesh, China and on Nile – drought in US Midwest – earthquakes in Armenia & India; 5–10m. worldwide are HIV positive	'vernacular' styles. **Film:** Coco Fusco pubs *Young, Black, and British* [on black film in UK]; Coppola, 'Tucker: The Man and His Dream'; Greenaway, 'Drowning by Numbers' [J. Plowright, J. Stevenson, J. Richardson]; Jordan, 'High Spirits' [O'Toole]; Parker, 'Mississippi Burning' [Hackman, W. Dafoe]; Scorsese, 'The Last Temptation of Christ' [Dafoe, H. Keitel]; Wenders, 'Wings of Desire'; Zemeckis, 'Who Framed Roger Rabbit?' [Hoskins]; Pedro Almodóvar [Sp.], 'Women on the Verge of a Nervous Breakdown'; Charles Crichton & John Cleese, 'A Fish Called Wanda' [Cleese, Palin, J. L. Curtis]; Terence Davies [UK], 'Distant Voices, Still Lives'; Christine Ezard [UK], 'Little Dorrit' [all-star UK cast; adptn of Dickens]; Barry Levinson, 'Rain Man' [Hoffman, Cruise]; Mira Nair [Ind.], 'Salaam Bombay!'; Giuseppe Tornatore [It.], 'Cinema Paradiso' **Lit. Events:** RSC's production of 'The Plantaganets' [Shakespeare's history plays]; Peter Brook's adaptn of *The Mahabharata* for NT	Sebastian Faulks (b.1953) Alan Hollinghurst (b.1954) Glenn Patterson (b.1961; Ulster) **Dr:** Bennett Friel Hare Pinter Potter Stoppard Wertenbaker **Theory/Crit:** Jean Baudrillard Culler Jane Gallop Gates Gilbert & Gubar Greenblatt Linda Hutcheon Jameson Kermode Lyotard Spivak Janet Todd A. Walker R. Williams	*The Girl at the Lion D'Or* [novel] *The Swimming Pool Library* [novel] *Burning Your Own* [novel] *Single Spies* [double bill]; *Making History* *The Secret Rapture* [1st in 'state of the nation' trilogy *] *Mountain Language*; *Christabel* [on TV] *Hapgood* *The Love of the Nightingale* *America* [Eng. trans; (1986)] *Framing the Sign* *Thinking Through the Body* *The Signifying Monkey* *No Man's Land* [2 vols] *Shakespearian Negotiations* *A Poetics of Postmodernism* *The Ideologies of Theory* [2 vols] *History and Value* *The Differend* [(1984); Eng. trans] 'Can the Subaltern Speak?' *Feminist Literary History* *Living By the Word* *Resources of Hope*
	1989	House of Commons 1st televised; Nigel Lawson resigns as Chancellor – £20b. deficit in UK balance of payments – economy in dire straits; Community Charge ('Poll Tax') intro.d in Scotland in place of 'rates' [all adults in a district pay same sum] – bitterly resented [v.1990]; water industry privatised; White Paper, 'Working for Patients', outlines sweeping changes for NHS; Lab. Party review document, 'Meet the Challenge, Make the Change', discards left-wing policies & inclines towards free-market economics; [–1990] London ambulance workers dispute – troops drive ambulances; 10 marines killed by IRA bomb in Deal, Kent; convictions of 'Guildford Four' pub bombers overturned – freed after 14 yrs [for 'Birmingham Six' v.1991]; Delors Report on EC economic & monetary union suggests single currency; European Parliament elections: Green Party wins 15% of votes; Bush & Gorbachev meet off Malta & announce 'end of Cold War' [v.1946];	Kegworth plane crash on M1 kills 44; 94 Liverpool football fans crushed to death at Hillsborough stadium; 'Marchioness' pleasure-boat disaster – 51 drown in Thames; *OED*, 2nd edtn. pub.d [incls 'Supplements']; Rupert Murdoch launches satellite TV in UK. **Lit.:** Laura Esquivel, *Like Water for [Hot] Chocolate* [novel; Eng. trans, 1992]. **Music:** Tippett, 'New Year' [rock opera]; Madonna, 'Like a Prayer'. **Art:** Rauschenberg, 'Courtyard [Urban Bourbon Series]'; Stephen Campbell [pnt] 'Not You As Well Snowy' [Marlborough Gall.]. **Film:** Brook, 'The Mahabharata'; Disney, 'The Little Mermaid'; Gilbert, 'Shirley Valentine' [Conti, P. Collins et al; Willy Russell's adptn of his play]; Greenaway, 'The Cook, The Thief, His Wife and Her Lover' [Mirren, A. Howard, M. Gambon, R. Boringer]; Jordan, 'We're No Angels' [De Niro, S. Penn, D. Moore]; Lee, 'Do the Right Thing'; Weir, 'The Dead Poets Society' [Williams]; Tim Burton, 'Batman' [Nicholson, Basinger, M. Keaton]; Kenneth Branagh [UK], 'Henry	**P:** Carson D'Aguiar Nichols Redgrove Simon Armitage (b.1963) **Pr/F:** Ackroyd M. Amis Banks Banville Barnes Brookner Burgess Chatwin Drabble Frayn Golding Ishiguro Kelman	*Belfast Confetti* *Airy Hall* *Lazy Thoughts of a Lazy Woman* *The First Earthquake* *Zoom!* *First Light* *London Fields* *Canal Dreams* *The Book of Evidence* *The History of the World in 10½ Chapters* *Lewis Percy* *Any Old Iron* *What Am I Doing Here?* [essays] *A Natural Curiosity* [*] *The Trick of It* [novel] *Fire Down Below* [*] *The Remains of the Day* [Booker; James Ivory film, 1993] *A Disaffection*

1989

revolutions in Hungary, Poland, Czechoslovakia, E. Germany, Bulgaria, Romania bring down Communist regimes; Berlin Wall demolished; US troops invade Panama – oust Gen. Noriega; last Soviet troops leave Afghanistan after 10 yrs; huge-scale anti-apartheid protests in SA – 23 killed near Cape Town; Pakistan rejoins Commonwealth; Vietnam withdraws from Cambodia after 11 yrs; damaged tanker 'Exxon Valdez' creates huge oil spill in Alaska; earthquake wrecks San Fransisco; 'Voyager 2' transmits photos of Neptune

'V' [Branagh, D. Jacobi, S. Shepherd]; Ray Reiner, 'When Harry Met Sally' [M. Ryan, B. Crystal]; Jim Sheridan [Ir/UK], 'My Left Foot' [Day Lewis] **Theory/Crit:** Bill Ashcroft et al, *The Empire Writes Back*; Alex Callinicos, *Against Postmodernism*; Nancy Chodorow, *Feminism and Pyschoanalytic Theory*; Steven Connor, *Postmodernist Culture*; Jonathan Dollimore, *Radical Tragedy*; hooks, *Talking Back. Thinking Feminist, Thinking Black*; Hutcheon, *The Politics of Postmodernism*; Emmanuel Lévinas, *The Lévinas Reader* [ed. Sean Hand]; Marjorie Levinson et al (eds), *Rethinking Historicism*; Laura Mulvey, *Visual and Other Pleasures*; Trinh, T. Minh-ha, *Woman, Native, Other: Writing Postcoloniality and Feminism*; Patricia Waugh, *Feminine Fictions: Revisiting the Postmodern*; R. Williams, *The Politics of Modernism* **Lit. 'Events':** Samuel Beckett & Laurence Olivier die; Muslims in Bradford burn Salman Rushdie's *The Satanic Verses* – Iran declares a fatwa on him & Penguin Books – Rushdie in hiding under death threat

Author	Work
Le Carré	*The Russia House*
Lively	*Passing On*
McIlvanney	*Walking Wounded*
Murdoch	*The Message to the Planet*
Tennant	*Two Women of London: The Strange Case of Ms Jekyll and Mrs Hyde*
Townsend	*True Confessions of Adrian Mole*
Winterson	*Sexing the Cherry*
Julie Burchill (b.1960)	*Ambition* [b-s. novel]
Janice Galloway (b.1956; Scotland)	*The Trick is to Keep Breathing* [novel]
Rose Tremain (b.1943)	*Restoration* [novel]
Robert McLiam Wilson (b.1964; Ulster)	*Ripley Bogle* [novel]
Dr: Churchill	*Icecream*
Hare	*Racing Demon* [*]
Russell	*Shirley Valentine* [film, same year]

1990

Recession in UK – inflation highest since Tories came to power in 1979; Thatcher gvnmt replaces rates with Community Charge – anti-'Poll Tax' riot in London; further Employment Act restricts trades unions [v. 1988]; [>] NHS & Community Care Act intros notion of 'internal market' & 'cost-effectiveness'; gvnmt intros student loans in HE – Student Loan Co. set up; gvnmt will join Europe's exchange rate mechanism (ERM), but not a single European currency – Deputy PM, Geoffrey Howe, resigns – Cons. Party leadership elections: Thatcher falls from power – John Major, PM; SDP wound up after 9 yrs; electricity industry privatised; Mary Robinson, 1st woman President of Eire; 6 soldiers killed in 'human bomb' attacks by IRA in Ulster – Ian Gow, Cons. MP, killed by IRA car bomb; 'supergun' bound for Iraq seized in UK; Fr. & British tunnel workers join up under Channel; Brian Keenan, Beirut hostage, freed after 1597 days; UK resumes diplomatic relations with Iran & Argentina; reunification of Germany; Israelis shoot dead 21 Palestinians in Jerusalem; 30-yr ban on ANC lifted in SA – Nelson Mandela freed from gaol – meets Pres. de Klerk; Gorbachev wins Nobel peace prize – Boris Yeltsin elected Pres. of Russian republic – resigns from Communist Party; 1st 'McDonald's' opens in Moscow; Iraq invades Kuwait – superpowers condemn Saddam Hussein & begin sending troops to Gulf

John Gummer, Agriculture Minister, & 4-yr-old daughter eat hamburgers on TV to stem concern about BSE; [>] all new cars in UK to run on lead-free petrol; [>] Internet use becomes widespread; Paul Gascoigne ('Gazza') weeps at England's defeat by W. Germany in World Cup. **Int. Lit.:** Smiley, *Ordinary Love* [2 novellas]; Coetzee, *Age of Iron*; Walcott, *Omeros* [Trinidadian 'homeric' poem]. **Music:** Royal Opera House has £3m. deficit – cancels new productions – West End musicals also in trouble; World Cup concert of 'The Three Tenors' in Rome. **Film:** Coppola, 'The Godfather III' [Pacino, D. Keaton, A. Garcia, E. Wallach, J. Mantegna]; Loach, 'Riff-Raff' [R. Carlyle, E. McCourt]; Lynch, 'Wild at Heart' [Dafoe, N. Cage, L. Dern]; Scorsese, 'Goodfellas' [De Niro, J. Pesci]; Chris Columbus, 'Home Alone'; Tim Burton , 'Edward Scissorhands' [J. Depp, W. Ryder]; Kevin Costner, 'Dances with Wolves' [Costner, M. McDonnell]; Garry Marshall, 'Pretty Woman' [Gere, J. Roberts]; Anthony Minghella [UK], 'Truly, Madly, Deeply' [J. Stevenson, A. Rickman]; Mike Ockrent [UK], 'Dancing thru' the Dark' [screenplay by Willy Russell]; Jean-Paul Rappeneau [Fr.], 'Cyrano de Bergerac' [Depardieu]; Zhang Yimou [Chin.], 'Raise the Red Lantern' [Gong Li]; Jerry Zucker, 'Ghost' [Moore, P. Swayze, W. Goldberg]. **Theory/Crit:** Baudrillard, *Seduction* [(1979); Eng. transl]; Homi Bhaba [ed.], *Nation and Narration*; Bourdieu, *In Other Words*; Thomas Docherty, *After Theory: Postmodernism/ Postmarxism*; Eagleton, *The Ideology of the Aesthetic* & [with Jameson & Said] *Nationalism,*

Author	Work
P: Agard	*Mangoes and Bullets*
Duffy	*The Other Country*
MacCaig	*Collected Poems* [posthm.]
Morgan	*Collected Poems*
Eavan Boland (b.1944; Ireland)	*Outside History*
Glyn Maxwell (b.1962)	*Tale of the Mayor's Son*
Robert Crawford (b.1959; Scotland)	*A Scottish Assembly*
Pr/F: Bainbridge	*An Awfully Big Adventure*
Bolger	*The Journey Home*
Boyd	*Brazzaville Beach*
Bragg	*A Time to Dance* [screenplay for TV ser., 1992]
Byatt	*Possession* [Booker]
Doyle	*The Snapper* [*]
Kureishi	*The Buddha of Suburbia* [novel; TV adptn., 1993]
McEwan	*The Innocent*
Moore	*Lies of Silence*
Mortimer	*Titmuss Regained*
Rankin	*Westwind*
Louis de Bernières (b.1954)	*The War of Don Emmanuel's Nether Parts* [novel]
Justin Cartwright (b.1945; SA)	*Look at it This Way* [novel]
A.[lison] L. Kennedy (b.1965; Scotland)	*Night Geometry and the Garscadden Trains* [stories]
John McGahern (b.1934; Ireland)	*Amongst Women* [novel]
Sara Maitland (b.1950; Scotland)	*Three Times Table* [novel]

PERIOD	YEAR	INTERNATIONAL AND POLITICAL CONTEXTS	SOCIAL AND CULTURAL CONTEXTS	AUTHORS	INDICATIVE TITLES
			Colonialism, and Literature; Greenblatt, *Learning to Curse*; hooks, *Yearning: Race, Gender and Cultural Politics* [incls 'Postmodern Blackness']; Jakobson, *On Language*; Jameson, *Late Marxism & Signatures of the Visible*; Kermode, *Poetry, Narrative, History*; J.H. Miller, *Tropes, Parables and Performatives*; Spivak, *The Post-Colonial Critic*; Young, *White Mythologies* **Lit. 'Events'**: RSC with £4m. deficit closes Barbican for winter; Seamus Deane (ed.), *The Field Day Anthology of Irish Writing*	Joseph O'Connor (b.1963; Ireland) Colm Tóibín (b.1955; Ireland) **Dr:** Barker Churchill Friel David Lan (b.1952)	*Cowboys and Indians* [novel] *The South* [novel] *Scenes from an Execution* *Mad Forest: A Play from Romania* *Dancing at Lughnasa* *Desire*
CONTEMPORARY	1991	Gvnmt substitute property tax for 'Poll Tax' & launch 'Citizen's Charter'; IRA mortar attack on Downing Street – bombs at Victoria & Paddington stations; convictions of 'Birmingham Six' pub bombers overturned – freed after 16 yrs; Major declares UK to be 'at the very heart of Europe' in Bonn – EC proposes single currency by Jan. 1999 – UK retains get-out clause & 'social chapter' removed from treaty – Maastricht Treaty signed; in Eire, 'X' case: 14-yr-old rape victim prevented from returning to UK for an abortion; 'Operation Desert Storm' launches Gulf War – USA & UK attack Iraq – huge oil slick in Gulf – Iraq fires 'Scud' missiles at Israel & Saudi Arabia – Allies defeat Iraqi troops & liberate Kuwait – harsh sanctions imposed on Iraq – 500,000 Kurdish refugees flee Iraq; START treaty signed after 9 yrs of negotiations; civil war begins in 'old' Yugoslavia – Serbians fight Croatia & Slovenia to prevent independence – besiege & capture Dubrovnik; Gorbachev ousted in hardline Communist coup – coup collapses – 'perestroika' means dissolution of USSR into independent states [e.g. Russia (with re-elected Pres. Yeltsin), Ukraine, Georgia, etc.] – Gorbachev resigns – USSR effectively finished; 7m. at risk of famine in Sudan; cyclone kills 125,000 & leaves 10m. homeless in Bangladesh; Beirut hostages, Terry Waite & Thomas Sutherland freed after 2353 days in captivity – John McCarthy, after 5 yrs & 3 mths	Media tycoon Robert Maxwell's body found in sea – publishing empire collapses; 1st 'league tables' of 7-year-olds' educational achievements pub.d; CNAA [v.1964, 1966] disbanded [dissolved by Act of Parliament, 1993]; the comic *Viz* becomes b-s. magazine. **Int. Lit.:** Smiley, *A Thousand Acres* ['re-vision' of *King Lear*]. **Music:** Freddie Mercury of pop group 'Queen' dies of AIDS; Mozart bicentennial celebrations; Pavrotti's free 30th-anniversary celebration concert in Hyde Park – Princess Di attends – Placido Domingo sings in Windsor Great Park; Bryan Adams's single, 'Everything I do) I do it for you', has record-breaking 16 weeks at Number 1. **Art:** Lichtenstein, 'Interior with Built-in Bar'; Blake, 'H.O.M.A.G.E – JJ MM RR KS' [collage on Japanese screen]; Damien Hirst, 'The Physical Impossibility of Death in the Mind of Someone Living' [preserved shark in tank; Saatchi Coll.]; Helmut Newton, 'Margaret Thatcher' [photo; NPG]. **Film:** 'Nubian Tales' distribution network fnd.d for black cinema; Cameron, 'Terminator II – Judgment Day' [Schwarzenegger]; Greenaway, 'Prospero's Books' [Gielgud; based on *The Tempest*]; Jarman, 'Edward II'; Lee, 'Jungle Fever' [W. Snipes, A. Sciorra]; Merchant-Ivory, 'Howards End' [V. Redgrave, Hopkins, H. Bonham-Carter, E. Thompson; adptn of Forster; script by Jhabvala]; R. Scott, 'Thelma and Louise' [Keitel, S. Sarandon, G. Davies]; Stone, 'JFK' [Costner]; Leos Carax [Fr.], 'Les Amants du Pont Neuf' [J. Binoche, D. Lavant]; Jonathan Demme, 'Silence of the Lambs' [Hopkins, Foster; adptn of Thomas Harris novel]; Kevin Reynolds, 'Robin Hood: Prince of Thieves' [Costner, Rickman, G. McEwan]; John Singleton , 'Boyz N the Hood'; Charles Sturridge [UK], 'Where Angels Fear to Tread' [Mirren, H. Bonham-Carter, R. Graves, B. Jefford; adptn of Forster]; Mario Van Peebles, 'New Jack City' [Snipes]; Gus Van Sant, 'My Own Private Idaho'. **Theory/Crit:** Adorno, *The Culture Industry & Notes to Literature* [both Eng. trans]; Dollimore, *Sexual Dissidence*; Baudrillard, 'The	**P:** Heaney Kwesi Johnson Longley Mitchell Motion Muir Paulin Helen Dunmore (b.1952) Jackie Kay (b.1961; Scotland) **Pr/F:** M. Amis Barnes Carter de Bernières Dabydeen Doyle Drabble Galloway Gardam S. Hill Kelman Lively Lodge McIlvanney Mo Phillips Rankin Pat Barker (b.1943) Gordon Burn (b.1948) Ben Okri (b.1959; Nigeria) Tim Parks (b.1954) Will Self (b.1961) Iain Sinclair (b.1943) **Dr:** Bennett Bleasdale Hampton	*Seeing Things* *Tings an Times* [also record album] *Gorse Fires* *Adrian Mitchell's Greatest Hits* *Love in a Life* *The Complete Poems* *Selected Poems 1972–1990* *Short Days, Long Nights: New and Selected Poems* *The Adoption Papers* *Time's Arrow* *Talking It Over* *Wise Children* *Senor Vivo and the Coca Lord* *The Intended* [novel] *The Van* [*] *The Gates of Ivory* [*] *Blood* [stories] *The Queen of the Tambourine* *Air and Angels* *The Burn* [stories] *City of the Mind* *Paradise News* *Strange Loyalties* *The Redundancy of Courage* *Cambridge* [novel] *Hide and Seek* *Regeneration* [1st novel in trilogy * (–1995)] *Alma Cogan* [novel] *The Famished Road* [novel; Booker] *Goodness* [novel] *The Quantity Theory of Insanity* [stories] *Downriver* [novel] *The Madness of George III* *GBH* [on TV] *White Chameleon*

Hare | *Murmuring Judges* [*]
Wertenbaker | *Three Birds Alighting on a Field*
Lit. 'Events': | Graham Greene dies

Gulf War Did Not Take Place' [Eng. trans]; Derrida, *A Derrida Reader* [ed., Peggy Kamuf]; Eagleton, *Ideology: an Introduction*; F. Fukuyama, *The End of History*; Diana Fuss (ed.), *Inside/Outside: Lesbian Theories*; *Gay Theories*; Greenblatt, *Representing the English Renaissance*; Harraway, *Simians, Cyborgs and Women*; Jameson, *Postmodernism, or, The Cultural Logic of Late Capitalism*; McGann, *The Textual Condition*; Nancy Miller, *Getting Personal*; Tania Modleski, *Feminism Without Women*; Chandra Talpade Mohanty et al (eds), *Third World Women and the Politics of Feminism* [incls 'Under Western Eyes']; Norris, *What's Wrong with Postmodernism?*; Sedgwick, *Epistemology of the Closet*; Showalter, *Sister's Choice*

1992

Gen. Elec.; Cons. re-elected for 4th time – Major, PM; John Smith succeeds Kinnock as Lab. leader; Betty Boothroyd, 1st woman Speaker of Commons in 600 yrs; Heritage Secretay, David Mellor, resigns over sex scandal; [–1993] severe recession in UK – over 3m. unemployed by Jan. 1993 – economic crisis on 'Black Wednesday' (16 Sept.) – UK suspends membership of ERM – interest rates rise to 15% to defend £; [–1993] Further & Higher Education Act grants Polytechnics university status & name ['Incorporation' – e.g. Liverpool John Moore's University, Nottingham Trent, Manchester Metropolitan, etc.]; IRA bomb kills 7 Protestant workers near army barracks at Omagh – 1000lb IRA bomb wrecks Baltic Exchange, City of London – UDA banned – 3000th victim of N. Irish 'Troubles' killed; European free trade area created – largest in world; Danish referendum rejects Maastricht Treaty; Bill Clinton elected US Pres.; EC recognises independence of Croatia & Slovenia – end of 'old' Yugoslavia – Serbs besiege Serajevo – UN troops deployed – Serbia's 'ethnic cleansing' of Muslims in Bosnia; Australia rejects oath of allegiance to Queen; SA constitutional reforms give legal equality to blacks; US marines enter Somalia to secure Mogadishu from warlords; radical Muslim mujahedeen attack Kabul, Afghanistan; ferocious Hindu v. Muslim religious riots in India; USA & UK to phase out use of CFCs as ozone layer depletes

Worst drought in UK since 1745; Andrew Morton's controversial *Diana: Her True Story* pub.d; Prince Charles & Princess Diana separate; C of E Synod votes to ordain women priests; Department of National Heritage created; Windsor Castle severely damaged by fire; *Punch* magazine closes after 150 yrs; **Int. Lit.:** Morrison, *Jazz*; Cormac McCarthy, *All the Pretty Horses* [US novel]; Michael Ondaatje, *The English Patient* [Canadian novel; Booker Prize; film, 1996]; Hope, *Serenity House*. **Music:** Madonna pubs *Sex* [photos]; 'Kiss of the Spider Woman' [musical]; BBC TV & Channel 4 show the whole of 'Tosca'. **Film:** Allen, 'Husbands and Wives' [Farrow]; Altman, 'The Player'; Coppola, 'Bram Stoker's Dracula' [Hopkins, Ryder, G. Oldman]; Disney, 'Aladdin'; Eastwood, 'Unforgiven' [Hackman, R. Harris]; Lee, 'Malcolm X' [D. Washington, A. Bassett; adptn of Alex Haley book]; R. Scott, '1492: Conquest of Paradise' [Depardieu, Weaver]; Yimou, 'The Story of Qiu Ju' [Li]; Ernest R. Dickerson, 'Juice' [O. Epps, T. Shakur]; Baz Luhrmann [Austrl.], 'Strictly Ballroom'; Michael Mann, 'The Last of the Mohicans' [Day Lewis; adptn of Fenimore Cooper]; Sally Potter [UK], 'Orlando' [T. Swinton, Q. Crisp; adptn of Woolf]; Quentin Tarantino, 'Reservoir Dogs' [Keitel, T. Roth]; Gregg Araki, 'The Living End' [M. Dytri, C. Gilmore]. **Theory/Crit:** Judith Butler, *Gender Trouble*; Robert Crawford, *Devolving English Literature*; Derrida, *Acts of Literature* [Eng. trans]; Gates, *Loose Canons: Notes on the Cultural Wars*; Jonathan Goldberg, *Sodometries: Renaissance Texts: Modern Sexualities*; hooks, *Black Looks*; Morrison, *Playing in the Dark: Whiteness and the Literary Imagination*; Norris, *Uncritical Theory: Postmodernism, Intellectuals and the Gulf War*; Camille Paglia, *Sex, Art, and American Culture*; Tom Paulin, *Minotaur: Poetry and the Nation State*; Alan Sinfield, *Faultlines: Cultural Materialism and the Politics of Dissident Reading*;

Author	Work
P: Armitage	*Kid & Xanadu* [film poem]
Cope	*Serious Concerns*
Crawford	*Talkies*
Fanthorp	*Neck-Verse*
Gunn	*The Man with Night Sweats*
Harrison	*The Gaze of the Gorgon* [long poem for TV]
Kay	*Two's Company*
Mahon	*Selected Poems*
Maxwell	*Out of the Rain*
McGough	*Defying Gravity*
McGuckian	*Marconi's Cottage*
K. Raine	*Living with Mystery, Poems 1987–91*
Shapcott	*Phrase Book*
Zephaniah	*City Psalms*
Pr/F: Banks	*The Crow Road* [TV adptn, 1996]
Barnes	*Porcupine*
Bradbury	*Doctor Criminale*
Brookner	*Fraud*
Byatt	*Angel and Insects* [2 novellas; Philip Hass film, 1995]
de Bernères	*The Troublesome Offspring of Cardinal Guzman*
Crace	*Arcadia*
A. Gray	*Poor Things*
Larkin	*Selected Letters 1940–85* [posthm; ed. Anthony Thwaite]
McEwan	*Black Dogs*
Roberts	*Daughters of the House*
Self	*Cock & Bull* [2 novellas]
Swift	*Ever After*
Tóibín	*The Heather Blazing*
Warner	*Indigo*
Winterson	*Written on the Body*
Andrew Greig (b.1951)	*Electric Brae: A Modern Romance* [novel]
Nick Hornby (b.1957)	*Fever Pitch* [novel]

PERIOD	YEAR	INTERNATIONAL AND POLITICAL CONTEXTS	SOCIAL AND CULTURAL CONTEXTS	AUTHORS	INDICATIVE TITLES
			Waugh, *Practising Postmodernism /Reading Modernism*; Wittig, *The Straight Mind* [title essay (1980)]. **Lit. Events**: Derek Walcott, Nobel Prize for Literature	Patrick McCabe (b.1955; Ireland)	*The Butcher Boy* [novel]
				Shena Mackay (b.1944; Scotland)	*Dunedin* [novel]
				Adam Thorpe (b.1956)	*Ulverton* [novel]
				Jeff Torrington (b.1935; Scotland)	*Swing Hammer Swing!* [novel]
				Barry Unsworth (b.1930)	*Sacred Hunger* [novel; Booker]
				Dr: McGuinness	*Someone Who'll Watch Over Me*
				Osborne	*Déjà Vu*
				Tony Kushner (b.1956)	*Angels in America*
				Phyllis Nagy (b.USA; nda)	*Weldon Rising*
CONTEMPORARY	**1993**	Major dismisses Norman Lamont as Chancellor – Michael Mates, N. Ireland Minister, resigns over secret funding scandal – [–1995] Tory disasters in local elections [in 1993, control retained in only 1 county council]; Trade Union Reform & Employment Rights Act estabs postal voting for strike ballots & 7-day 'cooling-off' period; UK finally ratifies Maastricht Treaty – EC Single Market inaugurated; British Rail privatised; Stella Rimmington, 1st woman head of MI5, reveals how it works; black teenager, Stephen Lawrence, murdered in Eltham, SE London, by white racists – 4 tried & acquitted [v.1997–99]; IRA bombs Warrington & Bishopsgate, City of London – bomb in Shankill Rd, Belfast, kills 10 – 1st IRA ceasefire – UK & Irish PMs sign 'Downing Street Declaration' & 'Joint Initiative' for peace in N. Ireland – Eire Pres., Mary Robinson, meets Queen in Ireland [1st such meeting for 71yrs]; 'old' Czechoslovakia splits into Slovakia & Czech Republic; FBI siege of David Koresh's Branch Davidian cult HQ at Waco, Texas, ends in inferno; 150,000 flee as Israel bombards S. Lebanon; Pres. Clinton brokers peace accord between PLO & Israel – allows limited Palestinian autonomy in Gaza Strip & West Bank; Pres. Yeltsin & Russ. army bombard & storm parliament building in Moscow to rout hardline rebellion; SA Communist Party leader, Chris Hani, assassinated; Australia confirms Aborigines' right to claim for land taken by European colonisers 200 yrs ago; 300 killed in Bombay bombings; wrecked tanker 'Braer' causes oil disaster on Shetland Isles	Two 11-year-old boys convicted of murdering 2-year-old James Bulger; ballet-dancer Rudolf Nureyev dies of AIDS. **Int. Lit.:** Toni Morrison wins Nobel Prize for Literature; Atwood, *The Robber Bride*; Vikram Seth, *A Suitable Boy* [Ind. novel]. **Music:** 'Sunset Boulevard' [musical] opens in London. **Art:** Whitney Biennial Exhibition, NY – postmodernist landmark; Hirst, 'Mother and Child Divided' [cow & calf cut in half & preserved in glass case – e.g. of 'Britart']; Glynn Williams [sculpt.] 'Lord [Noel] Annan' [NPG]; Glenys Barton [sculpt.] 'Glenda Jackson' [ceramic; NPG]; Michael Barton [pnt] 'Derek Jarman' [NPG]. **Film:** Altman, 'Short Cuts' [Lemmon, A. MacDowell; adptn of Raymond Carver stories]; Columbus, 'Mrs Doubtfire' [R. Williams, S. Field, P. Brosnan]; Jarman, 'Wittgenstein' [script partly by Terry Eagleton]; Leigh, 'Naked' [D. Thewlis, L. Sharp]; Scorsese, 'The Age of Innocence' [Day Lewis, Ryder, M. Pfeiffer; adptn of Edith Wharton novel]; Spielberg, 'Schindler's List' [Kingsley, R. Fiennes, L. Neeson, C. Goodall; adptn of Keneally's *Schindler's Ark*] & 'Jurassic Park' [R. Attenborough]; Weir, 'Fearless' [Rossellino, J. Bridges]; Jane Campion [Austrl.], 'The Piano' [Keitel, H. Hunter, S. Neill]; Leslie Harris, 'Just Another Girl on the IRT' [A. Johnson]; Harold Ramis, 'Groundhog Day' [MacDowell, B. Murray]; Jean-Marc Poiré [Fr.], 'Les Visiteurs'; Chen Kaige [Chin.], 'Farewell My Concubine'. **Theory/Crit:** Henry Abelove et al (eds), *The Lesbian and Gay Studies Reader* [incls De Laurentis, 'Sexual Indifference and Lesbian Representation']; Baudrillard, *Symbolic Exchange and Death* [Eng. trans; (1976)] & *The Transparency of Evil* [Eng. trans; (1990)]; Bourdieu, *The Field of*	**P:** Armitage	*Book of Matches*
				D'Aguiar	*British Subjects*
				Carson	*First Language*
				Duffy	*Mean Time*
				Dunn	*Dante's Drum Kit*
				Paulin	*Selected Poems 1972–1990*
				R.S. Thomas	*Collected Poems 1945–1990*
				Carol Rumens (b.1944)	*Thinking of Skins: New and Selected Poems*
				Pr/F: Ackroyd	*The House of Doctor Dee*
				P. Barker	*The Eye in the Door* [*]
				Boyd	*The Blue Afternoon*
				Burgess	*A Dead Man in Deptford* [about Christopher Marlowe]
				Doyle	*Paddy Clarke Ha Ha Ha* [Booker]
				Dunmore	*Zennor in Darkness* [novel; re. D.H. Lawrence in Cornwall in WWI]
				Faulks	*Birdsong*
				Kennedy	*Looking for the Possible Dance*
				Le Carré	*The Night Manager*
				Murdoch	*The Green Knight*
				Phillips	*Crossing the River*
				Roberts	*During Mother's Absence* [stories]
				Self	*My Idea of Fun*
				Mary Morrissy (b.1957; Ireland)	*A Lazy Eye* [stories]
				Irvine Welsh (b.1958; Scotland)	*Trainspotting* [novel; Danny Boyle film, 1996]
				Dr: Hare	*The Absence of War*
				Pinter	*Moonlight*
				Russell	*Terraces* [on TV]
				Stoppard	*Arcadia*
				Terry Johnson (b.1955)	*Hysteria*

Cultural Production; Butler, Bodies That Matter; Gilroy, The Black Atlantic & Small Acts; Mandy Merck, Perversions: Deviant Readings; Norris, The Truth about Postmodernism; A. Rich, What I Found There: Notebooks on Poetry and Politics; Said, Culture and Imperialism & Representations of the Intellectual; Cornel West, Race Matters

1994

Tim Yeo, Environment Minister, resigns over 'love-child' – 'sleaze' undermines Major's 'Back to Basics' ['family values'] campaign; what is left of coal industry privatised; John Smith dies – Tony Blair elected Lab. Party leader; Parliament lowers age of consent for homosexuals from 21 to 18; IRA announces complete ceasefire after 25 yrs of 'The Troubles' in N. Ireland – Loyalist paramilitaries follow suit; over 900 die as car-ferry 'Estonia' sinks in Baltic Sea; Russia signs NATO peace accord; Queen visits Russia; artillery shell kills 68 in Serajevo central market; US elections create Republican majorities in both houses of Congress – Pres. Clinton handicapped; major earthquake hits Los Angeles; O.J. Simpson, US football star, arrested on murder charge; Israeli zealot shoots dead 30 Palestinians in Hebron mosque; Yassir Arafat returns to Palestine after 27 yrs in exile; [–1996] Russia invades breakaway territory of Chechnya; battles in Johannesburg between ANC supporters & Zulus; Nelson Mandela inaugurated as President of new SA; inter-tribal massacres in Rwanda begin – 100,000 killed in 2 weeks; Angolan gvnmt & UNITA rebels sign peace treaty to end civil war

1st women priests ordained in C. of E; 1st draw in UK National Lottery; UK shops can open on Sunday; England v. W. Indies: Brian Lara becomes highest-scoring batsman in Test history; BM pays £1m. for Tyndale Bible. **Int. Lit.:** Coetzee, *The Master of Petersburg*. **Music:** 350,000 people attend 25th anniversary of original Woodstock concert at Saugerties, NY State; Oasis, 'Definitely Maybe' [album]; Blur, 'Park Life' [album]. **Art:** Institute of International Visual Arts (inIVA) launched at Tate. **Film:** Bertolucci, 'The Little Buddha'; Disney, 'The Lion King' [20m. copies of video sold by 1995]; Levinson, 'Disclosure' [M. Douglas, Sutherland, D. Moore]; Richardson, 'Blue Sky' [J. Lange, T. Lee Jones]; Tarantino, 'Pulp Fiction' [Travolta, U. Thurman]; Zemekis, 'Forrest Gump' [Hanks, Field, R. Wright, Penn]; Peter & Bobby Farrelly, 'Dumb and Dumber'; Krzysztof Kieslowski [Fr/Pol.], 'Three Colours Red'; Mike Newell [UK], 'Four Weddings and a Funeral' [MacDowell, H. Grant, S. Callow]; Stephan Elliot [Austrl.], 'The Adventures of Priscilla Queen of the Desert' [T. Stamp, H. Weaving, G. Pearce]; Shekar Kapur [Ind.], 'Bandit Queen' [S. Biswas]; Rose Troche, 'Go Fish' [G. Turner, V.S. Brodie]; P.J. Hogan [Austrl.], 'Muriel's Wedding' [T. Colette, R. Griffiths, B. Hunter]

Theory/Crit: Baudrillard, *The Illusion of the End* [Eng. trans]; Bhaba, *The Location of Culture*; P. Brooks, *Psychoanalysis and Storytelling*; Chodorow, *Femininities, Masculinities, Sexualtities*; Derrida, *Spectres of Marx* [1993]; Eng. trans]; hooks, *Outlaw Culture*; Jameson, *The Seeds of Time*; Kobena Mercer, *Welcome to the Jungle: New Positions in Black Cultural Studies*; Lynne Pearce, *Reading Dialogics*; Sedgwick, *Tendencies*; Sinfield, *Cultural Politics – Queer Reading & The Wilde Century*; Spivak, *Outside in the Teaching Machine*

P: Boland — *In a Time of Violence*
Dabydeen — *Turner* [long poem]
Duffy — *Selected Poems*
Jamie — *The Queen of Sheba*
Jennings — *Familiar Spirits*
McGuckian — *Captain Lavender*
Muldoon — *The Annals of Chile*
Paulin — *Walking a Line*
C. Raine — *History: The Home Movie* [long poem]

Pr/F: Ackroyd — *Dan Leno and the Limehouse Golem*
D'Aguiar — *The Longest Memory* [novel]
Banks — *Feersum Endjin*
de Bernières — *Captain Corelli's Mandolin* [film, 2001]
Crace — *Signals of Distress*
Caute — *Dr Orwell and Mr Blair: a novel*
Galloway — *Female Friends*
Gray — *A History Maker*
Hollinghurst — *The Folding Star*
Kelman — *How Late It Was, How Late* [Booker]
Kennedy — *Now That You're Back* [stories]
Naipaul — *A Way in the World*
Roberts — *Flesh and Blood*
Rushdie — *East West*
Self — *Grey Area*
Sinclair — *Radon Daughters*
Tennant — *Tess*
Trevor — *Felicia's Journey*
Welsh — *The Acid House*
Winterson — *Art and Lies: a piece for three voices and a bawd*

Jonathan Coe (b.1961) — *What a Carve Up!* [novel]
Emma Donoghue (b.1969; Ireland) — *Stir-fry* [novel]
Kathleen Ferguson (b.1958; Ulster) — *The Maid's Tale* [novel]

Dr: Churchill — *The Skriker*
(Sue) Townsend — *The Queen and I*
Kevin Elyot (b.1951) — *My Night with Reg*
Jonathon Harvey (b.1968) — *Babies*
Stephen Jeffreys (b.1950) — *The Libertine*

Period	Year	International and Political Contexts	Social and Cultural Contexts	Authors	Indicative Titles
	1995	Queen's 1st visit to SA since 1947; Major resigns & re-wins Cons. Party leadership; Blair wins fight to remove Clause Four [commitment to state ownership of means of production] from Lab. Party constitution; Lord Nolan reports on 'sleaze' in public life; UK & Ir. gvnmts present framework document for future of N. Ireland – broadcasting ban on IRA lifted [v.1988] – Sinn Fein leader, Gerry Adams, received at White House; race riots in Brixton & Manningham, Bradford; Rosemary West goes on trial for Cromwell Street murders, Gloucester [Fred West found hanged in his cell, Jan.]; Nick Leeson detained after his financial dealings in Singapore bankrupt Barings Bank; Channel Tunnel & Eurostar terminal, Waterloo, open; huge car bomb destroys federal building in Oklahoma City – 167 killed – Timothy McVeigh arrested; O.J. Simpson trial in USA ends with controversial not-guilty verdict; Serbs attack Zagreb, bombard & overrun UN 'safe haven' of Srebrenica & seize 350 UN peacekeepers at Gorazde – NATO bombs Serbs – Bosnian peace accord signed in Paris – NATO to police peace; Israeli PM, Yitzhac Rabin assassinated; Russians continue invasion of Chechnya & bombard capital, Grozny; [–1996] radical Islamic Taliban fighters in Afghanistan beseige Kabul; 4000 killed by earthquake in Kobe, Japan; Sarin nerve gas released on 5 underground trains in Tokyo – many casualties; Ebola virus kills 150+ in Zaire; Nigeria executes dissident writer, Ken Saro-Wiwa; Hutu massacred in Rwanda; [–1996] French recommence nuclear tests in Pacific – international protests; US 'Discovery' space shuttle docks with Russ. 'Mir' station; world population grows by 100m. to 5.7b. in 1995; World Conference on Women in Beijing; low ozone levels discv.d over N. Hemisphere – hottest year on record – assumed result of global warming	1st nationwide DNA database estab.d in Birmingham; scientists announce pigs' organs could be transplanted into human beings; breast cancer gene discv.d; Microsoft launch 'Windows 95' – Bill Gates wealthiest man in the world; Princess Diana interviewed about her m. to Prince Charles on BBC TV's 'Panorama' – Queen calls for royal divorce. **Int. Lit.:** Smiley, *Moo*; Hamilton, *A Map of the World*; David Guterson, *Snow Falling on Cedars* [US novel]. **Music:** Oasis, 'Morning Glory' [album] & 'Roll With It' [single] – released on same day in August as Blur's 'Country House' [single] – height of 'Britpop'. **Art:** Tracey Emin, 'Everyone I Have Ever Slept With, 1963–1995' [tent installation]; Bhupen Khakhar [pnt] 'Salman Rushdie' [NPG]; Paula Rego, 'Germaine Greer' [pastel; NPG]. **Film:** Disney, 'Toy Story' & 'A Kid in King Arthur's Court' [J. Ackland, A. Malik, K. Winslet]; Gibson, 'Braveheart' [Gibson, S. Marceau]; Loach, 'Land and Freedom' [I. Hart, R. Pastor]; Scorsese, 'Casino' [De Niro, Pesci, Woods, S. Stone]; Joel Schumaker, 'Batman Forever' [L. Jones, V. Kilmer, N. Kidman, J. Carrey, C. O'Donnell]; Pedro Almodovar [Sp.], 'Flower of My Secret'; Ron Howard, 'Apollo 13' [Hanks]; Scott Kalvert, 'The Basket Ball Diaries' [L. DiCaprio, L. Bracco]; Tim Robbins, 'Dead Man Walking' [Sarandon, Penn]; Kathryn Bigelow, 'Strange Days' [Fiennes, A. Bassett]. **Theory/Crit:** Ashcroft et al (eds), *The Post-Colonial Studies Reader*; Hans Bertens, *The Idea of the Postmodern*; Bloom, *The Western Canon*; Eagleton, *Heathcliff and the Great Hunger*; Fish, *Professional Correctness: Literary Studies and Political Change*; Young, *Colonial Desire: Hybridity in Theory, Culture and Race*. **Lit. 'Events':** Seamus Heaney, Nobel Prize for Literature; Martin Amis signs 2-book deal with Harper Collins for £500,000	**P:** Armitage Boland Fanthorpe Maxwell Muldoon O'Brien Rumens Zephaniah **Pr/F:** M. Amis P. Barker Brookner Burgess Burn Carter Cartwright Donaghue Dunmore Golding Hornby Ishiguro Kennedy Kureishi Le Carré Lodge McLiam Wilson Mo Murdoch Rushdie Thorpe Welsh Winterson Kate Atkinson (b.1951) Nicholas Evans (b.1950) **Dr:** Hare Nagy Stoppard Wertenbaker Sebastian Barry (b.1955) Jez Butterworth (b.1969) Sarah Kane (1971–99) Patrick Marber (b.1964)	*The Dead Sea Poems* *Collected Poems* *Safe as Houses* *Rest for the Wicked* *New Selected Poems 1968–1994* *Ghost Train* *Best China Sky* *Talking Turkeys* *The Information* *The Ghost Road* [* Booker] *Incidents in the Rue Langier* *Byrne* [verse novel] *Fullalove* *Burning Your Boats* [stories; posthm.] *In Every Face I Meet* *Hood* *A Spell of Winter & Burning Bright* *The Double Tongue* [posthm.; unfinished] *High Fidelity* *The Unconsoled* *So I Am Glad* [stories] *The Black Album* *Our Game* *Therapy* *Eureka Street* *Brownout on Breadfruit Boulevard* *Jackson's Dilemma* *The Moor's Last Sigh* *Still* *Marabou Stork Nightmares* *Art Objects: essays on ecstasy and effrontery* *Behind the Scenes at the Museum* [novel] *The Horse Whisperer* [novel] *Skylight* *The Strip & Disappeared* *Indian Ink* *Break of Day* *The Steward of Christendom* *Mojo* *Blasted* *Dealer's Choice*
	1996	Gvnmt loses majority in Commons; BSE crisis: EC bans export of British beef worldwide [later revoked] – gvnmt to cull all cattle over 30 mths old; [–1997] NHS costs over £42 billion to run: Lab.	Prince Charles & Princess Diana agree to divorce; Duke & Duchess of York divorced; Stone of Scone returned from Westminster to Scotland [stolen by King Edward I, 1296: record lottery jackpot to date	**P:** Carson Crawford Heaney G. Hill	*Opera Et Cetera* *Masculinity* *The Spirit Level* *Canaan*

CONTEMPORARY

promises referendum before entering single European currency; all-party talks on future of N. Ireland at Stormont collapse – arms decommissioning the crucial issue – huge bomb explosions at Canary Wharf in London Docklands & later Manchester end 17-mth IRA ceasefire – RUC & Unionists clash at Dumcree, Portadown; gunman shoots dead 16 primary-scool children & a teacher in Dunblane, Scotland; UK retains ban on gays in armed forces; US troops enter Bosnia as peace-keeping force – mass graves discv.d near Srebrenica – war crimes tribunal opens at The Hague – [–1997] pro-democracy demonstrations in Serbia call for resignation of Pres. Slobodan Milosevic; UN endorses Comprehensive Test Ban Treaty for nuclear weapons; Bill & Hillary Clinton embroiled in 'Whitewater' fraud case – Clinton re-elected US Pres.; Yasser Arafat victorious in elections to create Palestinian Authority – becomes 1st Pres. – PLO deletes destruction of Israel from its charter; bomb & rocket attacks on Israel by Hamas & Hezbollah guerrillas – troops enter West Bank & Beirut in retaliation; 18 tourists killed by Islamic terrorists near Pyramids, Egypt; Russia signs peace agreement with Chechnya – last troops withdraw; Taliban capture Kabul – intro. strict Islamic regime; offensive by Tutsis in Rwanda drives millions of Hutu refugees into Zaire; WHO to combat worldwide obesity problem; Hubble space telescope shows 5 times more galaxies in universe

– £42m; fire on freight train in Channel Tunnel. **Int. Lit.:** Anon, *Primary Colours* [US political novel; Mike Nichols film, 1998]; Atwood, *Alias Grace*; Hope, *Darkest England*; Kincaid, *The Autobiography of My Mother* [novel]; Rebecca Wells, *Divine Secrets of the Ya-Ya Sisterhood* [US b-s. novel]. **Art:** Mona Hatoum, 'Deep Throat' [mixed media; Saatchi Coll.]. **Film:** Leigh, 'Secrets and Lies'; Parker, 'Evita' [Madonna, A. Banderas, J. Pryce; adptn of Tim Rice stage musical]; Wes Craven, 'Scream'; Roland Emmerich, 'Independence Day' [M. MacDonnell, B. Pullman]; Michael Winterbourne [UK], 'Jude' [Winslet, C. Ecclestone, R. Griffiths, J. Whitfield; adptn of Hardy]; Anthony Minghella [UK], 'The English Patient' [Dafoe, Fiennes, Binoche; adptn of Michael Ondaatje novel]; Hettie MacDonald [UK], 'Beautiful Thing' [G. Barry, S. Neal, L. Henry]; Deepa Metha [Ind.], 'Fire' [S. Azmi, N. Das]; Baz Luhrman, 'Romeo and Juliet' [DiCaprio]; Scott Hicks [Austrl.], 'Shine' [L. Redgrave, N. Taylor, G. Rush] **Theory/Crit:** Docherty, *Alterities*; Eagleton, *The Illusions of Postmodernism*; Gates & Cornel West, *The Future of the Race*; Elizabeth Grosz, *Space, Time, Perversion*; S. Hall, *Critical Dialogues in Cultural Studies* **Lit. 'Events':** replica Globe Theatre opens on London's South Bank

Author	Work
Muldoon	*New Selected Poems 1968-1994*
C. Raine	*Clay: Whereabouts Unknown*
Anne Stevenson	*The Collected Poems 1955-1995*
Zephaniah	*Funky Chickens* [children's poems] & *Propa Propaganda*
Pr/F: Bainbridge	*Every Man for Himself*
Barnes	*Cross Channel*
Byatt	*Babel Tower*
Chatwin	*Anatomy of Restlessness* [posthm.; misc. writings]
Dabydeen	*The Counting House* [novel]
Doyle	*The Woman Who Walked Into Doors*
Drabble	*The Witch of Exmoor*
Dunmore	*Talking to the Dead*
Galloway	*Where You Find It* [stories]
Gray	*Mavis Belfrage* [series of stories]
Lessing	*Love, Again*
Morrissy	*Mother of Pearl*
Raban	*Bad Land* [travel]
Swift	*Last Orders* [Booker]
Torrington	*The Devil's Carousel*
Trevor	*Death in Summer*
Welsh	*Ecstasy*
Neil Bartlett (b.1958)	*Mr Clive & Mr Page* [novel]
Seamus Deane (b.1940; Ulster)	*Reading in the Dark* [novel]
John Lanchester (b.1962)	*The Debt to Pleasure* [novel]
Deirdre Madden (b.1960; Ireland)	*One by One in the Darkness* [novel]
Frank McCourt (b.1930; Ireland)	*Angela's Ashes* [novel]
Dr: Pinter	*Ashes to Ashes*
Potter	*Karaoke & Cold Lazarus* [pf.d posthm. on TV]
Marina Carr (b.1964; Ireland)	*Portia Coughlin*
Ayub Khan Din (b.1961)	*East is East* [Damien O'Donnell film 1999]
Martin McDonagh (b.1970; Ireland)	*The Beauty Queen of Leenane, A Skull in Connemara & The Lonesome West* [pf.d as *The Leenane Trilogy*] & *The Cripple of Inishmaan*
Mark Ravenhill (b.1966)	*Shopping and Fucking*
Nigel Williams (b.1948)	*Harry and Me*

1997

'New Labour' win Gen. Elec.: majority, 179: Tony Blair, PM; Gordon Brown, Chancellor, accepts European single currency in principle, but UK will not join before 2002; William Hague, Cons. Party leader; Scotland & Wales vote in referenda to have devolved Assemblies [v.1999]; judicial enquiry

Princess Diana involved in anti-land-mine campaign [incls visits to Angola & Bosnia] – 31 Aug: killed in Paris car crash; 'Dolly' the sheep – 1st live animal from cloned cell; 10m. 'Tamagotchi' toys sold; US judge orders Microsoft to sell internet software separately from 'Windows' to avoid creating Web

Author	Work
P: Armitage	*CloudCuckooLand*
Hughes	*Tales from Ovid*
McGough	*Bad Bad Cats*
Mitchell	*Heart on the Left: Poems 1953-1984*
Morgan	*Virtual and Other Realities*
Motion	*Salt Water*

PERIOD	YEAR	INTERNATIONAL AND POLITICAL CONTEXTS	SOCIAL AND CULTURAL CONTEXTS	AUTHORS	INDICATIVE TITLES
		announced into police handling of racist attacks [eg. murder of Stephen Lawrence; v.1993, 1998–99]; Neil Hamilton, Cons. MP, in 'Cash for Questions' scandal; Dearing Report on HE – independent body created to provide integrated quality assurance; IRA bombimg campaign continues in Midlands & North – Grand National postponed by bomb threats – Sinn Fein wins 17% of vote in Ulster elections – violence at Drumcree during Unionist July marches – Gerry Adams announces new IRA ceasefire – accepted by gvnmt – 1st face-to-face peace talks between Sinn Fein & Unionists – Blair 1st PM to meet Sinn Fein leaders; Mary McAleese, President of Eire; NATO & Russia sign Founding Act on Mutual Relations, Co-operation & Security – ends 50 yrs of hostility in Europe; Oslo & Ottawa international treaties totally ban landmines [USA, Russia & China abstain]; Hong Kong handed over to China after 156 yrs British rule – 'End of Empire'; Israel begins withdrawal from Hebron after 30 yrs occupation – Palestinian suicide bombers attack Israeli cities; terrorists shoot 70 tourists in Valley of the Kings, Luxor, Egypt; international tension mounts as Saddam Hussein expels 6 US weapons inspectors working for UN in Iraq; 200+ Muslim pilgrims killed in encampment fire at Mecca, Saudi Arabia; Taliban offensive to estab. control over remaining 3rd of Afghanistan; rebels victorious in Zaire – Pres. Mobuto forced to resign – Laurent Kabila, President of [renamed] Democratic Republic of Congo; 'Pathfinder' space probe lands on Mars; bitter winter thro'out Europe, but 1997 is world's warmest yr on record; spring now starting 8 days earlier – further assumed result of global warming; scientists claim 40m. will be infected by AIDS before 2000	access monopoly. **Int. Lit.:** Walcott, *The Bounty*; Charles Frazier, *Cold Mountain* [US novel]; Carey, *Jack Maggs*. **Music:** music stars give concert in Mostar, Bosnia; Elton John, 'Candle in the Wind' [tribute to Princess Diana – over 30m. copies sold in a month – b-s. single ever – knighted in New Years Honours]. **Art:** British & Arts Councils hold 'Re-inventing Britain' conference on identity. **Film:** Cameron, 'Titanic' [Winslet, DiCaprio]; Lee, 'The Ice Storm' [Weaver, Kline]; Lynch, 'Lost Highway' [Pullman, P. Arquette]; Paul Thomas Anderson, 'Boogie Nights' [Reynolds, M. Wahlenberg, J. Moore]; Gillian Armstrong [Austrl.], 'Oscar and Lucinda' [Fiennes, C. Blanchett; adptn of Peter Carey novel]; James. L. Brooks, 'As Good As It Gets' [J. Nicholson, H. Hicks]; Barry Sonnenfeld, 'Men in Black' [L. Jones, W. Smith, L. Fiorentina]; John Woo, 'Face/Off' [Travolta, N. Cage]; Sally Potter [UK], 'The Tango Lesson'. **Theory/Crit:** Genette, *Paratexts* [Eng. trans]; Hall, *Representation: Cultural Representations and Signifying Practices*; Pearce, *Feminism and the Politics of Reading*	Redgrove Lavinia Greenlaw (b.1962) **Pr/F:** M. Amis Banville Crace Dunmore MacLaverty McEwan Moore Phillips Roberts Sinclair Tóibín Tremain Weldon Winterson J.[oanne] K. Rowling (b.1965) Arundhati Roy (b.1946; India) Rupert Thompson (nda) **Dr:** Churchill Hare Marber Stoppard Conor McPherson (b.1971; Ireland)	*Assembling a Ghost* *A World Where News Travelled Slowly* *Night Train* *The Untouchable* *Quarantine* *Love of Fat Men* [stories] *Grace Notes* *Enduring Love* *The Magician's Wife* *The Nature of Blood* *Impossible Saints* *Lights Out for the Territory* *The Story of the Night* *The Way I Found Her* *Big Women* *Gut Symmetries* *Harry Potter and the Sorcerer's Stone* [1st in sequence of 7 novels; film, 2001] *The God of Small Things* [Booker] *Soft* [novel] *Blue Kettle/Heart's Desire* [pf.d together as *Blue Heart*] & *This is a Chair* *Amy's View* *Closer* *The Invention of Love* *The Weir*
1998		N. Ireland: peace process culminates in 'Good Friday Agreement' (10 Ap.) – initiates power-sharing Assembly [1st meeting, July] to re-estab. provincial self-gvnmt – endorsed by 71% of people in May referendum – Gerry Adams & David Trimble in historic private meeting – Unionist violence against Agreement – 'Real IRA' bomb in Omagh kills 29 people & injures 310 – Trimble & John Hume awarded Nobel Peace Prize for contribution to N. Ireland process; Blair announces inquiry into 'Bloody Sunday' in Ulster in 1972; London referendum votes for elected mayor & assembly; riots as 5 suspects of black teenager Stephen Lawrence's murder attend public inquiry – Metropolitan Police Commissioner apologises to	£2 coin intro.d in UK; 2 doctors at Bristol Royal Infirmary struck off – responsible for deaths of 29 children after heart surgery; 'Viagra', anti-impotence drug, sells in huge quantities; MCC lifts 200-yr-old ban on women members. **Int. Lit.:** Hamilton, *The Short History of a Prince*; Morrison, *Paradise*; Seth, *An Equal Music*; Smiley, *The All-True Travels and Adventures of Lidie Newton*. **Music:** Royal Opera House, Covent Garden, in financial crisis – closes for a yr; 'Ginger Spice', Geri Halliwell, leaves 'Spice Girls' pop-group. **Art:** Emin, 'My Bed' [installation]. **Film:** Farrelly Bros, 'There's Something About Mary' [M. Dillon, C. Diaz]; Kapur, 'Elizabeth' [Blanchette, Rush, J. Fiennes]; Spielberg, 'Saving Private Ryan' [Hanks, M. Damon]; Weir, 'The Truman Show' [J...	**P:** Armitage & Crawford Heaney G. Hill Hughes Jennings Longley McGuckian Motion Muldoon Rumens Shapcott **Pr/F:** M. Amis Bainbridge	[eds] *The Penguin Book of Poetry from Britain and Ireland since 1945* [anthol.] *Opened Ground: Poems, 1966–1996* *The Triumph of Love* *Birthday Letters* *Praises* *Selected Poems* *Selected Poems 1976–1997* *Hay* *Holding Pattern* *My Life Asleep* *Experience* [autobiog.] & *Heavy Water* [stories] *Master Georgie*

CONTEMPORARY

parents over failure to solve the case [v.1993, 1997, 1999]; gvnmt abolishes maintenance grants & intros basic tuition fees in HE; Peter Mandelson, Cabinet Minister, forced to resign over secret house loan; Jonathan Aitken, former cabinet minister, on trial for perjury [gaoled, 1999]; former Chilean dictator, Gen. Pinochet, under arrest in London clinic – legal battle to extradite him; Kosovo-Serb conflict begins – ethnic Albanians massacred – NATO threatens air-strikes on Serbia – Milosevic allows NATO peacekeepers into Kosovo; 'Zippergate' scandal in USA – Pres. Clinton & Monica Lewinsky – Clinton impeached but remains Pres.; Saddam Hussein refuses full access to UN missile inspectors – 'Desert Fox' air-strikes by allies on Iraq; US embassies in Nairobi, Kenya & Dar-es-Salaam, Tanzania bombed – 257 killed – Osama bin Laden prime suspect – cruise missile strikes on Afghanistan & Sudan in retaliation; Australian vote to become a republic fails; conflict in Burundi – 100s killed; Pres. Mugabe of Zimbabwe orders confiscation of white-owned farms

Carrey, E. Harris, L. Linney]; Phil Agland [UK], 'The Woodlanders' [E. Woof, R. Sewell, C. Macaninch, T. Haygarth; adptn of Hardy]; John Madden, 'Shakespeare in Love' [Fiennes, G. Paltow et al; wrtn by Tom Stoppard]; Tony Kaye [UK], 'American History X'; Josiane Balasko [Fr.], 'Gazon Maudit'; Mani Rathman [Ind.], 'Dil Se'; Guy Ritchie [UK], 'Lock Stock and Two Smoking Barrels' [V. Jones]; Nicole Garcia [Fr.], 'Place Vendome' [Deneuve, E. Seiger]; Tom Twyker [Ger.], 'Run Lola Run'; Todd Haynes, 'Velvet Goldmine' [Colette, E. MacGregor, J. Rhys-Meyers, E. Izard]. **Theory/Crit:** Crawford, *The Scottish Invention of English Literature.*
Lit 'Events': Ted Hughes dies; Fatwa on Salman Rushdie lifted [v.1989]

Barnes	*England, England*
Boyd	*Armadillo*
Dabydeen	*Disappearance*
Faulks	*Charlotte Gray*
S. Hill	*The Service of Clouds*
Hollinghurst	*The Spell*
Jackie Kay	*Trumpet* [novel]
Kelman	*The Good Times*
Kureishi	*Intimacy*
McEwan	*Amsterdam* [Booker]
Thompson	*The Book of Revelation*
Trevor	*Death in Summer*
Weldon	*A Hard Time to be a Father* [stories]
Welsh	*Filth*
Winterson	*The World and Other Places* [stories]
Zephaniah	*Face* [novel]
Nicola Barker (b.1966)	*Wide Open*
Lucy Ellman (b.1956)	*Man or Mango?* [novel]
Lisa Jensen (b.1959)	*Ark Baby* [novel]
Dr: Frayn	*Copenhagen*
Hare	*Via Dolorosa* [one-man play pf.d by Hare] & *The Judas Kiss*
T. Johnson	*Dead Funny* & *Imagine Drowning*
Kane	*Cleansed* & *Crave*
Liz Lochhead	*Perfect Days*
Nagy	*Neverland*
Lee Hall (b.1966)	*Cooking with Elvis*

1999 Elections for Scottish & Welsh Assemblies – Lab. gains no overall majority in either; devolved gvnmt for N. Ireland restored to Stormont after 25 yrs, but Good Friday Agreement under threat as Unionists & Sinn Fein disagree about Executive & arms decommissioning – Patten Report recommends setting up a N. Ireland Police Service; Paddy Ashdown resigns as leader of Lib. Dems; Macpherson enquiry into police handling of Stephen Lawrence murder finds London police force institutionally racist [v.1993, 1997, 1998]; nail-bomb campaign against racial & other minority communities in London; [1 Jan.]: 'Euro' launched as single European currency in 11 countries; UK & Iran exchange ambassadors after 10-yr break over Rushdie Fatwa; Serbs 'cleanse' ethnic Albanians from Kosovo – 500,000 refugees flee – NATO launches air-strikes on Serbians – errors cause many civilian casualties [incls Chinese Embassy in Belgrade] – Pres. Milosevic indicted as war criminal – Kosova peace plan finally agreed – Federal Republic of Yugoslavia [Serbia] withdraws troops – Kosovo an international protectorate with 50,000

Solar eclipse; TV presenter, Jill Dando, gunned down at London home; 23m. UK homes have 55m. TV sets; 200m. worldwide watch wedding on TV of Prince Edward & Sophie Rhys-Jones [Duke & Duchess of Wessex]; gvnmt stops BSkyB's takeover bid for Man. Utd – Man. Utd 1st team to win 'treble' [FA Cup, Premiership & European Champions Cup]; troubled Millennium Dome, London, opens just in time. **Int. Lit.:** Coetzee, *Disgrace* [Booker]. **Music:** Sir Simon Rattle becomes conductor of Berlin Symphony Orchestra. **Films:** Lucas, 'Star Wars: Episode 1: The Phantom Menace' [remake]; Wenders, 'The Buena Vista Social Club' [C. Segundo, R. Cooder]; Frank Darabont, 'The Green Mile' [Hanks]; David Fincher, 'Fight Club' [Pitt, H. Bonham-Carter, E. Norton]; Spike Jonze, 'Being John Malkovitch' [C. Diaz, J. Cusack, D. Mantini]; Sam Mendes, 'American Beauty' [K. Spacey, A. Bening, T. Birch]; Wachowski Bros, 'The Matrix' [K. Reeves, L. Fishburne, C.-A. Moss]. **Lit 'Events':** Iris Murdoch dies; Andrew Motion, Poet Laureate

P: Duffy	*The World's Wife*
Heaney	*Beowulf* [trans]
G. Hill	*The Triumph of Love*
Jamie	*Jizzen*
Paulin	*The Wind Dog*
Prynne	*Poems*
Pr/F: Armitage	*All Points North* [social comment]
Banks	*The Business*
Bartlett	*Ready to Catch Him Should He Fall*
Bragg	*The Soldier's Return*
Brookner	*Undue Influence*
Crace	*Being Dead*
Dabydeen	*A Harlot's Progress*
Doyle	*A Star Called Henry*
Dunmore	*With Your Crooked Heart*
Frayn	*Headlong* [novel]
Kennedy	*Everything You Need* [novel]
Le Carré	*Single and Single*
Lessing	*Mara and Dann: an adventure*
Mo	*Renegade or Halo*
Raban	*Passage to Juneau: A Sea and Its Meanings* [travel]
Rushdie	*The Ground Beneath Her Feet*

PERIOD	YEAR	INTERNATIONAL AND POLITICAL CONTEXTS	SOCIAL AND CULTURAL CONTEXTS	AUTHORS	INDICATIVE TITLES
CONTEMPORARY		NATO peace-keeping troops; Pres. Clinton acquitted in US impeachment trial; Europe imports Caribbean not S. American bananas – USA imposes sanctions on EU luxury goods; fire in Mont Blanc Tunnel between France & Italy kills 40; Col. Gaddafi of Libya agrees to trial in Netherlands of 2 Libyians Suspected of Pan Am 103 bombing over Lockerbie in 1988; conflict in Sierra Leone; conflict mounts between India & Muslim guerrillas in Kashmir; devastating earthquake in Columbia; Russia attacks Chechnya; WHO warns of worldwide tuberculosis crisis; worldwide anxiety grows about 'Millennium Bug' affecting computers as new year begins [proved groundless]		Tóibín Tremain Christopher Hart (nda) Laura Hird (b.1966, Scotland) David Mitchell (b.1969) **Dr:** Ayckbourn Bennett McPherson Ravenhill Wertenbaker	The Blackwater Lightship Music and Silence The Harvest [novel] Born Free [novel] Ghostwritten [novel] Comic Potential The Lady in the Van Dublin Carol Some Explicit Polaroids Dianeira
	2000	The 3rd millennium: and so it goes on …			

Works Used for Reference

Michael Alexander, *A History of English Literature*, Basingstoke and London: Macmillan – now Palgrave Macmillan, 2000

Simon Armitage and Robert Crawford (eds), *The Penguin Book of Poetry from Britain and Ireland since 1945*, Harmondsworth: Viking, 1998

Jeremy Black, *Modern British History since 1900*, Basingstoke and London: Macmillan – now Palgrave Macmillan, 2000

Bodleian Library, University of Oxford, on-line catalogue

John Brannigan, *Orwell to the Present: Literature in England, 1945–2000*, Basingstoke and New York: Palgrave Macmillan, 2003

Julia Briggs, *This Stage-Play World: English Literature and its Background, 1580–1625*, Oxford and New York: Oxford University Press, 1983

Peter Brooker, *A Concise Glossary of Cultural Theory*, London and New York: Arnold, 1999

D. C. Browning (ed.), *Everyman's Dictionary of Literary Biography* [English and American], (Dent, 1958) London: Pan Books, 1972

Ronald Carter and John McRae, *The Routledge History of Literature in English: Britain and Ireland*, 2nd edtn, London and New York: Routledge, 2001

Chronicle of the 20th Century (Editor-in-Chief, Derrik Mercer), London: Dorling Kindersley, 1995

Stephen Coote, *The Penguin Short History of English Literature*, Harmondsworth: Penguin Books, 1993

Elizabeth Cowling, *Interpreting Matisse Picasso*, London: Tate Publishing, 2002

Simon Dentith, *Society and Cultural Forms in Nineteenth-Century England*, Basingstoke and New York: Macmillan – now Palgrave Macmillan, 1998

DK Millennium 20th Century Day by Day, CD Rom, Dorling Kindersley/GSP, 2001

Mary Eagleton (ed.), *Feminist Literary Theory: A Reader*, 2nd edtn, Oxford: Blackwell, 1996

Roger Fowler (ed.), *A Dictionary of Modern Critical Terms*, London and Boston, MA: Routledge & Kegan Paul, 1973

Paul Goring, Jeremy Hawthorne and Domhnall Mitchell, *Studying Literature: The Essential Companion*, London: Arnold, 2001

Phyllis Hartnoll (ed.), *The Concise Oxford Companion to the Theatre*, Oxford and New York: Oxford University Press, 1972

Phyllis Hartnoll, *A Concise History of the Theatre*, London: Thames and Hudson, 1968

Jeremy Hawthorn, *A Glossary of Contemporary Literary Theory*, 3rd edtn, London and New York: Arnold, 1998

Geoffrey Holmes, *The Making of a Great Power: Late Stuart and early Georgian Britain, 1660–1722* ['Foundations of Modern Britain' series], London and New York: Longman, 1993

Geoffrey Holmes and Daniel Szechi, *The Age of Oligarchy: Pre-industrial Britain, 1722–1783* ['Foundations of Modern Britain' series], London and New York: Longman, 1993

Maggie Humm, *The Dictionary of Feminist Theory*, Hemel Hempstead: Harvester Wheatsheaf, 1989

Maggie Humm (ed.), *Feminisms: A Reader*, Hemel Hempstead: Harvester Wheatsheaf, 1992

Internet Movie Data Base UK @ www.imdb.com

Martin Kemp (ed.), *The Oxford History of Western Art*, Oxford: Oxford University Press, 2000

Edna Longley (ed.), *The Bloodaxe Book of 20th-Century Poetry from Britain and Ireland*, Tarset, Northumberland: Bloodaxe Books, 2000

Longmans English Larousse, Harlow and London: Longmans, Green and Co, 1968

Edward Lucie-Smith (ed. with intro.), *British Poetry Since 1945*, Harmondsworth: Penguin Books, (1970), rev.d edtn, 1985

Donald M. MacRaild and David E. Smith, *Labour in British Society, 1830–1914*, Basingstoke and New York: Macmillan – Now Palgrave Macmillan, 2000

Magnus Magnusson and Rosemary Goring (eds), *Chambers Biographical Dictionary*, 5th edtn, Edinburgh: Chambers, 1990

Roger Manvell et al, *The International Encyclopedia of Film*, London: Rainbow Reference Books, 1972

Tom McArthur (ed.), *The Oxford Companion to the English Language*, Oxford and New York: Oxford University Press, 1992

Kathleen McCoy and Judith Harlan, *English Literature from 1785* ('HarperCollins College Outline'), New York: Harpercollins, 1992

Michael Payne (ed.), *A Dictionary of Cultural and Critical Theory*, Oxford: Blackwell, 1996

David Parkinson, *History of Film*, London: Thames and Hudson, 1995

L. C. Pascoe et al, *Encyclopaedia of Dates and Events*, (2nd edtn revised by Brian Phythian, 1974), 3rd edtn, London: Hodder and Stoughton, 1991

Phaidon Encyclopedia of Art and Artists, Oxford and New York: Phaidon Press, 1978

Alex Preminger et al (eds), *Princeton Encyclopedia of Poetry and Poetics*, Basingstoke and London: Macmillan – now Palgrave Macmillan, enlarged edtn, 1974

Philip Rice and Patricia Waugh (eds), *Modern Literary Theory: a Reader*, 4th edtn, London and New York: Arnold, 2001

Julie Rivkin and Michael Ryan (eds), *Literary Theory: An Anthology*, Oxford: Blackwell, 1998

Keith Robbins, *The Eclipse of a Great Power: Modern Britain, 1870–1992* ['Foundations of Modern Britain' series], London and New York: Longman, (1983) 1994

David Robinson, *World Cinema: A Short History*, London: Eyre Methuen, 1973

Stanley Sadie (ed.), *The New Grove Dictionary of Music and Musicians*, 20 vols, London: Macmillan, 1980

Andrew Sanders, *The Short Oxford History of English Literature*, Oxford and New York: The Clarendon Press, 1994

Raman Selden, Peter Widdowson and Peter Brooker, *A Reader's Guide to Contemporary Literary Theory*, 4th edtn, Hemel Hempstead: Prentice Hall/Harvester Wheatsheaf, 1997

Alan G. R. Smith, *The Emergence of a Nation State: The Commonwealth of England, 1529–1660* ['Foundations of Modern Britain' series], London and New York: Longman, 1984

Charles Saumarez Smith, *The National Portrait Gallery*, London: National Portrait Gallery, rev.d edtn, 2000

S. H. Steinberg, *Historical Tables: 58 BC–AD 1985*, (11th edtn updated by John Paxton), Basingstoke: Macmillan – now Palgrave Macmillan, 1986

Jane Turner (ed.), *The Grove Dictionary of Art*, 34 vols, London: Macmillan – now Palgrave Macmillan, 1996

Neville Williams, *Chronology of the Modern World, 1763–1965*, (1966), rev.d edtn, Harmondsworth: Penguin Books, 1975

Duncan Wu (ed.), *Romantic Women Poets: An Anthology*, Oxford: Blackwell, 1997

Marion Wynn-Davies (ed.), *Women Poets of the Renaissance*, London: Dent, 1998

[Also referred to: scores of modern editions of texts, etc. which include 'chronologies' or 'timelines']

Index A

British Authors

(With their dates, and referenced by year of first citation in the timeline tables [**bold**])

Index B

Key Terms and Concepts Glossed in Chapter Headnotes

(Referenced by chapter and page number)